INSURANCE AGAINST POVERTY

Insurance Against Poverty

Edited by
STEFAN DERCON

*A study prepared by the World Institute for Development Economics
Research of the United Nations University (UNU-WIDER)*

*This book has been printed digitally and produced in a standard specification
in order to ensure its continuing availability*

OXFORD
UNIVERSITY PRESS

Great Clarendon Street, Oxford OX2 6DP

Oxford University Press is a department of the University of Oxford.
It furthers the University's objective of excellence in research, scholarship,
and education by publishing worldwide in

Oxford New York

Auckland Cape Town Dar es Salaam Hong Kong Karachi
Kuala Lumpur Madrid Melbourne Mexico City Nairobi
New Delhi Shanghai Taipei Toronto
With offices in
Argentina Austria Brazil Chile Czech Republic France Greece
Guatemala Hungary Italy Japan South Korea Poland Portugal
Singapore Switzerland Thailand Turkey Ukraine Vietnam

ISBN 978-0-19-927683-7

Contents

Part I. **Risk and Insurance: Evidence**

Part II. **Risk and Poverty: Theory**

Part III. **Risk and Poverty: Persistence**

Part VII. **Developing Better Protection for the Poor**

Part VIII. **Conclusion**

List of Tables

List of Figures

List of Figures

List of Abbreviations

BMI	body mass index (also known as the Quetelet Index)
BMR	basal metabolic rate
CGAP	Consultative Group to Assist the Poorest
CIDA	Canadian International Development Agency
CILSS	Côte d'Ivoire Living Standards Survey
CSA	Central Statistical Authority (Ethiopia)
CUBOS	Cupones de Bonificacion (Chile)
FDRE	Federal Democratic Republic of Ethiopia
FFW	food-for-work
FGT	Foster–Greer–Thorbecke
FONDEN	Fondo de Desastres Naturales (Mexico)
GMM	generalized method of moments
ICRISAT	International Crops Research Institute for Semi-Arid Tropics
IFC	International Finance Corporation (of the World Bank group)
IFPRI	International Food Policy Research Institute
IMF	International Monetary Fund
IV	instrumental variables
MFE	maternal fixed effects
MFEs	microfinance entities
NBS	National Bureau of Statistics (China)
NPDPM	National Policy on Disaster Prevention and Management (Ethiopia)
PROGRESA	Programa de Educación, Salud y Alimentación (Mexico)
REST	Relief Society of Tigray (Ethiopian NGO)
RHS	Rural Household Surveys (China)
ROSCAs	Rotating Savings and Credit Associations
UNCDF	United Nations Capital Development Fund
UNDP	United Nations Development Programme
WHO	World Health Organization
WIDER	World Institute for Development Economics Research

Notes on Contributors

Pedro Albarran is an Assistant Professor at the Department of Economics, Univ. Carlos III de Madrid (Spain). His research interests include microeconometrics, income risk, and consumption.

Orazio P. Attanasio is Professor of Economics at UCL, Research Fellow at IFS where he directs the Centre for the Evaluation of Development Policies (EDePo). He is also research associate of the NBER and Research Fellow of the CEPR.

Abhijit V. Banerjee is Ford Foundation International Professor of Economics at MIT and President of BREAD, the Bureau for Research in Economic Analysis and Development. He is currently involved in setting up the Poverty Action Laboratory at MIT, which is intended to promote greater use of high quality evidence in the design of anti-poverty policies.

Christopher B. Barrett is a Professor of Applied Economics and Management, co-director of the African Food Security and Natural Resources Management Program at Cornell University, Ithaca, NY, and co-editor of the *American Journal of Agricultural Economics*.

Daniel C. Clay is Director of the Institute of International Agriculture at Michigan State University.

Paul Collier is Professor of Economics and Director of the Centre for the Study of African Economies, at Oxford University. During 1998–2003 he was Director of the Development Research Group at the World Bank.

Jonathan Conning is Assistant Professor of Economics at Hunter College and at the Graduate Center of the City University of New York, USA. His research has focused on the economics of contracts and incentives in microfinance and the political economy of property rights and factor market imperfections in Latin America.

Alain de Janvry is a Professor of International Economic Development at the University of California at Berkeley with expertise on issues of rural poverty and rural development.

Joachim De Weerdt is based in Tanzania where he heads the research arm of Economic Development Initiatives Ltd., a local company with headquarters in Bukoba providing consultancy, research and training services to a diverse clientele ranging from international organizations to local governments and NGOs. Academically he is affiliated to Katholieke Universiteit Leuven in Belgium.

Stefan Dercon is the Professor of Development Economics at the University of Oxford and a Fellow of Wolfson College. He is the director of the UNU-WIDER project on 'Insurance against Poverty'. His research and policy work focuses on risk, poverty and growth, and on non-market institutions for risk coping.

Marcel Fafchamps is Reader in the Department of Economics and Professorial Fellow at Mansfield College, Oxford University. He also serves as Deputy Director at the Centre for the Study of African Economies. Marcel has just completed two book projects—one on Market Institutions in Africa with MIT Press, and one on Rural Poverty, Risk, and Development with Edgar Elgar.

Markus Goldstein is a Lecturer in Development Economics at the London School of Economics.

John Hoddinott is a Senior Research Fellow at the International Food Policy Research Institute, Washington DC; his current research interests include poverty dynamics, particularly as they relate to nutrition.

Stein Holden is Professor in Development Economics in the Department of Economics and Resource Management, Agricultural University of Norway. His area of research is on rural development, natural resource management, and food security in LDCs.

Jyotsna Jalan is an Associate Professor in the Department of Economics at the Indian Statistical Institute, New Delhi, India. Her current research interests include program evaluation, and role of information in social sectors.

Gisele Kamanou is a Statistician, Office of the Director, United Nations Statistics Division. She currently coordinates the division work programme on poverty statistics and manages a United Nations Development Account Project in Statistics for the Economic Community of West Africa States (ECOWAS) Region in support of the Millennium Development Goals.

Michael Kevane is Associate Professor of Economics at the Leavey School of Business, Santa Clara University, and author of *Women and Development in Africa: How Gender Works* (Lynne Rienner, 2003).

Pramila Krishnan is on the Faculty of Economics and Politics, University of Cambridge and Jesus College, Cambridge. Her current research interests lie in applied microeconomics, and in particular, household behaviour and the interaction of markets with non-market institutions in rural economies.

Donald F. Larson is Senior Economist with the Development Research Group, World Bank. He works on rural development and policy issues.

Ethan Ligon is an Associate Professor in the department of Agricultural and Resource Economics at the University of California, Berkeley, where he conducts research on risk-sharing and inequality.

Jonathan Morduch is Associate Professor of Public Policy and Economics at New York University. His research focuses on poverty and finance.

Jean-Philippe Platteau is Professor of Economics and member of CRED (Centre de Recherche en Economie du Developpement) at the University of Namur, Belgium. Most of his work has been concerned with the understanding of the role of institutions in economic development, and the processes of institutional change. Recent books include *Halting Degradation of Natural Resources—Is There a Role for Rural Communities?* (Oxford: Clarendon Press, 1995) with J.M. Baland, and *Institutions, Social Norms, and Economic Development* (London: Harwood Publishers and Routledge, 2000).

Martin Ravallion is Senior Manager in the World Bank's Research Department. His main research interests over the last 20 years have concerned poverty and policies for fighting it. He has written extensively on this topic and advised numerous governments, as well as teaching economics at a number of universities.

Elisabeth Sadoulet is Professor of Agricultural and Resource Economics at the University of California at Berkeley. Her research focuses on development policy and the impact of poverty alleviation programmes.

Loïc Sadoulet is assistant professor at ECARES at the Free University of Brussels. His research focuses on the enhancement of private sector activity in underdeveloped markets. Much of his recent work has centered on financial intermediation, and in particular on ways to extend the range of financial services for the poor (savings and insurance rather than just credit).

Paul Siegel has in recent years been working as a consultant at the World Bank on issues related to social risk management and on innovative finance and insurance instruments. He has worked widely in Latin American and Asia, and written extensively on social risk management, risk, vulnerability, and diversification in rural development.

Jerry Skees is the H.B. Price Professor of Agricultural Policy and Risk in the Department of Agricultural Economics at the University of Kentucky. He is also president of GlobalAgRisk, Inc. which provides public policy consulting advice to governments on agricultural risk policy.

Panos Varangis is a Lead Economist at the Agriculture and Rural Development department at the World Bank. His primary responsibilities and areas of interest include commodity risk management, including price, weather and yield related risks, commodity marketing and financing systems, and broader agricultural policy issues.

Foreword

The poor in developing countries are regularly exposed to risk and shocks such as drought, floods, illness, pests, commodity price changes, and recession. The usual policy response has been to develop some form of safety net, as a supplement to more general long-term economic growth-oriented policies; but the prevailing view in developing countries is that these safety nets are insufficient to avoid recurrent hardship.

Economists have long been interested in the welfare implications of risk and its consequences for poverty. However, the potential of risk and shocks to contribute towards low growth, persistent poverty and even poverty traps, has only recently received serious attention in the applied theoretical literature. More importantly, rigorous testing of these models has only become feasible recently with the availability of panel data in developing countries.

This study brings together new contributions that address these theoretical and empirical challenges. The book focuses on crucial questions for policymakers: how strong is the case for more public action? What can be done? What can be learned from existing informal institutions? Can we build on them? What initiatives could be taken to provide more protection?

Overall, the answer is that much can be achieved if policies are carried out with renewed commitment and credibility: providing insurance against poverty is not impossible.

Tony Shorrocks
Director, UNU-WIDER
December 2003

Acknowledgements

UNU-WIDER gratefully acknowledges the financial contribution to the project by the Ministry for Foreign Affairs of Finland. UNU-WIDER also gratefully acknowledges the financial contributions to the 2002–3 research programme by the governments of Denmark (Royal Ministry of Foreign Affairs), Finland (Ministry for Foreign Affairs), Norway (Royal Ministry of Foreign Affairs), Sweden (Swedish International Development Cooperation Agency—Sida), and the United Kingdom (Department for International Development).

'The Two Poverties', by Abhijit Banerjee is reproduced with the kind permission of the *Nordic Journal of Political Economy*, from where the original version of this chapter was published (vol. 26 no. 2).

Work on this WIDER project allowed me to engage closely with a number of colleagues working on issues related to risk and poverty, and trying to go a step further in teasing out the implications from this growing body of work. For me it has been a very illuminating experience and I am very grateful to all of the project participants for their work, comments, and support. Thanks are due to James Foster, who was a stimulating discussant and resource person during the workshop in preparation of this book. I am grateful to Andrea Cornia, previously director of WIDER, for recruiting me for a project that at first only seemed to have a catchy title. Thanks are also due to Tony Addison for helpful coaching in the beginning of the project and to Barbara Fagerman for her patient support. I am grateful to Tony Shorrocks, director of WIDER, and the entire staff at WIDER, for creating such a stimulating work place during two long summers in Helsinki. Adam Swallow deserves special thanks for his patience and perseverance to see the manuscript completed. Finally, allow me to thank Pramila Krishnan for first encouraging me to get involved in this project and her intellectual and emotional partnership.

Stefan Dercon
December 2003

Overview

STEFAN DERCON

This book is a collection of papers, offering new economic research and insights on the relationship between risk and poverty in developing countries, and the most effective policies to avoid that risk which continues to contribute to widespread poverty. The chapters are structured around three key questions: How important is risk for poverty? What lessons can be learned from studying existing, often informal, risk-sharing institutions for the design of broad-based social protection? What is the scope for designing new instruments for social protection?

In addressing the first question, contributions in the book present a review of the evidence on how risk affects the welfare of the poor in developing countries and the strategies they use to cope with risk; methodological insights on how to measure risk-related vulnerability to poverty and to identify vulnerable groups; and new theoretical and empirical work on the link between uninsured risk and poverty persistence. Contributions on existing risk-sharing arrangements highlight the strengths and weaknesses of these social institutions and the impact of social protection initiatives on them. The book also contains a number of contributions presenting evidence on successful safety nets and on new instruments such as microcredit contracts with insurance provisions, and drought insurance.

In recent years, ambitious targets to reduce poverty in the world have been approved by the international community. A renewed focus on increasing economic growth in the developing world has also emerged. Growth is clearly an important condition for large-scale poverty reduction, at least provided that the poor can benefit from these increases in growth. Creating opportunities for economic progress and empowering the poor to participate in this process are widely recognized mechanisms to achieve these objectives (World Bank 2000; UNDP 2002).

This process of growth and poverty reduction has to take place in a risky environment where shocks often threaten any gains in the living standards of the poor. Natural disasters, drought, conflict, and insecurity continue to disrupt local economies. The high incidence of health problems hinders many of the poor to take advantage of opportunities. Economic shocks, including currency crises, commodity price shocks, and the contagion effects of worldwide recession, undermine growth and contribute to continuing high poverty. Indeed, the very process of economic reform creates in any case losers, even if it may only be temporary. The extent of shocks and risk do not appear to be reducing in recent decades. Risks seem to be changing, with demographic shifts, AIDS, and globalization shifting risk to different regions, age groups, or different occupational and social classes.

These pressures on growth and poverty reduction have not gone unnoticed in the policy debate. The importance of providing more secure living conditions as an important dimension of poverty reduction has been recognized (World Bank 2000). Many international agencies, governments, and non-governmental agencies (NGOs) have developed programmes for more widespread social protection. Most of these programmes take the form of safety nets, ways of providing some protection from the worst effects of shocks.

Few would deny that this type of intervention is important and that there is a genuine role for public action and for development aid in assisting these programmes. However, the arguments for such programmes are often largely cast in humanitarian or equity terms. They are considered part of social programmes without much *economic* rationale. In this book, many of the authors take a different stance: that beyond humanitarian concerns, these programmes make *economic* sense. In particular, there is an *instrumental* role for better social protection, since it would facilitate a growth process that will also deliver poverty reduction. In other words, social protection may well be good for growth. Since the poor are least able to cope with risk and shocks, and therefore would benefit most from protection, the result is public action contributing to broader equity *and* efficiency.

This conclusion is *not* reached because the authors in this book reject the standard paradigm of mainstream 'neoclassical' economic theory, in which competitive forces and incentives are considered the foundations for efficiency and growth. On the contrary, most of the contributors effectively rely on these tools for their research. But the normative prescriptions of basic neoclassical economics, to let the markets work freely without interference, have weak foundations in the presence of risk and uncertainty, since it would require that competitive markets should exist that allow anyone to insure themselves for all contingencies. While even in developing countries some insurance markets exist, their scale and functioning seem far removed from the idealised theoretical construct, suggesting widespread market failure, opening the door for public action even within a simplified textbook world where efficiency is all that matters.

The focus in this book is on risk and its consequences, and our discussion on public action has to be seen in this light. We use vulnerability as referring to the stress on the livelihoods and welfare of the poor arising from risk. Social protection refers to public actions taken to reduce levels of vulnerability that are deemed unacceptable within a society. Public action is not limited to the state: these actions can be taken by the state or NGOs, and may also involve local social institutions and the private sector. We typically use the term social protection, rather than social security. Social security systems are typically identified with highly formalized and extensive systems with specific redistribution and poverty alleviation functions beyond the provision of different forms of insurance and protection. Our focus on the latter is not meant to signify that we do not consider the other functions important—on the contrary—but rather that we want to have a more narrow focus to allow us to draw more specific conclusions for policy from the analysis. Indeed, one of our arguments is that well-designed schemes could have relatively low cost and high social benefits, including in efficiency terms.

The case and scope for broader social protection has been made before by many aca-demics. One contribution in particular should be highlighted, the collection edited by Ahmad *et al.* (1991), not least since it was an earlier book in the Oxford University Press UNU-WIDER Studies in Development Economics series. It made a strong case for more widespread and broadly conceived social security in developing countries as well for the role of public action in achieving it. Many of the conclusions reached remain valid, including that we can only draw limited lessons from systems in developed coun-tries for developing countries and that specific schemes such as employment guarantee schemes, may have substantial benefits. Besides a more narrow focus on protection from vulnerability linked to risk, the current volume takes a different approach. Rather than a broad survey of the key issues related to social protection, it contains a number of new and specific theoretical contributions, as well as new empirical work based on detailed microlevel data, all of them with important implications for policy design. There is no attempt to be comprehensive in the analysis and conclusions, but rather, it aims to present new insights and inspire further thinking.

Still, there are some close links with the Ahmad *et al.* (1991) volume. For example, one particular chapter in that book, by Platteau, focuses on traditional social institutions for social security. It provides a starting point for a number of contributions in the current volume as well. Indeed, the emphasis on the understanding of the existing social institutions to build better social protection, is an important conclusion from the current volume. Historically, it is helpful to remember that the highly formalized, but quite diverse systems of social security in Europe or the United States have deep roots in community organizations, trade unions, and religious institutions. Sustainable systems in developing countries will need to have a strong local institutional basis.

The starting point for the analysis in this book is that the link between risk and poverty can then be seen as directly related to missing insurance markets and market failure. A number of contributions in this book explore this relationship theoretically and empirically. Superficially, the theoretical relationship may seem straightforward: if risk is uninsured, living standards will go down if a bad shock hits. Living standards may fall below some acceptable minimal level and poverty will result, at least until better times arrive. However, this ignores that the poor try to adapt their livelihoods in sophisticated ways to handle risk and shocks. Much of the focus of recent economic research in developing countries, not least by the contributors to this book, has focused on whether and how poor people try to cope with risk and shocks, typically and rather successfully applying insights from savings and portfolio analysis to developing country settings with widespread market failure as well as diverse local institutions to cope with risk. Households use their savings and assets, as well as transfers from friends and family to cope with the consequences of risk. They also address their vulnerability to such hardship by changing their exposure to risk by adapting their livelihoods, for example, via diversification or low risk activities, by migration or network formation.

The first chapter in this book, by Dercon, reviews some of the key theoretical con-cepts and evidence on responses to risk and their effectiveness, largely drawing on case studies from Africa and Asia. Morduch, in Chapter 2, focuses specifically on the evidence from one specific setting, a number of villages in Southern India. Due to the unique data available from these villages in the public domain, these villages have been intensively and independently studied by a large number of eminent researchers. Morduch's study has the additional feature of critically consolidating our knowledge on risk and its consequences in this particular setting. Both studies highlight that despite sophisticated strategies at the level of individuals and groups, much risk remains uninsured. Especially those with limited assets or support networks—typically the poorest—seem to be most exposed. The two chapters aim to consolidate much of the existing literature, focusing on the lessons learned and the new agenda that is emerging in the analysis of risk, insurance, and poverty. The rest of the book contributes to this agenda.

Two contributions in the book focus on designing measures of the welfare losses linked to uninsured risk, and identify those most exposed to risk. A literature on measuring vulnerability to poverty is growing, and Kamanou and Morduch provide a review in Chapter 8. Vulnerability refers to potential states, not actual outcomes, so a measure of vulnerability should be forward-looking. They propose a measure of vulnerability for a group or a population based on the difference expected future poverty and current poverty. Their application to Côte d'Ivoire highlights that substantial vulnerability may exist even if poverty did not materialize afterwards. Ligon, in Chapter 9, proposes an approach, nested within the expected utility framework, to identify the extent to which different individuals are exposed to different types of risk and applies it to Indian data.

The strategies employed by households and individuals to respond to risk, come at a cost in terms of long-term earnings. Low risk activities often give a lower return. Keeping liquid savings to cope with shocks may imply that fewer productive assets are acquired, again resulting in lower incomes. In the long-run, lower incomes are obtained, and this may be a cause of poverty persistence. In this situation, the lack of insurance results in an efficiency loss, while under reasonable circumstances any initial inequality will be exacerbated due to the missing insurance market. In Chapter 3, Banerjee shows how failures in the insurance market may result in a poverty trap. In Chapter 4, Fafchamps explores different scenarios of how risk affects the evolution of inequality over time. It provides a helpful reminder of the limits of risk-sharing and social protection.

Widespread poverty persistence and traps would give a strong argument to increase social protection, since it could unlock the income growth potential of the poor, contributing to growth and poverty reduction. Several contributions explore this empirically. In Chapter 1, evidence is presented that strategies in response to risk contribute to lower income and wealth levels. Jalan and Ravallion, in Chapter 5, test directly for the persistence of poverty due to uninsured risk by looking at the income dynamics in data from China. They find no evidence for poverty traps, but it takes a number of years before household income recovers fully from a negative shock. Dercon and Hoddinott, in Chapter 6, focus on the persistence of poor health outcomes after shocks in adults and children in Ethiopia and Zimbabwe. They find that shocks have big impacts and for children these effects are persistent, resulting in stunting, poor educational outcomes, and lower earnings. They also look at the intrahousehold impact of shocks. Boys and girls do not seem to be differentially treated but adult women in particularly poor households are worse protected from shocks. Collier, in Chapter 7, looks at the macroeconomic impact of uninsured agricultural price risk in developing countries. He quantifies the negative externalities of these shocks and suggests that they are sufficiently large to justify subsidies to increase efficiency.

In short, the case for increased social protection in the form of *insurance against poverty* seems strong, with potentially high returns for poverty reduction and growth. What form should it take? It is not necessarily clear that the appropriate public action should be intervention by the state. The causes for the failings of market-based insurance provision, including problems of imperfect and asymmetric information and enforcement problems, are not necessarily straightforwardly solved by direct state action. Furthermore, other agents, including NGOs or community organizations, may well be better placed to handle these challenges. Existing risk-coping networks—often very informal and based on family, neighbourhoods, or ethnic linkages—may contain useful lessons for the organization and implementation of better social protection. Finally, public action may displace these informal systems, and the extent and consequences of this displacement should be understood.

A number of contributions look into these existing mutual support systems. Most of the economics literature, as reviewed in Chapters 1 and 2, focuses on how effective these mutual support systems are to cope with risk. However, the contributions take another perspective. To look explicitly at the composition of these networks for mutual support De Weerdt in Chapter 10 studied one village in Tanzania extensively. Some of the factors determining who links up with whom are as expected: similar clan, religion, or kinship all increase the likelihood of forming a mutual support group. But strikingly, he finds that the poor in the village have less dense networks than the rich. Goldstein, de Janvry, and Sadoulet, in Chapter 11, study inclusion and exclusion in networks, by focusing on the type of shocks and extent of support that is offered to individuals within households and within the community. Gender and wealth matter at the household level for mutual support; lineage, social interactions, and expected inheritance matter at the community level. Exclusion from 'traditional' support is a distinct possibility, and strengthens the case for a careful design of interventions, focusing on specific vulnerable groups. Platteau, in Chapter 12, focuses on another important issue related to informal support systems: that over time, they are changing and they may become weaker. In particular, he focuses on support systems that involve needbased access to productive resources, in his case land. Changes in land tenure arrangements towards more individualized forms of property rights remove this support system in land allocation.

These studies confirm the relative weaknesses of informal mechanisms. They tend to overcome partly the market failures in insurance, by exploiting the information and enforcement possibilities of social proximity. However, by necessity they are typically small scale, and the scope for expanding them may well be limited. Their scale limits the risk they can handle to individual-specific risk, while covariate risk, affecting all individuals at the same time cannot be insured. Still, it leaves important possibilities for risk-pooling unexploited. Trying to introduce widespread private or social insurance is not self-evident in such a context. Conning and Kevane, in Chapter 15, study some of the impediments to the development of more linkages and intermediation with local financial and mutual support networks. Issues considered include monitoring costs, social norms, and power relations.

The presence of informal insurance systems may also affect the impact of transfers as part of social protection measures. First, there is the standard problem of crowding-out: public transfers may reduce private transfers, so that the net welfare impact may be lower than the value of the transfer. Albarran and Attanasio, in Chapter 13, analyse the impact of public transfers on private transfers using a unique data set from Mexico. In the presence of informal insurance networks, crowding-out may take a specific form, whereby public transfers may have externalities on others not covered by the public safety nets, and it could lead to undermining or even destroying the informal support system. They find that crowding-out of informal transfers is indeed taking place.

However, the interaction between informal insurance and formal safety nets has another dimension as well. Formal social protection measures may be able to exploit the presence of informal insurance, even if the latter is imperfect. Ligon, in Chapter 9, explains how targeting would be irrelevant if risk-sharing is perfect. Dercon and Krishnan, in Chapter 14, take this up. Even if risk-sharing is imperfect, poorly tar-geted transfers may well be shared in the community, and they find evidence that informal insurance systems compensate for relatively poor targeting of food aid by redistribution in villages in Ethiopia. They nevertheless also find evidence consistent with crowding-out of the informal arrangements due to the formal safety net.

A final set of chapters focus on improving the effectiveness of existing interventions and the design of new instruments. Barrett, Holden, and Clay provide a discussion of the case for employment programmes in the form of food-for-work. They provide rules-of-thumb for when and how these programmes can serve effectively as short-term insurance as well as contributing to longer-term development. Loïc Sadoulet, in Chapter 17, discusses the design of an incentive compatible insurance mechanism to improve on existing microcredit contracts, providing suggestive evidence for its potential from Guatemala. Skees, Varangis, Larson, and Siegel, in Chapter 18, discuss the scope for introducing forms of weather insurance contracts, providing protection against an important source of covariate risk. Such contracts are superior in terms of incentives and data requirements for monitoring to *ex post* mechanisms such as disaster relief or alternative insurance contracts such as crop insurance. In the last chapter, some of the findings from the book are brought together, in a broader discussion of the scope and limitations for successful public action to provide insurance against poverty.

REFERENCES

Ahmad, S. E., J. Drèze, J. Hills, and A. K. Sen (1991). *Social Security in Developing Countries.* UNU-WIDER Studies in Development Economics, Oxford: Oxford University Press.

UNDP (2002). *Human Development Report 2002: Deepening Democracy in a Fragmented World.* Oxford: Oxford University Press.

World Bank (2000). *World Development Report 2000/01: Attacking Poverty.* Washington, DC: World Bank.

PART I

RISK AND INSURANCE: EVIDENCE

1

Risk, Insurance, and Poverty: A Review

STEFAN DERCON

High-income risk is part of life in developing countries. Climatic risks, economic fluctuations, and a large number of individual-specific shocks leave these households vulnerable to severe hardship. In Ethiopia, for example, rural households are exposed to a variety of risks, including harvest failure as a result of drought, floods, frost, and other climatic events; policy shocks, such as changes in taxation and bans on migration; and the death and illness of their livestock (Table 1.1).

Many studies have reported high-income variability related to risks of various forms. Using the ten-year panel data for one of the three International Crops Research Institute for Semi-Arid Tropics (ICRISAT) villages in India, Townsend (1994) reports high yearly yield fluctuations (in monetary terms) per unit of land for the dominant

Table 1.1. *Risk-related hardship faced by rural households in Ethiopia*

Events causing hardship	Percentage of households reported to have been seriously affected, 1974–94
Harvest failure (drought, flooding, frost, pests)	78
Policy shock (forced labour, ban on migration, new levies or taxes)	42
Labour problems (illness or deaths)	40
Oxen problems (diseases, deaths)	39
Other livestock (diseases, deaths)	35
Land problems (villagization, land reform)	17
Assets losses (fire, loss)	16
War	7
Crime/banditry (theft, violence)	3

Source: Author calculations based on Ethiopian Rural Panel Data Survey (1994–7).

An earlier version of this chapter was written as a background paper for the *World Development Report 2000/01*. Much of the research was carried out as part of the UNU-WIDER project, 'Insurance against Poverty'. An early draft of the parts dealing with informal insurance was presented at the Annual Bank Conference in Development Economics in Europe, in Paris in May 1999. The current version is an updated and expanded version of Dercon (2002a). All errors and opinions are my own.

crops. Kinsey *et al.* (1998) report a high frequency of harvest failures in a twenty-three-year panel of rural households in a resettlement area in Zimbabwe. Bliss and Stern (1982) estimate that in Palanpur, India, a two-week delay in the onset of production is associated with a 20 per cent decline in yields. Morduch (1995) provides many other examples.

This chapter reviews the strategies, households, and individuals use to avoid consumption shortfalls caused by risk. It draws on a growing empirical economic literature, based mainly on panel data studies, supplemented by work on Ethiopia. This is not the first survey on this topic. Alderman and Paxson (1994), Morduch (1995, 1999), Townsend (1995), and Fafchamps (1999) have also published surveys. This chapter is different from those studies because it focuses on the constraints households face in using these strategies and on the policies needed to strengthen the ability of communities, households, and individuals to avoid severe consumption shortfalls caused by risk. Most of the examples cited are from Africa and Asia. Lustig (2001) provides relevant examples from Latin America.

The next section introduces the risk problem faced by households. In the following section, the focus is on asset strategies. Section 1.3 reviews income-based strategies, while Section 1.4 examines informal and formal safety nets. Finally, I review ways of defining and monitoring vulnerability to poverty.

1.1. RISK, HOUSEHOLD RESPONSES, AND CONSEQUENCES

The responses to risk by households are diverse. To understand them it is helpful to first consider the nature of the different sources of risk faced by households. Income risk is caused by a variety of factors. Common, or aggregate, risks are covariate risks that affect all members of a community or region. Individual, or idiosyncratic, risks affect only a particular individual. In practice, even within well-defined rural communities, few risks are purely common or idiosyncratic. Data from a three-period panel data set on Ethiopia reveal that most of the shocks experienced by households included both idiosyncratic and common risk features (Table 1.2).[1]

Other studies also find that the idiosyncratic part of income risk is relatively large. Deaton (1997) finds that common components explain very little of the variation in household income for particular villages in Côte d'Ivoire in 1985–6. Townsend (1995) reports evidence from Thailand which suggests that there are few common regional components in income growth. The Indian ICRISAT data also suggest relatively limited correlation in incomes within villages. Morduch (Chapter 2) concludes that idiosyncratic risk (inclusive of measurement error) accounts for 75–96 per cent of the total variance in income within these villages. Udry (1991) reports similar magnitudes for Northern Nigeria.

Other characteristics of income risk include the frequency and intensity of shocks and the persistence of their impact (see also Morduch 1999). Relatively small but frequent shocks, such as transient illness, are easier to deal with than large, infrequent

---

[1] The term 'shock' is used to mean a realization of the risky process: what is considered a risk *'ex-ante'* could become a shock *'ex post'*. In the literature reviewed in this chapter, it is used to reflect rather large deviations from expected outcomes, usually negative ones, although positive shocks may exist as well.

Table 1.2. *Shocks affecting income 1994–5 (n = 1450, 15 communities)*

	1994[a]	1994[b]	1995	Village level variance as % of total variance[a]	F-test of analysis of variance[b]
Village rainfall (% above long-run mean)	0.06	0.12	0.12	100	
Rain index (individual)	0.57	0.57	0.63	40.6	64.6
Total non-rain shock index	0.65	n.a.	0.80	28.2	37.2
Non-rain shock					
Low temperature, frost, storm, or other climatic event	0.71	n.a.	0.82	34.4	49.9
Crop pests and diseases	0.59	n.a.	0.77	28.9	38.7
Animal damage, trampling, or related shock	0.68	n.a.	0.85	30.9	42.6
Weed damage	0.29	n.a.	0.14	13.8	15.3
Crop index	0.33	0.65	0.43	34.0	49.1
Livestock affected by animal disease	0.72	0.86	0.89	24.6	30.6
Livestock affected by lack of water and grazing land	0.71	0.78	0.78	31.7	25.3
Number of days lost by adults in past month, per adult	0.66	0.45	0.39	5.2	5.3
Number of adults who died in past six months	n.a.	0.04	0.02	5.6	5.8
Smaller harvest linked to not having labour due to illness	0.19	n.a.	0.13	15.9	17.8
Smaller harvest due to not finding labour when needed	0.18	n.a.	0.13	14.4	15.7

[a] Results on the variance decomposition are obtained allowing for time-varying village-level means on the pooled data set across rounds. In practice, this village-level variance is the R^2 of a regression on a full set of time-varying village-level dummies. The lower the contribution of the village-level variance to total variance, the more idiosyncratic is the shock.

[b] All tests are significant at the 5 per cent level. The higher the F-statistic, the higher the contribution of village-level shocks to total shocks.

Notes: n = 1450 households in fifteen communities. Data collected in 1994 and 1995, with about six months between survey rounds. Index data are based on reported problems: 1 = no problems reported, 0 = all possible problems occur. Rain index (individual) is based on problems for own activities from rainfall, including whether it rained during harvest and whether the pattern of rainfall was irregular. Crop index is based on reported moderate or severe crop failures. n.a. = Not available.

Source: Dercon and Krishnan (2000*a*).

negative health shocks, such as disability or chronic illness. Gertler and Gruber (2002) find that, in terms of consumption levels, households in Indonesia can protect themselves against only 30 per cent of low-frequency serious health shocks, with severe long-term effects. In contrast, they are able to insure their consumption against about 70 per cent of high-frequency, smaller health shocks. If there is persistence in shocks, coping is more difficult. In a theoretical exploration, Deaton (1991) examines the effects of autocorrelation in income on consumption smoothing when credit markets are missing. Using panel data from Pakistan, Alderman (1998) shows that successive shocks make consumption smoothing more difficult than single shocks. Some shocks, such as health problems, may also have persistent effects.

Identifying the nature of the shock helps identify the possibilities for dealing with its consequences. Idiosyncratic shocks can be insured within a community. Common shocks cannot, since if everyone is affected, the risk cannot be shared. Formal or informal insurance transfers (credit or insurance) from outside the community or inter-temporal transfers (such as depletion of individual or community-level savings) are therefore necessary to deal with common shocks.

Households do not just undergo the consequences of high risk. Households in risky environments have developed sophisticated strategies to reduce the impact of shocks. Alderman and Paxson (1994) distinguish risk-management from risk-coping strategies.[2] Risk-management strategies attempt to reduce the riskiness of the income process *ex ante* (income smoothing). Examples include income diversification, achieved by combining activities with low positive covariance, and income skewing, achieved by taking up low-risk activities, even at the cost of low returns. Risk-coping strategies include self-insurance (through precautionary savings) and informal group-based risk-sharing. They deal with the consequences of income risk (consumption smoothing). Households can insure themselves by building up assets in good years, which they deplete in bad years. Alternatively, informal arrangements can be made among members of a group or village to support each other in case of hardship. These mechanisms are observed within extended families, ethnic groups, neighbourhood groups, and professional networks.

Risk-coping strategies may also involve attempting to earn extra income when hardship occurs. Kochar (1995) reports increased labour supply as the key response in the ICRISAT villages in South India. The literature on coping strategies when famine strikes also regularly report attempts to earn additional income through the reallocation of labour, including temporary migration, earning income from collecting wild foods, gathering activities (such as increased firewood collection), and so on.[3] During famines in Ethiopia or Sudan, these responses were all observed (De Waal 1987; Dercon 2002*b*).

---

[2] The *World Development Report 2000/01* uses an alternative, more policy-focused classification of strategies, the Social Risk-Management framework (Holzmann and Jørgensen 2000), taking the response to risk as its focus. It distinguishes risk reduction, risk mitigation, and risk coping strategies. The classification used in this chapter follows the economics literature and focuses on welfare outcomes, such as consumption and other dimensions, and distinguishes risk strategies on the basis of whether they take income as given or not (World Bank 2000). These different ways of structuring responses effectively yield similar insights.

[3] The social science literature on household strategies dealing with shocks often uses a different terminology. Davies (1996) uses the term 'coping strategies' to describe strategies employed during crises. In her terminology, 'coping' refers to success in dealing with the crisis. 'Adaption' is a characteristic of a 'vulnerable' household, using 'coping' strategies as part of standard behaviour. Adaptive strategies are then defined as a permanent change in the mix of ways in which households make a living, irrespective of the year in question. For a good review, see Moser (1998). I adopt a framework in which households develop strategies to deal with contingencies. The distinction between adaption and coping seems less relevant. Any coping strategies will require *ex ante* actions, such as forming informal networks or building up savings.

High risks are not easily insured by formal market mechanisms. Credit and insurance markets are typically absent or incomplete in developing countries, either for good theoretical reasons or because of bad policy (for surveys, see Besley 1994, 1995 or Bell 1988). Consumption loans are rare. Traditional credit systems (*roscas, susu, tontines*), however, often extend loans, which may be used for consumption purposes. Formal loans or loans in microfinance programmes also often finance consumption, since the funds they provide are fungible.

Informal credit markets appear to adjust to high-risk environments. Udry (1994) reports that informal loans in rural Nigeria appear to take the form of state-contingent loans. Repayment is conditional on income outcomes of both borrowers and lenders, with negative shocks translated into more favourable terms for the party experiencing them.

Despite these strategies for managing and coping with risk, vulnerability to consumption shortfalls remains high in developing countries. Further development of safety nets is therefore necessary. Townsend (1995) notes that income variability remains high in the ICRISAT villages in South India, where diversification and other income strategies are used only to a limited extent and are in any case inadequate. Risk-coping strategies are also typically insufficient. Rosenzweig (1988) estimates that transfers in India amount to less than 10 per cent of typical income shocks. Other studies also suggested imperfect risk-sharing or consumption smoothing (Deaton 1991, 1992, 1997; Paxson 1993; Chaudhuri and Paxson 1994).

The experiences during the famines in the Horn of Africa in the mid-1980s also illustrate the limitations of these coping strategies. Despite complex coping strategies, as documented by Rahmato (1991), the effects of the famines were severe. Dercon (2002*b*) reports that ten years after the famine, cattle holdings were still only two-thirds what they were just before the famine. Reardon *et al.* (1988) report that transfers in the aftermath of the 1984 drought were equivalent to only 3 per cent of the losses for the poorest households in the Sahel. Events in East Asia during the financial crisis of the late 1990s also exposed the limitations of informal insurance and self-insurance. In Indonesia, for example, consumption poverty increased substantially, but evidence suggests that the reductions in household investment in health and education were even more important, affecting future generations (see Chaudhuri *et al.* 2001; Thomas *et al.* 2004).

Rose (1999) finds that in rural India negative rainfall shocks are associated with higher child mortality rates in landless households but not in households with significant landholdings. Jacoby and Skoufias (1997) find that households in some villages in South India withdraw their children from school after adverse shocks. Beegle *et al.* (2003) find that credit-constrained households use child labour to smooth their income in response to shocks. Alderman *et al.* (2002) find that a drought shock in Zimbabwe had serious long-term implications for children aged 12–24 months,

---

Consequently, all households will have adapted their livelihood to serve their own objectives as well as possible. Whether they do so using traditional coping strategies is conceptually irrelevant, although, as will be seen, it has analytical and policy implications (regarding long-term incomes, for example).

lowering stature and grade attainment in later life (see also Chapter 6). Foster (1995) shows that child growth was affected during and after the severe floods in Bangladesh in 1988. He does not find evidence of a sex bias, but other studies do. Using ICRISAT data, for example, Behrman (1988) shows that the inability to smooth consumption negatively affects child health in the period before the major harvest, with girls affected more than boys. Using data on individual nutrient intakes from India, Behrman and Deolalikar (1990) report that estimated price and wage elasticities of food intake are substantially and significantly higher for females than for males, suggesting that women and girls share a disproportionate burden of rising food prices.

Dercon and Krishnan (2000*b*) examine risk-sharing by rural households in Ethiopia. They studied adult nutrition to investigate whether individuals are able to smooth their consumption within the household over the seasons. Poor households in the southern part of the country do not engage in complete risk-sharing between husbands and wives: women in these households bear the brunt of adverse shocks. Because of imperfect risk-sharing, women in poor households lose an average of 1.6–2.3 per cent of their body weight as a result of the loss of labour caused by illness.

1.2. ASSET STRATEGIES

Saving in good times and depleting assets when the going is tough are commonly observed strategies to smooth consumption. However, its effectiveness as a strategy is restricted in the typical circumstances faced by the poor in developing countries. Deaton (1991) describes the benefits of self-insurance through savings when credit markets are imperfect. In his model, the household maximizes expected utility over time. The household is risk averse and has a precautionary motive for savings, so that it will save more if risk increases. Households can save, receiving a safe return on asset, which is assumed to be relatively low. Income is risky, and in the basic model, independently identically distributed. Households are impatient, so that they have a preference to consume today rather than in the future. The result is that interest rates are lower than the rate of time preference.

Deaton assumes further that households behave as if they have an infinite planning horizon. In that case, they will build-up assets in good years to deplete in bad years. As a result of impatience, assets are not systematically accumulated to very large levels. High levels of fluctuations are observed in savings, and consumption is smoother than income. Severe crises are not easily insured, however: despite these strategies, a sequence of bad draws can still mean that consumption is very low. Deaton argues that for many developing countries, this model fits well with some of the stylized facts of occasional low consumption, low asset holdings, and high frequency of asset transactions. It is not easy to draw immediate policy conclusions from this work, however. The key result—imperfectly smooth consumption—follows largely from the impatience of households: if only they were patient, they could build-up sufficient assets to cope with future stress.

To understand household savings behaviour in risky environments in developing countries, one needs to acknowledge that assets are risky. Deaton's model assumes that savings can occur in a safe form with a positive rate of return. In practice, this may not be possible. The lack of integration of asset markets and the difficulties the poor face in obtaining access to internationally traded assets means that the portfolio of assets available to them is limited. When a common negative shock occurs, incomes are low and returns to different assets are also low, often even negative. As a consequence, just when assets are needed, net stocks could be low as well. For example, if assets are kept in the form of livestock (as they are throughout most of the developing world), a drought causes both a decline in crop incomes and the death of and drop in fertility of livestock. The consequence is a smaller herd or even loss of all livestock just when these assets are needed as part of the self-insurance scheme.[4] Similarly, stock market returns may be low when crisis hits an economy, as they were during the 1997 Asian financial crisis. The likely covariance of asset values and income as a result of common shocks thus reduces the usefulness of self-insurance.

Another problem with holding assets to buffer consumption is that the terms of trade between goods for consumption and assets change as a result of a common shock. If a negative common shock occurs, households would like to sell some of their assets. However, if everyone wants to sell assets at the same time, asset prices will collapse and the amount of consumption that can be purchased with the proceeds will fall. Similarly, when a positive shock occurs, everyone will want to buy assets for future protection, pushing prices up.

There is a lot of evidence, albeit some of it anecdotal, that this effect is common. During the famine in Ethiopia in 1984–5, terms of trade between livestock and food collapsed (Rahmato 1991). Relative food prices rose by a factor of three, reducing the purchasing power of assets by two-thirds. More recently, housing prices in Indonesia and other Asian countries collapsed, after a boom in the early 1990s. The same phenomenon occurs following positive shocks. Bevan *et al.* (1991) describe the construction boom that took place in Kenya during the coffee boom in the mid-1970s, when prices for construction materials and other durables increased markedly. Households tried to put some of their positive windfall into more assets, but their choice set was sharply restricted by macroeconomic policies, such as foreign exchange and capital controls.

While risk in asset returns and in the terms of trade may reduce the usefulness of assets for smoothing consumption, holding assets can nevertheless help smooth consumption. Rosenzweig and Wolpin (1993) show that bullock sales contribute to consumption smoothing in the South Indian ICRISAT villages, although Lim and Townsend (1994) argue that crop inventory appears to be the main strategy used by these households. Access to relatively safe and profitable assets may be limited, however. The lumpiness of assets may partly explain why the poor cannot protect themselves easily by holding assets. For example, buying and selling cattle is generally recognized as a common strategy for coping with income fluctuations in many rural areas

---

[4] This type of risk in returns to assets is not limited to commodity-based assets. The risk of bank failure and a run to withdraw deposits during an economic crisis means that seemingly safe assets are also risky, with covariate returns with incomes.

(Binswanger and McIntire 1987; Davies 1996). But large proportion of households often do not own livestock. Dercon (1998) finds that only half the households in a sample in Western Tanzania own cattle, even though cattle are important in the farming system and the culture. The explanation is not that half of all households choose to engage in other activities but that investing in livestock requires a sizeable surplus: livestock are lumpy. A cow, for example, costs about a one-fifth of the mean annual crop income. Cattle ownership is generally determined by endowments in male labour and land. Households with small endowments cannot accumulate sufficient means to purchase cattle, leaving them more exposed to income risk.

The consequences of risky or lumpy assets are easily illustrated via simulations. The Appendix to this chapter gives some results. Risk in asset returns, terms of trade risk, and lumpiness have substantial impacts. The largest effects stem not from risk per se, but from the covariance between asset values and income. Positive covariance is not unrealistic: when an economy-wide shock occurs incomes are likely to decline but so also will asset values. This results in a large reduction in the opportunity to effectively self-insure.

There is some evidence that household behaviour is consistent with these predictions. During the 1984–5 famine, households in Ethiopia cut their consumption to dangerously low levels rather than sell their assets when asset terms of trade had collapsed (Rahmato 1991). Czukas et al. (1998) find that livestock sales (both cattle and small stock) offset at most 30 per cent and probably closer to 15 per cent of the crop income shortfall during severe drought in Burkina Faso.

Policies that reduce asset market risks could help households deal with shocks. Maintaining macroeconomic stability during income downturns, for example, would allow self-insurance to function better. Providing households with access to more attractive and more diversified assets could also help them deal with shocks. Integrating asset markets with the wider economy could prevent much of the often-observed covariance between asset prices and incomes. In rural Africa or India, for example, facilitating the holding of assets other than animals—low-cost financial savings held in post office accounts, for example—could help households weather shocks. Introducing a focus on savings for self-insurance in the booming number of initiatives related to microfinance operations could also help.

Macroeconomic policy could also reduce the effects of shocks in the terms of trade. For example, a worsening of the terms often coincides with inflationary increases in consumer prices relative to asset prices, as occurred during the famines in Bangladesh in 1974 and Ethiopia in 1985. Low inflation and exchange rate stability could limit large shocks in relative prices when incomes are low. Policies that reduce the macroeconomic impact of common shocks would enhance self-insurance.

1.3. INCOME SMOOTHING STRATEGIES

Income smoothing refers to strategies that reduce risk and fluctuations in income. They are commonly observed in developing countries, but they may come at a cost in terms of persistent poverty. Income smoothing often involves diversifying income sources. Theoretically, as long as the different income sources are not perfectly covariate (i.e. they have a correlation coefficient less than 1), combining two income sources with the same mean and variance will reduce the total income risk. Stated in this way, there appears to be no cost to diversifying, since mean income remains unchanged. A more realistic scenario is one in which mean income is reduced in order to lower risk. This strategy can be called income skewing, since it involves allocating resources to low-risk, low-return activities. It is different from diversification, since it is possible that households specialize in only one activity, with low-risk and a low return.

Widespread diversification of income sources is observed in developing countries. Across the developing world, farm households receive a substantial share of income from non-farm activities. Reardon *et al.* (1994) report an average share of 39 per cent of income from non-farm activities in eight countries in rural West Africa. In addition to engaging in non-agricultural activities, households fragment their landholdings into many plots, grow different crops, and engage in local farm wage employment. Is diversification effective? Townsend (1995) notes that in the ICRISAT villages in South India, substantial scope for diversification exists. Relatively little appears to take place, however, and income remains highly variable.

Diversification does not always result in income smoothing, for several reasons. First, combining different income sources is not always intended to manage risk. Different activities may be conducted at different times of the year, providing income throughout the year by smoothing labour over time. Secondly, while farm and off-farm activities may be relatively uncorrelated in normal years, during crises they may move together. In a severe downturn, this would severely limit the usefulness of diversification. There is evidence that this is the case. Czukas *et al.* (1998) show that non-farm income is positively correlated with shocks affecting crop income: drought adversely affects not only crop income but also non-farm income. This finding is consistent with Sen's analysis of famine, in which crop failure sometimes leads to a collapse in demand for local services and crafts, limiting the usefulness of diversification to reduce risk.

There are also important constraints to entering into profitable and risk-reducing diversification. Non-agricultural activities or profitable alternative agricultural activities are not easily accessed. Entry constraints could take the form of working capital, skills, or other requirements (see Reardon *et al.* 1988; Reardon 1997). Dercon and Krishnan (1996) look explicitly at the role of different constraints in Tanzania and Ethiopia. They find that the poor typically enter into activities with low entry costs, such as collecting firewood and dungcakes, making charcoal, and working as casual agricultural wage earners. Entry into high-return non-crop activities, such as cattle-rearing or shop-keeping, which most households would like to engage in, is restricted to richer households, presumably with access to capital. Non-agricultural wage employment is restricted to people with education.

Recent data from Ethiopia on the investments needed to enter non-farm business activities indicate that relatively high levels of capital are required for some activities (Dercon 2002*b*). The median investment needed to enter into charcoal making, dungcake collection, handicraft production, weaving, or food processing—activities with relatively low returns—was 0–20 birr (up to US$3). More lucrative activities, such as starting a shop, trading livestock, or providing transport services, required 300–550 birr (US$45–80). A mature cow costs about 400 birr (US$60). These are large sums in an economy in which mean per adult income is less than US$200 a year. Dercon (1998) shows that barriers to entry were more important than comparative advantage in determining entry into high-return activities in rural Tanzania.

Reducing income risk often comes at a cost, because it is difficult to diversify the sources of income without reducing the level of mean income. Although they face more severe consequences from risky incomes (because of more limited insurance and credit market imperfections), the poor are often less diversified than wealthier households. The reason may be that many diversification or income-skewing strategies reduce mean income, making them less attractive for poor households. Capital and other entry constraints exclude the poor from diversification into activities with a higher return. This unwillingness (or inability) to accept lower returns may partly account for the limited income smoothing observed in developing countries. The long-term consequences for the asset-poor are lower average incomes and a higher income gap relative to asset-rich households.

Another reason why the poor have less diversified sources of income than other households is that income-based strategies are directly linked to asset-based strategies (and other forms of protections, such as those provided by informal insurance). As Eswaran and Kotwal (1989, 1990) show, credit can serve as an insurance substitute, but credit market imperfections usually imply collateralized lending. The consequence is that asset-poor households cannot enter into high-risk activities, since downside risks are too high. Asset-rich households do not face this problem. Households with access to (liquid) assets can borrow in times of crisis, or, if credit is not available, sell assets as part of a buffer stock strategy. In contrast, to reduce their income risk, asset-poor households have to enter low-risk, low-return activities. The consequence is further impoverishment, or at least increased inequality. This result only depends on risk-aversion, *not* on differential risk aversion between the rich and the poor.

Evidence suggests that this is indeed happening. Morduch (1990), using the ICRISAT sample, shows that asset-poor households devote a larger share of land to safer traditional varieties of rice and castor than to riskier but higher-return varieties.[5] Dercon (1996) finds that Tanzanian households with limited liquid assets (livestock) grow proportionately more sweet potatoes, a low-return, low-risk crop. A household with an average livestock holding allocates 20 per cent less of its land to sweet potatoes than a household with no liquid assets. The crop portfolio of the wealthiest quintile yields 25 per cent more per adult than that of the poorest quintile. Choosing a less risky crop portfolio thus has substantial negative consequences for incomes.

Rosenzweig and Binswanger (1993) suggest that the portfolio of activities (and investments) in the ICRISAT villages is affected by high-risk. Increasing the coefficient of variation of rainfall timing by one standard deviation reduces farm profits of the poorest quartile by 35 per cent; for the richest quartile the effect is negligible.

---

[5] Morduch finds a significant effect on plot diversification but not on a crop diversification index, which may well be linked with some of the points made here, related to constraints on access to some activities.

Efficiency is affected, and the average incomes of the poor decline. Wealthier farmers are not affected and are therefore able to earn higher incomes. This phenomenon affects the wealth distribution: 54 per cent of wealth is held by the top 20 per cent of households. Jalan and Ravallion (2001) cite other examples, although their evidence is more mixed.

These results do not follow from differences in risk preferences: controlling for preferences, the poor select a low-risk, low-return portfolio while the rich take on a riskier set of activities. These results reflect the constraints on the options available to poor households. As Kochar (1995: 159) notes, 'the set of options faced by farmers offers little role for preferences'. The behaviour of the poor may *look* as if they have more (innate) risk-averse preferences, but it is the lack of insurance and credit, and the set of options available to them that forces them to take less risk and therefore forgo income (see Eswaran and Kotwal 1990, for a careful theoretical discussion).

Several income-based strategies are invoked only when a crisis looms. These coping, or survival, strategies are especially important when the shock is economy-wide. Examples of economy-wide shocks include drought, floods, and large economic shocks, such as those affecting parts of Asia in recent years. When a large negative shock occurs, the usual household activities may not yield sufficient income. If all households in a community or region are affected, local income-earning activities are unlikely to be sufficient.

Kochar (1995) argues that labour supply adjustments, rather than asset or other strategies, are the main strategy used by households in India to cope with negative idiosyncratic shocks. Increased labour force participation in response to economic shocks is also found elsewhere. Moser (1998) reports increased female labour market participation and child labour in Ecuador and Zambia. Jacoby and Skoufias (1997) find that children in the ICRISAT villages in South India were taken out of school in response to adverse income shocks to work, reducing the accumulation of human capital. Beegle *et al.* (2003) found increases in child labour in response to income shocks. In Indonesia female labour participation rose and children were withdrawn from school to help households weather the recent crisis (Frankenberg 1999; Thomas *et al.* 2004). During a severe crisis, such as a famine, additional action is often taken to prevent destitution. These actions include temporarily migrating in order to obtain work, working longer hours, and collecting and selling wild foods and forest products (De Waal 1987; Corbett 1988; Rahmato 1991; Davies 1996).

To conclude, the poor are likely to engage in low-risk–low return activity portfolios. This is not because the poor have different innate preferences—a psychological trait that makes them less entrepreneurial. Rather, failing insurance and credit markets may make income smoothing optimal. Diversifying income sources is useful but for the poor it may come at a high cost, in terms of levels of income.[6] Nevertheless, observing specialization does not necessarily imply that the household follows a high-risk strategy. Also, entry constraints may limit the diversification that can be achieved, leaving

---

[6] This does not necessarily mean that the *growth* rate of income of the poor is lower. The link between growth and risk, and an emerging literature related to it, is briefly discussed in the conclusions.

only low-return activities free to the poor. Income portfolios must be seen in relation to the asset portfolio and other options available: a risky, specialized portfolio may mean lower consumption risk than a diversified portfolio, depending on the asset position. One important policy implication is that just promoting diversification is not necessarily a solution. Finding ways of reducing entry constraints into profitable low-risk activities is crucial.

1.4. INFORMAL RISK-SHARING AND SAFETY NETS

Beyond income-based strategies and self-insurance, households use a variety of informal risk-sharing arrangements to cope with the consequences of risk. Typically, these arrangements involve a system of mutual assistance between family networks or communities. There has been growing interest in the empirical analysis of informal risk-sharing and in the modelling of the sustainability and consequences of these arrangements (see Morduch 1999). Empirical studies have sought to determine whether there is evidence of complete risk-sharing in developing countries and other settings, including the United States, and to understand how (partial or complete) risk-sharing is achieved. Results from the United States, communities in India, and nuclear households in Ethiopia suggest that complete risk-sharing is not taking place but that partial risk-sharing may be occurring (Townsend 1994; Hayashi *et al.* 1996; Dercon and Krishnan 2000*b*).

These studies test the presence of outcomes similar to those obtained by risk-sharing. The tests cannot distinguish between the effects of self-insurance (i.e. accumulating and depleting assets) and informal insurance (or insurance-like behaviour through transfers or credit). Nevertheless, they reveal evidence of partial risk-sharing through transfer behaviour or state-contingent (quasi)-credit. Udry (1994) presents evidence of state-contingent loans in Northern Nigeria. Fafchamps and Lund (2003) show that loans and transfers within networks play an important role in risk-sharing. Dercon and De Weerdt (2002) find no village-level risk-sharing but some risk-sharing via networks in Tanzania. Grimard (1997) appears to have found more stable consumption by tribes in Côte d'Ivoire than for the full data set, suggesting that tribal networks facilitate consumption smoothing, including through transfers. Evidence of full risk-sharing was not found, however.

More direct evidence on the extent of risk-sharing also reveals its limitations. Using detailed data on Northern Ghana, Goldstein *et al.* in Chapter 11 show that many idiosyncratic shocks are not insured by community contacts or even spouses. De Weerdt (Chapter 10) uses a detailed survey of all networks in a Tanzanian village to show that poorer households have fewer contacts to turn to in times of need and that they can typically rely only on other poor households.

Theoretical work also reveals the limits of risk-sharing arrangements. Hoff (1996) has highlighted the possible negative consequences of informal risk-sharing on poverty. Fafchamps (Chapter 4) discusses the persistence of inequality and patronage linked to risk-sharing arrangements. Coate and Ravallion (1993), Platteau (1997),

Ligon *et al.* (2002), and Attanasio and Rios-Rull (2000) examine the nature and sustainability of (partial or complete) risk-sharing arrangements given the lack of formal enforcement. Ligon *et al.* (2002) present evidence that the constrained risk-sharing model fits the data on household food consumption in the ICRISAT villages in India better than the perfect risk-sharing model.

Even if imperfect, for many poor households in developing countries, these risk-sharing networks are crucial in helping them cope with misfortune. Such groups can insure only idiosyncratic shocks, however, not common shocks. Savings or public safety nets could be developed to cope with common risks and to protect against idiosyncratic shocks not covered by communities. Informal risk-sharing arrangements can complement public safety schemes. For example, targeting the most needy is notoriously difficult. But if a risk-sharing arrangement is present within a community, poorly targeted transfers would be redistributed within the risk-sharing group (Ligon, Chapter 9). Dercon and Krishnan (Chapter 14) discuss evidence from Ethiopia suggesting that despite poor targeting of food aid, some of this aid reaches a large part of the community. But such programmes often have other unintended consequences, which need to be clearly understood.

Much attention has been paid in the public transfer literature to the problems of crowding-out. The impact of public transfers for the poor is typically smaller than the total transfer, since net private transfers to the poor are reduced (see Cox and Jimenez 1992). Public safety nets can also crowd out informal arrangements. If the safety net provides full protection to all vulnerable households and individuals, this is hardly a serious problem from a welfare point of view (even if the budgetary cost may be high). However, the problem is more complicated in the case of informal risk-sharing arrangements in which enforcement is not self-evident.

Some households may have incentives to leave a risk-sharing arrangement if they feel that staying in the arrangement—supporting others when the going is good in order to receive support when the going is bad—may not be in their interest. For example, following a series of lucky income draws, individuals may prefer to hold on to and invest their income themselves rather than use it to support others. If some households in the network have access to a new source of risk reduction or protection, the arrangement may also come under pressure. Sometimes renegotiating the reciprocal arrangement may allow the arrangement to continue, albeit on new terms. When that is not possible, the arrangement may break down (Platteau 1997; Ligon *et al.* 2002).

Public safety nets create a change of circumstances that may have undesired welfare effects by putting pressure on informal arrangements. Information, budget, or other constraints often mean that some needy households are excluded from these programmes, even if targeting methods, including self-targeting, are used. The result may be a specific type of crowding-out. Some households covered by the safety net may have incentives to leave their informal risk-sharing arrangements, leaving other households less protected. As a result of the safety net, then, some households may be made more vulnerable.[7] This problem is not limited to public safety nets: any policy

---

[7] This may happen even if everyone is covered by the safety net, as Attanasio and Rios-Rull (2000) show. Since insurance of some part of the total risk faced by households improves the households' autarky

intervention that improves an individual's position outside a private group-based informal risk-sharing arrangement may provide incentives to break down the informal arrangement (Ligon, Chapter 9; Dercon and Krishnan, Chapter 14). Some researchers have suggested that this form of crowding-out is significant (Albarran and Attanasio, Chapter 13). However, large the effect may be, it is important that policymakers recognize that informal schemes for dealing with idiosyncratic risk may be negatively affected by other interventions, including better-functioning safety nets for common shocks or support for more self-insurance activities.

One way of avoiding these problems is to target groups rather than individuals— by creating employment schemes for an entire group or community involved in an informal scheme, for example. Of course, doing so requires detailed information about the informal schemes in place. Another alternative could be to encourage and support groups involved in informal insurance arrangements to develop group-based self-insurance mechanisms. The notion that individual-based self-insurance can deal best with common shocks while informal arrangements are suitable for idiosyncratic shocks is misleading. Groups have incentives to self-insure, especially if there are economies of scale in asset holdings (lower transactions costs, for example, or better opportunities for risk-pooling of assets). Groups could build-up assets in good years to deplete in bad years for the benefit of their members, adopting the same trans-fer rules and mechanisms used to manage idiosyncratic shocks.[8] Policy interventions could provide incentives for this type of behaviour. Better savings instruments, access to banking, and macroeconomic stability would facilitate this process. Policymakers could also try to include a stronger savings-for-insurance component in group-based credit programmes, a current favourite in donor interventions. Group-based targeting and insurance schemes have their own problems, however (Conning and Kevane 2002, and Chapter 15).

1.5. MONITORING INCOME RISK, VULNERABILITY, AND COPING STRATEGIES

The presence of significant income risk in developing countries and the limited ability of poor households to smooth the resulting shocks have implications for measuring poverty. Furthermore, it begs the question whether alternative measures, capturing risk, and vulnerability should be developed.

Using income as a measure of welfare to identify poverty has long been recognized as problematic. As an alternative, current consumption, as found in cross-sectional surveys, has been used for most quantitative poverty analysis. The argument is

---

position, it is possible that more than one-to-one crowding-out occurs and total welfare is reduced by the safety net. Self-targeted schemes may not necessarily solve the problem, since they also affect the individuals' outside options. Of course, the lower the payments in the scheme, the less they will affect the enforceability constraints. This is equivalent to providing lower insurance.

[8] Indeed, in some traditional societies, this type of group behaviour is common. In Western Tanzania a community food stock, run by the village head, provides protection for the village when a large-scale crisis occurred (Sukumaland) (Dercon 1998).

that because risk-averse households prefer less variable consumption, consumption is smoother than income. However, the combination of high-income risk and the observed inability of households to smooth consumption through risk-management or coping strategies, especially when faced with severe shocks, would suggest that alternative measures are needed.[9]

If time series data are available, dynamic poverty definitions can be used. If data on consumption over time are available, it is possible to take into account the fact that some households may be poor only in some years.[10] One could distinguish those who are poor in every period from those who are poor in only some of the periods sampled. In all panel data sets on developing countries currently available, large consumption fluctuations mean that a large number of households move in and out of poverty. For example, in the Indian ICRISAT data set, about 25 per cent of the poor in each period move out of poverty in the next period. Gaiha and Deolalikar (1993) report that only 12 per cent of households in the ICRISAT sample were never poor. Jalan and Ravallion (2000) report that about half the poor in each year were not poor on average in their sample from rural China. Using data from rural Ethiopia, Dercon and Krishnan (2000*a*) report that while poverty remained essentially unchanged between 1994 and 1995 (at about 40 per cent), about a third of the poor were different households each year. More evidence can be found in Baulch and Hoddinott (2000) and other articles in the same special issue of the *Journal of Development Studies*.

One need to be cautious in interpreting the evidence on widespread poverty transitions and fluctuations. Measurement error in the data would show up as increased movement above and below the poverty line, increasing the apparent mobility. Still, since most studies find variables correlated with fluctuations that are unlikely to be correlated with measurement error in consumption, it is likely that a substantial part of the observed consumption fluctuations are genuine.

Ravallion (1988) proposes a way of measuring chronic and transient (including risk-related) poverty. Using consumption as the underlying welfare measure, he defines the chronically poor as those with average consumption below the poverty line. A measure of transient poverty for an individual is then derived as the average value of the period by period poverty level of this individual minus chronic poverty. Additive poverty measures can then be decomposed into transient and chronic components. For example, using the squared poverty gap, Jalan and Ravallion (2000) report that roughly half of total poverty observed in their rural Chinese panel data set covering 1985–90 is transient poverty. Transient poverty is highest for households with average consumption near the poverty line, with about 40 per cent of transient poverty

---

[9] This is a problem for non-monetary dimensions of poverty as well. Alternative welfare measures, such as nutrition, food expenditure, expenditure on specific commodities (such as health or education), and even health or school enrolment, would suffer from the same problem. For evidence on the effect of risk on education and nutrition, see Jalan and Ravallion (2001), Jacoby and Skoufias (1997), Dercon and Krishnan (2000*b*), and Foster (1995).

[10] Risk need not be the only reason for fluctuations in poverty: if credit and asset markets are imperfect, even predictable fluctuations in income may cause fluctuations in consumption and poverty. An example is seasonality.

found among households that are not poor on average. Almost all-transient poverty is experienced by households whose mean consumption is no more than 50 per cent above the poverty line. This evidence implies that in any given year, the measured poverty level will exclude some people at risk of being poor in the near future.[11] Dercon and Krishnan (2000*a*) look explicitly at the link between shocks and poverty transitions, using panel data from Ethiopia. They use a fixed-effects model of consumption in which changes in consumption are linked to idiosyncratic and common shocks, such as rainfall, other crop shocks, illness, and the death or sickness of livestock. They find that some of the fluctuations appear to be seasonal responses to prices and labour requirements but that shocks matter. Most areas in the sample experienced a fairly good harvest in the sample period. In the best period of the year (the post-harvest period), the incidence of poverty was about 33 per cent; in the worst period, it was about 40 per cent. During the worst period of the year, up to 60 per cent of the population could be poor. This estimate is substantially larger than poverty estimates from the (relatively good) 1990s would suggest.

Work on poverty dynamics, including work on transient poverty, has highlighted the limitations of current static poverty measures (see Baulch and Hoddinott 2000 for a review). In response, researchers are currently developing measures of vulnerability to poverty. These measures, however, remain backward-looking: they describe the past consequences of shocks and fluctuations. Information on the characteristics of households experiencing poverty transitions may help identify those most at risk for consumption shortfalls, but it does not provide a measure of vulnerability to poverty. Such a measure should be *ex-ante* (forward-looking), and provide a statement on welfare based on information on potential outcomes of individuals and populations. Two key methodological issues can be distinguished. First, how to predict potential outcomes? And secondly, how to capture information on all possible outcomes in one statistic, both at the individual or household level as well as for a population?

To address the first issue, most contributions use econometric models to construct a prediction model. In practice, most work has been driven by the actual data availability. Some researchers have proposed prediction models based purely on cross-sectional household data (Chaudhuri *et al.* 2001), but the assumptions needed to identify common and idiosyncratic risk are very strong. Ligon (Chapter 9) uses panel data to identify aggregate and idiosyncratic shocks, using the ICRISAT data from India—Ligon and Schechter (2003) develop this approach further using data from Bulgaria. Panel data have the advantage that recent shocks and responses to risk can be modelled and households less able to cope with risk identified (Dercon and Krishnan 2000*b*; Christiaensen and Boisvert 2000; Amin *et al.* 2003). Kamanou and Morduch (Chapter 8) discuss this further, applied to data from Côte d'Ivoire. Elbers and Gunning (2003) take an alternative route, and explicitly consider growth dynamics linked to risk. They impose additional structure on the empirical model, allowing for

[11] More precisely, given that Jalan and Ravallion (2000) use the squared poverty gap (P_2), the non-poor in any given year will contribute to poverty in other years.

ex ante and *ex post* responses to risk, and estimate the model using simulation-based econometric techniques and panel data from Zimbabwe.

This still leaves the issue of how to express the welfare loss due to vulnerability, and it is not self-evident to obtain an agreed upon measure, not least since the term vulnerability is rather loosely used in economics and other disciplines (Alwang *et al.* 2001). One could define 'vulnerable households' as those likely to fall below an agreed upon poverty line in the future with a particular probability. Some non-poor households could be classified as vulnerable to poverty, while some poor households could be classified as not vulnerable to poverty in the future. These measures can be referred to as 'expected poverty' measures. Measures of this nature have been proposed in Christiaensen and Boisvert (2000), Chaudhuri *et al.* (2001), Pritchett *et al.* (2000). More generally, one could construct measures of vulnerability for different dimensions of poverty (such as health or nutrition) or measures that take into account the extent to which households are likely to fall below the poverty line (Kamanou and Morduch, Chapter 8). An alternative way of expressing vulnerability is closely linked to standard expected utility approaches (Ligon and Schechter 2003). Vulnerability is then the welfare cost related to the sum of the welfare loss from deviations of mean consumption relative to an agreed level ('the cost of poverty') plus a measure of the cost of risk, the difference of expected utility from the utility related to expected consumption. Its key advantage is its direct link with standard economic theory related to the behaviour towards risk, although the close link of expected poverty with standard poverty measures may be appealing to policymakers. In any case, vulnerability measures and profiles based on these measures could help policymakers design better policies.

Analysing vulnerability goes beyond deriving and estimating measures of vulnerability. Assessing in more detail the effectiveness of risk-management and coping strategies is just as important, not least for policymakers. The quantitative analysis of the effectiveness of households' risk strategies requires detailed panel data. In the economics literature, most analysis of risk and its consequences in developing countries is based on a handful of data sets, with most stylized facts entering into textbooks based on data from the three villages in South India covered by ICRISAT. It is not realistic to expect this level of detail for many developing countries.

While more work is needed on detailed panel data sets, household surveys, including cross-sectional surveys, could be used to derive insights into vulnerability and the strategies used by households to reduce it. Most panel data studies find that vulnerability to shocks is closely linked to human and physical capital assets (Deaton 1997; Baulch and Hoddinott 2000; Jalan and Ravallion 2000). These factors are similar to those identified as determining long-term poverty, although the extent to which they matter is usually different. Households with limited landholdings, few assets that can be liquidated, and limited education are typically most affected by the consequences of income risk. Their more limited ability to deal with risk is reflected in a lower mean level of consumption (due to consumption risk-averting actions, such as income skewing) or higher consumption fluctuations. Most cross-sectional household surveys contain information on physical and human capital, although in recent years, some of the instruments promoted for monitoring welfare changes appear to have been cutting back on these measures.

The total value of assets alone may not provide sufficient information on the ability to use self-insurance. It may not be possible to liquidate some assets. Other assets may lose their value during a crisis due to covariate risk. For these reasons, current asset values may not be a good indicator of the ability of an asset to buffer consumption. At least, information is needed on how well asset and food markets function in times of crisis.

Information on physical and human capital may not be sufficient for another reason. Households may be unable to enter into profitable diversification because of physical and human capital constraints or the lack of opportunity to use their capital. Well-functioning markets, facilitated by infrastructure and demand for the products the poor produced, are just as important. Individuals, for example, may possess the physical capital or skills needed to enter into handicrafts or trade as part of a coping strategy, but they may live in areas that are too remote for them to pursue these activities profitably.

Entry constraints and incentives to skew income towards low-risk activities imply that indexes measuring the degree of diversification (number of activities, share of off-farm income) are unlikely to be good measures of vulnerability. There is, for example, no reason why a household specializing in a low-risk activity faces higher risk than a household having a diversified portfolio of two very risky correlated activities. Furthermore, it is important to look at the income portfolio in conjunction with other risk-coping strategies, including self-insurance and informal insurance. Indeed, one important lesson from the literature surveyed is that the degree of diversification is endogenous to the other strategies used, including self-insurance, irrespective of constraints on diversification.

In short, data on physical and human capital, combined with information on the functioning of and opportunities in product, labour, and asset markets, could provide a good basis for identifying vulnerable households. Standard household surveys, including cross-sectional surveys, may include much of the relevant information at the household level.

Data on household involvement in informal insurance systems are also necessary to analyse vulnerability to poverty. The lack of such information is an important shortcoming of most standard household surveys. Understanding vulnerability and designing programmes to address these problems require information on the networks households can fall back on. Household surveys could include questions about households' association with other households and whether these associations include any insurance elements. Observing transfers and other linkages is one way of identifying these networks; direct questioning about opportunities for help in times of crisis is another (see Goldstein *et al.*, Chapter 11; Fafchamps and Lund 2003). Simple enumeration of networks may be useful, but care has to be taken to interpret any linkage or network as proof of the existence of informal insurance mechanisms. Insurance and support networks form part of social capital, but all social capital cannot be assumed to serve insurance purposes.

A full description of the opportunities available to households to cope with shocks also requires information on formal safety nets. All formal safety net programmes (including, for example, safety nets provided as part of a social security policy and public employment schemes) need to be taken into account in monitoring vulnerability or designing policy. In addition to the amount of support offered, the timeliness, targeting, and overall impact on household vulnerability need to be looked at. The impact of these programmes may be more limited than expected. Taking these factors into account may reveal that these programmes have less impact than they appear to have (Barrett *et al.*, Chapter 16; and Dercon and Krishnan, Chapter 14).

The different forms of capital and the opportunities to use them to reduce consumption risk can be identified by studying how households respond to shocks. It is useful, for example, to ask households how they handled idiosyncratic and common shocks in recent years. Questions could cover the impact of the shocks, whether the household adjusted its income-generating activities, how it used its assets, and whether it could rely on other people for support during the crisis. Households could also be surveyed about how they would respond if particular shocks hit them now. While qualitative in nature, these direct questions, combined with information on assets, could provide rich information on strategies to cope with risk and could inform policy design (e.g. see Udry 1994; Goldstein *et al.*, Chapter 11).

Economic reform programmes are bound to affect the opportunities and the ability of households to cope with risk—and not necessarily in a positive way. While more economic opportunities or better-functioning asset and product markets are likely to strengthen households' strategies, they may also expose households to other risks. For example, market liberalization may spread local price risk over larger geographical areas, but shocks in other areas would now be reflected in local prices as well. Vulnerability analysis should also take these factors into account.

Even new safety net programmes may have unwanted impacts, as a result of imperfect targeting or the crowding-out of households not covered by the programme. Policy design should require study of the informal links and insurance mechanisms that exist between the targeted group and other vulnerable groups that depend on informal arrangements. In general, if policies cannot be assumed to be exogenous to household behaviour and networks, detailed analysis of the shocks experienced by households and the way households cope with income risk should be conducted to inform policy. Such analysis is rarely conducted, however.

Households' ability to cope with risk by using assets and informal insurance can be gauged using both quantitative approaches, such as household surveys, and qualitative approaches, such as participatory assessment (see Moser 1998). The emphasis in both approaches on monitoring different forms of capital (human, physical, and social) and households' ability to use that capital when necessary. Both types of methodology view households as managers of complex portfolios of assets and suggest that policy should seek to improve their opportunities to use their assets.

I do not believe, as some researchers have proposed, that only qualitative methods should be used to study vulnerability and risk-coping strategies. Integrating qualitative data collection into quantitative household surveys is likely to yield less contradictory evidence than that provided by studies adopting one approach or the other. National household surveys are likely to be needed to measure the scale of vulnerability and its regional spread and diversity as well as to inform decisions about policies and priorities. The local nature of qualitative studies is likely to provide a more detailed understanding of vulnerability, but the results of such studies are difficult to aggregate and compare across areas.

1.6. CONCLUSIONS

Households in developing countries continue to face considerable risk, threatening their livelihood. In this chapter, I have discussed the different strategies households use to cope with this risk. I have focused on income-based strategies, on assets as self-insurance and on informal insurance arrangements. Households are constrained in using these strategies. Income-based strategies are limited because of entry-constraints into profitable activities, leaving the poor to concentrate on low-return, low-risk activities. Self-insurance is limited by access to assets and poor functioning of asset markets when a crisis hits the household. Informal insurance arrangements are affected by sustainability constraints, often excluding the poor from these arrangements; furthermore, economy-wide shocks cannot be handled by these arrangements.

The available evidence would suggest that there are substantial welfare losses linked to missing insurance and credit for the poor, via their impact on income and probably also on asset portfolios. It results in efficiency losses, more inequality, and higher current poverty. The losses in income levels may well translate into lower growth rates over time, and forms of poverty traps. Work on this long-run impact is under way using different methodologies, including Jalan and Ravallion (Chapter 5), Barrett (2003), Dercon (2004), and Elbers *et al.* (2003), but more work is definitely needed on this issue.

Economic policies could contribute to better protection against risk. Improved working of asset markets and macroeconomic stability would contribute to the usefulness of self-insurance. Increased access to alternative economic activities and increased opportunities could allow income-based strategies to be strengthened. Public safety nets could be a useful alternative, although initiatives to develop safety nets should take into account existing risk-coping strategies to understand their overall effects. Strengthening self-insurance may remain an insufficiently explored alternative, such as via group-based savings. More empirical research, however, is necessary to assess the functioning of informal risk-sharing arrangements and the consequences of interventions thereupon.

Obtaining estimates on the vulnerable population rather than the currently poor is very data-intensive, most likely requiring panel data to ensure that they reflect genuine vulnerability. Cross-section surveys could also provide useful insights. In particular, they could provide information on the underlying determinants of the risk-reducing strategies, in the form of physical, human, and social capital. They also could inform about the risk faced by households and the opportunities available to households, currently and during past crises. Qualitative studies could provide useful insights but incorporating some of these concerns in large quantitative household surveys is likely to yield important pay-offs in terms of better understanding of changes in welfare and vulnerability, and in terms of optimal policy design.

Appendix

1.A1. *The impact of asset market imperfections on the effectiveness of savings as insurance*

By extending Deaton's model and using some simulations, one can illustrate some of the problems arising from asset market imperfections in this context. Let the household maximize a standard intertemporally separable utility function u. Instantaneous utility v is defined over consumption c and strictly concave. Let δ be the rate of time preference. So at t, the household maximizes:

$$u_t = E_t \left[\sum_{\tau=t}^{T} (1 + \delta)^{t-\tau} v(c_\tau) \right]. \tag{1.A1}$$

Let y_t be risky income and A_t, the stock of assets. Assets have a risky return r_t. However, we also introduce the complication that assets are kept in another form than consumption units. With consumption prices as the numéraire, transforming consumption into assets is at a price p_t per unit of the asset. Asset prices are also risky. We can think of p_t as the terms of trade or the exchange rate between the asset and consumption, or equivalently, a measure of the purchasing power of assets at t. See above for some examples where this may be relevant.

The asset equation linking period t and $t + 1$ can be written as:

$$p_{t+1}A_{t+1} = \frac{p_{t+1}}{p_t}(p_tA_t + y_t - c_t)(1 + r_{t+1}). \tag{1.A2}$$

We introduce credit constraints in a simple way, stating that assets can never be non-negative, or

$$A_t \geq 0, \quad \forall t. \tag{1.A3}$$

Restricting c_t, y_t, p_t, and $(1 + r_t)$ to non-negative values only, we can write the optimal decision rule for consumption and savings between t and $t + 1$ as:

$$v'(c_t) = \max \left[v'(p_tA_t + y_t), E_t \left[\frac{p_{t+1}}{p_t} \frac{(1 + r_{t+1})}{(1 + \delta)} v'(c_{t+1}) \right] \right]. \tag{1.A4}$$

Households will consume and not save until intertemporally, appropriately discounted and valued expected marginal utility is equated to current marginal utility (second term on the right-hand side); however, if liquidity constraints bind, then the first term will be higher, so that all assets and income are used for consumption. Equation (1.A4) is standard, except for the relative prices of assets. Note that in this formulation, the path of prices (p_{t+1}/p_t) is relevant for evaluating expected future utility relative to current marginal utility, while only r_{t+1} matters, not r_t.[12] This allows us to consider different ways risk can enter into asset values over time.

Further analytical results on the consequences of risk in asset values are not obviously obtained. Using (1.A4), we can, however, conduct some numerical simulations using different assumptions about risk. We consider a finite lifecycle with $T = 20$ and assume that at the beginning of the first year, assets are equal to zero. Utility is logarithmic in consumption ($v(c_t) = \ln c_t$). Income is risky and we assume that income is identically and approximately normally distributed with mean 50 and a standard deviation of 10.[13] We use a rate of time preference of 5 per cent per period t. We can deploy different assumptions about the risk related to assets; however, in all cases, households know the distributions and moments of the random variables, but not the actual draw when making decisions (rational expectations). We also use different assumptions about the covariance between the risk in assets and the income risk.

To evaluate the consequences of different risk processes and their covariance, we simply calculate a *risk premium*. We define this as the consumption the household is willing to give up in the first year to obtain the optimal path of consumption without liquidity constraints (i.e. with perfect credit and insurance markets).[14] If the household did not have access to any form of savings or credit, in other words if consumption and income are equal in each period, then we find that, under our assumptions, the risk premium implied is 19.8 per cent. Obviously, access to savings instruments, however imperfect, could improve on this percentage. The success of self-insurance can be measured by the reduction in the risk-premium via savings and assets. We therefore also give the percentage of the total risk premium (i.e. of 19.8 per cent) that is *recovered* through using self-insurance.

We need to specify the different possible risk processes of assets and the covariance with income. Table 1.A1 summarizes the cases considered. In general we assume approximately normally distributed risk processes, using power points. We distinguish three cases. Case 1 considers a safe asset—no risk in terms of trade or in return. Case 2 considers a risky return to the asset, although no risk in the terms of trade. We assume a (approximately) bivariate normal distribution with correlation coefficient ρ_{yr} taking on different values to allow for different forms of covariance. For simplicity, all variables are independently and identically distributed over time.[15] Note that the values chosen imply a coefficient of variation in asset returns and in income of 0.20. Case 3 considers a safe return to the asset, but risk in the

---

[12] Formally, this means that current prices p_t are a state variable in the dynamic programming problem, besides the current value of assets plus income. When evaluating the future value of our assets, we need to take into account the current rate of exchange (terms of trade) between assets and consumption. The reason is that any reduction in consumption today needs to be transformed into assets using p_t, so that assets can be carried over to the future; in the future, to consume the asset, it should be transformed again into consumption units using p_{t+1}. Consequently, the current state at t is not fully described by the current means on hand, but we also need to consider the current price p_t.

[13] In particular, we approximate the normal distribution using 10 power points taken as mean values for each of the corresponding deciles of the distribution. In this way, we allow the computations to converge rather faster, but also avoid the problem of negative incomes, inherent if we assume the normal distribution.

[14] It is evaluated at zero assets and with income and asset prices equal to mean values.

Table 1.A1. *Values for simulations used*

Case	Assumptions used	Description
Case 1 Safe asset	$y_t \sim N(\mu_y, \sigma_y) = N(50, 10)$ $p_t \equiv 1,\ \forall t = 1, \ldots, 20.$ $r_t \equiv 0.05,\ \forall t$	Safe assets, with constant exchange rate between consumption and assets
Case 2 Covariate risk in asset returns	$((1 + r_t)y_t) \sim$ i.i.d. $N_2(\mu_r, \mu_y, \sigma_r, \sigma_y, \rho_{yr})$ $= N_2(1.05, 50, 0.21, 10, \rho_{yr})$ $\rho_{yr} \in \{-1, -0.5, 0, 0.5, 1\}$ $p_t \equiv 1,\ \forall t = 1, \ldots, 20.$	Bivariate normally distributed asset returns r_t and income y_t. Asset terms of trade p_t constant. Covariance between income and asset returns possible
Case 3 Covariate terms of trade risk	$(p_t, y_t) \sim$ i.i.d. $N_2(\mu_p, \mu_y, \sigma_p, \sigma_y, \rho_{yp})$ $= N_2(1.00, 50, 0.20, 10, \rho_{yp})$ $\rho_{yp} \in \{-1, -0.5, 0, 0.5, 1\}$ $r_t \equiv 0.05,\ \forall t = 1, \ldots, 20.$	Bivariate normally distributed asset terms of trade p_t and income y_t. Asset return r_t safe. Covariance between terms of trade and income possible
Case 4 Covariate risk in asset returns, lumpy assets	As in 2 but $A_t \in$], $p_t = 10$	Case 2 but lumpy asset to be bought and sold in units of 10 (1/5 of mean income)
Case 5 Covariate terms of trade risk, lumpy assets	As in 3 but $A_t \in$], $\mu_p = 10$	Case 3 but lumpy asset to be bought and sold in lumpy units with mean price of 10

terms of trade. Again, a (approximately) bivariate normal distribution with correlation coefficient ρ_{yp} is assumed. All variables are independently and identically distributed over time. The coefficient of variation of the terms of trade is also assumed to be 0.20. (Cases 4 and 5 are discussed below.)

The results of the numerical simulations using these assumptions are given in Table 1.A2. In each period, there is a draw of income and if applicable, of the terms of trade of assets and of the rate of return. On the basis of this information and assets carried over from last period, the household will decide its optimal consumption and asset holding. The algorithm uses the optimal programme, based on the backward solution of condition (4). The results show the consequences of risk in assets and

---

[15] Deaton (1992) introduces another complication: autocorrelation in income over time. In general, he finds that this makes self-insurance via savings far more costly, since much higher asset holdings have to be kept to obtain the same insurance (since bad years will come in sequence). We can expect that introducing autocorrelation in our simulations would have given exactly this effect, increasing the risk premium that remains after self-insurance.

Table 1.A2. *Risk premia with imperfect assets under liquidity constraints*

Case	Correlation coefficient between the asset and income risk process (ρ)	Risk premium as a percentage of the mean of the income process y[a]	One minus the risk premium, as a percentage of risk premium of the benchmark[b]

Benchmark
  Income risk, $y_t = c_t$
  (no assets)
	n.a.	19.8	0.0

Case 1 Safe asset	None	6.4	67.6
Case 2	−0.5	5.7	71.3
Covariate risk in	0	7.0	64.7
asset returns	0.5	8.2	58.7
Covariate risk in	1	9.4	52.5
asset returns			
Case 3	−0.5	−0.7	103.7
Covariate terms of	0	9.9	49.9
trade risk	0.5	16.7	15.7
	1	19.8	0.1
Case 4			
Case 2 with	0	9.6	51.4
lumpy asset	0.5	10.6	46.7
	1	11.5	41.9
Case 5	−0.5	1.7	91.5
Case 3 with	0	12.5	36.8
lumpy asset	0.5	19.0	4.1
	1	19.8	0.0

[a] The amount the household is willing to give up in the first period to get rid of all uncertainty.
[b] The percentage of the risk premium that is recovered by savings, that is, the value in column (3) divided by 19.8%.

Note: Simulations using equation (1.A4), (backward solution) with logarithmic utility, $T = 20$, $\delta = 0.05$.

covariance with income. First, comparing the benchmark with the case of a safe asset, we notice that two-thirds of the risk premium is recovered through self-insurance. However, if we introduce risk in the returns to assets, then this risk premium goes up, unless income and asset returns are negatively correlated. Negative correlation ($\rho_{yr} < 0$) simply means that whenever one wants to sell assets to smooth consumption due to a bad income draw, asset returns happen to be higher, so they are obviously more attractive and useful. Positive covariance gradually reduces the effectiveness of the asset as a buffer for consumption. When income and asset returns are perfectly correlated ($\rho_{yr} = 1$), the risk premium has increased by almost half. Self-insurance is still useful—the risk premium is still less than half than in the benchmark.

The situation changes when the risk is in the terms of trade or exchange rate between assets and consumption or income. Recall that positive covariance means pricy assets whenever income is high (and households want to buy), and very low exchange rates when income is low (and households want to sell). It is clear that terms of trade risk reduces the ability to smooth consumption via self-insurance. Even without covariate income and asset prices, this source of risk is very costly, increasing the risk-premium by half relative to the case of a safe asset: the non-zero probability that you may need to sell cheap and buy at high prices is causing this. Also, with a positive covariance between income and the asset terms of trade, self-insurance quickly loses its attractiveness— even with a correlation coefficient ρ_{py} of 0.5, very little benefit can be obtained from savings in this form. Although these are results based on numerical solutions, the difference is between risk in the returns to assets and in the terms of trade of assets is intrinsic, and not just dependent on the numerical example used. In the latter case, with positive covariance, not only results a bad draw for low asset values when you would want to sell them (this is also the case when there is a bad draw in asset returns). Also, when income is high, windfall income is transformed into assets only at a high price, when terms of trade risk is present (which is not the case when we have risk in asset returns). In other words, the current asset terms of trade affect the effectiveness of transforming income into assets.

The consequences of lumpy assets are also easily illustrated via simulations. In Tables 1.A1 and A2 we have added two more simulations: Cases 2 and 3 are repeated but with lumpy assets, so that they cost (on average) one-fifth of mean income. One can see that the risk premium increases quite significantly, and that the effectiveness of using the asset is reduced, especially if positive covariance is present. Dercon (1998) presents other simulations, such as on the number of periods that a poor household may have no assets left to use as a buffer stock, exposing it to the consequences of bad shocks.

REFERENCES

Alderman, H. (1998). 'Saving and Economic Shocks in Rural Pakistan'. *Journal of Development Economics*, 51(2), 343–66.

—— and C. Paxson (1994). 'Do the Poor Insure? A Synthesis of the Literature on Risk and Consumption in Developing Countries'. *Proceedings of the 4th International Economics Association Meeting*, Moscow.

——, J. Hoddinott, and B. Kinsey (2002). 'Long Term Consequences of Early Childhood Malnutrition', mimeo, Department of Economics, Dalhousie University, Halifax.

Alwang, J., P. Siegel, and S. Jorgensen (2001). 'Vulnerability: A View from Different Disciplines', Social Protection Discussion Paper Series 0115. Social Protection Unit, Human Development Network, World Bank, Washington, DC. May.

Amin, S., A. Roi, and G. Topa (2003). 'Does Microcredit Reach the Poor and Vulnerable? Evidence from Northern Bangladesh'. *Journal of Development Economics*, 70(1), 59–81.

Attanasio, O. and J. Rios-Rull (2000). 'Consumption Smoothing and Extended Families', mimeo, University of Pennsylvania.

Barrett, C. B. (2003). 'Rural Poverty Dynamics: Development Policy Implications', mimeo, Cornell University.

Baulch, B. and J. Hoddinott (2000). 'Economic Mobility and Poverty Dynamics in Developing Countries'. *Journal of Development Studies*, 36, 6.

Beegle, K., R. Dehejia, and R. Gatti (2003). 'Child Labor, Income Shocks and Access to Credit', mimeo, World Bank, Washington, DC.

Bell, C. (1988). 'Credit Markets, Contracts and Interlinked Transactions', in H. Chenery and T. N. Srinivasan (eds), *Handbook of Development Economics*, Vol. 1, Amsterdam: North-Holland.

Behrman, J. (1988). 'Intrahousehold Allocation of Nutrients in Rural India: Are Boys Favored? Do Parents Exhibit Inequality Aversion'. *Oxford Economic Papers*, 40, 32–54.

—— and A. Deolalikar (1990). 'The Intrahousehold Demand for Nutrients in Rural South India: Individual Estimates, Fixed Effects and Permanent Income'. *Journal of Human Resources*, 25, 665–96.

Besley, T. (1994). 'Savings, Credit and Insurance', in J. Behrman and T. N. Srinivasan (eds), *Handbook of Development Economics*, Vol. IIIA, Amsterdam: North-Holland.

—— (1995). 'Nonmarket Institutions for Credit and Risk Sharing in Low-Income Countries'. *Journal of Economic Perspectives*, 9(summer), 115–27.

Bevan, D., P. Collier, and J. W. Gunning (1991). *Peasants and Governments*. Oxford: Oxford University Press.

Binswanger, H. and J. McIntire (1987). 'Behavioral and Materina Determinants of Production Relations in Land-Abundant Tropical Agriculture'. *Economic Development and Cultural Change*, 36, 73–99.

Bliss, C. and N. Stern (1982). *Palanpur: The Economy of an Indian Village*. Oxford: Oxford University Press.

Chaudhuri, S. and C. Paxson (1994). 'Consumption Smoothing and Income Seasonality in Rural India'. *Discussion Paper* 173, Princeton University Research Program in Development Studies.

——, J. Jalan, and A. Suryahadi (2001). 'Assessing Household Vulnerability to Poverty: A Methodology and Estimates for Indonesia', draft, Columbia University, New York.

Christiaensen, L. and R. Boisvert (2000). 'On Measuring Households Food Vulnerability: Case Evidence from Northern Mali'. *Working Paper* 2000–05 (March), Department of Agricultural, Resource and Managerial Economics, Cornell University.

Coate, S. and M. Ravallion (1993). 'Reciprocity without Commitment: Characterisation and Performance of Informal Insurance Arrangements'. *Journal of Development Economics*, 40, 1–24.

Conning, J. and M. Kevane (2002). 'Community Based Targeting Mechanisms for Social Safety Nets: A Critical Review'. *World Development*, 30(3), 375–94.

Corbett, J. (1988). 'Famine and Household Coping Strategies'. *World Development*, 16, 9.

Cox, D. and E. Jimenez (1992). 'Social Security and Private Transfers in Developing Countries: the Case of Peru'. *The World Bank Economic Review*, 6(1), 115–69.

Czukas, K., M. Fafchamps, and C. Udry (1998). 'Drought and Saving in West-Africa: Are Livestock a Buffer Stock'. *Journal of Development Economics*, 55(2), 273–305.

Davies, S. (1996). *Adaptable Livelihoods*. London: Macmillan.

Deaton, A. (1991). 'Savings and Liquidity Constraints'. *Econometrica*, 59(5), 1221–1248.

—— (1992). 'Household Saving in LDCs: Credit Markets, Insurance and Welfare'. *Scandinavian Journal of Economics*, 94(2), 253–73.

—— (1997). *The Analysis of Household Surveys: A Microeconomic Approach*. Baltimore, MD: Johns Hopkins University Press.

Dercon, S. (1996). 'Risk, Crop Choice and Savings: Evidence from Tanzania'. *Economic Development and Cultural Change*, 44(3), 385–514.

—— (1998). 'Wealth, Risk and Activity Choice: Cattle in Western Tanzania'. *Journal of Development Economics*, 55(1), 1–42.

—— (2002*a*). 'Income Risk, Coping Strategies and Safety Nets'. *World Bank Research Observer*, 17, 141–66.

—— (2002*b*). *The Impact of Economic Reform on Rural Households in Ethiopia*. Poverty Dynamics in Africa Series. Washington, DC: World Bank and Oxford University.

—— (2004). 'Growth and Shocks: Evidence from Rural Ethiopia'. *Journal of Development Economics*, 74(2), 309–21.

—— and J. De Weerdt (2002). 'Risk-sharing Networks and Insurance Against Illness'. *Working Paper Series* 2002-17. Oxford: Centre for the Study of African Economies.

—— and P. Krishnan (1996). 'Income Portfolios in Rural Ethiopia and Tanzania: Choices and Constraints'. *Journal of Development Studies*, 32(6), 850–75.

—— and —— (2000*a*). 'Vulnerability, Seasonality and Poverty in Ethiopia'. *Journal of Development Studies*, 36, 6.

—— and —— (2000*b*). 'In Sickness and in Health: Risk-Sharing within Households in Ethiopia'. *Journal of Political Economy*, 108(4), 688–727.

De Waal, A. (1987). *Famines that Kills: Darfur Sudan, 1984–85*. Oxford: Clarendon Press.

Elbers, C., J. W. Gunning, and B. Kinsey (2003). 'Growth and Risk: Methodology and Micro Evidence', mimeo, Free University, Amsterdam.

Eswaran, M. and A. Kotwal (1989). 'Credit as Insurance in Agrarian Economies'. *Journal of Development Economics*, 31(1), 37–53.

—— and —— (1990). 'Implications of Credit Market Constraints for Risk Behaviour in Less Developed Economics'. *Oxford Economic Papers*, 42, 473–82.

Fafchamps, M. (1999). 'Rural Poverty, Risk and Development'. *FAO Economic and Social Development Paper* No. 144.

—— and S. Lund (2003). 'Risk-Sharing Networks in Rural Philippines'. *Journal of Development Economics*, 71(2), 261–87.

Foster, A. D. (1995). 'Prices, Credit Markets and Child Growth in Low-Income Rural Areas'. *The Economic Journal*, 105(May), 551–70.

Frankenberg, E. (1999). 'The Real Costs of Indonesia's Economic Crisis', mimeo, RAND.

Gaiha, R. and A. Deolalikar (1993). 'Persistent, Expected and Innate Poverty: Estimates for Semi-Arid Rural South India 1975–1984'. *Cambridge Journal of Economics*, 17(4), 409–21.

Grimard, F. (1997). 'Household Consumption Smoothing through Ethnic Ties: Evidence from Côte d'Ivoire'. *Journal of Development Economics*, 53, 391–422.

Gertler, P. and Gruber, J. (2002). 'Insuring Consumption Against Illness'. *American Economic Review*, 92(1), 51–76.

Hayashi, F., J. Altonji, and L. Kotlikoff (1996). 'Risk-Sharing between and within Families'. *Econometrica*, 64(2), 261–94.

Hoff, K. (1996). 'Informal Insurance Schemes: An Equilibrium Analysis', mimeo, University of Maryland.

Holzmann, R. and S. Jørgensen (2000). 'Social Risk Management: A New Conceptual Framework for Social Protection and Beyond'. *Social Protection Discussion Paper Series* No. 6. Washington, DC: World Bank.

Jacoby, H. and E. Skoufias (1997). 'Risk, Financial Markets and Human Capital in a Developing Country'. *Review of Economic Studies*, 64(3), 311–36.

Jalan, J. and M. Ravallion (2000). 'Is Transient Poverty Different? Evidence from Rural China'. *Journal of Development Studies*, 36, 6.

—— and —— (2001). 'Behavioral Responses to Risk in Rural China'. *Journal of Development Economics*, 66(1), 23–49.

Kinsey, B., K. Burger, and J. W. Gunning (1998). 'Coping with Drought in Zimbabwe: Survey Evidence on Responses of Rural Households to Risk'. *World Development*, 26(1), 89–110.

Kochar, A. (1995). 'Explaining Household Vulnerability to Idiosyncratic Income Shocks'. *American Economic Review, AEA Papers and Proceedings*, 85(2), 159–64.

Ligon, E. and L. Schechter (2003). 'Measuring Vulnerability', *Economic Journal*, 113(486), C95–C102.

——, J. Thomas, and T. Worrall (2002). 'Informal Insurance with Limited Commitment: Theory and Evidence from Village Economies'. *Review of Economic Studies*, 69(1), 209–44.

Lim, Y. and R. Townsend (1994). 'Currency, Transaction Patterns, and Consumption Smoothing: Theory and Measurement in ICRISAT Villages', mimeo, University of Chicago.

Lustig, N. (ed.). (2001). *Shielding the Poor. Social Protection in the Developing World*. Washington, DC: Brookings Institution Press.

Morduch, J. (1990). 'Risk, Production and Saving: Theory and Evidence from Indian Households', manuscript, Harvard University.

—— (1995). 'Income Smoothing and Consumption Smoothing'. *Journal of Economic Perspectives*, 9(summer), 103–14.

—— (1999). 'Between the State and the Market: Can Informal Insurance Patch the Safety Net?'. *World Bank Research Observer*, 14(2), 187–207.

Moser, C. (1998). 'The Asset Vulnerability Framework: Reassessing Urban Poverty Reduction Strategies'. *World Development*, 26(1), 1–19.

Paxson, C. (1993). 'Consumption and Income Seasonality in Thailand'. *Journal of Political Economy*, 101(1), 39–72.

Platteau, J.-P. (1997). 'Mutual Insurance as an Elusive Concept in Traditional Rural Communities'. *Journal of Development Studies*, 33(6), 764–96.

Pritchett, L., A. Suryahadi, and S. Sumarto (2000). 'Quantifying Vulnerability to Poverty: A Proposed Measure, Applied to Indonesia'. *Policy Research Working Paper* 2437. Washington, DC: World Bank.

Rahmato, D. (1991). *Famine and Survival Strategies, A Case Study from Northeast Ethiopia*. Uppsala: Nordiska Afrikainstitutet.

Ravallion, M. (1988). 'Expected Poverty under Risk-Induced Welfare Variability'. *Economic Journal*, 98(March), 1173–83.

Reardon, T. (1997). 'Using Evidence of Household Income Diversification to Inform Study of the Rural Nonfarm Labor Market in Africa'. *World Development*, 25, 5.

——, A. A. Fall, V. Kelly, C. Delgado, P. Matlon, J. Hopkins, and O. Badiane (1994). 'Is Income Diversification Agriculture-led in the West African Semi-Arid Tropics', in A. Atsain, S. Wangwe, and A. G. Drabek (eds), *Economic Policy Experience in Africa: What have We Learned*. Washington, DC: IFPRI, pp. 207–30.

——, C. Delgado, and P. Matlon (1988). 'Coping with Household-Level Food Insecurity Drought-Affected Areas of Burkina Faso'. *World Development*, 16(9), 1148–70.

Rose, E. (1999). 'Consumption Smoothing and Excess Female Mortality in Rural India'. *Review of Economics and Statistics*, 81(1), 41–9.

Rosenzweig, M. (1988). 'Risk, Implicit Contracts and the Family in Rural Areas of Low Income Countries'. *Economic Journal*, 98(1), 148–70.

—— and H. Binswanger (1993). 'Wealth, Weather Risk and the Composition and Profitability of Agricultural Investments'. *Economic Journal*, 103, 56–78.

—— and K. Wolpin (1993). 'Credit Market Constraints, Consumption Smoothing, and the Accumulation of Durable Production Assets in Low-income Countries: Investment in Bullocks in India'. *Journal of Political Economy*, 101(2), 223–44.

Thomas, D., K. Beegle, E. Frankenberg, B. Sikoki, J. Strauss, and G. Teruel (2004). 'Education in a Crisis'. *Journal of Development Economics*, 74(1), 53–85.

Townsend, R. M. (1994). 'Risk and Insurance in Village India'. *Econometrica*, 62(3), 539–91.

—— (1995). 'Consumption Insurance: An Evaluation of Risk-Bearing Systems in Low-Income Economies'. *Journal of Economic Perspectives*, 9(summer), 83–102.

Udry, C. (1991). 'Credit Markets in Northern Nigeria: Credit as Insurance in a Rural Economy'. *World Bank Economic Review*, 4(3), 251–71.

—— (1994). 'Risk and Insurance in a Rural Credit Market: An empirical Investigation of Northern Nigeria'. *Review of Economic Studies*, 61(3), 495–526.

World Bank (2000). *World Development Report 2000/01: Attacking Poverty*. Washington, DC: World Bank.

2

Consumption Smoothing Across Space: Testing Theories of Risk-Sharing in the ICRISAT Study Region of South India

JONATHAN MORDUCH

2.1. THE ICRISAT VILLAGE LEVEL STUDIES AND MODERN DEVELOPMENT ECONOMICS

In the history of modern development economics, no single data set has yielded as many important microeconomic papers as the ICRISAT (International Crops Research Institute for the Semi-Arid Tropics) Village Level Studies. Of the twelve papers collected by Bardhan and Udry (2000) as highlights of recent empirical work on development issues, for example, one-quarter draw on the ICRISAT studies. Scores of doctoral dissertations and scholarly articles have taken advantage of the data, collectively shaping policy debate and research directions across the field.[1]

Household-level data sets typically have three relevant dimensions. First is the number of households interviewed each round. Second is the number of rounds repeated on the same households. And third is the richness and variety of questions asked. Most surveys are strong on cross-sectional size, weak on repeated rounds, and modest on the extent of substantive coverage. The ICRISAT surveys, in contrast, are weak in terms of number of households surveyed (just forty in each year from each village) but have until recently been unparalleled in the combination of length and breadth. Access to ten years of consumption and income data on many of the households and extensive modules on transactions and production have made possible an

The chapter is a substantial revision of work initially completed as the third chapter of my Ph.D. dissertation. That work profited from discussions with Anne Case, Madhur Gautam, Larry Katz, Masao Ogaki, Martin Ravallion, Mark Rosenzweig, Peter Timmer, and Tom Walker. Subsequent work has benefited from conversations with Debraj Ray, Angus Deaton, and Robert Townsend. Research was funded by the Alfred P. Sloan Foundation and the IRIS Center at the University of Maryland. The revision was supported by UNU-WIDER, Helsinki, Finland. Data was kindly provided by the ICRISAT. Views and errors are my responsibility.

[1] Much of the early work with the ICRISAT data is surveyed by Thomas Walker and James Ryan (1990), who along with R. P. Singh, Hans Binswanger, and Narpat Jodha, were instrumental in conceiving and implementing the longitudinal studies.

outpouring of work on dynamic issues. Despite a cross-section of just 120 households per year, the data are still yielding valuable new insights seventeen years after the last wave was collected in 1983–4 (e.g. Ligon *et al.* 2000).

The data were collected between 1974 and 1984 as a project of ICRISAT. The Institute serves mainly as an agronomic research station, and its center in India (another center is in Burkina Faso) is located amid experimental fields outside the city of Hyderabad. The surveyed villages are scattered across India's semi-arid tropics, an area of predominantly rainfed agriculture with considerable climatic variability from season to season and year to year. Levels of rainfall can fluctuate widely, and in parts droughts occur once a decade or more. But, while villages face common weather shocks, climatic and soil conditions are heterogeneous within villages such that much risk is idiosyncratic even in small regions. A simple decomposition of household income shows that as much as three-quarters of income variation in these villages is due to idiosyncratic shocks, suggesting substantial scope for risk-sharing even within villages. These conditions have made the ICRISAT study area a particularly promising environment for investigating communal risk-coping strategies.

As a result, the work to date allows a window on rural South India as well as critical perspectives on modern empirical development economics more broadly. I focus below exclusively on work surrounding risk-sharing and insurance, although the ICRISAT data have also yielded important work on nutrition, crop choice, tenancy contracts, labour supply, poverty dynamics, and financial institutions.

I draw two main lessons. The first is that while empirical work has been driven by the theory of communal risk-sharing, in this period the most important risk-coping mechanism by far appears to be self-insurance. The second is that self-insurance is limited and risk-coping strategies are costly, suggesting opportunities for institutions that can help households more effectively save, work, and accumulate buffer stocks to mitigate risk.

2.2. DATA

The surveys[2] cover ten villages in five districts spread across different agroclimatic zones of the ICRISAT study region (Mahbubnagar in Andhra Pradesh, Sholapur and Akola in Maharashtra, Sabarkantha in Gujarat, and Raisen in Madhya Pradesh), but complete consumption data is available from just three villages (one from each of the first three districts). Aurepalle is in Andhra Pradesh while Shirapur and Kanzara are in Maharashtra state. The villages are poor and the main economic activity is dryland farming, with some irrigation.

Forty households were sampled from each village every year: ten landless, ten small-scale farmers, ten medium-scale, and ten large-scale. In 1975 the largest village, Aurepalle, had just 475 people and the forty surveyed households make up 8, 12, and 21 per cent of the overall populations of Aurepalle, Shirapur, and Kanzara, respectively.

---

[2] The descriptive information on the villages in this section is from Walker and Ryan (1990). The data are available from the Center for Data Sharing at the Economic Growth Center at Yale University.

While the survey continued for ten years, few households stayed in the sample for the entire period. If attention is restricted to the eight years, 1976–83, for example, a complete series of annual food consumption data is available for just fifteen of forty original households in Aurepalle, three in Shirapur, and thirty-five in Kanzara. Since the panels are incomplete and unbalanced, estimates of fixed effects in Aurepalle and Kanzara are less precise than often assumed in the long panel. But much of the drop off is at the end of the period, so a full panel exists for the shorter period, 1976–81 for thirty-four households in Aurepalle and thirty-six each in Shirapur and Kanzara.

The original intent was not to collect consumption data as a primary focus. But, seeing its potential value, ICRISAT researchers formed consumption measures using the data collected on household transactions (special nutritional surveys were also completed, but only for a limited duration). The consumption data are thus not drawn from expenditure diaries of the sort routine in household surveys (e.g. the World Bank's Livings Standards Measurement Studies), and data reliability has been debated.

Figure 2.1 displays the most evident source of concern. As in many household studies (Deaton 1997), measured consumption is substantially lower than measured income in all years (except for Shirapur in 1980). In Aurepalle in 1976, for example, average measured income per capita is 394 rupees while average measured consumption is 281 rupees. In 1981, the ratio is 612 : 449. If true, the households here are saving and investing in huge quantities, but this is implausible given the levels of poverty and lack of appealing saving instruments. The discrepancies stem mostly from the data on richer households, with consumption of poorer households tending to be quite close to income levels. In addition, the first and last years suffered from start-up and shut-down problems, and the quality of non-food consumption data slips after 1981 (see Townsend 1994, for information on food coverage).

Ravallion and Chaudhuri (1997) draw on the work of Madhur Gautam (1992) to create an alternative consumption measure based on cash flow data. It corrects some problems but still shows an unexpectedly sharp drop in 1982–3, under-predicts consumption levels, and yields some predicted values that are negative. Ravallion and Chaudhuri use instrumental variables to address these problems and find that the instruments make a large difference.

Here, consistent with Townsend (1994), the focus rests with the data distributed by ICRISAT, but I narrow the focus to data collected between 1976 through 1981 for total consumption and 1976 through 1983 for food consumption only. In addition, three observations were deleted for which either consumption growth, income growth, or food consumption growth were implausibly large (larger than 300 per cent). The resulting samples are of the most even quality, and the most problematic results that emerge when using the entire series are avoided.

2.3. PERSPECTIVES ON VILLAGE ECONOMIES

Economists have considered villages to be 'natural' insurance units: locations conducive to insurance provided via informal, reciprocity-based, repeated relationships between neighbours. Giving 'gifts' to those in need (with expectation of reciprocity) is the most

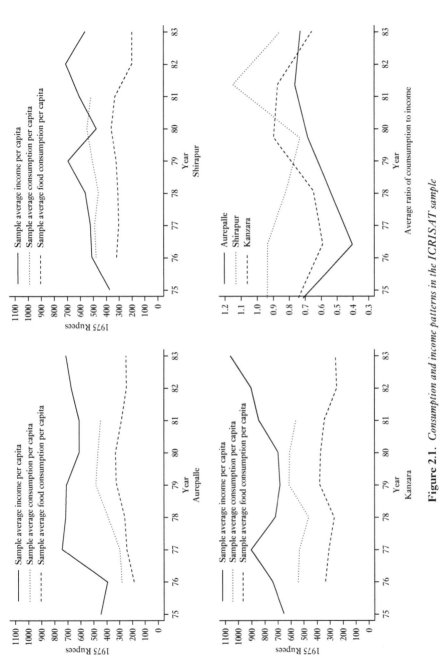

Figure 2.1. *Consumption and income patterns in the ICRISAT sample*

investigated phenomenon, but a range of more subtle relationships command attention as well. Gift-giving has also been much investigated by anthropologists (e.g. Malinowski 1922; Mauss 1967; Sahlins 1976), economic historians (e.g. Polanyi 1944), and political scientists (e.g. Popkin 1979; Scott 1986).

Not surprisingly, views are sharply divided. Anthropologists for the most part downplay the place of gifts and other transfers as a product of the rational calculus associated with informal insurance systems; instead they highlight roles in securing social status and signalling commitment to the community (e.g. Malinowski 1922; Mauss 1967). Other observers of village life in India suggest that the notion of an integrated village economy is often at odds with realities of segmentation, conflict, and discrimination (e.g. on South India, see Epstein *et al.* 1998). Polanyi (1944) stakes out a middle ground by arguing that, to the extent it occurred, redistribution was done to maintain a basic sense of 'justice' in a sense close to that of John Rawls (1971), but that more extensive redistribution was typically limited. Another view is that redistribution may occur partly out of self-interest, to raise the well being of the community as a whole and limit negative externalities such as disease and crime.

Still, the idea that a village should be a natural insurance unit remains powerful for most economists trained in the tradition of Coase. The problems of imperfect information and costly enforcement that hinder broad-based insurance markets are limited in small communities. Villagers tend to know a good deal about what their neighbours are up to, and they can fall back on 'informal' enforcement mechanisms like social sanctions when disputes arise. Experimental research has also shown that ICRISAT households care about risk and use a wide variety of instruments to reduce it (Binswanger 1981). Since supply and demand are both in force, it stands to reason that there ought to be a lot of insurance activity. And it is true that many insurance mechanisms exist within villages. Still, it remains unclear how effective these mechanisms are when taken together, where and how strongly constraints bind, and the extent to which gift-giving is an important feature of informal insurance systems (Morduch 1995, 1999). Rosenzweig (1988), for example, shows that reciprocal transfers within extended families (cutting across villages) are actively used to address risk, but the magnitudes are so small that insurance due to family-based transfers is not close to being complete (Morduch 1999). This evidence is not inconsistent with intra-village risk-sharing, but it suggests that the village may not be the most natural locus of insurance activity.

Robert Townsend's (1994) paper on the ICRISAT villages provides a structured way to ask how effective households' coping mechanisms are when taken together. Specifically, how well, in the end, can households protect consumption levels in the face of idiosyncratic income shocks? His insight was to derive testable implications from dynamic general equilibrium models, beginning with an explicit social planner's problem as a benchmark. Like other approaches built around testing exclusion restrictions, inability to reject the benchmark model is highly informative. On the other hand, rejecting the model when several plausible alternatives exist is less informative. Townsend's initial work was so striking because it came very close to *not rejecting* the full risk-sharing model.

Subsequent work with more elaborate models and alternative data has mainly rejected the full risk-sharing model, setting out a search for models that perform better with the data. Researchers inspired by Townsend have turned to identifying constraints that keep the full risk-sharing model from holding (following examples from Townsend's own work in Thailand). The two leading contenders are information asymmetries and enforcement problems that prevent effective long-term contracting between villagers. Specification errors and various forms of unobserved heterogeneity are plausible too, in isolation or in combination with the other concerns. On top of this, it is seldom easy to distinguish these newer models of imperfect village-based insurance from simpler models of imperfect self-insurance.

The newer work strengthens arguments for moving away from the village as the 'natural' level at which to organize informal insurance. In recent theoretical work that draws inspiration from the ICRISAT studies, for example, Genicot and Ray (2003) show that with imperfect enforceability of contracts, stable insurance groups at levels below *or above* the village-level can exist even when village-level arrangements break down. The counter-intuitive arguments do not require exogenous costs to group formation but hinge instead on the changing benefits of risk-pooling under self-enforcing insurance arrangements. The tension lies between the benefits of pooling risks with more people versus the tendency for larger groups to subdivide into smaller coalitions; they show that the stability of coalitions is highly non-linear as their size changes. The results reinforce the call to focus beyond the village-level.

The next section provides evidence on idiosyncratic versus aggregate shocks, and the concluding section returns to disentangling underlying mechanisms and policy implications. The approach and extensions are described in the sections in between, with particular attention to risk-sharing within groups identified by caste.

2.4. IDIOSYNCRATIC VERSUS COMMON INCOME SHOCKS

The notion of a 'common' income shock versus an idiosyncratic shock is often used loosely, but precision is essential. Shocks may be common to a neighbourhood, a village or town, a district, a province, a country, or a broader region. The degree of 'commonness' is critical to how easy it is to protect against the shock. Idiosyncrasy, in turn, only has meaning if framed with regard to a specific place in the hierarchy of scope. Here, the focus is just on shocks at the village-level, so idiosyncrasy is gauged relative to patterns in the village. A shock that is common to an entire caste, may thus be idiosyncratic within a given village—and it is that idiosyncrasy that is at issue here.

A simple decomposition of the income process for each village suggests that idiosyncratic risk accounts for as much as 75–96 per cent of income variation.[3] This can be seen by decomposing observed income (Y_{it}) of each household i in each period t as a multiplicative function of a base income level specific to the household (Y_i), a factor

---

[3] Throughout the chapter, 'income' refers to total income from all activities of the household (including non-market activities), less transfers received. Where noted, household income is deflated by measures of family size.

Table 2.1. *Idiosyncratic elements in income and consumption, 1976/7 to 1981/2*

Village	$(1 - R^2)^a$	Ratio of variance of consumption[b]	Standard deviation	$(1 - R^2)^c$
Aurepalle	0.75	0.57	(0.51)	0.60
Shirapur	0.96	0.09	(0.09)	0.96
Kanzara	0.84	0.50	(0.77)	0.77

[a] Here $1 - R^2$ is calculated from regression of total income on year fixed effects.
[b] Ratio of variance of consumption under complete risk-sharing of variance under autarky.
[c] Here $1 - R^2$ is calculated from regression of total consumption on year fixed effects.

Note: Data are in 1975 rupees, deflated by family size. Equations were estimated with fixed household effects and five-year dummies.

which scales the base level up and down for common shocks to the village (τ_t), a factor which does the same for idiosyncratic shocks to the household (τ_{it}), and measurement error (ε_{it}):

$$Y_{it} = Y_i \tau_t \tau_{it} \varepsilon_{it}.$$

With no other assumptions, this is an identity. By taking the logarithm, it can be estimated as a regression equation, where the household and common village factors are treated as fixed effects. Measurement error and idiosyncratic shocks are contained in the residual, and their combined magnitude can be inferred from $1 - R^2$ of the regression. This gives an upper bound on the variance of the uncorrelated idiosyncratic components as a fraction of the variance of total income.

Column 1 of Table 2.1 presents these statistics for regressions run on six-year samples in each of the three villages. The figures show that idiosyncratic elements explain as much as three-quarters of income variation in Aurepalle, up to 95 per cent in Shirapur, and up to more than 80 per cent in Kanzara. Even if half of residual variation is due to measurement error, these figures are striking.[4]

While there appears to be substantial scope for risk-sharing in the villages, what is its potential in reducing total household risk? The relative importance of the time and space components can be gauged by comparing the variation in consumption if risk-sharing is complete (but inter-temporal smoothing is not possible) to the variation of consumption with no smoothing at all. If consumption smoothing is impossible, neither across space nor time, consumption in each period equals income, $C_{it} = Y_{it}$ and the variance of household consumption (between period 1 and T) is:

$$\frac{1}{T}\sum_{t=1}^{T}(Y_{it} - Y_i)^2,$$

---

[4] When income is not deflated by household size, $1 - R^2$ is 0.80, 0.83, and 0.79 for Aurepalle, Shirapur, and Kanzara, respectively. Similar results are found for income disaggregated by source. See Morduch (1991).

where Y_i is the household's sample average. If there was complete pooling of idiosyncratic shocks, subject to the condition that there was no income redistribution on average (i.e. the average of household i's consumption over the sample is still Y_i), then $C_{it} = \theta_i Y_t$. Here, Y_t is total village income in period t and θ_i reflects the share of total income allocated to the household. Under these assumptions, the share is:

$$\theta_i = \frac{(1/T)\sum_{t=1}^{T} Y_{it}}{(1/T)\sum_{t=1}^{T}\sum_{i=1}^{N} Y_{it}} = \frac{Y_i}{\sum_{i=1}^{N} Y_i},$$

where there are N households in the village. This is the fraction of village income over the entire sample attributable to household i. A measure of the potential for risk-sharing in eliminating a household's total risk is then:

$$\frac{\sum_{t=1}^{T}(\theta_i Y_t - Y_i)^2}{\sum_{t=1}^{T}(Y_{it} - Y_i)^2}.$$

This is the variance of consumption over time under complete sharing for household i, as a fraction of the variance under autarky.

Column 2 of Table 2.1 reports the average of these statistics across households for each village. The calculations show that in Aurepalle the average variance of consumption under complete risk-sharing would be nearly 60 per cent of the variance under autarky. While a 40 per cent average reduction is relatively large, households still face most of the variation they would without risk-sharing. The situation is very different in Shirapur, where complete risk-sharing would reduce total income risk to less than 10 per cent. The calculations for Kanzara are closer to those for Aurepalle: on average half of total risk would remain under complete sharing.

Together, these results and the calculations suggest that risk-sharing can be important in reducing total income risk. How does this potential translate into practice? Column 4 of Table 2.1 reports on the extent of idiosyncratic components actually found in total consumption. The results are close to the figures in column 1 for income, suggesting that there is limited consumption smoothing in the villages, either across space or time. Only in Aurepalle do any of the idiosyncratic components in consumption appear to be mitigated. There, 60 per cent of total consumption variability is idiosyncratic, whereas this is true for 75 per cent of income variability. In Shirapur and Kanzara, 96 and 85 per cent of consumption variability is idiosyncratic, respectively. As with income, this is a great deal more than can be explained by measurement error.

These preliminary results leave little cause for optimism with regard to finding evidence of complete risk-sharing (or even substantial partial risk-sharing), but a more rigorous set of tests must be implemented before conclusions are drawn. In those tests, some instances of risk-sharing are evident, although the weight of the findings echoes those above.

2.5. THEORY

Household consumption decisions. Imagine a household that makes consumption and saving decisions while facing uncertain future income. The household derives utility from its consumption each period, such that consumption at time t, C_t, generates utility $U(C_t)$; this utility function is assumed to be time and state separable. A forward-looking household (with discount factor δ) will choose consumption in each period to maximize expected lifetime utility:

$$E_t \sum_{k=0}^{T-t} \delta^k U(C_{t+k}), \tag{2.1}$$

subject to the constraints that assets at the start of period $t + 1$, A_{t+1}, grow with net savings balances and income, Y_{t+1}; consumption is always non-negative; and the household is not in debt in the final period T (the transversality condition):

$$A_{t+1} = (A_t - C_t)(1 + r_{t+1}) + Y_{t+1},$$
$$C_{t+k} \geq 0 \quad \text{for } k = 0, \dots, T - t, \tag{2.2}$$
$$A_T \geq 0.$$

All uncertainty is introduced via stochastic income. No restrictions have been placed on the ability to borrow and save, but, even with perfect credit markets, households face risk due to unanticipated shocks.

Tests for risk-sharing. In principle, households can also reduce exposure to unanticipated shocks through state-contingent transfers and contracts that benefit those with bad luck, as set out by Townsend (1994). The optimal outcome corresponds to that determined by a fictional social planner who seeks to maximize the (socially weighted) sum of lifetime utilities across households:

$$\max \sum_{i=1}^{N} \theta_i \left[E_t \sum_{k=0}^{T-t} \delta^k U_i(C_{i,t+k}) \right], \tag{2.3}$$

(where i indexes households) subject to non-negativity and transversality constraints and the village resource constraint:

$$\sum_{i=1}^{N} A_{it+1} = \sum_{i=1}^{N}(A_{it} - C_{it})(1 + r_{t+1}) + \sum_{i=1}^{N} Y_{it+1}, \tag{2.4}$$

which is just the sum of equation (2.2) over all of the N households in the village. The social weights, θ, are bounded by zero and together they must sum to 1.

This framework could arise from several scenarios. Most directly, choices made by village leaders who are entrusted with basic allocation decisions for the village might look approximately like the problem in (2.3) and (2.4). This would be analogous to the extended family choice framework of Altonji *et al.* (1992), where the weights are determined according to the strength of altruism towards each family member. If the social planner is a utilitarian, the weights would be equal. Alternatively, such a framework could arise as a solution to a competitive game among self-interested actors, where the weights partly reflect bargaining power. Or, with the weights a function of household wealth, the framework could correspond to a decentralized competitive solution with complete insurance markets (Townsend 1994). Whichever the mechanism, the first best result is a full pooling of risks.

The first-order conditions of the problem yield that in every period:

$$\theta_i U'(C_{it}) = \theta_j U'(C_{jt}) = \alpha_t \tag{2.5}$$

for all households i and j, where α_t is the Lagrange multiplier on the village resource constraint—that is, the marginal utility of village income. Equation (2.5) says that at the optimum the weighted marginal utilities of all households are equal to each other (and equal to the marginal utility of village income). The social planner cannot transfer resources from one household to another and improve the weighted sum of their utility; at the optimum any further transfers reduce social welfare. Since equation (2.5) holds in all periods, it must then hold that:

$$\frac{U'(C_{it+1})}{U'(C_{it})} = \frac{U'(C_{jt+1})}{U'(C_{jt})} = \frac{\alpha_{t+1}}{\alpha_t}, \tag{2.6}$$

for any pair of periods and any pair of households. This means that the *growth* of marginal utilities for all households is also equal under the null hypothesis. Here, the social weights neatly cancel out, leaving a result that is potentially testable.

2.6. EMPIRICAL APPROACH

The formal tests for risk-sharing here follow from Townsend's (1994) approach, which, under additional assumptions about the form of utility functions, draws on equation (2.6) to exploit the fact that the consumption of households in each village can be described as a system of Frisch demands in which the marginal utility of village income is common to the sample. The first test of equation (2.6) is an exclusion restriction (or excess sensitivity) test similar to that common now in finance and macroeconomics. This is the main form of the tests used by Townsend (1994), Morduch (1991), and Ravallion and Chaudhuri (1997).

Deaton (1997) describes a second test, implemented in work on Taiwan, Britain, and the United States with Christina Paxson. If there is full risk-sharing, the cross-sectional variance of the growth of marginal utility (where the growth rate is measured for households across time, and the variance is then measured across households in the cross-section) should be zero since growth rates ought to be identical for all. But with imperfect sharing, some people do better and some do worse. Since the consumption shocks accumulate over time, the cross-sectional variance should increase over time too. Results from this test are not described here since the data set is too small to provide adequate reliability.

Instead, the first method above is extended here to provide a third test. The test pertains to common fixed time effects: if there truly is full village-level risk-sharing, the growth in marginal utilities should not differ across groups within the same village. The test examines whether failure of the village-level tests belies substantial risk-sharing within families or within members of a village subgroup (e.g. a caste).

Following Townsend (1994), constant relative risk aversion (CRRA) utility functions are assumed:

$$U_i(C_{it}) = \frac{C_{it}^{(1-\gamma)}}{1-\gamma}; \qquad U_i'(C_{it}) = C_{it}^{-\gamma} \tag{2.7}$$

and household consumption is adjusted for the size of the household and differences in the consumption needs of its members.[5] Substituting the assumed form of the marginal utility from equation (2.7) into (2.6) yields that

$$\left(\frac{C_{it+1}}{C_{it}}\right)^{-\gamma} = \left(\frac{C_{jt+1}}{C_{jt}}\right)^{-\gamma} = \frac{\alpha_{t+1}}{\alpha_t} \tag{2.8}$$

and taking the logarithm and simplifying gives a sharp, testable result:

$$\log \frac{C_{it+1}}{C_{it}} = -\frac{1}{\gamma} \log \frac{\alpha_{t+1}}{\alpha_t} \tag{2.9}$$

for all households and all periods. Although the term on the right is unobservable, it is a constant (i.e. the same for all households in any period) and can thus be captured with a set of time-specific fixed effects. Since (2.9) should hold exactly (except for random error picked up by the residual ε), an over-identification test can be employed:

$$\log \frac{C_{it+1}}{C_{it}} = \sum_{i=1}^{T} \beta_t D_t + \beta_y \log \frac{Y_{it+1}}{Y_{it}} + \varepsilon_{it}. \tag{2.10}$$

If there is full risk-pooling, the time-specific fixed effects, D_t, should fully explain systematic movements in consumption growth (i.e. the right-hand side of equation (2.9)). If that is so, the coefficients on the income growth term in (2.10) should not differ significantly from zero ($\beta_y = 0$). On the other hand, if the model is completely wrong and all income shocks translate into consumption variation then $\beta_y = 1$.

The test is narrow in that it can only reject (or not reject) evidence of complete risk-sharing within villages, but it is a helpful starting place. Thinking about partial risk-sharing is in many ways more natural, but a precise interpretation of $0 < \beta_y < 1$ is up for grabs. The test is mute on the ability to smooth consumption inter-temporally or to share risks with households outside the village (equation (2.6) holds equally well if there are extensive or absent credit or savings possibilities). Moreover, if say, $\beta_y = 0.5$, it is impossible to know immediately if this is because, say, households are able to protect half of the variance in income from translating into consumption shocks, or if, alternatively, half the population can find complete protection while the other half has none. Below, specific models of partial risk-sharing are described; like Townsend's approach, they assume that all households are able to partially insure to a common

---

[5] In the empirical work, consumption is deflated by the number of household members and by two measures of adult equivalence. The results are robust to parameterizing using the constant absolute risk aversion form, where $U(C) = -1/\sigma \exp\{-\sigma C\}$ and $U'(C) = C$.

degree. The strategy here instead is to analyse the coping abilities of village subgroups that might be thought to be able to insure themselves better than the village as a whole.

Homogeneity of fixed time effects

Equation (2.6) implies another test as well. Allowing different fixed time effects for subgroups of the sample should be redundant if equation (2.6) and the ancillary assumptions describe reality. The fixed time effects should be equal for all subgroups in each period, no matter how the sample is divided. If there are G subgroups in the village, $\beta_{gt} = \beta_{ht}$ for every group g and h:

$$\log \frac{C_{igt+1}}{C_{igt}} = \sum_{g=1}^{G} \sum_{i=1}^{T} \beta_{gt} D_t D_g + \beta_y \log \frac{Y_{it+1}}{Y_{it}} + \varepsilon_t. \tag{2.11}$$

The approach employed in the empirical section is to estimate the equation with a village-wide fixed time effect and additional fixed time effects for subgroups. Under the null hypothesis, the latter fixed time effects should equal zero.

Results following equation (2.11) are reported in Morduch (1991) for subgroups by landholding and by caste as identified by Victor Doherty (1982; see also Walker and Ryan 1990). Below, instead, results are presented for the more flexible specification of equation (2.10) estimated independently for subsamples defined by caste groupings.

2.7. RESULTS

This section describes results from Morduch (1991) and subsequent work. Table 2.2 provides evidence on risk-sharing following equation (2.10), using as dependent variables first total consumption and, second, food consumption only.

Coefficients on income growth tell just part of the stories: overall fit matters too. As expected, the fit of the equations is far weaker for total consumption than for food consumption. This is not surprising since non-food items are more likely to be

Table 2.2. *Risk-sharing tests by village*

	Growth of total consumption (1976–81)			Growth of food consumption (1976–83)		
	Coefficient on income growth	R^2	Observations	Coefficient on income growth	R^2	Observations
Aurepalle	0.27 (3.36)	0.18	193	0.24 (4.49)	0.32	272
Shirapur	0.19 (1.61)	0.09	192	0.25 (2.68)	0.26	268
Kanzara	0.24 (3.23)	0.05	191	0.21 (6.43)	0.32	270

Note: Data are in 1975 rupees, deflated by family size. Absolute values of t-statistics in parentheses. Equations are estimated with a full set of time fixed effects and are heteroskedasticity-corrected, taking into account the stratified sampling of the survey.

discretionary and thus volatile, leaving more variance to be explained. The levels of R^2 rise from 0.18 to 0.32 in Aurepalle, from 0.09 to 0.26 in Shirapur, and from 0.05 to 0.32 in Kanzara. If the model was right, we would expect better fits in all cases.

The coefficients on income growth are in all cases between 0.19 and 0.32. If consumption responded exactly to income, the coefficient would be 1.0. But this would only be so if there was no village-level insurance at all, nor any self-insurance by households. So households are a long way from simply consuming what they earn. On the other hand, the coefficient on income growth is large and statistically significant in all cases (but marginally significant in Shirapur for total consumption)—a clear rejection of the complete insurance model. What cannot be told from the results is whether the reason that the coefficients are relatively large but far below 1.0 has much to do with village-level activity (or any other group-level activity)—or whether it is mostly due to self-insurance. As Deaton (1997) and others have argued, the results could equally well be explained by households atomistically borrowing and saving while following the permanent income hypothesis under borrowing constraints.

Table 2.3 considers tests for groups where communal insurance seems more likely, relative to mutual insurance of the entire village. Here, insurance within castes is tested, with attention restricted to just the largest castes in the sample. The caste numbering follows the most disaggregated codes used by ICRISAT investigators. The codes follow a hierarchy by social status, with 1 being the highest caste in a village.

Table 2.3. *Risk-sharing tests by caste group*

	Growth of total consumption (1976–81)			Growth of food consumption (1976–83)		
	Coefficient on income growth	R^2	Observations	Coefficient on income growth	R^2	Observations
Aurepalle						
Caste 2	−0.12 (2.81)	0.18	33	−0.20 (2.69)	0.40	45
Caste 7	0.54 (4.24)	0.63	52	0.53 (5.00)	0.57	77
Caste 10	0.60 (4.94)	0.49	32	0.46 (6.24)	0.58	46
Caste 12	0.43 (1.81)	0.31	25	0.34 (1.95)	0.43	35
Shirapur						
Caste 1	0.20 (1.70)	0.09	100	0.26 (4.05)	0.21	138
Caste 5	0.009 (0.12)	0.27	47	0.07 (0.57)	0.37	66
Kanzara						
Caste 1	0.10 (0.68)	0.28	35	−0.04 (0.24)	0.29	49
Caste 4	0.22 (8.69)	0.14	67	0.19 (2.65)	0.58	97
Caste 11	0.32 (3.00)	0.41	35	0.42 (3.37)	0.61	48

Note: Data are in 1975 rupees, deflated by family size. Absolute values of *t*-statistics in parentheses. Equations are estimated with a full set of time fixed effects and are heteroskedasticity-corrected, taking into account the stratified sampling of the survey.

The theory described above implies that if complete village-level insurance exists, the finding should be replicated exactly when investigating the behaviour of any subgroup. Coefficients should be identical no matter how the sample is divided.

Table 2.3 shows clearly that coefficients are not identical, but interesting patterns emerge. In Morduch (1991), the results by caste provide evidence that food consumption (but not total consumption) appeared to be well insured for some castes, suggesting that the right model may be one where neighbours insure each other against dire events but are left to cope individually in the face of minor shocks. These findings are consistent with studies that describe distributive systems limited to subsistence needs (Polanyi 1944; Sahlins 1976; Scott 1986), rather than comprehensive arrangements characterized by tests for Pareto optima (Townsend 1994). Those findings do not hold up in the more flexible specification here, however. Instead, while coefficients vary between caste groups, they are remarkably consistent within caste groups, when the dependent variable is either growth in total consumption or growth in food consumption only.

In Aurepalle and Kanzara, the tests suggest that the highest ranked castes (lowest numbers) appear to be better 'insured' than others (although sample sizes are small and the Aurepalle coefficient is significantly negative). The castes classified as being of lower status show signs of weaker 'insurance' systems. The results (although they are not replicated in Shirapur) suggest that evidence of quite good insurance for some is being averaged in with evidence of weaker insurance for others. Disaggregating is critical to get a full picture.

The results caution against the temptation to interpret coefficients from village-level tests as yielding the extent to which the 'average' villager is protected from idiosyncratic shocks. There may be no 'average' villager in a meaningful sense. Instead, the results yield an average of protection levels across groups that may vary quite widely from each other.

2.8. RELATION TO PREVIOUS WORK

The results provide a context in which to view Townsend's evidence. He uses a 'mongrel' version of equation (2.10) to suggest that risk-sharing is important in the ICRISAT villages (β_y is small), although complete risk-sharing is statistically rejected and poorer households appear to have less access to risk reducing arrangements. In particular, Townsend finds that the marginal propensity to consume out of a household's own income is nowhere greater than 0.14. Ravallion and Chaudhuri's estimates of the marginal propensity to consume (using equation (2.10) and a variety of data sources) fall between 0.12 and 0.46. Their 'preferred estimates' are at the high end of the range. These results suggest that informal insurance exists, but it is not nearly perfect. Ligon *et al.* (2000) find similar results, as do I (Morduch 1991, and here). Results have been similar in other samples. Deaton (1997), for example, rejects the complete risk-sharing hypothesis in investigating consumption patterns in Côte d'Ivoire, using a framework similar to that of Townsend.

Townsend's results, however, are given support by Rosenzweig and Binswanger (1993). They find that in the ICRISAT sample, a 100 rupees decline in profits reduces food consumption by 7 rupees. But when the effect of common weather shocks is removed from the profit variable, the residual explains only 0.6 per cent of that of total profits. Idiosyncratic shocks thus appear to be almost completely smoothed away, while households must bear some of the impact of common weather shocks. But note that, as shown in Morduch (1991), results for total consumption can differ from those for food only (although Tables 2.2 and 2.3 here do not bear that out).

When disaggregating villages by agricultural status in Morduch (1991), I find evidence consistent with Rosenzweig and Binswanger for large-scale and medium-scale farmers, but not for small-scale farmers and landless labourers. I find that in investigating borrowing constraints, food consumption growth for the latter two groups is affected by idiosyncratic shocks, while such shocks do not affect food consumption growth of the larger-scale farm households. Similar results are reported by Bhargava and Ravallion (1993), also for the ICRISAT sample. Again, disaggregation within villages thus appears to matter.

Ogaki (1991) and Ogaki and Zhang (2001) shore up evidence for full risk-sharing by moving in a different direction. Rather than disaggregating or using alternative data sources, they turn to specification error. Specifically, they consider utility functions that explicitly allow for 'subsistence constraints', $U(C) = [(C - s)^{1-\gamma} - 1]/(1 - \gamma)$ where s is the subsistence parameter. Estimating using generalized method of moments techniques, they find that the more flexible specification yields stronger evidence of risk-sharing in the ICRISAT sample. The step is an important one, but the evidence would be even more revealing if the subsistence parameter could be imbued with sharper economic meaning. The parameter is not tied to an exogenous poverty line or other information on what it means to live at 'subsistence'. Rather, Ogaki and his co-authors remain agnostic about precise definitions.[6]

Ligon *et al.* (2000) take a different tack. They begin with the presumption that full risk-sharing does not describe the ICRISAT data adequately. They derive conditions expected to occur if contract enforcement is impossible. In that case, everything falls apart unless contracts are self-enforcing: the benefits to staying in must always exceed the benefits to reneging on obligations. The patterns that emerge will involve partial risk-sharing with transactions that have features of loans. Where contracts are fully enforceable, we expect that each period will be treated like a one-shot game. Without enforcement, history matters, so if A helps out B in period 1, then in future periods B remains obligated to A until conditions change or 'debts' are repaid. The model performs well against the alternatives offered by complete autarky, full insurance, and a static model of limited insurance (in which history does not matter). The model outperforms all three, and it has much to recommend it. As Ligon (1998) shows, however, asymmetric information can also undermine insurance in complicated ways. But incorporating both information asymmetries and imperfect enforcement in the same theoretical model is a difficult task. Deriving cleanly testable

---

[6] Other candidates for weakening are assumptions that leisure is separable from consumption in utility, that food is separable from other consumption, and that utility in different states and times is separable. All of these assumptions are reasonable, but they come at the cost of generality.

implications is even harder. More difficult still is finding a data set rich enough to deliver reliable results. At this point the ICRISAT set may have been stretched as far as it can go.

Considering imperfect information is, of course, just one path to pursue. Important (and very useful) simplifications are obtained by Ligon *et al.* (2000) by ruling out the ability to save or borrow. As Lim and Townsend (1998) and Chaudhuri and Paxson (1994) show, however, the detailed ICRISAT transaction files show that most insurance is obtained through building up and drawing down one's own buffer stocks of grain. Rosenzweig and Wolpin (1993) show how bullock purchases and sales appear to serve as risk-coping mechanisms as well—although Lim and Townsend (1998) fail to corroborate the evidence in the underlying transactions files.

Self-insurance, which is assumed away by Ligon *et al.* (2000), thus appears to be central in the raw data. Still, risk-sharing with others may in principle be critical on the margin, and their analysis takes us a step further in understanding a complex web of behaviours and constraints. As Ligon *et al.* (2000) conclude, figuring out how to take the blinders off with respect to self-insurance should be high on the list of research priorities.[7]

Youngjae Lim (1993) makes a start in this direction by attempting to disentangle risk-sharing models and the permanent income hypothesis under borrowing constraints. His test refines previous work by investigating how the unforecastable portion of consumption responds to unforecastable idiosyncratic income shocks. With no risk-sharing (i.e. under self-insurance only), the factor structure of the income shocks should be detectable in the factor structure of consumption. But where risks are pooled, expectation errors are smoothed away and the patterns should not translate. Like others, Lim (1993) is able to use the ICRISAT data to show that there is a fair amount of risk-sharing, but that it is incomplete.

Jacoby and Skoufias (1997) offer some promising leads in how to sharpen predictions. But rather than considering changes in consumption, they consider decisions about the enrolment of children in school. Still, the framework draws heavily on the consumption literature; an important question is: do enrolment decisions respond to idiosyncratic income shocks? To get adequate variation, they consider seasonal data—like Chaudhuri and Paxson (1994) but unlike the other researchers mentioned above. Their innovation is to use seasonal data on rainfall to disaggregate shocks both as idiosyncratic versus aggregate and as anticipated versus unanticipated. The predictability of the rainfall data allow insight into the latter relationships and provides a handle for distinguishing between credit market failure and insurance failure. Insurance failure is detected by seeing responses to idiosyncratic shocks, whether anticipated or not. Self-insurance failure is detected by seeing responses to anticipated shocks, whether idiosyncratic or not. Jacoby and Skoufias (1997) find that school enrolments respond to risk. Pushing further, they reject both perfect insurance and perfect credit markets (especially for

---

[7] Chapter 2 of Morduch (1991), on the other hand, tests models of borrowing and saving under borrowing constraints, while keeping on blinders to risk-pooling. The tests of risk-sharing and self-insurance are very close in form and identification comes from very similar sources of variation in the underlying data.

smaller farmers). Their evidence shows the importance both of disaggregation within villages and of explicitly modelling self-insurance as a risk-mitigation strategy in the ICRISAT sample.

2.9. CONCLUSION

Recent research has shown that rural households in developing economies use a wide variety of instruments to smooth consumption, some through the market and some through informal mechanisms. The ICRISAT studies have provided a rich source of data with which to probe the complexities of how this is accomplished. In doing so, their influence on policy and research has extended well beyond concern with South India or even the semi-arid tropics as a region.

The data have yielded many 'stylized facts', some of which have been replicated sufficiently to count as actual 'facts'. Most important: in these villages there is a lot of risk, but the bulk of idiosyncratic risk is mitigated. Second, poorer households are considerably more vulnerable than richer households. Neither complete autarky nor full risk-sharing are good characterizations of these villages.

None of this should be surprising, nor particularly comforting. The remaining idio-syncratic risk is not clearly innocuous, nor are risk-mitigating mechanisms necessarily inexpensive (Morduch 1999). Twenty years of work with these data offer little support for the contention that policy only needs to worry about limiting damages due to aggregate shocks since villagers seems to deal with idiosyncratic shocks on their own.

For the purposes of policy, it will be valuable to better target those households that are least able to cope with both aggregate and idiosyncratic shocks. The results shown here on risk-sharing by caste and previous work on risk-sharing by wealth take us a step in that direction.

Recent academic work on incomplete risk-sharing has focused on the role of imper-fect enforcement. Enforcement problems are a key part of the economic environment in the ICRISAT study region, but they are insufficient to explain the patterns in the data. Most important, evidence on incomplete risk-sharing may result as well (or, perhaps, instead) from imperfect information, heterogeneity in desires and ability to save and borrow, specification error, costly contracting, and a host of other factors including discrimination and social isolation.

While fundamental questions remain, it is remarkable how much we have answered in the process—and how much high-quality work has flowed from the use of these data. Sadly, the data remain the best available for many purposes, but they are starting to strain under the demands placed on them. With growing realism and subtlety of theoretical predictions, longer time series are required to put together with wide cross-sections. But it is the long time series that are especially critical. Remarkably, much fine work over two decades of development economics springs from evidence on just over 100 households. If this is a precedent, creating similar data sets in other regions will surely repay the effort many times over. Researchers will have to worry about limiting attrition, fatigue, measurement error, and other problems common to longitudinal data, but there is much to gain if the problems can be surmounted.

REFERENCES

Altonji, J. G., F. Hayashi, and L. J. Kotlikoff (1992). 'Is the Extended Family Altruistically Linked? Direct Tests Using Micro Data'. *American Economic Review*, 82(5), 1177–1198.

Bardhan, P. and C. Udry (2000). *Readings in Development Economics II: Empirical Microeconomics.* Cambridge, MA: MIT Press.

Bhargava, A. and M. Ravallion (1993). 'Does Household Consumption Behave as a Martingale: A Test for Rural South India'. *Review of Economics and Statistics*, 75(3), 500–504.

Binswanger, H. (1981). 'Attitudes Toward Risk: Theoretical Implications of an Experiment in Rural India'. *Economic Journal*, 91(364), 867–890.

Chaudhuri, S. and C. Paxson (1994). 'Consumption Smoothing and Income Seasonality in Rural India', draft, RPDS Princeton University, New Jersey.

Deaton, A. (1997). *The Analysis of Household Surveys.* Baltimore, MD: Johns Hopkins.

Doherty, V. S. (1982). 'A Guide to the Study of Social and Economic Groups and Stratification in Indian Village Level Studies,' draft, ICRISAT, Economics Program.

Epstein, T. S., A. P. Suryanaryana, and T. Thimmegowda (1998). *Village Voices: Forty Years of Rural Transformation in South India.* Walnut Creek, CA: Altamira Press.

Gautam, M. (1992). 'Sequential Decision-Making under Temporal Risk by Households in Dryland Agriculture'. Ph.D. dissertation, Department of Agricultural and Resource Economics, University of Maryland, Maryland, MD.

Genicot, G. and D. Ray (2003). 'Endogenous Group Formation in Risk-Sharing Arrangements'. *Review of Economic Studies*, 70(1), 87–113.

Jacoby, H. and E. Skoufias (1997). 'Risk, Financial Markets, and Human Capital in a Developing Country'. *Review of Economic Studies*, 64(3), 311–336.

Ligon, E. (1998). 'Risk Sharing and Information in Village Economies'. *Review of Economic Studies*, 65, 847–864.

——, J. Thomas, and T. Worall (2000). 'Informal Insurance Arrangements in Village Economies', draft, January, Department of Agricultural and Resources Economics, University of Berkeley.

Lim, Y. (1993). 'Disentangling Permanent Income from Risk Sharing: A General Equilibrium Perspective in Rural South India'. Unpublished Ph.D. dissertation, Department of Economics, University of Chicago, Chicago, IL.

—— and R. Townsend (1998). 'General Equilibrium Models of Financial Systems: Theory and Measurement in Village Economies'. *Review of Economic Dynamics*, 1(1), 59–118.

Malinowski, B. (1922). *Argonauts of the Western Pacific.* London: Routledge.

Mauss, M. (1967). *The Gift.* New York: W. W. Norton.

Morduch, J. (1991). 'Risk and Welfare in Developing Countries'. Unpublished Ph.D. dissertation, Department of Economics, Harvard University, Cambridge, MA.

—— (1995). 'Income Smoothing and Consumption Smoothing'. *Journal of Economic Perspectives*, 9(3), 103–114.

—— (1999). 'Between the Market and State: Can Informal Insurance Patch the Safety Net?'. *World Bank Research Observer*, 14(2), 187–207.

Ogaki, M. (1991). 'Subsistence Levels, Risk-sharing, and Saving: Evidence from Indian Panel Data', draft, June, University of Rochester, New York.

—— and Q. Zhang (2001). 'Decreasing Risk Aversion and Tests of Risk-Sharing', *Econometrica*, 69(2), 515–526.

Polanyi, K. (1944). *The Great Transformation*. Boston, MA: Beacon Press.

Popkin, S. (1979). 'The Political Economy of Peasant Society', reprinted in J. Elster (ed.) *Rational Choice*. New York: New York University Press, 1986.

Ravallion, M. and S. Chaudhuri (1997). 'Risk and Insurance in Village India: Comment'. *Econometrica*, 65(1), 171–184.

Rawls, J. (1971). *A Theory of Justice*. Cambridge, MA: Harvard University Press.

Rosenzweig, M. R. (1988). 'Risk, Implicit Contracts, and the Family in Rural Areas of Low Income Countries'. *Economic Journal*, 98(December), 1148–1170.

Rosenzweig, M. and H. Binswanger (1993). 'Wealth, Weather Risk and the Composition and Profitability of Agricultural Investments'. *Economic Journal*, 103(January), 56–78.

—— and K. Wolpin (1993). 'Credit Market Constraints, Consumption Smoothing, and the Accumulation of Durable Production Assets in Low-Income Countries: Investment in Bullocks in India'. *Journal of Political Economy*, 101(2), 223–244.

Sahlins, M. (1976). *Culture and Practical Reason*. Chicago, IL: University of Chicago Press.

Scott, J. C. (1986). *The Moral Economy of the Peasant*. Oxford: Basil Blackwell.

Townsend, R. (1994). 'Risk and Insurance in Village India'. *Econometrica*, 62(May), 539–592.

Walker, T. S. and J. G. Ryan (1990). *Village and Household Economies in India's Semi-Arid Tropics*. Baltimore, MD: Johns Hopkins.

PART II

RISK AND POVERTY: THEORY

3

The Two Poverties

ABHIJIT V. BANERJEE

3.1. INTRODUCTION

Are the poor just like you and me except in that they have less money, to invert Hemingway's famous line? Or is it useful to think of them as being subject to different pressures from the rest of the population and therefore sometimes making choices that are very different?

For a long time the dominant view in economics was that the distinction had only descriptive usefulness, that behaviourally the poor were much like anyone else.[1] One of the most important developments of the last two decades within formal economics, fuelled by attempts to rigorously study the evolution of the distribution of consumption and wealth, is a movement away from this position. There is growing emphasis on poverty as a distinct analytical concept rather than purely as a category of description.[2] That is, less 'who are the poor' and more 'what do they do and why'?

The roots of this shift are complex but an important part came from developments in microeconomics: a better understanding of preferences towards risk and the sources of asset market failures made it easier to see why there may be problems that affect the poor more than everybody else. The warning of the neo-Marxist and neo-Ricardian models, with their automatic assumption that the poor were workers and owned no assets, also made it easier to focus on the fact that the poor, like everybody else, make lifetime choices, albeit under less favourable circumstances.

It has been more than twenty years since this new literature was launched with the work of people like Kanbur (1979), Kihlstrom and Laffont (1979), and Loury (1981). It remains true, however, that the conceptualization of poverty in this literature is usually implicit, that is, in the form of an assumption in the model, rather than explicit: 'the right way to model poverty is...'. The goal of this chapter is to make the conceptualization explicit. In the process, it will emerge that there are at least two distinct and, prima facie, inconsistent views of poverty in these models, which I will call these 'poverty as desperation' and 'poverty as vulnerability'. These views have rather

I am grateful to Cesar Calvo, Esther Duflo, Campe Goodman, Karla Hoff, Omer Moav, and to the members of my 14.772/2390b class for many helpful comments.

[1] A very influential statement of this view is to be found in Schultz (1964).

[2] This is not to say that descriptions are unimportant. The work of Amartya Sen (see Sen 1999) and others on who we should think of as the poor have had an enormous impact on how we assess the effectiveness of anti-poverty policies.

different implications about anti–poverty policy and this makes it important that we confront the conflict between them.

3.2. POVERTY AS DESPERATION

The poor are different because they are desperate: they have too little to lose.[3] To give formal content to this idea, imagine a world where there is one good produced and a population of identical people who each live for one period and always have one child. Each person starts life with an endowment which her parent gave her. Her life is simple, verging on the drab. At the beginning of her life, she chooses among income earning opportunities (which we will describe later). At the end she decides on what to do with her realized income—she can leave it to her child or eat it herself. For simplicity, assume that she has Cobb–Douglas-like preferences over consumption (c) and bequest (b):

$$U(c,b) = \frac{A[c^{1-\beta}b^{\beta}]^{1-\alpha}}{1-\alpha}, \quad 0 < \beta < 1, \quad 1 > \alpha > 0, \quad A > 0.$$

Since she allocates her end-of-period wealth between these two uses, this immediately implies that if her end-of-period income (or wealth) is y:

$$c = (1-\beta)y, \quad b = \beta y.$$

It follows that her (indirect) utility from having an income of y is:

$$V(y) = \frac{\overline{A}y^{1-\alpha}}{1-\alpha}.$$

The end-of-period income, y, should clearly depend on beginning-of-period endowment, ω, though to understand the exact nature of the dependence, we would need to say something about the nature of income-earning opportunities in this economy. Moreover, choices made during the person's lifetime, C, and luck in the form of some random shock, θ, must play a role. For the time being, we just write the income function as:

$$y = y(\omega, \theta, C), \quad y_{\omega} > 0.$$

While we do not pretend that this is, or ought to be, all of life, this framework does capture important aspects of it. A large part of what we start out life with—health, education, land, money—comes from our parents, and is mostly a result of a choice that they make (or rather, one we make together). While the label we attach to the bequest[4]

---

[3] This idea is implicit in the models that draw the link between credit market imperfections and the persistence of poverty. See, among other papers, Aghion and Bolton (1997), Banerjee and Newman (1993), Galor and Zeira (1993), Piketty (1997), and Ghatak *et al.* (1998). It is explicit in Banerjee and Newman (1994).

[4] To the above list of possible types of bequest, we might add 'culture' where culture is interpreted narrowly as attitudes towards work and corruption. One 'learns' this kind of culture either from one's parents or from one's peer group, and in either case what we learn reflects choices made by our parents (which include our choice of peer group).

may vary (and, indeed, there are usually multiple types of bequests), to assume that one starts life with a bequest from one's parent and then makes choices about the kind of income one will get fits the pattern of most people's lives.

With this somewhat elaborate preamble, we are now ready to return to the problem of conceptualizing poverty. The simplest way to capture the idea that the poor are desperate is to assume that there is some bound on how low $V(\cdot)$ can get. That is to say, there is some effective utility function,

$$V^*(y) \equiv \max[\underline{V}, V(y)].$$

In other words, if the end-of-period income ends up being such that $V(y) < \underline{V}$, the person's utility will be $\underline{V}$, rather than $V(y)$.

There are several possible interpretations of $\underline{V}$. It could be the result of social policy: $\underline{V}$ may just embody the guarantees given by the welfare system. Or it may reflect private generosity (or the lack of it)—friends and neighbours will simply not allow anyone to fall below $\underline{V}$. Or, less obviously, it could reflect the failure of imagination: perhaps people cannot conceive of being worse off than $\underline{V}$. In other words, beyond some point, having less to eat either really stops mattering (perhaps because the body gives up) or stops mattering in the mind of someone who is not yet there but is thinking of it as a possibility.[5]

The interesting case for us, obviously, is the one in which for some choice c and some random realization θ:

$$V(y(0, \theta, c)) < \underline{V}.$$

That is, for someone who starts with wealth 0, and therefore for those close enough to 0 as well, the constraint that $V(\cdot) \geq \underline{V}$ is sometimes binding. To see what this can tell us about poverty, let us use this assumption in a model of credit.

Consider the following specialization of our basic model: Assume that once one gets one's bequest, one has the choice of putting it in the bank (where it earns a gross interest rate r) and going to work for a wage, W, or starting a business. If one starts a business, the rate of return on each dollar invested in the business up to $\overline{I}$ is $R > r$, the market interest rate, and there is never any reason to invest more than $\overline{I}$. Starting a business is, however, more work: let us assume that starting a business has disutility of effort, E, whereas working has no disutility.

It remains to say something about credit itself. Our typical agent has a wealth of ω but may want to invest an amount $I > \omega$. The constraint comes from the possibility of borrower misbehaviour. Once a borrower has borrowed and invested the money, he or she has no obvious reason to want to repay. What stops him or her from defaulting is the fact that the lender will come after him or her (legally or otherwise) and will try to

---

[5] The one place this last interpretation is different from the other two is that it leaves open the possibility that the realized income is much lower than the income actually corresponding to $\underline{V}$. From the point of view of the decision to invest or not, this distinction is obviously moot. However in Section 3.3, when we look at the dynamics of a dynasty that sometimes ends up with $\underline{V}$, we would need to specify what actually happened.

extract the money. Let us assume that a borrower who tries not to repay gets away with it with probability q. With probability $1 - q$, he or she gets caught and suffers having his or her entire income confiscated, that is, he or she ends up with an end-of-period income of 0. Assume $V(0) < \underline{V}$.

A borrower who defaults therefore has an expected utility of:

$$V^{*\text{dishonest}} = qV^*(IR) + (1 - q)\underline{V},$$

which he or she will compare with:[6]

$$V^{*\text{honest}} = V^*(IR - (I - \omega)r).$$

She will prefer not to default if:

$$V^{*\text{honest}} = V^*(IR - (I - \omega)r) \geq qV^*(IR) + (1 - q)\underline{V} = V^{*\text{dishonest}}.$$

Therefore, the maximum amount anyone can invest starting with wealth of ω is given by $I(\omega)$, defining $V^*(IR - (I - \omega)r) = qV^*(IR) + (1 - q)\underline{V}$.

To avoid keeping track of many cases, let us assume ω is large enough that $V(\omega r) \geq \underline{V}$. Using the expression for V^* we now have:

$$V(I(R - r) + \omega r) \geq q \max\{V(IR), \underline{V}\} + (1 - q)\underline{V}. \tag{3.1}$$

The two sides of this equation are drawn in Figs 3.1(a) and 3.1(b) as functions of I. The origin is chosen so that we focus on the region where the right-hand side is increasing in I, that is, $V(IR) > \underline{V}$.

These are the two cases: In Fig. 3.1(a) the two curves intersect, which gives us a finite investment cap $I(\omega)$. An increase in ω pushes $V^{*\text{honest}}$ up and therefore raises the investment cap. Richer people get to invest more. In Fig. 3.1(b) there is no intersection and consequently no limit to the amount he or she can borrow.

The basic logic behind this credit limit comes from the fact that for relatively low values of ω, the left-hand side may not be much greater than $\underline{V}$. As a result, the borrower cannot lose very much by trying to default, while he or she may indeed gain a lot. As ω becomes larger, she has more to lose and her investment cap moves up as a result.

This intuition is confirmed by looking at $\underline{V}$. Raising $\underline{V}$ raises $V^{*\text{dishonest}}$ and therefore exerts downward pressure on the investment cap. If the borrower has less to lose, he or she gets to borrow less.

A related point emerges when we look at the condition for getting our Fig. 3.1(a) rather than Fig. 3.1(b). For our assumed preferences, for the case where $\bar{I}$ is large enough, the condition turns out to be:[7]

$$R - r < q^{1/(1-\alpha)}R.$$

---

[6] Since he or she has wealth ω, $I - \omega$ is what he or she borrows.

[7] This follows from directly substituting the expression for the utility function into the inequality $V(I(R - r) + \omega r) < qV(IR) + (1 - q)\underline{V}$ and looking at the effect of making I large.

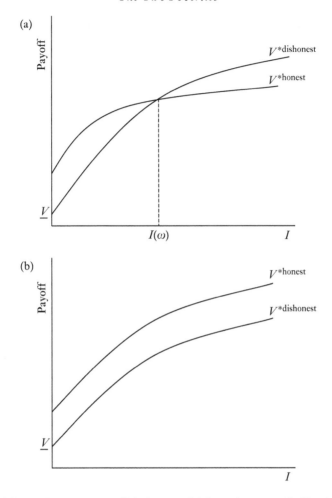

Figure 3.1. *(a) Intersecting payoffs for honest and dishonest borrowers. (b) Non-intersecting payoffs for honest and dishonest borrowers*

The reader will recognize α to be the coefficient of relative risk aversion. Note that as α goes up, this condition become harder and harder to satisfy, and for α close to 1, since $q^{1/(1-\alpha)}$ is close to 0, it cannot be satisfied.[8] In other words, the more risk averse the investor, the less likely it is that he or she faces a credit limit. Once again, this ought to make sense: the credit limit comes from the fact that he or she is too willing

[8] The reader will notice that we have only allowed α to be less than 1 whereas it is more usual to allow α to take all non-negative values. The reason is that for α greater than 1, utility is negative and therefore the $\underline{V}$ constraint always binds. This makes our exercise meaningless. We assume $\alpha \leq 1$ to avoid this problem.

to gamble. Making it costlier to gamble (by making him or her risk averse) acts as an obvious antidote.

We summarize this discussion in:

Claim 1 *People may face investment caps in this model. Richer people will face less stringent investment caps. Making the minimum guaranteed utility level higher makes the investment cap more stringent. Finally, more risk-averse people will face less stringent investment caps.*

The first, second, and third part of this result would hold in most models of imperfect credit markets. The fourth property is probably more specific to a class of models, though given that it is driven by the fact that defaulting increases risk, it ought to be relatively robust.

What does this model of credit limits and investment caps tell us about investment behaviour among the poor? To fix ideas, let $\alpha = 0$ so that $V(y) = y$ and assume $\underline{V} = 0$. It follows from equation (3.1) that $I = \lambda\omega$ where $\lambda = \lambda(\cdot) = r/(r - (1 - q)R)$. The investment cap is linear in wealth. Someone who has a wealth close to zero will only be able to invest a very small amount. Therefore, he or she will clearly not want to give up the wage income he or she could get if he or she did not invest. More specifically, anyone who has a wealth of ω will get a utility of $\lambda\omega(R - r) + \omega r - E$ if he or she invests and $W + \omega r$ if he or she goes to work for someone else. Clearly, he or she will not invest unless his or her wealth was more than $\underline{\omega} = (W + E)/\lambda(R - r)$.

For those who start with a wealth of $\omega_t < \underline{\omega}$ in period t, their end-of-period income will be $W + \omega_t r$ and their children will start life with $\omega_{t+1} = \beta(W + \omega_t r)$. Those who start with a wealth $\omega_t > \underline{\omega}$ will invest and their children will start life with $\omega_{t+1} = \beta[\lambda(R - r) + r]\omega$ unless $\lambda\omega > \overline{I}$,[9] in which case $\omega_{t+1} = \beta[\overline{I}(R - r) + \omega_t r]$.

Under the assumption that $\beta[\lambda(R - r) + r] < 1$ these dynamics can look like Fig. 3.2(a).

This is the classical poverty trap diagram. Poverty is a steady state and so is being rich. Both ω^* and ω^{**} are attractors with basins of attraction given by $[0, \underline{\omega}]$ and $[\underline{\omega}, \alpha]$ respectively, an extreme version of the poverty trap. At ω^*, no one starts a business, we think of ω^* as poverty. Poverty is self-sustaining because the poor are credit constrained and as a result choose not to invest. Consequently, they earn low rates of return on their investment and do not accumulate wealth fast enough to get out of the trap.[10]

---

[9] Recall that $\overline{I}$ is the maximum it is ever worth investing.

[10] The fact that the income shifts up discontinuously at $\underline{\omega}$ is a part of what makes the poverty trap possible. Otherwise, since $\beta[\lambda(R - r) + r] < 1$, the ω_{t+1} will not cross the 45° line again. This case is therefore only possible when E is sufficiently large since the jump in income is just the reward for the extra effort involved in running a business. One might wonder whether parents, faced with such a discontinuity in the outcome for their children would not always want to increase their bequest slightly, and therefore perhaps such an outcome cannot ever be an equilibrium if the parents were forward-looking. This is not, however, correct. The fact that the production technology is non-convex necessarily makes the parents' preferences over bequests non-quasi-concave and therefore even if the parents were forward-looking, their decision rule over bequests would be discontinuous and therefore the wealth of the next generation could be discontinuous as function of parental wealth.

This is the essence of the story told by many papers, including Galor and Zeira (1993), Dasgupta and Ray (1986), and Banerjee and Newman (1994), though they each give a different name to this investment: education in Galor–Zeira; health in Dasgupta–Ray; and capital in Banerjee–Newman. It is easy to see that this case is most likely to obtain when λ is small, which implies that raising $\underline{V}$ and reducing α, both of which, as we have seen, lower the investment cap, also make the poverty trap more likely.

It is easy, of course, to point to the aspects of reality that are missing from this narrative. For example, savings/bequests ought to be responsive to the rates of return. If we were to add this ingredient to our model, it would mostly reinforce the poverty trap since the poorest face the lowest return on their savings in this model and therefore should have the lowest β's. Adding more convexities to the production function (e.g. a set-up cost) also reinforces the poverty trap. Making wages endogenous has a more nuanced effect. On the one hand, an economy with lots of poor people will tend to have low wages and, all else being the same, low wages make it harder to get out of poverty. On the other hand, it also moves $\underline{\omega}$ down, which makes escape from poverty easier. An endogenous interest rate also cuts both ways: high interest rates reduce λ and make it less rewarding to invest, but they also raise the reward for those who put their money in the bank.

Of course we do not have to have a poverty trap. One alternative configuration, which is valid under the condition $\beta[\lambda(R-r)+r] > 1$ but $\beta r < 1$,[11] where everyone ends up rich, is depicted in Fig. 3.2(b).

Even if this were the economy, we would care about how long it takes to get out of poverty. Raising $\underline{V}$ and reducing α, by reducing $\underline{\omega}$ and moving the ω_{t+1} curve down (by lowering λ) makes it a longer process.

This is of course all based on a very specific model of the credit market. One can imagine many other ways in which a borrower could misbehave: he could borrow and fail to put effort into it on the assumption that if, as a result, the investment fails, he will not have to repay.[12] Or he or she could gamble on bad, high-risk projects, again with the view that if as a result he or she is left with very little, he or she will simply default.[13] Or he or she could try to hold up the lender once the investment is sunk, arguing that the lender needs his or her cooperation to get returns on his or her investment, thereby forcing the lender to lower the interest rate after the fact.[14] In each of these cases, richer people will find it easier to invest the same absolute amount simply because a larger part of the money at stake is their own, which makes them more likely to have the right incentives. Moreover, a lower $\underline{V}$ and a higher α will help the poor by making it easier for the lender to punish borrowers who misbehave. The rest of the story would therefore be more or less the same as what we have here.

---

[11] The latter assumption guarantees that no one accumulates an infinite wealth.

[12] This is the essential idea of the models of credit in Aghion and Bolton (1997) and Legros and Newman (1996).   [13] As in Bernanke and Gertler (1990), Hoff and Lyon (1995).

[14] As in Hart and Moore (1990).

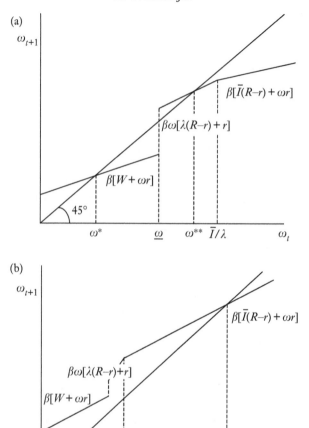

Figure 3.2. *Credit market failure: (a) with a poverty trap, (b) without a poverty trap*

3.3. POVERTY AS VULNERABILITY

The poor are vulnerable: they are afraid of any losses because losses cause them too much pain.[15] We can, fortunately, capture this idea using much the same framework as we had before. However, in order to avoid dealing with the credit market, assume that it is impossible to get away with not repaying, and as a result everyone repays. Everyone can therefore invest as much as they like and it is convenient to assume that everyone

[15] This conceptualization is more or less explicit in Kanbur (1979), Kihlstrom and Laffont (1979), and Newman (1995). It is also implicit in Banerjee and Newman (1991), Banerji (1997), Jacoby and Skoufias (1997), Morduch (1990, 1994), Ravallion (1988) and, in a much more applied context, in Walker and Ryan (1990).

who invests, invests all the way up to $\bar{I}$. Finally, add some risk to the investment by assuming that with probability q' the investor earned a return R' on his investment, with probability $1 - q'$ he or she earns r'.

As before, the alternative to investing is to put the money in the bank and to go and work for a wage W. Our decisionmaker now compares

$$V^{*\text{risky}} = q'V^*(\bar{I}R' + (\omega - \bar{I})r(\omega)) + (1 - q')V^*(\bar{I}r' + (\omega - I)r(\omega)) - E$$

with

$$V^{*\text{safe}} = V^*(\omega r + W),$$

where $r(\omega)$ is the (gross) effective interest rate. For those who have $\omega \geq \bar{I}$, since they do not borrow, $r(\omega) = r$. For those who have to borrow, that is, those with $\omega < \bar{I}$, there is the possibility of default: this happens when $\bar{I}r' + (\omega - I)r < 0$. We assume that in this case the borrower repays as much as he or she can, that is, he or she pays the lender $\bar{I}r'$. Therefore, for the lender to break even if it must be true that $q'r(\omega) + \bar{I}r' = r$ or $r(\omega) = (r - \bar{I}r')/q'$.

Assume that W is high enough that $V(W) > \underline{V}$. Our agent will choose to invest if:

$$V^{*\text{risky}} = q'V(\bar{I}(R' - r) + \omega r) + (1 - q')V^*(\bar{I}(r' - r) + \omega r) - E$$

$$\geq V(W + \omega r) = V^{*\text{safe}}. \tag{3.2}$$

The two sides of this equation are drawn in Figs 3.3(a) and (b) as functions of ω under the assumption that $\underline{V}$ is low enough that $q'V(\bar{I}(R' - r)) + (1 - q)\underline{V} - E < V(W)$.

The fact that the curves eventually cross is not automatic. It requires an additional assumption which says that there is some wealth level at which the investment project is worthwhile. In the case where $E = 0$, this assumption is equivalent to assuming that the investment would take place in the absence of any risk, that is, $q'R' + (1 - q')r' > r$. This follows from the fact that our utility functions have built-in constant relative risk aversion, which means that for ω large enough, the person must be almost risk neutral with respect to fixed absolute risks. The more rewarding risky investment should then dominate and should continue to dominate for all larger wealth levels. In other words, when $E = 0$, there is a $\underline{\omega}$ such that those above $\underline{\omega}$ take the risk and the rest do not. In the more general case where $E \neq 0$, this is not necessarily true: because richer people also value their leisure more relative to extra income, it may be that the richest people do not want to invest. In other words, the curves may cross again. In what follows we will ignore this effect, on the implicit assumption that no one in our population is rich enough for this effect to matter.

What does the effect of an increase in $\underline{V}$ have on $\underline{\omega}$? To answer this, note that a change in $\underline{V}$ only affects $\underline{\omega}$ if the person at $\underline{\omega}$ expects to end up at $\underline{V}$ when the project fails, that is, if $V(\omega r) < \underline{V}$. However, it is possible to show that the $V^{*\text{risky}}$ curve can only cut the $V^{*\text{safe}}$ curve from below if ω is large enough that

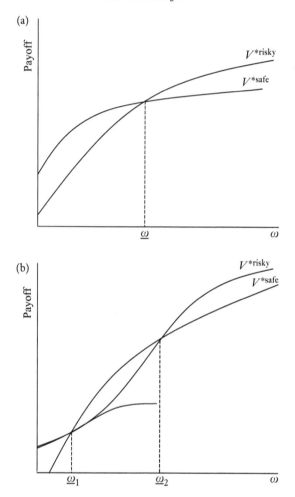

Figure 3.3. *(a) Possible payoffs for risky and safe activities. (b) Alternative payoffs for risky and safe activities*

$V(\omega) > \underline{V}$.[16] Therefore, if the configuration is as shown in Fig. 3.3(a), the $\underline{V}$ constraint can never bind at $\underline{\omega}$ and therefore changes in $\underline{V}$ have no effect on $\underline{\omega}$. A fall in risk aversion does, however, encourage people to take the risky option as one might have expected.[17]

---

[16] Intuitively, $V^{*\text{risky}}$ grows more slowly with respect to ω compared to $V^{*\text{safe}}$ as long as $V(\omega r) < \underline{V}$. In the case where $\omega - \overline{I} > 0$, this follows from the fact that under this condition $dV^{*\text{risky}}/d\omega = q'V'(\overline{I}(R' - r) + \omega r)$, which is less than $dV^{*\text{safe}}/d\omega = V'(\omega r + W)$ because $\overline{I}(R' - r) > W$, V is concave and $q' < 1$. In the alternative case a similar argument applies.

[17] The proof of the fact that increasing risk-aversion shifts people away from the risky option is more or less obvious, since it amounts to saying that the certainty equivalent has gone down. However, to do this

However, this is not the only possible configuration. For higher values of $\underline{V}$, the poor may be encouraged to invest because the distance between $\underline{V}$ and what they would get otherwise, $V(W + \omega r)$, may be small. This is obviously true, for example, in the case where $V(W + \omega r) < \underline{V}$, in which case it must pay to invest. In this case, if anyone does not invest it will be the middle classes, who can still lose a lot (for them $V(W + \omega r) - \underline{V}$ may still be large). This is the configuration shown in Fig. 3.3(b). In the case described by that figure, there are two critical values $-\underline{\omega}_1$ and $\underline{\omega}_2$. Those who are below $\underline{\omega}_1$ and above $\underline{\omega}_2$ choose the risky option. In this case, raising $\underline{V}$ will raise $\underline{\omega}_1$ without affecting $\underline{\omega}_2$ (for the same reason that it does not affect $\underline{\omega}$ in the previous case), and therefore increases the share of people taking the risk. In this case as well it remains true that less risk aversion encourages investment.

To summarize:

Claim 2 *For very low values of $\underline{V}$, the poor will not invest and the rich will. For higher values of $\underline{V}$, the poor will also invest but some sections of the middle class may still hold out for not investing. Also:*

i. *a higher $\underline{V}$ leads to more investment;*
ii. *more risk aversion leads to less investment.*

Once again, these are largely familiar points. The argument that risk aversion leads to underinvestment and that insurance helps promote investment goes back at least to Stiglitz (1969). Morduch (1990) provides some empirical evidence based on Indian agriculture suggesting that poorer people do shy away from adopting profitable but risky technologies, such as high-yielding varieties of crops.

There are also important caveats. We have not modelled why the risk does not get insured away. Once we allow for such insurance, it is not clear that the poor will be the ones who do not invest, since, as pointed out in Banerjee–Newman (1991) and more graphically in Newman (1995), the poor get the best insurance precisely because they are so vulnerable.

The evidence from many developing countries shows that the poor are often well insured against the kinds of risk they face.[18] It must be emphasized, however, that our interpretation of this evidence is constrained by the fact that we only observe the kinds of risk people have chosen to bear. In other words, we cannot control for the fact that people may have foregone investment opportunities in order to limit the risk they actually have to bear.[19] Moreover, there is some evidence that there is substantial variation in the kind of insurance that is available to people in different areas.[20] This

---

exercise correctly, we must ensure that the fall-back option remains $\underline{V}$ and the marginal rate of substitution between income and effort do not also change when α changes. For this reason, when we look at this question we assume $E = 0$ and also that when α changes $\overline{A}$ gets adjusted to ensure that $\overline{A}_z^{1-\alpha}/(1-\alpha) = \underline{V}$. In the more general case where $E \neq 0$, similar effects are to be found but there is no simple way to control for the direct effect of α on the marginal rate of substitution between income and effort.

[18] See Udry (1990), Townsend (1994), and Morduch (1995).
[19] As pointed out by Morduch (1990).
[20] See Townsend (1995).

is consistent with the fact that these informal systems of insurance have to be self-enforcing, and self-enforcing systems tend to be quite fragile.

It is straightforward to look at all the wealth dynamics implied by a model of this type, but we need to say a bit more about what exactly happens when someone hits the minimum utility constraint. The simplest assumption is that people get an income transfer that makes sure that their end-of-period income is $\underline{y}$, where $V(\underline{y}) = \underline{V}$. This transfer cannot be attached by the lender, but otherwise is just like any other form of income: it can be consumed or bequeathed. Focusing on the case where people invest if and only if they are rich enough (i.e. have $\omega_t > \underline{\omega} < \infty$), we have:

$$\omega_{t+1} = \beta[\omega_t r + W] \quad \text{for } \omega_t \leq \underline{\omega}$$

$$\omega_{t+1} = \beta[(\omega_t - \overline{I})r(\omega) + \overline{I}R'] \quad \text{with probability } q'$$

$$\omega_{t+1} = \beta[(\omega_t - \overline{I})r(\omega) + \overline{I}r'] \quad \text{with probability } 1 - q'.$$

Since $\omega_t - \overline{I}$ can clearly be negative and we would like to rule out negative bequests, assume that when $\omega_t - \overline{I}$ is negative the bequest is 0.

These dynamics are shown in Figs 3.4(a) and (b) under the assumption that $\beta r < 1$ and $\underline{y} = 0$. The curve AA represents the dynamics for those below $\underline{\omega}$, while the two curves BB and $B'B'$ represent the dynamics for those above it (the two curves represent the two outcomes).

Using standard techniques, the reader ought to be persuaded that in Fig. 3.4(a), the poor eventually converges to the point ω^* while the rich converge to a distribution with support $[\omega_1^*, \omega_2^*]$. In Fig. 3.4(b), the steady state is a single distribution. Figure 3.4(a), then, is a poverty trap driven entirely by the fact that the poor feel vulnerable and therefore do not invest, even though the returns are sufficiently rewarding that the rich, who do invest, stay rich. While not illustrated here, there is also the possibility that the poverty is an absorbing state. Those who invest and fail, fall into poverty and remain there, because the poor do not invest. The configurations with no mobility out of poverty are obviously more likely when $\underline{y}$ (and $\underline{V}$) are low and α is high.[21]

3.4. THE TWO POVERTIES

Both views of poverty give reasons why poverty may be persistent and why it might be inefficient. They are nevertheless very different. To see how different, consider the statements of Claims 1 and 2. In both of these (Parts 3 and 4 of Claim 1 and Parts 1 and 2 of Claim 2) we relate $\underline{V}$ and the extent of risk aversion to the extent of underinvestment, and through it to the persistence of poverty. However, the effects go in exactly the opposite direction in the two cases. When we emphasized desperation, a high value of $\underline{V}$ and low-risk aversion were both bad. If vulnerability is what we care about, the same things are both good.

[21] $\underline{y}$ being higher directly raises the incomes of the poor, making it less likely that they will stay poor. Moreover raising $\underline{y}$ and lowering α lowers $\underline{\omega}$, making it more likely that the poor will invest.

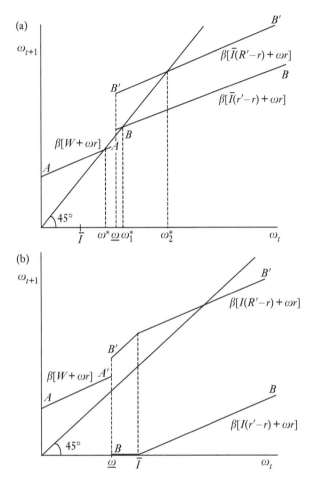

Figure 3.4. *(a) Vulnerability and a risk-induced poverty trap. (b) Vulnerability without a risk-induced poverty trap*

This ought not to surprise us: being vulnerable, after all, is almost the literal opposite of having too little to lose. While it is not impossible for someone to be both vulnerable and desperate (because she faces very different patterns of risk in the two situations), emphasizing one aspect of poverty will tend to make the other less relevant. To make matters worse, the extent of one's vulnerability is directly related to one's ability to borrow to smooth out short-run income fluctuations.[22] Since we have argued that what makes one vulnerable may also give one better credit access, this raises questions about who is really vulnerable.

---

[22] We have avoided this issue so far by having only very long-run fluctuations (everything in our model is on the scale of a generation). But in the world, sensitivity to short-run fluctuations is an important part of vulnerability.

These two very different views cannot but suggest rather different views of anti-poverty policy. If the poor are vulnerable, they will want to be protected from risk (a high value of $\underline{V}$) but that could make it harder for them to get credit. Conversely, lowering $\underline{V}$ makes borrowing easier, it also makes them more vulnerable.

Tradeoffs, of course, are the bread-and-butter of economics. What makes this particular tradeoff interesting is that while both the idea that the poor are vulnerable and the idea that they have limited access to credit are very much in the literature, the tradeoff between policies addressed towards them is not discussed. It is not mentioned, for example, in the otherwise excellent survey of the literature on poverty and anti-poverty policy by Lipton and Ravallion (1995), despite the fact that the survey has a place for both the idea that the poor may be credit-constrained and the idea that the poor may shy away from risk, and moreover has a discussion of the possible disincentive effects of anti-poverty policies.

Of course, it is possible that these concepts are ignored because they are not very useful. But both introspection and casual empiricism suggests otherwise. Moreover, both these ideas figure importantly in the fascinating evidence on how the poor view themselves, emerging from the recent work on participatory poverty mapping.[23]

It remains possible that there is no real conflict: one view applies to some people and the other to the rest. There is clearly no reason to presume that the poor are homogeneous. If this is right, it suggests that it is very important that we find observable correlates of these poverty characteristics and base policy on them: otherwise policies meant to help one set of poor people could end up hurting the rest. Alternatively, the conflict may have arisen from the specific formalization we have adopted here and a reconciliation may be possible. This is what we turn to now.

3.5. CONCLUSION: RECONCILING THESE VIEWS

The close connection between desperation and vulnerability comes from the fact that both are related to $\underline{V}$, which is the minimum socially accepted welfare level. One way to break the link is to have two separate values of $\underline{V}$ corresponding to the two views of what it is to be poor. In other words, there is one value of $\underline{V}$, which tells us what happens to a defaulter and another which tells us what happens to someone who simply had very bad luck.

One reason why these outcomes may be different is suggested by thinking about incentives. The fact that a defaulter ends up at $\underline{V}$ reflects an active choice by the lender, while the misery of someone whose investment has failed may not need anybody else's help. If collecting money from a defaulter is costly, the lender may not have the incentive to go after him or her, or at least go after him or her with enough gusto. This will be especially true if the borrower is poor, since the amount of money that can be extracted from him or her cannot be very large. In other words, at least in expectation,

---

[23] See Narayan *et al.* (1999). It is, however, also clear from this evidence that there are ways in which poverty gets conceptualized that are not in the formal literature. Examples of this include the idea that poverty is voicelessness (i.e. lack of control over public action), powerlessness (lack of control over one's own destiny), and stress (lack of ease, lack of leisure).

the borrower will not expect to be pushed all the way down to the minimum socially accepted level. In other words, the $\underline{V}$ that is relevant for the credit relationship is higher than the $\underline{V}$ that comes into play when we focus on risk-taking behaviour: the poor could be very vulnerable when they take on risks they have no control over and yet be protected from the wrath of the lender because the lender finds it too costly to go after them.

A related but less obviously economic argument stresses the fact that society may take different views of misery that people bring upon themselves and misery that others inflict upon them. Bankruptcy laws around the world do not allow creditors to attach someone's last bowl of food, and yet many of the same countries do not explicitly guarantee that no one will end up starving. This kind of moral schizophrenia may also give us two levels of $\underline{V}$.

Both these arguments, however, rely on making an excessively sharp distinction between bad luck and default. Bad luck for a farmer or a trader is not having enough money to pay their suppliers. In other words, the way bad luck unfolds is through a series of defaults. The two modes of poverty therefore remain connected, albeit perhaps less tightly.

Another approach to this question is to recognize that people may have different behavioural responses to the risk that comes from defaulting (which is something they choose) and the risk inherent in investments. Where they have control and actively choose the risk, they may have a tendency to underestimate how much it may cost them. By contrast, where it is a pure act of God, they may even overestimate the dangers that they are facing. As a result, despite the real $\underline{V}$ being the same, the agent will act as if he or she had two separate $\underline{V}$'s for the two decisions.

These more elaborate models do allow us to get away from the very stark conflicts we outlined above. However, these models also have important policy implications of their own. If, for example, the poor are actually vulnerable and the problem is commitment on the lender's side, the natural policy response would be to try to reduce the costs of collection. This may be an advantage, for example, of group lending schemes that shift a part of the burden of collection on to those who can easily do so (other members of the group). If, on the other hand, the problem is in the borrower's perceptions, the important step may be convincing the borrower that it is in his or her interest to repay. Dynamic incentives for borrowers like the ones built into many microcredit schemes may serve this purpose.

All this, of course, is necessarily speculative. In the end, only data can tell us whether any of these models are right or even interesting. However, without the theory being articulated, there cannot be data. Our hope is to have taken the first step on this question.

REFERENCES

Aghion, P. and P. Bolton (1997). 'A Theory of Trickle-Down Growth and Development'. *The Review of Economic Studies*, 64(2), 151–72.

Banerjee, A. and A. Newman (1991). 'Risk-Bearing and the Theory of Income Distribution'. *The Review of Economic Studies*, 58(2), 211–35.

—— and —— (1993). 'Occupational Choice and the Process of Development'. *Journal of Political Economy*, 101(2), 274–98.

—— and —— (1994). 'The Role of Poverty in Development Theory'. *American Economic Review Papers and Proceedings*, May, pp. 211–15.

Banerji, S. (1997). 'Financial Intermediary, Savings and Investment in a Macro Model with Imperfect Information', mimeo, Boston University.

Bernanke, B. and M. Gertler (1990). 'Financial Fragility and Economic Performance'. *Quarterly Journal of Economics*, 105, 87–114.

Dasgupta, P. and D. Ray (1986). 'Inequality as a Determinant of Malnutrition and Unemployment: Theory'. *Economic Journal*, 96, 1011–34.

Galor, O. and J. Zeira (1993). 'Income Distribution and Macroeconomics'. *Review of Economic Studies*, 60(1), 35–52.

Ghatak, M., M. Morelli, and T. Sjostrom (1998). 'Dynamic Incentives Occupational Mobility, and the American Dream', mimeo, Iowa State University.

Hart, O. and J. Moore (1994). 'A Theory of Debt Based on Inalienability of Human Capital'. *Quarterly Journal of Economics*, 109, 841–79.

Hoff, K. and A. Lyon (1995). 'Non-leaky Buckets: Optimal Redistributive Taxation and Agency Costs'. *Journal of Public Economics*, 58, 365–90.

Jacoby, H. and E. Skoufias (1997). 'Risk, Financial Markets, and Human Capital in a Developing Country'. *The Review of Economic Studies*, 64(3), 311–35.

Kanbur, S. (1979). 'Of Risk Taking and the Personal Distribution of Income'. *Journal of Political Economy*, 87, 769–97.

Kihlstrom, R. and J. Laffont (1979). 'A General Equilibrium Entrepreneurial Theory of Firm Formation Based on Risk Aversion'. *Journal of Political Economy*, 87, 719–48.

Legros, P. and A. Newman (1996). 'Wealth Effects, Distribution. and the Theory of Organization'. *Journal of Economic Theory*, 70(2), 312–41.

Lipton, M. and M. Ravallion (1995). 'Poverty and Policy', in J. Behrman and T. Srinivasan (eds), *Handbook of Development Economics, Volume 3B*. Amsterdam, New York, and Oxford: Elsevier Science, North Holland, 2551–657.

Loury, G. (1981). 'Intergenerational Transfers and the Distribution of Earnings'. *Econometrica*, 49, 843–867.

Morduch, J. (1990). 'Risk, Production and Saving: Theory and Evidence from Indian Households', mimeo, Harvard University.

—— (1994). 'Poverty and Vulnerability'. *American Economic Review*, 84(2), 221–5.

—— (1995). 'Income Smoothing and Consumption Smoothing.' *Journal of Economic Perspectives*, 9(3), 103–14.

Narayan, D., R. Patel, K. Schafft, A. Rademacher, and S. Koch-Schulte (1999). 'Can Anyone Hear Us? Voices from 47 Countries', in *Voices of the Poor*, Vol. 1. Poverty Group, PREM, World Bank, Washington, DC.

Newman, A. (1995). 'Risk-Bearing and 'Knightian' Entrepreneurship', mimeo, Columbia University.

Piketty, T. (1997). 'The Dynamics of the Wealth Distribution and the Interest Rate with Credit Rationing'. *The Review of Economic Studies*, 64(2), 173–89.

Ravallion, M. (1988). 'Expected Poverty under Risk-Induced Welfare Variability'. *Economic Journal*, 98(393), 1171–82.

Sen, A. (1999). *Development as Freedom*. New York: Knopf.

Shultz, T. (1964). *Transforming Traditional Agriculture*. New Haven, CT: Yale University Press.

Stiglitz, J. (1969). 'The Effects of Income, Wealth, and Capital Gains Taxation on Risk-Taking'. *The Quarterly Journal of Economics*, 83(2), 263–83.

Townsend, R. (1994). 'Risk and Insurance in Village India'. *Econometrica*, 62(3), 539–91.

—— (1995). 'Financial Systems in Northern Thai Villages'. *The Quarterly Journal of Economics*, 110(4), 1011–46.

Udry, C. (1990). 'Credit Markets in Northern Nigeria: Credit as Insurance in a Rural Economy'. *World Bank Economic Review*, 4(3), 251–69.

Walker, T. and J. Ryan (1990). *Village and Household Economies in India's Semi-arid Tropics*, Baltimore, MA and London: Johns Hopkins University Press.

4

Inequality and Risk

MARCEL FAFCHAMPS

There has been a lot of interest in the risk-coping strategies of the poor in the recent literature but little work on the relationship between these strategies and inequality (Fafchamps 1999). Some have begun to suspect that certain risk-coping strategies further impoverish the poor (e.g. Dasgupta 1993; Sen 1981). Labour bonding and debt peonage are examples that have been discussed in the literature (e.g. de Janvry 1981; Srinivasan 1989). Patronage, that is, the protection of the poor by the rich in exchange for labour and services, is also suspected of perpetuating poverty (e.g. Platteau 1995; Fafchamps and Quisumbing 1999).

The purpose of this chapter is to clarify the relationship between inequality and risk. Our objective is to understand how wealth accumulation and risk-sharing affect the evolution of inequality over time. Instead of analysing on a single model in detail, we provide a rapid overview of various modelling frameworks. This approach has the merit of identifying key tradeoffs. Results presented here should be seen as preliminary and tentative. To keep things manageable, we focus on a two-agent economy and ignore incentive issues and asymmetric information. Agents are infinitely lived. Returns to wealth are taken to be deterministic but, unlike many models of long-term inequality, income is stochastic. Five concepts of inequality are distinguished: wealth, income, consumption, cash-in-hand, and welfare. We ignore possible feedback effects between inequality and social choices (Benabou 2000).

We begin by showing that when risk-sharing is perfect, inequality in welfare is constant over time. This is hardly a novel result, but it implies that perfect risk-sharing eliminates social mobility. This might be a 'good' thing if welfare is distributed equitably. But it is hardly equitable if the constant distribution of welfare is highly unequal. We also examine the constraints that voluntary participation to mutual insurance imposes on redistribution.

Next, we assume risk-sharing away and examine how inequality evolves over time when agents accumulate an asset. We distinguish between three canonical situations. We first assume that asset accumulation is unbounded and the asset yields a positive return. In this case, wealth can be thought of as capital. We show that inequality converges to single value over time. If agents have different propensities to save, the share of total wealth in the hands of the more thrifty agent converges to 1. If agents have identical savings functions, inequality converges to an arbitrary level that depends on the path of income realizations.

We then consider what happens when the asset yields a zero or negative return. Grain storage is an example of such asset. Here, the only motive for holding wealth is precautionary saving. In this case, there is no persistent inequality; agents switch rank as a function of income realizations. Inequality is nevertheless correlated over time. This correlation is higher when the asset return is higher (i.e. less negative).

Next we examine the situation when wealth yields a positive return but is in finite supply. Land is an example of such asset. Manpower can also, in principle, be accumulated via indenture contracts. We find that, in this case, persistent inequality naturally arises if one agent is more thrifty than the other. Persistent inequality may also arise even if agents have identical savings functions provided their savings rate increases with wealth. In this case, multiple equilibria may obtain, especially if the return to the asset is high or the asset stock is large. Initial conditions or early realizations of income select, which equilibrium the economy gets locked into. Societies might seek to prevent this kind of polarization by closing down markets in such assets. One possible example is the prohibition of land sales that prevails over most of the countryside in sub-Saharan Africa (e.g. Atwood 1990; Platteau 1992). Another example is slavery, which is now prohibited everywhere but was legal in many places a couple of hundred years ago. Many European immigrants, for instance, financed their voyage to America through indenture contracts.

We then return to risk-sharing in the presence of assets. With perfect risk-sharing, welfare inequality is constant across time. But, as is well known, much indeterminacy arises in the definition (and packaging) of assets. For this reason, we focus on the accumulation of net wealth and ignore credit. We find that for continued participation to mutual insurance to be voluntary, welfare inequality must be consistent with agents' assets and incomes. A redistribution of assets may thus be necessary to support a particular level of inequality. This implies that asset inequality must remain 'close' to welfare inequality.

In the last section, we introduce imperfect commitment. The end result is a hybrid situation half-way between the risk-sharing model and the pure accumulation model. One interesting result is that, if risk aversion is high for poor agents but low for rich ones, risk-sharing with imperfect commitment is most likely to take the form of patronage. We find that, with imperfect commitment, patronage on average takes away from the poor. In this case, risk-sharing becomes a factor of polarization as it makes inequality more likely and more persistent.[1] Patronage does, however, protect the poor from starvation so that for the poor it is preferable to less wealth-inequality but no risk-sharing. This might explain why patronage relations tend to arise endogenously in a variety of contexts, even after asset redistribution (de Janvry *et al.* 2001).

---

[1] Here we do not use the term polarization to describe the distribution of income at a given point in time, as in Estaban and Ray (1994) and Zhang and Kanbur (2001), but as a differentiation process whereby persistent inequality endogenously arises among otherwise equal agents.

4.1. THE ECONOMY

We consider an infinitely-lived, two-agent economy. Throughout the chapter, we use the superscript $i \in \{1, 2\}$ to denote the agent and the subscript t to denote the time period. Aggregate variables appear without i superscript. Utility is written $U_i(c_t^i)$. For simplicity, we assume that the common discount factor is unity. Each agent i derives a random stream of income $\{y_t^i\}$ on a finite support $(0, \bar{y}]$ with $\bar{y} < \infty$. We also assume that the probability of zero income is 0. Aggregate income y_t is defined $y_t = \sum y_t^i$.

Each agent is endowed with a vector of assets. Some of these assets are market-able, such as grain; others cannot be traded, such as entrepreneurship. The value of marketable assets is called wealth and is denoted by W_t^i. Wealth can be accumulated. In contrast, non-traded assets denoted by Z^i cannot be accumulated and are constant over time. The institutional framework determines which assets are marketable and which are not. The prohibition of indenture contracts, for instance, means that man-power is not a marketable asset—although its product, work, can be traded. Wealth yields a return γ which, for simplicity, we assume constant over time and individuals. This return can be positive or negative. When $\gamma > 0$, we say that wealth is pro-ductive; when $\gamma \leq 0$, we say that wealth is storable but unproductive. Examples of productive wealth include land, manpower, and capital. Examples of storable but unproductive wealth include grain, water, and minerals.[2] Income is a function of marketable and non-marketable assets:

$$y_t^i = \omega^i(Z^i, \theta_t) + \gamma W_t^i, \tag{4.1}$$

where θ_t denotes the state of nature at time t. Income is random through the dependence of function $\omega^i(.)$ on θ_t. We assume here that θ_t is uncorrelated over time. In the remainder of this chapter, we refer to $\omega^i(Z^i, \theta_t)$ as labour income and to γW_t^i as wealth income. Cash-in-hand X_t^i is defined as $X_t^i \equiv y_t^i + W_t^i$.

The object of the chapter is to investigate how wealth accumulation and risk-sharing affect inequality. We distinguish five concepts of inequality: marginal utility, consump-tion, income, cash-in-hand, and wealth. Since there are only two agents, inequality can be represented as the ratio between the two agents. Inequality ratios are written as the letter N_t^z, where z denotes the variable over which the ratio is computed. For instance, inequality in income is written as

$$N_t^y \equiv y_t^2/y_t^1. \tag{4.2}$$

Similarly, inequality in consumption, cash-in-hand, and wealth are written as $N_t^c \equiv c_t^2/c_t^1$, $N_t^x \equiv X_t^2/X_t^1$, and $N_t^w \equiv W_t^2/W_t^1$. For reasons that will become apparent when we discuss risk-sharing, it is also useful to define a measure of welfare inequality as the ration of marginal utility:

$$N_t^u \equiv U_1'(c_t^1)/U_2'(c_t^2). \tag{4.3}$$

---

[2] Storable wealth can, over a short period, yield a positive return. But, unlike productive assets, it has to be destroyed in order to produce something else.

If $U(c) = \log(c)$, then $N_t^u = N_t^c$. In general N_t^c tends to track N_t^u and can thus be thought of as a money-metric measure of inequality in instantaneous welfare.[3] While four of the inequality measures are unproblematic, N_t^w is not defined when $W_t^1 = 0$.[4] This is taken into account in subsequent sections.

The purpose of this chapter is to characterize what long-term inequality looks like and how it evolves over time. We also seek to relate the different measures of inequality to each other. As is clear from the notation, inequality measures vary over time and with the state of nature. Much of this chapter is thus concerned with the probability distribution of inequality measures. We focus primarily on long-term— or steady state—inequality and thus seek to uncover the asymptotic (steady state) unconditional distribution of inequality measures. To reflect this fact, steady-state inequality measures written without time subscript. For instance, $\Pr[N^y]$ denotes the probability distribution of steady-state income distribution. The unconditional expected value of N^y is denoted $N_e^y \equiv E[N^y]$, and similarly for the other inequality measures.

We also wish to study the extent to which inequality endures over time. In particular we focus on the steady-state correlation between N_t^y and N_{t+1}^y or, more precisely, on the relationship between N_t^y and $E[N_{t+1}^y | N_t^y]$. Suppose that

$$E[N_{t+1}^y | N_t^y] = \rho N_t^y + \delta N^y. \tag{4.4}$$

If, for instance, $\delta = 0$ and $\rho = 1$,

$$E[N_{t+1}^y | N_t^y] = N_t^y, \tag{4.5}$$

inequality follows a random walk: inequality today is likely to persist tomorrow. If, in contrast, $\rho = 0$ and $\delta = 1$, we have

$$E[N_{t+1}^y | N_t^y] = N^y, \tag{4.6}$$

which implies that inequality is short-lived. In general, the closer to 1 ρ is, the more persistent inequality is.

We proceed as follows. We first examine a number of simple, limit cases. Then we introduce complications. Limited commitment is discussed in Section 4.5. To characterize the distribution of inequality measures, we rely on a combination of algebraic and simulation methods. In all cases, we seek to relate different types of inequality with each other.

---

[3] To be a satisfactory measure of inequality, N_t^u needs to be normalized in some way. One possibility is to set $U_1'(c)/U_2'(c) = 1$ for some level of consumption c, for example, average consumption. In practice, N_t^u is most useful when both agents have the same utility function.

[4] To ensure that income inequality is always defined, we assume that $\Pr[\omega^i(Z^i, \theta_t) = 0] = 0$. This also ensures that N_t^x is always defined. We also assume that $U(0) = -\infty$ so that zero consumption is never optimal. Since income is never 0, positive consumption is always feasible and N_t^c is always defined. Utility is assumed continuously differentiable so that N_t^u is always defined as well. In contrast, N_t^w need not be defined if $W_t^1 = 0$.

4.2. NO MARKETABLE ASSETS

We begin by assuming that marketable assets are absent and thus that accumulation is not feasible: $W_t^i = 0$ for all i and t.[5] Income is labour income only: $y_t^i = \omega^i(Z^i, \theta_t)$. It follows that $\Pr[N_t^y] = \Pr[N^y]$: the unconditional probability distribution of income inequality is at its steady state in all t; there is no transition period. It also follows that $N_t^x = N_t^y$ since $y_t^i = X_t^i$. The unconditional expectation of income inequality simply is

$$E[N^y] = E\left[\frac{\omega^2(Z^2, \theta_t)}{\omega^1(Z^1, \theta_t)}\right]. \tag{4.7}$$

This means that a more talented individual has a higher income on average. Since income is a function of never changing assets, there is no social mobility in incomes. We also see that, since we have assumed that the θ_t shocks are uncorrelated over time, conditional and unconditional income inequality are equal:

$$E[N_t^y | N_{t-1}^y] = E[N^y]. \tag{4.8}$$

Any deviation from expected income inequality $E[N^y]$ is short-lived.

Inequality in consumption depends on whether income risk is shared or not. If risk-sharing is not possible, then $c_t^i = y_t^i = \omega(Z^i, \theta_t)$. In this case, $N_t^c = N_t^y$ and shares all the properties of N_t^y. If, in addition, utility has the form $U(c) = \log c$, we also have $N_t^u = N_t^y$. In a world with no accumulable assets, no risk-sharing, and relative risk aversion close to unity (i.e. log utility), income inequality summarizes all there is to know about welfare inequality.

Suppose, in contrast, mutual insurance contracts are perfectly and costlessly enforceable. Perfect competition thus reaches an efficient allocation. Pareto efficiency in the sharing of risk dictates that

$$\frac{U_1'(c_t^1)}{U_2'(c_t^2)} = \frac{U_1'(c_{t'}^1)}{U_2'(c_{t'}^2)} \equiv k \quad \text{for all } t \text{ and } t', \tag{4.9}$$

where k is a constant equal to the ratio of welfare weights (e.g. Cochrane 1991; Mace 1991; Altonji *et al.* 1992). Since $U_1'(c_t^1)/U_2'(c_t^2) \equiv N_t^u$, it follows that welfare inequality N_t^u is constant over time with $N^u = k$. This is true even though N_t^y varies from period to period: welfare inequality is divorced from income inequality.

With perfect pooling of risk, individual consumption is only a function of aggregate income. This implies that, if aggregate income y_t is constant over time, consumption is constant as well. If the economy is subject to collective shocks, inequality in consumption varies in a deterministic fashion with aggregate income. But the distribution of welfare is unchanged, that is, there exist monotonic functions of individual consumptions c_t^1 and c_t^2 (the marginal utility functions) such that the ratio of these functions is constant across time and states of nature. Thus, even though individual consumption and welfare might change over time (as aggregate resources expand or dwindle), inequality remains constant in some fundamental sense.

---

[5] This means that N_t^w is not defined. Consequently, it is ignored in this section.

When agents have identical preferences with constant relative risk aversion, N_t^c remains constant over time even in the presence of aggregate shocks.[6] Consumption inequality $N_t^c = (N^u)^{1/R}$, with $N_t^c = N^u$ if $U(c) = \log(c)$. For other utility functions, N_t^c might change slightly over time and states of nature. But within this framework, N_t^c can be thought of as an approximation to N^u, which is the relevant welfare measure in our economy.

Although hardly novel, this result implies that perfect risk-sharing, as could be achieved for instance via a perfect insurance market, would freeze welfare inequality to a permanent level. This might be socially acceptable if this level is relatively egalitarian. There are many Pareto efficient allocations in our stylized economy. But nothing guarantees that the Pareto efficient allocation selected by a competitive market equilibrium would be socially acceptable. This probably explains why there is a lot of public intervention in social insurance and why many insurance schemes pursue redistribution objectives. Some are even worded not as insurance but as anti-poverty programmes. Because insurance also determines welfare inequality, it is likely to be combined with redistribution so that it does not itself become the source of inequality.

This raises the issue of how much redistribution can be sustained if participation to risk-sharing is voluntary. Not all risk-sharing arrangements can be sustained in a decentralized market. The main constraint imposed by a decentralized market equilibrium is *ex ante* voluntary participation: agents must find it in their interest to participate to a risk-sharing arrangement/to purchase an insurance contract. If this condition is not satisfied, agents would be better off by consuming their individual income.[7] This simple observation implies that agents who could guarantee themselves a higher utility in autarchy must in general have a higher level of utility with risk-sharing.

Risk-sharing does not preclude redistribution. Suppose we wish to achieve equality in expected consumption, that is, we wish to attain $E[N^c] = 1$. If $E[N^y] = E[N^c]$, attaining equality is unproblematic since reversion to autarky—$c_t^i = y_t^i$—would result in equality. We can thus define redistribution as the difference between $E[N^y]$ and $E[N^c]$. With taxation/forced participation in mutual insurance, any level of N^u is sustainable. This is not true of decentralizable arrangements. Voluntary participation to any mutual insurance contract puts bounds on how far N^u (and thus $E[N^c]$) can stray from $E[N^y]$ and thus on the level of equality that can be achieved.

For instance, if all agents have the same utility function, agents with higher expected earnings must be ensured higher consumption. This puts a bound on $E[N^y] - E[N^c]$. Consumption inequality is thus, in general, a function of unalienable assets Z^i. The only case in which voluntary participation might induce agents with higher expected earnings to accept less consumption than agents with lower expected earnings is if the former are much more risk averse than the latter. By the same reasoning, we see that the more risk-averse agents are, the more they are willing to accept a redistribution

---

[6] We have $U(c) = c^{1-R}/(1 - R)$. Differentiating with respect to c and replacing in the definition of welfare inequality, we obtain $N_t^u = (c^2/c^1)^R$. When $U(c) = \log(c)$, $N_t^u = c^2/c^1$. Since $N_t^c \equiv c^2/c^1$, we see that whenever N_t^u is constant, so is N_t^c.   [7] The allocation must be in the core (Hildenbrand 1974).

of average consumption in exchange for better insurance. We revisit these issues in Section 4.5.

These results are summarized in the following proposition:

Proposition 1   *In the absence of accumulable assets:*

(1) The distribution of income inequality is at its steady state in all periods: $\Pr[N_t^y] = \Pr[N^y]$ *for all t.*

(2) If income shocks are uncorrelated, conditional expected inequality in income is constant: $E[N_t^y | N_{t-1}^y] = E[N_t^y] = E[N^y]$.

Proposition 2   *Without risk-sharing:*

(1) Inequality in consumption is equal to inequality in income: $N_t^c = N_t^y$.

(2) Expected long-term inequality in consumption is constant: $E[N^c] = E[N^y]$.

(3) With log *utility, inequality in welfare is equal to inequality in income:* $E[N^u] = E[N^y]$.

Proposition 3   *With perfect risk-sharing:*

(1) $N_t^u = N^u$: welfare inequality is constant; there is no social mobility.

(2) $N_t^c = G(y_t)$: inequality in consumption is a deterministic function of aggregate income.

(3) $N_t^c = N^c$ if $y_t = y$ or if $U_i(c) = \log(c)$ or if $U(c) = c^{1-R}/(1-R)$ for $i = \{1, 2\}$.

Proposition 4   *With voluntary participation in risk-sharing:*

(1) $E[N^c]$ is a non-decreasing function of $E[N^y]$ if all agents share the same utility function (up to an affine transformation).

(2) The more risk-averse agents are, the more redistribution $E[N^y] - E[N^c]$ can voluntarily be achieved, and the closer $E[N^c]$ can be brought to unity (equality in expected ratio of consumption).

4.3. ACCUMULATION WITH NO RISK-SHARING

We now allow for wealth accumulation by assuming the existence of marketable assets. In this section, we focus on the case where explicit risk-sharing is not possible—perhaps because a market for insurance does not exist. Agents potentially have two motives for saving: precautionary saving and growth in consumption—prudence and patience (Kimball 1990). If the return on marketable assets is negative, prudence is only motive for saving (Deaton 1991). Throughout we assume that there is no borrowing.

4.3.1. *Unbounded Accumulation*

We first examine the case where $\gamma > 0$. Provided agents save enough, they can accumulate indefinitely. At the limit, their wealth becomes so large that it is entirely dominated by the return to wealth γW_t^i which, by assumption, is non-stochastic. Consequently, as wealth becomes large, income shocks have less and less effect on consumption.

This implies that inequality is asymptotically deterministic. We now show this more rigorously.

We first must establish conditions under which people save enough for wealth to grow indefinitely. We need $E[W^i_{t+1}|W^i_t] > W^i_t$. Suppose, for instance, that agents save a constant proportion s of their income $y^i_t = \omega^i + \gamma W^i_t$. We have:

$$
\begin{aligned}
E[W^i_{t+1}|W^i_t] &= E[s(\omega^i + \gamma W^i_t) + W^i_t] \\
&= sE[\omega^i] + s\gamma W^i_t + W^i_t > W^i_t,
\end{aligned}
\tag{4.10}
$$

which is satisfied for any $s > 0$. If each agent chooses its level of saving by maximizing its expected discounted utility subject to a budget constraint, we obtain an Euler equation of the form:

$$
U'_i(c^i_t) = (1 + \gamma)E[U'_i(c^i_{t+1})],
\tag{4.11}
$$

where the intertemporal discount factor drops out since, by assumptions, agents do not discount the future.[8] We see from the above equation that the marginal utility of income must fall, on average, over time—which implies that consumption must rise and thus that assets must be accumulated (Deaton 1991). This establishes that when $\gamma > 0$ and agents do not discount the future, indefinite accumulation obtains.

Having established that both agents accumulate, we now turn to the characterization of long-term inequality in wealth N^w_t. Since agents always hold positive assets, at least after a while, the distribution of N^w_t is well defined.[9] We note that, as both agents become wealthier, labour income becomes a vanishingly small proportion of their cash-in-hand. Savings thus becomes almost deterministic and the path of individual wealth converges to a deterministic path. This is illustrated in Fig. 4.1, which plots three possible paths of N^w_t for a fully symmetrical model with a constant saving rate. The only difference between the paths is the sequence of labour income shocks. To facilitate interpretation, we graph wealth shares $W^2_t/(W^1_t + W^2_t)$ instead of N^w_t. We see that all paths eventually converge to a single share.

How inequality evolves over time depends on the relative savings rate of both agents. If one agent saves faster than the other, wealth inequality N^w_t diverges permanently, either tending to infinity (if agent 2 saves more) or to 0 (if agent 1 saves more). If agents save at the same rate, their wealth asymptotically grows at the same rate: the ratio of their wealths tends to a constant. Wealth inequality tends to a constant (see Fig. 4.1). This is true even if their labour income processes are different because, when wealth is large enough, labour income does not matter anymore. This finding is reminiscent of Polya urn processes (Arthur *et al.* 1994). Wealth inequality N^w_t follows a random walk with smaller and smaller increments. Initial realizations of income determine the speed with which wealth is initially accumulated, and thus the process of initial

---

[8] If agents discount the future, indefinite accumulation obtains if the return on the asset is higher than the rate of intertemporal preference.

[9] Starting from zero assets, it is possible that low initial realization of income trigger no accumulation. We ignore these complications here and focus on the long-run distribution of N^w_t only.

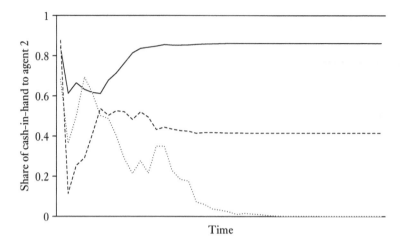

Figure 4.1. *Inequality over time for three realizations of labour income*

differentiation. As time passes, however, changes in wealth inequality (i.e. in the ratio of wealth levels) become smaller and smaller as income—and thus savings—become progressively dominated by wealth. Inequality in wealth converges to an asymptotic value N^w. This is illustrated in Fig. 4.1.[10]

This implies that the conditional distribution of N^w_{t+1} gets more and more narrowly defined around N^w_t as time passes. There is 'lock-in': changes in inequality becomes smaller and smaller over time. Even though both agents might have had the same economic opportunities *ex ante*, over time they diverge so that, with time, their economic prospects become highly contrasted. At the limit, relative prosperity becomes permanent. Social mobility—that is, the chance of changing one's rank—disappears over time.

Which value N^w_t converges to its path dependent: if agent 1 is lucky early on, he or she gets a headstart, and vice versa. *Ex ante*, there are many possible asymptotic values N^w can take—essentially any value between zero and infinity. Are all these values equally likely? In general the answer is no. To characterize the *ex ante* (unconditional) distribution of N^w we need to impose more structure on the model. The distribution of N^w is also complicated by the fact that it is a ratio. It is easier to characterize the distribution of the share of total wealth $S^w_t \equiv W^1_t/(W^1_t + W^2_t)$. By construction, $S^w_t \in [0, 1]$. Since N^w_t converges to a single value, so does S^w_t.

With identical non-traded assets $Z^1 = Z^2$, independent income shocks, identical initial wealth $W^1 = W^2$, and identical utility functions $U^1(.) = U^2(.)$, both agents are *ex ante* equivalent and their economic opportunities are the same. If agents have

---

[10] Figure 4.1 is constructed using a convex savings function (lower savings rate at low values of cash-in-hand). Both agents have the same savings function. Labour incomes are independent and uniformly distributed. Three paths are generated corresponding to three sets of labour income realizations. With a constant savings rate, the distribution of convergence shares S^w is more concentrated around 0.5. This is because lucky labour income early on provides less of a headstart in wealth accumulation.

equal initial endowments and identical preferences, it should be possible to show that $E[S^w] = 0.5$. The realized value of S^w, however, can take any value between 0 and 1. In the symmetric case, agents have equal opportunities *ex ante* but once inequality sets in it gets reinforced over time.

Having characterized the distribution of wealth inequality, we now turn to other inequality measures. By definition, we have $N_t^x = (\omega_t^2 + (1+\gamma)W_t^2)/(\omega_t^1 + (1+\gamma)W_t^1)$ and $N_t^y = (\omega_t^2 + \gamma W_t^2)/(\omega_t^1 + \gamma W_t^1)$. As W_t^1 and W_t^2 tend to infinity over time, both ratios tend to N_t^w. We thus have $\lim_{t\to\infty}||N_t^x - N_t^w|| = \lim_{t\to\infty}||N_t^y - N_t^w|| = 0$: inequality in cash-in-hand and in income tends to inequality in wealth. Of course, since wealth increases without bounds, inequality is not synonymous with poverty: at the limit, both agents are infinitely wealthy.

Given that there is no risk-sharing, each agent consumes exclusively from its own cash-in-hand $X_t^i \equiv y_t^i + W_t^i$. Let $c^i(X_t^i)$ denote the consumption function of individual i. We have $N_t^c = c^2(X_t^2)/c^1(X_t^1)$. Suppose that both consumption functions are asymptotically linear, for example, that $\lim_{X\to\infty} c^i(X) = k^i X$. In this case, $\lim_{t\to\infty}||N_t^c - (k^2/k^1)N_t^x|| = 0$: inequality in consumption tends to a multiple of wealth inequality.

More generally, there exist a function of wealth inequality $f^c(N_t^x)$ to which consumption inequality converges: $\lim_{t\to\infty}||N_t^c - f(N_t^x)|| = 0$.[11] This implies that, at the limit, the ratio of consumption is a function of the ratio of wealth. The same reasoning applies to welfare inequality, that is, there exist a function $f^u(N_t^x)$ such that $\lim_{t\to\infty}||N_t^u - f(N_t^x)|| = 0$. Inequality in wealth leads to inequality in consumption and in welfare. Other conclusions apply as well: path dependence; lock-in; *ex ante* unpredictability of long-term inequality. When both agents asymptotically save at the same rate, all inequality measures converge to a single number.

These results can be summarized as follows:

Proposition 5 *With unbounded accumulation ($\gamma > 0$), we have:*

(1) $\lim_{t\to\infty}||N_t^x - N_t^w|| = \lim_{t\to\infty}||N_t^y - N_t^w|| = 0.$
(2) *There exist a function* $f^c(N_t^x)$ *such that* $\lim_{t\to\infty}||N_t^c - f(N_t^x)|| = 0.$
(3) *There exist a function* $f^u(N_t^x)$ *such that* $\lim_{t\to\infty}||N_t^u - f(N_t^x)|| = 0.$
(4) $\lim_{t\to\infty} Var[N_{t+1}^w|N_t^w] = 0,\ \lim_{t\to\infty} Var[N_{t+1}^x|N_t^x] = 0,$
    $\lim_{t\to\infty} Var[N_{t+1}^y|N_t^y] = 0,\ \lim_{t\to\infty} Var[N_{t+1}^c|N_t^c] = 0,$
    $\lim_{t\to\infty} Var[N_{t+1}^u|N_t^u] = 0.$
(5) *Ex ante,* N^w *is a random variable* $\in (0, \infty)$. *By extension, the same applies to other inequality measures.*
(6) *If agents asymptotically save at the same rate, all inequality measures converge to a single number* $N^w \in (0, \infty)$.
(7) *If agents asymptotically save at a different rate, all inequality measures converge either to 0 (if agent 2 saves less than 1) or to* ∞ *(if agent 2 saves more than 1).*

---

[11] To see why, note that in the long run, the path of inequality depends less and less on income, that is, converges to a deterministic path. Consider the deterministic path of cash-in-hand inequality. Along this deterministic path, to each inequality ratio corresponds a ratio of consumption.

4.3.2. *Bounded Accumulation with Unproductive Assets*

The situation is very different if $\gamma < 0$. In this case, wealth accumulation is costly. Agents engage in it only to insure themselves against income shocks—the precautionary savings motive. This case is more relevant for poor or pre-industrial societies where opportunities to invest are few and returns to assets are low.

Accumulation in such models has been analysed elsewhere (e.g. Deaton 1990, 1991, 1992; Zeldes 1989) Assets are known to follow a renewal process. As long as accumulated wealth is positive, it follows a random walk. For sufficiently large negative shocks, agents deplete all their wealth, at which point the process is 'renewed', that is, it forgets the past and starts anew. How much accumulation takes place depends on the marginal propensity to save (MPS) out of cash-in-hand. Kimball (1990) has shown how the MPS is related to the third derivative of the utility function via what he calls 'prudence', defined as $\phi \equiv -U'''/U''$. Other things being equal, more prudent agents—higher ϕ—save more.

We seek to characterize the distribution of cash-in-hand, income, and consumption. In this model as in the previous one, all inequality measures are closely related. This is because, in the absence of risk-sharing, an agent's consumption depends exclusively on individual cash-in-hand X_t^i. Inequality in cash-in-hand thus translate into inequality in consumption and welfare. However, because agents use wealth to smooth consumption, inequality in consumption is typically much less than inequality in wealth (e.g. Paxson 1992; Townsend 1994).[12]

We begin by noting that, since income is bounded, wealth is also bounded. This is because $\gamma < 0$. To see why, let $\bar{\omega}^i$ denote the maximum level of labour income. The maximum rate at which wealth can accumulate is when agents save all and income is always at its maximum: $W_{t+1}^i = \bar{\omega}^i + (1 + \gamma)W_t^i$. Since $\gamma < 0$, we see that wealth cannot exceed $-\bar{\omega}^i/\gamma$.

Inequality in cash-in-hand N_t^x in general follows an AR1 stochastic process between 0 and ∞. This is because income realizations induce random changes in the wealth of both agents. If an agent gets a temporarily high cash-in-hand level, he saves and his wealth goes up. The opposite is true if realized cash-in-hand is low. Cash-in-hand inequality is thus a transient phenomenon: since each agents' wealth is bounded from above and from below, all agents eventually run out of funds in finite time. This implies that no agent can indefinitely stay ahead of the other. By this reasoning, the distribution of N_t^x is stationary. By extension, all inequality measures have stationary distributions. Unlike in the case with infinite accumulation, there is no lock-in here.

Can we be more precise and characterize the distribution of some of the inequality measures? Consider consumption inequality. If agents were perfectly able to smooth consumption thanks to precautionary saving, consumption would be constant as well as consumption inequality. This outcome, however, is generally not achievable. The next best outcome is if preferences are quadratic and households face no credit constraint.

---

[12] Because wealth can fall to 0 for both agents, the distribution of N_t^p is not strictly speaking defined. For this reason, we ignore it here and focus instead on inequality in cash-in-hand. The latter is always defined since income can never be 0.

In this case, certainty equivalence applies and agents respond to income shocks by consuming the annuity value of their total wealth (e.g. Hall 1978; Zeldes 1989).

In our case, the annuity value of a (finite) income shock is 0 since agents' rate of time preference is 0.[13] The annuity value of wealth is also 0 since, with $\gamma < 0$, wealth is expected to be eliminated in finite time. We therefore get the standard permanent income result: when the rate of time preference is 0, agents consume the average income $E[\omega^i(Z_t^i, \theta_t)]$ which is also the annuity value of wealth. In the more general case, Zeldes (1989) has shown that, when wealth is sufficiently large, consumption tends to the certainty equivalent level of consumption for a large enough level of wealth. This is true for any (reasonable) utility function and holds even if agents cannot incur a negative net worth. Applying these ideas to our economy, we see that when the wealth of both agents is large, N_t^c tends to $E[\omega^2(Z_t^2, \theta_t)]/E[\omega^1(Z_t^1, \theta_t)]$: consumption inequality is a function of inequality in expected labour income.

In general, N_t^c is not constant. When cash-in-hand is large for both agents, certainty equivalence approximately holds and fluctuations in consumption—and thus in consumption inequality—are quite small. As Zeldes (1989) and Carroll (1992) have shown, however, certainty equivalence is violated when wealth is small and agents cannot borrow (as we assume here). In this case, a shortfall in cash-in-hand results in a drop in consumption—and a temporary increase in consumption inequality. Since these shortfalls can affect both agents, we would expect consumption inequality to fluctuates around $E[\omega^2(Z_t^2, \theta_t)]/E[\omega^1(Z_t^1, \theta_t)]$ and to be correlated over time (through the dependence of current consumption on accumulated wealth). The precise distribution of consumption inequality, however, is difficult to characterize without imposing more structure on the model. Figure 4.2 illustrates how inequality in labour income, cash-in-hand, and consumption evolve over time.[14] We see that, thanks to precautionary saving, inequality in consumption is always less than inequality in cash-in-hand or in labour income.

Regarding correlation in inequality over time, we first note that, in the absence of correlation in labour income, correlation in cash-in-hand inequality depends on how much agents accumulate. If they accumulate a lot, the correlation is high; if they accumulate little, the correlation is low. Consequently, any factor that favours accumulation also favours the correlation of inequality over time. This means, for instance, that inequality is more persistent when the propensity to save is higher. By the same token, the correlation between N_t^x and N_{t+1}^x depends on γ. If γ is very negative, wealth dissipates rapidly and $Cor[N_t^x, N_{t+1}^x]$ is low: a wealth advantage does not last long. If γ is close to 0, the reverse is true. At the same time, if both agents accumulate more, they are better able to withstand shocks, and consumption inequality fluctuate less on average.

---

[13] Ignoring the case where labour income follows a random walk. Here the distribution of labour income is assumed stationary.

[14] As in Fig. 4.1, the savings function is convex (lower savings rate at low levels of cash-in-hand). This is meant to reproduce the shape Zeldes' consumption function. Both agents have the same savings function. Labour income is independently distributed.

M. Fafchamps

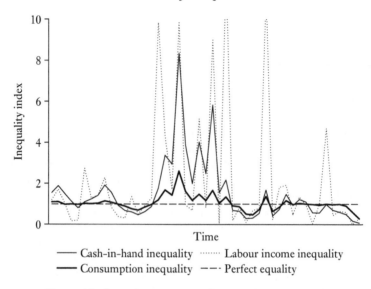

Figure 4.2. *Inequality over time with precautionary saving only*

Second, we note that the more cash-in-hand is correlated over time, the more consumption is correlated as well. This is because consumption is a monotonically increasing function of cash-in-hand: $c_t^i = c^i(X_t^i)$ with $c'(X) > 0$ for all X. As a result, a high correlation between X_t^2/X_t^1 and X_{t+1}^2/X_{t+1}^1 results in a high correlation between $c^2(X_t^2)/c^1(X_t^1)$ and $c^2(X_{t+1}^2)/c^1(X_{t+1}^1)$. Since welfare inequality depends on consumption, the same observation applies to N_t^u.

Combining the two above observations, we note that factors that raise accumulation reduce the variance of consumption and welfare inequality but raise persistence in inequality. This is illustrated in Fig. 4.3: when γ is lower—and accumulation less—consumption inequality is more variable but it is less correlated over time.[15]

Results can be summarized as follows:

Proposition 6 *With bounded accumulation ($\gamma < 0$) and no discounting, we have:*

(1) All inequality measures are stationary Markov processes.
(2) All inequality measures move together.
(3) N_t^c fluctuates around $E[\omega^2(Z_t^2, \theta_t)]/E[\omega^1(Z_t^1, \theta_t)]$.
(4) $Var[N_t^x]$, $Var[N_t^y]$, $Var[N_t^c]$, and $Var[N_t^u]$ are non-decreasing functions of γ.
(5) $Cor[N_t^x, N_{t+1}^x]$, $Cor[N_t^y, N_{t+1}^y]$, $Cor[N_t^c, N_{t+1}^c]$, and $Cor[N_t^u, N_{t+1}^u]$ are increasing functions of γ.

Part (1) means that inequality is a transient phenomenon. Part (2) means that inequality in non-traded assets Z^i has a permanent effect on inequality. Parts (3) and (4)

---

[15] Settings for Fig. 4.3 are identical to those of Fig. 4.2, except that the value of γ is varied.

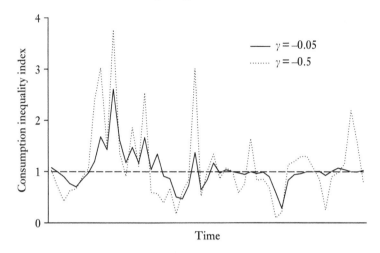

Figure 4.3. *Consumption inequality and return on savings*

mean that easier accumulation reduces fluctuations in inequality but raises persistence in inequality. There is a tradeoff between social mobility and vulnerability.

4.3.3. *Accumulation with Assets in Fixed Supply*

In the previous section, agents accumulate assets independently from each other. Grain storage is an example of wealth that fits nicely in this model. Other types of wealth, such as land, do not fit as nicely. In this section, we consider accumulable assets that are in fixed supply, that is, such that $W_t^1 + W_t^2 = \bar{W}$. Land is one possible example, provided there exists a sales market for land. Another possible example is manpower in societies that allow voluntary indenture contracts (Srinivasan 1989). In general, we assume that $\gamma \geq 0$, that is, that the asset is productive. The case where $\gamma = 0$ corresponds to the island economy discussed in Sargent (1987: Chapter 3).

We begin by focusing on asset inequality. Other inequality measures ultimately depend on how the fixed asset is shared. When the asset is in fixed supply, we can no longer ignore relative prices: the price p_t at which the asset is turned into consumption varies to clear the asset market. This singularly complicates the model because fluctuations in asset prices introduce uncertainty in real asset returns and generate a speculative motive for holding wealth. In the discussion that follows, we mostly ignore these complications.

Saving is now a function of cash-in-hand and asset price: $W_{t+1}^i = s^i(\omega_t^i, W_t^i, p_t)$. To simplify the presentation, we assume that the savings function is separable so that:

$$W_{t+1}^i = \frac{s^i(\omega_t^i, W_t^i)}{g(p_t)} \tag{4.12}$$

with $\partial s^i / \partial \omega^i \geq 0$ and $\partial s^i / \partial W^i \geq 0$. With this assumption, the market clearing condition $W_t^1 + W_t^2 = \bar{W}$ yields the following expression for asset inequality (expressed here as a share):

$$
\begin{aligned}
S^w_{t+1} &\equiv \frac{W^2_{t+1}}{W^1_{t+1} + W^2_{t+1}} \\
&= \frac{s^2(\omega^2_t, W^2_t)}{s^1(\omega^1_t, W^1_t) + s^2(\omega^2_t, W^2_t)} \\
&= \frac{s^2(\omega^2_t, S^w_t \bar{W})}{s^1(\omega^1_t, (1 - S^w_t)\bar{W}) + s^2(\omega^2_t, S^w_t \bar{W})}.
\end{aligned} \tag{4.13}
$$

For comparison with earlier sections, $N^w_t = S^w_t/(1 - S^w_t)$. The advantage of the above formulation is that the asset price has been factored out. What if the above expression shows is that future asset inequality depends on current inequality: when S^w_t is large, saving by agent 2 tends to be large relative to agent 1. This is because agents save from cash-in-hand and large wealth raises cash-in-hand. This process may lead to self-reinforcing inequality—what we call polarization. The question is under what conditions polarization arises.[16]

This can be answered by examining the law of motion of S^w_t given above. The analysis is complicated by the fact that the ω^i_t's are random variables so that the law of motion of S^w_t is stochastic. We focus on the relationship between S^w_t and $E[S^w_{t+1}]$. We note that

$$
E[S^w_{t+1}] \simeq \frac{s^2(E[\omega^2_t], S^w_t \bar{W})}{s^1(E[\omega^1_t], (1 - S^w_t)\bar{W}) + s^2(E[\omega^2_t], S^w_t \bar{W})}. \tag{4.14}
$$

Consequently the relationship between S^w_t and $E[S^w_{t+1}]$ can studied by studying the above difference equation. Figure 4.4 illustrates what it looks like depending on the curvature of the savings function.[17] The two agents are assumed to have the same savings function. Two curves are shown. The one with a nearly linear (low curvature) savings function intersects the 45-degree line at 0.5 from above. This means that if the fixed asset is shared equally at time t, it tends to be shared equally at time $t + 1$ as well. Deviation from equality tend to correct themselves over time: at low S^w_t leads to a higher $E[S^w_{t+1}]$, and vice versa. Income shocks push S^w_{t+1} up or down a bit, but inequality always gravitates around $S^w_t = 0.5$. There is a single steady state distribution of assets. Polarization does not arise. If agents have different savings rate, polarization arises: the thrifty agent eventually gets most of the asset. This finding is reminiscent of what we found with unbounded accumulation: the shave of total wealth owned by the thrifty agent rises over time, although in this case it does not converge to 1 unless

---

[16] In this model as in Banerjee and Newman (1991), the rich have a less risky income stream than the poor. But in contrast to their work, we do not consider risk-taking as an entrepreneurial activity.

[17] To compute this figure, we use a savings function of the form $S(\omega, W) = e^{\alpha(E[\omega]+(1+\gamma)W)} - 1$. Parameter α determines the curvature of the savings function: the higher it is, the more convex savings is. Values of α are respectively 0.02 and 0.2 for the low curvature and high curvature savings functions reported in the figure.

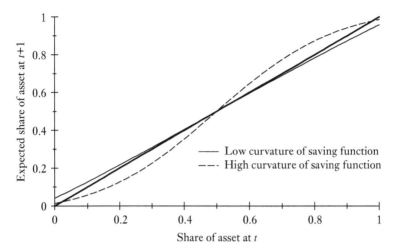

Figure 4.4. *Law of motion of inequality with fixed total asset*

the savings rate of the other agent falls to 0 for low enough wealth. However, there is still a single steady state distribution.

The story is different in the case of the high curvature savings function. Here, the curve intersects the 45-degree line three times, corresponding to three zeros of the difference equation.[18] The middle intersection is unstable because it is cut from below. This means that, starting from equal distribution of assets, small differences in income realizations induce differenciation: one agent is able to accumulate more than the other. There are therefore two steady state distributions of assets: one in which agent 1 owns most of the asset, and one in which agent 2 in the wealthy agent. There is polarization even though agents are symmetrical, that is, have the same preferences and the same expected labour income.

Multiple steady state distributions are illustrated in Fig. 4.5.[19] Two alternative paths of S_t^w are shown. The only difference between the two is the sequence of labour income shocks. Which long-term distribution of inequality is chosen depends on initial realizations of labour income. When agent 2 is lucky early on, he or she is able to accumulate more of the fixed asset and to gain a permanent advantage. The reverse is true if agent 1 enjoys high income draws at the beginning. There is path dependence. These results are similar to those reported by Carter and Zimmerman (2000) for a more complicated simulated economy. Multiple equilibria arise even if labour incomes are strongly correlated across agents, although this correlation may delay the polarization process starting from an egalitarian distribution.

---

[18] This curve resembles Azariadis (1996)'s analysis of country-level poverty traps (see his Fig. 4.2(c)). Our interpretation is quite different, however. In Azariadis, poverty traps exist for each country independently from any interaction between them. Here, the trap arises from the interaction between the two agents.

[19] The savings function is the same as for Fig. 4.4. Here $\alpha = 0.04$.

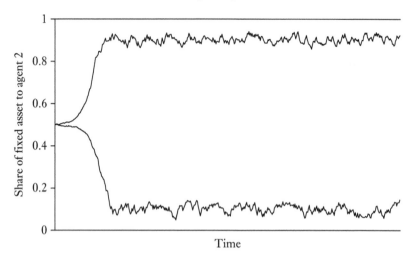

Figure 4.5. *Polarization*

The corollary of path dependence is that the starting point—'history'—matters. If, for exogenous reasons, an agent has most of the wealth to start with, multiplicity of equilibria disappears. The only steady state distribution is the one that favours this agent.

The above framework enables us to investigate the factors that favour multiple equilibria and thus polarization among otherwise identical agents. We have already seen that polarization is more likely when the savings rate increases sharply with cash-in-hand. In fact, polarization cannot arise if the savings rate is constant and identical for both agents. In this case we have:

$$E[S_{t+1}^p] \simeq \frac{sE[\omega_t] + sp_t(1+\gamma)S_t^p \bar{W}}{sE[\omega_t] + sp_t(1+\gamma)(1-S_t^p)\bar{W} + sE[\omega_t] + sp_t(1+\gamma)S_t^p \bar{W}}$$

$$= \frac{sE[\omega_t] + sp_t(1+\gamma)S_t^p \bar{W}}{2sE[\omega_t] + sp_t(1+\gamma)\bar{W}}, \tag{4.15}$$

which is linear in S_t^p. The intuition behind this result is that for multiple steady state distribution to arise, accumulation must get reinforced over time.

It can also be shown that all factors that increase wealth income relative to labour income favour multiple equilibria. This is true of an increase in γ or $\bar{W}$ or of a decrease in $E[\omega^i]$. The reason is that when the income from wealth is small, differences in wealth may not be sufficient to cause a large differentiation in savings rate. As a result, polarization does not arise.

Turning to the conditional (steady state) distribution of inequality, results from the previous section apply here as well: the more remunerative wealth is, the more correlated inequality is over time. The rationale is the same.

Having clarified how wealth evolves over time, the extension to consumption and welfare is straightforward. In the absence of risk-sharing, consumption is simply a function of individual cash-in-hand. Inequality in wealth results in inequality in cash-in-hand and thus in consumption and welfare. Consequently, all that has been said about polarization and multiple equilibria in asset inequality applies to consumption and welfare as well.

Our findings can be summarized as follows:

Proposition 7 *Suppose* $W_t^1 + W_t^2 = \bar{W}$ *and* $\gamma \geq 0$. *We have:*

(1) All inequality measures move together.

(2) Multiple steady state distributions of inequality can arise if the savings rate increases with wealth. This is true even if agents have identical savings function and distribution of labour income. This is true even if labour incomes are strongly correlated.

(3) When multiple steady state distribution exist, initial conditions may have a permanent effect on the distribution of inequality.

(4) Multiple steady state distributions are more likely if:

    (a) the savings rate increases more rapidly with wealth;

    (b) the return to wealth γ *is high;*

    (c) total fixed wealth $\bar{W}$ *is large;*

    (d) expected labour income $E[\omega^i]$ *is small.*

Although it is perilous to interpret the above results literally since they were obtained in a highly stylized model, they may provide an explanation for the apparent difficulty to durably affect land inequality. It has indeed been observed that land inequality often worsens after land reform. Using a complex simulation model, Zimmerman (1993) explains this outcome in terms of credit constraints and perverse fluctuations in land prices. The above model generalizes these insights.

In this section we have interpreted the accumulated factor as land. Other interpretations are feasible as well. If indenture contracts are allowed, then agents can sell their future labour force in exchange for immediate consumption. This has the effect of raising $\bar{W}$ and thus the likelihood of multiple equilibria and thus of polarization among otherwise identical agents. For this reason, certain societies might decide to 'close' or 'outlaw' markets for productive assets in order to prevent inequality. For such measures to be effective, however, alternative channels must exist that enable agents to smooth consumption. If such channels are inexistent, labour bonding and distress sales of land may be the next best alternative (e.g. Srinivasan 1989; Fafchamps 1999). Labour bonding contracts are revisited in the next section because indentured labourers would normally be insured against risk (i.e. they get a constant albeit low consumption) after they begin working as slaves.

4.4. ACCUMULATION AND RISK-SHARING

We now consider wealth accumulation and risk-sharing together. We begin by assuming that risk-sharing contracts are perfectly and costlessly enforceable. The case with unbounded accumulation is ignored since, in the long run, both agents have infinite wealth and self-insure perfectly. We therefore consider what happens if agents can save in the form of an unproductive asset such as grain stocks. This is the Arrow–Debreu world studied for instance by Udry (1994). With complete markets, the Pareto efficient outcome can be sustained. This outcome ensures that

$$\frac{U_1'(c_t^1)}{U_2'(c_t^2)} = \frac{U_1'(c_{t'}^1)}{U_2'(c_{t'}^2)} = k \quad \text{for all } t \text{ and } t', \tag{4.16}$$

where k is a constant that depends on the ratio of welfare weights of each agent. An immediate corollary of the above is that, with assets and perfect risk-sharing, welfare inequality is constant over time: $N_t^u = k$. Wealth and income distribution are inconsequential for welfare distribution.

We now turn to consumption inequality. Along the equilibrium path, individual consumption fluctuates only as a function of aggregate cash-in-hand $X_t \equiv X_t^1 + X_t^2$: if X_t is high, both agents consume a lot; if X_t is low, both agents consume little. Purely idiosyncratic fluctuations in income do not affect consumption. If the utility function takes a constant absolute risk aversion form, $N_t^c = N_t^u = k$ (e.g. Cochrane 1991; Mace 1991; Altonji et al. 1992). If the utility function has constant relative risk aversion, it is the ratio of the log of consumption that is constant. More generally, N_t^c is an increasing function of N_t^u.[20]

Next we note that if the economy is subject to collective income shocks, the precautionary savings motive applies: it is in the interest of all agents collectively to accumulate grain to protect themselves against future collective shortfalls. The rules governing the accumulation of precautionary savings are the same as those discussed earlier (e.g. Zeldes 1989; Kimball 1990; Deaton 1991), except that when they pool risk agents do not need assets to insure against idiosyncratic risk. The level of aggregate savings should, in general, be lower with risk-sharing. We denote the (efficient) aggregate savings function $s(X_t)$. The higher the collective risk, the more aggregate saving we expect (provided agents' preference are prudent; Kimball (1990)).

Can we say something about wealth inequality over time? To this we now turn. There is a difficulty because the distinction between credit, wealth, and insurance is indeterminate in equilibrium. All that matters is the level of cash-in-hand in the economy X_t, the aggregate savings function $s(X_t)$, and the consumption splitting rule k. Many different contract combinations can deliver the first-best solution: Arrow–Debreu securities/fully contingent contracts; a combination of credit and insurance contracts (Lucas 1978); and insured credit contracts (Udry 1994). This point has been made before and need not be revisited here. For the remainder of this section, we focus on the case with a combination of credit and insurance.

Even if we restrict our attention to a particular set of contracts, the distribution of wealth among agents is still indeterminate. This is because any distribution of wealth

---

[20] Conditional on the total cash-in-hand in the economy.

is compatible with any constant ratio of marginal utilities provided it is combined with the correct insurance contract. Put differently, it does not matter who 'owns' the wealth. This is because, whatever the distribution of wealth, insurance contracts can be found ensure that the existing cash-in-hand is distributed among agents so as to satisfy Pareto efficiency.

To reduce indeterminacy, we add a new incentive constraint, namely, that insurance contracts are renegotiation-proof. By this, we mean that at the beginning of each period, agents must regard insurance contracts as individually rational *ex ante*. (Commitment failure, that is, *ex post* voluntary participation is ignored here; it is discussed later.) An example of an insurance contract that violate this *ex ante* participation constraint is a contract that stipulate that agent 1 who transfers consumption to agent 2 in all states of the world. For agent 1 to accept to continue an insurance contract, it must provide agent 1 with some expected future benefits.

Formally, let $\tau(X_t^1, X_t^2)$ be the transfer from agent 1 to agent 2 that is stipulated in the contract if individual cash-in-hand are X_t^1, X_t^2. The continuation payoff of a participant is defined by the following Belman equation:

$$V_i(X_t^i) = \max_{W_{t+1}^i} U_i(X_t^i + \tau^i(X_t^1, X_t^2) - W_{t+1}^i)$$

$$+ EV_i(\omega^i(Z_i, \theta_{t+1}) + (1+\gamma)W_{t+1}^i), \qquad (4.17)$$

where transfers $\tau^i = -\tau$ if $i = 1$ and $\tau^i = \tau$ if $i = 2$.[21] The autarchy continuation payoff is:

$$\widetilde{V}_i(X_t^i) = \max_{\widetilde{W}_{t+1}^i} U_i(X_t^i - \widetilde{W}_{t+1}^i) + E\widetilde{V}_i(\omega^i(Z_i, \theta_{t+1}) + (1+\gamma)\widetilde{W}_{t+1}^i). \qquad (4.18)$$

Ex ante voluntary participation requires that:

$$E\widetilde{V}_i(X_t^i) \leq EV_i(X_t^i). \qquad (4.19)$$

Arrangements that satisfy the *ex ante* participation constraints belong to the core (Hildenbrand 1974).

This requirement somewhat restricts the range of insurance contracts, but not entirely. This is because, whenever all agents are risk averse, they are willing to pay for insurance. If all agents are risk averse, they are all willing to pay, which means that there are many insurance contracts that satisfy the *ex ante* participation constraint—that is, belong to the core. One category of contracts that always satisfy the participation constraint—even if one or more agents are risk neutral—is the set of contracts that are actuarially fair. For the purpose of this chapter, an actuarially fair contract is when the expected payment from one agent to the other is zero, that is, when $E[\tau(X_t^1, X_t^2)] = 0$. For the remainder of this section, we restrict our attention to actuarially fair contracts.

---

[21] Here we assume that savings decisions can be decentralized. This is because insured decisionmakers face the same returns to wealth as the group. Consequently, their savings decisions are consistent with the social planner's optimum.

This is still not sufficient to tie down wealth distribution. This is because, in the presence of assets, credit is redundant.[22] All that matters is agents' net wealth. This is immediately apparent from the above voluntary participation constraints: all that matters is net wealth/cash-in-hand X_t^i. Consequently, from now on we ignore credit and use the term 'assets' to refer to net wealth.

With all these additional assumptions, we now seek a characterization of insurance and wealth distribution as the level of transfers and current and future assets that satisfies voluntary participation constraints and ensures that $U_1'(X_t^1 - \tau(\theta_t) - W_{t+1}^1)/U_2'(X_t^2 + \tau(\theta_t) - W_{t+1}^2) = k$ for all θ_t and $E[\tau(X_t^1, X_t^2)] = 0$ in all periods. A full characterization of such plan is beyond this chapter (e.g. Lucas 1978; Prescott and Mehra 1980). But a few preliminary insights are worth mentioning.

First, voluntary participation to risk-sharing requires that wealth be aligned with desired consumption. Failure to align the two will either violate voluntary participation constraints or the actuarial fairness requirement. To see why, suppose that this is not the case: agent 1 is expected to enjoy more consumption but have less wealth. Since agent 1 has a lower income (wealth generates income), this means that on an average he will need to receive more from agent 2 in order to raise his consumption.

There are two cases to consider. First, suppose that future savings requirements remain unchanged. Giving more to agent 1 will violate the actuarial fairness requirement. Second, suppose that future saving is adjusted to satisfy the actuarial fairness requirement: agent 1 is asked to save less (to leave more for consumption); agent 2 is asked to save more. This solves the problem for the current period but results in a violation of the voluntary participation constraint in subsequent periods—a richer agent 2 is more likely to opt out of an insurance arrangement—or runs into a feasibility constraint when all the wealth of agent 1 is exhausted.

An immediate corollary is that wealth must be aligned with intended distribution of consumption for a risk-sharing arrangement to be renegotiation-proof. This is but an application of the second welfare theorem: initial wealth determines consumption inequality. Another way of saying this is that N_t^w is an increasing function of N_t^c. Since income is a function of wealth, we also have that N_t^y is an increasing function of N_t^c.

It is difficult to be more explicit given that the level of aggregate wealth varies with collective shocks. But one remarkable consequence of efficient risk-sharing is that welfare inequality N_t^u does not change over time. Inequality measures such as N_t^c, N_t^y, N_t^x, and N_t^w may change with X_t but rankings do not change.

The incompatibility of social mobility with efficiency in risk-sharing means that societies face a tradeoff between perfect insurance and equality of chances. Put differently, they must choose between permanent poverty for some and permanent prosperity for others but protection against idiosyncratic shocks; and social mobility, that is, the opportunity for ranks to change over time. This conflict should not come as a surprise: after all, the rich are not insured if they may lose their status. For them

---

[22] Agents who borrow to finance productive investments have a positive net worth. Most credit observed in practice goes to agents with positive net worth, that is, household to purchase a home or firms to purchase equipment.

social mobility is not Pareto efficient. Consequently an efficient risk-sharing system is always geared towards the preservation of the social status quo.

Our findings are summarized as follows:

Proposition 8 *With asset accumulation and perfect risk-sharing:*

(1) N^u is constant over time. Other measures of inequality may change over time.
(2) Credit is redundant; only net wealth matters.
(3) N_t^c, N_t^y, N_t^x, and N_t^w are all non-decreasing functions of N^u.
(4) N_t^c, N_t^y, N_t^x, and N_t^w must remain 'close' to N^u for risk-sharing to be renegotiation-proof.

4.5. IMPERFECT COMMITMENT

In the previous section we assumed that risk-sharing/insurance contracts can be perfectly and costlessly enforced. As argued by Posner (1980) and Platteau (1991), this need not be a reasonable assumption for poor communities. In the absence of external enforcement, risk-sharing must be self-enforcing. This requires adding *ex post* voluntary participation constraints of the form:

$$\widetilde{V}_i(X_t^i) \leq V_i(X_t^i). \tag{4.20}$$

Other sources of market imperfections (e.g. information asymmetries discussed in Fafchamps (1992) and Ligon (1998)) are ignored here. For a detailed analysis of risk-sharing with imperfect commitment, see Kimball (1988), Coate and Ravallion (1993), and Fafchamps and Quisumbing (1999). Ligon *et al.* (2000, 2002) present models with wealth accumulation. Our purpose here is not to present imperfect commitment models in detail but rather to discuss their implications for inequality over time.

We begin by noting that if *ex post* participation constraints are never binding, we are back to the previous section: risk-sharing is efficient and N_t^u is constant over time. Next, if participation constraints prevent any risk-sharing (i.e. all $\tau^i(X_t^1, X_t^2) = 0$ for all X_t^1, X_t^2), then we are back to Section 4.3. A world with imperfect commitment is thus in between the two.

Ligon *et al.* (2000) discuss how N_t^u evolves over time when commitment constraints are binding. Following Kocherlakota (1996), they show that N_t^u stays constant as long as constraints are not binding. When a constraint becomes binding for one agent, N_t^u changes so as to incite the agent to voluntarily remain in the risk-sharing arrangement. After this jump, N_t^u remains unchanged until another commitment constraint becomes binding. If there exist ratios of marginal utility such that constraints are never binding, then the economy converges to one of these ratios, after which time N_t^u remains constant. If not, then the economy stochastically cycles across a finite set of marginal utility ratios—and hence a set of N_t^u. To the extent that risk-sharing is optimized subject to commitment constraints, Kocherlakota (1996) and Ligon *et al.* (2001) further show that the set of N_t^u among which the economy randomly cycles is as close as possible given the constraints. Thus, even though inequality changes over time, it changes just by as much as is necessary to satisfy voluntary participation.

These results show that, the more efficient risk-sharing is, the more persistent poverty is. Any departure from efficient risk-sharing allows for social mobility, with the natural restrictions discussed in Section 4.3. Of course, if risk-sharing is initially egalitarian, imperfect commitment may take the economy away from an egalitarian distribution of welfare. In this sense, imperfect commitment can generate social differentiation. But the opposite is also possible: imperfect commitment and the rise of opportunism may erode asymmetric risk-sharing arrangements that traditionally guarantee more welfare to specific individuals, such as nobles, high castes, village chiefs, and the like.

One issue of interest is the emergence of patronage as a natural outcome of risk-sharing arrangements with imperfect commitment. To see how this is possible, first note that, in the presence of imperfect commitment, rankings may change over time. This means that certain agents accumulate more assets than others, even if the distribution was initially egalitarian. Suppose that absolute risk aversion falls with cash-in-hand. Then it can be shown that agents that have accumulated sufficient wealth will refuse actuarially fair contracts (Fafchamps and Quisumbing 1999). For their *ex post* participation constraint to be satisfied, they must receive more than they give on average. We call this situation 'patronage', that is, a situation in which a rich agent offers insurance and protection to poor agents in exchange for constant payments and services (e.g. Platteau 1995).

If we allow for patronage, *ex post* participation constraints should be easier to satisfy in sharply polarized societies provided that asset accumulation is sufficient to reduce absolute risk aversion to negligible levels among the rich while very poor households become extremely concerned by risk. To see why, consider our 2-agent economy and assume that agent 1 has all the economy's wealth W and sufficient income to be risk neutral. Agent 2, in contrast, faces a lot of income risk and is desperate to purchase insurance. It is clearly in the interest of agent 1 to become a patron and to serve as 'insurance company' for agent 2. If agent 2 is sufficiently patient, it is in her interest to pay agent 1 in exchange for the (credible) promise of protection against negative income shocks.

To demonstrate this point, consider the following example. Utility is linear except in the vicinity of 0 (e.g. below 1/4), where it falls to $-\infty$. This is meant to represent the fear of starvation. Incomes are (2,0) and (0,2) with probability 1/2. Total wealth is 100, return to wealth is 10 per cent. Here we assume that the rich agent has a discount factor of 0.5. First suppose that both agents have equal wealth. Since they can both insure themselves survival, they are unwilling to pay for future insurance. Consequently, risk-sharing does not take place. Next, suppose that agent 1 has all wealth and agent 2 has nothing. Now agent 2 is concerned about survival. His promise to pay for insurance is thus credible. The *ex post* participation constraint of agent 1 is:

$$\tau_1 \leq \left[-\frac{1}{2}\tau_1 + \frac{1}{2}\tau_2 \right] \frac{0.5}{1 - 0.5}, \tag{4.21}$$

where τ_1 is the transfer from agent 1 to agent 2 in the first state of the world (when agent 2 has an income of 0), and τ_2 is the transfer of agent 2 to agent 1 in state 2 (when agent 2 has an income of 2). The maximum transfer agent 1 agrees to pay must satisfy $\tau_1 \le \tau_2/3$. Given this constraint, the maximum agent 2 is willing to pay is an amount that ensures her constant consumption:

$$2 - \tau_2 = 0 + \tau 1. \tag{4.22}$$

The solution is $\tau_1 = 1/2$. This example illustrates that the fear of starvation by the poor may trigger patronage albeit imperfect commitment prevented risk-sharing among agents with equal wealth.

From the point of view of inequality dynamics, patronage is interesting because it enables the rich to accumulate more and the poor to accumulate less. This is because, on average, the rich receive net transfers from the poor. The precise form of inequality fostered by patronage depends on the returns to wealth and whether aggregate wealth is bounded or not. If returns to wealth are positive and unbounded, patronage is only a transient phenomenon: even poor agents save so that, in the long run, they no longer need to purchase insurance from the patron.

If returns to wealth is negative, patronage reinforces the tendency towards inequality. But polarization is not an absorbing state because aggregate wealth gets depleted in finite time with probability one. In this configuration, patronage arises and survives for a while until aggregate wealth is spent to deal with a large (or series of) collective shock(s), at which point it disappears because impoverished patrons cannot promise sufficient protection and extract net payments from others. If returns to wealth are positive but aggregate wealth is bounded, patronage makes polarization more likely.

A similar possibility arises if returns to wealth are positive but total wealth is fixed. In this case, patronage indirectly raises the return on wealth for the rich, hence making multiple equilibria more likely. This is but an application of Proposition 4.

These findings can be summarized as follows:

Proposition 9 *With imperfect commitment:*

(1) If ex post voluntary participation constraints are never binding, risk-sharing is efficient and there is no social mobility, that is, N^u is constant over time.

(2) If ex post voluntary participation constraints are always binding, models discussed in Section 4.3 apply.

(3) If risk aversion is high for agents without assets but low for agents with assets, risk-sharing is more likely in polarized societies, where it takes the form of patronage.

(4) Other things being equal, patronage makes inequality in wealth and consumption more likely and long-lasting, while protecting the poor from starvation.

4.6. CONCLUSION

In this chapter we have examined how risk, accumulation, and insurance affect inequality. The main findings are that there are tradeoffs between insurance and social mobility, and between asset markets and social polarization. We also find that, in the presence of imperfect commitment, mutual insurance might be easier to sustain in the form of patronage in unequal societies. These findings are hardly new but the contribution of this chapter is to show how they are related to each other within a coherent framework.

Perhaps our most novel result is the observation that, when wealth is made of assets in fixed supply, such as land or manpower, trade in these assets naturally leads to an unequal distribution of welfare and income. For this result to arise, the savings rate must increase with cash-in-hand. Factors that favour accumulation, such as a high return on wealth or large aggregate stock of wealth, also favour inequality.

From an equity point of view, there might therefore be a rationale for shutting down certain asset markets, that is, those for which supply is finite. This is because allowing accumulation is likely to result in polarization. This conclusion applies primarily to land, manpower, mineral resources, and the environment. With the possible exception of mineral resources, these are also the markets in which restrictions to market transactions are most widespread. In contrast, the accumulation of unbounded resources such as equipment, skills, and knowledge does not raise similar fears although, in the long run, they also lead to persistent inequality. These assets are also those that are essential for growth.

Developed societies are adamantly opposed to slavery—even if it is voluntary. Yet, the United States has a student loan programme that requires graduates to work in the army for a set number of years. Unlike other labour contracts for which employees can never be forced to work, military personnel who do not report for work are regarded as having deserted. Student loans by the military are thus a modern form of indenture contracts—with the caveat that they are used to accumulate education. These loans are acceptable while other indenture contracts are not. This suggests that society intuitively understands the distinction between bounded and unbounded assets and the implication for inequality.

This chapter also suggests that shutting down certain asset markets can only be effective in reducing inequality if it is combined with access to actuarially fair insurance. If a starving person cannot sell his future workforce in exchange for survival today, patronage is likely to arise as substitute (e.g. Srinivasan 1989; Platteau 1995). Given that patronage favours polarization, the end result is not very different. This implies that programmes to eradicate inequality must imperatively combine asset redistribution with access to fair insurance. This is particularly true in pre-industrial societies where aggregate accumulation is small or inexistent. Redistribution of assets is not, by itself, sufficient to durably eliminate inequality.

Our analysis also offers some caution to those who see the provision of insurance mechanisms as a solution to poverty. The theory is quite clear: perfect insurance freezes inequality. An insurance system based on voluntary participation—such as a market-based approach for instance—cannot eliminate inequality. It might raise the welfare of the poor by providing protection against shocks, but it will not in general eliminate inequality that is already there.[23] A tax-based system might be necessary to

---

[23] Unless the rich's willingness to pay was quite high to start with and they were asked to pay much more for insurance than the poor. With assets, this is unlikely to be the case because then the rich can self-insure.

build redistribution into the insurance system. Combatting inequality thus requires policy tools other than insurance. In some cases, organizing insurance might even worsen the long-term prospects of the poor by reducing social mobility.

This chapter leaves many questions unanswered. One issue of interest is the interface between accumulation, inequality, and growth. Most engines of growth require the accumulation of something—equipment, skills, knowledge. It is therefore widely recognized that economic development is intimately related to aggregate accumulation. The distribution of wealth across the population is also likely to affect the pace of growth (Aghion *et al.* 1999).

This issue has received a lot of attention in the literature as far as the accumulation of human capital is concerned (e.g. Becker and Tomes 1979; Galor and Zeira 1993; Maoz and Moav 1999; Mookherjee and Ray 2000). The literature has also examined the relationship between risk taking, credit markets, and growth (e.g. Banerjee and Newman 1991, 1993; Aghion and Bolton 1997; Piketty 1997). Less attention has been devoted to capital accumulation and returns to scale (e.g. Stiglitz 1969; Freeman 1996). For instance, if production is subject to increasing returns to scale, the concentration of capital in a few hands would ensure faster growth than a more egalitarian distribution. The same reasoning applies to human capital: if the highest returns are in technology transfer, a few highly trained individuals who can borrow technology from elsewhere might better favour growth than a large number of workers with a little bit of training. Factors that influence the evolution of wealth inequality over time, such as returns to assets, income correlation, and patronage, may thus affect growth.

REFERENCES

Aghion, P. and P. Bolton (1997). 'A Theory of Trickle-Down Growth and Development'. *Review of Economic Studies*, 64, 151–72.

——, E. Caroli, and C. Garcia-Penalosa (1999). 'Inequality and Economic Growth: The Perspective of the New Growth Theories'. *Journal of Economic Literature*, 37, 1615–60.

Altonji, J. G., F. Hayashi, and L. J. Kotlikoff (1992). 'Is the Extended Family Altruistically Linked? Direct Tests Using Micro Data'. *American Economic Review*, 82(5), 1177–98.

Arthur, B. W., Y. M. Ermoliev, and Y. M. Kaniovski (1994). 'Strong Laws for a Class of Path-Dependent Stochastic Processes' in *Increasing Returns and Parth Dependence in the Economy* Ann Arbor, MI: University of Michigan Press, pp. 185–201.

Atwood, D. A. (1990). 'Land Registration in Africa: The Impact on Agricultural Production'. *World Development*, 18(5), 659–71.

Azariadis, C. (1996). 'The Economics of Poverty Traps—Part One: Complete Markets'. *Journal of Economic Growth*, 1, 449–86.

Banerjee, A. V. and A. F. Newman (1991). 'Risk-Bearing and the Theory of Income Distribution'. *Review of Economic Studies*, 58, 211–35.

—— and —— (1993). 'Occupational Choice and the Process of Development'. *Journal of Political Economy*, 101(2), 274–98.

Becker, G. S. and N. Tomes (1979). 'An Equilibrium Theory of the Distribution of Income and Intergenerational Mobility'. *Journal of Political Economy*, 87(6), 1153–89.

Benabou, R. (2000). 'Unequal Societies: Income Distribution and the Social Contract'. *American Economic Review*, 90(1), 96–129.

Carroll, C. D. (1992). 'The Buffer-Stock Theory of Saving: Some Macroeconomic Evidence'. *Brookings Papers on Economic Activity*, 2, 61–156.

Carter, M. R. and F. J. Zimmerman (2000). 'The Dynamic Cost and Persistence of Asset Inequality in an Agrarian Economy'. *Journal of Development Economics*, 63(2), 265–302.

Coate, S. and M. Ravallion (1993). 'Reciprocity Without Commitment: Characterization and Performance of Informal Insurance Arrangements'. *Journal of Developmental Economy*, 40, 1–24.

Cochrane, J. H. (1991). 'A Simple Test of Consumption Insurance'. *Journal of Political Economy*, 99(5), 957–76.

Dasgupta, P. (1993). *An Inquiry into Well-Being and Destitution*. Oxford: Clarendon Press.

de Janvry, A. (1981). *The Agrarian Question and Reformism in Latin America*. Baltimore, MD: Johns Hopkins University Press.

——, G. Gordillo, E. Sadoulet, and J.-P. Platteau (eds) (2001). *Access to Land, Rural Poverty, and Public Action*. Oxford: Oxford University Press for UNU-WIDER.

Deaton, A. (1990). 'Saving in Developing Countries: Theory and Review'. *World Bank Economic Review, Proceedings of the World Bank Annual Conference on Development Economics*, 1989, pp. 61–96.

—— (1991). 'Saving and Liquidity Constraints'. *Econometrica*, 59(5), 1221–48.

—— (1992). 'Household Saving in LDCs: Credit Markets, Insurance and Welfare'. *Scandinaviun Journal of Economics*, 94(2), 253–73.

Estaban, J.-M. and D. Ray (1994). 'On the Measurement of Polarisation'. *Econometrica*, 62(4), 819–51.

Fafchamps, M. (1992). 'Cash Crop Production, Food Price Volatility and Rural Market Integration in the Third World'. *American Journal of Agricultural Economy* 74(1), 90–9.

—— (1999). 'Risk Sharing and Quasi-Credit'. *Journal of International Trade and Economic Development*, 8(3), 257–78.

—— and A. Quisumbing (1999). 'Human Capital, Productivity, and Labor Allocation in Rural Pakistan'. *Journal of Human Resources*, 34(2), 369–406.

Freeman, S. (1996). 'Equilibrium Income Inequality Among Identical Agents'. *Journal of Political Economy*, 104(5), 1047–64.

Galor, O. and J. Zeira (1993). 'Income Distribution and Macroeconomics'. *Review of Economic Studies*, 60, 35–52.

Hall, R. E. (1978). 'Stochastic Implications of the Life Cycle-Permanent Income Hypothesis: Theory and Evidence'. *Journal of Political Economy*, 86(6), 461–81.

Hildenbrand, W. (1974). *Core and Equilibria of a Large Economy*. Princeton, NJ: Princeton University Press.

Kimball, M. S. (1988). 'Farmers' Cooperatives as Behavior Toward Risk'. *American Economic Review*, 78(1), 224–32.

—— (1990). 'Precautionary Savings in the Small and in the Large'. *Econometrica*, 58(1), 53–73.

Kocherlakota, N. R. (1996). 'Implications of Efficient Risk Sharing Without Commitment'. *Review of Economic Students*, 63(4), 595–609.

Ligon, E. (1998). 'Risk Sharing and Information in Village Economics'. *Review of Economic Studies*, 65(4), 847–64.

——, J. P. Thomas, and T. Worrall (2000). 'Mutual Insurance, Individual Savings, and Limited Commitment'. *Review of Economic Dynamics*, 3(2), 216–46.

——, ——, and —— (2002). 'Informal Insurance Arrangements with Limited Commitment: Theory and Evidence from Village Economies'. *Review of Economics Studies*, 69(1), 209–44.

Lucas, R. E. (1978). 'Asset Prices in an Exchange Economy'. *Econometrica*, 46, 1426–46.

Mace, B. J. (1991). 'Full Insurance in the Presence of Aggregate Uncertainty'. *Journal of Political Economy*, 99(5), 928–56.

Maoz, Y. D. and O. Moav (1999). 'Intergenerational Mobility and the Process of Development'. *Economic Journal*, 109, 677–97.

Mookherjee, D. and D. Ray (2000). 'Persistent Inequality', mimeo, Boston University.

Paxson, C. H. (1992). 'Using Weather Variability to Estimate the Response of Savings to Transitory Income in Thailand'. *American Economic Review*, 82(1), 15–33.

Piketty, T. (1997). 'The Dynamics of the Wealth Distribution and the Interest Rate with Credit Rationing'. *Review of Economic Studies*, 64(2), 173–89.

Platteau, J.-P. (1991). 'Traditional Systems of Social Security and Hunger Insurance: Past Achievements and Modern Challenges', in E. Ahmad, J. Dreze, J. Hills, and A. Sen (eds), *Social Security in Developing Countries*. Oxford: Clarendon Press.

—— (1992). 'Formalization and Privatization of Land Rights in Sub-Saharan Africa: A Critique of Current Orthodoxies and Structural Adjustment Programmes', in *The Development Economics Research Programme*, Vol. 34. London: London School of Economics.

—— (1995). 'An Indian Model of Aristocratic Patronage' *Oxford Economic Papers*, 47(4), 636–62.

Posner, R. A. (1980). 'A Theory of Primitive Society with Special Reference to Law'. *Journal of Law and Economics*, XXIII, 1–53.

Prescott, E. C. and R. Mehra, (1980). 'Recursive Competitive Equilibrium: The Case of Homogenous Households'. *Econometrica*, 48(6), 1365–79.

Sargent, T. (1987). *Dynamic Macroeconomic Theory*. Cambridge, MA: Harvard University Press.

Sen, A. (1981). *Poverty and Famines*. Oxford: Clarendon Press.

Srinivasan, T. (1989). 'On Choice Among Creditors and Bonded Labour Contracts', in Pranab Bardhan (ed.), *The Economic Theory of Agrarian Institution*. Oxford: Clarendon Press.

Stiglitz, J. (1969). 'Distribution of Income and Wealth Among Individuals'. *Econometrica*, 37, 382–97.

Townsend, R. M. (1994). 'Risk and Insurance in Village India'. *Econometrica*, 62(3), 539–591.

Udry, C. (1994). 'Risk and Insurance in a Rural Credit Market: An Empirical Investigation in Northern Nigeria'. *Review Economic Studies*, 61(3), 495–526.

Zeldes, S. P. (1989). 'Optimal Consumption With Stochastic Income: Deviations from Certainty Equivalence'. *Quarterly Journal of Economics*, 104(2), 275–98.

Zhang, X. and R. Kanbur (2001). 'What Difference Do Polarisation Measures Make? An Application to China'. *Journal of Development Studies*, 37(3), 85–98.

Zimmerman, F. (1993). 'Structural Evolution under Imperfect Markets in Developing Country Agriculture: A Dynamic Programming Simulation', mimeo, University of Wisconsin.

PART III

RISK AND POVERTY: PERSISTENCE

5

Household Income Dynamics in Rural China

JYOTSNA JALAN AND MARTIN RAVALLION

5.1. INTRODUCTION

It is often argued that public transfers targeted to the currently poor provide a short-term palliative in the presence of uninsured risk. Clearly, this is a potentially important role for public action in poor, high-risk, settings. However, a body of recent theoretical work in economics has pointed to another potential role of a well-designed public safety net in such settings, namely in alleviating poverty in the longer term.

This new perspective stems from the realization that widespread credit and risk-market failures can entail efficiency enhancing functions for a well-designed safety net. With limited access to credit, or other forms of (formal or informal) insurance, a household will suffer from a transient shock—an unexpected but short-lived drop in income. However, it is also possible in theory that such a shock can cause a previously non-poor family to become poor indefinitely; or cause a moderately poor family to fall into persistent destitution. If this theoretical possibility is borne out by the evidence then there are important implications for knowledge about poverty and anti-poverty policies. Lack of a well-functioning safety net might well be a structural cause of persistent poverty. And there will be large long-term benefits from institutions and policies that protect people from transient shocks.

The long-run effect of a transient shock depends on properties of household income dynamics. And they are properties, which we currently know very little about. Granted, if household incomes follow the simplest type of linear auto-regression then a household that experiences a transient shock will see its income bounce back in due course. The serial dependence will mean that the family stays poor for a longer period than the duration of the shock. Incomes will not adjust instantaneously. Nonetheless, the household will recover from any adverse draw from a distribution of serially independent income shocks.

The research reported here would not have been possible without the help of the Rural Household Survey Team of China's National Bureau of Statistics and our colleague Shaohua Chen at the World Bank. Our thanks also go to the World Institute for Development Economics Research (UNU-WIDER) and the World Bank for their support of this research and to Stefan Dercon, Marcel Fafchamps, and participants at a WIDER conference for their comments. These views should not be attributed to the World Bank.

However, there is no theoretical reason why incomes would behave this way. Linear dynamics is an ad hoc assumption. Indeed, economic theory has pointed to the possibilities for non-linear dynamics, and special cases of such non-linear models can yield multiple equilibria in the dynamics, interpretable as 'poverty traps'. Then destitution can stem from short-lived shocks. This is not a new idea. Non-linear dynamic models with multiple equilibria have been widely used in explaining why seemingly similar aggregate shocks can have dissimilar outcomes.[1] A central feature of these models is the existence of a non-convexity in the dynamics of household incomes, giving rise to a low-level unstable equilibrium. The non-convexity can stem from effects of past consumption on current productivity, as in the Efficiency Wage Hypothesis (Mirrlees 1975; Stiglitz 1976). In such models, a vulnerable household may never recover from a sufficiently large but short-lived shock.

Whether such non-convexities in the dynamics are important in practice, and constitute a new case for safety net interventions, is a moot point. If multiple equilibria existed then there will be high social returns to arrangements that protect vulnerable households—arrangements that might well be implementable by private means, such as through repeated interaction in risky environments (Coate and Ravallion 1993). It can be conjectured that institutions will develop that assure—possibly imperfectly and at non-negligible cost—that most incomes exceed the low-level unstable equilibrium, thus avoiding the dynamic poverty trap.

Even without poverty traps, it is known that credit market failures can generate non-linear dynamics whereby the rate of growth in an economy depends critically on the initial distribution of income or wealth (Benabou 1996; Aghion and Bolton 1997; Aghion *et al.* 1999). By implication, redistributive policies can enhance long-term prospects of escaping poverty as long as they do not unduly jeopardize other determinants of growth. The arguments that initial distribution matters to future growth also rest on a type of non-linearity in the dynamics, such that individual income is a concave function of its own lagged value, that is, a concave recursion diagram. While there is some supportive evidence from cross-country regressions, this is arguably a rather weak basis for testing, given the known problems encountered, such as the potential for spurious correlations between growth and inequality arising from inconsistent aggregation across the underlying microeconomic relationships (Ravallion 1998).

This chapter tests for non-linearity in income and expenditure dynamics in rural China. The setting for our empirical work is rural south-west China in the period 1985–90. With Deng's reforms starting in the late 1970s, the collective mode of agricultural production had been disbanded in favour of a household-based responsibility system. These reforms brought rapid rural income growth—initially in agriculture, but in due course helping foster non-farm rural development. However, it is likely that the greater self-reliance that came with the break up of the collectives, and more heavy reliance on markets, also left many households facing greater risk.

---

[1] In macroeconomics, examples can be found in models of the business cycle (Chang and Smyth 1971; Varian 1979) and certain growth models (Day 1992; Azariades 1996). Similar ideas have been employed in modelling micropoverty traps (Dasgupta and Ray 1986; Banerjee and Newman 1994; Dasgupta 1997) and in understanding famines (Carraro 1996; Ravallion 1997).

We analyse a household-level panel data set spanning six years, 1985–90, in four contiguous provinces, Guangdong, Guangxi, Guizhou, and Yunnan. From past research (reviewed later) we know that poor farm-households in this setting are exposed to uninsured income and health risks. However, identifying the long-term effects of measured risks is clearly difficult. Six years is not long enough to confidently distinguish a slow process of adjustment after a shock—such that a unique long-run equilibrium is restored—from a more complex dynamic process with multiple equilibria arising from a non-convexity at low incomes.

We adopt a different approach that is feasible with the data. Instead of attempting to trace the long-run impacts of measured shocks, we directly study the process of income dynamics to see if it is consistent with the type of non-linearity postulated in the afore-mentioned theoretical work. With repeated shocks, we are presumably observing most households out of their steady-state equilibrium. The time series for each household can then reveal the dynamics of adjustment out of equilibrium. At any given long-run equilibrium, some households will simply be returning to that equilibrium. However, if there is also a low-level unstable equilibrium and sufficiently large uninsured shocks, then we should find both rising and falling incomes among the currently poor, with a tendency for incomes to fall among the poorest. To make this test feasible with only six years of data, the adjustment process is assumed to be common across households (though allowing for household-specific long-run equilibria). The specification allows the possibility of a low-level unstable equilibrium. In the process, we also see if the recursion diagram is concave, such that current distribution matters to future growth. Our estimation method allows for measurement error in observed incomes and other sources of correlation between lagged incomes and the error term.[2]

The following section describes the setting for our study. Section 5.3 puts the chapter in the context of our other recent work and Section 5.4 reviews the arguments as to why we might find non-linear dynamics. We then turn to our econometric model (Section 5.5), and results (Section 5.6).

5.2. THE SETTING AND DATA

The household panel used in this study was constructed from China's Rural Household Surveys (RHS) conducted by the National Bureau of Statistics (NBS) since 1984.[3] The data set covers four contiguous southern provinces. Three of the four provinces (Guangxi, Yunnan, and Guizhou) constitute one of China's poorest regions, while the fourth is the prosperous coastal province of Guangdong (Chen and Ravallion 1996). The panel consists of over 6000 households observed over the period 1985–90 (after which the sample was rotated).

---

[2] In a linear AR1 model, under (over) estimating the lagged income would lead to over (under) estimation of the subsequent change in income—a source of bias in OLS estimates of dynamic models commonly known as 'Galton's fallacy'. The problem is more complicated in a non-linear dynamic model, but the general concern with measurement error in lagged incomes remain.

[3] Further details on this survey, and the way it has been processed for this study, can be found in Chen and Ravallion (1996).

The RHS is a good quality budget and income survey, notable in the care that goes into reducing both sampling and non-sampling errors (Chen and Ravallion 1996). Sampled households maintain a daily record on all transactions, as well as log books on production. Local interviewing assistants (resident in the sampled village, or another village nearby) visit each sampled household at roughly two-week intervals. Inconsistencies found at the local NBS office are checked with the respondents. The sample frame of the RHS is all registered agricultural households except those who have moved to cities.

Our measure of consumption expenditure includes spending (either in cash or the imputed values of in-kind spending) on food, clothing, housing, fuel, culture and recreation, books, newspapers and magazines, medicines and non-commodity expenditures like transportation and communication, repairs, etc. The income variable includes both cash and imputed values for in-kind income from various sources (farm-household production, forestry, animal husbandry, handicrafts, gifts) as well as labour earnings and income received as a gift. It does not include borrowings from (or loans to) informal and/or formal sources.

There was very little sample rotation in the RHS between 1985 and 1990. The panel was formed from the sequence of cross-sectional surveys. From discussions with RHS staff we decided that the identifiers in the data could not be trusted for forming the panel. Fortunately, virtually ideal matching variables were available in the financial records, which gave both beginning and end of year balances. Relatively stringent criteria were used in defining a panel household, with extensive cross-checks to assure that the same household was being tracked over time. About one third of the original sample could not be matched by our criteria. Some of this is attrition, but probably the main reason was that the household changed sufficiently for it not to be classified as a panel household by our criteria.

In studying non-linear income dynamics using panel data, there is a concern that attrition may well be endogenous to shocks (Lokshin and Ravallion 2001); for example, with a sufficient negative shock, a household may become destitute and drop out of the panel. We cannot distinguish such households from those that changed too much to keep in the panel or those who were replaced by the surveyors for some other reason. It is unclear how much of a concern endogenous attrition is in this setting. Sampled households in the RHS do receive a small payment to participate, which would help somewhat in encouraging continuing participation by the poor. The results from Lokshin and Ravallion (2001) indicate that estimates of the non-linearity in income dynamics for Russia and Hungary are robust to allowing for endogenous attrition (through a non-zero correlation between the error terms in the attrition model and the dynamic income regression).

5.3. RISK AND POVERTY IN SOUTH-WEST CHINA

In past research, we have found considerable vulnerability to both idiosyncratic and (village-level) covariate risks in this setting. In Jalan and Ravallion (1999) we tested for systematic wealth effects on the extent of consumption insurance against income-risk.

Motivated by the theory of risk-sharing, our tests entailed estimating the effects of income changes on consumption (with current income treated as endogenous), after controlling for aggregate shocks through interacted village-time dummies. We also tested for insurance against covariate risk at village level. To test for wealth effects, we stratified our sample on the basis of household wealth per capita, and whether or not the household resides in a poor area. The full insurance model was convincingly rejected. The lower a household's wealth, the stronger was the rejection, in that the estimated excess sensitivity parameter on changes in current income (implied by the test equation for consumption changes) was higher for less wealthy households.[4] We interpret these results as indicating that, while there are clearly arrangements for consumption insurance in these villages, they work considerably less well for the poor.

It is not then surprising that we also find considerable transient poverty in this setting. Year-to-year fluctuations in consumption account for one-third of the mean poverty gap (Jalan and Ravallion 1998). About 40 per cent of the transient poverty is found among those who are not poor on average, but almost all of this is for households whose average consumption over time is no more than 50 per cent above the poverty line. A comparison with similar tests for three villages in semi-arid areas of rural India (Chaudhuri and Ravallion 1994) suggests that there is far more transient poverty in this region of rural China.

These findings tell us nothing about the long-term consequences of uninsured risk. We have also studied portfolio and other behavioural responses to idiosyncratic risk using the same data set (Jalan and Ravallion 2001). In keeping with past empirical work on precautionary wealth, we extracted a measure of income risk from a first-stage income regression estimated on household panel and then used this measure of risk as a regressor in attempting to explain liquid wealth holdings.[5] Our results suggest that wealth is held in unproductive liquid forms to protect against idiosyncratic income risk. However, we found this effect to be small; indeed, even if all income risks were eliminated, the mean share of wealth held in liquid forms would fall only slightly, from 26.5 to 25.8 per cent. We also found that there is an inverted U relationship between the precautionary wealth effect and permanent income, such that neither the poorest quintile nor the richest appear to hold liquid wealth because of income risk; it is the middle-income groups that do so. We suspect that the rich do not need to hold precautionary liquid wealth, and the poor cannot afford to do so. We have found some evidence that liquid wealth is also held as a precaution against risk to foodgrain yields (independently of income risk). We found no clear signs of a precautionary response to health risk, though our measure (based on medical spending) is far from ideal (Jalan and Ravallion 2001). Schooling and (hence) future incomes

---

[4] This conclusion was found to be robust to changes in the set of instruments, and to changes in the wealth measure. It holds for both total consumption and food consumption, although the latter is better protected. There is little sign, however, that living in a poor area enhances exposure to risk at a given level of individual wealth.

[5] We extended past methods by allowing for serial dependence in income shocks and by using quantile regression methods that are more robust to the evident non-normality in the data on liquid wealth holdings (Jalan and Ravallion 2001).

appear to be protected from both income and health risk. However, greater uncertainty about incomes at home does appear to constrain the temporary migration of family labour.

In the rest of this chapter, we turn to yet another possible longer-term implication of risk, such that vulnerable households can never escape from the adverse impact of a short-lived (serially independent) but sufficiently large uninsured shock. We first discuss how this might come about in theory.

5.4. THEORETICAL MODELS WITH NON-LINEAR DYNAMICS

Probably the simplest model that can generate a dynamic poverty trap assumes that a family cannot borrow or save and derives income solely from labour earnings, but with a non-convexity at low earnings arising from a dependency of the worker's productivity and (hence) wage rate on consumption. (We discuss alternative interpretations of this non-convexity below.) Non-linear dynamics can be introduced by simply assuming that the wage rate in any period is contracted at the beginning of the period. Finally, we assume that this dynamic process of income determination has at least one stable equilibrium.

Combining these assumptions, the process generating the current income of household $i(y_{it} \geq 0)$ with exogenous characteristics x_{it} can be written as the non-linear difference equation:

$$y_{it} = f(y_{it-1}, x_{it}), \tag{5.1}$$

where f is continuous and vanishing for all $y < y_0$ (>0) and the function is increasing and concave in y_{it-1} for all $y > y_0$. (The control variables x_{it} are of a sufficient dimension that the function f is the same across all i.) An equilibrium of this model is a steady-state solution that varies with x_{it} such that $y = f(y, x_{it})$. It is evident that if there is more than one such solution then there will be an unstable equilibrium. The recursion diagram in Fig. 5.1 illustrates a case of multiple equilibria. There are two attractors, at 0 and y^* ($>y_0$), while y^{**} is an unstable equilibrium. Consider a household at y^*. With any shock exceeding $y^* - y^{**}$, the household will be driven beyond the unstable equilibrium, and will then see its income decline steadily towards zero. Destitution will be the inevitable result.

One can propose more complicated models. For example, one can allow for some positive lower bound to incomes. Assuming that this lower bound is below y^{**} in Fig. 5.1 there will be a stable equilibrium at the lower bound. Again, with a large negative shock, a household at its high (stable) income will see its income decline until it reaches the lower bound.

There are several possible interpretations of the non-convexity. One is the Efficiency Wage Hypothesis (Mirrlees 1975; Stiglitz 1976; Dasgupta and Ray 1986; Dasgupta 1993). This assumes that labour productivity and earnings are zero at a low but positive level of consumption; only if consumption rises above some critical level, $y_0 > 0$, will the worker be productive. In the efficiency wage literature, y_0 is usually interpreted as

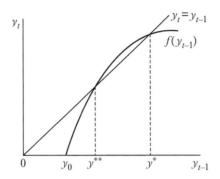

Figure 5.1. *Recursion diagram exhibiting non-linear dynamics*

the nutritional requirements for a basal metabolism, which account for about two-thirds of normal nutritional requirements (Dasgupta 1993).

Alternatively, one can assume that a minimum expenditure level is necessary to participate in society, including getting a job—in short, avoiding social exclusion requires a minimum consumption level for food and non-food commodities. Higher consumption permits social inclusion, but there are diminishing income returns to this effect. For example, earnings rise but at a declining rate until after some point the productivity effect of consumption vanishes.

Alternatively, we can think of a liquidity-constrained household that faces the choice of investing in (physical or human) capital or consuming all income in a given period. Suppose that the household is only willing to forgo current consumption in order to invest if its income exceeds a critical level y_0—at anything less than this amount, the need to assure maximum current consumption overrides all else. The investment yields an income at time t of $f(y_{t-1})$ where this function has the same properties as above.

Non-linearity in the dynamics also has implications for the growth rate of mean household income. Mean current income is:

$$\bar{y}_t = \frac{\sum_{i=1}^{n} f(y_{it-1}, x_{it})}{n}. \tag{5.2}$$

If the function f is non-linear in y_{it-1} then initial distribution will matter to future income at given current income. If f is strictly concave in y_{it-1} then the mean current income will be a strictly quasi-concave function of the levels of income in the previous period. By the properties of concave functions, higher initial inequality will entail lower future mean income for any given initial mean, $\bar{y}_{t-1} = \sum_{i=1}^{n} y_{it-1}/n$, holding x_{it} constant for all i. Recent theoretical papers have shown how concavity of the recursion diagram for income or wealth can arise from credit market failures, given decreasing returns to own capital (Benabou 1996; Aghion and Bolton 1997; Aghion *et al.* 1999; Banerjee and Duflo 2000).

This type of model has a powerful policy implication. A transfer payment not less than y^{**} will eliminate the low-income unstable equilibrium. The family will be fully protected from the possibility of a transient shock having an adverse long-term effect. Not only will the transfer help protect current living standards, but it will also generate a stream of future income gains. An effective safety net will then be a long-term investment, and with a potentially high return.

5.5. ECONOMETRIC MODEL

We now look for evidence in our data of the type of non-linear dynamics discussed above. We introduce the non-linearity in the form of a cubic function of the lagged dependent variable in a panel data model. (Lokshin and Ravallion 2001, further discuss this specification choice.) Another point to note is that we allow for only first-order autoregression in our model. This is done primarily to estimate a parsimonious model given that we have a very short time-series for each household. We also allow for an independent time trend. Thus our general econometric specification for i at date t is of the form:

$$y_{it} = \alpha + \gamma t + \beta_1 y_{it-1} + \beta_2 y_{it-1}^2 + \beta_3 y_{it-1}^3 + \mu_i + \varepsilon_{it}$$

$$(i = 1, 2, \ldots, N; \ t = 1, 2, \ldots, T), \tag{5.3}$$

where μ_i is an unobserved individual effect, and ε_{it} is an identically and independently distributed innovation error term. We estimate this model for both income and consumption. We eliminate the unobserved fixed effect μ_i, which is potentially correlated with lagged income (and its squared and cubed values) by taking the first differences of equation (5.3), giving:

$$\Delta y_{it} = \gamma + \beta_1 \Delta y_{it-1} + \beta_2 \Delta y_{it-1}^2 + \beta_3 \Delta y_{it-1}^3 + \Delta \varepsilon_{it}. \tag{5.4}$$

This model is estimated with and without the trend in income or expenditure, to see how this affects the estimated dynamics.

Least-squares estimation of equation (5.4) would still yield biased and inconsistent coefficient estimates due to correlation between lagged income changes and the differenced innovation error term. Assuming that the ε_{it}'s are serially uncorrelated, the generalized method of moments (GMM) estimator is the most efficient one within the class of instrumental variable (IV) estimators. In estimating (5.4), we follow standard practice in using y_{it-2} or higher lagged values (wherever feasible) as instrumental variables (Arellano and Bond 1991). (The Appendix gives further details, including on diagnostic testing.) Similar moment conditions are used for Δy_{it-1}^2 and Δy_{it-1}^3. We do not necessarily use all the moment conditions available to us. We choose the most parsimonious set of moment conditions based on the minimum value of the estimated objective function. In checking the validity of our instruments, the null hypotheses of the tests for over-identification and second-order serial correlation were accepted within standard levels of significance (Appendix). Notice that our GMM estimation method allows for serially independent measurement errors.

5.6. RESULTS

For purely descriptive purposes, Table 5.1 gives household recovery times following a drop in measured expenditure. We acknowledge that this is a crude indicator of 'shocks'; some of these income declines may simply reflect unusually high incomes in the first survey round. However, it is still of interest for descriptive purposes. We then categorized these households according to the time it took them to get back to at least 98 per cent of their expenditure in the first year of the survey.

We find that slightly more than half of the households that had a negative expenditure change recovered the loss within one year. However, 20 per cent had not recovered within five years. The time it takes to recover depends of course on the size of the initial expenditure contraction. Among households that experienced a decline in expenditure of less than 5 per cent between the first and the second year of the survey, 63 per cent recovered within one year. Among those that lost more than 10 per cent between the first two years of the survey, two-thirds had not recovered after five years.

These calculations might be interpreted as indicating that two types of dynamics exist. For the first type, an initial income shock leads to only a temporary drop in household income. For the second type, the shock appears to have been more devastating, putting them on a declining income path possibly leading to chronic poverty.

That interpretation is questionable, since there are other ways one might explain Table 5.1. Possibly the households that had not recovered, experienced other shocks in the intervening period. Or possibly they were returning more slowly to their steady-state equilibrium. Or possibly the first shock was not transient, and lasted for many years. Or the shock may have been transient, but the recursion process is linear with a slow speed of adjustment due to lagged effects of past incomes on current incomes.

For these reasons, one cannot conclude from Table 5.1 that short-lived shocks have long-lived impacts. We need to use our model of the dynamics to see if the structural process generating consumption and income is consistent with the type of non-linearity whereby sufficiently large shocks can create long-term poverty.

Table 5.1. *Recovery from an initial expenditure contraction (percentage)*

Recovery time after shock (years)	Any shock	Small shock	Medium shock	Large shock
1	54.53	63.23	31.35	14.39
2	15.14	15.58	14.05	9.35
3	6.24	5.57	8.84	5.76
4	4.38	3.44	7.88	4.32
Never recovered within the period	19.71	12.18	37.14	66.19

Note: Small shock: 5% or lower fall in household expenditure; medium shock: 5–10% fall in household expenditure; large shock: 10% or higher fall in household expenditure.

Table 5.2. *Non-linear dynamic model without trend*

	Expenditure	Income
Δy_{it-1}	0.2468 (11.989)	0.5441 (14.240)
Δy_{it-1}^2	0.0113×10^{-2} (4.067)	-0.0116×10^{-2} (-5.228)
Δy_{it-1}^3	-0.0146×10^{-6} (-1.1211)	-0.0376×10^{-6} (-5.439)

Note: *t*-statistics in parentheses; higher lags used as instruments.

Table 5.3. *Non-linear dynamic model with trend*

	Expenditure	Income
Trend	3.3894 (4.936)	-0.0316 (-0.027)
Δy_{it-1}	0.1613 (6.428)	0.5251 (13.339)
Δy_{it-1}^2	-0.0893×10^{-3} (-2.420)	-0.0101×10^{-2} (-4.539)
Δy_{it-1}^3	-0.0115×10^{-5} (-9.003)	-0.0481×10^{-6} (-7.246)

Note: *t*-statistics in parentheses; higher lags used as instruments.

Turning to the model of income dynamics, Table 5.2 gives our estimates of equation (5.4) without the trend (suppressing the constant term in 5.4).[6] Table 5.3 gives the results including the trend. The trend coefficient (i.e. the constant term) is not significantly different from zero for income, but it is for expenditure. Our preferred model for income is that without the trend while for expenditure it is the model with a trend.

Figures 5.2–5.5 give the recursion diagrams in all four cases. To retrieve the recursion diagram from the estimated parameters of (5.4) we treat the distribution of time-mean incomes and expenditures as the distribution of long-run (steady) state values. Thus the recursion diagram for the *p*'th percentile with income $\bar{y}_p$ is:

$$y_{pt} = \bar{y}_p + \beta_1(y_{pt-1} - \bar{y}_p) + \beta_2(y_{pt-1} - \bar{y}_p)^2 + \beta_3(y_{pt-1} - \bar{y}_p)^3. \qquad (5.5)$$

Figures 5.2–5.5 indicate that there is non-linearity in the range of the data, with concavity suggested in all cases except the expenditure model without trend. However, there is no sign of a non-convexity.

The concavity in the recursion diagram implies that higher initial income inequality (in the sense of mean-preserving spreads) will reduce future mean income at a given current mean. We can construct a natural measure of the contribution of inequality to growth as:

$$I_t = f[M(y_{it})] - M[f(y_{it})], \qquad (5.6)$$

---

[6] Pooling years and households, the sample mean annual income is 446 Yuan per capita at 1985 prices (with a standard deviation of 264), while the corresponding mean for expenditure is 345 Yuan (standard deviation of 166).

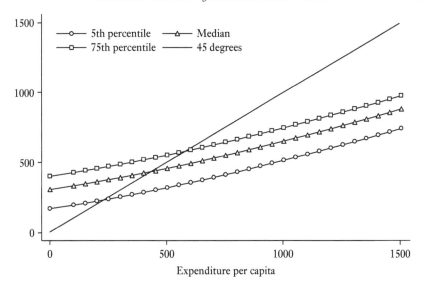

Figure 5.2. *Expenditure model without trend*

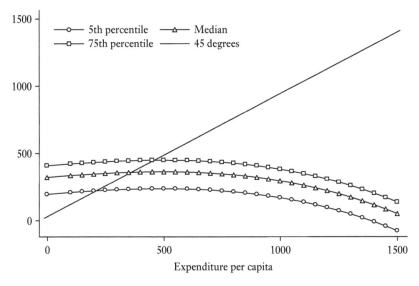

Figure 5.3. *Expenditure model with trend*

where $M[.]$ denotes the mean of the term in brackets (the mean being taken over all i at date t). This must be positive whenever f is concave. Using the models without trend, our estimates of (5.6) represent 4.1 per cent of mean income and 1.7 per cent of mean expenditure; in the models with trend, the corresponding numbers are 6.5 and 2.1 per cent.

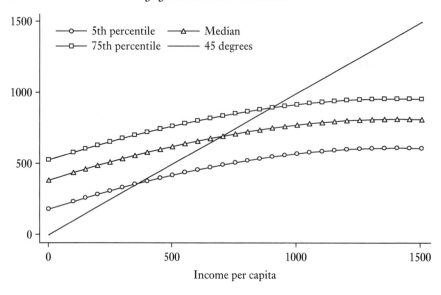

Figure 5.4. *Income model without trend*

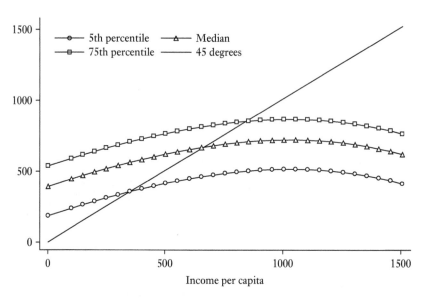

Figure 5.5. *Income model with trend*

A further implication of concavity in the recursion diagram is that the speed of adjustment will be lower for households with lower steady-state incomes. The speed of recovery from an income loss is $1 - \partial y_{it} / \partial y_{it-1}$. At one extreme, if a serially independent transient shock to a household at date $t-1$ has no impact on the household's period t

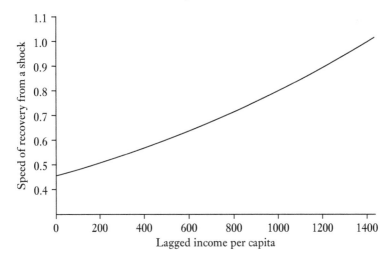

Figure 5.6. *Speed of recovery from a transient income shock*

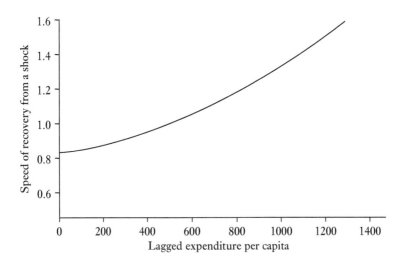

Figure 5.7. *Speed of recovery from a transient expenditure shock*

income then the speed of adjustment is unity. At the other extreme, if income at data t is lower than it would have been otherwise by the full amount of the shock at $t-1$ then the speed of recovery is zero. Given that f is strictly concave, the speed of recovery must be a strictly increasing function of y_{it-1}.

Figure 5.6 gives the speed of recovery as a function of y_{it-1} for income (using the preferred model without trend). For a household at zero income, the speed of recovery is 0.45. For a household with annual income of around 240 Yuan per capita (around the mean poverty line across the four provinces, as estimated by Chen and Ravallion 1996) the speed of recovery is 0.52. For household with an income of 900 Yuan per capita (roughly the 95th percentile) the speed of recovery from a shock rises to about 0.76, while it reaches unity at around 1400 Yuan (the 99th percentile is at 1441 Yuan), at which point the shock has no effect beyond the current year.

Figure 5.7 gives the corresponding figure for expenditures (based on the preferred model, with trend). At given y_{it-1}, the speeds of recovery are considerably higher for expenditures, reflecting consumption smoothing. The value of $\partial y_{it}/\partial y_{it-1}$ becomes negative at high expenditures (Fig. 5.3), implying speeds of recovery over unity, which would seem unlikely and may well reflect a problem with the model specification for consumption dynamics. However, the bulk of the data (about 90 per cent) is in the region with speeds of recovery below unity. As we saw for income, the speed of expenditure recovery is lower for households with lower initial per capita spending.

5.7. CONCLUSIONS

We have tried to assess whether existing (private and social) arrangements within a poor rural economy are able to avoid what is possibly the worst potential manifestation of uninsured risk, namely that a sufficiently large transient shock might drive a household into permanent destitution. This requires a specific kind of non-linearity in the dynamics of household incomes. Economic theory offers little support for the common assumption of linear dynamics, whereby households inevitably bounce back in time from a transient shock. Theoretical work has pointed to the possibility of a low-level non-convexity in the recursion diagram, such that a short-lived uninsured shock can have permanent consequences. It is an empirical question whether the dynamics found in reality exhibit such properties.

Our test entails estimating a dynamic panel data model in which income (or expenditure) is allowed to be a non-linear function of its own lagged values. As is invariably the case, we have had to impose a structure on the data. The most restrictive assumption we have had to make is that, while long-run-equilibria differ across households, the out-of-equilibrium adjustment process is common to all households. Our household panel is not short by developing-country standards, but in order to relax this restriction, more time-series observations would be needed to relax this restriction.

On calibrating the model to household panel data for rural areas southern China, we do find some evidence of non-linearity in the dynamics. However, we find no evidence of low-level non-convexities. The data are not consistent with the existence of an unstable equilibrium for the poor. This suggests that households in this setting tend to bounce back in due course from transient shocks. Our results are broadly consistent with those of Lokshin and Ravallion (2001) using panel data for Russia and Hungary. While we do not find evidence of a poverty trap arising from non-linear dynamics, in other work we have found strong signs of geographic poverty traps in these data, whereby location matters crucially to prospects of escaping poverty at given (latent and observed) household characteristics (Jalan and Ravallion 2002).

We find evidence of concavity in the recursion diagram. One implication of this finding is that the speed of recovery from a transient shock is lower for those with lower initial income. The differences in recovery speeds between the 'poor' and 'rich' appear to be sizable, particularly for incomes. So, while our results suggest that the poor eventually bounce back from short-lived shocks, the adjustment process is slower than for the non-poor.

The type of non-linearity that we find also suggests that the growth rate of household incomes in this setting will depend on higher moments of the initial distribution than its mean. Depending on the model specification, we find that inequality contributes 4–7 per cent to mean income and about 2 per cent to mean expenditure. These figures are appreciably lower than those obtained by Lokshin and Ravallion for Russia and Hungary, where inequality appears to be more costly to growth.

Appendix

GMM Estimation of the Non-Linear Dynamic Model

The GMM estimator for the parameter vector $\hat{v} = (\gamma, \beta_1, \beta_2, \beta_3)$ is defined as:

$$\hat{v} = (q'wa_nw'q)^{-1}(q'wa_nw'\Delta y),$$

where $q = [e, \ \Delta y_{-1}, \Delta y^2_{-1}, \Delta y^3_{-1}]N$, is the set of regressors with eN a vector of ones, w is the matrix of instrumental variables, a_n is the weighting matrix, and Δy is the $(NT \times 1)$ vector of the first differences of the dependent variable. The optimal choice of a_n (in the sense of giving the most efficient estimator asymptotically) is proportional to the inverse of the asymptotic covariance matrix (Hansen 1982).[7] Heteroscedastic consistent standard errors are computed using the residuals from a first-stage regression to correct for any kind of general heteroscedasticity.

Inferences on the estimated parameter vector $\hat{v}$ are appropriate provided the moment conditions are valid. Sargan's (1958) and Hansen's (1982) chi-square test of the over-identifying restrictions was implemented to check whether the exclusion restrictions are consistent with the data. The degrees of freedom for this test are calculated as the difference between the number of columns in the instrument matrix and the number of parameters to be estimated in the model. A second-order serial correlation test was also constructed, given that the consistency of the GMM estimators using twice (or higher) lagged dependent variables as instruments for the first differenced model depends on the assumption that $E(\Delta\varepsilon_{it}\Delta\varepsilon_{it-2}) = 0$ (the t-statistic is normally distributed).[8] Both tests passed at the 5 per cent level.

---

[7] In the just-identified case (i.e. in the case where the number of moment conditions are exactly equal to the number of parameters to be estimated), the parameter estimates do not depend on the weighting matrix and hence the choice of a_n is redundant.

[8] There may be some first-order serial correlation, that is, $E(\Delta\varepsilon_{it}\Delta\varepsilon_{it-1})$ may not be equal to zero since $\Delta\varepsilon_{it}$ are the first differences of serially uncorrelated errors.

REFERENCES

Aghion, P. and P. Bolton (1997). 'A Theory of Trickle-Down Growth and Development'. *Review of Economic Studies*, 64, 151–72.

——, E. Caroli, and C. Garcia-Penalosa (1999). 'Inequality and Economic Growth: The Perspectives of the New Growth Theories'. *Journal of Economic Literature*, 37(4), 1615–60.

Arellano, M. and S. Bond (1991). 'Some Tests of Specification for Panel Data: Monte-Carlo Evidence and an Application to Employment Equations'. *Review of Economic Studies*, 58, 127–34

Azariadis, C. (1996). 'The Economics of Poverty Traps. Part One: Complete Markets'. *Journal of Economic Growth*, 1, 449–86.

Banerjee, A. and A. F. Newman (1994). 'Poverty, Incentives and Development'. *American Economic Review, Papers and Proceedings*, 84(2), 211–15.

—— and E. Duflo (2000). 'Inequality and Growth: What Can the Data Say?'. *NBER Working Paper* 7793. Cambridge, MA: NBER.

Benabou, R. (1996). 'Inequality and Growth', in B. Bernanke and J. Rotemberg (eds), *National Bureau of Economic Research Macroeconomics Annual*. Cambridge, MA: MIT Press, pp. 11–74.

Carraro, L. (1996). 'Understanding Famine: A Theoretical Dynamic Model.' *Development Studies Working Paper* No. 94. Terion: Centro Sudi Luca d'Agiano.

Chang, W. and D. Smyth (1971). 'The Existence and Persistence of Cycles in a Non-linear Model: Kaldor's 1940 Model Re-examined'. *Review of Economic Studies*, 38, 37–44.

Chaudhuri S. and M. Ravallion (1994). 'How Well do Static Indicators Identify the Chronically Poor?'. *Journal of Public Economics*, 53(3), 367–94.

Chen, S. and M. Ravallion (1996). 'Data in Transition: Assessing Rural Living Standards in Southern China'. *China Economic Review*, 7, 23–56.

Coate, S. and M. Ravallion (1993). 'Reciprocity Without Commitment: Characterization and Performance of Informal Insurance Arrangements'. *Journal of Development Economics*, 40, 1–25.

Dasgupta, P. (1993). *An Inquiry into Well-Being and Destitution*. Oxford: Oxford University Press.

—— (1997). 'Poverty Traps', in D. M. Kreps and K. F. Wallis (eds), *Advances in Economics and Econometrics: Theory and Applications*. Cambridge: Cambridge University Press.

—— and D. Ray (1986). 'Inequality as a Determinant of Malnutrition and Unemployment'. *Economic Journal*, 96, 1011–34.

Day, R. H. (1992). 'Complex Economic Dynamics: Obvious in History, Generic in Theory, Elusive in Data'. *Journal of Applied Econometrics*, 7, S9–S23.

Hansen, L. P. (1982). 'Large Sample Properties of Generalized Method of Moments Estimators'. *Econometrica*, 50, 1029–54.

Jalan, J. and M. Ravallion (1998). 'Transient Poverty in Post-Reform Rural China'. *Journal of Comparative Economics*, 26, 338–57.

—— and —— (1999). 'Are the Poor Less Well Insured? Evidence on Vulnerability to Income Risk in Rural China'. *Journal of Development Economics*, 58(1), 61–82.

—— and —— (2001). 'Behavioral Responses to Risk in Rural China'. *Journal of Development Economics*, 66, 23–49.

—— and —— (2002). 'Geographic Poverty Traps? A Microeconometric Model of Consumption Growth in Rural China'. *Journal of Applied Econometrics*, 17(4), 329–46.

Lokshin, M. and M. Ravallion (2001). 'Nonlinear Household Income Dynamics in Transition Economies', mimeo, Development Research Group, World Bank, Washington, DC.

Mirrlees, J. (1975). 'A Pure Theory of Underdeveloped Economies', in L. Reynolds (ed.) *Agriculture in Development Theory*. New Haven, CT: Yale University Press.

Ravallion, M. (1997). 'Famines and Economics'. *Journal of Economic Literature*, 35(September), 1205–42.

——(1998). 'Does Aggregation Hide the Harmful Effects of Inequality on Growth?'. *Economics Letters*, 61(1), 73–7.

Sargan, J. D. (1958). 'The Estimation of Economic Relationships Using Instrumental Variables'. *Econometrica*, 26, 393–415.

Stiglitz, J. (1976). 'The Efficiency Wage Hypothesis, Surplus Labor and the Distribution of Income in LDCs'. *Oxford Economic Papers*, 28, 185–207.

Varian, H. (1979). 'Catastrophe Theory and the Business Cycle'. *Economic Inquiry*, 17, 14–28.

6

Health, Shocks, and Poverty Persistence

STEFAN DERCON AND JOHN HODDINOTT

6.1. INTRODUCTION

The starting point for many of the contributions in this book is that households in developing countries often experience weather-related and other shocks that drastically affect incomes. Much has been written before on how households respond to these shocks and on the effectiveness of these strategies in reducing fluctuations in consumption (see the survey in Chapter 1, this volume). A principal result that emerges is that some, but not all, households can smooth consumption. In particular, households facing liquidity constraints or without formal or informal support networks have limited smoothing ability. For these households, therefore, income fluctuations will generate a welfare loss.

This chapter complements studies on the effectiveness of these strategies, but differs in focus. Our interest is in exploring the impact of shocks on child and adult health, making particular use of recent studies undertaken in Ethiopia and Zimbabwe. One attraction of such a focus is that health status is, in its own right, a valid indicator of welfare. A second stems from the growing literature on allocation processes within the household (Behrman 1995; Haddad *et al.* 1997). This stresses that changes observed at the household level have different effects on individuals within the household, depending on intrahousehold allocation mechanisms. As health status is observed at the level of the individual, it is possible to observe directly the joint consequences of these shocks and the intrahousehold allocation processes.

A third reason for this focus follows from the apparent causal relationship between health status and other dimensions of well-being. Young children are believed to be especially vulnerable to shocks that lead to growth faltering (Waterlow 1988; Beaton 1993; Martorell *et al.* 1994; Martorell 1999). Children that experience slow height growth are found to perform less well in school, score poorly on tests of cognitive function, have poorer psychomotor development, and fine motor skills. They tend to have lower activity levels, interact less frequently in their environments and fail to acquire skills at normal rates (Lasky *et al.* 1981; Johnston *et al.* 1987; Grantham-McGregor *et al.* 1997, 1999). A small but growing literature, discussed below, explores

This chapter was completed as part of the programme on 'Insurance against Poverty', for the World Institute for Development Economics Research of the United Nations University. An anonymous reviewer provided useful comments.

whether health shocks have permanent or transitory effects on child health status. This is especially important in light of the epidemiological evidence that stature by age three is strongly correlated with attained body size at adulthood (Martorell 1995, 1999). Adult height is correlated with earnings and productivity, poorer cognitive outcomes, and premature mortality due to increased risk of cardiovascular and obstructive lung disease. Taller women experience fewer complications during childbirth, typically have children with higher birthweights, and experience lower risks of child and maternal mortality (World Bank 1993). In the case of adults, an increasing body of evidence links adult weight or body mass index[1] (the BMI, also known as the Quetelet Index) to agricultural productivity and wages (Pitt *et al.* 1990; Dasgupta 1993; Strauss and Thomas 1998; Dercon and Krishnan 2000). Low BMI is correlated with a large number of health-related indicators, including early onset of chronic conditions and increased risk of premature mortality (North 1999; Waaler 1984 cited in Higgins and Alderman 1997).

The common feature across both child and adult studies is that *temporary* shocks can have *permanent* effects. As such, conventional studies that focus on the short-term welfare losses associated with reduced consumption following shocks that are not fully insured against may *understate* the full consequences of these shocks.[2] Shocks affecting health may then even be a cause for a form of poverty trap: a permanently lower equilibrium income stream in the long-run following a negative shock, making previously feasible outcomes impossible.

6.2. SHOCKS AND CHILD HEALTH

We begin by sketching a model that links shocks and child health. A fuller development of these models is found in Behrman *et al.* (1995), Foster (1995), Alderman *et al.* (1994), and Hoddinott and Kinsey (2001).

Households are assumed to maximize intertemporal expected utility. Utility in each period is a function of consumption of goods (x), the number of surviving children (n), and a vector indicating the health or 'quality' of each child (q), and may also be affected by household characteristics (A) such as its lifecycle position and the education of household members that act as preference shifters. The (instantaneous or sub-)utility function for time period t is:

$$U_t = u_t(x_t, n_t, q_t; A). \tag{6.1}$$

Preferences are assumed to be intertemporally additive and individual sub-utility functions are increasing and concave in their arguments, so that individuals are risk-averse. Fertility decisions are taken as given and that there is no replacement response to

---

[1] The BMI is weight in kilograms, divided by the square of height in metres.

[2] The issue of persistent consequences from shocks is also discussed in Jalan and Ravallion Chapter 5, this volume (see also Lokshin and Ravallion 2000). Their focus is, however, different: they look at shocks to overall earnings and ask whether they can detect paths of intertemporal adjustment consistent with persistence. In this chapter, we directly look into the links between shocks and health outcomes in the short-run and long-run.

mortality and we ignore for the time being the complications involved in recasting this as a 'collective' model (Alderman *et al.* 1995). The household faces a budget constraint in each period. Wealth in period $t + 1$ (W_{t+1}) is the sum of wealth in the previous period (W_t) plus the difference between income (y_t) and expenditure (x_t). Denoting prices as p_t and the interest rate on both savings and debt as r_t yields:

$$W_{t+1} = W_t(1 + r_t) + (y_t - p_t x_t). \tag{6.2}$$

Next, we specify a health production function that allows for the impact of shocks. In a static context, child health is a function of physical inputs such as nutrients, time spent caring for children and illness (Behrman and Deolalikar 1988). The technology by which these inputs are combined will be affected by characteristics of the principal carer such as education and age. In a dynamic context, it is necessary to note that the production of current health is a function of past health (and thus shocks that affected health in previous periods). Consider a well-nourished, healthy girl that is growing along a biologically predetermined growth path. Now, suppose this child experiences an illness that temporarily reduces growth. Given the pre-ordained nature of this child's growth, she will grow faster, or 'catch up', in the post-illness period in order to return to her long-run growth path. Such a process may also reflect deliberate decisions made by the household, as where additional resources are provided to children who have recently suffered health shocks.

Accordingly, a general formulation of the determinants of child health in period $t + 1$ has two components: investments associated with increases in child health, the first term in (6.3), and initial child health, the second term:

$$H_{t+1} = h(H_t, g_t, c_t, M_t, A, Z_t, \varepsilon_C) + H_t, \tag{6.3}$$

where H_t is child health at period t; g_t includes physical inputs such as nutrients (which are a subset of x_t) and non-physical inputs such as child care used to produce health, c_t are child characteristics such as age and sex, M_t captures characteristics of the principal care giver, and Z_t refers to the health and sanitation environment which is assumed to influence illness and therefore growth. ε_C captures characteristics of the child such as inherent healthiness, growth potential, or inherited immunities.

We assume that at time t, these young children do not contribute to household income. But at some future date, children may contribute to household income via providing labour time, remittances, or other transfers. These contributions are a function of expected future wages that will vary by sex (given labour market discrimination), age, health (via the links between health–child quality and productivity reviewed in Strauss and Thomas 1998) and community or cultural factors (θ). For example, where bridewealth is practised, the groom and his family are required to transfer resources in the form of cattle and money to provide compensation for the woman. The present value of these contributions at time t can be expressed as (again suppressing the child subscript):

$$R_t = r(c_t, q_t, \theta). \tag{6.4}$$

This constrained maximization problem generates a set of first-order conditions that can be solved out to yield a set of reduced form commodity and child health demand functions. Maintaining the assumption of intertemporal separability, the discounted expected value of additional income is constant, implying as Alderman *et al.* (1994) and Foster (1995) note, that analogous to a consumer durable, households will seek to smooth fluctuations in child health, so that over time, the expected marginal utility of health is equal, up to appropriate discounting. In the case of height, this would imply a smooth growth path over time, provided there are no binding liquidity constraints. But unlike commodity demands, child growth is affected by the height of the child, since the extent to which child growth can be increased between t and $t + 1$ is itself affected by the level at t. It therefore takes the form:

$$H_{t+1} - H_t = h_t(H_t, c_t, M_t, W_t, A, Z_t, p_t, \theta_t, \varepsilon_C). \qquad (6.5)$$

A number of studies use this framework, or variants on it, to explore the links between shocks that affect child health at time period t and health states measured subsequently at period $t + 1$, including Behrman *et al.* (1995), Foster (1995), and Deolalikar (1996). A related literature, using a slightly amended version of this conceptual model, explores the relationship between child health at time period t and schooling attainments at period $t + 1$. Examples of this include Glewwe *et al.* (2001) and Alderman *et al.* (2001). Grantham-McGregor *et al.* (1999: 65–70 especially) provide an exhaustive summary of the epidemiological literature.

Hoddinott and Kinsey (2001) use this framework to examine the impact of the 1994/5 drought on the heights of children living in three resettlement areas in Zimbabwe. Using longitudinal data across five years (1993–7), they estimate a village fixed effects regression of the determinants of annual growth in stature of pre-school children by age cohort with controls for child (initial height, age, sex), maternal (height, age, education, relation to household head), household (livestock holdings, land quality). Their core results are replicated in Table 6.1. Children aged 12–24 months at the end of the drought—who are deemed to be at particular risk from shocks—grew more slowly than comparable children in non-drought years.

Table 6.1. *The impact of the 1994/5 Zimbabwean drought on growth in stature by age group*

Age group in months (children initially aged)	Estimated coefficient on period of observation being 1995–6 (drought cohort)	Asymptotic *t*-statistics based on Huber–White standard errors	Sample size
12–24	−1.727	2.029*	222
24–36	−0.745	0.910	209
36–48	0.068	0.142	239
48–60	−0.173	0.254	194

* Significant at the 5% level.

Note: Dependent variable is annual (12 months) growth rate in child height. Full results available on request.

The slowdown in growth, -1.73 cm, is equivalent to a loss of about 15–20 per cent in growth velocity. Running identical regressions for children in three older age groups: 24–36 months; 36–48 months; and 48–60 months show that the 1994–5 drought had no impact on the growth rates of these older children. These effects are robust to a variety of estimation issues, including the presence of maternal fixed effects, endogeneity of initial health states, and the method used to calculate the standard errors.

Hoddinott and Kinsey (2001) extend this analysis by estimating a maternal fixed effects model of the determinants of the stature of cohorts of children aged 60–72 months. Children who were initially aged 12–24 in the year after the 1994/5 drought have z scores for height-for-age that are about six-tenths of a standard deviation below that of comparable children not exposed to this drought. A refinement to their basic specification adds an interaction term between exposure to drought and a variable that indicates whether pre-drought, the household had livestock holdings below or above the sample median. Children from wealthier households appear to have suffered no long-term effects from this drought. Children from poorer households, by contrast, appear to have experienced a growth slowdown that has persisted to age 60–72 months.

Alderman *et al.* (2002) use a similar framework to examine the impact of the 1982–4 droughts in Zimbabwe, as well as exposure to the civil war preceding independence, on longer-term measures of child health and education. Exposure to the civil war lowers stature as does drought shocks if the child is in the critical 12–24-month age category. These children were interviewed again 13–16 years later. Using an instrumental variables–maternal fixed effects (IV–MFE) estimator, they also show that lowered stature as a pre-schooler leads to lowered in late adolescence as well as delays in school enrolment and reductions in grade completion. The magnitudes of these impacts are meaningful. The mean initial height-for-age z score for these children as pre-schoolers is -1.25. If this population had the nutritional status of well-nourished children, the median z score would be 0. Applying the IV–MFE parameter estimates, this would result in an additional 4.6 cm of height in adolescence, an additional 0.7 grades of schooling and starting school seven months earlier. Further, exposure to the 1982–4 drought reduced height-for-age z scores by 0.63. Using the IV–MFE estimates, this implies that this transitory shock resulted in a loss of stature of 2.3 cm, 0.4 grades of schooling, and a delay in starting school of 3.7 months. Using the values for the returns to education and age/job experience in the Zimbabwean manufacturing sector provided by Bigsten *et al.* (2000: table 5), the impact of these shocks translates into a 7 per cent loss in lifetime earnings.

In the model, A are preference shifters. It may well be that these preference also include preferences of the parents regarding preferential treatment of some of the children relative to others, allowing discrimination to be considered, even in a unitary household framework, using (6.5). Furthermore, analysing intrahousehold issues in non-unitary models would also be possible and under certain assumptions, (6.5) would still be valid. For example, let parents decide over the well-being of children, but allow each parent to have different preferences, which cannot be trivially resolved (i.e. there is no accepted dictator and no identical preferences). Assume further that they resolve their differences in the form of a cooperative bargaining solution, so that we can use a 'collective' model to represent their preferences. Let W be the aggregator function of preferences of each of the parents, $W(U_t^m, U_t^f)$, with U_t^m and U_t^f defined as in (6.1), for the male and female partner. If we then interpret A as variables reflecting the relative bargaining position of the male versus the female partner then (6.5) would still be the basis for testing the impact of shocks, even in a non-unitary model, such as the collective model.

While Hoddinott and Kinsey (2001) and Alderman *et al.* (2002) show that health shocks have differential impacts when pre-schoolers are disaggregated by age, they do not consider gender-differentiated impacts. However, this is straightforward to accomplish by interacting their drought shock variable with child sex. When we do so using their data, we find no evidence to indicate that either the 1982–4 or 1994–5 droughts have different effects on boys or girls health.

It is also possible to explore whether the impact of the 1994/5 differed according to the relationship of the child to the household head. In these resettlement areas, there are an increasing number of mothers in these households who are daughters or daughters-in-law of the head. The important distinction lies between children whose mothers are spouses or daughters-in-law of the household head, and those children whose mothers are daughters of the head. Rights and obligations regarding the former are clear-cut—these children belong to the family. But the position of children of daughters of the head who are born out of wedlock or whose parents have divorced is considerably more ambiguous. They may, or may not, be receiving support from the father and the father's family. They may be considered part of the father's or mother's family. If the mother marries, or remarries, these children will leave the household and the family will have no claim on them for future labour, transfers, or bridewealth payments (Armstrong 1997). Alternatively, these mothers may have little bargaining power within the household. These considerations provide an a priori reason for suspecting that, *ceteris paribus*, these children may have poorer access to household resources. When we interact child's relationship to the household head with the representation of the drought shock, we find that children whose mothers are daughters of the head have a greater loss in growth velocity than other children in the household, but this effect is not statistically significant.

These Zimbabwe data do not suggest a gender-specific impact of drought shocks on pre-schooler health and there is no evidence suggesting a differential impact of health shocks on long-term well-being of girls relative boys (as distinct from differential *levels* of health or other measures of well-being). While such findings are consistent with Svedberg's (1990) claim that, in sub-Saharan Africa, gender bias in health outcomes is largely absent, Foster (1995), using data from Bangladesh, does not find any sex bias in the evolution of child growth during and after the severe floods in Bangladesh in 1988. Still, using other health indicators, there is some evidence of sex bias in India in response to shocks in poor households: Rose (1999) finds that in rural India negative rainfall shocks are associated with higher mortality rates for girls and that this is more pronounced in landless households.

6.3. SHOCKS AND ADULT HEALTH

Modelling adult health is not fundamentally different from modelling child health. Individuals can be assumed to have a sub-utility function at time t, defined in terms of health q, consumption of goods x and, as before, some preference shifters A, such as educational background or other characteristics.

$$U_t = u_t(q_t, x_t; A). \tag{6.6}$$

In the context of adult health in this chapter, we could think of weight or BMI as a good indicator. Note that this implies using a 'stock' rather than a flow as argument in the utility function, implying again that the analysis is analogous to the analysis of durables or capital goods. The individual is assumed to maximize her expected intertemporal additive utility. As before, individual sub-utility functions are increasing in all arguments and individuals are risk-averse.

A first constraint is the adult health production function, which is similar to (6.3). Following Grossman (1972), adult health at $t + 1$ is determined by health in period t in the previous period plus net investment in adult health. Focusing on BMI, net investment in adult BMI includes the loss of weight even in a state of rest, which is similar to depreciation of capital goods,[3] as well as the addition of weight through nutrition, including via food consumption, and the impact of expending energy through working.[4] Other health variables, including morbidity and the general health and sanitation environment, will enter as well.

$$H_{t+1} = h(H_t, g_t, a_t, L_t, Z_t, \varepsilon_a) + \delta H_t, \tag{6.7}$$

where H_t is adult BMI at period t and $(1 - \delta)$ is the person's basal metabolic rate (BMR). The function $h(.)$ is the health production function, transforming nutrients g_t into BMI, net of energy expended by working L_t. The efficiency of this transformation is affected by individual characteristics a_t such as age and sex, Z_t capture morbidity status and the general health and sanitation environment, and ε_a captures specific health characteristics of the adult such as metabolism, inherent healthiness, or inherited immunities.

The budget constraint, linking period t and $t + 1$, is again similar to (6.2), but a direct link between earnings can be written by defining income at period t, y_t, as a function of market wages, labour expended and adult health, reflecting adult

---

[3] A person needs to assure a basal metabolic rate (BMR), that is, the food energy intake needed to support bodily functions at rest, otherwise one experiences net weight loss at rest.

[4] The concept of the body being used as a store of energy is well developed in the biomedical literature, see Dugdale and Payne (1987), Ferrro-Luzzi et al. (1994, 2001), and Payne (1989). Dasgupta (1993) extensively reviews this literature.

health and productivity links (Strauss and Thomas 1998).

$$W_{t+1} = W_t(1 + r_t) + y_t(w_t, L_t, H_t) - p_t x_t. \tag{6.8}$$

The assumptions imply that the interior solution for an optimum path of BMI involves constant expected marginal utilities over time, up to appropriate discounting, provided there are no credit constraints. To write the solution, define a user cost of additional weight, similar to the rental cost of durables or capital goods, that is, the marginal cost of boosting nutritional status for one period only. The optimal path of BMI will then involve equal expected marginal utility benefits from additional BMI in each period, up to discounted relative user costs. This user cost is affected by all the sources of individual heterogeneity described in the adult weight production function—suggesting that initial or past weight may well be a helpful predictor for changes in weight or BMI over time. Furthermore, in each period, prices of nutrients (such as food prices) and wages would also affect user costs. To the extent that relative user costs change over time, they could also be a source of variable BMI over time.

Dercon and Krishnan (2000) use a similar model to discuss adult BMI movements across seasons using panel data in Ethiopia. Their key results are summarized in Table 6.2. Predictable movements in relative prices and wages could affect the optimal path of nutritional status over the seasons, with price variability and differential returns to labour in off-peak and peak seasons encouraging the use of the body as a store of energy, provided that returns to other liquid assets are low, resulting in different 'optimal' weights across the seasons: feast when prices are low and fast when prices are high. They find indeed evidence that this is happening, with higher body weights in correlation with the peak season as well as with the post-harvest period: during: BMI increases by about 0.5 per cent during periods of peak labour needs, while up to 0.5 per cent in the period immediately after the harvest.[5] The effects are typically only significant and large for households with low landholdings, so that 'feast now, fast later' is a strategy typically used by poorer households.[6]

This use of body weight as a consumption smoothing device is consistent with imperfections in asset and food markets, suggesting that returns to assets, food stocks, and returns to using the body as a store of energy are not integrated and arbitrage is profitable. Given the aversion to fluctuations in nutrition by individuals (given concave utility), welfare improvements, especially for the poor, could be obtained by asset and food markets that function better. Evidence in Behrman and Deolalikar (1989), using the ICRISAT Indian data, on the impact of weight-for-height on wages, suggests that body fat may well be used to store energy for later use, suggesting possible failure in optimally smoothing nutritional status over the seasons. Evidence from Pakistan (Behrman *et al.* 1997) suggests that storing calories in the body does not result in an optimal allocation of energy over the seasons, with calorie consumption rising in the

---

[5] Dugdale and Payne (1987) discuss similar results using data from Gambia and Burma.

[6] Their empirical results are based on the generalized method of moments (GMM) estimation of the growth in BMI, using shock variables, lagged BMI and a number of controls as regressors, allowing for heterogeneity using fixed effects in the growth path.

Table 6.2. *The impact of shocks during 1994/5 on the Quetelet (or BMI) of Ethiopian adults (1787 adults)*

Source of shock and fluctuation (by group)	Estimated coefficient	t-statistic
Selected community and household level shocks		
Peak labour period for males	0.0039	1.70*
Peak labour period for females	0.0050	2.10**
Post-harvest period (land rich household)	0.0015	0.69
Post-harvest period (land poor household)	0.0049	2.45***
Rain shock (land rich households)	−0.0012	−0.14
Rain shock (land poor households)	0.0089	2.01**
Individual specific shocks		
Own illness if male in South (land rich household)	−0.0010	−0.95
Own illness if male in South (land poor household)	0.0001	0.04
Own illness if female in South (land rich household)	−0.0022	−1.17
Own illness if female in South (land poor household)	−0.0042	−5.90***
Own illness if male in North (land rich household)	0.0013	1.17
Own illness if male in North (land poor household)	−0.0016	−1.35
Own illness if female in North (land rich household)	0.0004	0.32
Own illness if female in North (land poor household)	−0.0007	−0.81

* Significant at the 10% level.
** Significant at the 5% level.
*** Significant at the 1% level.

Note: The dependent variable is the natural logarithm of BMI. The results are based on a model regressing the change in BMI on the previous level of BMI, shocks and a number of time-varying control variables, as well as controlling for fixed effects in the change in BMI. The Arrellano-Bond GMM estimator is used. Group-specific effects are obtained via interaction terms. Land poor households have less than the median level of land per adult per village. Further details and full results in Dercon and Krishnan (2000).

post-harvest period relative to peak labour periods such as the planting season, but the marginal return to calories is still very high, suggesting that more calories ought to be consumed during the planting season.

The evidence on the lack of optimal smoothing in nutritional status even across seasons—which imply relatively predictable fluctuations in prices and needs—suggests that shocks may have substantial effects as well. Dercon and Krishnan (2000) show that rainfall shocks significantly affect BMI. Even though rainfall was relatively favourable in the period of their study, relatively poor rainfall in some communities lowered BMI by about 0.9 per cent for households with low land holdings (Table 6.2).

Their study also investigates the intrahousehold effects of shocks, more specifically on whether husbands and wives protect each other from the effects of shocks to the earnings capacity of their partner. If the household were to operate as a perfect risk-sharing group, then there should be no separate effect from such shocks on a particular individual, beyond a general loss of resources to the household. While in most households this seems to be occurring, in poor households in the South of the country it does appear not to be the case. In particular, women seem not to be protected by the husbands, even though the reverse holds. The negative effects on women are substantial: for a typical length of an illness episode (5.5 days), BMI would go down by an additional 2 per cent for these women.[7] Hoddinott and Kinsey (1999) also explore the determinants of adult body mass, again using data from Zimbabwe. Controlling for individual, household, and community factors, and individual fixed, unobservable effects, they find women, but not men, are adversely affected by the 1994/5 drought. However, these effects are not borne equally by all women. The BMIs of daughters-in-law of the household head are unaffected by drought. Both wives and daughters are adversely affected, with a 10 per cent reduction in rainfall corresponding to a 2.2 and 3.9 per cent reduction in BMIs, respectively. Although higher livestock holdings protect wives of the household head from drought shocks, this is not true for daughters.

The question of persistence of low BMI after a substantial negative shock remains largely unanswered in both studies; the available evidence suggests that recovery in body weight can and does occur. In Hoddinott and Kinsey (1999), no persistence of the reduction in BMI is noted in Zimbabwe. In Dercon and Krishnan (2000) on rural Ethiopia, there is evidence of lags in adjustment to 'optimal' levels. In particular, they find that past levels of BMI significantly affect the growth path of adult BMI. But the adjustment or 'catching up' costs implied are empirically relatively small (i.e. weight can be increased and decreased relatively easily), making persistent effects unlikely in this context. However, the specification used does not answer the question of persistence directly (see for example Chapter 5). Furthermore, the rainfall and other community shocks observed in their data set were relatively small, so whether for large shocks persistent effects exist, remains to be seen. Still, since most evidence suggests that returns to labour and BMI are positively correlated, the lack of perfect insurance against fluctuations in BMI will in any case imply at least a temporary loss of earnings and therefore lower lifetime earnings.

6.4. CONCLUSION

In this chapter, we have explored the impact of shocks on health status, making particular use of evidence from Ethiopia and Zimbabwe on the impact of droughts and other serious shocks. We find that health status, as measured by height and body mass, is affected by these shocks, suggesting that they are imperfectly insured against. Livestock and other assets play a role in mitigating these shocks. The evidence also suggests that poor people are using their body as a store of energy, in ways consistent with poorly functioning asset and food markets. This implies welfare losses and puts them at risk of further ill-being.

---

[7] Table 6.2 only reports the results for the full sample of adults. Restricting the sample to couples only confirms these results, as did an alternative specification based on the risk-sharing model was estimated, whereby the impact of individual shocks on the relative path of BMI for husbands and wives was tested (Dercon and Krishnan 2000).

A commonality across these studies is that the impact of shocks is not uniform within the household. Younger pre-schoolers are more adversely affected than older pre schoolers. Adult women are more often adversely affected than adult men. Amongst adult women, daughters of the household head are more vulnerable than other women. Lastly, these shocks can have long-term consequences, reducing final attained stature and schooling outcomes. This adversely affects the employment prospects and productivity of these young people. Further, taller (and better educated) women have, on average, taller (and healthier) children, and so the impact of these transitory shocks may well be felt for several generations.

REFERENCES

Alderman, H., P. Gertler, J. Strauss, and D. Thomas (1994). 'Income, Economic Shocks, Infrastructure and Child Growth', unpublished project proposal.

——, P. A. Chiappori, L. Haddad, J. Hoddinott, and R. Kanbur (1995). 'Unitary versus Collective Models of the Household: Is it Time to Shift the Burden of Proof?'. *World Bank Research Observer*, 10, 1–19.

——, J. Hoddinott, and B. Kinsey (2002). 'Long Term Consequences of Early Childhood Malnutrition', mimeo. Department of Economics, Dalhousie University, Halifax.

J. Behrman, V. Lavy, and R. Menon (2001). 'Child Health and School Enrollment: A Longitudinal Analysis'. *Journal of Human Resources*, 36, 185–205.

Armstrong, A. (1997). *Struggling Over Scares Resources: Women and Maintenance in Southern Africa*. Harare: University of Zimbabwe Press.

Beaton, G. (1993). 'Which Age Group should be Targeted for Supplementary Feeding?', in *Nutritional Issues in Food Aid, Nutrition Discussion Paper* No. 12, *ACC/SCN Symposium Report*. Geneva: ACC/SCN.

Behrman, J. (1995). 'The Contribution of Improved Human Resources to Productivity', mimeo, Department of Economics, University of Pennsylvania, Philadelphia, PA.

—— and A. Deolalikar (1988). 'Health and Nutrition', in H. Chenery and T. N. Srinivasan (eds), *Handbook of Development Economics*, Vol. 1. Amsterdam: North Holland.

—— and —— (1989). 'Wages and Labor Supply in Rural India: The Role of Health, Nutrition and Seasonality', in D. Sahn (ed.), *Seasonal Variability in Third World Agriculture: The Consequences for Food Security*. Baltimore, MD: Johns Hopkins University Press.

——, ——, and V. Lavy (1995). 'Dynamic Decision Rules for Child Growth in Rural India and the Philippines: Catching Up or Staying Behind?', mimeo, University of Pennsylvania, Philadelphia, PA.

——, A. Foster, and M. Rosenzweig (1997). 'The Dynamics of Agricultural Production and the Calorie-Income Relationship: Evidence from Pakistan'. *Journal of Econometrics*, 77, 187–207.

Bigsten, A. *et al.* (2000). 'Rates of Return on Physical and Human Capital in Africa's Manufacturing Sector'. *Economic Development and Cultural Change*, 48, 801–28.

Dasgupta, P. (1993). *An Inquiry into Well-being and Destitution*. Oxford: Oxford University Press.

Deolalikar, A. (1996). 'Child Nutritional Status and Child Growth in Kenya: Socioeconomic Determinants'. *Journal of International Development*, 8, 375–94.

Dercon, S. and P. Krishnan (2000). 'In Sickness and in Health: Risk-sharing within Households in Rural Ethiopia'. *Journal of Political Economy*, 108, 688–727.

Dugdale, A. and P. Payne (1987). 'A Model of Seasonal Changes in Energy Balance'. *Ecology of Food and Nutrition*, 19, 231–45.

Ferro-Luzzi, A., F. Branca, and G. Pastore (1994). 'Body Mass Index Defines the Risk of Seasonal Energy Stress in the Third World'. *European Journal of Clinical Nutrition*, 48(Suppl. 3), S165–S178.

——, S. Morris, S. Taffesse, T. Demissie, and M. D'Amato (2001). *Seasonal Undernutrition in Rural Ethiopia: Magnitude, Correlates and Functional Significance*. Research Report 118, Washington, DC: International Food Policy Research Institute.

Foster, A. (1995). 'Prices, Credit Markets and Child Growth in Low-income Rural Areas'. *Economic Journal*, 105, 551–70.

Glewwe, P., H. Jacoby, and E. King (2001). 'Early Childhood Nutrition and Academic Achievement: A Longitudinal Analysis'. *Journal of Public Economics*, 81, 345–68.

Grantham-McGregor, S., L. Fernald, and K. Sethuraman (1999). 'Effects of Health and Nutrition on Cognitive and Behavioral Development in Children in the First Three Years of Life: Part I'. *Food and Nutrition Bulletin*, 20, 53–75.

——, C. Walker, S. Chang, and C. Powell (1997). 'Effects of Early Childhood Supplementation With and Without Stimulation on Later Development in Stunted Jamaican Children'. *American Journal of Clinical Nutrition*, 66, 247–53.

Grossman, M. (1972). *The Demand for Health: A Theoretical and Empirical Investigation*, Occasional Paper No. 119, New York: Columbia University Press, for NBER.

Haddad, L., J. Hoddinott, and H. Alderman (1997). *Intrahousehold Resource Allocation in Developing Countries: Models, Methods and Policy*. Baltimore, MD: Johns Hopkins University Press.

Higgins, P. and H. Alderman (1997) 'Labor and Women's Nutrition: The Impact of Work Effort and Fertility on Nutritional Status in Ghana'. *Journal of Human Resources*, 32, 577–95.

Hoddinott, J. and B. Kinsey (1999). 'Adult Health in the Time of Drought', mimeo, International Food Policy Research Institute, Washington, DC.

—— and —— (2001). 'Child Health in the Time of Drought'. *Oxford Bulletin of Economics and Statistics*, 63, 409–36.

Johnston, F., S. Low, T. de Baessa, and R. MacVean (1987). 'Interaction of Nutritional and Socioeconomic Status as Determinants of Cognitive Achievement in Disadvantaged Urban Guatemalan Children'. *American Journal of Physical Anthropology*, 73, 501–6.

Lasky, R., R. Klein, C. Yarborough, P. Engle, A. Lechtig, and R. Martorell (1981). 'The Relationship between Physical Growth and Infant Development in Rural Guatemala'. *Child Development*, 52, 219–26.

Lokshin, M. and M. Ravallion (2000). 'Short-Lived Shocks with Long-Lived Impacts? Household Income Dynamics in a Transition Economy', *World Bank Working Paper Series* No. 2459. Washington, DC: World Bank.

Martorell, R. (1995). 'Results and Implications of the INCAP Follow-up Study'. *Journal of Nutrition*, 125(Suppl.), 1127S–1138S.

—— (1999). 'The Nature of Child Malnutrition and its Long-term Implications'. *Food and Nutrition Bulletin*, 20, 288–92.

——, K. L. Khan, and D. G. Schroeder (1994). Reversibility of Stunting: Epidemiological Findings in Children from Developing Countries'. *European Journal of Clinical Nutrition*, 48(Suppl.), S45–S57.

North, D. (1999). 'Catching up with the Economy'. *American Economic Review*, 89, 1–21.

Payne, P. (1989). 'Public Health and Functional Consequences of Seasonal Hunger and Malnutrition', in D. Sahn (ed.), *Seasonal Variability in Third World Agriculture: The consequences for Food Security*. Baltimore, MD: Johns Hopkins University Press.

Pitt, M., M. Rosenzweig, and M. D. Hassan (1990). 'Productivity, Health and Inequality in the Intrahousehold Distribution of Food in Low Income Countries'. *American Economic Review*, 80, 1139–56.

Rose, E. (1999). 'Consumption Smoothing and Excess Female Mortality in Rural India'. *Review of Economics and Statistics*, 81, 41–9.

Strauss, J. and D. Thomas (1998). 'Health, Nutrition, and Economic Development'. *Journal of Eocnomic Literature*, 36(2), 766–817.

Svedberg, P. (1990). 'Undernutrition in sub-Saharan Africa: Is There a Gender Bias?'. *Journal of Development Studies*, 26, 469–86.

Waaler, H. (1984). 'Height, Weight and Mortality: The Norwegian Experience'. *Acta Medica Scandinavia*, 77, 279–303.

Waterlow, J. (1988). *Linear Growth Retardation in Less Developed Countries. Nestle Nutrition Workshop Series*, Vol. 14. New York: Raven Press.

World Bank (1993). *World Development Report: Investing in Health*. New York: Oxford University Press.

7

The Macroeconomic Repercussions of Agricultural Shocks and their Implications for Insurance

PAUL COLLIER

7.1. INTRODUCTION: DISSIPATION VERSUS CONTAGION

This chapter investigates the transmission of shocks from the agricultural households that are initially effected by them to other parts of the economy. Some types of shock are transmitted, and indeed, to an extent *shifted*, whereas other types of shock have no effects on other households. The analysis has two implications for the impact of shocks on poverty. First, those shocks that are 'contagious' are likely, dollar-for-dollar, to have more detrimental effects on poverty than those that are not. There is some evidence that the contagion effect can be large, reducing incomes elsewhere in the economy by considerably more than the value of the initial shock itself. Hence, abstracting for a moment from the incidence of the shocks, the poverty impact of contagious shocks is a multiple of equivalently sized non-contagious shocks. Second, because contagious shocks are not just transmitted but shifted, their ultimate incidence may be more heavily concentrated upon poor households than the apparent, or initial incidence. I argue that this is indeed likely to be the case.

In the microeconomics of agricultural households, the distinction between idiosyncratic and systemic shocks is of interest because of their different implications for local insurability. The risks from idiosyncratic shocks can profitably be pooled locally, whereas those from systemic shocks cannot. From the macroeconomic perspective the distinction is, however, even sharper. Idiosyncratic risks, whether insured or not, net out at the aggregate level, whereas systemic risks cumulate and so have macroeconomic effects on consumption and savings. When changes in the demand for consumer goods and assets are sudden and large, they can generate non-pecuniary externalities, which effect output in the rest of the economy. In this case, the full impact

A previous draft of this chapter was presented at the UNU-WIDER project meeting 'Insurance against Poverty', 15–16 June 2001, Helsinki, Finland. The findings, interpretations, and conclusions expressed in this chapter are entirely those of the author. They do not necessarily represent the views of the World Bank, its Executive Directors, or the countries they represent. I would like to thank Tony Addison and Stefan Dercon for comments on a previous draft.

Table 7.1. *The paradox of insurance provision*

	Nature of shock	
	Idiosyncratic	**Systematic**
Insured	Common, but no external benefits	Rare, but large external benefits
Uninsured	Rare	Common

of systemic agricultural shocks is not confined to producers: the decisions of producers have externalities for other agents. Potentially, these second round repercussions of systemic agricultural shocks are more important than their direct effects. Hence, whereas idiosyncratic shocks are dissipated at the macroeconomic level, systemic shocks are potentially contagious.

Table 7.1 illustrates the *paradox of insurance provision* from the perspective of the macroeconomy. Since synchronized shocks are likely to have repercussions for other agents in the economy, the desirable pattern of insurance is for these shocks to be insured, whereas the insurance of idiosyncratic shocks is unimportant. In fact, the economy will generate precisely the opposite pattern: idiosyncratic shocks will be insured, while systemic shocks will be uninsured.

Systemic agricultural shocks obviously occur both for prices and for quantities: world prices for many agricultural products are volatile, and supply at the national level is subject to shocks from climate and disease. However, price shocks are usually more extreme than quantity shocks. Just as idiosyncratic shocks net out when aggregated, so modest systemic agricultural shocks net out against other systemic disturbances. Hence, it is only the large systemic agricultural shocks, which have important macroeconomic effects, and these are mostly generated by price changes rather than by quantity changes. In Section 7.2, I consider the repercussions of large negative agricultural price shocks. The price changes that are for those agricultural products, which are not traded internationally, generate only transfers between domestic agents. Whether these transfers have a net impact upon consumption and savings depends upon differences in behavioural responses between types of agent and hence on the particularities of each case. Hence, I focus on agricultural exports. Price changes for exports generate a net income effect and so necessarily have an impact on consumption and savings.

A fall in the price of agricultural exports gives rise to an income shock to the household, the locality, and the nation. Usually, the income shock will change aggregate demand, but by less than the shock because consumption will be partially cushioned by changes in liquid assets. The fall in aggregate demand potentially causes changes in aggregate supply. The extent of such an effect depends upon the degree of flexibility of prices and initial spare capacity. The Keynesian model assumes fixed prices. With fixed prices, negative shocks will reduce output through underemployment and the Keynesian multiplier. If there is initial spare capacity, positive shocks will also affect output in the opposite direction. The neoclassical model assumes fully flexible prices and hence full employment. There will nevertheless be an output multiplier as a result of changes in savings and investment: for example, a windfall will be invested and this will augment subsequent output. In most developing countries, especially in rural areas, prices are highly flexible and there is little spare capacity. However, complete price flexibility in response to large and sudden shocks is unlikely since, in effect, it would imply that information costs were zero. Hence, the actual extent of an output multiplier is an empirical matter.

In Section 7.3, I turn to positive price shocks for agricultural exports. Large and sudden increases in prices are likely to cause a sharp and temporary increase in the demand for financial assets. However, private agents cannot in aggregate change their net financial asset position without accommodation by the central bank. Hence, inept policy by a central bank can frustrate the asset strategies of private agents. Finally, in Section 7.4, I briefly consider agricultural quantity shocks.

7.2. MACROECONOMIC REPERCUSSIONS OF NEGATIVE AGRICULTURAL PRICE SHOCKS

In work with Jan Dehn (Collier and Dehn 2001), I investigate the extent to which price shocks for primary commodity exports are transmitted onto output. Although we consider all primary commodity exports other than oil, including those that are non-agricultural, the effects of price shocks for agricultural exports are not significantly different from the general pattern. We consider only large annual price shocks, defined as price changes, which are in one or other of the 2.5 per cent tails of the frequency distribution of price changes. The sample is for 113 developing countries over the period 1957–97 and is described in Dehn (2000: 232). There are 179 large positive shocks and 99 large negative shocks.

We then analyse the effect of these shocks within the framework of the Burnside–Dollar model of how aid affects growth (Burnside and Dollar 2000). Their analysis is for fifty-six countries during the period 1970–93, with the period divided into six growth episodes each of four years.

In this Section, I consider only the effect of the large negative shocks. Within the Burnside–Dollar sample there are thirty-eight episodes during which there was at least one year of severe negative terms of trade shock (i.e. in the bottom 2.5 per cent tail of the distribution of price shocks). The mean for these severe negative shocks was a fall in the world price of 40 per cent between one year and the next. The mean direct income loss from these price shocks is around 6.8 per cent of GDP, where the income loss is defined as the price change times the prior volume of exports.

If prices were fully flexible, this fall in income would only affect constant price GDP through reduced investment. The change in relative prices would induce some resource reallocation, but measured at constant prices this would only have second-order effects on aggregate GDP and indeed even the sign of such second-order effects would be ambiguous.[1] At the other extreme, were prices fixed and the income shock could

---

[1] If the constant prices used to measure GDP were those prevailing in the year prior to the price shock then necessarily aggregate output would appear to decline as a result of reallocation, however, in practice constant price GDP is measured at relative prices which prevailed several years prior to the price shock and so the induced resource reallocation could even raise the valuation of aggregate output.

not be cushioned by dissaving, the change in output would be the familiar Keynesian multiplier of $1/(1 - c - m)$, times the income shock. For plausible ranges of the marginal propensities to consume (c) and import (m), the likely multiplier would be well in excess of unity.

The price shock can occur in any year of the four-year episode, while the effect on growth is estimated over the entire episode. Hence, any output effects of the price shock are observed both for the year in which it occurs, and for between zero and three further years. The output effects of the typical shock are thus observed for eighteen months beyond the year in which it occurs. We find that the these severe negative price shocks have significant and substantial effects, reducing the growth rate of aggregate output by around 1.4 per cent per annum over the episode. Thus, by the end of the episode, output is around 5.6 per cent lower and the total loss of output as a per cent of initial annual income is around 14 per cent. Recalling that the average severe shock in our sample constitutes a loss to the income terms of trade of 6.8 per cent of initial GDP, the pure income shock causes a loss of output of approximately double its own value. Thus, the implied multiplier from the initial loss of income to the total loss of income is around three: the economy loses three times in terms of trade loss. Such a large multiplier cannot credibly be fully accounted for by disinvestment. Even if households fully protected consumption, so that investment declined by the full amount of the initial income loss, the capital-output ratio would need to be around unity to generate such a large loss of output over such a short period. An implication is that such price shocks cause contagious reductions in income, presumably at least in part due to less than complete price flexibility. If so, presumably the decline in output is not persistent, although the losses themselves are not recovered.

A multiplier of this magnitude has important implications for poverty. Unless the shock happens to be transmitted to richer households, its impact on poverty among the households producing the affected export commodity will considerably understate its true impact in the society.

With such large and rapid output losses resulting from a severe fall in the price of agricultural exports, it is implausible that most of the reduction in output comes from agricultural exports or other output produced by the producers of agricultural exports. A more likely account is that the primary recipients of the income shock reduce their demand for domestically produced goods and that, due to less-than-full price flexibility elsewhere in the economy, this in turn reduces output. In this case, the second round fall in output would not reflect an optimal response to relative price changes, but rather would be the result of information failures. The income loss to the society from the price shock would be triple the direct effect of the shock: the direct income loss due to the diminished value of exports, plus double that loss through the induced reduction in output across the economy. Instead of the shock being dissipated, it is contagious.

What can be done to remedy such shocks? Dehn and I explore the effect of compensatory changes in aid inflows. We add an interaction term of the price shock and changes in the aid inflow to the Burnside–Dollar regression. We measure the change in the aid inflow as the average during the four-year period being analysed relative to the average in the preceding four-year period. We find that the interaction term is significant and positive: increased aid offsets the adverse effect on output of a sharp decline in export prices. This approach also constitutes an indirect test of the channels by which the reduction in output is generated. Since aid does not restore the domestic price of the export crop, if the reduction in output were directly a labour supply decision of exporters, then aid would not be able to offset the reduction in output. In fact, we find that increases in aid compensate for the effect of the income loss from exports approximately one-for-one. That is, for the average 40 per cent price fall and resulting 6.8 per cent direct decline in income, were donors to increase aid by an equivalent amount to this direct income loss there would be no second round loss of output. Since the Burnside and Dollar growth regression already includes aid as an explanatory variable (and its interaction with policy), the compensatory output effect of aid during negative shocks is over and above its normal effect on growth. Hence, the result is not simply that aid projects are productive. Rather, it shows that precisely at times of falling aggregate demand due to terms of trade losses, additional aid is unusually productive. Since both other effects of aid and the effects of policy are controlled for, the most plausible explanation for this is surely that it is preventing the fall in aggregate demand and thus preventing the adverse output responses to it.

To summarize, we find that large negative export price shocks have two adverse effects on income, a direct effect, which accrues to producers of export goods and an indirect effect of about double the magnitude which presumably accrues to those who supply them with consumer goods. We have found that a temporary increase in aid, of the same order or magnitude as the price shock, will on average fully neutralize the second of these effects. Of course, the aid does not accrue to the producers of exports, it accrues to the government. Thus, while a donor-run insurance scheme providing compensation to the government could fully rectify the contagion-type feature of export price shocks, it would obviously not directly compensate exporters.

The dilemma in providing such a donor insurance arrangement arises from the distributional consequences of donor intervention. Far from directly compensating exporters, a temporary aid inflow would actually amplify the income shock to them despite neutralizing it to the economy as a whole. The reason for this is that aid, like exports, is an inflow of foreign exchange and so tends to appreciate the real exchange rate. Aid competes with exports to supply imports to the rest of the economy. In the absence of compensatory aid, the decline in export revenue will depreciate the real exchange rate. The price of non-tradable goods declines relative to the price of imports. This cushions the decline in the overall purchasing power of exports in units of consumption. The real exchange rate depreciation acts as an automatic insurance mechanism for exporters, shifting the income decline to other parts of the society. Because of the depreciation of the real exchange rate, and the second round multiplier effects on output, the structure of risk-bearing from the typical export price shock is complex. Table 7.2 sets out an estimate in which I assume arbitrarily that due to exchange rate depreciation the initial 6.8 per cent income loss is shared equally between exporters and producers of non-tradable goods. That is, the decline in demand for local goods on the part of exporters lowers the price of those goods sufficiently to cushion half of their income loss, thereby shifting it on to the rest of the society. I assume that

Table 7.2. *Distributional effects of negative agricultural export price shocks with and without compensating aid (losses (−), gains (+) in percentage points of GDP)*

	Fall in export price = 6.8% of GDP	Aid = 6.8% of GDP	Induced decline in output	Total (%)
Without aid				
Effect on export producers	−3.4	—	0	−3.4
Effect on rest of economy	−3.4	—	−14	−17.4
Total effect	−6.8	—	−14	−20.8
With aid				
Effect on export producers	−6.8	0	0	−6.8
Effect on rest of the economy	0	6.8	0	+6.8
Total effect	−6.8	6.8	0	0

the second round decline in output of 14 per cent is likely to be concentrated among producers of non-tradable goods who face excess supply.

The implications of the shock for poverty depend not just upon its scale—the fact that it is multiplied beyond the direct decline in export income—but also upon its incidence. On the assumptions of Table 7.2, agricultural export households end up bearing less than a fifth of the shock, the rest being borne by households selling non-tradable goods. These households experience both lower prices for their produce and an overall contraction in output—in the absence of full price flexibility the decline in demand is partly met by cuts in production. The non-tradable sector typically covers a wide spectrum of activities and household income levels. However, as an approximation, workers in the more flexible price component of the sector—such as self-employed service workers—have low incomes, often lower than agricultural exporters. By contrast, workers in activities with less flexible prices may be wage-earners in formal employment with relatively high incomes. This conjunction does not bode well for the poverty incidence of contagious shocks. The fall in incomes in the flexible price activities would affect a particularly poor group of households. The fall in output in the less flexible price activities would admittedly accrue to better-off households, but it would accrue as unemployment. Thus, instead of being spread fairly evenly across a wide group of relatively well-off households, it would leave most unaffected and cause drastic reductions in the incomes of a few households, pushing some of them into poverty.

Were this shock to be fully compensated by increased aid, there would be no depreciation in the real exchange rate. The structure of risk-bearing would then be that exporters would bear the full 6.8 per cent loss from the terms of trade decline, while those agents who were direct beneficiaries of the aid inflow would gain by an equivalent amount. To heighten the dilemma, in the table I assume that the beneficiaries of the extra aid are entirely distinct from the producers of agricultural exports. However, this seems quite a reasonable assumption. The only type of aid which could be disbursed sufficiently quickly to compensate for fall in export prices is programme aid: hence donors do not have the time to design and implement additional aid projects targeted at export producers. The government is itself unlikely to be able to target the aid towards export producers and presumably does not even have the incentive to do so.

To summarize the donors' dilemma, compensation to the society is a highly efficient use of aid: aid is atypically productive when it is used to offset negative terms of trade shocks. However, it involves the opposite of insurance for the primary recipients of the shock.

This dilemma was seen in practice in the Stabex scheme of the European Union. The initial version of this scheme provided compensation to governments for periods of low prices of agricultural exports. However, sensitive to the critique that the effects on the real exchange rate were having adverse effects on precisely the farmers who were hit by the price shock, the revised version of the Stabex scheme required that all Stabex aid should be used for projects, which benefited farmers. Inevitably, such projects have very long lead times and so Stabex funds could not be disbursed during the period of the price shock. Indeed, the delays in disbursement were so long that the receipt of funds tended to be pro-cyclical with export prices rather than counter-cyclical. Thus, Stabex sacrificed the aggregate demand compensation effects for which compensatory aid appears to be highly effective.

What is the way out of this dilemma? One implication is that because negative export price shocks have large externalities beyond their impact on export produ-cers, the producers will under-insure relative to the social optimum. To the extent that export producers do insure locally, they may even make the problem worse. Domestic insurance does not prevent the impact of a term of trade decline on aggregate income, it simply shifts the income loss to some other agents in the economy. Since the agents to whom the risk is shifted are better placed to bear shocks, the impact upon aggregate demand of a given income shock will be more muted. However, offset-ting this, insurance induces farmers to increase their exposure to export price shocks, thereby increasing the exposure of the society. Thus, improved domestic insurance arrangements may increase the need for aid to compensate the rest of the society.

The first best is to supply international insurance for export prices direct with farmers. If farmers could fully insure internationally, the rest of the economy would not suffer the decline in demand when export prices fell and so donors would not need to compensate. Hence, donors could potentially justify subsidizing such an insurance arrangement to try to offset the externalities generated when exporters suffer income losses. However, any scheme, which is more generous than is actuarially justified, raises the overall return to export production and thereby involves moral hazard: producers will increase output. Donors can, however, cover the administrative costs of an insurance scheme without encountering moral hazard. A scheme established without donor assistance would need to be self-financing, covering its own administrative costs. To recover these costs, the prices paid to farmers would on average need to be below prices without insurance. Hence, the insurance scheme would lower the mathematical expectation of the producer price. The avoidance of moral hazard only requires that the expected price should not be increased by the scheme. As the Grameen Bank credit schemes have shown, while poor people are willing to take up and repay credit at significantly positive interest rates, the administrative costs of such schemes are very high. It is sometimes argued that if these schemes can be self-financing, subsidy of administrative costs is unnecessary, whereas if the schemes cannot be self-financing, subsidy of administrative costs is unjustified: the cost to donors exceeds the value to users. However, in the case of crop price insurance, the private benefits to the producer appear very substantial to understate the social benefits. Hence, where price insurance is unviable without donor subsidy of administrative costs, even though the cost to donors will exceed the direct cost to users, they may still be justified by the large external benefits to society. Indeed, in the presence of such an externality, even where a price insurance scheme is viable without subsidy, producers will not insure to the extent that is socially efficient, and so subsidy of administrative costs is desirable.

In the absence of international insurance direct to producers, domestic insurance of export prices for producers can be combined with international insurance direct to the government. The domestic insurance spreads the shock across the society, and the international insurance to the government then prevents the aggregate demand decline. Note that international subsidy of domestic insurance arrangements does not provide the necessary neutralization of the aggregate demand shock: the insurance has to be external. A third best is for international insurance of the government, combined with domestic insurance of farmers more generally, although not targeted to export prices.

7.3. MACROECONOMIC REPERCUSSIONS OF POSITIVE AGRICULTURAL PRICE SHOCKS

For idiosyncratic shocks, whether positive or negative, agents can cushion consumption by using community insurance and credit arrangements, as well as by accumulating and decumulating assets. However, for shocks, which are systemic at the national level, such as export price shocks, national or sub-national level insurance is not feasible and so the society must rely upon asset accumulation and decumulation. This introduces a potential asymmetry in response to positive and negative shocks. Agents may individually choose to accumulate assets, but they can only decumulate to the extent that they already hold assets in liquid form. The holding of large liquid balances is costly and is likely to be unnecessary to guard against idiosyncratic shocks, which are a great deal more common than systemic shocks. Hence, we would expect that unlike idiosyncratic shocks, systemic shocks would produce asymmetric effects depending upon whether they were positive or negative. Large positive shocks would disproportionately induce asset accumulation, whereas large negative shocks would necessarily have to be absorbed predominantly by reductions in consumption.

In the short term, the increased demand for assets would predominantly take the form of financial assets: the acquisition of real assets requires time both to plan investments and to implement them. Hence, this asymmetry would be manifest in the impact on aggregate demand: large negative shocks would reduce demand more than large positive shocks would increase them. In Section 7.2, I investigated the multiplier from large negative shocks: the typical negative shock reduced output by twice the decline in initial income, and I interpreted this as evidence for powerful Keynesian-type effects on aggregate demand. Dehn and I also investigate the effects of large positive shocks. The typical positive shock is even larger than the typical negative shock—the mean price increase is of 47 per cent as compared with the mean price decrease of 40 per cent. Further, as might be expected from the basic theory of commodity price determination (Deaton and Laroque 1992), there are more large positive shocks than large negative shocks. Despite the fact that the positive shocks are both larger and more numerous, we find that they have no significant effects, positive or negative, on short-term growth. Whereas large negative shocks severely reduce output, large positive shocks do not increase it. This asymmetry has two interpretations consistent with the Keynesian aggregate demand story proposed for negative shocks. First, it might be that the economy is normally operating at full employment of resources, so that increases in aggregate demand simply translate into higher prices rather than additional output. Second, it might be that savings rates out of positive shocks are sufficiently high that the demand effects are quite modest.

Both of these interpretations might be correct. There is considerable microeconomic evidence that farmers have high savings rates out of agricultural price windfalls (Collier *et al.* 1999), commonly around or even above 50 per cent. Such high dissaving rates from large negative windfalls are implausible simply because they would require poor people to hold very large liquid assets. Hence, the aggregate demand shock from large price increases might indeed be considerably smaller than from price decreases. These more modest aggregate demand shocks might then have less impact on output because the economy is normally close to full utilization of resources.

I will assume that the high savings rate from positive windfalls is at least part of the story of such shocks. Since in normal times savings rates of poor agricultural households are typically very low, the episodes of high savings out of windfalls are of considerable importance for them. These often-brief opportunities are when a disproportionate amount of asset formation on the part of poor households can take place. It is therefore incumbent upon the government authorities to manage the macroeconomy in such a way as to facilitate the asset strategies of these households. I now turn to the macroeconomic consequences of this sudden synchronized increase in the demand for assets.

First, consider the effect of a large increase in the world price of the export crop in a fully dollarized economy. Typically, there are large wedges between borrowing and lending rates in the financial markets to which small farmers have access. As a result, we would expect the increased savings should in the medium term translate predominantly into an increase in productive assets in the enterprises in which the farmer is engaged, rather than an accumulation of financial assets. Yet, in the short term such an increase in real assets will usually not be feasible. Time will be needed, both to assess the overall scale of the windfall, and to identify and implement investment plans. During this interval, windfall income must be accumulated in financial assets. In a dollarized economy, these financial assets will, by definition, be foreign assets. As each farmer accumulates financial assets, the economy as a whole accumulates claims abroad. During this period, the holdings of dollars in the economy will increase both absolutely and relatively to income. Conversely, when farmers reach the phase of implementing their investment plans, they will convert these financial assets into real assets and so dollar holdings in the economy will decline again. In such a dollarized economy, an export price boom therefore induces temporary changes in the aggregate demand for real money balances, which are automatically satisfied by the accumulation and decumulation of dollar holdings.

However, very few economies are fully dollarized. Many small, low-income countries have their own currencies with floating exchange rates against the dollar, but very limited markets in domestic debt. Central banks can intervene in the foreign exchange market, but cannot offset such interventions by transactions in domestic bond markets. Hence, they cannot effectively sterilize changes in the money supply brought about by their exchange rate interventions. These central banks nevertheless operate with a policy rule on monetary growth. A common policy rule, under arrangements with the IMF, is for the nominal money supply to be subject to a ceiling rate of increase. In the circumstances of an export price boom, such ceilings create a divergence between individual and aggregate asset behaviour. To see this, consider what happens if the demand for real money balances, necessarily in domestic currency, rises as a result of the shock by more than the increase permitted by the agreed ceiling. Exporters initially receive additional dollars, which they attempt in aggregate to convert into additional domestic currency. The central bank refuses to make net purchases of foreign currency because this would increase the domestic money supply beyond the ceiling. As a result, the domestic currency appreciates sharply against the dollar. This appreciation in turn lowers the price level: the nominal domestic currency price of importable goods falls. In turn, the decline in the price level brings about the desired increase in real money balances and, indeed, this is the point at which the exchange rate ceases to appreciate.

Such a rapid and dramatic sequence of events can be seen in the Ugandan coffee boom of 1994, the result of a frost in Brazil which damaged the Brazilian coffee crop and approximately tripled the world price. The increase in the world price of coffee was very largely passed on to coffee farmers. Since this was the first windfall for coffee farmers in almost twenty years it was recognized as exceptional and farmers saved accordingly. The Ugandan economy had a floating exchange rate, virtually no domestic bond market, and ceilings for monetary growth: hence, it had precisely the combination of shocks, markets, and policy rules discussed above. Within five months of the start of the coffee boom the exchange rate had strongly appreciated and the price level had declined absolutely by 6 per cent, reversing an inflation rate, which over the previous twelve months had been 16 per cent.

For the central bank to accommodate the increased demand of farmers for real money balances requires an equivalent increase in base money (M0). Increases in 'inside money' net out in aggregate as claims and liabilities: only base money is a net claim of private agents on the government. In turn, to be able to honour these claims, the government, through its central bank, must accumulate foreign financial assets. The increase in base money may itself trigger a much larger increase in bank lending and this could be inflationary. Ideally, the central bank should accommodate the desired increase in base money, but restrain credit expansion by raising the minimum cash ratio that banks must retain.

In Uganda, fear of increasing base money was influential in the decision to introduce a windfall export tax on coffee. Such a tax was doubly problematic. First, coffee farmers were even poorer than the average Ugandan, so that the tax was regressive. Second, coffee farmers had a high savings and investment rate from that part of the windfall, which they retained, and in retrospect, this investment proved to be highly productive. Hence, the tax reduced the scale of the largest investment episode, which rural Uganda has ever experienced. Fortunately, the Ugandan government rapidly repealed the tax and expanded the nominal money supply. Overall, during the first year of the boom the money supply in real terms grew by 23 per cent.

Up to this stage, it is of no consequence whether the accumulation of real money balances is directly in dollars, as in a dollarized economy, or in domestic currency as in Uganda. However, in the remaining stage of asset responses the difference can be crucial. Recall that in this second stage farmers convert their financial assets into real assets. For an individual farmer it evidently makes no difference whether the money, which he converts into real investment, is in dollars or domestic currency. The farmer simply buys the investment goods. However, in aggregate, if the financial asset which farmers are reducing is domestic currency, the outcome will only be a rise in the price level unless the central bank offsets the fall in demand for domestic currency by intervening in the foreign exchange market to sell dollars. In the absence of such intervention, farmers achieve their desired decline in real money balances not by converting them into real assets, but by an erosion in the real value of their nominal balances. In this event, the behaviour of farmers in aggregate frustrates their individual intentions: each asset switching decision inflicts a negative externality on others, because the economy in aggregate does not have the resources to expand investment. Precisely this phenomenon occurred in the wake of the cocoa boom in Ghana (Wetzel 1999). Cocoa farmers had a very high financial savings rate out of the windfall but these savings were entirely dissipated by post-windfall inflation. Their windfall was taxed at 100 per cent, not by a direct export tax on cocoa, but by a post-windfall inflation tax.

The key behaviour is thus that, of the central bank. Whereas in a dollar economy farmers automatically increase and then run down foreign financial assets, a domestic currency introduces a dual decision problem. The central bank must accumulate and then decumulate dollars to correspond to the changing demand by farmers for domestic currency. The demand for financial assets can change substantially, first upwards and then downwards. The lag between accumulation and decumulation is not necessarily related to the length of the windfall: decumulation may precede or occur after the end of the windfall. Rather, it may be related to the necessary lag for farmers to plan and implement substantial investments. Since these lags are not known, the central bank does not know either how much foreign exchange to accumulate, nor when to switch interventions to decumulation. If the central bank fails to accumulate enough foreign assets, or delays running them down, farmers' investment plans cannot in aggregate be fully implemented.

As is evident, were the central bank to stick to a pre-shock ceiling for nominal monetary growth it would completely frustrate farmers' plans. There is, however, a policy rule, which if the central bank follows, will enable farmers to fulfil their plans. This is to maintain an inflation rate, or price level, target rather than a money supply target. In order to keep to a price level target the central bank will need to offset changes in money demand with changes in supply, achieved through interventions in the foreign exchange market. Price level targeting rather than money supply targeting is often discouraged, for good reason. The timeliness and quality of information available to the central bank about changes in the price level is usually inferior to that on changes in the money supply. Money supply figures can be known with very little delay and a high degree of accuracy. Price level information depends upon an administratively complex data gathering system and an aggregation procedure, which between them introduce a range of uncertainty. If the data collection system is slow and the aggregation procedure weak, then short-term observed changes in prices have doubtful information content and so are unreliable as the basis for policy. However, at times of agricultural price shocks, targeting the money supply, no matter how accurately it can be observed, are simply an inappropriate policy rule. The correct strategy is therefore to recognize that in economies subject to agricultural price shocks it is important to have a reliable consumer price index. The Ugandan authorities recognized that in their economy the demand for money was unlikely to be stable, so that price level targeting was necessary, and for this they developed both fast collection of raw price data, and reliable aggregation based upon an up-to-date consumer expenditure survey. The consumer price index was available by the end of each month based on prices observed during the middle of the month.

While a central bank operating price-level targeting should correctly accommodate farmers' changing demand for real money balances, in practice central banks are subject to many countervailing pressures. The advice of international agencies and the demands of politicians may from time to time derail a price-level rule. Farmer's, accumulation of windfall financial savings is likely to depend upon their confidence in financial assets. A good way, and conceivably the only way, for the government to credibly pre-commit to the maintenance of the real value of windfall savings is to dollarize. Small economies, subject to agricultural price shocks should probably not have their own currencies.

Note that this conclusion is at variance with the traditional open economy macroeconomic literature on exchange rates and shocks. In that literature, a flexible exchange rate is preferable to a fixed exchange rate, and a fortiori to dollarization, because it permits price level stabilization during a boom. The rise in the relative price of non-tradables, 'Dutch disease', can be accommodated without an increase in the price level, by a fall in the nominal price of tradables through exchange rate appreciation. However, this analysis is entirely static. It was designed to analyse a once-and-for-all shock such as the rise in the price of oil in the mid-1970s. Agricultural price shocks are seldom of this nature. More commonly, they have a strong temporal element: producers respond by saving windfalls as if they viewed such windfalls as liable to be temporary. Hence, the main macroeconomic effects of positive agricultural price shocks are on asset demand rather than on the relative prices of consumer goods. A dollarized economy is disadvantageous if the main effects are in consumer markets, but is advantageous if the main effects are in asset markets.

7.4. MACROECONOMIC REPERCUSSIONS OF AGRICULTURAL OUTPUT SHOCKS

In work with Arne Bigsten (Bigsten and Collier 1995) I investigated the effect of agricultural quantity shocks on other sectors of the economy using time series for Kenya. Our proxy measure for output shocks was variations in national agricultural value-added measured at constant prices. While value-added and gross output series potentially need not be closely related, in view of the rules of thumb adopted in the Kenyan national accounts, the two series are likely to be very similar. We found that shocks to agricultural value-added measure had no effect on output in other sectors of the economy—with one exception. Output of the construction sector varied pro-cyclically with agricultural output. Further, a Granger causality test established that causality ran from agriculture to construction. A 1 per cent increase in agricultural value-added increased construction value-added by 0.8 per cent. Since agricultural value-added measure was considerably larger than construction value-added, this converted into an investment rate into construction value-added of around 20 per cent. However, note that construction value-added is only a proportion of construction expenditure, so that the true investment rate would have been somewhat higher. This is consistent with the evidence that farmers invest windfalls. However, the absence of an effect on the rest of the economy suggests that, at least in Kenya, quantity shocks were not as important as price shocks. None of the negative value-added shocks were as large as the price shocks analysed in Section 7.2. Outside the Sahel it may be that output shocks are simply less important at the systemic level than price shocks, although they are presumably far more important at the idiosyncratic level.

A second piece of evidence on the effects of quantity shocks is the series of studies of rural Asia by Peter Hazell. He indeed found evidence of a larger multiplier from agricultural income onto the local non-agricultural economy (see Rosengrant and Hazell 2000: 108). On average, an increase in agricultural income raised non-agricultural income by between 50 and 100 per cent of the initial increase. However, Hazell was not investigating temporary deviations from the path of growth of agricultural output, but rather permanent large increases in output. Hence, we would expect a smaller proportion of the income gains to be saved, so that they would have a larger impact on aggregate demand in the rest of the economy. Hazell's work is not, therefore, pertinent for arguments concerning risk and insurance.

7.5. CONCLUSION

I have looked at three types of systemic agricultural shock: negative price shocks, positive price shocks, and output shocks. Export price shocks are intrinsically systemic and so have macroeconomic repercussions: I have cited evidence that when price shocks are extreme, these repercussions are highly adverse. These repercussions imply that, abstracting from distributional considerations, the systemic shocks have a considerably larger impact on poverty, dollar-for-dollar, than idiosyncratic shocks. Further, I have suggested that agricultural export price shocks are likely to get substantially shifted to two groups with a high-risk of poverty. One is workers in the flexible price part of the non-tradable sector, who are often even poorer than agricultural exporting households. The other is workers in the less-flexible part of the non-tradable sector who become unemployed and so suffer a sharp drop in income.

The negative externality created by farmers' aggregate response could be offset were farmers to take out international insurance. The *paradox of insurance provision* is that farmers are far more likely to insure idiosyncratic shocks than systemic shocks. Idiosyncratic shocks are more common, and local informal and even private formal insurance arrangements are radically more feasible. Hence, to the extent that macroeconomic considerations matter, public insurance provision should concentrate upon export price shocks rather than on quantity shocks. However, macroeconomic considerations are only part of the picture. Indeed, in conventional analyses of farmer insurance they do not even make it into the picture. The usual case for public insurance rests partly on the growth-sacrificing measures that farmers otherwise adopt to reduce risk, and partly on the humanitarian need to target resources to people during transient adverse shocks. Such insurance rightly focuses on quantity shocks. My point is not to call into question the importance of public insurance for quantity shocks, but rather to raise the question of whether price insurance can be made feasible by a modest level of subsidy of administrative costs that thereby does not create moral hazard. If such insurance is feasible, it would be useful because it is price shocks where the large externalities are to be found. To the extent that it is not feasible, it is better to provide the insurance to the economy as a whole, through temporary reallocations of aid, than to leave it uncompensated. I have suggested that concerns that such compensating aid would further hurt export farmers through Dutch disease are probably exaggerated: the costs of the terms of trade shock are large and probably spread widely over the economy. It is more important to reduce these costs than to compensate export farmers themselves.

Negative price shocks appear to have very large externalities, around double their direct effects. Hence, there is a strong case for subsidizing insurance arrangements, subject to the avoidance of moral hazard considerations. Positive price shocks do not create large externalities for aggregate output, but farmers themselves have high savings rates and so use the opportunities well to the extent that macroeconomic policy permits. Hence, income stabilization through government price smoothing appears highly undesirable. Farmers need insurance from negative shocks for the sake of the macroeconomy, whether or not they need it for themselves. By contrast, it is the government, which usually needs to be protected from positive shocks since windfall revenue often destabilizes the budget. While positive shocks retained by farmers do not create large externalities for the rest of the economy, they do often create large externalities among farmers themselves. As each individual farmer saves and dissaves in financial assets, there is a danger that in aggregate they will generate changes in the price level, which neutralize their efforts. To avoid this damaging externality requires that the central bank really understands how to accommodate farmers' rapidly changing asset demands. Since this is quite unlikely, a better strategy might be for the government to dollarize.

REFERENCES

Bigsten, A. and P. Collier (1995). 'Linkages from Agricultural Growth in Kenya', in J. Mellor (ed.), *Agriculture on the Road to Industrialization*. Washington, DC: IPFRI.

Collier, P. and J. Dehn (2001). 'Aid, Shocks and Growth'. *Policy Research Working Paper* 2688. Washington, DC: World Bank.

——, J. W. Gunning, and Associates (1999). *Trade Shocks in Developing Countries*. Oxford: Clarendon Press.

Burnside, C. and D. Dollar (2000). 'Aid, Policies and Growth'. *American Economic Review*, 90(4), 847–68.

Deaton, A. and G. Laroque (1992). 'On the Behaviour of Commodity Prices'. *The Review of Economic Studies*, 59(1), 1–23.

Dehn, J. (2000). 'Commodity Price Uncertainty and Shocks: Implications for Investment and Growth'. D.Phil. thesis, December, Oxford University, Oxford.

Rosegrant, M. W. and P. B. R. Hazell (2000). *Transforming the Rural Asian Economy: The Unfinished Revolution*. Hong Kong: Oxford University Press.

Wetzel, D. (1999). 'The Ghanaian Cocoa Boom', in P. Collier, J. W. Gunning, and Associates (eds), *Trade Shocks in Developing Countries*. Oxford: Clarendon Press.

PART IV

IDENTIFYING THE VULNERABLE

8

Measuring Vulnerability to Poverty

GISELE KAMANOU AND JONATHAN MORDUCH

8.1. INTRODUCTION

The notion of 'vulnerability to poverty' remains elusive. It is a condition that may be easy to recognize in oneself or one's neighbours, but there is no consensus about how to define the concept and measure it in a broad cross-section of people. In surveys, poor households often identify vulnerability as a condition that takes into account both exposure to serious risks and defenselessness against deprivation. Defenselessness in turn is often seen as a function of social marginalization that ultimately results in economic marginalization (see, for example, Kanbur and Squire 2001).

While this is a start, for quantitative researchers, the problem is to isolate a simple measure (or set of measures) of vulnerability that is comparable across time and location—that is, something akin to poverty measures. Not only have the principles underlying such a measure been hard to pin down, but practical applications are demanding of data and turn up challenges posed by a variety of forms of measurement error. Given the complexities, we focus here only on vulnerability to low consumption in order to shed light as sharply as possible. To focus even more sharply, we restrict attention to measures that can be constructed using quantitative data drawn from large, representative household surveys. Our concern is with statistical properties, and in that pursuit, we necessarily sacrifice the richness of narratives emerging from qualitative approaches like participatory poverty assessments (e.g. Narayan *et al.* 2000). This is thus a first step towards an approach that we hope would ultimately combine some of that richness as well.

We begin by discussing the economic context in Côte d'Ivoire in the late 1980s, to provide context for the illustration in Section 8.5. Section 8.3 then discusses data issues including measurement error, changing household compositions, and attrition bias. Section 8.4 offers critical perspectives on existing approaches to measuring vulnerability, and Section 8.5 suggests a new framework that combines Monte Carlo and bootstrap statistical techniques. An application to Côte d'Ivoire in 1985–6 shows that by our definition there was considerable vulnerability in the cities outside of

We are grateful to the Direction de la Statistique in Côte d'Ivoire and to the Living Standards Measurement Surveys programme of the World Bank for access to the data used here. The data are available for download at www.worldbank.org/lsms. Kristin Mammen kindly shared Stata code that greatly facilitated assembly of the data. Stefan Dercon and James Foster provided helpful comments on the first draft. All views and errors are our own.

Abidjan, a finding obscured by existing methods. The conclusion highlights possible extensions of the approach.

8.2. CÔTE D'IVOIRE 1985–8

8.2.1. *Economic Context*

The 1980s were a period of sharp economic challenge, and we summarize the context, drawing on Husain and Faruqee (1994). Faced with the pressure of financial crisis in the early 1980s, the government of Côte d'Ivoire turned to the World Bank and International Monetary Fund (IMF) for financial assistance. The first round of financing, coupled with a structural adjustment programme, covered 1981–6 with the objectives of stabilization through fiscal and monetary restraint. The programme entailed raising taxes on petroleum products, alcoholic beverages, and tobacco. Despite the programme (and in part as a result of it), investment expenditures fell from 23 per cent of GDP in 1979 to just 5 per cent in 1986. Current expenditures were also cut, although to a lesser extent, and civil service wages were frozen between 1984 and 1986. Agricultural reforms under structural adjustment mainly aimed at raising export production. The consumer price of rice was raised, leading to price increases of all other food crops.

Improved terms of trade brought a slight economic recovery in 1984–6, but in 1987, the international prices of cocoa and coffee fell sharply. The country then plunged into another severe economic crisis. Agricultural policies in 1988 were designed to retain part of cocoa crops. This policy disrupted the agricultural marketing cycle: exporters were not reimbursed by the Agricultural Price Stabilization Fund and were unable to obtain export permits. Consequently, they were unable to repay crop credit, which in turn aggravated the liquidity problems of the banking system. At the same time, the country withdrew from adjustment programmes and bank lending to Côte d'Ivoire was interrupted between 1987 and 1989. The burden of adjustment fell on public investment expenditures, which declined from 18 per cent of GDP in 1978–83 to just 3 per cent 1988–91.

8.2.2. *Data*

We consider vulnerability using the 1985–8 rounds of the Côte d'Ivoire Living Standards Survey (CILSS). Using the CILSS for illustration is particularly helpful as the data have been used by others to study poverty dynamics, allowing us to draw on related studies of consumption patterns, poverty, and household behaviour (see, for example, the studies cited in Deaton 1997).

The sample selection process for the CILSS household surveys yielded a nationally representative cross-section of Ivorian households. Each year 1600 households were sampled, half of which were revisited the following year; the other half was replaced with new households. The net result is four cross-sectional data sets and three two-year panels (for 1985–6, 1986–7, and 1987–8). Consumption and income have been deflated

Table 8.1. *Poverty measures and per capita consumption (CFA), all households*

	1985	1986	1987	1988
Headcount	0.31	0.34	0.35	0.48
Normalized poverty gap	0.094	0.094	0.099	0.157
Squared poverty gap	0.041	0.036	0.041	0.073
Expenditure per capita	223,226	206,872	216,179	175,327
Household size	11.8	10.8	9.8	9.7

Note: Sample is restricted to households with consumption changes between 2 and −2.

to capture regional price variation and overall inflation (anchored by 1985 Abidjan prices).

The poverty line is set here at 128,600 CFA, following Deaton (1997: 155) and Grootaert and Kanbur (1995). The line corresponds roughly to the dollar-a-day poverty line used often in international comparisons. Using this poverty line, we find that the headcount poverty rate rises from 31 per cent in 1985 to 48 per cent in 1988.[1]

The economic crisis in Côte d'Ivoire of the 1980s is echoed in the household survey data. Per capita consumption fell sharply between 1985 and 1988 and households faced considerable uncertainty. Table 8.1 shows that real per capita consumption fell from 223,226 CFA in 1985 to 175,327 in 1988 in our sample.

8.3. DATA ISSUES

Our main focus is on conceptual frameworks, but before turning there, we begin by reviewing three important data problems that can be particularly acute when studying consumption and income dynamics: attrition bias, changing household consumption, and measurement error.

8.3.1. *Attrition*

Even if data quality is high, biases emerge when panel data are incomplete. The most extreme form occurs when households leave the panel. In the three two-year panels, the attrition rates are 8, 13, and 5 per cent for poor households in 1985–6, 1986–7, and 1987–8, respectively. The rates for non-poor households are somewhat higher (11, 14, and 15 per cent, respectively). The numbers are in the range of those for surveys of this kind. For the purposes here, attrition is particularly problematic when those who leave the survey are differently vulnerable than others. Those who leave may be among the most vulnerable, or, since migration can be a coping mechanism, they

---

[1] Here, as in much below, the sample is restricted to households with proportional consumption changes between 2 and −2 (i.e. those who report changes by less than 200 per cent up or down). The restriction removes outliers and restricts attention just to households in complete two-year panels. Results without the restriction are similar. In the unrestricted sample, poverty increases from 31 per cent to 44 per cent and per capita consumption drops from 231,971 CFA to 178,641 in 1985–8.

Table 8.2. *Mean changes in household size (%), panel households only*

	Members			Adult equivalents		
	1985–6	1986–7	1987–8	1985–6	1986–7	1987–8
Poor	−7	−20	−4	−6	−17	−3
Non-poor	−3	−6	−3	−3	−6	−2

may be less vulnerable. Regression analyses show that rates of attrition are negatively associated with increased age of the household head and larger household size. On average, smaller, younger (and presumably more mobile) households are more likely to leave the sample, but without follow-up surveys, it is impossible to discern the exact nature of biases.

8.3.2. *Changing Household Composition*

Table 8.1 shows that in the CILSS household size fell from 11.8 in 1985 to 9.7 in 1988. Partly this is due to a change in sampling frame procedures between the first and second panel in 1987 (Coulombe and Demery 1993). Table 8.2 shows this shift clearly. But even without a change in the sampling frame, households often change sharply in size and composition. For the poor population, for example, the household size fell on average by 7 per cent between 1985 and 1986. The changes are generally less sharp for the non-poor.

The changes are partly due to family splits and to migration, some of which was induced by the economic crisis. Counter-balancing the losses, many households also report births and the arrival of relatives and others. We show below that analysing the data in terms of adult equivalence rather than per capita values goes some distance in addressing the problem, but the net effect on results is modest here.

The bigger issue concerns interpretation. Throughout the chapter we take changes in per capita income and consumption (or adult equivalents) to signal 'shocks' (like price changes or low rainfall). But variance decompositions suggest that as much as a quarter of the variation in per capita consumption is due to the denominator—to changes in household size. These are typically not 'shocks' as we commonly think of them. Instead, they are often the product of deliberate choices made by households. Decreasing per capita consumption associated with the birth of children may reasonably be deemed desirable in many cases—not a 'negative shock' at all (Anand and Morduch 1999). In principle, the bootstrap Monte Carlo approach discussed below could be extended to allow prediction of shocks after conditioning on changing demographic structure, and this is left here as a caveat on interpreting our results.

8.3.3. *Measurement Error*

Measurement error poses a serious challenge for analysts of vulnerability (Baulch and Hoddinott 2000). The error can come in several forms: first, errors in forming measures of consumption aggregates; second, inappropriate price deflations; third, inappropriate deflations for household size; and fourth, errors in matching households in different waves of panel data. Measurement error can exaggerate the apparent degree of vulnerability by adding noise to measured incomes, but it can also introduce a number of more subtle biases, including spurious evidence of mean reversion.

Grootaert *et al.* (1997: 645–648) argue that these problems are apt to be minimal in the CILSS. Their assertion rests on several claims. First, the average consumption declines in the household data match quite closely with the declines in private consumption seen in the (independently derived) national accounts. Second, if there is misreporting in transitory income, it is apt to be underreported, leading to an underestimation of vulnerability not exaggeration. Third, first-differencing the data will eliminate all measurement error that is fixed from period to period. Fourth, changes in consumption appear to be systematically related to human capital variables and household composition, suggesting that consumption variation is not due mainly to error. And, fifth, the quality control of the CILSS fieldwork was excellent, with many built-in cross-checks on data quality (Ainsworth and Munoz 1986).

Unfortunately, we cannot assume that other data sets are of similar quality. And, even here, there are reasons for concern. Table 8.3, for example, shows mean reversion of a sort that is consistent with substantial measurement error. The Table gives average proportional changes in per capita income and consumption in the three two-year panels. (Table 8.4 shows that accounting for changing household composition through the use of adult equivalents and modest returns to scale does not change the picture very much—although in other contexts it might.) The data are disaggregated by poverty status and, within that, by quartile. The top half of Table 8.3 shows that average income improved for poor households in each panel, while consumption improved for all but the third and fourth quartiles of the poor in 1987–8. The early improvements are often large: on the order of 30 per cent per year for the poorest groups. But the

Table 8.3. *Average proportional changes in income and consumption*

	Income			Consumption		
	1985–6	1986–7	1987–8	1985–6	1986–7	1987–8
Poor						
Quartile 1	0.287	0.286	0.309	0.516	0.370	0.109
Quartile 2	0.439	0.136	0.301	0.332	0.159	0.041
Quartile 3	0.188	0.151	0.185	0.235	0.146	−0.067
Quartile 4	0.167	0.203	0.066	0.088	0.118	−0.113
Non-poor						
Quartile 1	0.143	−0.022	0.141	0.030	−0.022	−0.067
Quartile 2	0.027	−0.059	0.027	−0.156	−0.048	−0.133
Quartile 3	0.051	0.026	−0.010	−0.189	−0.076	−0.176
Quartile 4	−0.054	−0.076	−0.069	−0.315	−0.091	−0.250

Note: Sample is restricted to households with consumption and income changes between 2 and −2.

Table 8.4. *Standard deviations of proportional changes in income and consumption per capita*

	Income			Consumption		
	1985–6	1986–7	1987–8	1985–6	1986–7	1987–8
Poor						
Quartile 1	0.609	0.559	0.580	0.629	0.363	0.523
Quartile 2	0.688	0.576	0.712	0.451	0.429	0.490
Quartile 3	0.678	0.593	0.589	0.612	0.386	0.406
Quartile 4	0.506	0.608	0.589	0.439	0.439	0.339
Non-poor						
Quartile 1	0.627	0.604	0.605	0.449	0.445	0.322
Quartile 2	0.652	0.546	0.566	0.339	0.438	0.397
Quartile 3	0.630	0.604	0.546	0.348	0.396	0.353
Quartile 4	0.590	0.572	0.695	0.259	0.384	0.358

Note: Sample is restricted to households with consumption and income changes between 2 and −2.

improvements do not hold for the better-off households, where average consumption almost uniformly declined (by as much as 25 per cent in 1987–8 for the highest quartile). Figure 8.1 shows the results in a simple graph. For all years, average changes turn from positive to negative close to the poverty line (the vertical line at 128,600 CFA).

Note that the richest households have disproportionately large negative consumption changes, and the poorest have disproportionately large increases. This is consistent with measurement error in the base period, where error makes the 'rich' too rich and the 'poor' too poor. In the subsequent period, they tend to be closer to where they should have been. Some of the changes, of course, may be real, but Table 8.3 shows the changes to be too large to be fully credible as true variation. One of the ways that the problem could be approached is to use an alternative wealth measure to generate base-year categorizations; one possibility is the housing index of Kamanou (1999), which uses principal components methods to create alternative measures of well-being using CILSS data.

8.4. CONCEPTUAL FRAMEWORKS

With those empirical issues in mind, we turn to conceptual frameworks.

8.4.1. *Expected Utility Theory*

To capture the idea of vulnerability, we could start with the microeconomic theory of risk and uncertainty. The theory of expected utility tells us that the expected utility of risk-averse individuals falls as the variability of consumption rises, holding all else the same. If we knew the utility functions and expected consumption patterns of

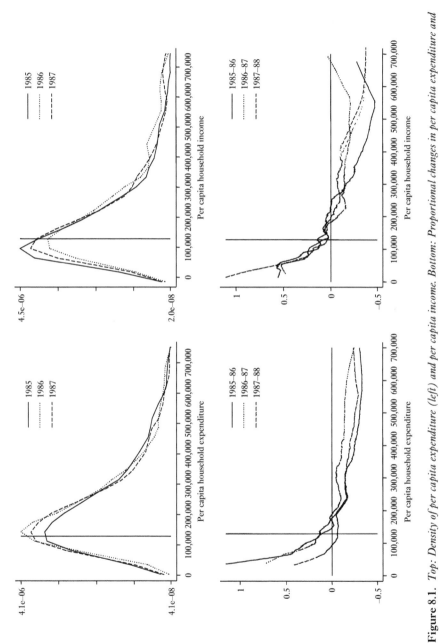

Figure 8.1. *Top: Density of per capita expenditure (left) and per capita income. Bottom: Proportional changes in per capita expenditure and income versus base year levels*

all individuals, we could then analyse poverty in terms of certainty-equivalent consumption (the level of consumption which, if unvarying, would yield an equivalent level of expected utility as a household's actual—higher mean but more variable—consumption levels). The theory allows the integration of consumption variability in a natural way, but the data requirements are too high to be of much practical use here. Not only are utility functions unobservable, but there are just a handful of longitudinal data sets from low-income countries with an adequate time dimension to yield precise measures of household-specific consumption variability. In addition, the tradition of poverty measurement has always had just a loose relationship with cardinal notions of utility, and introducing those notions via certainty-equivalent consumption introduces restrictions on measures that will create disjunctures with standard ordinal-based frameworks.

8.4.2. *Mobility Measurement*

An alternative, and more promising, starting point is the literature on income mobility (e.g. Shorrocks 1978; Fields and Ok 1999). The literature avoids cardinally comparable utility functions and evaluates the evolution of income rankings, focusing on the degree of path dependence. The starkest beginning point is the question: if you are born poor, are you more likely than others to die poor? Concern has tended to focus on long-term transitions across ranks (e.g. from generation to generation), rather than the short- and medium-term fluctuations considered here, but it provides a jumping-off point.

The mobility literature as a whole, though, has limitations with respect to our narrow interest. Most important, the literature is concerned primarily with changes in income rankings: it is relative movement that matters there. Here, though, the concern is with movements judged against an absolute standard given by official poverty lines. Given an absolute standard, simpler measures may suffice, where they would inadequately capture mobility. For example, Grootaert and Kanbur (1995) profitably employ Markov transition matrices in order to study changes in poverty status in the CILSS data.

Moreover, the mobility literature focuses on historical patterns, not prospective ones. This is a critical distinction. With just two observations on a set of households, for example, we can see which households became poor, which exited poverty, and which did not cross the line. But some among those that did not change status may well have been 'vulnerable' to a misfortune—however, good luck intervened to prevent a downturn. It is this condition of *possibility* that we are trying to capture. Measuring historical patterns is of course important, but for policy purposes the hope is to be able to generate measures that allow targeting of groups that are 'vulnerable' to loss, not just households that can be identified as actually having suffered in retrospect (a point stressed also by Chaudhuri 2000).

8.4.3. *Vulnerability as Variability*

If the history of shocks is a predictor of future shocks, a simple starting point for measuring vulnerability would be to compare standard deviations of consumption and income changes. Households or groups are judged to be more vulnerable if standard deviations of past consumption changes are higher. The approach is simple and draws on the association of vulnerability with variability.

An immediate practical problem here is that few data sets have a long enough time dimension to yield a reliable standard deviation for each household over time. Most, like the CILSS, have two repeated observations for a household at best. In practice, the standard deviation then must be estimated from cross-sectional variation. Thus, it picks up the dispersion of shocks not their average strength. A strong homogeneity assumption must also be made in order to interpret results of vulnerability, namely that all households observed in the cross-section receive draws from the same distribution of consumption changes. If this is so, measures of dispersion of the changes will then indicate the degree of exposure. One can do better by disaggregating further—by region, by income group, by education status, and so on. But, at the end of the day, some kind of homogeneity assumption must be made, leaving concern with unobserved heterogeneity.

Strengths and weaknesses are illustrated in Tables 8.4 and 8.5. The right half of Tables 8.4 and 8.5 show that, almost uniformly, the standard deviations of proportional consumption changes are lower than those of income, indicating considerable consumption smoothing in the limited sense above. In Table 8.5, for the top quartile of the non-poor in 1987–8, the difference is nearly half (0.695 for income versus 0.358 for consumption), but most differences are on the order of 20 per cent. Within consumption, variability is somewhat less for richer households than poorer, but the magnitudes are in the same range (roughly 0.35 to 0.45).

Comparison of the tables with Table 8.3 illustrates one immediate concern with using the standard deviation as a measure of vulnerability: downside risk is weighed the same as upside risk (see also World Bank 2001: 20, Box 3, based on Dercon 2001).

Table 8.5. *Means and standard deviations of proportional changes in consumption per adult equivalent*

	Mean			Standard deviation		
	1985–6	1986–7	1987–8	1985–6	1986–7	1987–8
Poor						
Quartile 1	0.528	0.315	0.091	0.624	0.307	0.479
Quartile 2	0.287	0.128	0.016	0.489	0.396	0.439
Quartile 3	0.228	0.131	−0.075	0.565	0.369	0.375
Quartile 4	0.075	0.093	−0.140	0.407	0.446	0.264
Non-poor						
Quartile 1	0.015	−0.023	−0.077	0.415	0.424	0.322
Quartile 2	−0.161	−0.050	−0.129	0.332	0.405	0.372
Quartile 3	−0.138	−0.070	−0.157	0.523	0.378	0.335
Quartile 4	−0.289	−0.060	−0.254	0.239	0.403	0.347

Note: Sample is restricted to households with per capita consumption changes between 2 and −2.

A 10 per cent upward shock affects the standard deviation identically to a 10 per cent downward shock. The tables show that the standard deviations for richer house-holds, while somewhat lower than for poorer households, are measured with respect to decreasing consumption. If standard deviations were all that we had to go by, it would be reasonable to conclude that variability is hurting the poor more than the non-poor. But vulnerability is not just about variability: most observers would argue that down-side risk is the chief concern and it may be that, with declining average consumption levels, down-side risk is greater for non-poor households. These statistics, while commonly employed, are not sufficient to discern the essence of vulnerability. Turning to coefficients of variation could help (standard deviation divided by the mean), but with some means at zero or very close to zero, the coefficients of variation blow up in some cells, obscuring comparisons.

A second concern is that the standard deviation can give odd results in times of persistent growth. Imagine that consumption is growing for a household, so that over eight periods their consumption is $(1, 2, 3, 4, 5, 6, 7, 8)$. Take another household with a consumption pattern of $(7, 5, 2, 6, 3, 1, 4, 8)$. The standard deviations of both series are identical, but the second appears to be buffeted by shocks while the first is on a steady upward path. Labelling them both as identically vulnerable misses the key part of their stories. (A related tension emerges when defining transitory poverty as deviation from mean consumption in rapidly growing regions like China; see, for example, Jalan and Ravallion 1998.)

A third, related concern is that the standard deviation offers no accounting for persistence of downturns—or negative serial correlation. Across eight periods, the pattern $(1, 0, 1, 0, 1, 0, 1, 0)$ has the same standard deviation as $(0, 0, 0, 0, 1, 1, 1, 1)$ but, if we interpret 1 as being poor and 0 being non-poor, the second pattern might suggest a more serious exposure to poverty. In terms of the standard deviation of the change in poverty status, the patterns above imply changes of the form $(1, -1, 1, -1, 1, -1, 1)$ and $(0, 0, 0, -1, 0, 0, 0)$. The former has a higher standard deviation, but again the latter flows from a situation, which many would associate with greater vulnerability. With just two-year panels, this concern underlies our work below as well, since persistence can only be addressed when more data are available.

8.4.4. *Risk of Change in Poverty Status*

Another starting point has been to identify the probability of becoming poor (or becoming poorer) in a given sample. For many, this implies that vulnerability is a condition of the *non-poor* only. The approach has appeal by highlighting the groups that could be helped by preventative measures before adverse events are realized.

Dercon and Krishnan (2000: 44–45) measure 'vulnerability' in rural Ethiopia, for example, by estimating determinants of consumption levels and then predicting the degree to which households would suffer severe consumption shortfalls given particularly poor rainfall (less than half the long-term mean). Their estimates suggest that the 'vulnerable' population (those that have a risk of falling below the poverty line) is 40–70 per cent higher than the observed poverty rate.

Pritchett *et al.* (2000) answer the question by estimating the standard deviation of consumption changes in the cross-section and then, given that variation, predicting the income level below which households are more than 50 per cent likely to be poor next period. The idea is clear and not particularly demanding of data (a two-year panel is sufficient). A limitation is that the problems with the standard deviation are unavoidable in this framework as well. In using the bootstrap Monte Carlo method in Section 8.5, it is possible to avoid relying on the standard deviation in this way (but, like Pritchett *et al.*, we are forced to use cross-sectional variation to predict intertemporal variation).

A refinement of this basic approach is suggested in Morduch (1994) and a related idea is applied in Jalan and Ravallion's (1999) work on China. The idea is to disaggregate the population into groups that are 'structurally poor' (in the sense of having fundamentally low earning power) and those that are not. Then within each group, subgroups that become poor due to bad shocks or that exit poverty due to good shocks are identified separately. In this way, the 'non-poor' in a base year are disaggregated according to those who appear to be 'fundamentally' not poor and those who, in a given period, appear to be above the poverty line through good fortune only. As a practical matter, though, more than two years of data are required.

8.4.5. *Ability to Cope*

Better data and new empirical methods have led to new studies on coping mechanisms and the efficacy of 'informal insurance' (see, for example, Morduch 2000 and Dercon 2001). Amin *et al.* (1999) use econometric methods for measuring the efficiency of informal insurance to form a measure of vulnerability. In their work, 'vulnerability' is associated with consumption fluctuations associated with imperfect risk-sharing as set out by Townsend (1994). A similar approach is taken by Jalan and Ravallion (1999); see Morduch (2002) for a discussion of the approach and empirical evidence.

In the Amin *et al.* (1999) study of two villages in rural Bangladesh, a household is considered vulnerable in proportion to the extent to which income shocks translate into consumption shocks. Specifically, they estimate the equation:

$$\Delta \ln c_t^h = \alpha^h \Delta \ln y_t^h + \sum_t \beta_t X_t + \varepsilon_t^h, \qquad (8.1)$$

where the change in log consumption at time t for household h is regressed on a set of time-specific dummy variables for the village (X_t) and the change in log income for the household. Full insurance is assumed if the household-specific parameter α is 0. Complete autarky is implied by $\alpha = 1$, and values of α approaching 1 are taken to imply heightened vulnerability. For a quarter of the households α is negative, which is perplexing but nevertheless interpreted as implying a lack of constraints and thus full insurance. Most households are determined to be somewhat vulnerable, with female-headed households taking a coefficient on α that is 0.35 higher than that of male-headed households.

The approach captures an important, but selective, element of vulnerability. In general the vulnerability of a population is the product of three elements:

- The pattern of possible 'shocks'. These may be losses due to, say, losing a job or experiencing a bad harvest. Included here are also increases in needs due, for example, to illness, childbirth, or costly social occasions.
- The strength of coping mechanisms. This is the degree to which provisions are not in place to fully address shocks (and is captured by the Amin *et al.* 1999, method).
- Structural and behavioural ramifications of consumption declines. Are they apt to lead to temporary shortfalls or to lead to poverty traps?

The estimate of α only captures the second element, and the decomposition suggests that the focus on α is apt to be incomplete for many policy purposes. First, the estimates only get at idiosyncratic risk (since α captures the role of income fluctuations over and above those picked up by the time-specific dummy variable for the village). In Côte d'Ivoire, though, covariant risk is a critical element of vulnerability. Second, the measure of vulnerability here captures the transmission of both positive and negative income shocks. In principle, a household could fend off all downward income shocks adequately well (so they do not translate into consumption declines) but then consume out of positive income shocks (making hay while the sun shines). This would lead to an estimated α between 0 and 1, but these households would not be 'vulnerable' in the sense assumed here. It is unlikely that this is the case in the Bangladesh sample, but it is a concern as we look for general approaches. (One way to address the tension is to distinguish between negative and positive shocks in the regression equation, following, for example, Jacoby and Skoufias 1997.)

In the same light, there are concerns that surround policy implications. Consider two populations. Both could have the same average standard deviation of consumption changes. In one, though, there may be quite good coping mechanisms (a low estimated α) but many shocks. In the other, coping mechanisms may be far weaker (high α), but the shocks may be much weaker too. In the first case, policy might most effectively attempt to reduce income variability. In the latter, it might best strengthen coping mechanisms. Here, the Amin *et al.* (1999) yields very useful information. But consider instead a situation where both populations have the same estimated α such that both seem equally 'defenceless'. In the first, again, assume that there are many income shocks and in the second, there are far fewer. Many would say that 'vulnerability' is greater in the first case, but the approach would view both cases identically.

One way to address this concern is to form an index from the product of α and a measure of income shocks. This, though, effectively leads us back to working with consumption fluctuations directly. All the same, estimating α provides a means to identify 'defencelessness' from 'vulnerability', and with a sufficiently long panel might profitably be used in conjunction with the ideas set out in Section 8.5 (see also Ligon (2002), which explores approaches to targeting vulnerable households in the relatively long International Crops Research Institute for Semi-Arid Tropics (ICRISAT) panel.)

8.4.6. *Asset Holding*

Another approach is to measure assets rather than consumption patterns (e.g. World Bank 2001: 20, Box 3). The idea addresses frustration at identifying vulnerability measures (and at often lacking panel data). The idea flows from what we know about coping mechanisms: having more assets generally makes coping easier and households work hard to hold onto particular assets. (It should be noted, though, that assets may lose much of their insurance value when shocks are strongly covariant; this happens when the supply of assets on the market rises dramatically in a crisis and/or demand rises dramatically in a surplus period—pushing up prices when households are trying to accumulate and depressing prices when households are trying to protect their welfare.) Prices thus may be high. An inventory of assets can show how much of a cushion households will have in time of crisis—and how costly addressing the crisis by selling assets is likely to be.

The approach has promise, and the first order of business is to better identify the exact relationship of assets and vulnerability. This, of course, requires having a clear measure of vulnerability to start with. As with the approach discussed above, where vulnerability is associated with the ability to smooth idiosyncratic shocks, an asset-based measure yields useful information about coping mechanisms conditional on shocks, but extra information is required to inform about the distribution of expected shocks.

8.5. A NEW FRAMEWORK

We set out a simple framework that combines elements of the approaches above and addresses some shortcomings. The framework developed here combines Monte Carlo simulations with the bootstrap, a nonparametric method for estimating the standard error of sample parameters (Efron and Tibshirani 1994). The idea is to generate a distribution of *possible* future outcomes for households, based on their observed characteristics and the observed consumption fluctuations of similar households. We are limited by having just two repeated observations on each household, but the approach could be refined if more data were available—in particular, a longer time series would allow consideration of persistent poverty versus shorter spells (see, for example, Morduch 1991).

8.5.1. *Preliminaries*

To be concrete, we follow Chaudhuri (2000) in employing the commonly used Foster–Greer–Thorbecke (FGT) (1984) class of poverty measures,

$$P_\alpha = \frac{1}{N} \sum_{i=1}^{G} \left(\frac{z - y_i}{z} \right)^\alpha, \tag{8.2}$$

where with $\alpha = 0$ we get the headcount index, with $\alpha = 1$ we get the (normalized) income gap, and with $\alpha = 2$ we get a measure that is sensitive to the distribution of consumption below the poverty line. Here, z is the poverty line, y is household income, N is the total population size, and households are ordered from bottom to top: $y_1, y_2, \ldots, y_G, z, y_{G+1}, \ldots, y_N$. Using the measure, we can gauge changes in poverty status across periods (generalizing earlier analysis of the CILSS by Grootaert and Kanbur 1995). More important, we can use the framework to derive a measure of vulnerability that applies to all households, both currently poor and not.

There is some debate over interpretation, and we pause to note the debate. First, Ligon and Schecter (2003) argue that the FGT measure has unappealing properties in this context. If you think of the index as a utility function, it is a somewhat odd one. First, no utility is accorded to any income increase beyond z. Second, the particular functional form (in the case in which $\alpha > 1$) would allow for risk aversion, but it implies that households have increasing absolute risk aversion, which is to say that people become more risk averse as they become wealthier. Most evidence suggests that in fact the opposite is true: households tend to exhibit declining absolute risk aversion instead. But this is to take the FGT too literally here. Our aim is to use the measure as a device to describe basic variability in the data; it is certainly adequate for that descriptive purpose. As we argue above, finding a utility-based approach presents its own complications, although Ligon and Schecter (2003) make headway.

Second, it can be argued that the most intuitive measure of vulnerability is the predicted value of the poverty measure for the coming period, predicted base on the probable pattern of shocks. As we show below, we start there but then net out the observed measure of poverty for the period (i.e. looking backward, what actually happened). This allows us to isolate those households that did not become poor (or that did not become as poor) but that might have. For other purposes, a fuller characterization of vulnerability would be the predicted value of the poverty measure for the coming period, since it includes those who actually became poor—and thus were vulnerable as well.

Before turning to the Monte Carlo bootstrap approach, we consider historical experience in the base data. To do this, we focus on a single measure, which with only two years of data is $(P_{\alpha t+1} - P_\alpha)$.[2] If attention was just accorded to transitions into poverty, attention could be restricted just to households that begin in the basis year above the poverty line (so that the measure is just $P_{\alpha t+1}$). In the present application, we consider only households with two complete years of data, with base year summary statistics provided in Table 8.6. Following the earlier tables, Table 8.7 provides measures for quartiles of the poor and quartiles of the non-poor (defined by status in base years), and Fig. 8.2 shows the relationship graphically. The first column of the table shows that 45 per cent of the first quartile of those who were not poor in 1985 were poor by 1986. For the next richest quartile, 18 per cent became poor, and for the third quartile, 10 per cent became poor. Just 1 per cent of the richest group was poor in 1986.

If we take this evidence alone, there appears to be a great deal of 'vulnerability' (as measured by worsening poverty status). Yet poverty overall increased by just

---

[2] Estimates of poverty changes are examined, for example, in Dercon and Krishnan's (2000) work on seasonality and poverty in Ethiopia.

Table 8.6. *Per capita consumption (1985 Abidjan CFA), first wave of households in two-year panels*

	1985	1986	1987
Poor			
Quartile 1	55,936	62,257	56,419
Quartile 2	82,552	90,400	85,615
Quartile 3	103,375	103,499	104,897
Quartile 4	120,724	119,682	120,152
Non-poor			
Quartile 1	153,921	149,990	153,154
Quartile 2	221,706	204,635	209,825
Quartile 3	326,669	295,264	293,815
Quartile 4	634,982	592,414	616,885
Total	222,727	225,583	210,394
Headcount index	0.302	0.300	0.345

Table 8.7. *Observed changes in measured poverty*

	Change in headcount index			Change in squared poverty gap		
	1985–6	1986–7	1987–8	1985–6	1986–7	1987–8
Poor						
Quartile 1	−0.145	−0.107	−0.042	−0.150	−0.132	−0.011
Quartile 2	−0.287	−0.287	−0.161	−0.037	−0.004	0.060
Quartile 3	−0.246	−0.392	−0.118	−0.043	0.014	0.088
Quartile 4	−0.406	−0.522	−0.183	−0.043	0.034	0.067
Non-poor						
Quartile 1	0.454	0.396	0.474	0.029	0.037	0.026
Quartile 2	0.177	0.194	0.249	0.012	0.016	0.012
Quartile 3	0.096	0.069	0.087	0.002	0.003	0.006
Quartile 4	0.013	0.010	0.007	0.002	0.000	0.000
Total	0.076	0.034	0.119	0.000	0.005	0.025

Note: Poverty rate in final year less the rate in the base year. Positive numbers reflect a worsening of conditions.

8 per cent. This is because (as seen in Fig. 8.1), many who were poor in 1985 exited poverty (from the poorest to least poor quartiles below the poverty line in 1985, the rate of exit was 15, 29, 25, and 41 per cent). The magnitude of changes should not be surprising once the frequency distributions of per capita consumption are seen in Fig. 8.1—much of the population is very close to the poverty line so a small tip one way or the other can lead to a change in measured poverty.

If these processes are independent, policymakers would want to encourage exit and discourage entry. But imagine that the processes stem from the same origin, that they

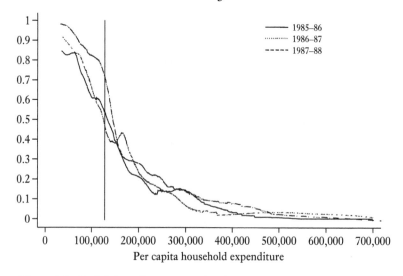

Figure 8.2. *Probability of being poor in the subsequent period versus base year levels*

are intrinsically linked. In that case, reducing the vulnerability of the non-poor may also reduce the chance for exiting poverty of the poor, an issue on which we can only speculate.

Considering the squared poverty gap in Table 8.7 offers a different story. Here, the top two quartiles of the poor also do worse from period to period. While some households are exiting poverty, others are becoming much worse off, and the downside outweighs the upside. The bottom lines are that: a large fraction of non-poor households face the risk of becoming poor in the next year, and; by the same token, many poor households will exit poverty. A key question (which is unanswerable in these data) is whether those that are poor are also likely to soon exit. If so, notions of 'vulnerability' take a very different cast than if spells were persistent.

8.5.2. *Monte Carlo Bootstrap Approach*

In a natural extension of the framework above, we define vulnerability in a population as the difference between the *expected* value of a poverty measure in the future and its current value. This yields a set of measures of vulnerability that expand the framework illustrated in Table 8.7. The measures take the form:

$$E\,P_{\alpha t+1} - P_{\alpha t} = \frac{1}{N}\sum_{i=1}^{G_{t+1}}\sum_{S}\Pr(s,y_{it+1})\left(\frac{z-y_{it+1}}{z}\right)^{\alpha} - \frac{1}{N}\sum_{i=1}^{G_{t}}\left(\frac{z-y_{it}}{z}\right)^{\alpha},$$

$$(8.3)$$

where E is the expectation operator, s is a given state of the world for which the joint probability distribution of y_{t+1} is $\Pr(s,y)$, G_t, and G_{t+1} are the number of poor households in the current and future periods respectively, and y_{it} and y_{it+1} denote the current and future consumption of household i. We assume that the true distribution of *possible* outcomes in the next period for households (y_{it+1}) could be known.

The practical implementation of this approach, however, is made difficult by the fact that the joint distribution of s and y_{it+1} is not known. In fact, the 'states of the world' might be latent variables with an unknown distribution. The idea is to make up for the unknown joint distribution $\Pr(s, y)$ by generating a distribution of possible future outcomes for households, based on their observed characteristics, and the observed consumption fluctuations of 'similar' households. In other words, the bootstrap technique enables us to construct several versions of possible future data by resampling the original data. The expected value is thus estimated by the mean of the bootstrap estimate of $P_{\alpha t+1}$.

The approach is implemented by starting with the base year of a panel and drawing a large number (say $B = 1000$) of independent bootstrap samples. (A bootstrap sample is a random sample of size n drawn with replacement from the empirical distribution of some observed data of size n.) With each bootstrap sample, a regression equation is constructed to predict the change in consumption based on its correlation with a set of household covariates. The linear part of the predicted value is then augmented with a shock drawn at random from the empirical distribution of the regression residuals.

This yields a predicted per capita expenditure of the future period for each household in each of the bootstrap samples. Using these samples we compute $P_{\alpha t+1}^{b}$ for each b from 1 to 1000, and we then estimate $EP_{\alpha t+1}$ as the mean of the bootstrap estimates $P_{\alpha t+1}^{b}$. The algorithm goes as follow for each region:

Step 1: Draw 1000 bootstrap samples from the original data. Let $X = (x_1, x_2, x_3, \ldots, x_n)$ be the data on a given region (n is the number of households in the region) with $x_i = (y_{i1}, y_{i2}, h_1, h_2, \ldots, h_p)$ and y_{i1} and y_{i2} are the first and second wave household consumption and $h_1, h_2, h_3, \ldots, h_p$ are p household covariates. Say $X^b = (x_1^b, x_2^b, x_3^b, \ldots, x_n^b)$, $b = 1, 2, 3, \ldots, 1000$ are the bootstrap samples drawn by resampling $X = (x_1, x_2, x_3, \ldots, x_n)$ with replacement.

Step 2: With each new bootstrap sample, run a regression of $\delta_i = (y_{2i}^b - y_{1i}^b)/y_{1i}^b$ on covariates $h_1, h_2, h_3, \ldots, h_p$ and form the Monte Carlo estimates of the future period consumption by: $\hat{y}_i^{\mathrm{mcb}} = y_{1i}^b (1 + \hat{\delta}_i + \varepsilon^{\mathrm{mc}})$ where $\hat{\delta}_i$ is the fitted values from the regression for the household i, and $\varepsilon^{\mathrm{mc}}$ is a random draw for the empirical distribution of the residuals from the regression. (While we do not do it here, the method can be refined by allowing residuals to have a household-specific component; see Chaudhuri 2000.) For the illustrative example shown below we constructed the prediction equation for second period consumption using the Generalized Linear Model to fit the proportional change in the per capita consumption (δ_i) on household covariates including first wave per capita consumption, household size, age of the head of the household, nationality, and indicators of whether the head of the household is literate and numerate. The independent variables also included an index of housing constructed using a combination of principal components analysis and the U-scores, a new statistical technique used for scaling discrete variables in the context of Principal Components (see Kamanou 1999).

Table 8.8. *Vulnerability index (based on poverty headcount) based on Monte Carlo bootstrap results, 1985–6 panel (713 observations)*

	Observed headcount 1985	Observed headcount 1986	Bootstrap headcount 1986	Change in observed headcount	Vulnerability index
Abidjan	0.05	0.16	0.17	0.11	0.12
Other Cities	0.25	0.23	0.35	−0.02	0.10
West Forest	0.11	0.22	0.28	0.11	0.17
East Forest	0.45	0.37	0.44	−0.07	−0.01
Savannah	0.46	0.48	0.43	0.02	−0.03

Step 3: Form an estimate of the future period's poverty measure of the bootstrap sample as:

$$\hat{P}^{mcb}_{\alpha t_2} = \frac{1}{n} \sum_{i=1}^{G_b} \left(\frac{z - \hat{y}_i^{mcb}}{z} \right)^{\alpha}.$$

This is the Monte Carlo estimate of the future period's poverty measure obtained from the bootstrap sample.

Step 4: The Monte Carlo bootstrap estimate of vulnerability for the population for the period (t_1, t_2) is then defined by: $V_{\alpha}^{mcb} = \hat{P}^{mcb}_{\alpha t_2} - P_{\alpha t_1}$.

To illustrate, we compared the five regions of the Côte d'Ivoire according to their vulnerability measures in the 1985–6 sample. Table 8.8 gives the observed poverty headcounts for the 1985 and 1986 waves for each region in the 1985–6 panel. Table 8.8 also gives the Monte Carlo bootstrap estimate of predicted poverty in 1986, $\hat{P}^{mcb}_{\alpha t_2}$.[3]

These data are used to calculate the change in the observed headcount in column 4 and the vulnerability index in the final column. The most striking difference between the two occurs for the cities outside of Abidjan. There, the observed change in the headcount is small (−0.02) while the vulnerability index shows a larger, positive value (0.10). The index shows that many more households were 'vulnerable' to poverty than actually became poor, a condition that played out in later years as the economy worsened, pushing richer households below the poverty line.

---

[3] Since the histograms of the proportional change in the bootstrap estimate of poverty headcount in all three panels show that they are very close to normally distributed, we could easily calculate the bootstrap confidence interval for $\hat{P}^{mcb}_{\alpha t_2}$. The 90 per cent confidence interval can be computed along the same lines as those of the bootstrap confidence interval, given that $P_{\alpha t_1}$ is a constant (and thus that the variability of $V^{mcb}_{\alpha t_2 t_2}$ depends only on that of $\hat{P}^{mcb}_{\alpha t_2}$) and that $\hat{P}^{mcb}_{\alpha t_2}$ is close to normal. The bootstrap confidence interval is the standard confidence interval (i.e. based on an asymptotic normal theory): $p \in \hat{p} \pm z^{(1-\alpha)} * s\hat{e}$ with probability $(1 - 2\alpha)$, where $\hat{p}$ is the estimated poverty measure obtained from the original data, $s\hat{e}$ is the bootstrap estimate of the standard error of the poverty measures obtained form the bootstrap samples ($\hat{p}^{mcb}$), and $z^{(1-\alpha)}$ is the $100(1 - \alpha)$th percentile of a standard normal distribution.

The illustration shows the power of the basic approach. As described above, the application can be extended to incorporate distributionally weighted poverty indices as well, yielding additional dimensions by which to view the changes in Côte d'Ivoire.

8.6. CONCLUDING COMMENTS

We have proposed a new definition of vulnerability, and we have developed an approach built around Monte Carlo bootstrap predictions of consumption changes. The approach both generalizes and extends previous approaches, and it avoids unappealing features of existing measures.

We have illustrated the methods using the two-year panels of the CILSS. Our method reveals substantial measured 'vulnerability' between 1985 and 1986 in cities outside of Abidjan, for example. The result is in contrast to impressions gleaned from viewing observed poverty outcomes in 1985 and 1986. Our method shows potential difficulties faced by households that are obscured when simply using the historical record as a guide to the extent of possible vulnerabilities. The method is a first step in targeting all households with a reasonable risk of worsening poverty status, not just those that in fact lose out.

To sharpen policy implications, the approach can be extended to test whether a specific condition common to a given group is likely to make the group more vulnerable than others. In particular, the effectiveness of a poverty alleviation programme can be measured by comparing the pre- and post-programme vulnerability along the same lines as those of the scheme presented above.

With panel data for just two consecutive periods available, we have not taken on longer-term issues. Those issues are apt to matter greatly when considering vulnerability more richly, though. Concerns that will immediately arise include how to judge the persistence of poverty. Second, how should variability be traded-off against changes in the mean? In the CILSS, poorer households on average saw increases in consumption, even while country-wide average consumption fell. While the approach can accommodate alternative poverty measures (and, hence, different social weights), it cannot resolve the deeper conceptual issues surrounding the tradeoffs between 'winners' and 'losers' involved. Real progress will require consideration of issues at the intersection of moral philosophy, policy analysis, and the broader social sciences.

REFERENCES

Ainsworth, M. and J. Munoz (1986). 'The Cote d'Ivoire Living Standards Surveys: Design and Implementation'. *Living Standards Measurement Study Working Paper* No. 26. Washington, DC: World Bank.

Amin, S., A. Rai, and G. Topa (1999). 'Does Microcredit Reach the Poor and Vulnerable? Evidence from Northern Bangladesh'. *CID Working Paper* No. 28, October. Cambridge, MA: Harvard University.

Anand, S. and J. Morduch (1999). 'Poverty and the 'Population Problem', in M. Livi-Bacci and G. de Santis (eds), *Population and Poverty in Developing Countries*. Oxford: Oxford University Press.

Baulch, B. and J. Hoddinott (2000). 'Economic Mobility and Poverty Dynamics in Developing Countries'. *Journal of Development Studies*, 36(6), 1–24.

Chaudhuri, S. (2000). 'Empirical Methods for Assessing Household Vulnerability to Poverty', preliminary draft, April, Department of Economics, Columbia University, New York.

Coulombe, H. and L. Demery (1993). 'Household Size in Cote d'Ivoire: Sampling Bias in the CILSS'. *Living Standards Measurement Study Working Paper* No. 97. Washington, DC: World Bank.

Deaton, A. (1997). *The Analysis of Household Surveys*. Baltimore, MD: Johns Hopkins.

Dercon, S. (2001). 'Income Risk, Coping Strategies and Safety Nets', draft, Centre for the Study of African Economies, Department of Economics, Oxford University, Oxford. See also *WIDER Discussion Paper* No. 2002/22. Helsinki: UNU-WIDER.

—— and P. Krishnan (2000). 'Vulnerability, Seasonality and Poverty in Ethiopia'. *Journal of Development Studies*, 36(6), 25–53.

Efron, B. and R. J. Tibshirani (1994). *An Introduction to the Bootstrap*. New York: Chapman & Hall/CRC.

Fields, G. and E. Ok (1999). 'The Measurement of Income Mobility: An Introduction to the Literature', in J. Silber (ed.), *Handbook on Income Inequality Measurement*. Boston, MA: Kluwer Academic Press.

Foster, J., J. Greer, and E. Thorbecke (1984). 'A Class of Decomposable Poverty Measures'. *Econometrica*, 52, 761–5.

Grootaert, C. and R. Kanbur (1995). 'The Lucky Few Amidst Economic Decline: Distributional Change in Côte d'Ivoire as Seen through Panel Data Sets, 1985–88'. *Journal of Development Studies*, 31(4), 603–19.

——, ——, and G.-T. Oh (1997). 'The Dynamics of Welfare Gains and Losses: An African Case Study'. *Journal of Development Studies*, 31(4), 635–57.

Husain, I. and R. Faruqee (eds) (1994). *Adjustment in Africa: Lessons from Country Case Studies*. Washington, DC: World Bank.

Jacoby, H. and E. Skoufias (1997). 'Risk, Financial Markets, and Human Capital in a Developing Country'. *Review of Economic Studies*, 64(3), 311–35.

Jalan, J. and M. Ravallion (1998). 'Transient Poverty in Postreform Rural China'. *Journal of Comparative Economics*, 26(2), 338–57.

—— and —— (1999). 'Are the Poor Less Well Insured? Evidence on Vulnerability to Risk in Rural China'. *Journal of Development Economics*, 58(1), 61–81.

Kamanou, G. (1999). 'An Index of Household Material Wealth Based on Principal Components of Discrete Indicators: An Inquiry into Family Support and Human Capital within the Household Dynamics during Structural Adjustment in Côte D'Ivoire'. Ph.D. dissertation, Department of Statistics, University of California, Berkeley, CA.

Kanbur, R. and L. Squire (2001). 'The Evolution of Thinking about Poverty: Exploring the Interactions', in G. Meier and J. Stiglitz (eds), *Frontiers of Development Economics: The Future in Perspective*. New York: World Bank and Oxford University Press, pp. 183–226.

Ligon, E. (2002). 'Targeting and Informal Insurance'. *WIDER Discussion Paper* No. 2002/8. Helsinki: UNU-WIDER.

—— and L. Schechter (2003). 'Measuring Vulnerability'. *Economic Journal*, 113(486), C95–C102.

Morduch, J. (1991). 'Risk and Welfare in Developing Countries'. Unpublished Ph.D. dissertation, Department of Economics, Harvard University.

—— (1994). 'Poverty and Vulnerability'. *American Economic Review*, 84(May), 221–5.

—— (2000). 'Between the State and the Market: Can Informal Insurance Patch the Safety Net?'. *World Bank Research Observer*, 14(2), 187–207.

—— (2002). 'Consumption Smoothing Across Space: Testing Theories of Consumption Smoothing in the ICRISAT Study Region of South India'. *WIDER Discussion Paper* No. 2002/55. Helsinki: UNU-WIDER.

Narayan, D., R. Patel, K. Schafft, A. Rademacher, and S. Koch-Schulte (2000). *Voices of the Poor: Can Anyone Hear Us?*. New York: World Bank and Oxford University Press.

Oh, G.-T. and M. Venkataraman (1992). 'Construction of Analytical Variables and Data Sets. Using the Data from the Côte d' Ivoire Living Standards Survey 1985–1988: Concept, Methodology and Documentation'. Technical Document. Washington, DC: World Bank.

Pritchett *et al.* (2000). 'Quantifying Vulnerability to Poverty: A Proposed Measure with Application to Indonesia'. *SMERU Working Paper*, May (www.smeru.or.id).

Ravallion, M. and S. Chaudhuri (1996). 'Risk and Insurance in Village India: Comment'. *Econometrica*, 65(1), 171–84.

Shorrocks, A. (1978). 'The Measurement of Mobility'. *Econometrica*, 46, 1013–24.

Townsend, R. (1994). 'Risk and Insurance in Village India'. *Econometrica*, 62, 539–92.

—— (1995). 'Consumption Insurance: An Evaluation of Risk-Bearing Systems in Low-Income Countries'. *Journal of Economic Perspectives*, 9, 83–102.

World Bank (2001). *World Development Report 2000/2001: Attacking Poverty*. Oxford: Oxford University Press.

9

Targeting and Informal Insurance

ETHAN LIGON

9.1. INTRODUCTION

To be successful, policies meant to target assistance to poor, vulnerable house-holds must do a reasonably good job of identifying the target population. Although here are a number of well-known measurement difficulties involved in this sort of identification, methods for identifying poor households are better developed than are methods for identifying households which bear disproportionate risk, beginning with an appropriate measure of risk.

The usual measure of poverty is just some scalar measure of wealth, perhaps adjusted for household composition or other circumstances, but still just a number. In contrast, the *risk* a household faces is related to an entire distribution of possible outcomes. Thus, while measures of poverty focus on summarizing a distribution across households, a measure of risk must summarize a distribution for *each* household, *as well* as providing a population summary.

Our approach here is motivated by some of the same concerns that have motivated other researchers to try and directly extend traditional measures of static poverty to a dynamic environment with uncertainty. Of particular note in this connection is Ravallion (1988) who, with a similar motivation and the same data set that we will use, tries and distinguishes between 'transitory' and 'permanent' components of poverty,[1] to better understand the effects of uncertainty on expected poverty.

In this chapter, we provide a natural, cardinal measure of risk which is consistent with the ordinal notion of risk developed in Rothschild and Stiglitz (1970). We give a simple method for decomposing this measure of risk into risk which is attributable to aggregate shocks, observable idiosyncratic shocks, and unobservable shocks. As a by-product, we develop an estimator for the kinds of risk-sharing regressions developed by Townsend (1994) and Deaton (1990) which allows consistent hypothesis testing and inference even in the presence of cross-sectional correlation of unspecified form.

We apply our techniques to a data set from the Indian ICRISAT (International Crops Research Institute for the Semi-Arid Tropics) villages explored by Townsend (1994) and many others. This Indian data is of particular interest because there

---

[1] Jalan and Ravallion (2000) do something similar, but with Chinese data; Dercon and Krishnan (2000) use Ethiopian data to measure households' movements in and out of poverty; and Baulch and Hoddinott (2000) provide a nice survey of the young but rapidly growing literature on dynamic poverty.

seems to be general agreement that these villages display a great deal of risk-sharing, yet there is relatively little direct evidence on just *how* this risk-sharing is accomplished. Information on risk-sharing networks can be gleaned from estimated correlations between household consumptions (or correlations in residuals from some prediction equation). We use this technique to identify, for example, two quite distinct risk-sharing groups in Aurepalle, one composed chiefly of households with substantial landholdings, and the other of households with little or no land.

The remainder of this chapter is organized as follows. In Section 9.2, we provide a precise definition of risk used in this chapter. The measure we provide is cardinal, and is consistent with the ordinal approach taken by Rothschild and Stiglitz (1970). This same measure of risk is combined with a measure of poverty to construct a measure of overall *vulnerability* in Ligon and Schechter (2003). In Section 9.3, we provide methods to estimate the risk borne by households, and show that this measure can be easily decomposed into risk from various sources. Once one has identified households, which one thinks may bear large amounts of risk, one may wish to ameliorate this risk. In Section 9.4, we discuss the problems that may arise from acting on these good intentions. Since the intervention of an outsider may be perceived by the community as yet another sort of shock, existing mechanisms for sharing risk within the village may also serve to undo targeted transfers. We consider the consequences of targeting transfers to villages under a sequence of different assumptions regarding existing markets and institutions. Section 9.5 concludes.

9.2. DEFINING RISK

We take a utilitarian approach to defining a measure of the risk households face. Suppose there to be a finite population of households indexed by $i = 1, 2, \ldots, n$, and let $\omega \in \Omega$ denote the state of the world. We focus on the distribution of household i's consumption expenditures, $c^i(\omega)$, rather than measures of income or wealth on the grounds that these kinds of expenditures are what most directly determines household welfare. To measure risk, for each household we first choose some strictly increasing, weakly concave function $U^i : \mathbb{R} \to \mathbb{R}$ mapping consumption expenditures into the real line. Given the function U^i, we define the risk faced by the household by the function

$$R^i = U^i(\mathrm{E}c^i) - \mathrm{E}U^i(c^i).$$

Taking expectations of an increasing, concave function of consumption expenditures has the effect of making risk depend not only on the mean of a household's consumption, but also on variation in consumption. Take, for example, the case in which consumption expenditures are bounded above by some b, and where we take $U^i(c) = -(c - b)^2$. In this case, the risk facing a household is simply equal to the variance of consumption expenditures.

The measure R^i, which measures the risk faced by household i, is consistent with the ordinal measures of risk proposed by Rothschild and Stiglitz (1970) (though any monotone transformation of R^i would do as well). Further, this risk measure can usefully be further decomposed into two distinct measures of risk, one aggregate, the other idiosyncratic. Let $E(c^i|\bar{c})$ denote the expected value of consumption c^i conditioned on knowledge of aggregate consumption $\bar{c}$. Then we can rewrite the risk facing household i as

$$R^i = [U^i(Ec^i) - EU^i(E(c^i|\bar{c}))] + [EU^i(E(c^i|\bar{c})) - EU^i(c^i)].$$

Here the first term expresses the *aggregate risk* facing the household, while the second filters out the aggregate component of risk to leave only the component of *idiosyncratic risk*.[2]

Of course the notation here is intentionally chosen to evoke comparisons with utility functions. If in fact our functions $\{U^i\}$ coincide with households' von Neumann–Morgenstern momentary (indirect) utility functions, then we can interpret our measure of risk as the loss of utility experienced from consumption risk. Further, if one were to adopt a utilitarian notion of welfare for some population of n households, then in principle one could use the set of functions $\{U_i\}$ in the objective function of a social planner, as in Townsend (1994); in this case a social planner who maximizes a weighted sum of these functions subject to some aggregate resource constraint would implicitly allocate resources so as to eliminate the idiosyncratic component of risk.

Despite the notation, our proposed procedure of maximizing the sum of the expected values of concave functions of expenditures need not be interpreted as a utilitarian social welfare function. One of several possible alternative interpretations would have a paternalistic donor or NGO choose some concave function, with the shape of the function reflecting the *donor*'s preferences over the distribution and uncertainty of consumption expenditures. One happy consequence of this sort of paternalism is that it is not necessary to be able to measure individual households' utility functions.

As a simple example, consider an environment with no uncertainty, and suppose that a donor with budget B wishes to make income transfers to a population of n households in such a way as to minimize poverty, as measured by the Foster *et al.* (1984) poverty index. This is equivalent to choosing functions $\{U^i\}$ such that

$$U^i(c) = \frac{|c - z|^\alpha}{\alpha} \operatorname{sgn}(c - z). \tag{9.1}$$

To interpret this as a measure of poverty, we may interpret z as a poverty line, and α is a parameter which could be chosen by the donor to place more or less emphasis on the consumption of the very poor.

Now suppose that this same function is used in an environment in which households face shocks which make their consumption expenditures uncertain. As a consequence, $U^i(c)$ is itself a random variable. What, then, should the objective of the donor be? One natural possibility (and the one which we will pursue here) would be for the donor to seek to minimize *expected* poverty, and now the functions $\{U^i\}$ should be chosen to reflect the donor's preferences over both the distribution of consumption expenditures

---

[2] Ravallion (1988) uses a different decomposition in order to distinguish between permanent and transitory *poverty*.

and over the risk that households face. The properties of (9.1) for evaluating the distribution of income are well understood when there is no uncertainty. However, if a donor were to use this function to evaluate expected poverty, what would be the consequences?

First, note that this function is non-decreasing in c^i for all real values of c, z, and α; a donor with these preferences always (weakly) prefers any given household to have more, rather than less, consumption. Second, note that (9.1) is concave if either of the following conditions hold:

(1) $\alpha > 1$ and $0 \leq c \leq z$;
(2) $\alpha < 1$ and $0 \leq z \leq c$.

The first case, under certainty, is considered by Foster *et al.* (1984), while Ravallion (1988) considers the same case under uncertainty. The second case really changes the function considered by these authors into a standard HARA utility function, with a coefficient of relative risk aversion equal to $(\alpha - 1)c/(z - c)$. As long as this quantity is positive, then the donor has a preference against exposing households to needless risk.

In the usual analysis (with no uncertainty), one's choice of the parameter α reflects one's sensitivity to inequality in distribution. As one might expect, in an environment with uncertainty, the choice of this parameter also has important consequences for the qualitative nature of the donor's preferences over risk. In particular, when $c < z$ and $\alpha > 1$ this index implicitly supposes that households with high levels of expenditures are more sensitive to risk than are poorer households, in the sense that if no household currently faced any consumption risk, but the donor had to assign a fair bet of fixed size to some household in the population, then it would prefer to assign that bet to a household with lower consumption, *ceteris paribus*. Interpreting U^i as a utility function, this is just a statement to the effect that households have increasing absolute risk aversion. Of course, this is precisely the reverse of what is usually assumed in research on households' tolerance of risk (for an early argument, see Arrow (1965)). To put the matter concisely, any donor who seeks to minimize the expected value of the Foster–Greer–Thorbecke poverty measure (minus one times the function defined in (9.1), with $\alpha > 1$ and $0 \leq c \leq z$) implicitly assumes that households with low consumption are better able to tolerate risk than are better-off households. A donor who wished to assign more risk to wealthier households should choose $\alpha < 1$ and $z \leq c$, thus maximizing a standard utilitarian social welfare function, with HARA utility functions.

9.3. MEASURING RISK

Among recent papers on risk-sharing, Townsend (1994) has arguably been the most influential. Assuming that agents are risk averse, with von Neumann–Morgenstern preferences with an exponential momentary utility function, Townsend derives the consumption function for each household in a village economy, which with exponential utility and complete markets can be written as a linear function of village aggregate consumption.

Thus, to test the hypothesis of complete markets, Townsend regresses deviations of household consumption from the village average on a set of household specific fixed effects and some set of other right-hand side variables. Under the null hypothesis such other variables should not have any additional ability to explain household consumption. Townsend rejects the null hypothesis; various measures of household income seem to be related to the residual from Townsend's consumption function. Nonetheless, the magnitude of the coefficients he estimates seem to be small, at least relative to some researchers' priors, and it seems fair to say that Townsend's research has convinced many people that consumption insurance is very important in at least three Indian villages.

Still, like much good empirical research, Townsend's paper raises more questions than it answers. He has, after all, *rejected* the most coherent theoretical model we have of village allocation—what should the complete markets model be replaced with? To answer a model with incomplete markets is fatuous, as this class includes far more models than it excludes. Also, if one takes as given that households are doing a great deal of consumption smoothing, then that raises the question of what sort of specific institutions are being employed at the village level to accomplish this smoothing. Certainly households are not participating in some spanning set of contingent claims markets in any formal sense, and one wonders what less formal mechanisms are taking the place of these textbook markets.

Here we take a different approach to measuring risk-sharing, which focuses on accurately inferring and accounting for the different kinds of risks households face, rather than on hypothesis testing. Nonetheless, a strong parallel with Townsend's regression emerges. In addition, though this chapter offers no conclusive evidence on either of these questions, we add some new information with which to inform the debate. First, we point out a qualification to the conclusions that many (though not Townsend himself) have drawn from Townsend's research—namely, that although in each of the three villages Townsend works with household income is not very highly correlated with consumption residuals (the main conclusion from Townsend's test), neither is it the case that household consumptions are very highly correlated with *each other*, which seems at odds with the idea that there's a great deal of consumption insurance in these villages. Where there is little insurance, the search for institutions which provide insurance seems less pressing. Second, by working directly with inter-household correlations, we are able to identify households that *do* have significantly correlated consumptions. In only one of the three villages we work with (Aurepalle) do there seem to be many such households; we turn our attention to the problem of trying to identify factors which help to predict whether a given household will be well-insured by this measure or not.

Our approach to measuring risk in the ICRISAT villages begins with an effort to operationalize the measures of risk developed in the previous section. We begin by supposing, as is usual in the literature on consumption-smoothing, that consumption is measured with error. Let z_t denote a vector of possibly time-varying village characteristics, let x_t^i denote a vector of observed, time-varying household characteristics, and let c_t^i denote the actual consumption of household i at date t, and let $\tilde{c}_t^i = c_t^i + \epsilon_t^i$

denote observed consumption, where ϵ_t^i is some measurement error, with the property that $E(\epsilon_t^i | z_t, x_t^i) = 0$ and $E(\epsilon_t^i | c_t^i) = 0$.

In the presence of measurement error, using observed consumption to measure risk as in Section 9.3 would lead the analyst to confute measurement error with idiosyncratic risk. To avoid this problem, we further decompose our measure of idiosyncratic risk into risk which can be attributed to variation in observed household characteristics x_t^i and a risk which cannot be explained by such variation, but which is due instead to variation in unobservables and to measurement error in consumption. Thus, rewriting the expression for risk yields

$$R^i = [U^i(Ec_t^i) - EU^i(E(c_t^i | z_t))] \qquad \text{(Aggregate risk)}$$

$$+ [EU^i(E(c_t^i | z_t)) - EU^i(E(c_t^i | x_t^i, z_t))] \qquad \text{(Explained idiosyncratic risk)}$$

$$+ [EU^i(E(c_t^i | x_t^i, z_t)) - EU^i(c_t^i)].$$

$$\text{(Unexplained risk and measurement error)}$$

Two additional steps are required before one can actually use data to compute the risk facing a household. First, one must choose the functions $\{U^i\}$. Second, one must devise a way to estimate the conditional expectations which figure in our risk measure. Here, we choose the risk evaluation function to take the simple form $U^i(c) = (c^{1-\gamma} - 1)/(1 - \gamma)$ for some parameter $\gamma > 0$; as gamma increases, the function U^i becomes increasingly sensitive to risk. We assume that $E(c_t^i | z_t, x_t^i) = \alpha^i + \eta_t + x_t^i \beta$, where $\theta = (\alpha^i, \eta_t, \beta')$ is a vector of unknown parameters, to be estimated.

We estimate the unconditional expectation of household i's consumption by $Ec_t^i = (1/T) \sum_{t=1}^T c_t^i$. For the present application, we wish to choose θ so as to optimally predict c_t^i in a least-squares sense. In the presence of measurement error, choosing parameters to predict consumption has the consequence that our estimates of total risk will not be unbiased. However, given our assumptions on the measurement error process ϵ_t^i, $E(c_t^i | z_t, x_t^i) = E(\tilde{c}_t^i | z_t, x_t^i)$, measurement error in consumption expenditures will influence only our measure of *unexplained* risk. This last measure will be incorrect by the difference

$$EU^i(\tilde{c}_t^i) - EU^i(c_t^i),$$

while our measures of aggregate and explained idiosyncratic risk will not be biased by this sort of measurement error.

Our parameterization of $E(c_t^i | z_t, x_t^i)$ suggests the linear estimating equation

$$\tilde{c}_t^i = \alpha^i + \eta_t + x_t^i \beta + v_t^i, \tag{9.2}$$

where the conditioning information (z_t, x_t^i) is understood to include the knowledge of the date and of the identity of the household,[3] where v_t^i is a disturbance term equal to

---

[3] Thus, $\{\eta_t\}$ captures the influence of changes in aggregates, and $\{\alpha^i\}$ captures the influence of fixed household characteristics on predicted household consumption.

the sum of both measurement error in consumption as well as prediction error, and where the household fixed effects α^i are restricted to sum to zero.

Our focus on risk-sharing strongly suggests that the disturbances $\{v_t^i\}$ may be correlated across households. This follows, for example, if a subset of the population is engaged in an otherwise perfect risk-sharing scheme. We assume that the cross-sectional correlation is governed by a time-invariant matrix $\Sigma = [\text{cov}(v_t^i, v_t^j)]$. Accordingly, we first construct point estimates of the parameters of (9.2) using ordinary least squares. Next, following Newey and West (1987), we use the estimated residuals $\{\hat{v}_t^i\}$ to estimate $X'(\Sigma \otimes I_T)X$, where the matrix X denotes the regressors employed in estimation, and where the (i,j) element of Σ is estimated by $\hat{\Sigma} = (1/T)\sum_{t=1}^{T} \hat{v}_t^i \hat{v}_t^j$. For this just identified estimator, the estimated covariance matrix of our parameter estimates is given by $(X'X)^{-1}X'(\hat{\Sigma} \otimes I_T)X(X'X)^{-1}$. This estimator of variance is consistent even in the presence of unspecified cross-sectional correlation, so long as this correlation is unchanging over time.

Using data on household consumption and income for the three Indian ICRISAT villages identical to that used by Townsend, we have estimated (9.2), using household income for the right-hand side variable x_t^i. Point estimates for the associated parameter β along with estimated standard errors are presented in the first lines of Table 9.1. The point estimates in this table very nearly replicate results reported in Townsend (1994).[4] As one might expect, in two of the three villages the OLS standard errors reported by Townsend are lower than are our estimates, as we correct these estimates for cross-sectional correlation in a way Townsend did not. However, in one village (Shirapur), our estimated standard errors are actually slightly *smaller* than are Townsend's estimates, and despite the correction, household income continues to have a pronounced, significant effect on household consumption in every village.

With an estimate of $E(c_t^i|z_t, x_t^i)$ in hand, we proceed to estimate the different components of risk. Following the suggestion of Arrow (1965), we choose the parameter $\alpha = -1$, implying a relative risk aversion of two. However, rather than reporting a measure of risk denominated in utilities, we find the certain transfer b necessary to just compensate the household for the risk it faces. So, for example, to measure the aggregate risk the household faces, we find some number b satisfying

$$U^i(Ec_t^i) = EU^i(b + E(c_t^i|z_t))$$

and similarly for explained idiosyncratic risk and unexplained risk. We call this transfer *risk compensation*. Both consumption expenditures and b are denominated

---

[4] The relevant results from Row 1 of table XIII(c) of Townsend's paper are

	Aurepalle	Shirapur	Kanzara
β	0.1362	0.0830	0.1398
	(0.0265)	(0.0218)	(0.0270)

We would replicate Townsend's point estimates exactly, except that we have used data only for households observed continuously over the period 1976–81.

Table 9.1. *Risk compensation for different components of consumption risk*

	Aurepalle	Shirapur	Kanzara
β	0.1075 (0.0332)	0.1015 (0.0237)	0.1417 (0.0363)
Aggregate risk	26.2984	1.8888	6.6943
Compensation	(17.6760, 35.7046)	(0.9651, 6.8974)	(4.3943, 12.9619)
Idiosyncratic risk	1.9049	2.3958	3.5221
Compensation	(0.2816, 3.2486)	(0.5356, 5.1289)	(0.5073, 6.7310)
Unexplained risk	17.2996	30.8564	15.0921
Compensation	(−0.3030, 50.1978)	(−5.2433, 72.1132)	(−13.2834, 53.3856)

Note: The first row reports point estimates for the coefficient associated with household income, in a regression of household consumption on income, a set of household fixed effects, and a set of time effects. Parenthetical numbers are the standard errors of these point estimates, taking into account possible cross-sectional correlation in disturbances. Subsequent rows report estimates and bootstrapped confidence intervals for the average risk compensation required (in every period) to compensate each household for facing each particular source of risk.

in 1975 Rupees; the mean of estimated risk compensations are presented in Table 9.1 by village and component.

From Table 9.1, the total risk faced by households in Aurepalle could be compensated by an annual per-household payment of between 27.42 and 44.77 1975 Rupees (depending on whether or not unexplained risk is included or not). From the perspective of a wealthy donor, this is a rather small sum, between about $10.50 and $17.50 in current US dollars. However, when compared to per household consumption expenditures of 787 Rupees in Aurepalle, the importance of risk springs into sharper focus: the *average* total risk compensation in Aurepalle amounts to between 7.6 and 12.3 per cent of consumption expenditures. Analogous figures for Shirapur are 0.9 and 7.1 per cent, and for Kanzara are 2.1 and 6.6 per cent.

Our largest estimate of risk compensation (12.3 per cent of average household expenditures in Aurepalle) seems considerable in welfare terms, but not enormous, particularly since much of this may be attributable to measurement error. In Shirapur and Kanzara estimates of explained risk compensations actually seem quite small. One explanation for may be that there is not actually a great deal of risk in the environment of these villages; an alternative is that households have developed effective means of reducing consumption risk, whether via risk-sharing, self-insurance, or some other sort of arrangement.

Table 9.2 is similar to Table 9.1, except that instead of measuring risk in consumption expenditures, it reports measures of compensation for *income* risk. Note that information on idiosyncratic consumption is used to predict income, so that (re-using the notation for parameters from above) we have $E(x_t^i|z_t, \tilde{c}_t^i) = \alpha^i + \eta_t + \tilde{c}_t^i$, estimated as before. Comparison of these two tables is informative. Total income risk seems considerable across all three villages, amounting to 58.54 1975 Rupees in Aurepalle, 108.50 Rupees in Shirapur, and 84.44 Rupees in Kanzara. The three villages differ

Table 9.2. *Risk compensation for different components of income risk*

	Aurepalle	Shirapur	Kanzara
β	1.0488 (0.3465)	0.7014 (0.1838)	1.1206 (0.2811)
Aggregate risk	30.4632	17.8811	19.0124
Compensation	(10.8093, 78.9837)	(8.3641, 48.0137)	(11.3652, 45.7730)
Idiosyncratic risk	11.6528	14.5646	12.2930
Compensation	(−1.3890, 20.9283)	(0.2103, 33.0543)	(−1.4376, 25.0382)
Unexplained risk	16.4296	76.0551	53.1372
Compensation	(−14.8286, 52.2384)	(49.3828, 103.8923)	(−174.3121, 221.1009)

Note: The first row reports point estimates for the coefficient associated with household consumption, in a regression of income on household consumption, a set of household fixed effects, and a set of time effects. Parenthetical numbers are the standard errors of these point estimates, taking into account possible cross-sectional correlation in disturbances. Subsequent rows report estimates and bootstrapped confidence intervals for the average risk compensation required (in every period) to compensate each household for facing each particular source of risk.

in interesting ways. Aggregate risk seems to be particularly important in Aurepalle, in both income and consumption—there appears to be little smoothing of aggregate consumption in this village. On the other hand, while there is considerable idiosyncratic risk in income, there's very little idiosyncratic risk in consumption, suggesting that mechanisms for sharing risk may be quite effective in Aurepalle. In Shirapur there is somewhat less aggregate income risk than in Aurepalle, but *both* aggregate and idiosyncratic consumption risk are negligible, suggesting that the village makes important use of some intertemporal technology, such as storage or transactions in credit markets outside the village. The possibility of this sort of financial integration means that the very small idiosyncratic risk in Shirapur may be due to village-level risk-sharing, or may alternatively be due to credit or insurance arrangements made outside the village. Kanzara is somewhat similar to Shirapur, in that both aggregate and idiosyncratic risk in consumption is considerably smaller than it is for income, which again implies the use of storage or credit, combined with some unidentified form of insurance against most idiosyncratic risk.

In order to shed some additional light on the mechanisms used to insure consumption in different villages, I have computed the simple correlation coefficients between the consumptions of different households, for each village. These are shown (using various shades of gray) in Fig. 9.1. The first column of these figures indicates the degree of correlation between different households. Note that the average correlation coefficient in Aurepalle is relatively large, compared to the other two villages. In the right-hand column, we report results of a bootstrap test of significance of the correlation coefficients to the left. If household consumptions were independent, then white squares would appear 2.5 per cent of the time (a false positive correlation), as would black (a false negative correlation). By this standard consumptions in Shirapur truly do appear to be nearly independent, as fewer than 2 per cent are significantly positive, and 2.4 per cent are negative. Households in these matrices are ordered according to

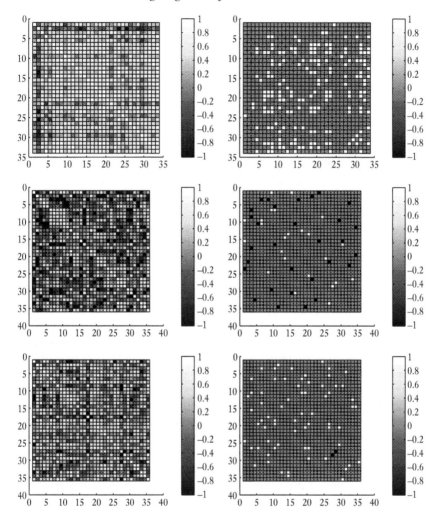

Figure 9.1. *Correlations between household consumptions and tests of significance*

Note: Figures in the first column show the complete matrix of correlation coefficients between household consumption. The second column presents tests of the significance of these coefficients (at a 95 per cent confidence level). A black square indicates a significant negative correlation; a white square indicates a significant positive correlation. The first row presents data from Aurepalle; the second from Shirapur; the third from Kanzara.

their household numbers. The survey which collected these data was designed so that low household numbers were assigned to households which owned no land in the initial year (1975) of the survey, while the remaining three-quarters of the sample households were selected according to a stratified sample design so that one quarter of the sampled households had landholdings in the bottom tercile the landholding distribution (by size of holding), a second quarter had holdings in the second tercile, and the final quarter had landholdings in the highest tercile. Household numbers were assigned in blocks corresponding to terciles, so that the ordering of households in Fig. 9.1 corresponds roughly to the size of their landholdings.

More interesting patterns of correlation emerge in Aurepalle and Kanzara. In Aurepalle there are no significant negative correlations, while 17 per cent of all correlation coefficients are significant and positive. There is weaker evidence of a meaningful number of significant correlations in Kanzara, where 5.8 per cent of all correlations are significant and positive.

To a considerable degree these differences across villages simply reflect differences in aggregate risk; since there is little common time-series variation in consumptions in Shirapur, it is difficult to detect possible correlation patterns. We would like to control for this aggregate variation, and then take a closer look at *which* households have significant patterns of correlation after removing purely aggregate changes in consumption (measured by the estimated $\{\eta_t\}$ in (9.2)). This amounts to looking at patterns of correlation in residuals from the regression (9.2). As it happens, we have already estimated the covariance matrix of these residuals; this is just the matrix Σ we used earlier to construct a consistent estimator of the covariance matrix of our parameter estimates in (9.2). Fig. 9.2 parallels Fig. 9.1, but presents correlations for these estimated residuals.

The patterns of correlation revealed in Fig. 9.2 are not obviously remarkable in Shirapur and Kanzara. However, a surprising and interesting feature of the data emerges from the plots for Aurepalle. It is apparent from the figure that residuals are correlated among the first 17 households, and among the last 17; however, correlations between these two groups of households are comparatively small. This neatly divides the plot in the upper left of the figure into quadrants. So how are the first 17 households different from the final 17? The first 17 households are precisely those who either had no land or had holdings in the bottom tercile in 1975; the ICRISAT investigators intended this as a measure to capture the landless and the poorest farmers. Thus, these correlations suggest that the landless and the poorest insure among themselves, while medium and large farmers (the remaining 17 farmers) form a similar risk–sharing group.

It is of some interest to think of this result in light of the findings of Lim and Townsend (1998), who found that saving (cash and grain) was the chief mechanism used to smooth consumption in Aurepalle. Our results indicate that the two different groups we have identified save at different rates. Unfortunately, our measurement of correlation in consumption residuals is silent as to the mechanism which induces this correlation, so it is not clear whether there are also contingent transfers among (but not between) the two different groups we have identified.

9.4. TARGETING

We now turn our attention to ways in which the foregoing analysis might be used to make targeted income transfers to particular households. We assume that the risk

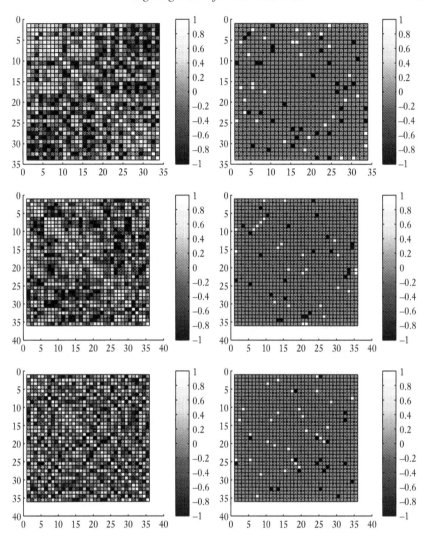

Figure 9.2. *Correlations between residuals and tests of significance*

Note: Figures in the first column show the complete matrix of correlation coefficients between the residuals from (9.2) for different households. The second column presents tests of the significance of these coefficients (at a 95 per cent confidence level). A black square indicates a significant negative correlation; a white square indicates a significant positive correlation. The first row presents data from Aurepalle; the second from Shirapur; the third from Kanzara

evaluation functions $\{U^i\}$ have been chosen to reflect the preferences of the donor. We also assume that the donor cannot observe shocks faced by the household, and does not offer any kind of contingent transfers (does not act as an insurer, in other words).

Now, *if* it were the case that transfers made to the different households were simply consumed by that household, then targeting households to compensate each for the risk it faces would be a simple matter; one could simply estimate the risk each household faces as above, compute the necessary risk compensation, and make a non-contingent transfer b^i to household i in every period. In this way, though each household would still bear risk, each household would be indifferent between its risky consumption plus transfers and a riskless consumption with the same mean. Provided that households consumed their transfers, then such a scheme would (weakly) improve the welfare of all households while at the same time preserving, largely intact, existing incentives to save, invest, and work.

Unfortunately, in general there is no reason to suppose that a household which receives a transfer b^i in every period will simply consume that transfer, without otherwise acting to change its intertemporal consumption profile (through saving, investment, or credit markets) or making contingent transfers to other households. To take one particularly simple case, suppose that the household regards the transfer it receives in the same way that it regards other forms of income, and suppose that the simple linear allocation rule proposed above holds, so that $c_t^i = \alpha^i + \eta_t + \beta(x_t^i + b^i) + v_t^i$ holds, with x_t^i equal to all income net of the transfer b^i. To induce the household to actually consume one additional unit in that period, one would have to transfer $1/\beta$ to the household. However, the extra resources presumably are not squandered; instead some share of the transfer will be given to some other household or somehow invested; this in turn will influence consumption realized by the household in other periods, or in other states.

The way in which an income transfer made to household i is treated may depend both on the opportunities the household has to invest or save. Somewhat less obviously, it will also depend on prior informal arrangements the household may have made with other households. Here we give a short list of models, along with the predictions regarding the disposition of income transfers associated with each model.

9.4.1. *Full Insurance*

This is the model of Wilson (1968), Townsend (1994), and many others. The basic prediction of the model is that any collection of risk-averse households will insure each other against any idiosyncratic shocks, so that household consumption at any date state can be written as a fixed, household-specific function of village aggregates, or

$$c_t^i = f^i(z_t).$$

In the case Townsend considers, households have Gorman-aggreable preferences, and so the relevant village aggregate is simply the total supply of the consumption good. However, even more general preferences deliver the result that household consumption should not depend on idiosyncratic events. This arrangement may be implemented via some *ex ante* income-pooling scheme.

The point here, of course, is that the arrival of a donor agency making 'targeted' transfers looks just like another source of idiosyncratic shocks. In the full insurance model, households with the exponential utility functions assumed by Townsend (and no intertemporal technology) would simply pool the total transfers received by the village as a whole. Each household would receive an equal share of this windfall to supplement the consumption they would have received in the absence of the transfers. If households instead have CRRA utility functions, then they would divide the pooled transfers into unequal (but predetermined) shares. Accordingly, the effect of a targeted transfer scheme on our measure of risk would be to slightly change the aggregate risk faced by every household. There would be no effect on idiosyncratic risk (though if there was really full insurance, there would be no idiosyncratic risk to begin with).

9.4.2. *Credit*

Consider a model in which households have access to perfect credit markets, but make no arrangements to insure their consumption. These same households may or may not be constrained with respect to their borrowing, as suggested in Morduch (1995), Lim (1992) provides a test of this hypothesis using these same data). Now, by assumption households make no contingent transfers to other households, so we need to concern ourselves only with how the transfer will affect savings and investment. Since the household had access to credit markets prior to the targeting programme, it would have chosen its savings behaviour to satisfy the Euler equation

$$U^{i\prime}(c_t^i) = \mathrm{E}_t H_{t+j}^i U^{i\prime}(c_{t+j}^i),$$

$j = 1, 2, \ldots$, where E_t denotes the household's expectations at time t, and where H_t^i denotes the discounted realized returns on an investment of a single rupee at $t - 1$. Note that here we conflate the risk evaluation function U^i with the household's utility function, to avoid additional notation.

Now, how receipt of a transfer affects the households consumption profile hinges critically on the households expectations. If the receipt of the transfer is entirely unanticipated, the household has quadratic utility as in Hall (1978), and $H_t^i = 1$ for all t then household consumption will increase by exactly b^i in every period, as this represents a change in permanent income. However, if the scheme is anticipated, household consumption will increase by less than b^i, though the earlier anticipation of the scheme may have raised consumption earlier. This raises an important practical point. If one were to canvass a village, trying to measure risk so as to implement a scheme of targeted transfers, then the very act of measurement may lead the villagers to infer that future transfers may be forthcoming. This inference, in turn, will influence consumption *at the very time* that one is attempting to measure it.

9.4.3. *Private Information (Hidden Actions)*

We next turn our attention to a dynamic model of hidden actions described by Ligon (1998). In this model, households supply labour or make costly investments which cannot be observed by others in the village. However, the total output of each household *can* be observed. As a consequence, in a constrained-efficient arrangement, household consumption does not depend directly on labour effort, but does vary with the realized output of the household. Though not strictly correct, an intuition is that observing output allows other households to infer what effort may have been, and to compensate the household accordingly. Thus, consumption expenditures in this model may respond to income shocks, in much the same way as the model of credit sketched in Section 9.4.2. However, and this is key, household compensation depends on output or other idiosyncratic shocks to the extent that these shocks provide information regarding unobserved behaviour of the household, or to the extent that these shocks affect the aggregate resource constraint of the village.

As a consequence, publicly observable shocks to income, such as an observable transfer from a donor, will have no direct influence on the households' consumption expenditures, just as in the case of full insurance. In particular, suppose that all households in the village derive utility from an exponential function of consumption expenditures and disutility from an additively separable function of effort. Suppose also that household one has no private information, while household two takes some hidden labour effort a_t^2 to produce output x_{t+1}^2. Then in a constrained efficient arrangement, consumptions of the two households will satisfy

$$c_{t+1}^1 - c_{t+1}^2 = c_t^1 - c_t^2 + \mu \frac{\ell_a(x_{t+1}^2 | a_t^2)}{\ell(x_{t+1}^2 | a_t^2)},$$

where μ is a non-negative constant, the function ℓ is the likelihood of observing output x_{t+1}^2 given action a_t^2, and ℓ_a is the partial derivative of the likelihood with respect to labour effort. Note that the ratio ℓ_a/ℓ is a likelihood ratio, which measures the usefulness of information x_{t+1}^2 in inferring labour effort. Adding some other random variable b^2 distributed independently of labour effort to household two's income would only increase two's consumption by an equal share of b^2, b^2/n. This is the same impact such a transfer would have on the consumption of every household in the village, and will be no different from the impact of making precisely the same public transfer, but to a completely different household.

9.4.4. *Limited Commitment*

Finally, we turn our attention to another dynamic model, but one in which the relevant friction is limited commitment, as in Kocherlakota (1996) or Ligon et al. (2002), and discussed at length in Platteau (1997). In this model, households make risk-sharing arrangements, but the institutions to enforce these contracts are missing or imperfect, so that any household can choose to renege on the mutual insurance arrangement *ex post*.

The consequences of reneging are that the household is henceforth excluded from risk-sharing opportunities with all other households, and so non-trivial risk-sharing will emerge if households are not too impatient. Households never actual renege in equilibrium. However, households who receive sufficiently large positive shocks (relative to other households) may try to renegotiate, using the (credible) threat that they will otherwise renege as leverage in their negotiations. A household which succeeds in renegotiating the risk-sharing arrangement will negotiate a larger share of consumption both in the present period *and* in all future periods (subject to another shock to some household possibly resulting in a subsequent renegotiation). In this way, a positive income shock even in a single period can lead to a permanent change in household expenditures, even in the absence of formal credit markets or an intertemporal technology.

The would-be donor seeking to make transfers to households in villages where risk-sharing is limited by imperfect enforcement is faced with both an opportunity and a challenge. By making a sufficiently large transfer to household *i*, the donor can effect a permanent change in the distribution of consumption expenditures. However, if the donor seeks to target households who are particularly vulnerable to risk, she may reduce the ability of those households to benefit from local informal insurance arrangements, and may actually increase the idiosyncratic risk the household faces.[5] At the same time, the donor may reduce the effectiveness of the household's insurance of *other* households. This follows because a households' future demand for insurance may be reduced by transfers from the donor. If the household benefits less from informal insurance arrangements, then that makes it more likely that the household will threaten to renege in future periods, and limits the indemnity of the household both in the present period *and* in the future.

Finally, the point made earlier about the expectations aroused by a donor surveying a village has a parallel here. If a donor visits a village, leading locals to believe that the donor will effectively target vulnerable households in the future, then those same vulnerable households may be immediately excluded from existing risk-sharing arrangements.

9.5. CONCLUSION

In this chapter we have proposed a utilitarian measure of risk, related it to existing measures of poverty, and given a method for both estimating household-specific risk and also decomposing it into aggregate and idiosyncratic components. In addition, we develop a simple estimator of risk-sharing regressions which delivers correct inference, even when estimated residuals are correlated across households (as they would be if households participated in distinct insurance networks).

We have used this technique to explore the risk faced by households in the three main Indian ICRISAT villages. Of the three villages, we infer that Aurepalle has the best intra-village insurance, but the least access to mechanisms for smoothing aggregate consumption. In contrast to Aurepalle, households in Shirapur bear almost no aggregate risk, but do face a large amount of unexplained idiosyncratic risk. Kanzara is somewhere in between, though it is the wealthiest village.

An exploration of the structure of residuals from risk-sharing regressions reveals two strikingly distinct risk-sharing networks in Aurepalle, one among the landless and smallholders; the other between medium and large holders. Risk-sharing networks are

---

[5] An example of this is discussed in Attanasio and Rios-Rull (2000).

not identifiable in the other two villages, but then evidence for any effective risk-sharing in these villages is relatively weak.

Finally, we discuss a sequence of models, which might explain the apparently imperfect risk-sharing we observe in these villages, along the consequences for a benevolent donor seeking to target non-contingent transfers to particular households. In two of these three models (full insurance and dynamic moral hazard), targeting attempts seemed doomed to failure, as the 'shock' of a donor making transfers is itself fully insured away. In the remaining models (credit and limited commitment) targeted transfers can change the distribution of resources in the village, but may actually tend to *increase* the risk targeted households face—it is possible to compensate these risk-bearing households by making them wealthier, but a more sophisticated mechanism than targeted lumpsum transfers would be necessary to reduce the risks borne by these households.

REFERENCES

Arrow, K. J. (1965). *Aspects of the Theory of Risk Aversion*. Helsinki: Yrjö Jahnssonin säätiö.

Attanasio, O. and J.-V. Rios-Rull (2000). 'Consumption Smoothing in Island Economies: Can Public Insurance Reduce Welfare? *European Economic Review*, 44(7), 1225–58.

Baulch, B. and J. Hoddinott (2000). 'Economic Mobility and Poverty Dynamics in Developing Countries'. *Journal of Development Studies*, 36(6), 1–24.

Deaton, A. (1990). 'On Risk, insurance, and Intra-Village Consumption Smoothing', Manuscript.

Dercon, S. and P. Krishnan (2000). 'Vulnerability, Seasonality and Poverty in Ethiopia'. *Journal of Development Studies*, 36(6), 25–53.

Foster, J., J. Greer, and E. Thorbecke (1984). 'A Class of Decomposable Poverty Measures'. *Econometrica*, 52(3), 761–6.

Hall, R. E. (1978). 'Stochastic Implications of the Life Cycle–Permanent Income Hypothesis: Theory and Evidence'. *Journal of Political Economy*, 86, 971–87.

Jalan, J. and M. Ravallion (2000). 'Is Transient Poverty Different? Evidence for Rural China'. *Journal of Development Studies*, 36(6), 82.

Kocherlakota, N. R. (1996). 'Implications of Efficient Risk Sharing Without Commitment'. *The Review of Economic Studies*, 63(4), 595–610.

Ligon, E. (1998). 'Risk-Sharing and Information in Village Economies'. *Review of Economic Studies*, 65, 847–64.

—— and L. Schechter (2003). 'Measuring Vulnerability'. *Economic Journal*, 113(486), C95–C102.

——, J. P. Thomas, and T. Worrall (2002). 'Informal Insurance Arrangements with Limited Commitment: Theory and Evidence from Village Economies'. *Review of Economic Studies*, 69(1), 209–44.

Lim, Y. (1992). 'Disentangling Permanent Income from Risk Sharing: A General Equilibrium Perspective on Credit Markets in Rural South India'. Ph.D. thesis, University of Chicago.

—— and R. M. Townsend (1998). 'General Equilibrium Models of Financial Systems: Theory and Measurement in Village Economies'. *Review of Economic Dynamics*, 1(1), 59–118.

Morduch, J. (1995). 'Income Smoothing and Consumption Smoothing'. *Journal of Economic Perspectives*, 9(3(summer)), 103–14.

Newey, W. K. and K. D. West (1987). 'Hypothesis Testing with Efficient Method of Moments Estimation'. *International Testing with Efficient Method of Moments Estimation*, 28(3), 777–87.

Platteau, J.-P. (1997). 'Mutual Insurance as an Elusive Concept in Traditional Rural Societies'. *Journal of Development Studies*, 33(6(August)), 764–96.

Ravallion, M. (1988). 'Expected Poverty Under Risk-Induced Welfare Variability'. *Economic Journal*, 98(393), 1171–82.

Rothschild, M. and J. E. Stiglitz (1970). 'Increasing Risk: I. A Definition'. *Journal of Economic Theory*, 2, 225–43.

Townsend, R. M. (1994). 'Risk and Insurance in Village India'. *Econometrica*, 62(3), 539–91.

Wilson, R. (1968). 'The Theory of Syndicates'. *Econometrica*, 36(January), 119–32.

PART V

RISK AND SOCIAL
INSTITUTIONS

10

Risk-Sharing and Endogenous Network Formation

JOACHIM DE WEERDT

10.1. INTRODUCTION

In much of the economic literature an insurance network is treated as an exogenous institution. Frequently, the assumption is made that all households who are members of an easily identifiable group (e.g. the village, the extended family, and so on) form one single network. There are, however, both theoretical and empirical grounds for being sceptical about this approach. Bala and Goyal (2000) theoretically model network formation as a non-cooperative game. Although the specifics of their model are geared towards explaining the formation of information networks, the basic principle can also be applied to risk-sharing networks: self-interested individuals can form or destroy links with others, trading off the costs and the benefits of doing so. Numerous factors will determine whether agents are able to exploit the gains of cooperation in the context of an informal insurance market. In an economy with heterogeneous agents these factors will differ across dyads.[1] This makes some pairs of households more suitable insurance partners than others.

First, there are factors related to information. Agents who have smooth information flows between each other are more likely to enter into an insurance arrangement. This means, for example, that we expect close neighbours or households engaged in similar income-generating activities to form insurance links with each other. Note that even

Research funded by the National Science foundation (FWO-Vlaanderen). I am indebted to Abigail Barr, Stefan Dercon, Micheal Kevane, Markus Goldstein, Els Lievois, Katleen Van den Broeck. Also to the participants at the UNU-WIDER project meeting on 'Insurance against Poverty', the NEUDC 2001 conference at Boston University, the 'understanding poverty and growth in sub-Saharan Africa' conference at Oxford University, and a seminar at the University of Dar es Salaam, for their comments and help. I thank Philemon Charles, Augustina John, Obadiah Kyakajumba, Respichius Mitti, George Musikula, Isaya Mukama, Adelina Rwechungula, and Taddeo Rweyemamu for their excellent work on the field, Julius Majula for taking charge of the data entry and all the people of the community of Nyakatoke for their continuous hospitality and willingness to provide us with the data. This chapter is based on my doctoral thesis on 'Social Networks, Transfers and Insurance in Developing Countries'.

[1] A dyad is a pair of households. When we say 'cross dyads', we mean across all possible combinations of two households in the village.

between members of the same village or extended family information flows are likely to be heterogeneous.

Second, there are factors related to trust, norms, and the ability to punish (Platteau 1991; Fafchamps 1992). Kinship, clan membership, and religious affiliation might be important in this respect, because they help to impose strict norms on members. Deviant behaviour of group members can be punished with disgrace or ostracism. *Ceteris paribus*, this creates an incentive to form links within one's group.

Third, if dyads are heterogeneous with respect to the correlation of their income flows, then the potential gains of cooperation may differ greatly across dyads. Two households engaged in different activities may have weakly correlated income streams and may thus be better insurance partners (if we abstract from any informational concerns). Households, who have similar activities or, in an agricultural setting, are close neighbours, might have more covariate income streams and are less suitable as insurance partners. Grimard (1997) points to the tradeoff that agricultural households are forced to make regarding the geographical proximity of their insurance partners. Informational flows are smooth between close neighbours, but income streams are likely to be covariate. Households living further away might have less covariate incomes, but informational problems can be large. Our data suggest that the information constraints outweigh the non-covariance of income.

Fourth, non-cooperative, game theoretic models (e.g. Coate and Ravallion 1993; Spinnewyn and Wijaya 1996) stress the importance of the discount factor. Agents need to be sufficiently concerned about future income flows to engage in risk-sharing arrangements.

The fact that the creation of insurance links depends on such a wide range of factors and that dyads are heterogeneous with respect to these factors suggests that insurance networks will not be identical to groups delineated on the basis of just one factor. For example, there is no a priori reason to assume that the whole village forms a network. Indeed, in many societies a single village is spread over a substantial area and information flows are, *ceteris paribus*, better between close neighbours than between villagers living, say, 1 km apart. Typically, there will also be different clans, religions, kinship, and professional groups within a single village, making the likelihood of forging an insurance link unequally distributed across all possible dyads in the village.

Researchers have offered other compelling evidence that there are bounds on the size of an insurance group, even when agents are homogenous. Murgai *et al.* (2000) argue that there are increasing costs to group size. As the network becomes larger the task of coordinating transfers, gathering information, and enforcing contracts becomes more difficult. In such an environment, full insurance at village level becomes an extreme case. They back this argument up with an empirical study of water exchanges along irrigation canals in Pakistan. Genicot and Ray (2000) show that one does not even have to impose increasing costs to have bounded group size. They consider a non–cooperative risk-sharing model, which is robust not only to single-person deviations, but also to subgroup deviations. They show that introducing this (quite natural) assumption is sufficient to put bounds on the size of the network. In both these studies, community level (or family level) insurance can be seen as an extreme case.

The little empirical work that has been done on these issues all suggests that networks should not be treated as exogenous. Fafchamps and Lund (2000) and Murgai *et al.* (2000) find that risk is shared within the confines of small clusters of households and not at the level of the community (and neither at any other clearly demarcated level). Murgai *et al.* (2000) find that kinship, geographical proximity, and the degree of risk exposure are important in explaining network formation. Goldstein (2000) notes that networks are formed among kin, neighbours, and gender groups.

This chapter builds on these theoretical and empirical findings and suggests an approach by which one can present stylized facts on the determinants of network formation. Our unit of analysis will be the dyad, a pair of households. Dyads are often studied in the literature on network analysis, because of their intuitive appeal and their versatility in statistical tests (e.g. Wasserman and Faust 1995). Applied to a data set collected in a small Haya village in rural Tanzania, we find that kinship, geographical proximity, the number of common friends, clan membership, religious affiliation, and wealth strongly determine the formation of risk–sharing networks.

10.2. THE DYADIC DATA

The basic procedure of the dyadic approach is to make a data set of all possible unique combinations of two households in the village. For each of these pairs we construct a value for the 'degree of connection', or 'the strength of the insurance link' between them. This will be the endogenous variable, which can be explained by exogenous variables (e.g. the strength of the kinship tie) through multiple regression analysis. This chapter does not analyse any issues related to the *direction* of the link.

We make use of data collected in the community of Nyakatoke, a small Haya village in the Kagera region of Tanzania. We interviewed *all* of the 119 households in the community in household interviews and *all* of the 220 adults in these households in individual interviews. Although some of the data has been collected at individual level, our analysis will be done at household level. Note that in a village of 119 households there are $\binom{119}{2} = 7021$ unique combinations of two households (also called dyads) possible.

We want to attach a value of degree of connection to each of these 7021 dyads. Because of time constraints, we did not query each of the 220 individuals about their relation with each of the other 219 individuals in the survey. Instead we asked them: '*Can you give a list of people from inside or outside of Nyakatoke, who you can personally rely on for help and/or that can rely on you for help in cash, kind or labour.*'[2]

The persons mentioned are called the 'network members' or the 'network partners'. The respondents listed a total of 1126 network members. About two-thirds of them (738 in total) live in Nyakatoke. The other one-third (388 in total) live outside of Nyakatoke. Given the set-up of our approach, we are only able to make use of the 738 links inside Nyakatoke.

---

[2] Of course, who exactly is mentioned as an insurance partner depends on the framing of this question. As long as answers are not systematically biased to certain types of network members, this should not influence our results.

We want to make two remarks concerning the weight that will be attached to each link. First, although our analysis is at household level,[3] one might argue that if more than one member of the household mentions a particular other household, this link should have a higher weight. Second, respondents often unilaterally mention each other as network partners.[4] This should not be taken to mean that there are false expectations or the relation is not reciprocal. Remember that the question was framed as 'who can you rely on and/or who relies on you', so no directional meaning can be attached to it. In this chapter, we take the view that the interviews administered to each side of the dyad complement one another. We consider unilaterally mentioned links to be weaker than bilaterally mentioned links.

Taking account of the two previous remarks, we construct three different specifications for the LHS variable, summarized in the first three rows of Table 10.1. First, we have the total number of links that were reported between two households. For example, if two members of household A mention someone from household B and one member of B mentions a member of A, then the total number of links is three. The second measure also counts the links, but now under the assumption that each household can only send one link to (and receive one link from) each of the other 118 households. If several members of household A send a link to household B, then this is counted as a single link. In the above example, this variable would be equal to two. The variable is equal to two when the link between A and B is reciprocal, equal to one when it is unilateral, and equal to zero when neither of the two households mentions each other. The third specification is simply a dummy indicating whether there exists at least one link between the two households. We will perform an ordinal logit regression for the first two variables and a logit regression for the third.

The fourth measure for our LHS variable is the 'geodesic distance' between two households. Because we interviewed every household in the village we can, quite literally, draw the complete network inside the village, with lines joining the households which have mentioned each other as network members (this graph is given in Appendix 1, Figure 10.A1). The 'geodesic distance' between two households is the minimum amount of steps one has to take to go from one household to the other on the network graph (Wasserman and Faust 1995).

For example, in the picture given above A has a link with B and D; C is not linked to anyone. The geodesic distance is 1 between A and B and between A and D. It is two between B and D and it is infinity between C and any other household. The geodesic distance is more convincing for those who believe that one does not only benefit from one's own direct network members, but also from the vast network lying behind

---

[3] An analysis at individual level would have 24,090 dyads, of which 23,352 have the endogenous variable equal to zero. This would give us too little variation for the econometric analysis.
[4] Fafchamps and Lund (2000) find the same for households in the Philippines.

Table 10.1. *Four different specifications of the endogenous variable*

Endogenous variable	Definition	Distribution across the 7,021 dyads	
Total number of links reported by individuals	The number of times a member of household A mentions a member of household B + the number of times a member of household B mentions a member of household A	0 1 2 3 4 5	6,531 308 129 42 9 2
Number of household level links	0 if there is no link between the households 1 if there is a unilateral link 2 if there is a reciprocal link	0 1 2	6,531 350 140
Dummy	0 if there is no link between the households 1 if there is at least one link	0 1	6,531 490
Geodesic distance	Shortest distance between the households on the network graph	1 2 3 4 5	490 1,996 2,900 1,275 360

Source: Nyakatoke Household Survey.

one's own direct network members. Of course, there are costs attached to each node that is crossed in the network (Bala and Goyal 2000). The geodesic distance is an ordinal measure for these costs and thus a natural measure of how well connected two households are. The last row of Table 10.1 shows how the geodesic distance is distributed across the dyads. We use an ordinal logit to explain the geodesic distance between two households.

The survey has data on religion, clan, schooling, income-generating activities, age of the household head, and wealth. Tables 10.2 and 10.3 present summary statistics for these variables. Out of the three religions in the village, the Muslims form the smallest group. There are 26 clans in Nyakatoke. The Bayango form the biggest clan (23 members), followed by the Basimba (20 members), the Bahimba (12 members), and the Bahunga (10 members). There are 10 clans which have only one household in Nyakatoke. Schooling is very low in this village, with only 72 household heads having completed primary school. There are 93 households in which at least one member has completed primary education. Almost all households are engaged in crop production. Note that very few people get any income out of assets. Livestock and landholdings are good indicators of wealth in Haya society (Reining 1967).[5]

---

[5] Land size is the best proxy available in the survey to capture the value of land.

Table 10.2. *Distribution of attribute variables*

Variable	Category	Frequency	n
Distribution of religion	Muslim	24	
	Lutheran	46	
	Catholic	49	119
The number of clans with the specified number of members[a]	1 member	11	
	2 members	5	
	3 members	2	
	4–10 members	5	
	12–23 members	3	119
Household has at least one member who has completed primary education	No	26	
	Yes	93	119
Income-generating activities. Number of households engaged in each activity	Casual labour	57	
	Trade	41	
	Crops	108	
	Livestock	31	
	Assets	8	
	Processing	45	
	Other off-farm	40	116

[a] The exact distribution, specified per clan, can be found in Mitti and Rweyemamu (2000).
Source: Nyakatoke Household Survey.

Table 10.3. *Distribution of attribute variables, quintiles*

Quintile	Mean age of household head (years)	Mean livestock value (TSh)	Mean area of land (ha)
1st (lowest)	27	0	0.29
2nd	35	1,867	0.62
3rd	41	7,400	0.98
4th	54	23,544	1.45
5th (highest)	70	254,018	3.45
Total	45	53,354	1.34
n	119	119	119

Source: Nyakatoke Household Survey.

Table 10.3 shows how unequally distributed wealth is in the village, especially livestock.

The above-mentioned variables are all *attribute variables*. They can only take on a value for a single household. We cannot sensibly talk about the religion of two

Table 10.4. *Distribution of relational variables across the dyads*

Variable	Category	Frequency	n
Kinship	Parents, children, and siblings	109	
	Nephews, nieces, uncles, aunts, cousins, grandparents,		
	and grandchildren	102	
	Other blood bond	172	
	No blood bond	6,638	7,021
Number of common friends	0	4,696	
	1	1,421	
	2	563	
	3	209	
	4	69	7,021
	Between 5 and 11	63	
Same religion	Yes	2,487	
	No	4,534	7,021
Same clan	Yes	659	
	No	6,362	7,021
Do both households have at least one member who has completed primary education?	No, neither of them has	325	
	No, only one of them has	2,418	
	Yes, both of them have	4,278	7,021

Source: Nyakatoke Household Survey.

households. However, the observations for the regression analysis are dyads, so we can only enter *relational variables* as explanatory variables. There are some variables that are intrinsically relational (e.g. kinship ties) and others that can be created by transforming attribute variables. We enter the following relational variables in our regressions (summary statistics are given in Tables 10.4 and 10.5).

10.2.1. *Kinship*

Kinship might be important because of history, norms, and trust. Typically, one has had a long-lasting relationship with family members and, as Hayami and Kikuchi (cited in Platteau 1991) put it, 'performances in past transactions comprise a reliable data set for prediction of future performances'. Furthermore, the family as a group is likely to criticize or punish uncooperative behaviour, thus inducing norms and trust. From a Darwinist point of view, helping family members is good for the expansion of the gene pool. There are data on the kinship ties between all the households in Nyakatoke. We use these to create three dummy variables. The first is equal to one for parents, children, and siblings. The second is equal to one for nephews, nieces, uncles, aunts, cousins, grandparents, and grandchildren. The third is equal to one for any other blood relation. The reference category is having no blood bond. There are

Table 10.5. *Distribution of relational variables across dyads, quintiles*

Quintile	Distance (m)	Activity overlap (%)	Age of household head (years)		Livestock value (TSh)		Land (ha)		Number of respondents
			Diff.	Max.	Diff.	Max.	Diff.	Max.	Max.
1st (lowest)	161	0.19	3	35	678	927	0.12	0.64	2
2nd	325	0.45	9	44	6,496	9,464	0.41	1.05	2
3rd	466	0.57	16	53	16,805	23,482	0.75	1.46	2
4th	645	0.66	24	63	36,947	44,680	1.40	2.30	2
5th (highest)	1,016	0.85	40	78	403,638	436,736	3.39	4.41	3
Total	522	0.53	18	54	92,727	99,718	1.21	1.94	4
n	6,670	6,670	7,021	7,021	7,021	7,021	7,021	7,021	7,021

Source: Nyakatoke Household Survey.

383 blood-bond relations between the households of Nyakatoke. We do not include relations that are through clan membership only. The influence of clan membership in network formation will be captured by a separate variable. The Haya have a patrilineal society, so it would make sense to create kinship dummies that take this into account. However, because the wife usually moves to the husband's village when she marries, there are very few matrilineal links in the village. For example, in the second category (uncles, cousins, and so on) there are only eight matrilineal links, which is too little to enter as a separate variable.

10.2.2. Geographical Distance

Neighbours have clear information advantages, which we expect to have a positive effect on the emergence of risk-sharing arrangements. On the other hand, they are likely to have covariate agricultural risk, which we expect to hamper the formation of a link. Haya homesteads are typically surrounded by dense fields of banana trees, intercropped with other crops. These form a natural barrier with their closest neighbour, who can only be reached by a short walk through the field or along a path. Houses are never built adjacent to each other. All the homesteads were plotted on an electronic map and the distance between each pair was calculated.[6] The average distance between the households is 522 m; the maximum distance is 1,738 m.

[6] Geographical distance is a good proxy for accessibility as people will take shortcuts through the fields if a path does not go directly. Attribute variables influencing accessibility, like health or the ability to walk, will be controlled for by dummies in the regressions.

10.2.3. *Number of Common Friends*

Households having many common friends are likely to have more information channels (e.g. through the grapevine) between them than households without common friends. It may also be true that these common friends act as observers of the relation between the two households and will frown upon any deviant behaviour. Falling out with someone might impose the extra punishment of falling out with some common friends, especially if you are the one considered to be behaving in the wrong way. We measure this variable as the number of common network members both households have. If A is linked with B, C, D, and E and B is linked with C, E, F, G, and H, then A and B have two common 'friends' (C and E). In the data this variable ranges from 0 to 11.

10.2.4. *Same Religion*

One might argue that religious gatherings ease information transfers, but the control and mediating functions the church or mosque have are probably more important. We expect that, *ceteris paribus*, links form within the same religious groups. 'Same religion' is a dummy, which is one if both households are of the same religion and we expect it to have a positive coefficient. We have information on affiliation to the three main religions (Muslim, Roman Catholic, and Lutheran), but unfortunately the data do not allow us to identify any heterogeneity within these three groups.

10.2.5. *Same Clan*

Although it is in the process of losing its significance, the clan is still an important institution in Haya culture, for example, in matters regarding land rights. The clan elders can, in effect, function as a court of law. They could easily reprimand younger clan mates when they think their behaviour is bad for the clan. Everybody wants to avoid falling out with their clan. 'Same clan' is a dummy, which is one if both households are of the same clan. We expect this dummy to have a positive sign.

10.2.6. *Education*

Do households link up with others who have the same educational achievement as them, or are insurance partners mixed in terms of education? With respect to this, note that there may be interhousehold externalities to education, which make it interesting for a non-educated person to befriend an educated person. Green *et al.* (1985) and Basu and Foster (1998) argue that the benefits of education are shared *within* the same household. For example, a literate family member may help a non-literate member to fill in a form or read a brochure left behind by the extension officer. Along the same line of thinking, households who have no literate members may find it interesting to befriend households with literate members. We create two dummy variables to test for the effect of education on link formation. The first dummy takes on a value of one when one household has no members who have completed primary and the other household has at least one member who has completed primary education. The second dummy indicates that neither of the two households have any household members who have completed primary education. The reference is the category in which both households have at least one educated member. Of course we have to bear in mind that education can proxy for other variables, like wealth.

10.2.7. *Activity Overlap*

Households who are engaged in similar activities are likely to have covariate income streams, which we expect to be an impediment to link formation. To test for this we create an index that measures how similar the income portfolio of two households is. All the income-generating activities the household engages in, were placed into seven categories (casual labour, trade, crop production, livestock rearing, assets, and processing farm produce, other off-farm activities). Each household can have several activities within the same category. By dividing the number of activities in each category by the total number of activities the household is engaged in, we get a rough measure of the spread of activities expressed in percentages of the total portfolio (it is only rough because we take no account of the income each activity generates). The activity overlap between two households is taken to be the sum of the minimum percentages in each category. For example, if the portfolio of A is (30, 0, 40, 0, 30, 0, 0 per cent) and of B is (0, 20, 70, 0, 10, 0, 0 per cent) then the overlap will be 0% + 0% + 40% + 0% + 10% + 0% + 0% = 50% . The overlap will always lie between 0 and 100 per cent. In our sample, the mean and median activity overlap are both 0.55 and the standard deviation is 0.25.

10.2.8. *Difference in the Age of the Household Heads*

We want to know whether insurance partners are chosen within one's own age category, outside one's own age category, or whether age does not matter. The neediness of a household and its possibilities to reciprocate in the future might depend on its age. We use the age of the household head to proxy for the age of the household. A possible measure of how heterogeneous two households are with respect to age is the age difference between the two heads.

10.2.9. *Differences in Wealth*

We would like to know whether networks form between households of similar wealth. If so, we expect that the wealth differences between two households have a negative effect on link formation. Table 10.5 shows the distribution of livestock and land differences across the dyads.

10.3. ECONOMETRIC ISSUES

This section first describes the three different sets of regressions that were performed on the data and then goes on to discuss possible problems of autocorrelation. In a first set of regressions we only enter relational variables. Still, attribute variables might play an important role in explaining the degree of connection between two households. For example, older households have had more time to build-up links, so we might expect them to have more links than younger households. In this case, not only the difference in age between the two households matters, but also the absolute age of both parties.

To control for all attribute variable we run a second set of regressions in which we control for household fixed effects. To this end we introduce a special kind of dummy variable. There are 119 of these dummies in total, one for each household in the sample, and each of them indicates whether that specific household is part of the pair or not. This means that every row of the data always contains two dummy variables equal to one (not taking account of the reference category). On the one hand, we control for observable attribute variables. For example, we will find that richer households typically have more links than poorer households. On the other hand, by including dummies we will also control for unobserved attribute variables. For example, a very communicative and cheerful person might be likely to have more links than an introvert. Related, how many network partners you choose, might be correlated with unobservables. Once dummies are included in the regression we have control for these effects.

We also run a third set of regressions in which, instead of entering dummies, we enter the maximum age of the household head, livestock value, landownership, and the number of respondents. This has essentially the same effect as the inclusion of the dummies. Now we do not perfectly control for all non-relational variables, but we do get information on which non-relational effects are at work. The number of respondents is entered to control for the fact that aggregating individual interviews to household level causes households with many respondents to have more links. The mean and median number of respondents is two. The distribution of the maximum values across dyads is summarized in Table 10.5.

Before reporting the regression results, we want to draw attention to the issue of autocorrelation. Say u_{ij} is the error term associated with the dyad formed by household i and household j. We should be particularly wary of possible correlation between u_{ij} and all $u_{.i}, u_{i.}, u_{.j}$, and $u_{j.}$ (i.e. all other dyads in which i or j appear). The unobserved attributes of i feature in the error terms of all the dyads containing i. For example, if household i consists of grumpy, ill-tempered individuals, then all other households may avoid having insurance links with them for reasons beyond anything we observe in the data. This would make all $u_{.i}$ and $u_{i.}$ correlated. Thus, in the first set of regressions which has no controls for attributes, autocorrelation may bias our results. In the second set of regressions, household fixed effects purges out the effects of all attribute variables and therefore eliminates the autocorrelation in the example.[7] In the third set of regressions, only observed attribute variables are controlled for. To be sure, even in the household fixed effects regressions we need to make an assumption about the

---

[7] In the literature on network analysis this autocorrelation problem has long been recognized and is solved by running QAP regression instead of using dummies (e.g. Krackhardt 1988).

error structure: the error terms of two dyads, which contain no mutual members are assumed to be uncorrelated to each other.

10.4. REGRESSION RESULTS

Tables 10.6–10.8 report the three different sets of regression results. The coefficients of the logit regressions in the third column of each table are marginal effects, so we can interpret them as the increase in probability of a link after a unitary increase in the explanatory variable at the sample mean. Throughout all the different regression specifications there are four variables which stand out because of the consistency of their sign and their high significance. These are the kinship dummies, the geographical distance, being of the same religious affiliation and the number of common friends.

Kinship has the strongest effect on link formation. Compared to having no blood bond, sharing 50 per cent of one's genetic material (parents, children, and siblings) raises the chances of having a link with 39 per cent in the household fixed effects logit regressions. As the genetic distance increases, the effect diminishes.

Increasing the distance between two households with 1 km, reduces the probability of having a link with approximately 9 per cent. Enforcement constraints seem to outweigh issues related to the non-covariance of income here. To put these numbers into perspective, remember that the two furthest neighbours in the village live 1.7 km away from each other.

It is common practice in economics to use the term 'the network of family, neighbours and friends'. Our results confirm that family and neighbours do indeed go far in explaining group formation. 'Friends', I believe, is supposed to be the rest-term for all who are neither neighbour nor kin, but still network members. The remainder of this section studies what the network looks like once kinship and geographical proximity are controlled for.

Being of the same religious affiliation has a significant, but small effect on network formation. Clan membership has no influence in the regressions which concentrate solely on direct links. This may be because there are 25 clans amongst 119 households, which leaves few possibilities for direct matching along clan lines. It is perhaps not surprising that the variable does become significant in the geodesic distance regression. Once we make more comprehensive use of the network graph, by also considering what lies *beyond the direct links* clan does become significant; that is, clan mates do lie closer to each other on the network graph. However, we should be cautious about this result as the significance disappears in the fixed effects regressions.

Having many common friends increases the possibility that two households are also linked. The size of this effect is smaller in the household fixed effects regression than in the others, which may indicate that it is correlated to unobserved fixed effects.

Both education dummies have negative coefficients. Although the effects only become significant in the geodesic distance regressions, the sign of the first education dummy does seem to suggest that households without any educated members avoid having insurance links with each other. At the same, the second education dummy tells us that dyads that are mixed in terms of education also have less chance of being

Table 10.6. *Regressions excluding attribute controls*

	Total no. of links reported by individuals (ordered logit)		Total no. of household level links (ordered logit)		Dummy (logit)[a]		Geodesic distance[b] (ordered logit)	
	Coeff.	p	Coeff.	p	Coeff.	p	Coeff.	p
Parents, children, and siblings	2.502	0.00	2.371	0.00	0.346	0.00	2.921	0.00
Nephews, nieces, uncles, aunts, cousins, grandparents, and grandchildren	1.497	0.00	1.468	0.00	0.129	0.00	1.132	0.00
Other blood bond	1.182	0.00	1.230	0.00	0.083	0.00	0.486	0.01
Distance (km)	−1.999	0.00	−2.003	0.00	−0.090	0.00	−0.763	0.00
No. of common friends	0.445	0.00	0.444	0.00	0.020	0.00	2.059	0.00
Same religion	0.344	0.00	0.336	0.00	0.016	0.00	0.147	0.00
Same clan	0.146	0.37	0.120	0.46	0.006	0.41	0.215	0.02
Neither of the two households has a member two who completed primary	−0.337	0.24	−0.413	0.15	−0.015	0.17	−0.717	0.00
Only one household has a member who completed primary	−0.167	0.14	−0.167	0.14	−0.007	0.14	−0.313	0.00
Activity overlap	−0.065	0.80	−0.063	0.81	−0.003	0.77	0.695	0.00
Difference in age of household head (10 years)	−0.087	0.03	−0.098	0.01	−0.004	0.02	0.005	0.79
Difference in livestock value (/100,000 TSh)	0.044	0.01	0.040	0.02	0.002	0.03	0.043	0.00
Difference in land (ha)	0.061	0.12	0.050	0.20	0.002	0.16	0.001	0.95
Pseudo R^2	0.16		0.17		0.20		0.24	
p-value of chi^2 test	0.00		0.00		0.00		0.00	
n	6,555		6,555		6,555		6,555	

[a] Marginal effects at the sample means.

[b] The coefficients in the ordered logit for geodesic distance have been multiplied by −1. This makes it easier to compare them to the coefficients from other regressions. Thus, a positive coefficient here means that the variable REDUCES the geodesic distance, that is, they are better connected.

Source: Nyakatoke Household Survey.

Table 10.7. *Regressions including attribute controls: household fixed effects*

	Total no. of links reported by individuals (ordered logit)		Total no. of household level links (ordered logit)		Dummy (logit)[a]		Geodesic distance[b] (ordered logit)	
	Coeff.	p	Coeff.	p	Coeff.	p	Coeff.	p
Parents, children, and siblings	2.880	0.00	2.739	0.00	0.391	0.00	3.277	0.00
Nephews, nieces, uncles, aunts, cousins, grandparents, and grandchildren	1.749	0.00	1.694	0.00	0.143	0.00	1.053	0.00
Other blood bond	1.387	0.00	1.426	0.00	0.087	0.00	0.560	0.00
Distance (km)	−2.641	0.00	−2.627	0.00	−0.092	0.00	−1.174	0.00
No. of common friends	0.210	0.00	0.203	0.00	0.008	0.00	1.775	0.00
Same religion	0.408	0.00	0.401	0.00	0.015	0.00	0.183	0.00
Same clan	0.130	0.46	0.081	0.65	0.003	0.70	0.026	0.80
Neither of the two households has a member who completed primary	−1.216	0.32	−1.239	0.31	−0.026	0.31	−3.652	0.00
Only one household has a member who completed primary	−0.613	0.31	−0.590	0.33	−0.019	0.33	−1.739	0.00
Activity overlap	−0.344	0.36	−0.321	0.39	−0.013	0.33	0.291	0.08
Difference in age of household head (10 years)	−0.151	0.00	−0.164	0.00	−0.005	0.00	−0.027	0.27
Difference in livestock value (/100,000 TSh)	−0.132	0.06	−0.169	0.02	−0.008	0.01	−0.051	0.51
Difference in land (ha)	−0.088	0.21	−0.095	0.18	−0.003	0.16	−0.025	0.52
Pseudo R^2	0.20		0.22		0.25		0.34	
p-value of chi^2 test	0.00		0.00		0.00		0.00	
n	6,555		6,555		6,555		6,555	

[a] Marginal effects at the sample means.
[b] The coefficients in the ordered logit for geodesic distance have been multiplied by −1. This makes it easier to compare them to the coefficients from other regressions. Thus, a positive coefficient here means that the variable REDUCES the geodesic distance, that is, they are better connected.
Source: Nyakatoke Household Survey.

Table 10.8. *Regressions including attribute controls: maximum values*

	Total no. of links reported by individuals (ordered logit)		Total no. of household level links (ordered logit)		Dummy (logit)[a]		Geodesic distance[b] (ordered logit)	
	Coeff.	p	Coeff.	p	Coeff.	p	Coeff.	p
Parents, children, and siblings	2.573	0.00	2.444	0.00	0.352	0.00	2.955	0.00
Nephews, nieces, uncles, aunts, cousins, grandparents, and grandchildren	1.549	0.00	1.517	0.00	0.135	0.00	1.150	0.00
Other blood bond	1.108	0.00	1.165	0.00	0.074	0.00	0.439	0.01
Distance (km)	−2.111	0.00	−2.114	0.00	−0.091	0.00	−0.790	0.00
No. of common friends	0.392	0.00	0.391	0.00	0.018	0.00	2.035	0.00
Same religion	0.357	0.00	0.350	0.00	0.016	0.00	0.153	0.00
Same clan	0.167	0.31	0.134	0.42	0.007	0.37	0.232	0.01
Neither of the two households has a member who completed primary	−0.194	0.52	−0.288	0.34	−0.009	0.42	−0.588	0.00
Only one household has a member who completed primary	−0.102	0.41	−0.113	0.36	−0.004	0.46	−0.221	0.00
Activity overlap	−0.087	0.74	−0.077	0.76	−0.004	0.70	0.689	0.00
Difference in age of household head (10 years)	−0.173	0.00	−0.194	0.00	−0.008	0.00	−0.054	0.05
Difference in livestock value (/100,000 TSh)	−0.182	0.14	−0.232	0.08	−0.015	0.02	−0.174	0.20
Difference in land (ha)	−0.286	0.00	−0.284	0.00	−0.012	0.00	−0.280	0.00
Maximum age of household head (10 years)	0.124	0.01	0.134	0.01	0.005	0.02	0.078	0.00
Maximum livestock value (/100,000 TSh)	0.205	0.09	0.252	0.05	0.016	0.01	0.201	0.14
Maximum land (ha)	0.320	0.00	0.309	0.00	0.013	0.00	0.257	0.00
Maximum no. of respondents	0.132	0.13	0.109	0.21	0.006	0.13	0.137	0.00

Table 10.8. (*Continued*)

	Total no. of links reported by individuals (ordered logit)		Total no. of household level links (ordered logit)		Dummy (logit)[a]		Geodesic distance[b] (ordered logit)	
	Coeff.	p	Coeff.	p	Coeff.	p	Coeff.	p
Pseudo R^2	0.17		0.18		0.21		0.25	
p-value of chi^2 test	0.00		0.00		0.00		0.00	
n	6,555		6,555		6,555		6,555	

[a] Marginal effects at the sample means.

[b] The coefficients in the ordered logit for geodesic distance have been multiplied by -1. This makes it easier to compare them to the coefficients from other regressions. Thus, a positive coefficient here means that the variable REDUCES the geodesic distance, that is, they are better connected.

Source: Nyakatoke Household Survey.

linked to each other. This implies that interhousehold externalities to education do not play a role in network formation. On the contrary, households with educated members seem to lie closer to each other on the network graph. We will find a similar result with respect to wealth.

The variable 'activity overlap' is significantly positive in the geodesic distance regressions, which suggests that non-covariance of income is less of an issue than information constraints here. The effect becomes smaller in the fixed effects regressions. The most likely cause of this difference is correlation between the fixed effects and the activity overlap. Households with many activities are likely to have a high activity overlap. At the same time, the regressions in Appendix 2 show that households with many activities have many links. Thus, in the regressions without attribute controls the activity overlap picks up some of the effect of the number of activities. Indeed, running the third set of regressions (attribute controls through maximum values) with a new variable 'maximum number of activities' included, gives results which are very similar to the fixed effects results (results are not shown). Still, it is worrying that in the regressions for direct links the effect of activity overlap is no longer significant. One reason might be that we have defined the income categories too broadly and that even within one category there might be very non-correlated income streams. Age differences between households have a very small, significant effect. There is a slight tendency for households to choose network partners close to their own age. In the third set of regressions, we see that the maximum age of the household has a small, but significant effect on link formation. This might be because older households have, through the years, established more links than younger households have.

The differences across households in livestock value and landholdings, are measures of how heterogeneous a pair of households is with respect to wealth. The coefficients are positive in the regressions without attribute controls. This would suggest that larger disparities in wealth enhance network formation and the network is redistributive. This is, however, not what is really going on. Fafchamps (1992) notes that wealthier people are more desirable to befriend and this is also apparent in the Nyakatoke data. The total number of links a household has correlates with its livestock and landholdings (regression results are given in Appendix 2, Table 10.A1): the rich have denser networks than the poor. This popularity effect implies that a dyad with a rich person in it has more chance of being linked. At the same time, such a dyad will also have a large wealth disparity. This is obviously so if the other half of the dyad is a poor person, but is also true in combination with another rich person, because of scale effects—in absolute terms the rich have bigger wealth gaps between each other than the poor.

Including household dummies purges the regression of household fixed effects, so also any popularity effect. We can see that all the wealth variables get reverse signs once dummies are included. Including the maximum (across the two households) livestock value or landholdings gives the same results, as they will also pick up any popularity effect of wealthy households. The picture we then get is that rich households choose each other as network partners, but poor households avoid each other as network partners.

10.5. CONCLUDING REMARKS

On the basis of household and network data collected in a Haya village in rural Tanzania, we found that kinship, geographical proximity, the number of common friends, clan membership, religious affiliation, and wealth strongly determine network formation.

We would like to point to some of the shortcomings of our analysis. First, we have excluded links to households living outside Nyakatoke and it is difficult to determine how this influences the results. Second, we conduct the analysis at household level, so we abstract from any intrahousehold issues. Third, the identification of which we call a network partner may depend on the framing of the question.

Insights in endogenous network formation are important for assessing vulnerability of households. A vulnerability assessment should distinguish between households that are likely to experience network shocks (everyone in their network is hit at the same time) and those who are not. Note that a shock might be common in the sense that everyone in the economy is hit (e.g. harvest failure in a large area), but still it can affect different networks in a different way. We might find that there are weak networks that collapse under this shock and strong networks that can cope with the shock. This is likely if households tend to link up with others of similar wealth, occupation, and place of residence.

Better insight in the determinants of group formation might also point to categories of vulnerable households who fail to enter into risk-sharing arrangements. Our data suggest that poor households have less dense networks than the rich, making them more vulnerable in the face of idiosyncratic risk.

Appendix

10.A1. *Appendix 1*

Figure 10.A1. *The network graph of Nyakatoke*

Note: Each dot is a household, each line a link. Households are *not* positioned according to geographical location. The map has been drawn using a programme called DOTTY from Graphiz.

10.A2. *Appendix 2*

Table 10.A1. *OLS for the total number of household links* (n = *116*)

	Coeff.	p-value of t-stat.	Coeff.	p-value of t-stat.	Coeff.	p-value of t-stat.
Constant	−1.037	0.56	0.443	0.80	0.502	0.77
No. of activities	0.376	0.02	0.554	0.00	0.539	0.00
One member completed primary	0.779	0.44	0.922	0.38	1.507	0.13
Age household head	0.059	0.02	0.063	0.02	0.069	0.01
Livestock[a]	0.652	0.00			0.760	0.00
Land	0.134	0.72	0.811	0.03		
No. of respondents	1.771	0.01				
R^2		0.35		0.23		0.28
p-value of F-stat.		0.00		0.00		0.00

[a] Coefficient multiplied by 100,000.

REFERENCES

Bala, V. and S. Goyal (2000). 'A Non-cooperative Model of Network Formation'. *Econometrica*, 68(5), 1181–229.

Basu, K. and J. Foster (1998). 'On Measuring Literacy'. *Economic Journal*, 108(451), 1733–49.

Coate, S. and M. Ravallion (1993). 'Reciprocity without Commitment: Characterisations and Performance of Informal Risk-sharing Arrangements'. *Journal of Development Economics*, 40, 1–24.

Fafchamps, M. (1992). 'Solidarity Networks in Preindustrial Societies: Rational Peasants with a Moral Economy'. *Economic Development and Cultural Change*, 41(1), 147–74.

—— and S. Lund (2000). 'Risk-sharing Networks in Rural Philippines', mimeo, Oxford University, Oxford.

Genicot, G. and D. Ray (2000). 'Endogenous Group Formation in Risk-sharing Arrangements', mimeo, University of California and New York University.

Goldstein, M. (2000). 'Intra-household Allocation and Farming in Southern Ghana'. Ph.D. dissertation, University of California, Berkeley.

Green, S., T. Rich, and E. Nesram (1985). 'Beyond Individual Literacy: The Role of Shared Literacy for Innovation in Guatemala'. *Human Organization*, 44, 313–21.

Grimard, F. (1997). 'Household Consumption Smoothing Through Ethnic Ties: Evidence from Côte d'Ivoire'. *Journal of Development Economics*, 53, 391–421.

Krackhardt, D. (1988). 'Predicting with Networks: Nonparametric Multiple Regression Analysis of Dyadic Data'. *Social Networks*, 10, 359–81.

Mitti, R. and T. Rweyemamu (2000). 'Taswira ya Kijamii na Kiuchumi ya Kitongoji Nyakatoke', mimeo, KU Leuven.

Murgai, R., P. Winters, E. Sadoulet, and A. de Janvry (2000). 'Localized and Incomplete Mutual Insurance', mimeo, World Bank and University of New England and University of California.

Platteau, J. P. (1991). 'Traditional Systems of Social Security and Hunger Insurance: Past Achievements and Modern Challenges', in E. Ahmad, J. Drèze, J. Hills, and A. Sen (eds), *Social Security in Developing Countries*. Oxford: Clarendon Press, pp. 112–70.

Reining, P. (1967). 'The Haya: The Agrarian System of a Sedentary People'. Ph.D. dissertation, University of Chicago, Chicago, IL.

Spinnewyn, F. and M. Wijaya (1996). 'Voluntary Reciprocity and Income Mobility'. *CES Discussion Paper*. KU Leuven.

Wasserman, S. and K. Faust (1995). *Social Network Analysis*. Cambridge: Cambridge University Press.

11

Is a Friend in Need a Friend Indeed? Inclusion and Exclusion in Mutual Insurance Networks in Southern Ghana

MARKUS GOLDSTEIN, ALAIN DE JANVRY, AND
ELISABETH SADOULET

11.1. THE PUZZLE OF INCOMPLETE INSURANCE IN VILLAGE COMMUNITIES

Theory predicts that, when there is perfect information and perfect enforcement, risk-averse members of a community that face risks in their sources of income should engage in mutual insurance to completely insure idiosyncratic income shocks. If it holds true, changes in individual consumption across states of nature would be unaffected by changes in individual income and proportional to changes in average community consumption. Empirical tests of this hypothesis have rejected full insurance, but they have also shown that some degree of mutual insurance does indeed exist (Deaton 1992; Townsend 1994; Gertler and Gruber 1997). This has opened the door to a series of analyses to find out: what limits complete insurance, and; who gets to be included and excluded in mutual insurance schemes.

Analyses of factors that limit the quality of insurance have focused on problems of monitoring and enforcement. If there are observability problems, households have private information that cannot be obtained by their insurance partners. Ligon (1998) shows that, in this case, inducing truthful revelation and a high level of effort requires a contract that offers a higher utility for revealed good outcomes than for bad ones, and therefore results in less than full insurance in some states of nature. Unless this

We thank Stefan Dercon, Michael Kevane, Loïc Sadoulet, Chris Udry, and seminar participants at LSE and UNU-WIDER for useful comments. Markus Goldstein thanks STICERD for support during the writing phase of this project. Data collection was funded by the National Science Foundation (SBR-9617694), the Fulbright Commission, the World Bank Research Committee, the International Food Policy Research Institute, the Institute for the Study of World Politics, the Social Science Research Council, and the Institute of Industrial Relations at UC Berkeley. The data collection team was led by Ernest Appiah and consisted of Robert Ernest Afedoe, Patrick Selorm Amihere, Esther Aku Sarquah, Kwabena Moses Agyapong, Esther Nana Yaa Adofo, Michael Kwame Arhin, Margaret Harriet Yeboah, Issac Yaw Omane, Peter Ansong-Manu, Ishmaelina Borde-Koufie, Owusu Frank Abora, and Rita Allotey.

is done, partial insurance will be observed at the community level. If there are enforcement problems, binding commitments cannot be specified, and insurance partners must rely on self-enforcing agreements. In this case, risk-sharing will be incomplete in states of nature with large shocks since a household will only provide a transfer if the discounted expected future benefits from participating in the insurance agreement exceed the one-time gains from defection (Kimball 1988; Coate and Ravallion 1993). As an alternative to self-enforcement, transfers can be secured by incurring extraction costs. If these costs are variable, increasing with the level of transfer requested from partners, the community may choose partial insurance as the optimum level of insurance (Murgai *et al.* 2002).

Mutual insurance may, however, be practiced over networks of individuals other than the community as a whole, raising the question of who insures with whom, and if some individuals are left uninsured, who are the included and who are the excluded. To answer this question, research has focused on identifying the configuration of networks of reciprocal exchange between self-selected individuals (Platteau 1991; Fafchamps 1992; Fafchamps and Lund 2000). When there are association costs, insurance may be better provided in small sub-coalitions of individuals with high levels of insurance as they have low extraction costs (Murgai *et al.* 2002). Empirical studies show that these groups tend to form on the basis of a number of criteria including kinship, neighbourhood, ethnicity (Grimard 1997), and gender (Goldstein 2000). If mutual insurance is only practiced among members of sub-coalitions, leaving some individuals outside insurance networks, tests of mutual insurance at the community level will show imperfect insurance.

This broad characterization of the formation of networks and sub-coalitions is, however, not fine enough to predict inclusion and exclusion of specific individuals in a community. This is serious if the excluded are vulnerable poor people left without insurance coverage. Inclusion/exclusion should be looked at from the angle of individuals in need of insurance because they have been exposed to a shock, which they are not fully able to absorb themselves. As a consequence, they find themselves short of cash to cover specific expenditures, either to meet household needs or to acquire personal items. This is what we study in this chapter.

Critical to undertaking this task is an understanding of the social connections that underpin networks and social coalitions, and thus the next section frames the hypotheses we examine using anthropological work done on the area under study. Section 11.3 discusses the data we use for our analysis. Section 11.4 lays out the logical framework we use to organize the empirical analysis. We then proceed in Section 11.5 to analyse econometrically the responses obtained by a person short of cash for the desired purchase of a household item. The same analysis is repeated in Section 11.6 for the desired purchase of a personal item. In Section 11.7, we analyse the differential quality of insurance among those we have identified as included in insurance networks versus the rest of the population. We characterize the coping mechanisms which, in the end, are being used by different categories of households to cope with shocks. We also look at the differences in access to insurance for the poor and the non-poor. Section 11.8 concludes.

11.2. FRAMING THE QUESTION

Answering the question of inclusion–exclusion at the individual level takes us into psychological analysis of the relations among individuals in a household, and sociological analysis of the relations between individuals in a community. We investigate two hypotheses:

H1: In a traditional agrarian community, many individuals who are short of cash to meet an expenditure do not ask their spouse for help, and some who ask do not get it. When this happens, this is due to poor marital relationships as perceived by the demanding party for asking, and as measured by the difference in perceptions between spouses for receiving help.

H2: Many individuals who are short of cash do not ask others or do not obtain help from others. When this happens, this is due to lack of social capital or to fear of social stigma and loss of reputation if they ask.

Our grounding for these hypotheses draws on the anthropological literature that analyses how networks of individuals form and what the functions of these networks are. The primary 'network' is composed of spouses. In a Western perspective, we may expect the household to be the logical unit of insurance, given the communal nature of many expenses and the ease with which spouses can observe each other's activities. However, evidence from Ghana and nearby countries seems to indicate that this is not the case—West African households tend to operate more as a collection of separate individual economies. For example, Vercruijsse *et al.* (1974) discuss the coastal Fante communities in Ghana.[1] They note that 'women are economically active in their own right as much as the men are and this is not affected by being married and having children. Accordingly, their income does not have the character of a supplement and cannot even be conceived as being part of "family income"' (1974: 36). Numerous writers such as Kwamena Poh (1974) argue that, for the Akan (the dominant ethnic group in the study area), marriage is an economic and procreative 'contract', not a spiritual union. Oppong, characterizing the traditional Akan norm of marriage, notes that: 'according to custom, the Akan husband and wife do not own, manage, or inherit together any exclusive or substantial property of their own' (1974: 328). She finds (in her sample of civil servant couples) that

more than twice as many husbands own property together with their kin as with their wives, and fewer than one in ten couples have joint accounts. . ... The new urban norm thus follows the traditional pattern to some extent in that responsibility for day to day maintenance of the family seems to be shared by most husbands and wives, while the majority maintain separate financial arrangements for spending, owning, and saving (1974: 329–330).[2]

---

[1] While the area under study is composed primarily of Akwapim Akan, there has probably been some Fante influence.

[2] Oppong is studying civil servants. We might expect them to be the most divergent from the Akan tradition of separate economies, both because of their relatively observable salaries and their urban/'modern' lifestyles. The fact that they are not is evidence of the deep-seated nature of this feature of marital relations.

This practice of maintaining separate economies while jointly providing for communal consumption can be a source of significant frictions. Oppong, in documenting economic practices among civil servants in Accra, writes that:

In discussions, spouses commonly state that they insulate most of their cash and property dealings from observation and control by their partners on purpose.... In some cases, the separation of interests is itself a matter of mutual agreement by husbands and wives, who consider the arrangement to be the most suitable adaptation to their domestic situation. In other cases, the arrangement is a continual source of friction, each spouse repeatedly attempting to gain more knowledge of and control over the other's spending (1974: 330).

While we will not be able to explain why levels of friction differ among spouses, we will examine their implications for the provision of assistance from one spouse to the other.

A natural venue for insurance outside of the household is the ethnic group. Indeed, this was the approach taken by Grimard (1997) in a study of mutual insurance in Côte d'Ivoire. He found that mutual insurance, even if only partial, is practiced among members of a same ethnic group. The area under study here is fairly homogenous in terms of ethnic groups—most of the respondents are Akwapim, a subgroup of the Akan. Within the Akan, however, the lineage has a central role in social life. As Smith (1972: 113) puts it, 'whatever he wishes to do in life, the Akan turns to his lineage (*abusua*) for help; kindred consciousness is the most important fact in his life'. These lineages are matrilineal; a child belongs to the lineage of his or her mother. Some authors (e.g. Fortes 1950) argue that it is the clan's association with local chiefs (often the chief was the head of the dominant clan) that was the most relevant unit of government in the Ashanti confederacy. In addition to political association, the lineage is an important locus of economic rights. For example, the traditional form of access to land was through the lineage, and property was passed to matrikin, not to one's own children (who would presumably inherit from their mother's brothers). The economic and political rights conferred by lineage may also be useful in building the stock of social capital, which enables individuals to command assistance from others than kin.

Lineages may also provide insurance directly as they provide a strong social network in times of trouble. Brokensha (1972: 78) explains that 'we are concerned with this lineage, which is most important in matters of land tenure, inheritance, and any sort of "trouble", including debt, arrest by the police, help in school fees, or finding employment'. Fortes documents the role of lineage in providing assistance in times of trouble:

Ashanti link this with the obligation of the lineage to help a member who is in debt or extreme distress. A lineage could not and cannot be held responsible for the private debts of any of its members. But it is incumbent on the head to take action to save a member from being driven to desperation by debt or misfortune (Fortes 1969: 188).

Using the broad definition of these lineages, the resulting groups are generally quite large. While there is some debate in the literature about this, there are probably less than ten of these that encompass the Ashanti population. Such dispersed groups are probably not the relevant unit for an analysis of local economic activity. Fortes provides some insight into how these units may be disaggregated when he writes, 'the lineage has a segmentary structure, each segment being defined in relation to other segments of a like order by reference to common and to differentiating ancestresses. This allows of both accretion to and differentiation within lineages' (Fortes 1950: 255).

This local segmentation is particularly important for informal insurance. Fortes writes that 'mutual aid—as when a member gets into debt or funeral expenses have to be met—is extended throughout the lineage, but the heaviest responsibility falls on this segment' (1950: 257). The local segment that he refers to is descendents of four to five generations from the same ancestresses.[3]

Fortes' characterization of local segments seems to be what we observe in the villages under study here. He notes that there are generally two or three dominant lineages in a village which account for about half of the population. This is roughly in accordance with what we observed in our four village clusters. Based on the evidence above, we can expect these local lineages to serve as networks that provide assistance to members.

In addition to the spouse and the lineage, membership in a variety of social organizations may be important as they either provide insurance directly (see Goldstein 2000 for an example of the importance of these groups) or serve as vehicles that build the stock of social capital used in securing insurance (e.g. reputational effects for contract formation). Some data on the purpose and structure of organizations were collected from these villages but they do not provide us with enough information to differentiate organizations along these lines. Hence, in the analysis that follows, we will use total organizational membership rather than membership in a specific organization.

11.3. DATA

The data we use come from a two-year household survey carried out from November 1996 to October 1998 in the Akwapim south district of the eastern region of Ghana. Initially, four village clusters were selected based on their varying degree of market integration and diverse cropping patterns. As we will use social indicators in our analysis, it is worth discussing the history of these villages in some detail. 'Village 1' is a pair of adjacent villages 5 km west of the large market town of Nsawam. Both villages were settled by Ashanti migrants during the 1850s. 'Village 2' lies about 15 km east of Nsawam and 6 km southwest of Aburi (an older larger town that was home to one of the first Christian missions in Ghana) on a road joining the two large towns. It is made up of two towns, 150 and 80 years old that joined together 50 years ago. This village has the largest population of the four clusters with about 2030 people.[4]

---

[3] As regards to terminology, Fortes (1950) and Brokensha (1972) state that the Twi word *abusua* denotes both the larger lineage and the more local clan segment, while Ayisi (1974) provides a technical discussion of the nomenclature. Fortes (1969) provides a detailed discussion of the political and social organization of the lineage.

[4] Population figures are calculated using the number of houses multiplied by the average household size (5.6) in our data, adjusted for a joint occupancy rate of 37 per cent (Ghana Statistical Service 1995) in this region.

Eight kilometres north of Village 2 (and, at the time of the survey, a 45 min journey by vehicle) lies 'Village 3'. It is made up of a central town and two surrounding hamlets. The central town is fairly small (population is around 340) and it is the youngest of our four villages as it was settled in 1939. People were farming this area long before, however, as one of the neighbouring hamlets (population 110) was settled 200 years ago. With limited access to non-farm income opportunities, Village 3 is by far the most agriculturally active community among the four. Three kilometres south of Aburi, and 2 km from the road from Aburi to the capital of Accra, is 'Village 4'. Settled in 1821, it has a population of around 990 people today. Twenty-five years ago, cocoa farming was the major livelihood in Village 4, and the village was fairly well off. Today, no one is growing cocoa and farming has shifted to food crops. Despite this shift in agricultural income, the village has continued to grow, nearly doubling in size since the early 1970s.[5]

Within each village cluster, sixty married couples or triples were selected at random for the survey.[6] Men and women were interviewed separately by an enumerator of the same gender. The survey was conducted in fifteen rounds, about four to six weeks apart during 1996–8. A common set of agricultural questions was asked at each round and specialized modules (including on expenditures, shocks, transfers, and social interactions) were asked during different rounds. Information on the data and questionnaires is available at www.econ.yale.edu/~udry/ghanadata.html.

The data that we use in this chapter are mainly drawn from the later rounds of the survey (rounds 14 and 15) when respondents were given a detailed transfers questionnaire. This questionnaire (which evolved from round 14 to round 15 but contains a core set of questions asked of each respondent in each round) gives us a detailed characterization of:

- Who in the community is, at a particular moment, short of cash to meet expenditures to acquire household items and personal items?
- Whether a person in this situation asks for assistance from his/her spouse or not.
- Whether a person in this situation asks for assistance from someone besides his or her spouse.
- Whether a person who asked for assistance from his or her spouse gets approved or rejected.
- What are the coping instruments that a particular person short of cash uses in addition to transfers from their spouse, family members, or friends?

To complement this information, we also use data from earlier rounds that give us a characterization of the quality of spousal relations. These relations are characterized under a number of aspects. Importantly, they are appraised separately by each side of the relation, which allows us to characterize how one party to the relation assesses its quality, and also how this quality assessment diverges between the two parties.

---

[5] These histories are based on information from the village level questionnaires that also include social organizations, market infrastructure, and political and social organizations.
[6] About 5–10 per cent of the households in the sample are polygamous.

The variables on which we have information indicate the degree of trust each member has in the other, the degree to which the respondent thinks that his or her spouse treats him or her fairly, how well the respondent is getting along with her or his spouse, and whether there is a history of domestic violence in the relationship or not. Aside from domestic violence, which is binary, all relationship variables are ranked on a 1–5 scale, with 5 being the best.

We also use two other questionnaires for information on the social standing and interactions of individuals. The family background questionnaire provides us with a large number of variables that characterize the individual's social standing in the community. We add to this data using one of the learning questionnaires. In an effort to understand how agricultural technology was spread through these villages, respondents were asked if they knew seven people in the community selected at random. We use this to measure the probability that the individual knows any other individual in the village. We also know how often they talk with these individuals, so we can construct a variable of intensity of social interactions using these data.

11.4. A PROPOSED LOGICAL FRAMEWORK TO ANALYSE RESPONSES TO A CASH SHORTAGE

This section lays out the framework we use to analyse how people go about securing assistance. The way in which the questionnaire was structured was to elicit who provided the assistance in times of shortage, but not the order in which the consultations occurred (asking the spouse first, then others, or the reverse). Hence, part of our task will be to examine alternate structures of this process. Before turning to this problem, we examine in greater depth the determinants of who is short of funds in an effort to map the realized shortage to some of the underlying processes that may have caused it.

11.4.1. *Understanding Who is Short of Cash*

We start by discussing what may cause the declared shortage and by speculating on how the respondent's report of a shortage is associated with unexpected income shocks. Reports of shortages come from the transfers' questionnaires where respondents were asked if they have been short of cash to buy a household or a personal item. This shortage could come from a number of causes (e.g. idiosyncratic income shocks, consumption smoothing difficulties, and the like) so our first task is to see if we can shed light on the causes and correlates of the shortage.

Table 11.1 provides a probit estimate of who is short of cash when needing to buy an item for the household. In addition to the village dummies, the two significant variables are a measure of agricultural shocks (lagged one survey round, about six weeks) and the level of personal wealth. The agricultural shock variable indicates that some of the reported shortages are due to the unexpected income shocks we associate with conventional insurance tests. The fact that wealth is negative and significant is

Table 11.1. *Explaining who is short of cash to buy a household item*

Variables	dF/dx	P > |z|	Mean
Income shock			
Value of damage due to agricultural shock (10^6 cedis)	0.07	0.08	0.0063
Individual asset position			
Size of inherited land area (ha)	0.06	0.11	0.19
Size of land area anticipated to be inherited (ha)	0.05	0.41	0.06
Number of plots owned	−0.01	0.50	3.50
Value of non-land assets (10^6 cedis)	−0.01	0.01	0.75
Received other assistance to get started = 1	0.05	0.30	0.19
Individual characteristics			
Gender: female = 1	−0.04	0.35	0.52
Has other sources of income = 1	−0.04	0.21	0.52
Household characteristics			
Member of major village clan = 1	0.03	0.41	0.47
Location			
Village 2 = 1	−0.06	0.28	0.23
Village 3 = 1	0.19	0.00	0.27
Village 4 = 1	0.16	0.00	0.24
Goodness-of-fit			
n	743		
Pseudo R^2	0.07		

Probit analysis, sequence SO, node SO1.
Dependent variable: individual is (yes/no) short for the purchase of a household item.

Table 11.2. *Reasons for being short of household item* (n = 212)

Reason	Percentage of responses
Did not sell crops	28
Illness (other family members)	12
Crop was not ready when expected (delayed harvest)	11
Unexpected loss in business	10
Did not get paid for work when expected	7
Illness (self)	7
Unexpected household expense	7
Other	18

consistent with general difficulties with consumption smoothing for individuals with lower levels of liquid assets.

We can also get a sense as to the cause of these shortages by asking the respondents directly. Table 11.2 presents their answers. These responses are broadly consistent with our probit results. Respondents indicate that shortages come from not having

Table 11.3. *Incidence of cash shortage to buy household and personal items (percentage of total,* n = *799 observations)*

		Household item		
		No	Yes	Total
Personal item	No	65.7	7.6	73.3
	Yes	20.4	6.3	26.7
	Total	86.1	13.9	100

sold crops (28 per cent) and delayed harvest (11 per cent). But they also show that the realm of income shocks is wider than just agriculture—shocks associated with illness (12 per cent) and losses in non-farm businesses (10 per cent) are important.

Respondents were asked separately if they were short of cash when they needed to buy an item for themselves. Table 11.3 presents the results of a cross tabulation of the responses to this and the household item shortage. Data show that, while some respondents were short for both household and individual items (6.3 per cent), many were short for only one or the other (with household items dominating (20.4 per cent)). This separation of types of shortages gives a preliminary indication that it is worth considering the two events separately.

Table 11.4 provides a probit estimate of who is short of cash to buy a personal item. In these results, agricultural shocks are not a significant predictor, but individual wealth and whether or not the respondent had received financial assistance from their family or parents in starting their household are.[7] Table 11.5 shows the respondents' explanations of why they were short. As with household items, the main reason is that they did not sell crops, either because of a marketing failure or a crop failure. Self-illness seems to play a more important role than it does in the household item shortage. There is also a larger dispersion across different minor reasons leading to a large group of 'other' responses.

We thus conclude by observing that individuals self-declare as being short of cash in meeting an expenditure when they were exposed to a shock that they were not able to cope with through their own accumulated wealth. Agricultural shocks play a major role in creating a shortage to meet an expenditure for a household item, and self-illness is particularly important in creating a shortage for individual items. Having established the origins of shortages, we now proceed to study how individuals use mutual insurance with kin and others to cope with these two types of shortages.

11.4.2. *Frameworks for Analysis*

We have seen that individuals face a number of causes of financial shortfalls that create unexpected variations in their consumption. The question is: how do they

---

[7] For both Tables 11.1 and 11.4 we are unable to test for reported illness as a cause of the shortage as the timing of our illness data (other than that reported as a direct cause of the shortage) does not coincide with the two rounds of shortage reports. Our agricultural shock data spans the entire survey.

Table 11.4. *Explaining who is short of cash to buy a personal item*

Variables	dF/dx	P > |z|
Income shock		
Value of damage due to agricultural shock (10^6 cedis)	0.02	0.33
Individual asset position		
Size of inherited land area (ha)	0.03	0.21
Size of land area anticipated to be inherited (ha)	0.03	0.51
Number of plots owned	0.01	0.04
Value of non-land assets (10^6 cedis)	−0.00	0.01
Received other assistance to get started = 1	−0.05	0.04
Individual characteristics		
Gender: female = 1	−0.01	0.92
Has other sources of income = 1	0.01	0.67
Household characteristics		
Member of major village clan = 1	−0.00	0.85
Location		
Village 2 = 1	−0.01	0.41
Village 3 = 1	0.32	0.00
Village 4 = 1	0.20	0.00
Goodness-of-fit		
n	741	
Pseudo R^2	0.20	

Probit analysis, sequence SO, SO1.
Dependent variable: individual is (yes/no) short for the purchase of a personal item.

Table 11.5. *Respondents' reasons for being short of cash for self-items (n = 111)*

Reason	Percentage of responses
Did not sell crops	32
Illness (self)	13
Did not get paid for work when expected	7
Did not get expected job	7
Crop was not ready when expected (delayed harvest)	6
Unexpected loss in business	6
Other	29

cope? We examine what would appear to be a likely option: transfers from spouse and/or from others who are members of their social networks. Figures 11.1 and 11.2 show the outcomes of the process of requesting assistance, combining data from both round 14 and round 15. Figure 11.1 provides the data for cash shortages to acquire a

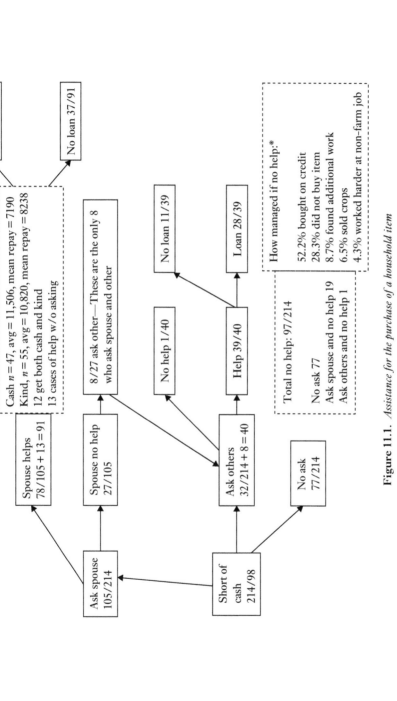

Figure 11.1. *Assistance for the purchase of a household item*

* Based on questions in Round 15 only with 402 observations.

Note: Rounds 14 and 15, 245 households; 798 observations.

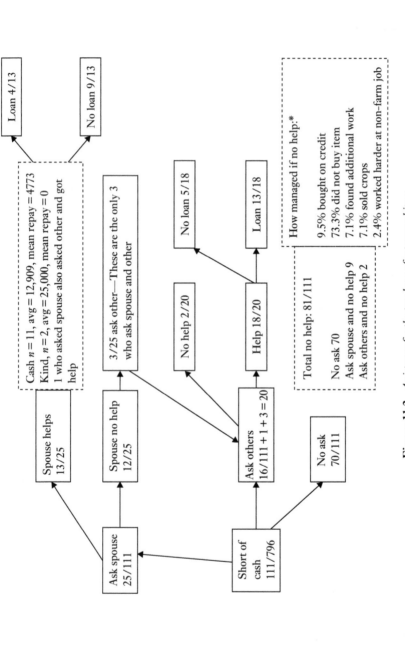

Figure 11.2. *Assistance for the purchase of a personal item*

* Based on questions in Round 15 only with 402 observations.

Note: Rounds 14 and 15, 245 households; 796 observations.

household item, by individual respondent.[8] Figure 11.2 provides similar information for cash shortages to acquire a personal item. The figures below each response or action are the number of observations we have at each point. They provide an overview of how the requests and responses are distributed across the types of items.

The data show that being short of cash is a frequent state of nature. On average, 26.8 per cent of the observations show a shortfall for household expenditures and 13.9 per cent for personal expenditures. A total of 34 per cent of the households experienced a shortage of some type, including 6 per cent who were short of cash for both types of expenditures.

Among the 214 cases where respondents were short of cash for household items, 49.1 per cent asked their spouse for help, 18.7 per cent asked others (some asked both), and 36 per cent did not ask anyone (Figure 11.1). Of those who asked their spouse for help, 74.3 per cent received the assistance they were requesting. The data indicate that only one person who asked for assistance for a household item from persons other than his or her spouse was turned down. Ultimately, only 54.7 per cent of those who were short of cash for a household item received assistance. Of the 45.3 per cent who did not get help, 79.4 per cent did not ask and 20.6 per cent asked but were turned down.

There are 111 cases of individuals reporting a shortage of cash needed to acquire a personal item (Figure 11.2). Of those, 22.5 per cent asked their spouse for assistance, 18 per cent asked others, and 63.1 per cent did not ask anyone. Of those who asked their spouse for assistance, only 52 per cent received help. Between those who got assistance from spouses and from others, only 27 per cent of those in need received transfers.

We can thus safely conclude that mutual insurance systems through transfers do not work for all individuals in need: 45 per cent of those short of cash to acquire a household item and 73 per cent for a personal item did not receive assistance, either because the individual did not ask for help, or because the demand was denied. Note that not asking largely reflects internalizing rejection, or not wanting to incur the transactions costs associated with asking, as opposed to being able to cope through one's own accumulated wealth since the individual declared being short of cash. Not asking, like having one's request rejected, reflects the failure of deriving benefit from mutual insurance when in need. Showing the relative urgency of needs, assistance for shortfalls to buy household items is more prevalent than for personal items. With such a large gap in coverage, it is important to explain who is successful in getting assistance and who is not, and from what source the assistance comes for those who succeed.

We also need to understand (at least from an econometric standpoint) how individuals go about making their requests for assistance. In our data, we observe that individuals do not obtain assistance from both spouse and community members, but from either one or the other. Based on this, we can postulate two decision trees in seeking assistance. One is to proceed first with asking the spouse and then, if rejected, asking other community members. In this case, we have the sequence spouse-others (SO) in Figure 11.3 the alternative is to first ask others. If this fails, the individual

---

[8] Each individual reported the number of times he/she was short. These figures define an individual as short of cash if he or she reported at least one shortage.

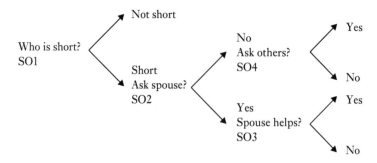

Figure 11.3. *Decision nodes in sequence (SO)*

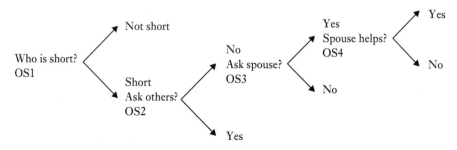

Figure 11.4. *Decision nodes in sequence (OS)*

can then turn to his/her spouse in a quest for help. In this case, we have the sequence others-spouse (OS) in Figure 11.4.

11.4.3. *The Empirical Strategy*

Given that there are very few observations of assistance being requested from both the spouse and others, we estimate both decision trees portrayed in Figures 11.3 and 11.4. In our initial examination of the data, we suspected that selection bias might be a problem. Running the different nodes as selection bias corrected probits, however, yielded the result that the errors between the selection and the final probit were nowhere significantly different from zero.[9] Moreover, the general tenor of the selection corrected results were the same as those discussed here. Hence, we report the uncorrected probits in what follows.

It also might be that both decisions are taken simultaneously, not sequentially. The most general representation of this is a bivariate probit of the two decisions. This model would allow for all four options in asking for help: asking spouse, asking others, asking both, or asking no one. Table 11.6 shows the results when we compare the log

[9] Note that the different sets of variables in each regression allow sufficient flexibility to identify the first stage in all cases.

Table 11.6. *Comparison of alternate decision structures*

	Likelihood ratios	
	Help asked for household item	Help asked for personal item
Bivariate probit	−1,130	−42.6
Sequential decision		
SO	−1,078	−41.1
OS	−1,040	−41.8

likelihood of the bivariate estimate with the two different sequential models. As can be seen, the sequential models give a slightly better fit. In addition, the bivariate results indicate that the same coefficients are significant as in the sequential models. Hence, in what follows, we will report the results of the two sequential models, indicating differences across the two models when appropriate.

11.5. RESPONSES TO A CASH SHORTAGE FOR HOUSEHOLD ITEMS

11.5.1. *Requests to the Spouse*

Table 11.7 shows the results of probit estimates of asking or not the spouse for assistance conditional on being short of cash for a household item. It corresponds to node SO2 in Figure 11.3.

In an effort to get a qualitative feel for how respondents viewed their union, we asked whether they trusted their spouse, how fairly they thought their spouse treated them, and how well they got along overall. We have included these variables in the regression in an effort to measure some of the intangibles of the recent history of the relationship.[10] One of the more striking result is the fact that better quality of spousal relations (as perceived by the respondent who is facing a cash shortage) are significantly associated with an increased probability of asking the spouse. This is true at the 1 per cent significance level for fairness, trust, and overall getting along. Domestic violence is less robust, showing an effect only at the 9 per cent significance level and it is not significant in the estimation of node OS3.

How should we understand these results? Before turning to any interpretation, we need to address the potential for endogeneity. Indeed, the most obvious explanation for these results is that the quality of relationship variables are determined by the response of the spouse to the request for help. While this critique is more germane to the next section where we discuss the spouse's response, we are partially protected from this

---

[10] We should note that these responses seem to be correlated with gender and village and hence we control for these effects (possibly in the administration of the questionnaire) with the inclusion of gender and village dummies. There is also some degree of collinearity among the reports of these variables, which is why we include each one in a separate regression.

source of endogeneity though the use of marital quality data from the round preceding the two rounds in which we measure shortages.

One explanation for not asking for help when spousal relations are poor is that the respondent is less likely to ask a spouse because he/she assumes that the spouse holds the same view and he/she will be turned down. Another explanation is that the respondent does not take his/her spouse's views of the relationship into account, but will not ask because of fears that the bad state of trust or unfair relations will lead to problems with reciprocity in the future. Yet, another explanation is simultaneity—that the marital quality variables are indicative of the failure of a larger process that drives insurance-type transfers by spouses, be it a commitment failure, the outcome of a non-cooperative bargaining process, or the like. The problem with this result is one highlighted by Manski (2000)—while we can show a correlation with the state of relations, we cannot isolate the cause of the state of relations and rule out alternate explanations.

Another factor that is important in determining whether or not the spouse is asked for assistance is ownership of non-land assets. This measure of wealth encompasses a wide range of assets including traditional cloth, livestock, and farm equipment (but not cash, where we failed to get reliable data). We might expect that, if there is a cost associated with asking for assistance, individuals prefer to use their own assets rather than seek assistance. Results show that wealthier individuals are less likely to ask their spouse for assistance. This result confirms that declaring oneself short of cash for an expenditure is *ex post* relative to using one's own instruments for coping. The probability of asking is also increasing in the wealth of the spouse. This result that individual asset positions matter is consistent with the separateness of spouse's economic lives highlighted by the anthropological literature on this area.[11]

Table 11.7 also indicates that two other factors are related to seeking assistance from the spouse. First, women are more likely to ask their spouse for assistance than men. This is consistent with their roles as coordinators of much of the expenditures on children and household meals. Second, is the somewhat puzzling result that the longer a couple has been married, the less likely the respondent is to seek help from his or her spouse. This would suggest either increased separation in economic activities and insurance networks over the course of a relationship, or that the need to ask decreases during the course of the relationship, perhaps because we did not fully account for the accumulation of own assets. The results in the next section will shed some further light on this issue.

We thus conclude that who asks for help to a spouse when short of cash to meet an expenditure for a household item can be explained by a number of factors. One major factor is the quality of the relationship with the spouse as seen by the one who would be asking. Also important is the relative wealth position of the partners. Finally, women are more likely to ask their spouse than men when the household is in need. Who asks is thus characterized by considerable heterogeneity across individuals, explaining both inclusion and exclusion from mutual insurance schemes.

---

[11] Although not reported here, spouse shocks were not significant.

Table 11.7. *Explaining who asks spouse for money when short of cash to buy household item*

Variables	dF/dx	P > |z|
Individual asset position		
Value of non-land assets (10^6 cedis)	−0.01	0.05
Individual characteristics		
Quality of marital relations as seen by the demanding party: fair	0.17	0.00
Gender: female = 1	0.17	0.10
Household characteristics		
Value of spouse assets (10^6 cedis)	0.03	0.01
Years married	−0.01	0.01
Number of household members	−0.03	0.05
Location		
Village 2 = 1	−0.39	0.00
Village 3 = 1	−0.34	0.01
Village 4 = 1	−0.65	0.00
Goodness-of-fit		
n	174	
Pseudo R^2	0.29	
Partial results with other variables characterizing the quality of marital relations as seen by the demanding party		
Trust	0.17	0.00
Get along	0.19	0.00
Domestic violence = 1	−0.17	0.09

Probit analysis, sequence SO, node SO2.
Dependent variable: individual asks spouse for money (yes/no) when short of cash to purchase a household item.

11.5.2. *Who Gets Help from His/Her Spouse?*

In the majority of cases where the spouse is asked for help for a household item, he or she delivers (74 per cent). Table 11.8 shows the results of probit estimations of a spouse's positive response for the SO sequence.

In explaining success in getting help, we use the absolute difference between the perceived quality of marital relation as seen by each spouse. These differences can be interpreted in various ways. For example, the difference in 'getting along' (the answer to the question 'over all, how well do you get along with your spouse') is illustrative of communication—the answer would be determined by how well the respondent saw the relationship and this would depend on perception of the spouse's views. Answer to the questions on 'how fair' the spouse treats the respondent and how much the respondent trusts his/her spouse are more indicative of a psychological asymmetry in the relationship—these are answers that are not likely to be tainted by the respondent's perception of the spouse's view of the relationship.

Estimates from both decision trees (nodes SO3 in Table 11.8 and OS4 (not reported)) indicate that the difference in perceived fairness of treatment is significantly negatively

Table 11.8. *Explaining whether spouse helped with cash when asked for a household item*

Variables	dF/dx	P > |z|
Income shock		
Value of damage due to agricultural shock (10^6 cedis)	−1.80	0.30
Individual characteristics		
Gender: female = 1	0.05	0.67
Household characteristics		
Absolute difference in spouses' perceptions of fairness	−0.08	0.04
Value of spouse assets (10^6 cedis)	0.00	0.76
Years married	0.01	0.17
Location		
Village 2 = 1	−0.14	0.07
Village 3 = 1	−0.09	0.46
Village 4 = 1	−0.16	0.07
Goodness-of-fit		
n	81	
Pseudo R^2	0.22	

Probit analysis, sequence SO, node SO3.
Dependent variable: spouse was helped (yes/no) when asked for cash for a household item.

correlated with the decision to render assistance. The difference in responses to getting along and trust are not significant. Results (not reported here) show that this result is being driven by the spouse's report of fairness. Hence, we can conclude that those who do not receive insurance from their spouse are in the first instance those who do not ask because they have a low view of the trust, fairness, or quality of the relationship in general, and (given that they ask) those who get turned down are those whose spouse has a dim view of the fairness of the relationship.

A number of intriguing possibilities is suggested by this two-tiered result. For example, the fact that people with a positive view of fairness ask, only to be turned down by a spouse with an opposing view, suggests a lack of communication or information between the pair. It is also consistent with a gambling view of the decision to ask: given a low cost of asking, even those who know that their spouse does not share their opinion about fairness of the relationship might take the chance in case they get lucky. In the end, we cannot rule out these competing explanations of the dynamics that leads to these characteristics being correlated with the transfer process. However, the fact that difference in perception of fairness is important in explaining success when asking suggests that communication in marital relationships is far from perfect and that this is correlated with increased probability of rejection.

11.5.3. *Who Gets Help from Others?*

In examining who seeks and receives assistance from persons outside the household, the results change somewhat depending on which decision tree we are using.

Table 11.9. *Explaining who asked others for help when short to buy a household item*

Variables	dF/dx	P > [z]	Mean
Individual asset position			
Size of inherited land area (ha)	−0.01	0.89	0.42
Size of land area anticipated to be inherited (ha)	0.49	0.09	0.05
Value of non-land assets (10^6 cedis)	0.01	0.88	0.72
Individual social capital			
Probability of knowing any person in the community	−0.72	0.19	0.90
Years respondent or family lived in the village	−0.00	0.25	75.28
Number of fostering episodes	−0.17	0.04	0.77
Number of organizations respondent belongs to	0.10	0.10	1.21
Individual characteristics			
Gender: female = 1	0.26	0.07	0.46
Household characteristics			
Member of major village lineage = 1	0.21	0.06	0.59
Location			
Village 2 = 1	−0.30	0.13	0.10
Village 3 = 1	−0.53	0.01	0.37
Village 4 = 1	−0.55	0.01	0.44
Goodness-of-fit			
n	111		
Pseudo R^2	0.28		
Partial result with other variables characterizing the individual's social capital instead of probability of knowing others			
Probability of talking to others	0.04	0.91	0.19
Partial result in OS sequence, node OS2			
Probability of knowing any person in the community	−0.45	0.08	0.91

Probit analysis, sequence ask spouse–ask others, node SO4 (and partial result for sequence ask others–ask spouse, OS2 node).
Dependent variable: individual asks others (yes/no) when short of cash to purchase a household item.

Table 11.9 provides the results for estimating the probability of asking others using the sample provided by the SO sequence (node SO4).

The sample associated with the SO tree (the 111 individuals who did not ask their spouse) shows a number of social capital variables to be significantly associated with the probability of asking others. Belonging to the major lineage in the village is positively associated with asking others. We include lineage because, as indicated earlier, it plays an important role in Akan economic and social life. The result is consistent not only with possible assistance rendered by lineage members, but also in the associated social standing that comes from being a member of the lineage that controls access to the largest amount of land and holds a number of local political and ceremonial positions. The number of local organizations that an individual belonged to is also significantly correlated with the probability of asking others for assistance. We know that a few of these organizations exist specifically for insurance reasons (e.g. one group pays out for funeral expenses), so it is natural that this would be related to the probability that an individual could ask others for insurance for a variety of shocks. Village effects are also significant for two of the villages. This is indicative of inherent differences in organizational and social life (among other factors) that we cannot capture with our set of variables. Indeed, in our work in the villages, we discovered many differences that defy categorization in simple quantitative variables. For example, one village was without a chief and, instead, authority was vested in a council of elders. This difference in power structure made the resolution of disputes (say over the reneging on a reciprocal assistance agreement) markedly different in this village compared to others.

Among individual characteristics, gender is an important determinant of seeking assistance outside the household. This is consistent with the results obtained by Goldstein (2000) which indicate that women tend to insure outside the household and family, doing so instead with other women. For women, mutual insurance networks in the villages studied thus run by gender rather than kinship. The number of fostering episodes that an individual experienced while growing up is negatively related to the probability that he/she will ask others for assistance. Fostering is quite common in these villages, as in much of West Africa. This variable is capturing two main effects. First, fostering usually takes place outside the village and thus the respondent's absence while growing up curtails his or her ability to develop networks. Second, it is likely indicative of a lower status within the family, resulting in lower willingness of extended family members to help. In this specification, personal wealth matters as the anticipated land inheritance is positively related with the probability of asking others. As future access to land provides capital to guarantee the future reciprocity of favours (as well as serving as an indicator of family wealth and status), this is not surprising.

In an effort to examine the effects of broader social interactions, we include a measure of the probability of knowing any random person in the village as an independent variable. We included this measure because the level of social connection that it indicates would provide a natural vehicle for not only identifying more effectively possible sources of assistance, but also providing the greater social connections to enforce mutual insurance arrangements.[12] While not significant in the SO4 analysis, this effect is significantly negative in the OS2 specification. This result is counter to what we would expect. However, one plausible explanation for the underlying relationship is that there is a reduction in social standing associated with asking others for help. This loss of social standing comes from revealing that you (or your partner) cannot make ends meet. Revealing this inability to cope will lead to being recognized as a risky person to deal with and is likely to curtail future access to credit and other forms of capital, as well as incurring a broader loss of status. The more people the individual knows, the higher the cost will be, as knowledge of this failure will spread more broadly

[12] An alternative to this hypothesis might revolve around the 'big man' hypothesis. A 'big man' is someone who is well known and usually wealthy. While this informal position confers added prestige, it also brings responsibility to respond to the needs of others. Big men might seek to avoid others in order to avoid unilateral claims for assistance. However, given the high average value of probability of knowing variable, this does not seem to be what is captured by this variable.

through the village. Hence, these individuals are more likely to avoid asking, unless it is absolutely necessary. Social connections can thus be a curse in calling on others for mutual insurance. A complementary explanation draws on the fact that the ability to provide for one's spouse is a major criterion by which a relationship is judged. Hence, admitting an inability to provide one's share of the household items reveals a weakness in the relationship that will harm future bargaining positions, both within the relationship and also in case of divorce.

We thus conclude that asking others when not asking a spouse is limited by a number of factors that are indicative of the individual's standing in the community. Lineage position is important, both in support that comes directly from membership or from the anticipated access to resources through inheritance. Relations conferred by growing up in the community (fostering) and gender also appear to be important. However, social connections in the community may be a curse for mutual insurance if asking others is a signal that undermines social capital.

11.6. RESPONSES TO A CASH SHORTAGE FOR A PERSONAL ITEM

The response to a cash shortage when needing to buy a personal item seems to generate a different type of response.[13] We can see part of the picture from the data in Figure 11.2 as compared to Figure 11.1. In this section, we estimate probits to examine the two possible decision trees when seeking assistance for a personal item.[14] Results show that not only the patterns in seeking assistance differ, but also different characteristics are associated with the choice of whom to ask. This is particularly true for the decision to ask someone other than the spouse.

11.6.1. *Requests to the Spouse*

Results of these estimates for the SO sequence are given in Table 11.10. Results for the OS sequence are essentially identical and not reported. The request to the spouse is strongly associated with gender in estimates of both decision paths (nodes SO2 and OS3). Women are much more likely to ask their spouse for help than the other way around.

The variables we use to measure quality of the conjugal relationship are not significant. However, a history of domestic violence is significant and negative. The most frequent causes of domestic violence cited by male respondents were insults from their spouse (17 per cent) and disobedience (11 per cent). These do not suggest direct economic causes (in fact very few of the other responses were centred around directly economic reasons). Hence, the effect of domestic violence on the propensity to ask is

---

[13] These data were collected under the instruction that this was a good to be consumed solely by the individual. Feedback from the field staff indicated this was a fairly straightforward concept.

[14] Note that, because of the low number of observations, we do not estimate the spouse response to a request for assistance.

Table 11.10. *Explaining who asks spouse for money when short of cash to buy a personal item*

Variables	dF/dx	$P > |z|$
Individual asset position		
Value of non-land assets (10^6 cedis)	0.00	0.30
Individual characteristics		
Quality of marital relations as seen by the demanding party: fair	−0.03	0.48
Gender: female = 1	0.46	0.00
Household characteristics		
Value of spouse assets (10^6 cedis)	−0.01	0.40
Years married	0.00	0.90
Number of household members	−0.01	0.63
Location		
Village 2 = 1	NA	NA
Village 3 = 1	−0.15	0.63
Village 4 = 1	−0.17	0.33
Goodness-of-fit		
n	86	
Pseudo R^2	0.28	
Partial results with other variables characterizing the quality of marital relations as seen by the demanding party		
Trust	−0.02	0.50
Get along	−0.03	0.55
Domestic violence = 1	−0.19	0.04

NA, Village predicts failure perfectly.
Probit analysis, sequence SO, node SO2.
Dependent variable: individual asks spouse for money (yes/no) when short of cash to purchase a personal item.

likely to be through the tenor of the relationship, in particular how it affects the bargaining process, as well as the bargaining outcomes. Since a spousal transfer for a personal item is more likely to be a gift than a transfer for a household item, the importance of domestic violence is suggestive of the role of the tenor of the relationship in explaining the ease with which spouses may approach one another with a request for a gift.

11.6.2. *Requests to Others*

In seeking assistance for a personal item, a different set of social relations and individual characteristics matter than for a household item. Table 11.11 provides these estimates for the SO sequence (node SO4). Four results are notable.

First, belonging to the major village lineage is significantly and positively associated with seeking outside assistance. This is similar to what we observed in seeking help for a household item. Second, the number of years a respondent or his or her family has been in the village is negatively related to the probability of asking others. We included this

Table 11.11. *Explaining who asked others for help to buy a personal item*

Variables	dF/dx	$P > [z]$
Individual asset position		
Size of inherited land area (ha)	−0.04	0.51
Value of non-land assets (10^6 cedis)	0.03	0.37
Individual social capital		
Probability of knowing any person in the community	−0.34	0.43
Years respondent or family lived in the village	−0.00	0.01
Number of fostering episodes	−0.03	0.60
Number of organizations respondent belongs to	0.02	0.65
Individual characteristics		
Gender: female = 1	0.06	0.43
Household characteristics		
Member of major village lineage = 1	0.13	0.07
Location		
Village 3 = 1	−1.00	0.00
Village 4 = 1	−0.63	0.00
Goodness-of-fit		
n	80.0	
Pseudo R^2	0.43	
Partial results with other variables characterizing the individual's social capital instead of probability of knowing others		
Probability of talking to others	0.38	0.06

Probit analysis, sequence ask spouse–ask others, node SO4.

variable given the social standing that the anthropological literature attributes to the length of time an individual or his or her family has lived in a village. This social standing might provide greater access to informal insurance. Our result here is consistent with the fact that long-established families have better access to modes of insurance other than mutual transfers. If there is a social cost incurred in obtaining the transfer needed (and this is perhaps more pronounced for personal items which the transferor might not approve of), then these individuals would prefer to use other modes to obtain the needed item—be it credit, use of reciprocal labour arrangements, or the like.

Our third common result is that the variable for the probability of knowing others is not significantly related to with seeking help from others. However, when we use the probability of talking to others (a measure of the quality or depth of relationships), this is significantly and positively related to the probability of asking others. This result might seem to be at odds with the household item result where the signs on the probability of knowing others is negative. This may indicate that, for a personal item, there is no reflection on the intra-household relationship when one seeks help from others. In the case of a personal item, our respondents prefer individuals that they know well because the strength of their relationship with the person they are asking to for assistance helps overcome problems of information and enforcement and thus allows for better mutual insurance.

Overall, the fact remains that asking others for help with a personal expenditure is more difficult than asking for a household expenditure. Social connections (major lineage, talking to others) help, but social capital is clearly harder to mobilize for this purpose, leaving many excluded from insurance to cope with this type of shock.

11.7. A FRIEND IN DEED? THE QUALITY OF INSURANCE AND THE IMPLICATIONS OF EXCLUSION

The previous sections have identified the factors that are associated with asking for and receiving help from others. This section examines the 'help' in more detail, examining the terms of the assistance and the implications for consumption smoothing. We also discuss the strategies used by those that are rejected or never ask others for assistance. The final part of this section looks more explicitly at the question of how the poor manage shortages and examines whether their access to this type of mutual insurance is different from the rest of the population.

11.7.1. *The Quality of Insurance*

On what terms is help given by the spouse and by others? Figures 11.1 and 11.2 indicate that, even when help is forthcoming from a spouse or another individual, it is often an explicit (albeit interest free) loan.[15] Table 11.12 summarizes these figures. What is clear is that the spouse treats household items differently from personal items, while individuals outside the household do not. Spouses are more likely to provide assistance for a household item in the form of a loan, and to do this in kind rather than in cash. According to discussions with respondents, this is often for fear of fungibility—that is, that the cash will not go to the designated household expense, which suggests contract enforcement problems.

Personal items appear to follow a different pattern altogether, with 69 per cent of the assistance from the spouse taking the form of a gift. Assistance from others for both types of items, on the other hand, is usually a loan. This is different from those who buy items on credit in that there is usually no interest charged. Items bought on credit (according to anecdotal evidence) incur an implicit interest rate, as the credit price is different from the cash price once repayment spans a certain period of time.

Ultimately, what we care about is how this shortage of cash affects consumption. One way to test for the quality of the insurance received by those who obtained assistance is to look at the variation in their consumption relative to other members of the community. Given the data we have from earlier rounds of the survey, we can conduct a test of the type developed in Townsend (1994) and others on a different configuration of these data for full insurance. If we assume that people who are helped in rounds 14

---

[15] This is what distinguishes these loans from the response to the question of how individual's managed (after being turned down or not seeking help). The latter are likely to be consumer loans of shorter duration and with implicit interest.

Table 11.12. *Forms of assistance*

	Type (%)		Form (%)			
	Gift	Loan	Cash	Kind	Both	*n*
Spouse assistance						
Household item	40.7	59.3	38.5	48.4	13.2	91
Personal item	69.2	30.8	84.6	15.4	0.0	13
Assistance from others						
Household item	28.2	71.8				39
Personal item	27.8	72.2				18

and 15 were also helped in these earlier rounds (i.e. they are usually helped), we can test whether this population and/or the rest of the village exhibits full insurance. Our econometric test is to estimate:

$$c_{ist} - c_{ist-1} = a(\bar{c}_{st} - \bar{c}_{st-1}) + b(y_{ist} - y_{ist-1}) + e$$

where c_{ist} is the consumption of individual i in state s at time t, $\bar{c}_{st}$ is the village average consumption, and y_{ist} is the individual idiosyncratic income shock.[16] Theory predicts that, in the case of full insurance, β should equal zero and α should equal 1, that is, the change in individual i's consumption should be unaffected by own income shocks and move with the community's average change in consumption.

Table 11.13 presents the results of this regression for the entire sample, and then separately for those who received help and those who did not,[17] using consumption and shock data from the same survey.[18] The income shock data consist of agricultural plot level unexpected events and illnesses. The consumption data presented is for private consumption—goods that can be clearly assigned to individuals for their own consumption based on their own expenditure reports. Thus, we define those who received help only as those who received help for a personal item outside of the household. We estimate this equation (in parts B and C of Table 11.13) only for those who expressed a shortage as we cannot be certain about the classification of the rest of the population.

When we estimate this equation for the entire sample (Table 11.13, Part A), a joint F-test of the coefficients fails to reject the hypothesis of full insurance. When we estimate this equation for the sample restricted to those who received help in rounds 14 and/or 15, we also fail to reject the hypothesis of full insurance. However, when we estimate this equation for the sample of individuals who were short of cash for a personal item and received no assistance, we can reject the hypothesis of full insurance at the 3 per cent level. Although these results come from a small sample, they provide

---

[16] There are better ways to test this hypothesis (e.g. Ravallion and Chaudhuri 1997), but data constraints make this our best option.

[17] See Goldstein (2000) for a discussion of the data and the errors in variables estimation.

[18] Note that we face two sources of attrition here: missing consumption data in all panels, and those for whom we cannot identify help/no help in panels B and C.

Table 11.13. *Errors in variable regression: change in private consumption*

Dependent variable: change in private cons.	Coefficient	*t*-stat	95% conf interval	
A. Whole sample ($n = 203$)				
Village mean consumption	−0.57	−0.75	−2.10	0.93
Change in illness shocks	−0.01	−0.05	−0.36	0.34
Change in agricultural shocks	0.02	1.04	−0.02	0.05
Constant	5214	−0.71	−9303	19,732
F-test of perfect insurance coefficients	$F(3,199) = 1.96$		Prob $> F = 0.12$	
B. Those who received assistance for personal items ($n = 14$)				
Village mean consumption	−2.18	−0.91	−7.52	3.16
Change in illness shocks	−0.17	−0.71	−0.71	0.36
Change in agricultural shocks	−0.03	−0.37	−0.20	0.14
Constant	33,851	1.74	−9501	77,204
F-test of perfect insurance coefficients	$F(3,10) = 0.70$		Prob $> F = 0.57$	
C. Those who were short but received no assistance ($n = 49$)				
Village mean consumption	−1.53	−1.58	−3.48	0.42
Change in illness shocks	−0.16	−0.80	−0.57	0.25
Change in agricultural shocks	−0.01	−0.80	−0.03	0.01
Constant	21,979	1.85	−1928	45,887
F-test of perfect insurance coefficients	$F(3,45) = 3.20$		Prob $> F = 0.03$	

evidence that receiving assistance is consistent with full insurance, while failing to receive assistance when short is associated with a rejection of full insurance.

11.7.2. *How do the Excluded Manage?*

In round 15, the questionnaire included a component which asked those who received no help how they coped with their cash shortage. We can see this data summarized in Figures 11.1 and 11.2 for the household item and the personal item, respectively. The patterns of coping were different across the two items.

In the case of a household item, the major response was to find some way to buy the item. Most respondents (52 per cent) bought the item on credit, followed by seeking additional work (9 per cent) and selling crops from the farm (7 per cent). A minority, but not insignificant number of individuals, responded by not buying the item (27 per cent). Overall, a larger fraction of those who were short of cash for a personal item received no help whatsoever (73 per cent compared to 45 per cent of those short of cash for a household item). The main mode of coping was to not buy the item (74 per cent), followed by credit (10 per cent), and finding additional work and selling crops from the farm (7 per cent each). Unlike the response to the shortage of cash for a household item, there was a difference in how each gender managed the shortage for a personal item, with women more likely to buy the item on credit. However, the dominant choice for both genders was to not buy the item.

11.7.3. *How do the Poor Manage?*

In examining which groups might be excluded from mutual insurance, we can take inspiration from Jalan and Ravallion (1997). Using data from China, they find that non-land wealth is positively correlated with a household's ability to insure consumption. This leads them to conclude that the poor are less well insured. We can use two measures to examine whether or not the poor have less effective insurance. One option is to use the wealth variable included in many of the regressions discussed above. This is measured by non-land assets. As our earlier results have shown, wealth matters at two junctures. First, people with higher levels of average non-land assets during the two-year survey period are less likely to have a shortage of cash for both household and personal items.[19] This suggests that they chose to smooth consumption using their assets. Second, people with lower assets are more likely to ask their spouse for assistance with a household item. However, wealth is not significantly correlated with the probability of asking others for assistance.

Another approach would be to measure poverty in terms of per capita food expenditure. We created two poverty lines: one based on 80 per cent of the US$1/day benchmark, and the other, which is about half that amount, is defined as the bottom quartile of the expenditure distribution. Data came from an average of the thrice-administered expenditure questionnaires.[20] Using these two poverty measures, we recalculated the estimates of who were short, using the specification of Table 11.1. Both measures were not significantly correlated with the probability of being short of cash for a household item. Similarly, when we estimate the probability of asking one's spouse, the probability of the spouse helping, and the probability of asking others, we do not find that either measure of poverty is significant at the 10 per cent level or better.[21] Mutual insurance thus seems to work equally well for the poor.

We can also examine those who end up without help in Figures 11.1 and 11.2 to see if the poor are disproportionately represented in this group. An analysis of each group shows that, for the household item, 33 per cent of the poor (using the first definition here and for the discussion that follows) receive no help, while 38 per cent of the non-poor receive no help. While there is no major difference in representation, coping strategies are slightly different. The poor are more likely to use credit (63 per cent of poor) than the non-poor (40 per cent). The non-poor were more likely not to buy the item (35 per cent) than the poor (26 per cent) but we need to keep in mind that we are dealing with a small number of responses. In terms of a shortage when needing to buy a personal item, the poor were more likely to defer consumption (80 per cent) than the non-poor (70 per cent), and more likely to buy things on credit (20 per cent) than the non-poor (5 per cent).

---

[19] Note that two measures of land assets (inherited land and the number of plots owned) are not significantly correlated with the probability of being short of cash.

[20] We use the sum of the respondent's own reports of expenditures to determine poverty at the household (per capita adjusted) level.

[21] The closest result comes with the difference in fair specification of spouse helping where the first measure of poverty is negative with a z-statistic of 1.60.

Thus, for the region under study, poor individuals seem to have equal access to transfers from their spouse, family, and friends. By contrast to the inference made by Jalan and Ravallion (1997) for China, mutual insurance is here equally accessible to poor and non-poor. Being poor matters, however, in two ways. First, low wealth endowments are more likely to be associated with an initial cash shortage for both personal and household items. Second, the poor utilize different alternate mechanisms when they are rejected from mutual insurance support or do not seek this assistance, relying more on credit or accepting not to buy the item and to defer consumption.

11.8. CONCLUSIONS

This chapter attempted to bring together the anthropological, sociological, and psychological dimensions of intra- and extra-household relations with the work on risk and insurance in economics. What we show is that the shape of social relations matters: personal relations within the household and social status and connections within the community are important for receiving transfers in times of shortage. Within the household, the gender of the demanding party (+ for women), the quality of the relationship, and the wealth of the other partner are all associated with the likelihood of asking for assistance. Among those who asked, and hence with good quality spousal relationships as seen by the demanding party, receiving assistance depends on equality in perception of this relationship between spouses. Those who had a mistaken appreciation of the relationship are turned down. Outside the household, membership in the major lineage, participation in secular organizations, the individual's fostering history (−), and anticipated land inheritance are all related to receiving assistance from others. Gender is also associated with receiving assistance outside the household, with women more likely to get help for a household item.

We also showed that the patterns of requests for assistance and responses to requests differ according to the item for which insurance is sought. People are overall less likely to ask for help with a personal item. Those who do capitalize on the strength of their social relations in seeking help outside the household. However, individuals with high levels of active connections in the village seem to be reticent to ask others for help with a household item, possibly to avoid losing social status in exposing weakness. Domestic violence, rather than other measures of relationship quality, appears to be important in whether or not assistance for a personal item is sought within the household. These contrasts suggest that there are different categories of people who are unable to access mutual insurance for specific types of shortages.

These characteristics can help identify individuals who are likely to be excluded from insurance via transfers. As we have shown, these individuals' consumption shows that they are not perfectly insured, by contrast with those who received assistance. In addition, we also examined the correlation of poverty with access to transfers in times of shortage. We found that individuals who are asset poor are more likely to be short of cash for household and personal items and are more likely to ask their spouse for assistance with the household item. However, they do not appear to face different responses to requests for transfers from others. Hence, mutual insurance is more needed by the poor, but equally accessible to them.

Incomplete insurance in rural communities, as observed in most empirical tests reported in the literature, can thus be due to the social exclusion of many community members with specific individual, household, and community characteristics. In fact, we have shown that inability to rely on mutual insurance in the face of cash shortages is surprisingly pervasive. Mutual insurance thus works for some, but not for many. And for whom and for what it does not work can be predicted, potentially helping target remedial assistance to the excluded individuals.

REFERENCES

Ayisi, E. (1974). 'Kinship and Local Community in Akwapem', in C. Oppong (ed.), *Domestic Rights and Duties in Southern Ghana, Legon Family Research Papers*, Vol. 1. Legon: Institute of African Studies.

Brokensha, D. (1972). 'Society', in D. Brokensha (ed.), *Akwapim Handbook*. Accra: Ghana Publishing Company.

Coate, S. and M. Ravallion (1993). 'Reciprocity without Commitment: Characterization and Performance of Informal Insurance Arrangements'. *Journal of Development Economics*, 40(1), 1–24.

Deaton, A. (1992). 'Household Savings in LDCs: Credit Markets, Insurance, and Welfare'. *Scandinavian Journal of Economics*, 94(2), 253–73.

Fafchamps, M. (1992). 'Solidarity Networks in Preindustrial Societies: Rational Peasants with a Moral Economy'. *Economic Development and Cultural Change*, 41(1), 147–74.

—— and S. Lund (2000). 'Risk-Sharing Networks in Rural Philippines', mimeo, University of Oxford, Oxford.

Fortes, M. (1950). 'Kinship and Marriage Among the Ashanti', in A. Radcliffe-Brown and D. Forde (eds), *African Systems of Kinship and Marriage*. London: Oxford University Press.

—— (1969). *Kinship and the Social Order: The Legacy of Lewis Henry Morgan*. Chicago, IL: Aldine Publishing Company.

Gertler, P. and J. Gruber (1997). 'Insuring Consumption Against Illness', mimeo, University of California, Berkeley, CA.

Ghana Statistical Service (1995). *Ghana Living Standards Survey: Report on the Third Round*. Accra: Ghana Statistical Service.

Goldstein, M. (2000). 'Intra-Household Allocation and Farming in Southern Ghana'. Ph.D. dissertation, University of California, Berkeley, CA.

Grimard, F. (1997). 'Household Consumption Smoothing through Ethnic Ties: Evidence from Cote d'Ivoire'. *Journal of Development Economics*, 53(2), 391–422.

Jalan, J. and M. Ravallion (1997). 'Are the Poor Less Well Insured? Evidence on Vulnerability to Income Risk in Rural China'. *Policy Research Working Paper* No. 1863. Washington, DC: Development Research Group, World Bank.

Kimball, M. (1988). 'Farmers' Cooperatives as Behaviors Towards Risk'. *American Economic Review*, 78, 224–32.

Kwamena Poh, M. (1974). 'Church and Change in Akuapem', in C. Oppong (ed.), *Domestic Rights and Duties in Southern Ghana, Legon Family Research Papers*, Vol. 1. Legon: Institute of African Studies.

Ligon, E. (1998). 'Risk Sharing and Information in Village Economies'. *Review of Economic Studies*, 65(4), 847–64.

Manski, C. (2000). 'Economic Analysis of Social Interactions'. *Journal of Economic Perspectives*, 14(3), 115–36.

Murgai, R., P. Winters, E. Sadoulet, and A. de Janvry (2002). 'Localized and Incomplete Mutual Insurance'. *Journal of Development Economics*, 67(2), 245–74.

Oppong, C. (1974). 'Domestic Budgeting Among Some Salaried Urban Couples', in C. Oppong (ed.), *Domestic Rights and Duties in Southern Ghana, Legon Family Research Papers*, Vol. 1. Legon: Institute of African Studies.

Platteau, J. P. (1991). 'Traditional Systems of Social Security and Hunger Insurance: Past Achievements and Modern Challenges', in E. Ahmad, J. Drèze, J. Hills, and A. Sen (eds), *Social Security in Developing Countries*. Oxford: Clarendon Press.

Ravallion, M. and S. Chaudhuri (1997). 'Risk and Insurance in Village India: Comment'. *Econometrica*, 65(1), 171–84.

Smith, N. (1972). 'Religious Beliefs', in D. Brokensha (ed.), *Akwapim Handbook*. Accra: Ghana Publishing Company.

Townsend, R. (1994). 'Risk and Insurance in Village India'. *Econometrica*, 62(3), 539–91.

Vercruijsse, E., L. Vercruijsse-Dopheide, and K. Boakye (1974). 'Composition of Households in some Fante Communities: A Study of the Framework of Social Integration', in C. Oppong (ed.), *Domestic Rights and Duties in Southern Ghana, Legon Family Research Papers*, Vol. 1. Legon: Institute of African Studies.

12

The Gradual Erosion of the Social Security Function of Customary Land Tenure Arrangements in Lineage-based Societies

JEAN-PHILIPPE PLATTEAU

INTRODUCTION

In our paper 'Traditional Systems of Social Security and Hunger Insurance: Past Achievements and Modern Challenges', published under the WIDER programme of studies in development economics (Platteau 1991), the need had been emphasized to distinguish between two central mechanisms of social security in traditional village societies, namely voluntary state-contingent reciprocal transfers and access rules for vital resources. While the first of these mechanisms has received considerable attention in the economic literature, the second one has been largely ignored. To what extent rules of access to vital resources can be considered as an effective way to cope with adverse shocks is a pending question that will need to be elucidated.

Evidence indicates that informal mutual insurance arrangements are an imperfect mechanism of social security. Not only have they a restricted scope, but they are also fragile, unreliable in protecting the poorest households, and susceptible of retarding capital accumulation and economic growth (Platteau 1991, 2000: chapter 5; Alderman and Paxson 1992; Morduch 1995). As regards the first point, from the observation that reciprocal transfers are frequent it is not legitimate to infer that they provide effective insurance to villagers. For one thing, such transfers may involve only a limited fraction of the village population and, for another thing, they may represent only a low proportion of the income shocks in bad periods (Cox and Jimenez 1990, 1997; Platteau 1997; Czukas et al. 1998; Rosenzweig 1988; Goldstein 1999). Risk characteristics are an important determinant of the feasibility of group- or community-based informal insurance. Thus, low frequency events as well as repeated shocks (shocks strongly correlated over time) and covariate risks are difficult to insure against on a local level. This observation carries the unfortunate implication that informal village mechanisms may be particularly fragile when needed most (Morduch 1999).

More importantly, the effectiveness of informal risk-sharing schemes is likely to decline as economic mobility and differentiation increase with development. As a matter of fact, widening wealth differentials, say, as a result of newly emerging outside income-earning opportunities, create incentives for the better-off households to leave the risk-sharing scheme. As they exit, the welfare gains from the scheme to those remaining in the system fall, and it can unravel (Fafchamps 1992; Hoff 1997).

In the present chapter, we intend to argue in the same vein that the effectiveness of the second mechanism is also subject to erosion under the impact of economic development and population growth. Public intervention from central agencies is therefore all the more justified as market development is more advanced. In Section 12.1, the operation of the customary rules of access to vital resources is described. Also, their potential role as a social security mechanism is subsequently discussed, carefully distinguishing between social security for the poor in the sense of protection against the risk of chronic poverty, on the one hand, and insurance against adverse shocks, on the other hand. Section 12.2 is the central part of the chapter where attention is drawn to the dynamic evolution of these rules as the value of land and water resources increase as a result of economic development and population growth. As for Section 12.3, it will summarize the main findings and draw policy implications.

12.1. CUSTOMARY RULES OF ACCESS TO VITAL RESOURCES AND THEIR ROLE AS SOCIAL SECURITY PROVIDER

12.1.1. *Central Features of the Customary System of Land Tenure*

Under the traditional land tenure system in Africa and other regions with a long tradition of extensive land use patterns associated with high land–man ratios, land and other natural resources are held under a system of corporate ownership. This implies that the right to allocate land is vested in the heads of collectives which claim to be its ultimate rightful owners, typically ward or village chiefs, earth priests, masters of fire or masters of the axe. The general principle is that a member of the group or community is entitled to be allocated land for cultivation. The term 'member', it must be pointed out, includes not only those who can claim descent, actual or putative, from the founding lineages but also strangers and migrants who have been accepted as members of, and reside with, the group (Popkin 1979: 43; Noronha 1985: 182). Yet, access to land may be unequal as it is usually qualified by rules relating both to the period of residence in the area and the member's ancestry: thus, members who are recent residents are likely to be entitled only to marginal lands while those who can trace back their ancestry to the founders of the village often get the best lands (whenever they are in scarce supply) or parcels of greater size (Noronha 1985: 182).[1]

---

[1] Among the Moose of the north-central region of Burkina Faso, we learn that, 'if a "stranger" obtains high yields or if rainfall circumstances during the past seasons favoured for example farming on lowland, the (low)land can be withdrawn for use by a *tengbiiga* [that is, an elder of the village's founding kin group]' and the 'stranger' 'will be asked to choose another plot to farm in the village territory' (Breusers 2001: 56). The point of the matter is that, in the village's hierarchy of control and access rights to land, relative 'strangers' occupy a low position. This is reflected in the fact that they are entitled only to land not wanted by any member of an earlier arrived kin group (Breusers 2001: 58–60). It is actually inconceivable that a 'stranger' fares better, in the long run at least, than a member of the autochtonous population.

It must moreover be pointed out that the relationship between membership and access to land is reciprocal: on the one hand, group membership is the basis of social rights and, on the other hand, access to a share of the corporate productive assets serves to validate membership in the group (Berry 1984: 91). The latter holds especially true for members of late arrived kin groups who have to obtain prior authorization of local land authorities to have access to land (Breusers 2001: 54–58). Such authorization is refused or withdrawn only when the 'stranger' behaves incorrectly, typically when he violates the local rules and traditions.

As a matter of principle, the land which a group member is allowed to receive from the community to which he belongs must be sufficient to provide for his own livelihood and that of his family (see, for example, Cohen 1980: 353). In such a need-based logic, since the size of the family is subject to fluctuations over the life cycle, the size of the land allotted to the head of a household must also be susceptible of being adjusted. In Lesotho, for example, till recently, 'village chiefs had the power to acquire lands deemed surplus to requirements of a household and redistribute these among the more needy members' (Noronha 1985: 186). Likewise, in the villages of Niger, there exists a pool of community land entrusted to the village chief, known as *hawjou* land, which he has the right to put at the disposal of farmers who are short of land (Gavian and Fafchamps 1996). Another principle that follows from the need-based logic of land allocation is that the allottee has possession and use of the lands only as long as they can be cultivated with the help of the family workforce (Noronha 1985: 183). Nonetheless, a man is entitled 'to keep some land for his sons if they are old enough to establish themselves as heads of their own families within the next few years. If he abandons his fields permanently, the land reverts to the ward or the tribe' (Schapera 1943: 44; Ault and Rutman 1979: 170).

It is therefore evident that a guaranteed access to land and other natural resources is a 'general right' granted to all members of the group as distinct from the 'specific rights' to a particular portion of the resource. While the former is 'an inseparable element of the status as member of the tribe' and can only be lost through formal expulsion from the group, the latter can be reshuffled according to circumstances. For instance, in a system of slash-and-burn agriculture, when the period of fallow is so long that all traces of previous cultivation are lost, a household does not automatically return to the same parcel (Boserup 1965: 79–80; Ault and Rutman 1979: 172).[2]

In many instances, it must be noted, different types of tenure coexist in the same location, a feature known as multiple tenure that results from the presence of lands of

---

Still, it remains possible for latecomers to gradually enlarge their claims over local plots through prolonged presence and use of the land—'Consolidating their presence at a particular place is their only way to ever root territorially in the village'—and through ritual collaboration and the establishment of kin relations with founding lineages (Breusers 2001: 60–62). Breusers uses the expression autochtonization to characterize this process of gradually securing tenure rights in a village in which a kin group has been a latecomer.

[2] By abandoning land under cultivation, an individual actually forsakes his right to cultivate it. This is a rational step to take so long as the net return from newly cleared land exceeds the net return from cultivating previously cleared land. This happens when the fertility of the land has been exhausted and 'is restored by allowing the land to remain fallow while newly cleared land is cultivated' (Ault and Rutman 1979: 172).

varying quality and therefore subject to varying modes of exploitation. Leaving aside common-property lands, such as grazing lands, to which we shall soon return, we find, at one extreme, the intensively cultivated garden lands situated near dwellings and over which households have close to permanent rights and, at the other extreme, lands devoted to slash-and-burn cultivation over which rights granted are only temporary, as explained above.[3] In addition, unlike what is observed in more developed agricultural societies, rights over land are usually not exclusive, meaning that various overlapping rights may prevail over a given portion of the community territory. This is especially noticeable in the case of societies that combine agriculture and grazing: it is indeed a common practice that farmers open their fields after the harvest so that herder groups or other farmers including themselves can feed their cattle on the remaining stubble. In such circumstances, the definition of tenure rights varies through time (see, for example, Cohen 1980; Dahlman 1980; Noronha 1985; Platteau 1992).

The same principles essentially apply to herder societies as well: in particular, members are entitled to own a stock of animals deemed sufficient for subsistence and, when any of them falls into destitution, he or she can rely on his community to have his or her ownership position restored and thus escape the poverty trap. In Somali traditional pastoral communities, for example, poor or destitute individuals (known as *maskiin* or *ceer*) are given a collection of animals by members of their lineage (the *reer*) so that they can re-enter the pastoral economy as full-fledged owners (Nunow 2000: 151).

As regards access to land for women, the guiding principle in (patrilineal) lineage-based societies is that women can have only rights over the land. Upon marriage, they are typically expected to work some part of their husband's land, and their degree of autonomy varies considerably according to whether they work on a family (collective) field, on a husband's field, or on a parcel specially earmarked for them. In the latter case, women enjoy most autonomy, particularly under the form of the right to freely dispose of the land's produce. Nevertheless, even when working on their own fields, women remain placed under the authority of their husband acting as household head. This is notably reflected in the fact that the time schedule of women's work is laid down by the husband and, when they have access to a woman's plot (which is not necessarily true), it is usually during the hottest time of the day (in the afternoon) that they are allowed to work on it.

In the event of separation or divorce, the rule is that women have the right to return to their native village where they are granted use rights over the family land, or are accommodated in the farm of a close relative (father, brother, or uncle). This is with a

---

[3] In Bechuanaland (presently Botswana), for example, the chief, with the support of the tribal assembly and the notables (among whom the headmen of 'wards' figure prominently), acts as a trustee for his tribe. He determines 'what land shall be used for dwellings, for grazing, for cultivation, and what land shall be temporarily or permanently withdrawn from usage; also, what land shall be used in common by the tribe and what should be parceled out for use to families. The land to be distributed is allocated to the wards, and the headmen of the wards then assign the plots to individuals. From the headman every married man in the ward can claim enough land for residence and cultivation to accommodate his family. Once land has been taken for cultivation, the family to which it has been assigned remains in possession as long as it continues the use' (Landauer 1964: 497, quoting Schapera 1943: 44).

view to ensuring their livelihood until they hopefully find a new husband. Of course, when the woman is deemed responsible by her family for the marriage break-up, acute pressure is exercised to drive her back to her husband and intense efforts are deployed to reconcile the couple. It is only when a woman has been chased away by her husband or when she has left him but the fault is clearly on the husband's side—generally on account of impotency or ill-treatment of his wife—that she has an automatic right to go back to the parental farm.

In the case of the death of her husband, a widow is neither abandoned nor denied access to land. Depending on the circumstances, she will either remain on the husband's land (in the case she accepts a levirate marriage or is old enough to have grown-up children to take care of her), or go back to her father's farmland and draw her livelihood from it as long as necessary to find a new husband. As for unwed mothers, they also have the right to stay on the parental land during the time needed for them to find a man willing to marry them and take charge of their child or children.

As our own field studies in Senegal (in the Senegal river valley) and Burkina Faso (various districts) have shown, the aforementioned mechanisms of women's social protection are still well alive in West Africa (see Abraham and Platteau 2001).

12.1.2. *The Village Commons*

We have so far considered situations in which land is parcelled out among household units for cultivation purposes. In actual fact, some portion of the natural resource endowment of a tribal community is typically kept as a commons to which every member has an automatic right of access. Common-property resources generally have the following characteristics: their division would involve high transaction costs because they are highly spread out, possibly of a low quality, or it would entail high opportunity costs in terms of lost scale economies and/or foregone insurance benefits (such as happens when their returns are highly variable across time and space). In the latter case, indeed, a system offering access to a large area within which rights-holding users (think of herders or fishermen) can freely move appears as a desirable arrangement from a risk-reducing perspective (Dasgupta 1993: 288–289; Baland and Platteau 1998; Platteau 2000: Chapter 3; Breusers 2001).

Village commons can benefit all members of the community or mainly the local poor, and they can be used either on a permanent or a transient basis. Regarding the former aspect, there is abundant evidence that poor villagers tend to derive a substantial fraction of their incomes from the local commons, which then have a clear social security function in the sense of providing protection against the risk of chronic poverty (Jodha 1986; McKean 1986; Dasgupta 1987; Hecht *et al.* 1988; Humphries 1990; Agarwal 1991).

Turning to the latter aspect, the commons are used as a permanent basis when they are a vital resource that everybody depends upon for everyday livelihood. And they are used on a transient basis when they serve as a fall back resource that provides all members with partial protection in times of unusual economic stress. It is evident that the more aggregate the risks, or the more common the (downside) shocks hitting the community, the larger the externalities created in the use of the commons and the lower the (average) return extracted by the villagers. If risks are idiosyncratic rather than collective, it is important that people in the community are left free to access the commons depending upon their needs of the moment. In such conditions, the absence of exclusive property rights means that risks are more effectively pooled (Bromley and Chavas 1989: 730).

12.1.3. *Land Loans and Non-Land Exchange Arrangements*

Clearly, village commons can be effective not only in helping the vulnerable members of the community to escape chronic poverty, but also in helping them and probably other members of the community to tide over periods of unusual economic stress. The first function is equally evident in the case of privately appropriated land (or water) resources insofar as a corporate system of landownership guarantees an access to portions of these resources that enables all member households to earn a decent livelihood in different phases of their lifecycle. Whether such a system allows people to cope with adverse shocks in the short or medium term will depend on the presence of other institutional arrangements. Indeed, because land is not the only factor that plays a critical role in production, a guaranteed access to land does not properly insure a household or a person confronted with a sudden shortage of a complementary input. Just consider the case of a dearth of labour, say due to illness or a temporary absence from the village. In this case, customary land tenure rules must be complemented by labour exchange mechanisms in order to provide effective protection against income shortfalls. In actual fact, the supply of emergency labour assistance to a needy household within the framework of voluntary reciprocal transfers (in kind) is frequently observed in tribal communities.

What applies to labour also holds true for other production factors such as draught animals: in order to allow a field to be cultivated even when the possessor has lost his cattle, neighbours can possibly come to his rescue by bringing their own animals to that field. Since well-known moral hazard considerations prevent them from simply lending their stock to the needy farmer, assistance is here provided in the form of a joint input associating labour with draught power.

If the risk lies in a shortage of land rather than labour or cattle, the customary system of land tenure can be considered to effectively perform as a social security mechanism provided that land adjustments are rapid enough. The above-described rules that apply to women who find themselves without the support of a man are a good illustration of this possibility. Also, as pointed out by Boserup (1965: 80): 'If a family does not need to use a given plot for a certain period it may pledge it to another family... subject to the condition that the land must be returned upon request.' In other words, the operation of a flexible system of land loans or pledges usually provides the necessary safeguard against short-term imbalances in land distribution. Among the Chagga and the Kikuyu (Kenya), for example, 'tenants' could be accepted on lineage land, and they used (before registration of land was undertaken towards the end of the colonial period) to pay a fee up front for use of the land. The lineage could redeem the land at any time by repaying the original amount, but the redeemer had to reimburse the tenant for any improvements made to the land (Pinckney and Kimuyu 1994: 12; see also Schapera 1943).

Long-term loans of land can also be observed if this resource is unequally distributed because villagers belong to different ethnicities, castes, lineages, or family units that are unequal in social status (think, for example, of the persisting social differentiation between descendants of slaves and slave owners in West Africa, which dates back to the Islamic conquest). Traditional land loans can sometimes extend over several generations, thus reflecting the existence of patronage relations through which land-rich households put at the secure disposal of land-poor households the amount of land necessary for their subsistence. Typically, in such cases, land borrowing and lending transactions, at least among native farmers, are often part of a wider relationship between two families or lineages, and the desire to keep such a relationship going ensures that borrowing arrangements are frequently renewed or not easily ended.

For instance, as has been observed in the particular case of Burkina Faso by Matlon (1994) and De Zeeuw (1997), use rights over borrowed lands can actually be bequeathed to descendants when the borrower and the lender have struck a sort of long-term socio-political alliance (the borrower owes loyalty to the family of the lender) and land has thus been lent for an indefinite period. In the words of Matlon:

> Because of the strong tradition of transfer of intergenerational use rights, inheritable use rights prevail even for fields on long-term borrowing arrangements [borrowed by ancestors and subsequently passed down to current users through inheritance]. ... Most farmers consider withdrawal of use rights unthinkable for long-term borrowings that have been within the current user's household for more than one generation (Matlon 1994: 52–54).

Nowadays, this long-term borrowing of land (traditionally known as *mokwala doudou*) has become rather rare owing to the growing scarcity of land. It is to this kind of dynamic considerations that attention is turned in the following section.

12.1.4. *Summary*

Before turning our attention to dynamic processes, let us pause for a moment in order to relate the above facts to the central theme of the chapter. The customary land tenure system prevailing in lineage-based societies appears to be guided by both insurance and equity considerations. The insurance motive is evident from the fact that membership in a rural community automatically ensures proper access to land be it in the form of use rights over privately apportioned land plots or over the village commons. Thus, for instance, a member who emigrated and later decides to return to his native village because of economic difficulties or other reasons is entitled to obtain enough land to make a living.

As for the equity motive, it is reflected in the fact that, for example, people with smaller privately held landholdings have the same rights of access to the village commons than those with large landholdings—and may actually use them more intensively than the latter. Equality is not necessarily perfect, though, since descendants of the founding lineage(s) are generally guaranteed a better access to valuable lands. What deserves to be emphasized is that the efficiency costs of redistributive or insurance-motivated rules of land allocation are nil or negligible. When land use patterns are extensive, indeed, the need for land improvements simply does not exist as a result of which no particular advantage would be derived from the granting of permanent rights over well-delimited parcels of land.

12.2. THE GRADUAL EROSION OF THE SOCIAL SECURITY FUNCTION OF INDIGENOUS LAND TENURE ARRANGEMENTS

When population grows rapidly and when market integration proceeds at a significant pace, such as we have observed in Africa especially during the postcolonial period, land becomes more scarce and therefore more valuable. This new situation is bound to cause substantial transformations in the indigenous system of land tenure. In point of fact, observation of evolving arrangements in many African regions amply confirm the economic prediction that the nature of property rights in land must change in the direction of increased privatization and allocation processes must increasingly resemble market mechanisms (see Platteau 2001: Chapters 3 and 4, for detailed references). In the following, we intend to elaborate upon the dynamics of this evolution, especially with a view to highlighting its impact on the traditional role of land tenure arrangements as a provider of social security.

Our analysis proceeds in three successive stages where three different effects of land tenure evolution are being discussed. These effects are taken up separately in each of the following sections. In the order of their presentation, they are: the growing incidence of exclusionary practices, including the collapse of social security through land access rules for single adult women (Section 12.2.1); the gradual disappearance of the village commons as well as their diminishing role as fall-back options for the poor (Section 12.2.2); and the increasing individualization of land tenure rights (Section 12.2.3).

12.2.1. *The Growing Incidence of Exclusionary Practices*

When population pressure on village-level natural resources intensifies, growing competition causes an increasing incidence of externalities among users that get reflected in declining individual incomes. A common response to this situation consists of restricting access by outsiders to these resources (see, for example, Noronha 1985; Downs and Reyna 1988; Bassett and Crummey 1993; Berry 1993; Laurent *et al.* 1994). Thus, for example, in the case of the Orma pastoralist communities of northeastern Kenya, elders responded to increasing land pressure by prohibiting nomadic (Somali and other Orma) herders from grazing their herds on the village common pasture. Over the years, they strengthened this prohibition by gradually extending the period during which the local common pasture is made inaccessible to outsiders. Eventually, the restricted zone was declared out of bounds to the outsiders year round. Interestingly, however, Orma villagers continued to use the common pasture as much as they liked and this lack of restrictions applied to insiders was not seen by them as problematic in spite of the quick degradation of the resource that ensued (Ensminger 1990: 667–669).

Exclusion takes place not only with respect to common-property resources but also with respect to individually held portions of land. Thus, an immediate upshot of the growing scarcity of land is that stranger farmers are being increasingly denied their rights of access to land, especially to plots of relatively high quality. In the Senegal river valley, for example, the local Haalpulaar (Toucouleur) communities have become concerned that land will not be available in sufficient amounts for their children and grandchildren. As a result, they have started closing access to the good inundable lands (known as *waalo*) located near the river for all strangers and immigrant farmers, confining them to the poor-quality drylands (the *jeeri* soils), which are still plentiful (Rodenbach 1999). Similar events have occurred in many places in sub-Saharan Africa and violent conflicts have resulted in not a few cases (as in Côte d'Ivoire, in the Senegal river valley, in Guinea, in the Kivu state in Congo, and so on).

Another form of exclusion that is increasingly resorted to is the calling into question of the secondary or derived rights of access to land that are usually reckoned under the customary system of land tenure. With land becoming increasingly scarce, derived rights thus tend to be denied to secondary rightsholders for fear that they might stake ownership claims and/or simply because continuous cultivation practices are being introduced with a view to making land exploitation more intensive (see, for example, Coldham 1978; Ault and Rutman 1979; Noronha 1985; Bruce 1986; Green 1987; Barrows and Roth 1989; Bruce and Fortmann 1989; Atwood 1990; Platteau 1992, 1996, 2000: Chapter 4; Mackenzie 1993).

In West Africa, for example, gradual demarcation of parcels for cultivation in what were communal pastures previously arouses the anger of those groups such as the *Tuaregs* and the *Fulanis* who primarily depend on animal grazing for their daily live-lihood (see, for example, Lund 1998). The outcome, of course, depends upon the configuration of power relations, including possible alliances with state authorities. In actual fact, 'the farmers often have the upper hand in conflicts over pastures', and 'the extension of cultivated fields into the pastoral areas is the main trend' (Lund 1998: 142, 145). Revealingly, access to grazing lands is more easily open to influential and wealthy farmers who know with whom to forge tactical alliances, how to approach and mobilize authorities, how to read a sequence of contingent opportunities, and how to use economic resources at their disposal to influence the result of an arbitration.[4]

Women are a special category of insiders because, even though they have been born in the village, they are destined to leave it and reside in their husband's location (at least, this is so in societies following the patrilocal system of marriage). It is therefore not surprising that they are an especially vulnerable lot when land resources are lacking.

---

[4] As Christian Lund points out, 'some money always change hands during an audience. Economic resources, therefore, play a central role. While the difference between a token of respect, a fee and a bribe can be difficult to discern since the gesture holds several meanings depending on the position of the "giver", the "receiver", and the "onlooking opposing litigant", money or other tangible goods are necessary prerequisites for accessing the politico-legal institutions' (Lund 1998: 161).

Perceived as strangers in their husband's village and as a threatening additional claimant on family land in their native village, they tend to be rejected from every quarter when in difficulty.

Thus, in the course of a field study on the role of self-help groups in Kibera slum, Nairobi, Kenya (see Abraham *et al.* 1998), it was observed that nearly half of the members of such groups are single women: divorced or separated women, unwed mothers, eloping women, and widows. Interviews revealed that many of these women have been denied access to land, whether in the village of their husband or in their native place where the parental farm is located, and were compelled to migrate to cities and survive on precarious employments, including prostitution. Young beggars in Nairobi and other big cities are actually the children of these destitute women.

Observations in Central and Western Kenya (as well as in the Kilimanjaro region in Tanzania, and to Western Rwanda) confirm that the growing number of women falling into the above categories are confronted with livelihood problems owing to their inability to accede to land (Hakansson 1988; Rocheleau *et al.* 1994; Rocheleau and Edmunds 1995; Hunt 1996; personal field observations). Thus, brothers-in-law may harass a widow because her rights to use the land of her ex-husband and to bequeath it to her children compete with their claims on the family land assets. If she wants to escape from such an atmosphere of conflict, she may have no other solution than to migrate to a city or a plantation because a return to her parents' home may prove equally difficult due to the opposition of her own brothers.

The same opposition may be manifested by the brothers towards a sister seeking haven on the family land following the break-up of her marriage, or towards an unmarried sister with children who stays in the parental home for lack of marriage proposals. Thus, parents have generally become unwilling to accept a separated daughter back home even when she has truly suffered from living with her husband. If she refuses to return to him, she is pushed out of the family on the ground that the home of a married woman is in her husband's village and that it is the duty of a woman to put up with her husband and in-law family. In fact, marriage gifts offered to a woman, such as bed and mattress, serves to carry the point that once married she has no place in her parental home. The fact that the brideprice must be repaid to the husband's family if the woman is considered responsible for the break-up of the marriage compounds the problem still further.

Finally, the growing frequency of elopements as a result of the spreading of love marriages (girls elope with boys whom they love because the latter are unable to pay the customary brideprice) can easily lead to the same predicament as unwed motherhood. In the event of separation, indeed, women who did not go through a customary marriage find themselves in the position of unwed mothers. Moreover, if their companion dies, they will be denied any use rights over his land and their children will be barred from inheriting their father's property. On the other hand, the premature death of a co-habiting woman can lead to problems for her burial since her customary right of being buried in her husband's land can be denied when the union has not been legitimized. This is a serious problem insofar as the burial in the parent's land of married daughters, whether their marriage is legitimate or not, brings shame to the family. Therefore, such a prospect is likely to be resisted by the woman's own family which usually prefers to forego the payment of the brideprice and have the union legitimized post-mortem on the basis of a symbolic marriage payment so that the customary burial ceremony can take place.

According to our informants in Kenya, marriage is becoming a problem for uneducated and unemployed daughters belonging to economically better-off families that are engaged in non-agricultural activities, such as trade, business, and professions. Such women have a relatively low value in the marriage market as they do not have the necessary education to find a job in the modern sector nor do they have any experience in agriculture. Thus, young men in the countryside tend to rate them low because they do not know how to till the land and manage a farm. Failure to find a marriage partner after having waited for a long period has the effect of pushing these uneducated and unemployed women into unwed motherhood or elopement.

On the other hand, due to the impossibility of returning to the parental home for help in case of marital problems, women are more and more obliged to put up with unbearable tensions within their couple and the in-law family. According to our informants from Tanzania, parents and close relatives keep a close watch over their married daughters and invest emotionally in young couples to make sure that conjugal conflicts do not escalate to the point of marriage breakdown. This is done by paying repeated visits to them and advising them in difficult moments.

Finally, it must be remarked that when population pressure becomes very acute exclusionary practices may not only affect female but also male members of the narrow family group. Thus, in our study of Rwanda, we found that old parents were harassed by their boys on the ground that they had reserved for themselves more land than could be justified by their subsistence needs in old age. Despair among old people was sometimes reflected in a longing for death, or it led them to select a poor caretaker outside the family circle in order to help them work their piece of land on the understanding that he would inherit it upon their death (André and Platteau 1998).

12.2.2. *The Diminishing Role of the Commons*

The role of the village commons as an institutional arrangement providing social security can decrease as a result of either their sheer physical disappearance or their reduced economic significance under the impact of population growth, possibly mitigated by growing market integration. For the sake of clarity, we consider these two distinct situations in turn.

Privatization of the commons
The first effect occurs when the commons are being privatized because the efficiency costs of a common-property regime become too high (see Baland and Platteau 1996 for a formal elaboration) and people want to complement their privately inherited lands, which have become too small, with a share of the resources that used to be jointly held in the past. Division of the commons may be made in an rather egalitarian and

democratic manner or in a coercive way under the initiative of a village elite eager
to appropriate them for their private benefit (see Platteau 2000: Chapter 3, for more
details).

In the latter instance, even allowing for the combined fact that (i) the villagers now
deprived of access to the local commons may possibly be hired as labourers by the new
exclusive owner; and that (ii) the privatized resource will be more efficiently managed
because externalities are better internalized under private than collective ownership,
the distributional consequences of privatization may be undesirable. As Weitzman
(1974) has shown, indeed, dispossessed resource users are necessarily worse off after
privatization when they lose the rent associated with the resource.[5] This follows from
the fact that the wage earned in the newly created labour market is always lower than
the income obtained under communal ownership. Former resource users thus lose not
only in terms of employment (not all the joint owners of the resource in the previous
situation will be hired by the appropriator after it has been privatized) but also on
account of reduced individual labour earnings. In point of fact, the rent collected by
landlords exceeds the extra output society achieved by shifting from common property
to the private ownership equilibrium (Samuelson 1974).

The result obtained by Weitzman is not quite robust, however. As a matter of
fact, even without a share of the rents, it is possible that the returns to labour rise
with privatization if complementary inputs to labour are variably provided (De Meza
and Gould 1985, 1987). Moreover, in general equilibrium, as the output obtained
in the commons is expected to fall after privatization due to better internalization of
externalities, its price will increase resulting in a rise of the marginal product of labour
and the real wage. The same result of increasing real wages following privatization
of a commons can be achieved by assuming that workers are heterogeneous in skills
(Brito *et al.* 1997).[6] Last, it is noteworthy that all these arguments are static: if the
exclusive owner responds to privatization by adopting technical innovations and if
these innovations are labour-intensive (this assumption is purely gratuitous as we have
no particular reason to believe that it would be true), the level of employment could be
higher than assumed by Weitzman.

What needs to be emphasized now is the following: the above-illustrated indeterminacy in the predicted distributive outcome of privatization comes out of works that
overlook the insurance role that common-property resources might play, as underlined
in the previous section. In order to properly assess the possible insurance gains that
common property allows, it is essential to take into account the possibility that after

---

[5] For a simple graphical proof of Weitzman's theorem under the assumption of quasi-linear preferences,
see Baland and Platteau 1987: 47–48.

[6] When workers are heterogeneous, indeed, institutional arrangements associated with ownership as well
as the technology that creates the externality become crucial and the outcome of privatization (whether it is
Pareto-improving) is highly sensitive to the particular assumptions made. More precisely, the institutional
arrangements of a licensor (the private owner charges a fixed fee for the use of the fixed factor) or a two-part
tariff on effort or output (a linear tax with a fixed entry fee) can lead to an increase in the income of the
variable factor after privatization (since, in those cases, the owner is not able to appropriate all the gains from
privatization).

privatization other institutions may emerge to provide similar consumption insurance. If contracting were complete, we know from general equilibrium theory that outcomes under privatization would dominate those under the common-property regime. Yet, in the rural areas of developing countries, contracting if it is typically incomplete so that the result of the comparison between the two property regimes is not straightforward. Baland and François (1999) have recently addressed this problem rigorously by considering two sources of contracting incompleteness: the first one arises out of informational asymmetries while the second one is due to limited enforcement. In the first situation, individuals have private productivity information but contracts conditioned on commonly known events can be fully enforced. By contrast, the second situation is characterized by widely shared information about individuals but poor enforcement prevents compliance with the terms of contracts *ex post*.

In the presence of such contracting limitations, and a full tragedy of the commons, the authors show that if individuals face independently distributed risks and are sufficiently risk averse, privatization of the common-property resource, even when perfect, costless, and equitable, can reduce welfare. In other words, common property has desirable consumption insurance features, which are not present under private property and 'cannot be replicated by the establishment of a private insurance market under equivalent informational assumptions' (Baland and François 1999: 3). In the first situation (private information and full enforcement), the insurance advantage of common property is all the more likely to exist as the income derived from the use of the common property is higher and the labour earning possibilities of the adversely affected agents are lower. In the second, opposite situation, this advantage is all the more likely to occur as both the efficiency gains from privatization and the opportunity costs from exploiting the resource for agents of the high type (those with relatively attractive income opportunities outside the commons) are lower.

In general, one should therefore expect widespread opposition to privatization of common-property resources, except by those individuals who are able to appropriate them. Opposition may nevertheless dwindle if the cost of insurance rises so much, owing to the growing efficiency costs resulting from greater externalities, that it comes to exceed the benefit.

Reduced economic significance of the commons: the distributive aspect
A common-property resource may be kept whole because it is prohibitively costly to divide, or because the community concerned wants to maintain it in that state for insurance or other purposes. In these circumstances, a significant increase in the number of rightsholders (the 'insiders') will produce two distinct effects. First, it will cause the average return from the use of the resource to fall, which may jeopardize the livelihood of the poor. The threat is all the more ominous if the resource is subject to gradual degradation over time under conditions of excessive pressure. In the second place, growing numbers of participants may erode the insurance capacity of the common-property resource in the sense that the vulnerability or exposure to risk of the individuals depending on it may become larger. As for increasing market integration, it may mitigate and even outweigh the negative effect of population growth on

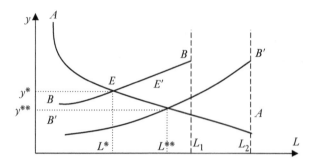

Figure 12.1. *Impact of population growth and market integration on average incomes*

average incomes while it is likely to fail to mitigate the negative effect of population growth on income variations. Let us now substantiate these results in greater detail.

The negative effect of population growth on average income obtains as soon as we assume that the resource is subject to decreasing returns, an inescapable outcome of scarcity. Consider a situation in which two income sources are available to community members: farming incomes derived from privately held land, on the one hand, and incomes obtained from a common-property resource, say a fishing space, on the other hand. To begin with, we assume that all households are equally endowed in privately held land. For the sake of simplicity, we make the additional inconsequential assumption that the two activities, farming and fishing, are exclusive in the sense that a given individual cannot be simultaneously engaged in both. All households choose the proportion of their workforce that is going to work on the commons and, since they are equally endowed, this proportion is identical across all households. Furthermore, all villagers operating on the commons are assumed to be equivalently productive and to receive the average product therefrom.

This situation is depicted in Fig. 12.1 where the average income earned per individual, denoted by y, is measured along the vertical axis while the total number of individuals occupied on the common fishery, denoted by L, is measured along the horizontal axis.

The number of individuals remaining to work on the family farms is measured residually from right to left as the distance between the initial size of the population, L_1 and L^*, the equilibrium number of individuals engaged in the common fishery in the initial situation. This initial equilibrium is derived by intersecting the downward-sloping curve AA with the upward-sloping curve BB. The curve AA describes the way the average income derived from the fishing sector falls as the number of workers involved increases. As for the curve BB, its shape reflects the fact that the marginal and also the average productivity of labour in agriculture are decreasing with the number of farmers actively working the land. (For the sake of simplicity, all non-labour costs are assumed to be negligible.) Corresponding to the intersection point E is y^*, the average equilibrium individual income in the initial situation.

Comparative statistics enables us to highlight the effects of population growth and market expansion. The first effect is depicted by a shift rightwards of the perpendicular to the horizontal axis corresponding to population size, now set at L_2. As a result of this move, the upward-sloping curve shifts downwards from position BB to position $B'B'$. The new intersection point, E', therefore implies a lower equilibrium average individual income, y^{**}, and a higher equilibrium number of people working in the common fishery, L^{**}. The number of people working in agriculture has also increased, from $(L_1 - L^*)$ to $(L_2 - L^{**})$.

The second effect, that of market integration, may consist of an increase in the price of agricultural products that get translated in an upward shift of the BB curve. The outcome of this change is, as expected, an increase in the number of people engaged in agriculture, the sector which has become relatively more attractive, and a subsequent fall of the number of those engaged in the common fishery. Unlike what was observed in the case of population growth, the average individual income rises. If the produce collected from the commons is marketed rather than being largely self-consumed, the AA curve may also undergo an upward shift and the net change in the equilibrium number of people exploiting the common fishery will of course depend on the relative sizes of the two parallel shifts. In any event, the individual average income increases.

More interesting is the case where both population growth and market penetration occur at the same time. In such circumstances, two opposite forces are in operation and their net impact on the average individual income is impossible to predict a priori. Thus, if price increases affect only the agricultural sector, the curve BB undergoes a downward shift as a result of population growth and an upward shift as a result of market penetration. Bear in mind that increased rates of use of the village commons following a shift in the internal terms of trade in favour of the products extracted from them (relative to the price of agricultural products) imply a particular risk, namely that of causing their gradual degradation over time. We may now relax the simplistic assumption according to which all community members are equally endowed in private landholdings. Adopting the formalization used by Baland and François in their afore-mentioned paper, let us consider a continuum of agents each of whom is endowed with one unit of labour. Each agent i can allocate labour to his private farm, with returns θ_i, or work in the common fishery. Returns to labour on the farm, θ, are continuously distributed over $[0, \infty]$, by the density $f(\theta)$. The fixed amount of the common-property resource is denoted by R while, as above, L is the aggregate labour used in the common fishery. The commons' production function, $Y(R, L)$, is homogeneous of degree one, strictly increasing and concave in L. It is then easy to see that an equilibrium allocation of labour in this sector is given by

$$L^0 : \frac{Y(R, L^0)}{L^0} = \theta^0 \qquad \text{with} \int_0^{\theta^0} f(\theta)\, d\theta = L^0.$$

With such an allocation, all agents i, for whom $\theta_i \leq \theta^0$, work in the common fishery and receive $Y(R, L^0)/L^0$ while all agents with $\theta_i > Y(R, L^0)/L^0$ work on their private landholdings obtaining payment θ_i.[7]

---

[7] By assumption, the distribution of θ is such that $L^* > 0$. Concavity of $Y(.)$ in L ensures that the equilibrium allocation, L^*, is unique.

Equilibrium allocations on the common-property resource therefore imply that those villagers with smallest land endowments obtain a larger proportion of the rents generated by this resource. As pointed out by Baland and François (1999), a commons 'thus provides a form of income targeting to the poor', in line with the empirical evidence reviewed in Section 12.1. A presumed effect of population growth is that the absolute number of community members with $\theta_i \leq \theta^0$ increases, putting added pressure on the commons and causing a fall in the average product therefrom. The allocation of labour to the common fishery, L^0, rises in the new equilibrium and the incomes of the poor are lower. On the other hand, if it causes the value of incomes from private landholdings to rise relatively to those obtained on the common-property resource, market integration reduces the pressure on this resource and the situation of the poorest members of the community improves. If prices rise in both sectors, that pressure may not be relieved, yet the poor are still better than before.

Reduced economic significance of the commons: the insurance aspect
In order to illustrate the insurance effect of the evolution of the commons, a convenient method is to posit a resource characterized by a fixed number of exploitable spots that are continuously occupied as soon as population pressure begins to bear. Think, for example, of a beachseine fishery. Beachseining is a fishing technique that requires a substantial water space located close to the shore to operate. This follows from the fact that the beachseine is a large bag-shaped net with coir-wings of extensive length which, although necessitates the help of a boat to be put out at sea, is essentially handled from the shore itself. Note that the sea bottom must be sandy and free from rocks and other obstructions so that the net can be dragged smoothly. These two constraints have the obvious effect of limiting the number of fishing spots that are available to any given coastal community (Alexander 1980; 1982; Platteau *et al.* 1985; Amarasinghe 1989).

Let n be the number of community members who need to work on the resource to earn a living, m the number of available fishing spots, y_i the (certain) daily return yielded by spot i, and $Var(y_i)$ the variance of such returns. Let us also have that $p = n/m$, the number of users per available resource spot. When p exceeds one, there is a queuing problem resulting from an effective pressure of the user group on the commons. The value of p can therefore be construed as a measure of the intensity of that pressure. We are essentially interested in the way household vulnerability to hunger evolves as population pressure increases. Household vulnerability, denoted by V, is defined here as the proportion of annual time during which the income earned by the household falls below an accepted standard of minimum consumption. It obviously varies between a minimum zero value and a maximum unitary value. Incomes are assumed to be earned on a daily basis. Finally, the distribution of location-specific yields is such that the yield falls short of the minimum subsistence level, labelled c, in some fishing sites but not in others. Let us denote by F the relative number of sites such that $y_j < c$ ($0 \leq F \leq 1$).

The general formula describing household vulnerability as a function of population pressure is:

$$V = \frac{n - (m - mF)}{n} = 1 - \frac{1}{p}(1 - F).$$

Table 12.1. *Evolution of household vulnerability as population grows under two different assumptions regarding the variation of location-specific yields*

n ($m = 4$, given)	V with $F = 1/4$	V with $F = 1/2$
6	4/8	8/12
8	5/8	9/12
12	6/8	10/12

In accordance with the anthropological literature, a rotation rule has been posited to exist that allows the limited locations available on each fishing day to be equally shared among the rightsholders.[8] More precisely, the rule provides that fishermen with access rights should be shifted from day to day from one spot to another so that income-earning opportunities are perfectly equalized (see Baland and Platteau 1996: 199–209).

Polar cases obtain when (i) $p = 1$ and $F = 0 \Rightarrow V = 0$ (all fishermen can be continuously occupied and returns are uniform across all fishing spots at a rewarding level); (ii) $p > 1$ and $F = 0 \Rightarrow V = 1 - 1/p$ (fishermen are deprived of income on certain days owing to a lack of available spots); and (iii) $p = 1$ and $F > 0 \Rightarrow V = F$ (there are enough spots yet some of them do not provide enough yield to allow subsistence). The general case obtains when the number of claimants exceeds that of the available fishing spots and the quality of these spots varies significantly, so that fishing incomes vary on a double count. This is the situation described by Alexander in his study of beachseine fishing communities in Sri Lanka (1982), by Berkes in his inquiry about Alanya fishermen in Turkey, or by Béné *et al.* (2002) with reference to Ghanaian small-scale fisheries. The signs of the first derivatives are straightforward: $\mathrm{d}V/\mathrm{d}p > 0$ and $\mathrm{d}V/\mathrm{d}F > 0$. Furthermore, $\mathrm{d}(\mathrm{d}V/\mathrm{d}p)/\mathrm{d}F < 0$.

In Table 12.1, we present a simple numerical example that illustrates the aforementioned results. We assume that $m = 4$ while n takes on three different values and F two different ones.

If we now consider the possibility that growing population pressure on the common-property resource causes its gradual degradation, we must recognize the existence of a relationship of the form $F = f(p)$, with $f'(p) > 0$. The impact of population pressure on household vulnerability then includes both a direct and an indirect effect:

$$\frac{\mathrm{d}V}{\mathrm{d}p} = \frac{(1 - F) + pf'(p)}{p^2} \geq 0,$$

where $pf'(p)$ corresponds to the indirect effect.

---

[8] Note that, if no rotation rule exists and access to fishing locations is anarchic, welfare losses are likely to occur because fishermen will tend to flock in the most promising spots (those with the best income prospects) while a more balanced distribution of them among the available sites would have been more socially efficient (see Platteau and Seki 2001: 397–9, for a proof). Moreover, the costs of large congregations of boats in the best locations (collisions entailing damages and injuries) will have to be borne.

Instead of assuming that yields of the resource vary from one location to another, we could alternatively assume that yields are identical (like in the second case considered above) yet fluctuate seasonally. To the problem of unemployment is now added the risky prospect that fishermen will have their turn during the lean season when yields are uniformly low. In the aforementioned work by Alexander (1982), only 25 per cent of the beachseines thus received turns during the flush period in 1970–1. It is true that over the medium or long term incomes are expected to even out as the rotation rule ensures that every fisherman will operate his net during the flush period if a sufficiently long period is considered. In the short term, however, the pressing question remains as to how fishermen will succeed in buffering the year-to-year fluctuations in income that are the direct result of their growing numbers (Platteau 1991: 125–129).

In the most complex case, interseasonal fluctuations in yields are added to variations between locations. Household vulnerability is likely to be quite large in such circumstances insofar as there is no reason to expect that the different types of risks will cancel each other out.

A last and important remark is in order. If the expansion of market opportunities is accompanied by a process of socio-economic differentiation that is reflected in unequal asset endowments, and if rights to have turns in a rotation scheme are defined on the basis of asset units (in this instance, fishing units) rather than of household units or individuals, the rich will improve their ability to insure in the commons at the expense of the poor. Indeed, by raising the number of their turns in the sequence of access rights and by spreading them over the entire net cycle, the former can stabilize their incomes. The latter find themselves in the opposite situation insofar as their shares or participation rates in the sequence of net turns are more diluted than before, thereby causing an erosion of their insurance capacity. For the poor, increasing inequality has actually the same effect as population growth. This is exactly the story told by Alexander (1982) for the village of Gahävalla in south Sri Lanka (see Bardhan *et al.* 2002 for a similar story about forestries in Nepal).

Clearly, the old rotational arrangement aimed at equalizing income-earning opportunities is perverted under the joint impact of rising pressure on the resource and private accumulation strategies by the rich. When so perverted, it may quickly become inferior to the private property outcome from the standpoint of the poor. (For an illustration of the adverse effects on household exposure to risk of combined inter-seasonal and inter-location fluctuations of yields as well as inequality in the distribution of assets, see Platteau 2002.)

12.2.3. *Increasing Individualization of Land Tenure Rights*

We have already noted (see above, Section 12.2.1) that population growth breeds exclusionary practices initiated by the strongest customary rightsholders in village societies. The gradual demise of secondary rights traditionally enjoyed by the weaker segments of the rural population (herders, old slaves, artisans, . . .) and the withdrawal of rights of land occupancy for members of late-arrived kin groups are an illustration of these marginalization processes that directly reflect the growing individualization of land rights under conditions of increased land pressure. The trend towards more exclusive possession of the land is not the only manifestation of such individualization, however. Two other ingredients that are especially relevant to our topic are (i) the increasingly permanent use rights that individual possessors enjoy over the land; and (ii) the enlarging scope of their rights to transfer it relatively freely. They are both mentioned in the following statement of Robert Bates who draws a pessimistic picture of their effects on social security:

Membership in the community is no longer sufficient to guarantee access to land; nor is it a necessary condition. Thus, land can be alienated to persons outside the community. Moreover, land that is not in use does not revert to the community; it can be held for purposes of speculation, transferred to other private individuals, or bequeathed to persons of the owner's choosing. It is a consequence of this system, of course, that even in the presence of abundant land, people may starve for want of access to it; primary attraction of a communal system of land rights is that under similar circumstances such deaths would not occur (Bates 1984: 243).

In the remainder of this section, we will examine the claim made by Bates by looking at the impact of the two aforementioned components of tenure individualization on the effectiveness of social security via land access rules. We will then be in a position to critically assess his judgement of the 'primary attraction of a communal system of land rights', which will be done in the conclusive section.

(i) An immediate consequence of population pressure on land resources is the shortening of the fallow period. When this period becomes sufficiently short, actual cultivators are prompted to claim the continued possession of their parcels. They thereby call into question the erstwhile practice according to which the land once fallow must return to the community to be reallocated later when its fertility will have been naturally restored. To enforce their claim, as noted by Boserup, they may even 'wish to begin to recultivate a given plot before the normal period of fallow has elapsed . . . lest the cultivation right be forfeited by desuetude'. As a result, smaller amounts of land will be available for redistribution by the chief, and 'valuable land for redistribution will become available mainly when a family dies out or leaves the territory. . . . Redistribution of land thus becomes a less important and less frequently exerted function of the chief, and in the end it disappears altogether' (Boserup 1965: 79–81; see also Cohen 1980: 359).

Since less land returns periodically to the village pool, there are also fewer possibilities to adjust the endowments of community members when the need arises. The scope of the social security mechanism that operates through such adjustments is correspondingly reduced to eventually vanish when all land plots are under the permanent control of their individual possessors. Note that this tendency is accelerated when the right to plant trees and to bring other improvements to the land are being recognized since such improvements are a well-established method of enhancing tenure security and establishing private property rights (see, for example, Noronha 1985; Bruce 1988; Robertson 1987; Besley 1995; De Zeeuw 1997; Sjaastad and Bromley 1997; Brasselle *et al.* 2002).

(ii) An important feature of indigenous land systems in sub-Saharan Africa is the existence of extremely tight restrictions on transfer rights. In particular, possessors are not allowed to alienate the land that belongs to the community considered as a corporate entity. Land gifts and land loans may be permitted when individual use rights to specific plots are established but only provided that the donee or the loanee belongs to the same community (of common descent or residence) as the donor or the lender. As for land sales, they are strictly forbidden as a matter of principle.

As land becomes more scarce and therefore more valuable, however, customary prohibitions regarding land transfers are gradually relaxed. At one end of the spectrum, concomitantly with the establishment of more permanent rights over the land, the right to bequeath land to children is increasingly asserted. At the other end, the right to sell the land individually held remains circumscribed, although in a less strict manner than before. There are thus several steps through which prescriptions concerning land sale prerogatives evolve as land scarcity increases.

At first, any land parcel sold is redeemable by the seller as soon as he gets the wherewithal to repurchase it (see, for example, Ault and Rutman 1979: 170). Indeed, as possession becomes more individualized, land is increasingly viewed as part of a family patrimony and it forms the substance of its social identity and prestige. As a result, it is an asset that may not be parted with: it belongs to the sphere of gifts—or, in the words of Godelier (1999), the sphere of 'inalienable possessions'—as opposed to commodity exchanges (Gregory 1982), implying that it can only be temporarily entrusted, but never really given away, to another individual or family. Moreover, sales are sanctioned only among members of the local community, since only they can be expected to keep their promise to give back the plot of land acquired if the above possibility arises.

Thereafter, sales become subject to a right of preemption by the seller (or his family): in the event that the present owner wants to dispose of the land purchased in the past, the land must go back to the original owner (or his family) provided that the latter is willing and able to repurchase it. If he is unwilling (say, because he has emigrated with his family) or unable to do so, the land may be sold but only with the approval of village elders. As a matter of fact, the elders have the responsibility to ensure that nobody within the group wants to acquire the land proposed for sale before allowing its disposal.

Finally, a stage is reached when all prohibitions fall into decay and land sales become completely free (see, for example, Bruce 1986: 38–40, 1993: 42). When the right to sell thus includes sales to members outside the community and the individual possessor of the land does not need any approval, 'the last vestiges of general cultivation rights are lost and private property rights are complete. General rights survive only as grazing and collection rights on communal grazing areas and forests, whose soils are usually unsuitable for crop or intensive pasture production' (Binswanger et al. 1995: 2669).

It bears emphasis that allowing the land to fall into the hands of outsiders is generally a consequence of the fact that land markets are often activated through distress sales (André and Platteau 1998). As has been pointed out by Bohannan and Dalton (1962), indeed, villagers would feel bad if they were to take advantage of the plight of their neighbors or kin in order to enlarge their own farms. As indicated above, it is only under the understanding that they would immediately release the plots to the distress seller would he become able to repurchase them (at the original selling price) that farmers would accept to buy plots disposed of under duress by another member of their community.

If farmers want to make permanent acquisitions (an expected feature given the increasing scarcity of land and the necessity to undertake long-term land improvements), and if there is no hope that the distress seller can retake possession of his land in a foreseeable future, the passing of village lands into the hands of outsiders is a likely outcome. Note incidentally that distress sales are a natural way in which a land market can establish itself despite customary prohibitions. This is because such prohibitions are generally suspended in cases of emergency (Dalton 1962), and rule violations become the norm when emergency conditions tend to persist.[9]

A similar evolution can be detected for land alienations through mortgaging. To begin with, what is permitted are traditional land pledges whereby a household obtains credit against temporarily foregoing the use of the land offered as a security to the lender. Upon repayment of the loan, the land is automatically redeemed to the pledgor. Revealingly, there is a common understanding that, even if the repayment is repeatedly postponed or delayed (sometimes over successive generations), ownership of the land is never transferred to the credit-giver, only the right to collect the proceeds derived from its exploitation. Later, this intrinsic right of the pledgor to retrieve his land is called into question and lenders—first discreetly and almost shamefully, then more openly— assert their willingness to set a time limit beyond which they can claim the right to keep the pledged land in full ownership (as I could observe in the highly populated district of Anloga, Ghana; or in the high value lands of the irrigation schemes of Yalogo, Burkina Faso).

With a mortgage, the lender does not have the right to use the land offered as security but, precisely for that reason, he will be all the more keen to exercise his right to seize upon it if the debt is not cleared in due time. The main question is how long the borrower may delay his loan repayment before the threat of foreclosure becomes effective. Like in the case of land pledges, evolution towards free alienability of land assets is reflected in the shorter grace periods granted to the borrower, in the diminished role of the group in negotiating such grace periods in order to rescue him, and in the increasingly recognized right of the lender to stipulate precise terms regarding repayment conditions.

On the other hand, since the same kind of prohibitions as found in the case of land sales also traditionally applied to land mortgages, the individualization of land rights also gets reflected in the gradual relaxation of these prohibitions. Yet, given the enormous stake involved in such an evolution, it is not surprising that loans are often taken against other securities than the land itself, for example, the security of standing crops. It may nevertheless happen, as has been observed on irrigation schemes in Burkina Faso (Yalogo region), that the credit-giver reserves to himself in the event

---

[9] Traditional prohibitions against land sales are more easily subverted when the land and money exchanged are in the form of gifts and counter-gifts rather than trade, as observed by Espen Sjaastad (1998) for Zambia.

of crop failure the right to take hold of his borrower's land if the latter is unable to return the loan after a more or less protracted span of time (Baland *et al*. 1998). In such circumstances, the risk of crop failure is entirely borne by the borrower and loans are ultimately secured by his land.

There is an evident rationale behind restrictions on free land sales or free land mortgaging by individual rightsholders and this rationale is based on obvious social security considerations. As a matter of fact, heads of a lineage or a family, and elders in general, are concerned that if land becomes freely disposable they will have eventually to bear the negative consequences that can follow from the granting of such a freedom. In Kenya, for instance, we learn that it is mainly elders who reject the idea of land mortgage while younger men tend to be more attracted by the prospect of ready cash and, as a result, they are more liable to have their lands foreclosed (Shipton 1988: 106, 120). 'Urgent' consumption needs, which elders may well regard as luxury, can easily drive young people into landlessness, whether inadvertently or not (Green 1987: 7; *The Economist* 21–27 January 1995: 49). Attractive but risky investment projects may have the same effect.

Once deprived of their land assets, since there is no state social security system to fall back on and since alternative employment opportunities are rare and labour markets risky, the venturesome or myopic youngsters are tempted to rely on the elders for their subsistence needs. To avoid being involved in such rescue operations, elders prefer that land sales by youngsters be made subject to their approval. In other words, restrictions on the free play of land markets eventually arise from the absence of a centralized social security mechanism as well as from all sorts of market imperfections (including risky labour markets and imperfect credit and insurance markets) that make people dependent on their native community or social group for a guaranteed livelihood.

It is interesting to point out that in Kenya (the only country in sub-Saharan Africa with several decades of experience with systematic registration and titling of rural lands), District Land Control Boards in charge of approving land sales are frequently reluctant to permit transactions which would leave families (and their descendants) landless and destitute. That is why they insist that all adult members of the household (including women) of the title-holder are to be present at the hearing to indicate their agreement with the sale. The government has actually sanctioned this de facto situation since a presidential directive aimed at minimizing land disputes requires the agreement of family members in addition to that of the title-holder prior to any sale or use of land as collateral (Haugerud 1983: 84; Mackenzie 1993: 200; Pinckney and Kimuyu 1994: 10).

In Zimbabwe, likewise, a proposal by a land tenure commission appointed by the government (October 1994) provides that individual farmers should be given the right to own their land, but their right to buy and sell it should be subject to the approval of the traditional village council (the *sabuku*) which in pre-colonial days used to be vested with the prerogative of allocating local lands (*The Economist* 21–27 January 1995: 49).

The lesson to draw from the above evidence is that, although there is an unmistakable trend towards the assertion of the right to permanently transfer land in African rural areas, resistance is still pervasive against unhibited land sale and mortgage transactions (see Platteau 2000: Chapter 4, for a more detailed account). This is apparently because of the social security risk involved. Revealing of the resistance that people can put up against such unfettered transactions is the fact that in Kenya lenders have had great difficulty foreclosing on land mortgages chiefly because 'the presence of many kin around mortgaged land makes it politically unfeasible to auction the holdings of defaulters' (Shipton 1988: 120). In urban peripheries, notes another study, 'although some banks have accepted titled land as collateral and auctioned it off in cases of default, in some cases purchasers were not able to take occupation of the land for fear of reprisals' (Migot-Adholla *et al.* 1991: 170).

In a recent study conducted in thirty-six villages of East-Central Uganda, probably the African country with the strongest tradition of land market activity (which dates back to colonial times), two results achieved by the authors are particularly relevant to our discussion. On the one hand, rural land markets are remarkably active as indicated by the fact that almost half of the total land area owned has been purchased. And, on the other hand, people who are native of a given location and did not inherit any land from their father have a privileged access to the local land sale market: other things being equal, they are able to purchase significantly larger areas than other residents, which enables them to eventually hold a sufficient amount of land to start a sustainable farming activity (Baland *et al.* 2001).[10] In addition, for autochthonous villagers with a positive land endowment inherited from the father, there is an inverse relationship between initial land endowment and the amount of land purchased in the village.

Such a positive discrimination in favour of landless or quasi-landless members of the community is mirrored in the fact that land sale transactions are typically subject to restrictions in the form of requirement of prior notification or approval by lineage authorities. Revealingly, a recent study done in the same region has concluded that 'despite the high proportion of parcels that had been acquired through purchase, the unfettered individual right of sale is relatively uncommon' (Place *et al.* 2001: 219). Such restrictions are usually driven by social security considerations, meaning concretely that (i) land is not being sold by people who may later need it, and (ii) priority is given to land-hungry people in the disposal of the land.[11]

In the Ziz valley (Morocco, see above), by contrast, customary restrictions on land transactions were aimed at barring people with a low and subservient status (the *Haratine*, of dark complexion) from acquiring land.[12] There, liberalization of the land sales market caused by the inflow of foreign remittances in the hands of the *Haratine*

---

[10] Note that in estimating the effect of landlessness on access to local land parcels offered for sale, the possibility that landless farmers expect to receive land in the future when their (presently living) father will have died has been explicitly allowed for.

[11] For a reason explained above, this priority is more easily given when the land sale is caused by the owner's emigration (a frequent occurrence in Uganda) or his desire to consolidate his land assets in the village than when it is caused by distress conditions.

[12] The concept of *shafa'a*—preemption rights in favour of the Berber clans or lineages—ensured that land would remain in their hands 'because a lineage member's price and blood negated those of a stranger or a *Haratine*'. As a matter of fact, 'in the Berber villages, any land transactions or selling of trees had to be made public so that the right of *shafa'a* could be applied by distant clan and lineage members who might be away from the village during the sale' (Ilahiane 2001: 104).

and the multiplication of distress sales by traditional landowners had beneficial effects on the distribution of land assets (Ilahiane 2001: 104–108).

In Rwanda, unlike what has been observed in Uganda, land sale transactions have had the effect of concentrating land in the hands of a minority of people lucky enough to enjoy access to the few non-agricultural employment opportunities available (see the in-depth study of André and Platteau 1998). Others, who did not have the required political connections to get access to these scarce jobs, have often been forced to resort to distress sales of land parcels in order to make ends meet. In this country, customary restrictions on land sale transactions have completely collapsed, giving rise to extremely bitter reactions on the part of landless people towards those who have purchased significant amounts of land thanks to their discriminatory access to ample non-agricultural incomes. The centrifugal tendencies operating in the Rwandan countryside are so strong that one can no more speak of 'village communities' and 'village customs', a consequence of extreme and continuing land pressure combined with an acute dearth of off-farm employment opportunities. These accumulated resentments, frustrations, and hatred manifested themselves in the crudest manner on the occasion of the 1993 civil war since there was a selective killing of large landowners even after controlling for ethnic affiliation.

The central lesson from the above two contrasted studies is therefore that rural land sale markets, provided that their functioning is limited by social security-driven considerations inspired by traditional norms, are susceptible of mitigating rather than accentuating inequalities in initial endowments. If such restrictions have vanished, on the other hand, one may fear that land sale transactions have a disequalizing impact.

It is time to recap our central argument. When a household head is allowed to sell land to another member of his community, it is because he can thus tide over a difficult period and is expected to redeem his land in the future. And it is because it wants to ensure that such repurchase will indeed be feasible that the social group does not approve land sales to people outside of its confines. Only upon its own members can it exercise the necessary pressure to prevent any reneging on the promise to give back the land purchased when the seller will be in better straits. Yet, beyond a point, presumably, land becomes such a valuable asset that promises to part with the land purchased once the seller is able to buy it again becomes non-credible, even when they have been made by fellow community members.

At this stage, the granting to the land seller of a preemption right to later repurchase his land if offered for sale constitutes the expected next step in the gradual emergence of a free land sale market. The rule according to which landless members of the community should have priority access to the local land sale market whenever a land is supplied participates in the same logic of providing whatever feasible support to deserving community members. This said, insofar as the social group does not really provide the landless or the land-hungry or the distress seller with the wherewithal needed to buy land, the above rules constitutes only an imperfect mechanism. Witness to it is the fact that distress sales do occur in the first place. Incidentally, the fact that poor people sell land under duress also attests to the imperfection of mutual insurance networks based on state-contingent reciprocal transfers, or to the presence of important aggregate risks.

12.3. CONCLUSION

The problem with the judgment made by Robert Bates in the beginning of this section is that it mistakenly assumes that the customary system of corporate landownership can be maintained intact under changing conditions of land availability (*'under similar circumstances* such deaths would not occur'—my italics). It is as though such a system would be the outcome of a cultural evolution conceived as an autonomous process cut-off from the sphere of material determinants of human life. We believe, on the contrary, that values, norms, and institutions are devices that answer the need to coordinate human behaviour in the specific context of a given technological, ecological, and economic environment. In other words, they are profoundly influenced by a particular set of material determinants of human life.[13]

Thus, as Ester Boserup (1965) and others (e.g. Johnson 1972: 271; Ault and Rutman 1979: 171–178) have convincingly argued, a communal system of land rights is conceivable only under conditions of relatively high land–person ratios.[14] When land becomes so scarce as to require a shift to intensive land use patterns, several processes are set in motion.

As far as common-property resources are concerned, three main evolutions are discernible. First, the growing incidence of externalities (economic and ecological) that results from increasing land scarcity has the effect of raising the cost of insurance provided through a guaranteed access to the village commons. The cost may rise so much as to exceed the benefit and rightsholders may therefore wish to divide the commons among themselves. This is all the more likely to happen if alternative, self-insurance opportunities have become available to them, for example, under the form of non-agricultural incomes. Second, the growing scarcity of cultivable lands tempts powerful people or the rural elite to privately appropriate the more valuable commons at the expense of other members of the local community. Third, for non-divisible common-property resources, by accumulating capital assets functioning as entry tickets richer rightsholders are able to increase their relative share of the product flows at the expense of poorer participants, thereby perverting the old rotational arrangements.

---

[13] The causal chain running from material determinants to norms, values, and institutions need not be deterministic, however. As a matter of fact, it may well be the case that different sets of norms, values, and institutions fit in with one given set of material constraints. This corresponds to the case where there exist multiple equilibria in the social game. Under these conditions, culture does not simply reflect the constraints of material life but serves the purpose of selecting one particular equilibrium among several possible ones. It remains true, however, that the material environment plays a critical role insofar as the set of possible equilibrium positions is narrowed down under its impact.

[14] Thus, 'As long as a tribe of forest-fallow cultivators has abundant land at its disposal, a family would have no particular interest in returning to precisely that plot which it cultivated on an earlier occasion. Under these conditions a family which needed to shift to a new plot would find a suitable plot, or have it allocated by the chief of the tribe' (Boserup 1965: 79).

Regarding private landholdings, three additional processes can be observed. First, as land becomes scarcer, overlapping rights tend to be denied and exclusive ownership tends to be asserted by those groups that wield more power. In point of fact, the insurance benefit arising from the flexibility of a multiple tenure system is bound to become outweighed by the growing efficiency costs entailed by that system, especially dynamic efficiency costs (the long-term land improvements that are forsaken). Second, as the fallow period is being continuously shortened as a consequence of population pressure, there is a smaller pool of land available for (periodic) redistribution in favour of the most needy villagers. And, lastly, increasing land scarcity unavoidably causes the emergence of an enlarged scope of transfer rights. Marginalization processes duly follow unless persisting prohibitions against unfettered land sales enforced by sufficiently strong village communities operate as a countervailing force.

Yet, to the extent that rural communities do not provide unlucky members with financial resources in order to help them avoid distress sales of land assets or to repurchase lost parcels of land, they cannot be considered as an effective provider of social security: preemption rights of repurchase to the benefit of the previous owner can thus be ineffective. Moreover, insofar as it is deemed socially unacceptable to take advantage of the plight of neighbours and kin, land offered for sale under duress is likely to be acquired by outsiders lest the land should remain without purchaser.

All these channels through which population growth exerts its influence compound their effects to make equity and insurance considerations recede into the background. As for market integration, it can also be expected to threaten customary insurance arrangements, mainly because by making new risk diversification opportunities available, it tends to enhance the self-insurance capacity of the elite. By causing the value of land and other natural resources to grow, it also accelerates the process of land tenure individualization and possibly intensifies the pressure on the commons thereby raising the risk of their eventual degradation (if the internal terms of trade turn against the products harvested on private landholdings). Finally, the opening up of new market opportunities, by inducing the village elite to follow a path of individualist capital accumulation, may lead them to call traditional sharing norms into question and to favour asymmetrical patron–client relationships.

The central conclusion emerging from the above is that redistributive and insurance concerns are predominant in the land allocation rules applied in rural societies as long as the resulting efficiency costs are moderate or insignificant. Once efficiency costs associated with corporate ownership increase significantly following a shift from extensive to intensive patterns of land use triggered by population growth and market integration, tenure arrangements undergo a major transformation towards more individualized rights. Such a transformation implies that property rights in land are increasingly defined without regard for equity and insurance concerns.

Short of creating a full-fledged centralized social security system, which can be only a distant objective given the informal character of the agricultural sector in most poor countries, there are many things that a state can do to supplement failing village-level insurance mechanisms. In particular, it can stimulate, rather than stifle, the development of land rental markets and it can reinforce protection of the tenants in ways that are not self-defeating, in the sense of discouraging the supply of land rental contracts. It can also encourage the penetration of the market into rural areas by building up the required communication infrastructure, overcoming informational deficiencies, combating rural monopolies and state patronage in the distribution of public employment, and providing basic social services to the population. Lastly, it can intervene to actively negotiate with rural communities with a view to minimizing exclusionary processes, especially when they take on an ethnic dimension. There is a link between this third policy avenue and the first one mentioned above. Indeed, a good way to avoid exclusion is precisely by encouraging the granting of land to strangers under rental contracts formally backed by a state or a joint state-community agency.

REFERENCES

Abraham, A., and J. P. Platteau (2001). 'Two Cultural Approaches to the Problem of Women's Land Inheritance', mimeo, Centre de Recherche en Economie du Développement (CRED), Department of Economics, University of Namur.

——, J. M. Baland, and J. P. Platteau (1998). 'Groupes informels de solidarité dans un bidonville du Tiers-Monde: le cas de Kibera, Nairobi'. *Non Marchand*, 2, 29–52 (Editions De Boeck Université, Bruxelles).

Agarwal, B. (1991). 'Social Security and the Family: Coping with Seasonality and Calamity in Rural India', in E. Ahmad, J. Drèze, J. Hills, and A. Sen (eds), *Social Security in Developing Countries*. Oxford: Clarendon Press.

Alderman, H. and C. H. Paxson (1992). 'Do the Poor Insure? A Synthesis of the Literature on Risk and Consumption in Developing Countries'. *Policy Research Working Papers* No. 1008. Washington, DC: World Bank.

Alexander, P. (1980). 'Sea Tenure in Southern Sri Lanka', in A. Spoehr (ed.), *Maritime Adaptations—Essays on Contemporary Fishing Communities*. Pittsburgh, OH: University of Pittsburgh Press.

—— (1982). *Sri Lankan Fishermen—Rural Capitalism and Peasant Society*. Canberra: Australian National University Press.

Amarasinghe, O. (1989). 'Technical Change, Transformation of Risks and Patronage Relations in a Fishing Community of South Sri Lanka'. *Development and Change*, 20(4), 701–33.

André, C. and J. P. Platteau (1998). 'Land Relations under Unbearable Stress: Rwanda Caught in the Malthusian Trap'. *Journal of Economic Behavior and Organization*, 34(1), 1–47.

Atwood, D. A. (1990). 'Land Registration in Africa: The Impact on Agricultural Production'. *World Development*, 18(5), 659–71.

Ault, D. E. and G. L. Rutman (1979). 'The Development of Individual Rights to Property in Tribal Africa'. *Journal of Law and Economics*, 22(1), 163–82.

—— and J. P. Platteau (1996). *Halting Degradation of Natural Resources: Is There a Role for Rural Communities?* Oxford: Clarendon Press.

—— and —— (1998). 'Dividing the Commons—A Partial Assessment of the New Institutional Economics of Property Rights'. *American Journal of Agricultural Economics*, 80(August), 644–50.

——, D. Dubuisson, and J. P. Platteau (1998). 'Dynamique des mécanismes informels d'assurance en milieu rural : Le cas du Burkina Faso', research Report for the General

Administration of Development Cooperation, Centre de Recherche en Economie du Développement (CRED), University of Namur.

Baland, J.M. and P. François (1999). 'Commons as Insurance and the Welfare Impact of Privatization', mimeo, Centre de Recherche en Economie du Développement (CRED), Department of Economics, University of Namur.

——, F. Gaspart, F. Place, and J. P. Platteau (2001). 'The Distributive Impact of Land Markets in Central Uganda', mimeo, Centre de Recherche en Economie du Développement (CRED), Department of Economics, University of Namur.

Bardhan, P., J. M Baland, S. Das, D. Mookherjee, and R. Sarkar (2002). 'Household Firewood Collection in Rural Nepal: The Role of Poverty, Population, Collective Action and Modernisation', in J. M. Baland, P. Bardhan, and S. Bowles (eds), *Inequality, Collective Action and Environmental Sustainability*. New York and New Jersey: Russell Sage Foundation and Princeton University Press.

Barrows, R. and M. Roth (1989). 'Land Tenure and Investment in African Agriculture: Theory and Evidence'. *Land Tenure Center Paper* No. 136. Madison, WI: University of Wisconsin-Madison.

Bassett, T. J. and D. E. Crummey (eds). (1993). *Land in African Agrarian Systems*. Madison, WI: University of Wisconsin Press.

Bates, R. H. (1984). 'Some Conventional Orthodoxies in the Study of Agrarian Change'. *World Politics*, 26(2), 234–54.

Béné, C., E. Bennett, and A. E. Neiland (2002). 'The Challenge of Managing Small-Scale Fisheries With Reference to Poverty Alleviation', in A. E. Neiland and C. Béné (eds), *Small-Scale Fisheries, Poverty and the Code of Conduct for Responsible Fisheries*. Centre for the Economics and Management of Aquatic Resources (CEMARE), University of Portsmouth.

Berry, S. (1984). 'The Food Crisis and Agrarian Change in Africa: A Review Essay'. *African Studies Review*, 27(2), 59–112.

—— (1993). *No Condition is Permanent—The Social Dynamics of Agrarian Change in Sub-Saharan Africa*. Madison, WI: University of Wisconsin Press.

Besley, T. (1995). 'Property Rights and Investment Incentives: Theory and Evidence from Ghana'. *Journal of Political Economy*, 103(5), 903–37.

Binswanger, H. P., K. Deininger, and G. Feder (1995). 'Power, Distortions, Revolt and Reform in Agricultural Land Relations', in J. Behrman and T. N. Srinivasan (eds), *Handbook of Development Economics*, Vol. III. Amsterdam: North-Holland.

Bohannan, P. and G. Dalton (eds). (1962). *Markets in Africa*. Evanston, IL: Northwestern University Press.

Boserup, E. (1965). *The Conditions of Agricultural Growth: The Economics of Agrarian Change under Population Pressure*. London: Allen & Unwin.

Brasselle, A. S., F. Gaspart, and J. P. Platteau (2002). 'Land Tenure Security and Investment Incentives: Puzzling Evidence from Burkina Faso'. *Journal of Development Economics*, 67, 373–418.

Breusers, M. (2001). 'Searching for Livelihood Security: Land and Mobility in Burkina Faso'. *Journal of Development Studies*, 37(4), 49–80.

Brito, D. L., M. D. Intriligator, and E. Sheshinski (1997). 'Privatization and the Distribution of Income in the Commons'. *Journal of Public Economics*, 64, 181–205.

Bromley, D., and J. P. Chavas (1989). 'On Risks, Transactions and Economic Development in the Semiarid Tropics'. *Economic Development and Cultural Change*, 37(4): 719–36.

Bruce, J. W. (1986). 'Land Tenure Issues in Project Design and Strategies for Agricultural Development in Sub-Saharan Africa'. *Land Tenure Center Paper* No. 128. Madison, WI: University of Wisconsin-Madison.

—— (1988). 'A Perspective on Indigenous Land Tenure Systems and Land Concentration', in R. E. Downs and S. P. Reyna (eds), *Land and Society in Contemporary Africa*. Hanover, NH and London: University Press of New England.

—— (1993). 'Do Indigenous Tenure Systems Constrain Agricultural Development?' in T. J. Bassett and D. E. Crummey (eds), *Land in African Agrarian Systems*. Madison, WI: University of Wisconsin Press.

—— and L. Fortmann (1989). 'Agroforestry: Tenure and Incentives'. *Land Tenure Center Paper* No. 135. Madison, WI: University of Wisconsin-Madison.

Cohen, J. M. (1980). 'Land Tenure and Rural Development in Africa', in R. H. Bates and M. F. Lofchie (eds), *Agricultural Development in Africa—Issues of Public Policy*. New York: Praeger.

Coldham, S. (1978). 'The Effect of Registration of Title upon Customary Land Rights in Kenya'. *Journal of African Law*, 22(2), 91–111.

Cox, D. and E. Jimenez (1990). 'Achieving Social Objectives Through Private Transfers—A Review'. *World Bank Research Observer*, 5(2), 205–18.

—— and —— (1997). 'Coping with Apartheid: Inter-household Transfers over the Life-cycle in South Africa', mimeo, Boston College and World Bank.

Czukas, K., M. Fafchamps, and C. Udry (1998). 'Drought and Saving in West Africa: Are Livestock a Buffer Stock?'. *Journal of Development Economics*, 55, 273–305.

Dahlman, C. J. (1980). *The Open Field System and Beyond: A Property Rights Analysis of an Economic Institution*. Cambridge: Cambridge University Press.

Dalton, G. (1962). 'Traditional Production in Primitive African Economies'. *Quarterly Journal of Economics*, 76(3), 360–78.

Dasgupta, M. (1987). 'Informal Security Mechanisms and Population Retention in Rural India'. *Economic Development and Cultural Change*, 36(1), 101–20.

Dasgupta, P. (1993). *An Inquiry Into Well-being and Destitution*. Oxford: Clarendon Press.

De Meza, D. and J. R. Gould (1985). 'Free Access Versus Private Ownership: A Comparison'. *Journal of Economic Theory*, 36, 387–91.

—— and —— (1987). 'Free Access Versus Private Property in a Resource: Income Distributions Compared'. *Journal of Political Economy*, 95(6), 1317–25.

De Zeeuw, F. (1997). 'Borrowing of Land, Security of Tenure and Sustainable Land Use in Burkina Faso'. *Development and Change*, 28(3), 583–95.

Downs, R. E. and S. P. Reyna (eds) (1988). *Land and Society in Contemporary Africa*. Hanover, NH and London: University Press of New England.

Ensminger, J. (1990). 'Co-opting the Elders: The Political Economy of State Incorporation in Africa'. *American Anthropologist*, 92, 662–75.

Fafchamps, M. (1992). 'Solidarity Networks in Preindustrial Societies: Rational Peasants with a Moral Economy'. *Economic Development and Cultural Change*, 41(1), 147–74.

Gavian, S. and M. Fafchamps (1996). 'Land Tenure and Allocative Efficiency in Niger'. *American Journal of Agricultural Economics*, 78, 460–71.

Godelier, M. (1999). *The Enigma of the Gift*. Cambridge: Polity Press.

Goldstein, M. (1999). 'Chop Time, No Friends, Intrahousehold and Individual Insurance Mechanisms in Southern Ghana', mimeo, University of California at Berkeley, Berkeley, CA.

Green, J. K. (1987). 'Evaluating the Impact of Consolidation of Holdings, Individualization of Tenure, and Registration of Title: Lessons from Kenya'. *Land Tenure Center Paper* No. 129. Madison, WI: University of Wisconsin-Madison.

Gregory, C. A. (1982). *Gifts and Commodities*. London: Academic Press.

Hakansson, T. (1988). *Bridewealth, Women and Land: Social Changes Among the Gusii of Kenya*. Uppsala Studies of Cultural Anthropology, University of Uppsala.

Haugerud, A. (1983). 'The Consequences of Land Tenure Reform among Smallholders in the Kenya Highlands'. *Rural Africana*, 15–16(winter–spring), 65–89.

Hecht, S., A. B. Anderson, and P. May (1988). 'The Subsidy from Nature: Shifting Cultivation, Successional Palm Forests and Rural Development'. *Human Organization*, 47(1), 25–35.

Hoff, K. (1997). 'Informal Insurance and the Poverty Trap', mimeo, University of Maryland.

Humphries, J. (1990). 'Enclosures, Common Rights, and Women: The Proletarianization of Families in the Late Eighteenth and Early Nineteenth Centuries'. *Journal of Economic History*, 50(1), 17–42.

Hunt, D. (1996). 'The Impacts of Individual Land Titling in Mbeere, Eastern Kenya'. *Discussion Papers in Economics* No. 01/96. Brighton: University of Sussex.

Ilahiane, H. (2001). 'The Ethnopolitics of Irrigation Management in the Ziz Oasis, Morocco', in A. Agrawal and C. C. Gibson (eds), *Communities and the Environment*. New Brunswick, NJ and London: Rutgers University Press.

Jodha, N. S. (1986). 'Common Property Resources and Rural Poor in Dry Regions of India'. *Economic and Political Weekly*, 21(27), 1169–82.

Johnson, O. E. G. (1972). 'Economic Analysis, the Legal Framework and Land Tenure Systems'. *Journal of Law and Economics*, 15(1), 259–76.

Landauer, C. (1964). *Contemporary Economic Systems—A Comparative Analysis*. Philadelphia and New York: J. B. Lippincott Company.

Laurent, P. J., P. Mathieu, and M. Totte (1994). 'Migrations et accès à la terre au Burkina Faso', *Cahiers du Cidep* 20, Louvain-la-Neuve.

Lund, C. (1998). *Land, Power and Politics in Niger—Land Struggles and the Rural Code*. Hamburg: Lit Verlag.

Mackenzie, F. (1993). 'A Piece of Land Never Shrinks: Reconceptualizing Land Tenure in a Smallholding District, Kenya', in T. J. Bassett and D. E. Crummey (eds), *Land in African Agrarian Systems*. Madison, WI: University of Wisconsin Press.

Matlon, P. (1994). 'Indigenous Land Use Systems and Investments in Soil Fertility in Burkina Faso', in J. W. Bruce and S. E. Migot-Adholla (eds), *Searching for Land Tenure Security in Africa*. Dubuque, IA: Kendall/Hunt Publishing Company.

McKean, M. A. (1986). 'Management of Traditional Common Lands (Iriaichi) in Japan'. *Proceedings of the Conference on Common Property Resource Management*, National Research Council. Washington DC: National Academy Press.

Migot-Adholla, S. E., P. Hazell, B. Blarel, and F. Place (1991). 'Indigenous Land Rights Systems in Sub-Saharan Africa: A Constraint on Policy?'. *World Bank Economic Review*, 5(1), 155–75.

Morduch, J. (1995). 'Income Smoothing and Consumption Smoothing'. *Journal of Economic Perspectives*, 9(3), 103–14.

—— (1999). 'Between the Market and the State: Can Informal Insurance Patch the Safety Net?'. *World Bank Research Observer*, 14(2), 187–207.

Noronha, R. (1985). 'A Review of the Literature on Land Tenure Systems in Sub-Saharan Africa'. *World Bank Report* No. ARU 43. Washington, DC: Research Unit of the Agriculture and Rural Development, World Bank.

Nunow, A. A. (2000). 'Pastoralists and Markets—Livestock Commercialization and Food Security in North-Eastern Kenya'. Ph.D. thesis, University of Amsterdam.

Pinckney, T. C. and P. K. Kimuyu (1994). 'Land Tenure Reform in East Africa: Good, Bad, or Unimportant?'. *Journal of African Economies*, 3(1), 1–28.

Place, F., J. Ssenteza, and K. Otsuka (2001). 'Customary and Private Land Management in Uganda', in K. Otsuka and F. Place (eds), *Land Tenure and Natural Resource Management: A Comparative Study of Agrarian Communities in Asia and Africa*. Baltimore, MD and London: Johns Hopkins University Press.

Platteau, J. P. (1991). 'Traditional Systems of Social Security and Hunger Insurance: Past Achievements and Modern Challenges', in E. Ahmad, J. Drèze, J. Hills, and A. K. Sen (eds), *Social Security in Developing Countries*. Oxford: Clarendon Press.

—— (1992). 'Land Reform and Structural Adjustment in SubSaharan Africa: Controversies and Guidelines'. *FAO Economic and Social Development Paper* No. 107, Rome: FAO.

—— (1996). 'The Evolutionary Theory of Land Rights as Applied to SubSaharan Africa: A Critical Assessment'. *Development and Change*, 27(1), 29–86.

—— (1997). 'Mutual Insurance as an Elusive Concept in Traditional Rural Communities'. *Journal of Development Studies*, 33(6), 764–96.

—— (2000). *Institutions, Social Norms, and Economic Development*. London: Harwood.

—— (2002). 'Solidarity Norms and Institutions in Agrarian Societies: Static and Dynamic Considerations', in S. C. Kolm, G. Varet, and J. Mercier-Ythier (eds), *Handbook on Gift-Giving, Reciprocity and Altruism*. Amsterdam: North-Holland and Elsevier.

——, J. Murickan, and E. Delbar (1985). *Technology, Credit and Indebtedness in Marine Fishing—A Case Study of Three Fishing Villages in South Kerala*. Delhi: Hindustan Publishing Co.

—— and E. Seki (2001). 'Community Arrangements to Overcome Market Failures: Pooling Groups in Japanese Fisheries', in M. Aoki and Y. Hayami (eds), *Communities and Markets in Economic Development*. Oxford: Oxford University Press.

Popkin, S. L. (1979). *The Rational Peasant: The Political Economy of Rural Society in Vietnam*. Berkeley and Los Angeles, CA: University of California Press.

Robertson, A. F. (1987). *The Dynamics of Productive Relationships—African Share Contracts in Comparative Perspective*. Cambridge: Cambridge University Press.

Rocheleau, D., P. Steinberg, and P. Benjamin (1994). 'A Hundred Years of Crisis? Environment and Development Narratives in Ukambani, Kenya'. *Working Papers in African Studies* No. 189. Boston, MA: African Studies Center, Boston University.

—— and D. Edmunds (1995). 'Women, Men and Trees: Gender, Power and Property in Forest and Agrarian Landscapes'. *World Development*, 25(8), 1351–71.

Rodenbach, E. (1999). 'La transformation des droits fonciers dans la vallée du fleuve Sénégal: Etude de trois villages'. Unpublished M.A. thesis, Department of Economics, University of Namur.

Rosenzweig, M. (1988). 'Risk, Implicit Contracts, and the Family in Rural Areas of Low-Income Countries'. *Economic Journal*, 98(1), 1148–70.

Samuelson, P. A. (1974). 'Is the Rent Collector Worthy of his full Hire?' *Eastern Economic Journal*, 1(1), 1–7.

Schapera, I. (1943). *Native Land Tenure in the Bechuanaland Protectorate*. Lovedale, Cape Town: The Lovedale Press.

Shipton, P. (1988). 'The Kenyan Land Tenure Reform: Misunderstandings in the Public Creation of Private Property', in R. E. Downs and S. P. Reyna (eds), *Land and Society in Contemporary Africa*. Hanover, NH and London: University Press of New England.

Sjaastad, E. (1998). Land Tenure and Land Use in Zambia. Unpublished Ph.D. thesis, Department of Forest Science, Agricultural University of Norway.

——and D. W. Bromley (1997). 'Indigenous Land Rights in Sub-Saharan Africa: Appropriation, Security, and Investment Demand'. *World Development*, 25(4), 549–62.

Weitzman, M. (1974). 'Free Access vs. Private Ownership as Alternative Systems for Managing Common Property'. *Journal of Economic Theory*, 8(2), 225–34.

PART VI

SAFETY NETS AND SOCIAL INSTITUTIONS

13

Do Public Transfers Crowd Out Private Transfers?: Evidence from a Randomized Experiment in Mexico

PEDRO ALBARRAN AND ORAZIO P. ATTANASIO

13.1. INTRODUCTION

An important issue that is often neglected in the design of programmes targeted to the poor in developing countries is that of the interaction of the proposed programme with existing private arrangements. This issue is relevant for poverty alleviation programmes, for insurance programmes, for education subsidies, and virtually any intervention and has implications not only for the private sector activities that are close substitute for the programme intervention, but also for other aspects. The neglect of these effects is lamentable, as a proper cost–benefit analysis, and the consideration of alternative programmes should recognize that such interventions do not happen in a vacuum. The 'side' effects of a public intervention programme do not need to be negative: while it is possible that some private activities might be 'crowded out' by the intervention, it is possible that others (and possibly unrelated ones) would grow as a consequence of it.

Many studies have considered whether the introduction of public transfers affects private transfers among the households targeted by the public scheme. From a theoretical point of view, as clearly stated by Cox (1987), there are several reasons to expect an effect of public transfers on private ones. As we discuss below, several models predict a negative relationship between public and private transfers. There are also models that predict negative effects of the introduction of insurance schemes on private transfers: the intuition here is that the latter play an insurance role that can be crowded out, for a variety of reasons, by the introduction of public insurance.

From an empirical point of view, the challenge to test for the presence and the empirical relevance of these effects is that the recipients of many of the programmes on which data are available are not a random sample of the population. It is therefore very tricky to compare recipients and non-recipients to identify the effect of the programme.

We would like to thank Patricia Muniz and Ana Santiago for many conversations about the data and Susan Parker for some useful suggestions. This chapter would not have been possible without the inspiration of Jose Gomez de Leon who first stimulated our interest in the PROGRESA programme.

Our chapter is a contribution to the analysis of the interaction of public programmes and private transfers. We analyse a large welfare programme in rural Mexico: PROGRESA—Programa de Educación, Salud y Alimentación (the Education, Health, and Nutrition Program of Mexico). As we discuss in detail below, PROGRESA is a programme aimed at fostering the accumulation of human capital by increasing school enrolment, improving nutrition, and health practices. It should be stressed that the PROGRESA is not a pure transfer programme. The subsidies poor households receive are not unconditional, but depend on a number of other choices. Indeed, the programme is better described as a change in the relative prices of education and health services rather than a pure income subsidy. However, the programme has a sizeable unconditional component and is, overall, perceived as having a positive income effect. These considerations, however, should be kept in mind when evaluating and interpreting our findings.

Even more importantly, our findings should not be interpreted as an evaluation of the programme: PROGRESA's main objective is the improvement of the process of human capital accumulations among poor families in rural Mexico: in what follows we do not evaluate how successful PROGRESA was in achieving its stated goals but only whether the programme has affected a specific aspect (intrahousehold transfers) of the life of the households living in the villages where the programme is affected.

From an empirical point of view, the PROGRESA data set has a big advantage: the evaluation sample we use has a randomized component, which introduces genuinely exogenous variation that can be used to identify the parameters of interest.

13.2. A THEORETICAL FRAMEWORK

Whether the presence of public transfers affects private transfers has been the topic of a large number of studies. As pointed out by Cox (1987), there are several reasons why public transfers could affect private ones. Some models, initiated by Becker (1974), explain transfers with altruism. Other models, such as Bernheim *et al.* (1985), instead, appeal to intrahouseholds informal exchanges whereby a transfer is motivated by the provision of some kind of service that the recipient performs for the donor. Finally, it is possible, that transfers are part of insurance schemes by which participants share idiosyncratic risk. All these models predict that the occurrence and size of private transfers are affected by the presence of public transfers that change the income of the recipient or of the donor. However, different models have different implications and stress different mechanisms for the interaction of private and public transfers.

The implications of altruism are quite unambiguous: if public transfers are directed to the recipient of a transfer, both the probability of observing a transfer and its size conditional on occurrence are likely to decrease. The opposite is true for a public transfer targeted to the net donor of a private transfer.

If, instead, private transfers occur as a payment for some sort of service, it can be shown that an increase in the income of the recipient, could give rise either to a decrease or to an increase in the amount transferred (see Cox 1987). In particular, it is possible that transfers are the outcome of a Nash bargaining mechanism involving both sides of the transfer and possibly some services given from the recipient to the donor. In such a situation, it is possible that the relationship between the amount of transfers, conditional on a positive transfer, and the recipient's income is non-monotonic. Cox *et al.* (1998), for instance, show the results of some simple simulations of a parent–child model where at low levels of income, an increase in the children's income raises her threat point and therefore, raises the transfer. Past a certain level of income, however, further increases will cause the effect to become negative.

Private transfers can also be part of insurance schemes through which households are linked in order to share idiosyncratic risk. If this is the case, both under perfect risk-sharing and under imperfect risk-sharing (due to the presence of imperfect enforceability or asymmetric information), public transfers will be partly undone by private transactions, even though the mechanisms at play might be slightly different and depends on whether the government transfer targets a segment of the population and whether they are contingent on some observable state (such as is the case for government insurance). Under perfect risk-sharing, which effectively implies income pooling, targeted public transfers will enter the pool of resources available to the agents sharing risks and, therefore, are likely to be shared. They are also bound to affect the size and direction of private transfers. If they do not change the Pareto weights in the social planner problem (or to be more concrete the particular competitive equilibrium that is selected) and if they are targeted towards the net receivers of private transfers, they are likely to reduce them. In models with imperfect information, if the public transfers are observed and the targeting is done on the basis of observable variables, private transfers will be reduced via essentially the same mechanism at play under perfect risk-sharing.

Under imperfect enforceability, on the other hand, the introduction of a public unconditional transfer that will move agents away from situations where the marginal utility of consumption is very high, will induce a reduction in the amount of equilibrium risk-sharing and, therefore, the amount of private transfers that happen in equilibrium for any given income shock. These effects are discussed at length and illustrated with numerical simulations by Attanasio and Rios-Rull (2000*a*,*b*). In general the properties of this model depend on the specific utility function and the features of the economic environment. With power utility, one gets that the introduction of non-contingent public transfers, of the kind studied in the empirical application below, reduce the amount of private transfers.

Many studies have looked at the relationship between private transfers and recipient income. In particular, Cox (1987) and his co-authors (Cox *et al.* 1997, 1998) have tested in a variety of contexts both the presence of crowding-out and alternative models of transfers. In most situations, Cox and his co-authors find that while the likelihood of receiving a transfer is negatively related to income, as predicted both by altruistic and exchange models, more often than not, the relationship between transfers conditional on a positive transfer and income is non-monotonic, being positive at low levels of income and negative at larger levels. That is transfers first increase with income and then decrease. The fact that transfers increase as a function of income is consistent with the exchange model where the transfer is provided in exchange of a service: as the income of the recipient of the transfer increases, this is likely to increase the implicit price of the recipient's 'services' (see Cox 1987, for example).

Schoeni (1997), has looked at transfers in the US PSID to find that, while poorer households are more likely to receive transfers both in money and in time, the altruistic model does not fully explain the patterns observed in the data.

More recently, Jensen (1998) has looked directly at the effects on migrant remittances of the introduction of a public pension scheme in South Africa. Jensen's is one of the few studies that looks at the crowding-out effect directly.

Foster and Rosenzweig (2001) consider the altruistic motive in a model in which transfers across individuals constitute the only mechanisms for sharing idiosyncratic risk in a situation in which borrowing is limited and contracts cannot be enforced perfectly. Foster and Rosenzweig (2001) test one of the implications of a model with imperfect enforceability, namely that, conditional on the current shock an individual receives, current transfers are negative related to the cumulative level of past transfers. They find support for this hypothesis in data from Bangladesh and Pakistan.

Most studies of the crowding-out effect suffer from an important endogeneity problem: public policy programmes are typically targeted towards households that are in particular need of transfers. It is therefore difficult to identify the effect that public transfer programmes have on private transfers and in particular, to assess what the level of private transfer would have been in the absence of a given programme comparing beneficiaries to non-beneficiaries of the programme. In this respect, our study is unique as it exploits the randomization component in our data: a set of villages in our sample were randomly excluded from the programme we are studying for two years. This allows us a direct evaluation of the effect of the programme on private transfers. We now turn to a description of the data set we use and of the programme it refers to.

13.3. THE PROGRESA PROGRAMME AND THE EVALUATION DATA SET

13.3.1. *The PROGRESA Programme*

In 1997, the Mexican government decided to start a new and large welfare programme targeted to rural Mexico. The programme had three components: health, nutrition, and education. The health component consists of a number of initiatives aimed at improving information about vaccination, nutrition, contraception and hygiene, and of a programme of visits for children and women to health centres. Participation into the health component is a pre-condition for participating into the nutrition component that, in addition to a basic monetary subsidy received by all beneficiary households, gives some in kind transfers to households with very young infants and pregnant women. The largest component of the programme is the education one. Beneficiary households with school age children receive grants conditional on school attendance. The size of the grant increases with the grade and, for secondary education, is slightly higher for girls than for boys. Finally, all the transfers are received by the mother in the household.

The programme first targeted the poorest communities in rural Mexico. Roughly speaking, the two criteria communities had to satisfy to qualify for the programme were a certain degree of poverty (as measured by what is called an 'index of marginalization') and access to certain basic structures (schools and health centres). Once a locality qualifies, individual households could qualify or not for the programme, depending on a single indicator that is affected by a number of poverty variables (income, house type, and so on). Eligibility was determined in two steps. First, a general census of the PROGRESA localities measured the variables needed to compute the indicator and each households was defined as 'poor' or 'not-poor' (where 'poor' is equivalent to eligibility). Subsequently, in March 1998, an additional survey was carried out and some households were added to the list of beneficiaries. This second set of households is called 'densificados'.

The programme was phased in slowly and is currently very large: at the end of 1999 its budget was US$777 million and was implemented in more than 50,000 localities. At that time, about 2.6 million households, or 40 per cent of all rural families and one-ninth of all households in Mexico, were included in the programme. The cost of the programme is about 0.2 per cent of Mexican GDP. The programme has received a considerable amount of attention and publicity and similar programmes are currently being implemented in Honduras, Nicaragua, and Argentina. (See IFPRI 2000 for additional details on the programme and its evaluation.)

The programme represents a substantial help for the beneficiaries. The nutritional component was 100 pesos per month (or US$10) in the second semester of 1998, which corresponds to 8 per cent of the beneficiaries' income in the evaluation sample. The education component, which is conditional to school enrolment of children between third and ninth grade, can be added up to a maximum total amount of 625 pesos per month (or US$62.5) or 52 per cent of the beneficiaries' income. The average grant in the sample we use was 348 pesos per month for households with children and 250 for all beneficiaries or 21 per cent of the beneficiaries' income. In addition to the (bi)monthly payments, beneficiaries with children in school age receive a small annual grant for school supplies.

It should be stressed that the education component, which is the largest component in the programme, is not a pure transfer, as it is conditional on school attendance. It is therefore better described as a change in the relative price of education. The education component, however, is likely to have a substantial wealth effect. For instance, according to IFPRI (2000) there is not much evidence of a decrease in beneficiaries' income as a consequence of a reduction of child labour. This wealth effect and the presence of an unconditional component (the nutritional supplement) justify our attempt to identify the crowding-out of private transfers.

The agency running the programme used the fact that, for logistic reasons, the programme could not be started everywhere simultaneously, to start an evaluation sample. Among the beneficiary localities, 506 where chosen randomly and included in the evaluation sample. Among these, 320 randomly chosen were assigned to the communities where the programme started early, while 186 were assigned to the communities where the programme started almost two years later (December 1999 rather than May 1998). An extensive survey was carried out in the evaluation sample: after the initial data collection between the end of 1997 and the beginning of 1998, an additional four instruments were collected in November 1998, March 1999, November 1999, and April 2000. Within each village in the evaluation sample, the survey covers all the households and collects extensive information on consumption, income, labour supply, school enrolment, transfers, and a variety of other issues. While each instrument contained a core questionnaire, they differed in that some of them also contained some additional modules. There are also some minor differences in the way some questions are formulated across waves.

The randomization through which the villages were assigned to the treatment and control groups seems well executed: Behrman and Todd (1999) present evidence in this respect. In particular, most variables seem to be not statistically different between the treatment and control villages. As one should expect to get around 5 per cent of rejections, we feel comfortable in using explicitly the randomization to identify the crowding-out of private transfers.[1]

13.3.2. *The Data*

The data set we use is the wave collected in October/November 1998 and contains information on 25,846 households. After loosing, for various reasons, some observations, we are left with 23,268 households.[2]

As we mentioned in Section 13.3.1, not all households within a village qualify for PROGRESA and eligibility was determined in two steps. Fortunately, we observe eligibility status (in both steps) both in the treatment and in the control variables. We therefore have four groups of households: poor and non-poor living in treatment villages and poor and non-poor living in control villages. Here and in the econometric application we do not distinguish between households that gained eligibility in the first and second round, that is we do not distinguish between 'densificado' poors and households that were designed as poor in the first survey. In Table 13.1, we show how many of the households included in the sample live in treatment (PROGRESA) and control villages and how they split between 'poor' and 'non-poor', where 'poor' is a household that was defined as such by PROGRESA and therefore entitled to the programme.

Unfortunately, matters are further complicated by the fact that not all poor in the treatment villages receive the programme. It is not clear why this was the case. It was probably due to a combination of administrative delays, non-compliance with the programme and so on. In Table 13.1, therefore, as in the econometric specifications

---

[1] For studies that consider the effect of the programme on enrolment, it is a bit worrying that one of the few variables that appear to be significantly different between control and treatment villages is pre-programme school enrolment.

[2] We discarded 2361 households who did not fully answer the questionnaire, so that relevant information (on transfers, consumption, household characteristics, and so on) was missing; additionally, we found and dropped 223 households having more than one household head and/or household head's spouse: these are multiple families living in a single household.

Table 13.1. *Distribution of households, October 1998*

	Treatment 320 villages	Control 186 villages	All 506 villages
Non-poor	3,176 (22.12)	2,011 (22.57)	5,187 (22.29)
Poor			
Beneficiaries	8,304 (57.83)	6,898	18,081
Non-beneficiaries	2,879 (20.05)	(77.43)	(77.71)
	14,359 (100)	8,909 (100)	23,268 (100)

Note: Percentage of households in parentheses.

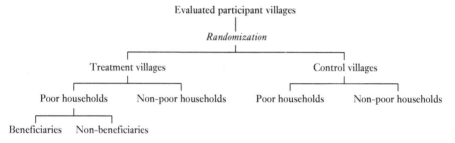

Figure 13.1. *Summary of the structure of the sample*

we estimate below, we divide eligible (or poor) households between those who actually receive the programme and those who do not.[3]

Figure 13.1 summarizes the structure of our evaluation sample: as it should be clear from the final branches of the tree, there are a total of five groups to consider: in control villages there are eligible and non-eligible households (which we call poor and non-poor); in the treatment villages there are the same two groups, but the eligible are divided into beneficiaries and non-beneficiaries. In what follows, for consistency with the evaluation literature, we will be occasionally referring to this last group as 'non-compliers' with a slight abuse of language. From an econometric point of view, the existence of such a group is a problem because we cannot identify 'non-compliers' in control villages.

That is, in control villages we do not know which of the 'poor' households would fail to become beneficiaries were the programme implemented.

---

[3] Most of these poor non-beneficiaries are 'densificado' households (so, they might have not fully incorporated to the programme yet); see Table 13.A1 in the Appendix, where we extend Table 13.1 to distinguish the 'densificado' poor.

On the other hand, Table 13.A2 reports some descriptive statistics for our sample in October 1998. Similarly to Behrman and Todd (1999), we do not find statistically significant differences between treatment and control villages for several characteristics (mainly demographics) that are not expected to have been affected by the implementation of the programme.

If the 'non-compliers' were a random subset of the poor households, the problem would not be too serious. Unfortunately, this is not the case. It turns out that, among poor households in treatment villages, 'non-compliers' are significantly (but not perfectly!) predicted by several observable variables. For instance, 'densificado' households, or households with no children are much more likely to be non-compliers. This prevents a direct comparison of poor, beneficiary households in the treatment villages with the poor households in the control villages.

The questionnaire in the November 1998 wave included two sections on private transfers received by each household member. In the first, the respondent was asked about monetary and non-monetary transfers obtained during the month preceding the interview from friends, neighbours, and relatives living either in or outside the village. The second section, instead, included information about support provided during the last six months by former family members who left the household within the last five years ('migrants'). In both sections, we know if each transfer is in money or in kind (food, clothes, and so on), but the latter are not given a monetary value. In what follows, we aggregate this individual information, thus focusing on households as our unit of analysis. We build two types of household variables on transfers: an indicator that takes the value one if any family member has received some transfers, and, for monetary transfers, the total amount of transfers (by adding up individual transfers received by each member). We build such variables separately for transfers from friends and transfers from migrants. We also convert migrant's monetary transfers (reported for the last six months) into a monthly basis, so as to be comparable with monetary transfers from friends.

Table 13.2 shows the relative importance of these inter-household transfers in our sample by computing the percentage of households receiving some transfers for each of the five groups we consider. We found remarkably few households receiving private transfers, as compared to other data sets (see, for instance, Foster and Rosenzweig 2001). The proportion of households receiving transfers from friends and relatives is particularly low. This might be due to the fact that the question focuses on the month preceding the interview. Notice that the proportion of 'non-poor' households in treatment and control villages is not statistically different. Notice also that, while 'poor' households are more likely to receive transfers from family and friends (at least in the control villages), 'non-poor' are (both in treatment and control villages) more likely to receive remittances from migrants.

The large majority of transfers received by households were in money: around 90 per cent of the households supported by migrants and three-quarters of those obtaining help from anyone else were being given monetary transfers. In Table 13.3, we show the average monetary amount received by households: that is, the average among those actually getting some monetary transfer. Remarkably, conditional on receiving a transfer, 'non-poor' households receive much larger transfers than poor ones. This is true both in treatment and control village and is particularly true for transfers from friends and relatives.

If all the poor households in the treatment villages were receiving grants, Tables 13.2 and 13.3 could give a first simple test of crowding-out. One could simply compare 'poor'

Table 13.2. *Percentage of households receiving transfers*

	Non-poor	Poor		
		Beneficiaries		**Non-beneficiaries**
From friends, neighbours, and relatives (but not migrants)				
Treatment villages	0.0532	0.0442		0.0785
			0.0523	
Control villages	0.0462		0.0567	
t-statistic for difference	1.1328		−1.0640	
(*p*-value)	(0.257)		(0.287)	
From migrants				
Treatment villages	0.0784	0.0497		0.0660
			0.0539	
Control villages	0.0766		0.0560	
t-statistic for difference	0.2393		−0.5964	
(*p*-value)	(0.811)		(0.551)	
From either of them				
Treatment villages	0.1228	0.0890		0.1344
			0.1006	
Control villages	0.1154		0.1051	
t-statistic for difference	0.8074		−0.9670	
(*p*-value)	(0.420)		(0.334)	

households in treatment and control villages and check whether those in treatment villages receive smaller and less frequent transfers. Unfortunately, as we discussed above, the fact that a non-random subset of households in treatment villages does not receive (for a reason or another) the treatment makes such a straightforward test unfeasible. While we discuss this problem and our proposed solution below, at this stage it is nonetheless interesting to notice that both among the poor and non-poor and for both transfers from migrants and others, the treatment and control villages do not exhibit any differences in the percentage of households receiving a transfer and in the quantity received. The only significant difference is shown between the amount of transfer received by poor households from anyone (i.e. aggregating migrants and others). In interpreting these results, however, it should be considered that among the poor in treatment villages, only some households receive transfers, and that the tables indicate that these households receive less often and smaller amounts. Interestingly, the poor who do not receive the programme in the treatment villages (the 'non-compliers') seem to receive more often and larger amounts. In our more formal analysis below we will use these differences to unravel the effect of the programme.

Before we start our formal analysis, it is worth considering some of the features of the households in the villages, distinguishing programme participants and household receiving transfers.

Families in the survey were asked about their total consumption on different goods in the last week before the survey; we know how many of these consumed goods have been

Table 13.3. *Average monthly amount of received monetary transfers (in pesos, conditional on positive transfer of each type)*

	Non-poor	Poor	
		Beneficiaries	Non-beneficiaries
From friends, neighbours, and relatives (but not migrants)			
Treatment villages	784.23	403.18	422.05
		410.47	
Control villages	704.35	465.21	
t-statistic for difference	0.5074	−1.1363	
(p-value)	(0.613)	(0.256)	
From migrants			
Treatment villages	259.53	191.40	202.13
		194.61	
Control villages	254.59	225.31	
t-statistic for difference	0.0929	−1.4404	
(p-value)	(0.926)	(0.150)	
From either of them			
Treatment villages	472.54	292.17	329.81
		305.21	
Control villages	433.20	359.37	
t-statistic for difference	0.5220	−1.9441	
(p-value)	(0.602)	(0.052)	

bought and how many have been produced by the household (i.e. 'self-consumption'). Thus, we compute the weekly expenditure on food for households in our sample by summing up across the different items; 'self-consumption' is valued at market prices.[4] Summary statistics are reported in Table 13.4, which presents the weekly expenditure on food for households in our sample; we have included consumption from goods produced by the household valued at market prices.

Table 13.5 reports the average household income in our sample. We added up self-reported income (by each household member) from the following sources: wages, net profits from self-employment, pensions, interest, community earnings, and income from rental (of land, animals or machinery);[5] we have also included self-consumption. Therefore, our measure of household income does not include either the private transfer received or the programme support. Notice that there seems to be no important differences between treatment and control villages. However, we can reject the hypothesis that beneficiaries in treatment villages and poor households in control

[4] The market value of self-consumption was computed using information from a locality survey, carried out by PROGRESA and which is parallel to the main household survey. Among other local information, it provides the prices of consumption goods in the two closest shops.

[5] As the respondent can report daily, weekly, biweekly, monthly, or annual income, all reported income is first converted into weekly income; we used information on the number of days worked in the previous week to compute this weekly income when daily earnings were reported.

Table 13.4. *Average (and median) weekly household expenditure in food (in pesos)*

	Non-poor	Poor		
		Beneficiaries		Non-beneficiaries
Households not receiving transfers				
Treatment villages	156.39 (133)	145.57 (127)		130.62 (112)
Control villages	168.37 (143)		137.64 (119)	
Households receiving transfers				
Treatment villages	156.97 (130)	142.56 (116)		128.96 (99)
Control villages	146.50 (129)		134.35 (109)	
All households				
Treatment villages	156.46 (133)	145.23 (126)		130.40 (111)
Control villages	165.84 (142)		137.29 (118)	

Table 13.5. *Average (and median) weekly household income (in pesos)*

	Non-poor	Poor		
		Beneficiaries		Non-beneficiaries
Households not receiving transfers				
Treatment villages	370.36 (231)	262.33 (189)		289.18 (188)
Control villages	395.68 (258)		326.89 (200)	
Households receiving transfers				
Treatment villages	321.92 (214)	299.10 (177)		474.19 (180)
Control villages	325.72 (211)		258.82 (175)	
All households				
Treatment villages	365.78 (230)	264.68 (189)		306.45 (188)
Control villages	389.15 (254)		321.54 (195)	

villages have the same average income (for households not receiving transfers and for all households, but not for households receiving transfers): the income of beneficiaries seems to be lower than those of the control households. It is tempting to interpret this as an effect of the programme arising from a reduction in child labour supply. However, Gomez de Leon and Parker (1999) find no strong effects of the programme on child labour supply.

In Table 13.6, we show that transfers are quite important relative to household food expenditure and household income. Transfers can expand the budget by 15–30 per cent and help to buy over one-third of the food consumed in the household.

13.4. AN ECONOMETRIC SPECIFICATION AND ECONOMETRIC PROBLEMS

In this section, we describe our econometric specification and some of the econometric problems we had to face.

Table 13.6. *Transfer receipts relative to income and consumption*

	Non-poor	Poor	
		Beneficiaries	Non-beneficiaries
A: Median of ratio monthly monetary transfer/food expenditure			
Treatment villages	0.4021	0.3127	0.4130
Control villages	0.3302	0.3708	
B: Median of ratio monthly monetary transfer/household income			
Treatment villages	0.2901	0.1633	0.1832
Control villages	0.2239	0.2189	

13.4.1. *Econometric Specification*

As we discussed in Section 13.3, we have information both on monetary transfers and on transfers in kind. However, for the latter, we do not have information on the value of the transfer. For this reason, we specify a Probit model for the probability of receiving any transfers, be it in kind or monetary.[6] Such a variable does not consider the size of the transfer. Moreover, as some households might be giving *and* receiving transfers, we cannot assess whether such households are net givers or receivers. On the other hand, as shown in Appendix Table 13.A3, most of the families involved in inter-households transfers (around 10 per cent out of all households, both in treatment and in control villages) have just received some transfer, whereas less than 0.25 per cent have received but also given transfers. Likewise, it is interesting that the non-poor households are more likely to give transfers without receiving them than the poor ones.

For net monetary transfers, instead, we estimate a simple Tobit, truncated at zero. Again, few households in our sample are giving monetary transfers (25 out of 23,268), and only six of them are also receiving transfers from friends or migrants. So, we have finally only twenty-one net givers and the difference of analysing gross and net transfers is negligible.

As we found it difficult to think of a variable that would affect the probability of receiving a transfer while not affecting the size of the grant, we did not use a generalized Tobit, as it would only be identified through functional form assumptions.

13.4.2. *Some Econometric Problems*

As mentioned above, not everybody entitled to the programme gets it in the PROGRESA village. With a slight abuse of language, we call these households, which correspond to the 'treatment-poor-non-beneficiary' branch of the tree in Fig. 13.1, 'non-compliers'. Our understanding of this phenomenon is limited. However, it seems that it is due to a combination of factors, including administrative delays, non-compliance with the terms of the programme, and outright refusal of the programme. Whatever the reason

---

[6] In our Probit specification, the dependent variable is the indicator for receiving transfers commented in the previous section.

for the existence of non-compliers, two things are evident. First, we cannot identify them in the control villages. Second, they are not a random subset of the beneficiaries. If we try to predict 'non-compliers' among the beneficiaries in the treatment villages, we find many significant factors, even though, no combination of variables can predict them perfectly.[7] The issue is potentially a serious one and has been discussed in the evaluation literature, see Heckman *et al.* (1998) and Angrist *et al.* (1996). If we were willing to assume that the effect of the programme on the non-compliers is zero, it is easy to show (see Angrist *et al.* 1996) that the presence of non-compliers would not imply a problem, given the randomized nature of the treatment. However, we feel such an assumption is too strong in our context. As the non-compliers (and the non-beneficiaries) live in villages where other individuals receive the programme, it might be that, for these households, the probability of receiving a private transfer increases as a consequence of the programme. Such a scenario would violate the assumption that the programme has no effect on non-compliers and therefore invalidate the procedure proposed by Heckman *et al.* (1998) and by Angrist *et al.* (1996). In other words, general equilibrium effects are very likely to be operative in our context. It is therefore worthwhile to see if we could identify the effects of interest using alternative assumptions to those proposed in the literature. To make our point it is not necessary to focus on the non-linearities implied by the Probit and Tobit structure. To keep the discussion simple, therefore, we will discuss it within a linear system.

Let Y_t and Y_c denote the outcomes of interest in treatment and control villages, respectively. Let p take the value 0, 1 in both control and treatment villages indicating poor household entitled (in the treatment villages) or eventually entitled (in control villages) in the programme. For $p = 1$, let b take the value 0 or 1; $b = 1$ are beneficiaries and $b = 0$ are non-beneficiaries. Finally, let k be the fraction of beneficiaries. Proper randomization will guarantee that k is the same in treatment and control villages, even if complying (p) is a decision variable.

We are interested in estimating the effect of the programme, that is, the average effect of the treatment on the treated:[8] $E[Y_t \mid p = 1, b = 1] - E[Y_c \mid p = 1, b = 1]$. Notice that we do not observe or measure the second element because we do not know who would be a beneficiary in the control villages. Notice also that:

$$E[Y_t \mid p = 1] = kE[Y_t \mid p = 1, b = 1] + (1 - k)E[Y_t \mid p = 1, b = 0]$$
$$E[Y_c \mid p = 1] = kE[Y_c \mid p = 1, b = 1] + (1 - k)E[Y_c \mid p = 1, b = 0].$$

From this it follows that:

$$E[Y_t \mid p = 1, b = 1] - E[Y_c \mid p = 1, b = 1] = \frac{E[Y_t \mid p = 1] - E[Y_c \mid p = 1]}{k}$$
$$- \frac{1 - k}{k}\{E[Y_t \mid p = 1, b = 0] - E[Y_c \mid p = 1, b = 0]\}. \tag{13.1}$$

---

[7] It turns out that the non-compliers are much more frequent among the *densificado* households and among those with few or no children.

[8] It may also be of some interest to assess $E[Y_t \mid b = 1] - E[Y_c \mid b = 1]$, that is ignoring the compliers issue altogether. Given the randomization, this is trivial.

If one assumes that the second term on the right-hand side of this expression is zero, which would be the case if one assumes that the treatment has no effect on non-beneficiaries, then you obtain what Heckman *et al.* (1998) or Angrist *et al.* (1996) suggest.

However, if one not willing to make this assumption, it is necessary to rely on something else. The alternative and weaker assumptions we propose is the following:

$$E[Y_t \mid p = 1, b = 0] - E[Y_c \mid p = 1, b = 0] = E[Y_t \mid p = 0] - E[Y_c \mid p = 0],$$

$$(13.2)$$

that is, that the difference in the outcomes of non-compliers in treatment and control villages is the same as the difference in the outcomes for non-beneficiaries. That is, if one thinks that the treatment has an effect on non-beneficiaries because of general equilibrium effects, we assume that these effects are the same for the non-poor and for the non-beneficiaries. The right-hand side of equation (13.2) can be estimated.

In the next section, we present two estimates for the effect of the programme along the lines discussed here. We call Effect 1 to the effect of the programme estimated using equation (13.1) under the assumption that the treatment has no effect on non-compliers (thus the second term on the right-hand side of (13.1) vanishes). On the other hand, by substituting (13.2) into (13.1) you obtain what we call Effect 2 in the tables containing our empirical results.

In addition to these issues, one needs to worry about the computation of standard errors. First, one would like to use methods that are robust. Second, one would like to take into account the presence of correlation among observations at the village level. For this reason we use bootstrapped standard errors with cluster effects at the village level. In other words, we first estimate conventional Probit and Tobit models. Then we use bootstrapping allowing for village cluster effects, such that the sample drawn during each replication is a bootstrap sample of clusters. Therefore, we obtain with this procedure standard error for the parameters in the Probit and Tobit models, which are robust to village cluster effects. Furthermore, we report the bootstrapped mean of the two effects and their corresponding bootstrapped standard errors.

13.4.3. *Crowding-out and Grant Size*

If the grant was uniform across households (as is the case of the nutritional supplement), one would only be interested in the coefficient on the dummy variable indicating beneficiary households in treatment villages or in the estimated effect that takes into account the non-complier problem discussed above. In reality, however, different households are entitled to different amounts of grant and, *ex post*, receive different levels of support. It is therefore interesting to check whether private transfers are affected by the level of the public grant, that is, whether households receiving a larger public grant are less likely to receive a private transfer and, conditionally on getting it, receive smaller amounts.

As mentioned above, the amount each household is entitled to depends on the number of school age children living in the household and the last approved grade of each child. The amount they do receive depends on whether each child is enrolled or not. Therefore, what the household receives in addition to the basic nutritional subsidy is not an unconditional grant but is linked to specific actions (and depends on the household demographic structure). More than a transfer, a large proportion of the programme we consider should be interpreted as a change in the price of education for these households. However, for households that would have enrolled their children in school regardless of the presence of the grant, the grant represents a pure income transfer.

To have an idea of the effect of the size of the grant on private transfers, while side-stepping the issue of the possible endogeneity of the grant level, we add to our Probit and Tobit specifications the potential grant that 'poor' households (in a treatment or control village) would be entitled to receive. In particular, we consider six different levels of the potential grant and interact the corresponding dummies with the treatment-poor and control-poor dummies as well as with the 'treatment-poor-non-beneficiary' dummy to take into account the non-complier issue discussed in the previous section. Having computed the effect of the grant for each of the six grant classes, we then impose either a linear or a quadratic effect of the grant by minimum distance.

13.5. RESULTS

In this section, we present our estimation results for the probability of receiving a transfer and its amount. We show separate estimates for those transfers coming from 'migrants' and from friends or relatives.

First, we report the results for the transfers received from anyone but migrants. In particular, Table 13.7 reports the results of a Probit model for the probability of receiving any (in columns 1–3) and the results of a Tobit model for net monetary transfers (columns 4–6). All specifications in these tables include a set of controls (state dummies, shock dummies, individual illness, and days lost) whose coefficients are not reported to save space. In columns 1 and 4, we check the general effect of the programme on private transfers, that is, we introduce a dummy for the treatment villages but we do not distinguish between beneficiaries and non-beneficiaries. We find a very small negative effect that is not significantly different from zero.

In columns 2 and 3, we distinguish the programme's effects on households according to their entitlement status and also take into account if they are actually beneficiaries or not. In particular, we substitute the treatment villages dummy with a set of dummies that indicate the poor beneficiaries, the poor non-beneficiaries and the non-poor in the 'treatment' villages and the non-poor in the control villages. The excluded group, therefore, is that of the 'poor' in the control villages.

In the absence of 'non-compliers', one could read from the coefficient on the treatment poor (the beneficiary of the programme relative to similar households in control villages) the effect of the programme. However, as discussed in Section 13.4, the presence of non-compliers requires additional computations to unravel the effect of the programme. The effect estimated making the assumptions suggested by

P. Albarran and O. P. Attanasio

Table 13.7. *Transfers from friends*

	Probit			Tobit		
	(1)	(2)	(3)	(4)	(5)	(6)
Treatment villages	−0.0143			−46.3592		
	(0.0457)			(67.2524)		
Treatment villages		−0.1152	−0.1020		−188.4291	−174.7272
Poor		(0.0641)	(0.0569)		(97.1155)	(75.1016)
beneficiaries						
Treatment villages		0.1461	0.1278		174.0266	154.2646
Poor		(0.0651)	(0.0703)		(112.1027)	(101.3515)
non-beneficiaries						
Treatment villages		−0.0709	−0.0480		−71.0503	−43.6969
Non-poor		(0.0637)	(0.0663)		(110.1851)	(113.8477)
Control villages		−0.1356	−0.1178		−126.0521	−102.7882
Non-poor		(0.0651)	(0.0717)		(102.2041)	(98.7407)
Log consumption			−0.2270			−239.3304
			(0.0343)			(48.7671)
Effect 1		−0.0646	−0.0577		−128.1521	−121.2951
		(0.0636)	(0.0647)		(106.9990)	(102.7401)
Effect 2		−0.0870	−0.0819		−147.2029	−141.7623
		(0.0788)	(0.0798)		(86.0295)	(105.8298)
Observations	23,247	23,247	23,247	23,247	23,247	23,247

Effect 1: Treatment effect under the assumption that the effect on non-compliers in treatment and control villages is the same.

Effect 2: Treatment effect under the assumption that the difference in the effect on non-compliers in treatment and control villages is the same as the difference between non-beneficiaries. These effects and their standard errors have been computed by bootsraping.

Note: Robust standard errors in parentheses. Constant, state dummies, shock dummies, days of illness, days of work lost are always present.

Heckman *et al.* (1998) and by Angrist *et al.* (1996) are reported in the row labelled 'Effect 1'. The effect estimated the alternative assumption we suggest and discuss in Section 13.4 are in the row labelled 'Effect 2'.

The results in column 2 indicate that beneficiaries are less likely to get private transfers as compared with poor households in control villages; on the other hand, non-beneficiaries appears to receive more transfers. Although our alternative assumption concerning the importance of general equilibrium effects seems to be relevant; the negative impact is not too strong in both cases. These results are basically unchanged when, in column 3, we add to our basic specification the log of consumption. Such a variable is strongly significant and takes a negative sign: households who enjoy a higher level of consumption receive less transfers. The coefficients on the programme dummies, however, are substantially unaffected.

When considering net monetary transfers (columns 4–6), the negative effect appears strongly significant. The amount by which the public grant crowds out is less than one for one (140 is below the average grant obtained from PROGRESA) but is substantial.

As discussed in Section 13.4.3, we explicitly take into account the possibility that the effect of the programme on private transfers depends not only on whether a household receives the public transfer or not, but also on the 'intensity of the treatment', that is, on how much a household can (potentially) be paid. Thus, we fit a linear or quadratic relationship between the programme effect and the potential grant, whose coefficients are reported in Table 13.8. In particular, the coefficients that we report in Table 13.8 take into account the non-compliers issue, using both assumptions discussed in Section 13.2. As we mentioned in Section 13.4.3, the parameters are fitted by minimum distance on the coefficients corresponding to those we label 'Effect 1' and 'Effect 2' in Table 13.7, for each of six grant categories. A complete set of estimates is available upon request. In Table 13.8, we also report the effect of the programme, implied by the estimated coefficients in each specification, evaluated at the average grant in our sample (250 pesos).

Both in the Probit and Tobit case, the coefficients in the linear specifications do not appear to be individually significant, although the programme effect evaluated at the average grant are comparable with those displayed in Table 13.7 (in particular, they are negative and marginally significant). On the other hand, we find that the quadratic specification fits quite well: all coefficients are individually significant. As for the reported effects evaluated at the average grant, we find again that the programme has a significant negative effect on the probability of receiving a transfer and on the amount-received conditional on receiving a private transfer. In this case, our point estimate for the programme effect implies a large crowding-out. Although our estimates are higher than those in many existing studies, some papers also find that, for very poor households in developing countries, public transfers can induce a strong crowding-out. Cox and Jimenez (1995), for instance, report evidence that public pension programmes for the Philippines would result in a 92 per cent reduction of private transfers. In another recent paper, Cox *et al.* (1999) claim that, once the non-monotonicity in the transfer-income relationship is taken into account, public transfers are found to have a substantial negative effect on private transfers.

We now move to the consideration of the results that we obtain for transfers received from migrants. Table 13.9 reports the results of a Probit model for the probability of receiving any transfer and the results of a Tobit model for net monetary transfers. The set of controls common to all specifications and the different specifications (in each column) are the same as in Table 13.7. However, in estimating these equations we use only households that report having migrants. This explains the reduction in the number of observations. As we are estimating the effect of the programme off the variation induced by the randomization, we do not need to worry about the selection issues connected with the consideration of only households with migrants.

As in Table 13.7, the coefficients associated with the plain 'Treatment villages' dummy in columns 1 and 4 are negative but not statistically different from zero. Once again, however, once we control for who receives the programme, we found significant crowding-out effects, both in the Probit and in the Tobit specifications. Notice however, that the crowding-out of this kind of transfers seems to be less strong than that for

Table 13.8. *Treatment effects on transfers from friends, as a function of the grant size*

	Probit				Tobit			
	Effect 1		Effect 2		Effect 1		Effect 2	
Intercept	-0.0647	0.4658	-0.0801	0.4468	795.567	-184.159	803.471	-161.037
	(0.1053)	(0.1946)	(0.1025)	(0.1922)	(320.841)	(156.133)	(314.109)	(150.083)
Grant	-0.0002	-0.0044	-0.0002	-0.0044	-7.738	-0.034	-7.738	-0.034
	(0.0002)	(0.0013)	(0.0002)	(0.0013)	(2.236)	(0.377)	(2.236)	(0.377)
Grant^2	6.5E-06		6.5E-06		0.012		0.012	
	(2.0E-06)		(2.0E-06)		(0.003)		(0.003)	
Effect at mean grant	-0.1076	-0.2163	-0.1230	-0.2353	-397.093	-192.724	-389.189	-169.602
	(0.0810)	(0.0877)	(0.0785)	(0.0858)	(126.751)	(112.460)	(124.866)	(107.912)

Table 13.9. *Transfers from migrants (only for households with migrants)*

	Probit			Tobit		
	(1)	(2)	(3)	(4)	(5)	(6)
Treatment villages	−0.0364			−25.2468		
	(0.0462)			(22.8879)		
Treatment villages		−0.1134	−0.1113		−59.2782	−61.2460
Poor beneficiaries		(0.0639)	(0.0729)		(22.3539)	(30.4710)
Treatment villages		0.0083	0.0046		−28.4244	−24.8774
Poor non-beneficiaries		(0.0780)	(0.0810)		(34.8725)	(28.6178)
Treatment villages		0.0026	0.0047		−6.0889	−8.8712
Non-poor		(0.1054)	(0.0907)		(32.2626)	(33.4399)
Control villages		−0.0664	−0.0629		−43.3385	−46.4576
Non-poor		(0.0932)	(0.0667)		(30.6215)	(36.6859)
Log consumption			−0.0347			33.7289
			(0.0344)			(15.6499)
Effect 1		−0.1105	−0.1097		−69.1235	−69.8627
		(0.0778)	(0.0800)		(35.2458)	(34.2884)
Effect 2		−0.1344	−0.1331		−82.0255	−82.8814
		(0.0929)	(0.0778)		(35.7559)	(36.7581)
Observations	3,721	3,721	3,721	3,721	3,721	3,721

Note: Robust standard errors in parentheses. See also note in Table 13.7.

transfers received from friends and family. This result is consistent with the idea that people living in the village or near by, have better information on the nature of the grant and therefore can react more to its introduction. On the other hand, transfers from friends can be thought of as part of an informal insurance arrangement, whereas transfers from the migrated members of the household are more likely to be for altruistic reasons or as a payment for some sort of service. Therefore, the mechanism through which these two classes of private transfers are crowded out by the public programme is different.

Finally, we present in Table 13.10 the results of fitting a linear or quadratic relationship between the programme effect and the potential grant, whose coefficients are reported in Table 13.8; also we present the effect of the programme. In this case, both linear and quadratic specification fits very poorly, being insignificant all the estimated coefficients in the relationship. Nevertheless, the estimated effects, evaluated at the average grant, are similar to those in Table 13.9.

13.6. CONCLUSIONS

In this chapter, we have analysed the effect of a large welfare programme in rural Mexico, PROGRESA, on the private transfers received by the beneficiaries of such a

Table 13.10. *Treatment effects on transfers from migrants as a function of the grant size*

	Probit				Tobit			
	Effect 1		Effect 2		Effect 1		Effect 2	
Intercept	−0.1058	−0.3491	−0.1353	−0.3751	−60.189	−119.842	−70.744	−130.140
	(0.1362)	(0.2804)	(0.1344)	(0.2764)	(56.619)	(110.850)	(57.150)	(110.769)
Grant	5.0E−05	0.0018	0.0001	0.0018	−0.009	0.409	−0.009	0.409
	(3.4E−04)	(0.0018)	(0.0003)	(0.0018)	(0.133)	(0.681)	(0.133)	(0.6810)
Grant^2		−2.5E−06		−2.5E−06		−0.001		−0.001
		(2.5E−06)		(2.5E−06)		(0.001)		(0.001)
Effect at mean grant	−0.0932	−0.0623	−0.1227	−0.0883	−62.438	−55.704	−72.992	−66.002
	(0.0889)	(0.0942)	(0.0863)	(0.0930)	(36.463)	(38.017)	(36.732)	(38.392)

programme. While PROGRESA is not a pure transfer programme, as most of the subsidies the beneficiaries household receive are conditional on school attendance or other
specific actions the programme is meant to encourage, the evaluation sample we use
has the big advantages of having a pure randomization component. In particular, in
186 of the 506 villages included in the evaluation sample, the implementation of the
programme was delayed for two years. This allows us to overcome the endogeneity
problem that plagues many of the papers that have looked at the crowding-out of
private transfers induced by public programmes. While it is true that PROGRESA is
not a pure transfer, it is fair to say that it does have a positive income effect for the
beneficiary families, both because it has an unconditional component and because the
education subsidy probably more than compensate for the loss of income from child
labour. Moreover, the programme does not change the observed enrolment behaviour
of many households.

From a methodological point of view, we have to deal with the fact that some
beneficiary households in treatment villages do not receive the programme. This
feature of the programme prevents the simple comparison of treatment and control villages' poors, because some of the treatment villages' poors do not receive
the programme. On the other hand, those poor households who do receive the
programme in treatment villages are not strictly comparable to the poor in control
villages. We use two different sets of assumptions that allow us to identify the effect of
interest.

Our results indicate that the programme does crowd our private transfers. Both
the likelihood to receive a transfer and the amount-received conditional on receiving
private transfers are significantly and negatively affected by the programme. This
result is consistent with the implications of several theoretical models that have been
considered in the literature. We consider separately the transfers received from friends
and relatives other than migrant children and those received from migrants and find
that the crowding-out effects, especially in the amount received, are weaker for the
migrant transfers. This might be an indication that the mechanism through which
private transfers are crowded out by the public programme is different for the two
classes of transfers.

This evidence is particularly important, as the variation we use is, by construction,
exogenous. Our data therefore avoid some of the problems that have affected the
empirical literature on this subject. The general conclusion we draw from this exercise
is that this particular programme has a negative effect on private transfers. Some
of our estimates indicate that the crowding-out effects can be quite large. Having
said this, however, in interpreting our results it should be remembered that the main
objective of PROGRESA is that of fostering the accumulation of human capital among
poor rural households. Our results do not say anything about the effectiveness of the
programme in achieving such a goal. It should be clear, however, that when evaluating
a public programme, such as PROGRESA, one has to take into account the fact that such
programmes do not occur in a vacuum but interact with existing mechanisms within a
society.

P. Albarran and O. P. Attanasio

Appendix

Table 13.A1. *Distribution of households, October 1998*

	Non-poor	Poor		Total
		Beneficiaries	**Non-beneficiaries**	
Treatment villages				
Non-poor in 1997	3,176	1,380	1,977	6,533
Poor in 1997		6,924	902	7,826
	3,176	8,304	2,879	14,359
Control villages				
Non-poor in 1997	2,011	2,248		4,259
Poor in 1997		4,650		4,650
	2,011	6,898		8,909

Table 13.A2. *Descriptive statistics, October 1998*

	All		Poor		Non-poor	
	Treatment	Control	Treatment	Control	Treatment	Control
Sample size	14,359	8,909	11,183	6,898	3,176	2,011
Age of household head (HH)	47.120 (0.031)	47.585	45.894 (0.030)	46.433	51.437 (0.814)	51.533
Age of HH's wife	40.853 (0.182)	41.135	39.540 (0.264)	39.803	45.695 (0.543)	45.961
Sex of HH (=1 if male)	0.884 (0.622)	0.886	0.886 (0.627)	0.889	0.876 (0.869)	0.877
Sex of HH's wife (=1 if male)	0.017 (0.179)	0.015	0.017 (0.122)	0.014	0.018 (0.997)	0.018
Number of members	5.675 (0.104)	5.736	5.843 (0.716)	5.858	5.084 (0.002)	5.316
Number of babies (aged 0–6)	1.310 (0.630)	1.301	1.470 (0.558)	1.458	0.745 (0.548)	0.763
Number of children aged 7–16	1.416 (0.987)	1.417	1.535 (0.956)	1.534	0.997 (0.642)	1.014
Number of adults aged 17–64	2.533 (0.002)	2.594	2.451 (0.355)	2.471	2.823 (0.000)	3.018
Number of elderly (aged 65 or more)	0.389 (0.602)	0.394	0.361 (0.314)	0.371	0.489 (0.434)	0.472
Wage per day earned by HH	32.651 (0.163)	39.765	32.158 (0.193)	40.447	34.686 (0.080)	37.047
Wage per day earned by HH's wife	32.440 (0.328)	116.906	28.695 (0.182)	26.324	41.132 (0.319)	351.651
Hours per day worked by HH	8.002 (0.590)	7.988	8.025 (0.758)	8.016	7.910 (0.599)	7.879

Table 13.A2. (*Continued*)

	All			Poor			Non-Poor		
	Treatment		Control	Treatment		Control	Treatment		Control
Hours per day worked by HH's wife	7.669	(0.039)	7.254	7.533	(0.494)	7.376	7.982	(0.010)	6.929
Years of schooling (HH)	3.457	(0.889)	3.463	3.373	(0.707)	3.355	3.761	(0.426)	3.841
Years of schooling (HH's wife)	2.325	(0.543)	2.305	2.315	(0.208)	2.267	2.362	(0.259)	2.440
Weekly expenditure per capita on non-durables	31.227	(0.260)	30.780	29.442	(0.098)	28.746	37.511	(0.803)	37.756
Household weekly total income	294.637	(0.120)	336.719	274.944	(0.175)	321.538	365.778	(0.259)	389.151

Note: Numbers in parentheses are *p*-values of the *t*-test for the difference.

Table 13.A3. *Households involved in transfers (from friends and migrants) by entitlement*

	Non-poor	Poor		Total
		Beneficiaries	Non-beneficiaries	
Treatment villages				
Received not given	380	724	382	1,486
	(11.96)	(8.72)	(13.27)	(10.34)
Received given	10	15	5	30
	(0.31)	(0.18)	(0.17)	(0.21)
Not received given	37	33	21	91
	(1.16)	(0.40)	(0.73)	(0.63)
Not received not given	2,749	7,531	2,471	12,751
	(86.56)	(90.70)	(85.83)	(88.81)
Total	3,176	8,303	2,879	14,358
	(100.00)	(100.00)	(100.00)	(100.00)
Control villages				
Received not given	229		712	941
	(11.39)		(10.32)	(10.56)
Received given	3		13	16
	(0.15)		(0.19)	(0.18)
Not received given	25		33	58
	(1.24)		(0.48)	(0.65)
Not received not given	1,754		6,140	7,894
	(87.22)		(89.01)	(88.61)
Total	2,011		6,898	8,909
	(100.00)		(100.00)	(100.00)

REFERENCES

Angrist, J. D., G. W. Imbens, and D. B. Rubin (1996). 'Identification of Causal Effects Using Instrumental Variables'. *Journal of the American Statistical Association*, 91, 444–55.

Attanasio, O. P. and J. V. Rios Rull (2000*a*). 'Consumption Smoothing in Island Economies: Can Public Insurance Reduce Welfare?'. *European Economic Review*, 44, 1225–58.

—— and —— (2000*b*). 'Consumption Smoothing and Extended Families', in M. Dewatripoint and L. P. Hansen (eds), *Advances in Economic Theory—The World Congress of the Econometric Society—Seattle 2000*. Cambridge: Cambridge University Press.

Becker, G. (1974). 'A Theory of Social Interactions'. *Journal of Political Economy*, 82, 1063–1093.

Behrman, J. and P. E. Todd (1999). 'Randomness in the Experimental Samples of PROGRESA', mimeo, International Food Policy Research Institute, Washington, DC.

Bernheim, D., A. Schleifer, and L. H. Summers (1985). 'The Strategic Bequest Motive'. *Journal of Political Economy*, 93, 1045–76.

Cox, D. (1987). 'Motives for Private Transfers'. *Journal of Political Economy*, 95, 508–46.

—— and E. Jimenez (1995). 'Private Transfers and the Effectiveness of Public Income Redistribution in the Philippines', in D. van de Walle and K. Nead (eds), *Public Spending and the Poor: Theory and Evidence*. Baltimore, MD and London: Johns Hopkins University Press for the World Bank.

——, ——, and W. Okrasa (1997). 'Family Safety Nets and Economic Transition: A Study of Worker Households in Poland'. *Review of Income and Wealth*, 43, 191–209.

——, Z. Eser, and E. Jimenez (1998). 'Motives for Private Transfers over the Life Cycle: An Analytical Framework and Evidence from Peru'. *Journal of Development Economics*, 55, 57–80.

——, B. E. Hansen, and E. Jimenez (1999). 'How Responsive are Private Transfers to Income? Evidence from a *laissez-faire* Economy', manuscript.

Foster, A. and M. Rosenzweig (2001). 'Imperfect Commitment, Altruism, and the Family: Evidence from Transfer Behavior in Low-Income Rural Areas'. *Review of Economics and Statistics*, 83(3), 389–407.

Gomez de Leon, J. and S. Parker (1999). 'The Impact of Anti-Poverty Programs on Labor Force Participation', mimeo, PROGRESA.

Heckman, J., J. Smith, and C. Taber (1998). 'Accounting for Dropouts in Evaluations of Social Programs'. *Review of Economics and Statistics*, 80, 1–14.

IFPRI (2000). 'Is PROGRESA Working? Summary of the Results of an Evaluation by IFPRI', mimeo, International Food Policy Research Institute, Washington, DC.

Jensen, R. (1998). 'Public Transfers, Private Transfers, and the 'Crowding Out' Hypothesis: Evidence from South Africa'. *Research Working Paper R98-08*. Cambridge, MA: Harvard University, Kennedy School of Government.

Schoeni, R. F. (1997). 'Private Intrahousehold Transfers of Money and Time: New Empirical Evidence'. *Review of Income and Wealth*, 43, 423–64.

14

Food Aid and Informal Insurance

STEFAN DERCON AND PRAMILA KRISHNAN

14.1. INTRODUCTION

It is generally acknowledged that developing and transition economies need better safety nets (see, for example Drèze and Sen 1990; World Bank 2000*b*). Current provision often takes the form of direct transfer programme such as the distribution of food-aid and public employment programmes with in-kind wages. Their aim is to support the poor and vulnerable and to prevent current and future deprivation and insufficient nutrition.[1] Despite calls for more long-term safety nets, they remain largely relief programmes that swing in as a response to emergencies.

The problems with food-based support programmes and their efficiency in developing countries has received a lot of attention (for reviews see Clay 1986; Ravallion 1991; Barrett 2001). Much of this literature has been concerned with questions about the programme objectives, their long-run sustainability and dependency problems (Ruttan 1993; Barrett 2000) or the incentive effects of transfers on labour supply, food production and other productive activities (Maxwell *et al.* 1994; Dorosh *et al.* 1995; Sahn and Alderman 1996; Barrett 2001; Bezuneh *et al.* 1988). Other studies try to quantify the net transfer benefits, taking into account the opportunity cost of time spent on food-for-work (Datt and Ravallion 1994). There is a sizeable literature on the impact of ration systems and supplementary feeding programmes (Beaton and Ghassemi 1982; Kennedy and Alderman 1987; Alderman 1991). A few papers have directly addressed the issue of nutritional impacts of food distribution and food-for-work programmes (Athanasios *et al.* 1994; Jayne *et al.* 1999), while some have focused on the indirect effects, such as on-farm investment (Bezuhen and Deaton 1997; Bezuneh *et al.* 1988).

In recent years the focus has been on problems related to the targeting of transfers (Besley and Kanbur 1990; Sen 1995; van de Walle and Nead 1995). Building on

Financial support by the World Institute for Development Economics Research (WIDER) for developing this research is gratefully acknowledged by the authors. We received useful comments during presentations at the World Bank/IFPRI, Oxford, Gent and WIDER. All errors are our own.

[1] Different terms tend to be used to describe the objectives of these programmes. Often, they aim to promote food security, which can be defined as the freedom from the risk of insufficient nutrition, thereby avoiding current and future deprivation. Different authors use different definitions. Reduced 'nutritional risk' or 'vulnerability' are used in a similar sense (Beaton 1987; Morduch 1994; Maxwell 1996; Christiaensen 2000; Dercon and Krishnan 2000*a*; Barrett 2001).

the success of the Maharashtra Employment Guarantee Scheme, self-selection based employment schemes are often advocated as providing a partial solution to these targeting problems (Alderman and Lindert 1998; Drèze and Sen 1990; Ravallion 1990; Barrett 2001). Empirical work on rural data has tried to quantify these targeting issues and ask whether the poor do obtain the transfers (Ravallion 1991; von Braun 1995; Teklu and Asefa 1999; Jayne *et al.* 2001).

To the extent that empirical research has focused on the impact of transfers on the welfare of the poor, much of this work suffers from at least four problems. First, many studies, especially those on food aid and food-for-work, focus on whether the poor are reached or not, without directly evaluating the impact on the livelihoods of the poor. Second, even if they do, they rarely address the issue of the impact in terms of nutritional *risk*, and focus only on the direct effect on current incomes and nutrition, partly due to the lack of longitudinal data that can document vulnerability and welfare dynamics (Barrett 2001). Third, and linked to this, they do not consider the presence of alternative ways of coping with consumption or nutrition shortfalls, such as running down assets and relying on informal support networks (Deaton 1992; Morduch 1995). Any impact evaluation ought to take these alternatives into account for they will affect the sum total of support available: for instance, Attanasio and Rios-Rull (2001) demonstrate large crowding-out effects. Fourth, they fail to acknowledge the econometric problems related to programme placement effects (see Rosenzweig and Wolpin 1993 for a classic treatment). In particular, the recipients of support may receive it due to certain characteristics, unobserved to the researcher, that also affect the recipients' nutrition or consumption outcomes thus biasing the results of the impact evaluation.

In this chapter, we study food aid distribution in rural Ethiopia, and try to address some of these problems. As in other studies, we distinguish two questions. First, what determines the allocation rule of food aid in Ethiopia? By studying the allocation rule, we can also address the issue of whether food aid is indeed used as a form of insurance and so, is responsive to negative shocks. Second, what is the impact on consumption of food aid transfers? For this question, we explicitly tackle the issue of how food aid might interact with informal sharing arrangements within the village.[2] (Issues related to the long-term impact of the safety net, for instance, investment in productive assets, are discussed in Chapter 16.)

Per capita GDP is estimated at about US$140 per annum, child malnutrition (stunting) is estimated at well above 50 per cent during the 1990s and adult malnutrition is about 25 per cent (World Bank 2000*a*; Dercon and Krishnan 2000*a*; Christiaensen and Alderman 2001). Furthermore, its population lives in a highly risky environment: drought is a recurrent phenomenon, requiring large public responses (as in 1994 and 1999) or, in conjunction with failing public policy and war, triggering a large-scale famine in 1974 and in 1984–5. Ethiopia is also an important recipient of food aid, and is arguably increasingly dependent on it. The World Food Programme estimates

---

[2] This chapter is a companion to a previous piece (Dercon and Krishnan 2003) where we abstracted from issues about the allocation rule (and placement effects) to focus on the impact of food aid interventions for existing informal arrangements.

for 1994–8 suggest that Ethiopia is the second largest recipient of food aid in the world (after Bangladesh). In the 1990s, volumes of food aid accounted for about 5–15 per cent of production (Clay *et al.* 1998). Food aid is largely distributed via food-for-work programmes—the best estimate puts its share at 63 per cent of food aid, while the rest is largely distributed as direct (free) transfers. Food-for-work and direct food aid distribution are virtually the only publicly provided safety net in rural Ethiopia. A few recent studies have documented and analysed the effectiveness of food aid delivery, uncovering important deficiencies, although the focus has largely been on targeting issues (Sharp 1997; Clay *et al.* 1998; Barrett and Clay 2003; Jayne *et al.* 1999, 2001).

In the next section, we discuss food aid distribution in Ethiopia and the data used in this chapter. In the third section, the village-level and within village allocation rule for food aid is analysed. In Section 14.4, we present a theoretical framework to test the impact of a safety net on households faced with income risk. An empirical model is developed in Section 14.5 and this is used in Section 14.6. Section 14.7 concludes.

14.2. DATA AND DESCRIPTIVE STATISTICS

Ethiopia offers an obvious opportunity to study the impact of safety nets on the household's ability to keep consumption smooth. It is one of the highest recipients of food aid and faces a harsh and variable climate. Both donors and the government have committed themselves to forming a well-functioning safety net. The Food Security Strategy (FDRE 1996) distinguishes between food-for-work or other income generating labour schemes (supplementary employment and income schemes), aimed at able-bodied adults, and targeted interventions for especially vulnerable groups. They cover both interventions in large-scale crisis and programmes designed to reach particular groups over longer periods. In practice, most interventions involve food aid. In turn, food aid has long contributed to food supplies in Ethiopia. This dependence has been exacerbated by the food shortages during the famine in 1984–5, the increasingly desperate situation in many rural areas in the late 1980s, linked to civil war and political turmoil. The annual volume of cereal food aid has typically been about 2,000–6,000 metric tons per year in the period 1986–1995, representing about 5–15 per cent of production. Even in average years, the volume of cereal food aid in a given region can account for 25 per cent or more of total marketed supply of grain, increasing up to 50 per cent in drought years (Clay *et al.* 1998). A substantial portion (over 80 per cent in bad years) of food aid has been used for emergency relief purposes.

Food aid is usually distributed across regions and districts by the government while the actual allocation to beneficiaries at the local level is decided by local village officials. In rural areas, this will be the peasant association, which is a local government institution covering one or more villages. For food-for-work, self-targeting is not often used, but even if eligible, households must still make a decision of whether to work or not. Alternative opportunities are likely to influence this decision. Often, the workload related to food-for-work activities is not clear while wages are typically rather high, and probably higher than the opportunity cost of time. The result is that usually more people apply for food-for-work than can be accommodated. In effect, this means that the distinction between food aid and food-for-work is not as important as expected, even though allocation rules differ. This is investigated further below.

What is the evidence on the targeting of this food aid? Sharp (1997), who reviewed a large body of evaluation studies and conducted several new case studies, found that food aid has been spread too thinly over too many areas and too many people, particularly in recent years. There is little evidence of targeting specific areas. Furthermore, in most cases, participants are selected at the community level, but there is a clear reluctance to select some households while excluding others, so that much larger numbers are involved in the programmes than intended. The result is that, locally, targeting errors of inclusion (providing aid to people who are not in the intended target group) are a greater problem than errors of exclusion (failing to provide aid to the people who need it most). The result is that often too little aid is provided to the poorest to make much difference. A similar result was found in the sub-sample of the large nationally representative HICES/WMS survey for 1995/96. A number of related studies (Clay *et al.* 1999; Jayne *et al.* 2001) find that the most important factor determining access to food aid was whether there was a programme previously in the area, resulting in a serious regional bias of food aid allocation. Half the food aid distributed went to households with more than sufficient food from their own resources. It should be stressed that these types of findings are not uncommon across other developing countries. Nevertheless, they appear to have encouraged many donors to reassess their activities in these areas. Subsequent careful econometric studies of food aid in Ethiopia (Jayne *et al.* 2002) seems to confirm these patterns.

The data used in this chapter come from three rounds of the Ethiopian Rural Household Survey, collected in 1994 and 1995. This is a panel data survey collected by the Economics Department of Addis Ababa University in collaboration with the Centre for the Study of African Economies at Oxford University. It covers fifteen villages, representative for different areas across the country, and a total of 1,450 households were interviewed. The attrition rate in this panel is very low—about 2 per cent per year. The survey has detailed information on households, including consumption, assets and income, as well as the shocks they faced. Furthermore, it contains detailed information on participation in food aid and food-for-work programmes.

Consumption per adult equivalent[3] (in 1994 prices) is relatively low: about 80 birr on average, which was then about US$12 per month per adult. Using a local nutritional poverty line of 2200 kcal per adult, this suggests that about 40 per cent do not get sufficient calories on average. Shocks are very common, even in this short period and even, given that this was a relatively good year. In about a quarter of the villages, a serious drought occurred while diseases affected crops and livestock in many others. The average household lost several person days a month due to serious illness

---

[3] The consumption data are based on summing and valuing food and non-food consumption obtained via own production, the market and via gifts. It is expressed in real terms by using a consumer price index, using the average household in the first round as a base. It is expressed in adult equivalent units using nutritional equivalence scales based on WHO data for East Africa. All data issues are discussed in Dercon and Krishnan (2000).

(more details are in Dercon and Krishnan 2000*a*). Ability to cope with shocks is quite limited. Many households reported episodes of serious hardship linked to shocks in the last twenty years, related to drought, illness, policy changes, and other factors: 80 per cent of the sample suffered major economic hardship due to drought, mainly during the famine of the mid-1980s.

Efforts have clearly been made to supply the rural population with food aid. But how effective is it? First, in our sample we have a high percentage of households receiving food aid or benefiting from food-for-work in the six months before each round of the survey: about 20 per cent in both rounds 1 and 3, and even 39 per cent in round 2. However, the spatial and temporal spread is very large. In five villages (out of fifteen) programmes are always present, while in seven others, there was a programme in place some of the time and in three other villages, there was no food aid at all. Furthermore, the coverage in terms of households changed considerably over time. Table 14.1 gives the details for a few villages.

Clearly, one village (Ankober) had a programme with virtually complete coverage in the one period, to disappear in the other periods. In Geblen, the programme, very active in 1994, almost vanished. Only in Shumsha, (not far from the tourist destination Lalibela—a preferred destination of heads of missions and evaluation teams of donors and NGOs), coverage was always high: in round 1, six agencies are identified as giving food aid. Tables 14.2–14.4 give some indication about the targeting of the programme. First, we look at whether the poor in preceding period, labelled $t - 1$ received aid during the period between two rounds t and $t - 1$. The poor are identified using

Table 14.1. *Percentage of households receiving food aid per round in selected villages*

Village name	Round 1 (1994*a*)	Round 2 (1994*b*)	Round 3 (1995)
Atsbi	64	6	52
Geblen	79	97	5
Ankober	0	98	0
Shumsha	96	80	62
Yetmen	0	0	0

Source: Ethiopian Rural Household Survey.

Table 14.2. *Percentage of households receiving food aid by poverty status*

	Non-poor $(t - 1)$	Poor $(t - 1)$	Total $(t - 1)$
No food aid $(t, t - 1)$	52	22	74
Food aid $(t, t - 1)$	14	12	26

Source: Ethiopian Rural Household Survey.

Table 14.3. *Percentage of households receiving food aid by rainfall experience*

	Worst rains	Median rains	Best rains
No food aid $(t, t-1)$	28	27	21
Food aid $(t, t-1)$	8	2	13

Source: Ethiopian Rural Household Survey.

Table 14.4. *Is food aid targeted to the poor? Percentage of households receiving food aid by agricultural shock experience*

	Worst shocks	Median shocks	Best shocks
No food aid $(t, t-1)$	27	27	21
Food aid $(t, t-1)$	7	6	12

Source: Ethiopian Rural Household Survey.

a poverty line based on the cost of obtaining sufficient consumption to yield 2200 kcal per adult and with some allowance for non-food expenditures (details are in Dercon and Krishnan 2000*a*). Effectively about 40 per cent are poor in each round, although there is considerable mobilist among who might be labelled 'poor'. Table 14.2 shows that of the 26 per cent of households receiving aid, more than half were non-poor in round *t*-1. In short, targeting is rather more inclusive than might be intended.

Table 14.3 examines the effect of common shocks, namely village level rainfall, and divides the sample into groups according to whether the rains in the six months preceding a round are in the lowest tercile (worst rains), middle tercile (median rains), and the best rain tercile, and by whether food aid was received. The table suggests that, of those receiving food aid, most food aid went to those households in villages which experienced the best rains, while the people that did not receive food aid, also suffered worse weather. This description holds true even if the comparison is with rains in the previous period and current food aid. Finally, we also use information on overall shocks to crops, including plant diseases and other idiosyncratic shocks. Households were again divided into terciles by crop shocks and receipt of food aid and similar patterns emerge: using simple descriptive statistics, the evidence suggests that the poor and vulnerable are not clearly targeted. Of course, this is merely suggestive and a proper evaluation requires more analysis to which we now turn.

14.3. FOOD AID ALLOCATION

In this section, we present some regressions describing the allocation rule used for free food aid and food-for-work, by providing covariates of whether food aid is obtained and how much aid is received. We use a straightforward reduced-form regression, in which food aid is determined by a number of household and community characteristics, some time-varying, such as shocks, and others fixed over time. Jayne *et al.* (2002)

conduct a similar analysis using a relatively large nationally representative clustered sample collected in 1996. They have data on a large number of districts (343) and 2796 households. Within each woreda, a few clusters were selected from which households were chosen; these clusters are 5 on average and substantially larger than a village. The large number of districts allows detailed analysis of the allocation to districts but is less amenable in describing the allocation within villages, since only a relatively small number of households per cluster is selected. In contrast, our data consists of panel data on 1450 households from fifteen villages. The relatively limited number of villages limits our ability to describe the allocation rules to villages but the rather large random samples within villages allow us to describe allocation within villages with more confidence. The fact that we have panel data allows us to focus more closely on the role played by time-varying information. Since we ask the same questions, we can and do compare our findings to those in Jayne *et al.* (2002).

The variables of interest are, whether food-for-work aid has been received and whether free food aid has been received by the household. The model is specified as a probit. A subsequent set of regressions explores the amounts received (conditional on having received some aid). This is effectively a hurdle model.[4] The first set of regressions focus on within village allocation, controlling for village level effects. In particular, a set of village level time-varying dummies allows us to focus on the within-village allocation: given that the village gets food aid, how is it allocated? The explanatory variables used are the same for all specifications. We use real consumption per adult and a set of household characteristics, such as the number of male and female adults, total household size, whether the head has completed primary education, and the sex and age of the household head. Since real consumption per adult may well be endogenous, not least since it is measured at the same time as the receipt of the food aid, we use asset variables (land and livestock per adult) as identifying instruments. The use of consumption or asset variables allows us to investigate the extent of income or wealth targeting observed in the data. Furthermore, we use a number of idiosyncratic (or household specific) shock variables to explore the responsiveness of aid targeting to shocks: illness days lost per adult in the preceding four months, an index of whether livestock suffered from disease (where 1 is best) and an index of whether crops suffered in general from poor growing conditions (again, 1 is best). These indices were constructed using a number of questions related to specific problems experienced in the latest growing season (details are in Dercon and Krishnan 2000*a*). A second set of regression drops the time-varying village effects, and includes a number of characteristics at the village level. Also included are whether the village had any all-weather road and its distance to the nearest town, as well as the percentage deviation of rainfall in the particular year (normal is coded as 1). Table 14.5 provides descriptive statistics.

---

[4] An alternative would be to jointly estimate whether aid has been received and how much, by using a Tobit model or a sample selection model. However, the former would constrain coefficients to be the same for both the decisions on whether and how much aid has been received, while the latter would require identifying instruments to credibly estimate the first stage of the model, which we do not think exist, or identification by functional form which is also not preferable.

Table 14.5. *Descriptive statistics: mean and standard deviation* (n = 3,981)

	Mean	Std dev.
Does the household receive any aid?	0.29	0.45
Does the household receive free transfers?	0.18	0.39
Does the household receive food-for-work?	0.11	0.31
Free food aid per adult (1994 prices)	2.25	15.82
Food-for-work per adult (1994 prices)	0.76	5.66
Consumption per adult (1994 prices)	91.61	96.71
Livestock per adult (1994 prices)	333.97	501.63
Land per adult (1994 prices)	0.36	0.44
Household size (no.)	5.15	2.20
Number of male adults 15–65 years (no.)	1.55	1.16
Number of female adults 15–65 years (no.)	0.96	0.19
Male headed? (%)	0.77	0.42
Head completed primary education? (%)	0.10	0.29
Age head (years)	46.23	15.79
Illness days per adult	0.62	2.18
Rainfall index (normal = 1)	1.13	0.26
% suffering below normal rain	0.34	0.47
Crop shocks (%, best = 1)	0.48	0.41
Livestock disease (%, best = 1)	0.83	0.28
Village distance to nearest town (km)	9.18	5.06
Village has all weather road? (%)	0.53	0.50

Note: Consumption and aid per adult equivalent per month, in birr of 1994; aid is valued at consumer prices; illness days suffered by adults per adult in the household; the rainfall index is calculated as rainfall in the preceding agricultural year relevant to the survey round divided by mean rainfall, minus one, and is measured at the nearest meteorological station—mean values based on typically about twenty years of data; below normal rain is defined as rainfall below the long-term mean; crop shocks is a subjective (self-reported) index of whether main crops suffered moderately or severely from any type of damage (including pests or weather related), where no problem equals 1 and 0 is total failure; livestock disease is a self-reported measure of whether livestock suffered from serious disease between survey rounds, where 1 means no problem. Note that this means that for *all* shocks variables higher variables mean better outcomes, with the exception of illness.

The probability of receiving food aid or food-for-work is estimated using a standard probit model, using the pooled data, with robust standard errors corrected for village-cluster effects.[5] Since we have panel data, this was also estimated as a conditional fixed effect logit model. This allows a further focus on time-varying information, including whether food aid allocation is responsive to shocks. Where relevant, the results are discussed in the text. Table 14.6 provides the results for whether any aid is received.

[5] We estimated the models also as random effects probit models, and the results are virtually identical, including in terms of significance. Since the models with time-varying village level effects did not converge always using this estimation method, we report only the pooled regression results.

Table 14.6. *Determinants of receiving food aid (marginal effects from probit model with village-time fixed effects, robust standard errors)*

	Any free aid?		Any food-for-work?	
	Marg. effect	*p*-value	Marg. effect	*p*-value
Consumption per adult	−0.002	0.006	−0.002	0.183
Male adults 15–65 years (no.)	−0.035	0.000	0.007	0.621
Female adults 15–65 years (no.)	−0.017	0.783	0.012	0.904
Male headed? (%)	0.006	0.737	0.014	0.728
Household size (no.)	0.001	0.943	−0.009	0.439
Head primary education?	0.082	0.106	0.041	0.437
Age head (years)	0.000	0.969	−0.001	0.210
Illness days per adult	0.001	0.545	−0.003	0.359
Crop shocks (%, best = 1)	−0.013	0.570	−0.040	0.014
Livestock disease (%, best = 1)	−0.025	0.621	−0.032	0.164
Time-varying village dummies	Not reported		Not reported	
	Pseudo R^2	0.69	Pseudo R^2	0.46
	$n = 2,447$		$n = 1,595$	

Note: The underlying data set contains 3981 observations. However, since we use a binary left-hand side variable and time-varying fixed effects, all observations from villages that have no food aid at all in a specific period would be perfectly collinear with the village dummies and therefore cannot contribute to understanding the household level determinants, and are excluded. The table reports marginal effects as the derivative of the cumulative normal distribution at the mean of the right-hand side variables; for dummies the marginal effect is expressed as the discrete change from 0 to 1 is reported. Real consumption is treated as endogenous using a two-stage regression. Land per adult and livestock values per adult are identifying instruments.

There is evidence of income-based targeting within villages (controlling for whether the village received aid). Evaluated at the mean of all other variables, the probability of receiving free food aid increases from 5.8 per cent at the 75th percentile of consumption per adult, to about 18.6 per cent at the 25th percentile. Note that these marginal effects are somewhat larger than in Jayne *et al.* (2002: 273). One reason may be that they analysed *within-district* allocation, and that allocation from districts to villages was not as sensitive to incomes as the allocation within villages. The other significant effect is that households with more male adults are less likely to receive aid (with a 3.5 per cent lower probability per male adult), suggesting targeting towards children, elderly, and women. For food-for-work programmes, the marginal effect of consumption per adult on participating is only very weakly significant, even though the marginal effect is relatively high again, suggesting some targeting (and contrary to Jayne *et al.* 2002).[6] Participation in food-for-work is sensitive to idiosyncratic shocks to crops (at 1 per cent) or to livestock (significant at 16 per cent)—suggesting that food-for-work may perform

---

[6] Evaluated at the mean, the probability of receiving food-for-work goes up from about 2.5 per cent at the 75th percentile to 16.4 per cent at the 25th percentile.

some insurance function.[7] Whether this is because people are selected to participate on the basis of a recent misadventure or whether they are more likely to choose to participate if shocks occur cannot be assessed. We also offer two checks of the robustness of these results. First, the consumption data contain information on the source of food consumption items, including whether they were received as gifts from public sources. Since current consumption per adult (even if instrumented) may already be boosted by access to food aid, resulting in a spurious relationship, we used an alternative consumption measure, excluding all consumption from public gifts. The results were unaffected by this. Next, a conditional fixed effects logit model was run. The results related to livestock and crop shocks were confirmed; but we did not find a significant effect on consumption per adult. While this suggests that the effects on income targeting using pooled data are caused by missing 'fixed' attributes, correlated to consumption, the most plausible explanation is that these variables are wealth-related variables, and that targeting may still be sensitive to the levels of wealth or income, but not sensitive to fluctuations in income.[8]

Table 14.7 describes similar regressions but with the levels of aid received as the left-hand side variable and the sample restricted to those households receiving some aid of the relevant type. For those receiving aid, the amounts on average are 13 per cent of mean consumption in the case of free aid, and 10 per cent if food-for-work. The results suggest that although there is evidence of some targeting in terms of whether people get support, in terms of amounts, the better-off households do get more. At the mean, a 1 per cent increase in consumption results in 1 per cent more aid. Male headed households get more aid, although more male adults in the household reduces the transfer. For those participating in food-for-work, there is no evidence of income targeting either, in terms of the amounts received. The evidence suggests some targeting of households with more female adults, but this is weakly significant. In short, even though there is evidence that within villages, food aid and possibly access to food-for-work displays some targeting, the amounts received are typically higher for the better-off households. These results are unaffected when using an alternative definition of consumption, excluding food received as gifts from public sources. Using a household fixed effects panel estimator, the fixed effects are not significant for free food aid, so that the pooled sample result of higher amounts to the better-off stands, while for food-for-work, a significant positive relationship between the amounts received and consumption levels are obtained as well, providing further evidence that among those receiving food-for-work, the relatively better-off receive more.

Recall that all these results are conditional on village-level effects so that they only reflect the allocation rule conditional on a village receiving aid. Next, we consider the factors determining allocation across villages. We estimate the regressions investigating the determinants of who receives food aid or food-for-work again, but this

---

[7] Including shocks without consumption per adult or the reverse in the regression did not affect the results.

[8] An alternative explanation is that a significant part of the consumption fluctuations are related to random measurement error.

Table 14.7. *Determinants of how much food aid is received per adult (OLS with village-time fixed effects; only those receiving aid, robust standard errors with cluster effects)*

	How much food aid?		How much food-for-work?	
	Coeff.	*p*-value	Coeff.	*p*-value
Consumption per adult	0.140	0.013	0.163	0.187
Male adults 15–65 years (no.)	−0.553	0.028	0.240	0.600
Female adults 15–65 years (no.)	1.351	0.713	2.826	0.136
Male headed? (%)	1.669	0.030	−0.329	0.744
Household size (no.)	1.382	0.298	0.348	0.658
Head primary education?	−4.007	0.150	1.733	0.647
Age head (years)	0.190	0.160	0.119	0.155
Illness days per adult	−0.210	0.188	0.303	0.247
Crop shocks (%, best = 1)	−1.294	0.043	0.740	0.470
Livestock disease (%, best = 1)	2.149	0.010	−2.407	0.377
Constant	−29.470	0.191	−7.385	0.640
Time-varying village dummies	Not reported		Not reported	
	$R^2 = 0.16$		$R^2 = 0.76$	
	Mean = 13.01		Mean = 6.95	
	$n = 698$		$n = 363$	

Note: Only for those households receiving aid. Real consumption is treated as endogenous using a two-stage regression. Land per adult and livestock values per adult are identifying instruments.

time replacing the time-varying fixed effects with (instrumented) mean consumption per adult in the village in each period, village-level rainfall shocks and the means of the other shock variables.[9] Table 14.8 gives these results. The within-village effects are largely similar to those in Table 14.6—in any case, the results in that table offer the preferred interpretation, since they fully control for all possible village-level effects. While within the village, there is evidence of income targeting in the case of free transfers and no clear targeting for food-for-work, the evidence here suggests that *better-off* villages are more likely to receive free aid, while there is only very weak evidence of targeting poorer villages via food-for-work (both in terms of significance and size of the effect). The probability of receiving free food aid increases for a household living in a village with mean consumption around the 75th percentile by 18 percentage points, compared to a household living in a village with mean consumption around the 25th percentile. Furthermore, there is no correlation with rainfall, and a positive correlation between (fewer) problems with crops in the village, and receiving food aid. Households seem to be more likely to have access to food-for-work if on average the village had more problems with crops—suggesting that they are offered as a safety net when problems

---

[9] Adding the means of the other household level variables did not change the interpretation of the results substantially.

S. Dercon and P. Krishnan

Table 14.8. *Determinants of receiving food aid (marginal effects from probit model with village level variables, robust standard errors)*

	Any free aid?		Any food-for-work?	
	Marg. effect	*p*-value	Marg. effect	*p*-value
Village mean consumption	0.003	0.035	−0.001	0.198
Rainfall (normal = 1)	0.110	0.402	0.041	0.621
Village mean crop shocks	0.454	0.000	−0.221	0.007
Village mean livestock shocks	−0.177	0.403	0.055	0.623
Village mean illness days	0.225	0.001	0.082	0.002
Consumption per adult	−0.002	0.012	0.000	0.938
Male adults 15–65 years (no.)	−0.015	0.027	0.008	0.037
Female adults 15–65 years (no.)	−0.005	0.881	0.000	0.999
Male headed? (%)	0.019	0.291	−0.011	0.465
Household size (no.)	−0.018	0.093	0.001	0.833
Head primary education?	−0.004	0.916	0.014	0.210
Age head (years)	−0.001	0.073	0.000	0.891
Illness days per adult	−0.001	0.243	−0.001	0.362
Crop shocks (%, best = 1)	−0.010	0.243	−0.014	0.000
Livestock disease (%, best = 1)	−0.012	0.450	−0.004	0.505
	Pseudo R^2	0.41	Pseudo R^2	0.19
	$n = 3,981$		$n = 3,981$	

Note: The underlying data set contains 3,318 observations. The table reports marginal effects as the derivative of the cumulative normal distribution at the mean of the right-hand side variables; for dummies the marginal effect expressed as the discrete change from 0 to 1 is reported. Real consumption is treated as endogenous using a two-stage regression. Land per adult and livestock values per adult are identifying instruments.

occur. All these results appear robust to alternative specifications, such as changing the number of village-level characteristics, defining consumption so as to strictly exclude food aid itself and fixed effects specifications. Replacing consumption by assets, such as land and livestock, showed that areas with more land per adult were significantly more likely to receive free transfers, while they were significantly less likely to receive food-for-work programmes. In short, there is clearly no evidence in favour of targeting of free aid programmes to poorer areas in our sample, but there is some evidence of targeting food-for-work, albeit relatively weak.

These results obviously need careful interpretation. The sample of *villages* is relatively small, and although stratified to represent different typical types of villages, generalizing about the village-level effects has to be done with caution. However, the samples within villages are random and relatively large, so that the within-village processes may be well captured in this sample. Jayne *et al.* (2002) have a much larger and random sample of districts, and their district-level findings are likely to be stronger. They find some income targeting in both food-for-work and free food aid, but they find it also to be rather weak with very small increases in the probability of receiving food aid in a village with mean income near the 25th percentile, compared to villages at the 75th percentile. They discover some sensitivity to non-weather related crop shocks. Both our results and the results in Jayne *et al.* (2002) suggest that targeting is, at best, relatively weak, especially across villages. Within the villages, both data sets suggest targeting of (free) food aid, but the evidence on targeting of food-for-work is weaker. However, whether food aid is targeted or not does not necessarily measure fully the impact on households. In the rest of the chapter, we analyse this further, with a focus on the contribution of food aid on the consumption path over time and its interaction with alternative means of keeping consumption smooth such as informal reciprocal transfers between households, expanding on Dercon and Krishnan (2003). To this end, we provide a discussion of the theoretical framework for the analysis in the next section.

14.4. FOOD AID AND RISK-SHARING

In order to analyse the impact of the safety net provision, we focus on intertemporal behaviour in the face of risk and the existence of community and household-based mechanisms to cope with the consequences of risk.[10] As a basis for this analysis, we use standard risk-sharing tests (Townsend 1994). These tests investigate whether outcomes over time in a risky environment are consistent with those expected if markets were perfect, that is, as if all risk is insured *ex ante*. This literature is less concerned with *how* this full insurance occurs—it could occur through 'formalized' market mechanisms or via 'informal' sources, such as mutual support within families or villages. The basis of the most standard tests is to ask whether idiosyncratic shocks contain any information that could explain consumption growth—under perfect risk-sharing they should not. Typically, perfect risk-sharing is rejected: results from a variety of contexts, such as extended families in the United States, communities in India and nuclear households in Ethiopia have failed to find perfect risk-sharing but do find evidence of partial risk-sharing (Townsend 1994; Hayashi *et al.* 1996; Dercon and Krishnan 2000*b*). This in turn suggests that there might be a substantial role for interventions that might help households pool risk more effectively (Morduch 1999). This would provide the support for more widespread protection mechanisms, including via food aid or food-for-work. Clearly, investigating whether these programmes indeed contribute to smoother consumption and more risk-sharing is of importance.

However, standard models of transfers predict that private transfers will be reduced if public transfers are introduced and there is some empirical support for this proposition as well (Cox *et al.* 1998). The presence of informal risk-sharing arrangements has further consequences for the impact of formal transfers. If households share risk,

---

[10] Since for the empirical application, we specifically use household level data, we do not consider intra-household issues in this model. For an analysis of these issues in the context risk using the same Ethiopian data, see Dercon and Krishnan (2000*a*). The material in the next three sections is based on Dercon and Krishnan (2003).

public transfers to specific households might be treated like positive idiosyncratic shocks and hence, shared across households. If informal risk-sharing arrangements are self-enforcing, a formal safety net could undermine existing informal insurance: any scheme that changes the value of autarky relative to being in the scheme will affect the degree of risk-sharing. The result may be less informal insurance and even result in making some households worse off (Attanasio and Rios-Rull 2000; Ligon *et al.* 2002). In short, introducing public safety nets might not have completely benign effects and hence taking explicit account of alternative mechanisms becomes critical.

In what follows, we focus on the impact of food aid on consumption. We do so using a specification that explicitly allows for the existence of an (perfect or imperfect) informal risk-sharing arrangement in place. The null-hypothesis is that there is perfect risk-sharing. In that case, food aid at the level of the community will have an impact, while, controlling for this community-level effect, transfers to specific households will have no impact, since they will be shared across the members of the community. If food aid at the community level has an impact after controlling for household level transfers, then this would be evidence in favour for the existence of some sharing scheme within the community. Indeed, it is difficult to see why the consumption of all households in a community would increase if positive transfers occur to some members, unless it involves some sharing of these transfers within the community.

To test this formally, consider an endowment economy consisting of a community of N households, each household j with time-separable expected utility defined over instantaneous utility $u(c_{ts}^j; z_{ts}^j)$ in which c^j is a single consumption good and z_{ts}^j are taste shifters, varying across households; both c and z are defined across T periods t and S states s. Endowments in each period are assumed to be risky. There is no storage, or contracting outside the community. Let us assume that all households in this community efficiently share risk, without commitment or information constraints, so that the problem can be represented as if a social planner allocated weights θ_j to each household and maximizes the weighted sum of expected utilities (ignoring time preference for simplicity), subject to the community-level resource constraint in each period t and state s. Formally, at period 0, we can write this weighted sum as:

$$\max \sum_{j=1}^{N} \theta_j \sum_{t=0}^{T} \sum_{s=1}^{S} \pi_s u(c_{ts}^j; z_{ts}^j), \tag{14.1}$$

in which π_s is the probability of state s occurring. Denoting e_{ts}^j as the endowment of household j in state s in time t, and using c_{ts}^A and e_{ts}^A to denote aggregate consumption and endowments in the community in each state and time period, the community resource constraint in each period and state can then be defined as:

$$c_{ts}^A \equiv \sum_{j=1}^{N} c_{ts}^j \leq e_{ts}^A \equiv \sum_{j=1}^{N} e_{ts}^j. \tag{14.2}$$

More elaborate models including incomes, assets, and production could be defined, but the key predictions from a perfect risk-sharing model would not be affected

(Deaton 1992; Townsend 1994). Defining μ_{st} as the multiplier on the community resource constraint in each period and state, divided by the probability of the state occurring (π_s), then the first order condition for optimal allocation of consumption from this problem for household j at period t can be stated as:

$$\theta_j u_c^j(c_{ts}^j; z_{ts}^j) = \mu_{st} \qquad (14.3)$$

with $u_c^j(c_{ts}^j; z_{ts}^j)$ denoting the marginal utility of consumption of household j. Since the pareto weights are linked to a single consumption plan and since μ_{st} only depends on aggregate, not household consumption, then only considering interior solutions, this implies the standard perfect risk-sharing result: that the growth path of marginal utilities of all households ($u_{c_t}^{i'}$) is the same and that it is only influenced by changes in the aggregate resource constraint, or:

$$\frac{u_{c_{t+1}}^{i'}}{u_{c_t}^{i'}} = \frac{u_{c_{t+1}}^{j'}}{u_{c_t}^{j'}}. \qquad (14.4)$$

In other words, whatever state of the world materialized, relative marginal utilities are equal—with the lack of expectations operators the hallmark of full insurance. The other key prediction is that the relative marginal utilities of two households are a constant, the ratio of the pareto weights, irrespective of the state of nature.

This assumes that the risk-sharing arrangement is perfectly enforceable. There is a growing literature focusing on constrained efficient contracts, enforced by the threat to leave the arrangement and return to autarky (Attanasio and Rios-Rull 2000; Ligon *et al.* 2002). To characterize these arrangements, one could start from (14.1) and (14.2) above, but add an additional constraint for each household h, stating that in each period and state of the world, it must be in the interest of the household to stay in the arrangement rather than revert to autarky. These contracts still imply that risk-sharing will take place—so that changes in the community resource constraint will still affect the path of household marginal utilities. However, anything that increases the value of autarky relative to the value of staying in the contract will reduce the degree of risk-sharing. This means that shocks to individual endowments and incomes may affect the ratio of marginal utilities across individuals, despite the presence of a risk-sharing arrangement.

These theoretical predictions have important implications about the impact of transfers from a formal safety net (see also Ligon and Schechter 2003). Risk-sharing is not just concerned with negative shocks; the sharing predictions will hold for positive shocks as well. Transfers from outside, such as food aid delivery, are such positive shocks. Perfect risk-sharing implies that they are fully shared, based on the pareto weights; if risk-sharing is imperfect, transfers from outside will still be shared, but not necessarily fully. This has consequences for the impact of targeting the poor and needy in safety nets. Table 14.9 summarizes these effects. Suppose schemes target in order to reach the poor, evaluating targeting may be done by considering whether or not the poor are reached—if some of the poor are not reached, we will call this a problem of exclusion. An alternative way of evaluating targeting may be by considering the extent to which the non-poor are covered by the scheme—a problem of excess coverage.

Table 14.9. *Targeting and informal risk-sharing*

	Perfect targeting	Imperfect targeting	No targeting
Full risk-sharing	No exclusion full excess coverage	No exclusion full excess coverage	No exclusion full excess coverage
Imperfect risk-sharing	Possible exclusion possible excess coverage	Possible exclusion possible excess coverage	Possible exclusion excess coverage
No risk-sharing	No exclusion no excess coverage	Some exclusion some excess coverage	No exclusion full excess coverage

Note: Exclusion refers to poor households who did not benefit from the transfer scheme (in terms of higher living standards); excess coverage refers to non-poor households who benefited from the transfer scheme.

The table gives the matrix of possibilities: perfect targeting of the needy, imperfect targeting, and no targeting, when support is simply equally divided among households. We consider the impact when perfect, imperfect, and no risk-sharing takes place, assuming that imperfect risk-sharing is linked to enforcement problems.

If there is full risk-sharing, targeting becomes irrelevant: any transfer towards a household in the group, whether needy or not, is shared according to the sharing rule underlying the informal arrangement. If there is no risk-sharing, the 'standard' results related to targeting are obtained: perfect targeting results in full inclusion of all the needy in the scheme, and there are no non-poor included. If all households receive a transfer, so that there is no targeting, then there is no exclusion and full excess coverage. Under imperfect risk-sharing, the results are less clear-cut: if targeting is perfect, the risk-sharing arrangement may imply that some of transfer will need to be shared, although sharing will not be perfect. Under no targeting, partial risk-sharing may also imply that some of the transfer will be shared. In the end, who is covered or excluded is not clear a priori, especially if targeting is imperfect. However, there is a further issue: the incentives to leave the arrangement may result in exclusion still to take place even if there is full coverage of the poor as in both the perfect targeting or no targeting case, if some of the poor must use the positive transfer to pay some of the non-poor to remain in the arrangement. The conclusion is that the importance and consequences of targeting depend on the nature of the informal risk-sharing arrangements. For example, even if targeting is relatively poor, as appears to be the case in our data, and many of the needy are excluded, the impact of the transfer programme may be more positive due to the existence of the informal sharing mechanisms.

14.5. EMPIRICAL MODEL

Next, we derive an empirical model to investigate this further. Testable formulations of the perfect risk-sharing model can be obtained by assuming specific utility functions. Using a standard CRRA formulation, $u^j(c_t^j; z_t^j) = (z_t^j((c_t^j)^{1+\gamma} - 1)/(1 + \gamma))$

(in which subscript s is dropped so that conventional notation is used), using logarithms and allowing for measurement error ϵ_t^j in the logarithm of consumption, we can write (14.3) as:

$$\ln c_t^j = \frac{1}{\gamma} \ln \mu_t - \frac{1}{\gamma} \ln z_t^j - \frac{1}{\gamma} \ln \theta_j + \epsilon_t^j. \tag{14.5}$$

Equation (14.5) can be estimated using within (fixed effects) estimators, or first differences, so that the unobservable fixed pareto weights do not affect estimation of the parameters of interest equation (14.5) gives a useful basis for a standard test of perfect risk-sharing. Suppose one can identify a variable X_t^j that affects the income or endowment of household j, then provided X_t^j is cross-sectionally independent of z_t^j, θ_j, or ϵ_t^j, then under the null of perfect risk-sharing, $\ln c_t^j$, should be cross-sectionally independent of X_t^j.[11]

Idiosyncratic income shocks are thus useful candidates for testing risk-sharing, provided that they are independent of current consumption levels.[12] Most negative shocks typically used in the literature such as illness, job loss, and agricultural shocks would arguably satisfy this condition (Udry 1995; Dercon and Krishnan 2000a). In this chapter, we use positive shocks, in the form of food aid given to individuals in the village, as one of the idiosyncratic income shocks.[13] Under perfect risk-sharing, positive shocks should also be shared and not affect household consumption directly, but only do so through aggregate village resources. However, food aid is typically not randomly distributed so the assumption of cross-sectional independence of aid A_t^j with z_t^j and particularly, θ_j is untenable. This is the standard programme-placement problem of evaluating public programmes. If aid is targeted to specific types of households— for example, those in poor areas or those headed by females, then without further controls for programme-placement, the impact of aid on $\ln c_t^j$ would be inconsistently estimated in (14.5). However, if placement is determined by characteristics that do not change over time, then estimating (14.5) by fixed effects removes the source of inconsistency.

We begin with an estimation of (14.6), and regress the logarithm of consumption on a set of time-varying community dummies D_t and a set of time-varying taste shifters Z_t^j (which will be defined below). ϑ^j is assumed to contain all time-invariant taste

[11] The left-hand side measure of consumption used here includes food aid received. Note that this is because we are interested in evaluating the programme or treatment effect of food aid intervention. We assume away any behavioural (e.g. a move to a higher level of consumption because of the insurance effect on downside risk) response to the food aid, since we focus on a very short time horizon of about eighteen months.

[12] The advantage of using shocks to income, rather than just income is that in many alternative models, predictable changes would have been taken into account in the consumption path, and would therefore contain less information to reject perfect risk-sharing.

[13] In the evaluation of the impact of food aid, we do not distinguish between free food aid and food-for-work. While there may be different rules determining access to these different types of food aid, their impact on consumption is likely to be similar.

shifters, the fixed part of aggregate resources, fixed placement effects, and the Pareto weights.

$$\ln c_t^j = \alpha D_t + \beta Z_t^j + \delta Y_t^j + \lambda A_t^j + \vartheta^j + \epsilon_t^j. \qquad (14.6)$$

This regression is used to test perfect risk-sharing, using a set of variables measuring idiosyncratic events affecting income, such as illness, crop pests, and livestock disease Y_t^j, as well as aid A_t^j. The coefficient, λ, should be zero under perfect risk-sharing, as should be δ, the coefficient on idiosyncratic income. If the hypothesis that $\lambda = 0$ (or $\delta = 0$), is rejected, then perfect risk-sharing is ruled out. Does this then mean that no risk-sharing arrangement exists? Not necessarily, but (14.6) cannot clarify this point. To test this we can ask whether aid given to other people in the village affects a household's consumption. If so, this would provide strong evidence of some sharing arrangement, whether perfect or imperfect. In particular, it is unlikely that this effect is caused by correlated effects—all households responding to higher food aid to some households by independently increasing consumption, for example, by depleting assets. Actual transfers between households appears to be the most likely explanation in that case. Finally, a prediction of constrained efficient risk-sharing models, that a change in the value of autarky affects the degree of risk-sharing, can be tested by investigating whether the impact of a reduction in idiosyncratic income is higher in communities with substantial food aid compared to villages where there is little or no aid.

14.6. RESULTS

Tables 14.10 and 14.11 summarizes the econometric tests (discussed further in Dercon and Krishnan 2003). We report the fixed effects estimates, with robust standard errors. Idiosyncratic income determinants included are whether aid was received by the household as well as other indices of shocks, including the self-reported measure of shocks to crops, livestock disease, and illness. These alternative sources of shocks are introduced as control variables, to isolate the impact of aid. Household composition and the sex of the household head (with changes mainly due to seasonal migration or death) are used as taste shifters. We begin with a test of the perfect risk-sharing model, with all aggregate resources summarized as time-varying village-level dummies. We measure the impact of aid in two different ways: as a dummy for whether the household received any aid, as well as the logarithm of the level of aid received. Table 14.10, columns 1 and 2, suggest that the perfect risk-sharing model is rejected in either case, since controlling for time-varying community fixed effects, aid as well as other shocks affect consumption levels.[14] Column 2 suggests that a 10 per cent increase in aid increases consumption by 0.8 per cent.

Next we test whether there is actually *any* risk-sharing taking place. To do this, we replace the community level variables by time-varying variables proxying changes in common resources. Deviations from normal rainfall levels were included, expressed as

---

[14] Note that the positive sign on crop shocks implies that worse crop conditions reduced consumption.

Table 14.10. *Testing risk-sharing*

	1		2		3		4	
	Coeff.	p-value	Coeff.	p-value	Coeff.	p-value	Coeff.	p-value
Crop shocks (%, best = 1)	0.086	0.000	0.076	0.001	0.025	0.293	0.021	0.379
Livestock shocks (%, best = 1)	0.005	0.381	0.004	0.406	0.005	0.391	0.005	0.336
Illness days per adult	0.061	0.116	0.062	0.108	0.002	0.963	0.032	0.337
Rainfall index (normal = 1)					0.465	0.000	0.433	0.000
Rainfall index if bad (if <1)					0.316	0.000	0.240	0.000
Aid dummy	0.130	0.000			0.090	0.001		
ln aid per adult			0.082	0.000			0.051	0.009
Village aid dummy					0.090	0.000		
ln village aid per adult							0.124	0.001
ln relative price index							−0.590	0.000
Sex head (1 = male)	0.131	0.318	0.162	0.206	0.194	0.146	0.223	0.102
Household size (no.)	−0.119	0.000	−0.110	0.000	−0.131	0.000	−0.119	0.000
Crop shocks*village aid dummy								
Livestock*village aid dummy								
Time-varying village dummies	Yes		Yes					
R-squared	0.080		0.085		0.048		0.059	
Observations	3,987		3,985		3,987		3,987	

Note: Left-hand side variable is log real consumption per adult. Fixed effects estimator with robust standard errors.

Table 14.11. *Testing risk-sharing and crowding-out*

	1		2	
	Coeff.	*p*-value	Coeff.	*p*-value
Crop shocks (%, best = 1)	0.034	0.328	−0.029	0.426
Livestock shocks (%, best = 1)	0.005	0.379	0.005	0.295
Illness days per adult	0.066	0.123	0.052	0.251
Rainfall index (normal = 1)			0.425	0.000
Rainfall index if bad (if <1)			0.324	0.000
Aid dummy	0.111	0.000	0.053	0.054
ln aid per adult				
Village aid dummy			0.075	0.196
ln village aid per adult				
ln relative price index			−0.596	0.000
Sex head (1 = male)	0.133	0.310	0.240	0.135
Household size (no.)	−0.120	0.000	−0.119	0.000
Crop shocks*village aid dummy	0.084	0.068	0.107	0.025
Livestock*village aid dummy	−0.020	0.558	−0.069	0.243
Time-varying village dummies	Yes			
R-squared	0.080		0.061	
Observations	3,987		3,985	

Note: Left-hand side variable is log real consumption per adult. Fixed effects estimator with robust standard errors.

actual levels divided by long-term mean levels minus one. We allow for different effects on resources from 'better than normal' rainfall compared to 'worse than normal' levels. For example, if savings are possible, but credit markets suffer from imperfections, then it is easier to smooth in good years than in bad years (Deaton 1991). Therefore the regression includes rainfall in general, as well as a separate measure of rainfall interacted with a dummy variable that takes the value of one when the rainfall index is below 1, or below normal levels. Hence, in bad years, the effect of rainfall on consumption is the sum of the coefficient on rainfall and the coefficient on rainfall interacted with this dummy; both coefficients are expected to be positive. All the regression results confirm this: below normal rainfall has a significantly larger impact than above normal rainfall. However, both effects are substantial, consistent with large weather-induced fluctuations in consumption.

A further community characteristic included is whether more than 5 per cent of the households from a particular village in the sample received food aid. Testing its effect gave a strongly significant, positive effect. However, it could be argued that in areas with poorly functioning food markets, where arbitrage happens slowly or not at all, the addition of substantial amounts of food aid to supplies in a village may simply have relative price effects, so that the impact measured by this food aid at the village level is merely a price effect, and not evidence for risk-sharing transfers between households. To control for this possibility, we include a measure of the level of local food prices, compared to the average in the full sample: in short, as a control for local price movements beyond inflationary trends in national food prices. Column 3 shows that this has a strongly significant effect, and lowers the impact of the village aid dummy, but the latter remains strongly significant. This would suggest that some risk-sharing is taking place and evidence in favour of the use of transfers between households.

We explored this further using levels of food aid given to individuals and to the community. To construct a measure of the latter, we calculated the total volume of aid coming into the village per adult per month, using all reported levels by the households in the sample. Obviously, since we work with a sample of households (even if it typically constitutes about a quarter of the village), measurement error may bedevil this estimate. Even so, we found that both individual and community level aid have a positive impact on consumption, albeit that the community level impact is small (0.022) but it is only significant at 14 per cent. To address measurement error we can make use of an alternative measure of aid flows that might be used as an instrument to tackle the measurement issue further. Our measure of food aid coming in is based on a question asking for receipts of aid between the survey rounds—typically about 5 months. However, in the consumption questionnaire, food aid received from public sources is recorded again with a recall period of 7 days. Since this is an independent measure of the food aid variable, obviously correlated with the measure from the consumption files, we can use this measure as an identifying instrument for household and community level food aid received. The results are reported in column 4, and as expected, both the size and significance of the coefficients increases, especially the community level effect. In short, food aid coming into the village seems to be shared to some extent.

Finally, we test whether there is any evidence of pressure on informal risk-sharing arrangements due to the presence of food aid. (Note that we focus exclusively on the impact of interventions on consumption and it is plausible that formal safety nets do have a strong impact on other aspects of well-being such as health.) To investigate this, we use the same regression as in columns 1 and 3 of Table 14.10, but this time we include an interaction between idiosyncratic shocks that are clearly observable: namely, crop shocks and livestock shocks, and interact them with a measure of whether the village receives any food aid. Table 14.11 gives the results. The null hypothesis of no impact on informal arrangements from food aid is that the coefficient on the interaction term of food aid with the idiosyncratic shocks, is zero, that is, there is no additional information in this extra term to explain consumption (controlling for idiosyncratic shocks as before). Recall that in column 1 (Table 14.10), there was evidence of crop shocks not being fully insured within the community. Column 1 (Table 14.11) shows that the coefficient on the interaction term of crop shocks with food aid is positive and significant at 7 per cent, that is, there is a larger effect of idiosyncratic crop shocks in these communities than in those without food aid.[15] In fact, the evidence suggests that this lack of full insurance *only* occurs in villages receiving food aid, while for villages

---

[15] Given the definition of the interaction term, in villages with food aid, the total effect of crop shocks on consumption is the sum of the coefficient on idiosyncratic shocks *and* the coefficient on the interaction term.

without food aid the coefficient is not significantly different from zero, as if in localities
with safety nets some idiosyncratic shocks are not insured anymore. This result is
confirmed (and significant at 3 per cent) in column 2, where rainfall information
is used as a direct measure of time-varying village-level variables. This supports the
proposition that food aid crowds out local arrangements for insuring idiosyncratic risk.

14.7. CONCLUSIONS

The focus here has been the impact of food aid on household consumption in Ethiopia.
We begin with whether there is any evidence of targeting of the poor or of those suffering
bad shocks. Furthermore, we attempt to assess the impact of food aid on consumption
outcomes. Our study is different in that it specifically tests the impact of food aid in a
context of informal risk-sharing arrangements. In particular, if households form part of
such arrangement, the issue of targeting of food aid is either irrelevant (if the arrangement is perfect) or its consequences complex (if risk-sharing is incomplete). More specifically, with imperfect risk-sharing, some of the aid coming into a community is likely
to be shared in the community, but at the same time, it is possible that the food aid itself
may contribute to the breakdown of these arrangements, since it changes the autarky
situation, that is, the outcomes of households if they were to be outside the informal
arrangement. Furthermore, the fact that we have access to panel data with time-varying
food aid distribution allows us to deal with the econometric problems related to the
non-random placement of programmes across households and communities.

The evidence suggests relatively poor targeting. Our results imply that targeting
of free food aid is relatively sensitive to income within villages but the evidence of
targeting of food-for-work is much weaker within villages. Across villages, there is
some evidence of income sensitivity of targeting of food-for-work, but not of free food
aid. Note that the nature of our sample means that our results across villages are less
reliable than our within-village results.

Next, when looking at the impact of food aid, we find that there is some within-
village-sharing of this food aid. As a consequence, this implies that the relatively poor
targeting is less a problem then standard analysis would have implied. We find that
controlling for household level food aid, the fact that there is food aid to some in the
community has an additional effect on consumption and the most likely interpretation
of this effect that transfers indeed take place. Informal risk-sharing seems to result in
better outcomes of the food aid distribution scheme, compensating for some of the
poor targeting involved. Furthermore, we also evidence of some crowding-out. There
is evidence that villages with food aid seem to protect each other less for idiosyncratic
risk, compared to communities without food aid schemes. In other words, this evidence is consistent with weakening informal arrangements because of the presence of a
formal system.

This has some important implications for policy. In line with Jayne *et al.* (2002), it
would be helpful to improve targeting. Our evidence suggests that the better targeting of
communities will have to take precedence. Even if the actual local level distribution does
not appear to be based on self-targeting, the presence of informal arrangements seems

to contribute to some broader sharing of the benefits of food aid across a community. Note that this evidence of some shared benefits does not necessarily mean that the poor will in the end get most of the aid; rather that it will be spread over a relatively larger number of people than to whom it was initially given. Still, in our sample, we should remain aware that the problem of across-village targeting is also one of timing and of the volume of aid: the variation over time of food aid across communities (which community gets aid when and how much) suggests that there is much scope for improvement.

The issue of possible crowding-out of informal insurance arrangements by formal support programmes is complicated, not least to resolve via appropriate policy design. It is possible to design safety nets that would not induce welfare losses or to minimize crowding-out of idiosyncratic insurance. We can think of at least two examples. Both involve finding ways to reduce the incentives of participants to deviate from the arrangement due to the increase in autarky values. The solution would be to make the safety net conditional on participation in the mutual mechanism, so that the safety net would be lost if the household were to leave the arrangement. The simplest form would be to give the aggregate protection to the mutual insurance group. However, this would require the safety net operator to be able to identify the group and monitor its continued existence as a group. If the group cannot be observed or monitored, an optimal mechanism, may be designed to induce the group to stay together by allowing other group members to punish deviators by denying them aggregate insurance. Attanasio and Rios-Rull (2000) discuss some mechanisms, which could deliver this outcome. In any case, current practices are far removed from these optimal mechanisms.

REFERENCES

Alderman, H. (1991). 'Food Subsidies and the Poor', in G. Psacharopoulos (ed.), *Essays on Poverty, Equity and Growth*. Oxford: Pergamon.

—— and K. Lindert (1998). 'The Potential and Limitations of Self-targeted Food Subsidies'. *World Bank Research Observer*, 13(2), 213–29.

Athanasios, A., M. Bezuneh, and B. J. Deaton (1994). 'Impacts of FFW on Nutrition in Rural Kenya'. *Agricultural Economics*, 11, 301–9.

Attanasio, O. and J. V. Rios-Rull (2000). 'Consumption Smoothing in Island Economies: Can Public Insurance Reduce Welfare'. *European Economic Review*, 44(7), 1259–79.

—— and —— (2001). 'Consumption Smoothing and Extended Families: The Role of Government Sponsored Insurance', in N. Lustig (ed.), *Shielding the Poor*. Washington, DC: Brookings Institution Press.

Barrett C. (2001). 'Food security and food assistance programs', in B. Gardner and G. Rausser (eds), *Handbook of Agricultural Economics*, Vol. 2. Amsterdam: Elsevier.

—— and D. C. Clay (2003). 'How Accurate Is Food-For-Work Self-Targeting in The Presence of Imperfect Factor Markets? Evidence From Ethiopia'. *Journal of Development Studies*, 39(5), 152–80.

Beaton, G. H. (1987). 'Energy in Human Nutrition', in J. P. Gittinger, J. Leslie, and C. Hoisington (eds), *Food Policy: Integrating Supply, Distribution and Consumption*. Baltimore, MD: Johns Hopkins University Press.

Beaton, G. H. and H. Ghassemi (1982). 'Supplementary Feeding Programs for Young Children in Developing Countries'. *American Journal of Clinical Nutrition*, 35, 864–916.

Benuzeh, M. and B. Deaton (1997). 'Food Aid Impacts on Safety Nets: Theory and Evidence— A Conceptual Perspective on Safety Nets'. *American Journal of Agricultural Economics*, 79, 672–7.

Bezuneh, M., B. J. Deaton, and G. W. Norton (1988). 'Food Aid Impacts in Rural Kenya'. *American Journal of Agricultural Economics*, 70, 181–91.

Besley, T. and R. Kanbur (1990). 'The Principles of Targeting'. *Policy, Research and External Affairs Working Paper* No. 385. Washington, DC: World Bank.

Christiaensen, L. (2000). 'Measuring Vulnerability and Food Security: Case Evidence from Mali'. Unpublished Ph.D. thesis, Cornell University.

—— and H. Alderman (2001). *Child Malnutrition in Ethiopia*. Washington, DC: World Bank (www.worldbank.org/afr/et/health.htm).

Clay, E. J. (1986). 'Rural Public Work and Food-for-Work'. *World Development*, 14, 1237–1252.

Clay, D. C, D. Molla, and D. Habtewold (1998). 'Food Aid Targeting in Ethiopia: A Study of Household Food Insecurity and Food Aid Distributions'. *Working Paper* No. 12. Addis Ababa: Grain Market Research Project, MEDAC.

——, —— and —— (1999). 'Food Aid Targeting in Ethiopia: A Study of Who Needs It and Who Gets It'. *Food Policy*, 24, 291–409.

Cox, D., Z. Eser, and E. Jimenez (1998). 'Motives for Private Transfers over the Life-cycle: An Analytical Framework and Evidence from Peru'. *Journal of Development Economics*, 55, 57–80.

Datt, G. and M. Ravallion (1994). 'Transfer Benefits from Public-works Employment: Evidence for Rural India'. *Economic Journal*, 104, 1346–69.

Deaton, A. (1991). 'Savings and Liquidity Constraints'. *Econometrica*, 59(5), 1221–48.

—— (1992). *Understanding Consumption*. Oxford: Clarendon Press.

Dercon, S. and P. Krishnan (2000a). 'Vulnerability, Seasonality and Poverty in Ethiopia'. *Journal of Development Studies*, 36(6), 25–53.

—— and —— (2000b). 'In Sickness and in Health: Risk-Sharing within Households in Ethiopia'. *Journal of Political Economy*, 108(4), 688–727.

—— and —— (2003). 'Informal Insurance and Public Transfers'. *Economic Journal*, 113(March), C86–C95.

Dorosh, P., C. Ninno, and D. Sahn (1995). 'Poverty Alleviation in Mozambique: A Multi-market Analysis of the Role of Food Aid'. *Agricultural Economics*, 13, 89–99.

Drèze, J. and A. Sen (1990). *Hunger and Public Action*. Oxford: Clarendon Press.

FDRE (1996). *Food Security Strategy*. Addis Ababa: Ministry of Economic Development and Planning, Federal Democratic Republic of Ethiopia.

Hayashi, F., J. Altonji, and L. Kotlikoff (1996). 'Risk-Sharing Between and Within Families'. *Econometrica*, 64(2), 261–94.

Jayne, T. S., J. Strauss, T. Yamano, and D. Molla (2001). 'Giving to the Poor? Targeting of Food Aid in Rural Ethiopia'. *World Development*, 29(5), 887–910.

——, ——, Y. Yamano, and D. Molla (2002). 'Targeting of Food Aid in Rural Ethiopia: Chronic Need or Inertia?'. *Journal of Development Economics*, 68, 247–88.

Kennedy, E. T. and H. Alderman (1987). *Comparative Analyses of Nutritional Effectiveness of Food Subsidies and other Food-Related Interventions*. Washington, DC: International Food Policy Research Institute.

Ligon, E., J. Thomas, and T. Worrall (2002). 'Informal Insurance with Limited Commitment: Theory and Evidence from Village Economies'. *Review of Economic Studies*, 69(1), 209–44.

—— and L. Schechter (2003). 'Measuring Vulnerability.' *Economic Journal*, 113(486), C95–C102.

Maxwell, D. G. (1996). 'Measuring Food Insecurity'. *Food Policy*, 21, 291–303.

Maxwell, S., D. Belshaw, and A. Lirenso (1994). 'The Disincentive Effect of Food-for-Work on Labour Supply and Agricultural Intensificaton in Ethiopia'. *Journal of Agricultural Economics*, 45, 351–9.

Morduch, J. (1994). 'Poverty and Vulnerability'. *American Economic Review, Papers and Proceedings*, 84(2), 221-5.

—— (1995). 'Income Smoothing and Consumption Smoothing'. *Journal of Economic Perspectives*, 9(3), 103–14.

—— (1999). 'Between the State and the Market: Can Informal Insurance Patch the Safety Net?'. *World Bank Research Observer*, 14(2), 187–207.

Ravallion, M. (1991). 'Reaching the Rural Poor through Rural Public Employment: Arguments, Evidence and Lessons from South India'. *World Bank Research Observer*, 6(2), 153–75.

Rosenzweig, M. and K. Wolpin (1993). 'Credit Market Constraints, Consumption Smoothing and the Accumulation of Durable Production Assets in Low-income Countries: Investments in Bullocks in India'. *Journal of Political Economy*, 101(2), 223–44.

Ruttan, V. W. (1993). *Why Food Aid?* Baltimore, MD: Johns Hopkins University Press.

Sahn, D. and H. Alderman (1996). 'The Effect of Food Subsidies on Labor Supply in Sri Lanka'. *Economic Development and Cultural Change*, 45(1), 125-45.

Sen, A. (1995). 'The Political Economy of Targeting', in D. van de Walle and K. Nead (eds), *Public Spending and the Poor*. Baltimore, MD: Johns Hopkins University Press for the World Bank.

Sharp, K. (1997). *Targeting of Food Aid in Ethiopia*. Addis Ababa: Save the Children Fund.

Teklu, T. and S. Asefa (1999). 'Who Participates in Labor-Intensive Public Works in Sub-Saharan African? Evidence from Rural Botswana and Kenya'. *World Development*, 27(2), 431–8.

Townsend, R. M. (1994). 'Risk and Insurance in Village India'. *Econometrica*, 62(3), 539–591.

Udry, C. (1995). 'Risk and Saving in Northern Nigeria'. *American Economic Review*, 85(5), 1287–1300.

van de Walle, D. and K. Nead (eds) (1995). *Public Spending and the Poor*. Baltimore, MD: Johns Hopkins University Press for the World Bank.

von Braun, J. (ed.) (1995). *Employment for Poverty Reduction and Food Security*. Washington, DC: International Food Policy Research Institute.

World Bank (2000a). *Ethiopia: Country Assistance Evaluation*. Washington, DC: World Bank (www.worldbank.org/afr/et/poverty.htm).

—— (2000b). *Development Report 2000/01*. Oxford: Oxford University Press.

15

Why is there Not More Financial Intermediation in Developing Countries?

JONATHAN CONNING AND MICHAEL KEVANE

15.1. INTRODUCTION

Households in developing countries participate in labour and product markets that insert them directly into national and global markets, yet they often remain relatively cut-off from the opportunities for investing, risk-taking, and risk-spreading that is potentially available in a large integrated national or global financial market. Because financial institutions (FIs) are weak, and safety nets are often missing, people remain highly vulnerable to negative income shocks and other adverse events. Poor people are then forced to cancel or forego higher return activities that might have made better use of their talents and resources.

Development economists have spent much effort in recent years trying to measure the extent to which households appear to be insured against idiosyncratic shocks and the structure and performance of local financial contracts such as bilateral credit and insurance arrangements with landlords, moneylenders, family or friends, or group-based mutual savings and insurance arrangements such as Rotating Savings and Credit Associations (ROSCAs). While these studies have advanced our understanding of local *bilateral* financial contracting and mutual insurance within poor communities, the study of financial *intermediation* in developing countries has remained relatively neglected. Financial intermediaries expand and transform the set of trades that can take place both within communities and across communities by carrying out monitoring and control activities and providing asset transformation services at lower cost than what could be achieved under a system of local bilateral contracts or mutual insurance arrangements (Diamond 1996).

This chapter proposes to organize thinking about the opportunities for improving financial markets and safety nets for the poor. We are specifically interested in the question of what impedes more effective intermediation to link local financial networks and safety nets with the larger economy. Understanding impediments is the first step in proposing policies designed to promote more effective linkage. The rationale for policy is to have more comprehensive risk intermediation provided at lower cost to more of the poor. Public policy has both efficiency and redistributive rationales. In the longer run, a better supply of financial intermediation services will enable the poor to protect the value of consumption streams and to allocate their talents and resources to more productive, but risky or long-term, activities.

What retards the natural extension of national or urban financial institutions into poor rural and slum areas? Three important preliminary observations must be made. First, a large literature has made clear that financial repression resulting from interest rate caps, directed credit, and excessive regulation and state involvement in banking, has been a principal culprit of the relative lack of more effective intermediation in developing countries (McKinnon 1973; Adams *et al.* 1984). In this view, a movement away from bad policies is a far more important step than any pressing need for policy innovation. Nelson (1999: 1) summarizes the two principal liberalizing reforms that, in this view, would lead to more effective financial intermediation for the poor:

establishing permissive banking acts legalizing deposit-taking 'near-banks' but subjecting them to less onerous (and more participatory) regulatory, prudential, reporting and other requirements than major banks, and reforming usury laws on the basis of consumer information laws rather than quantitative interest rate caps.

A related theme in this literature is that the widespread history of government failure and political capture suggests that proposals that involve regulation or intervention in markets should meet stringent tests of imperviousness to interest group manipulation.

Second, the relative absence of intermediaries may be a simple function of the low-level income and wealth in developing countries. Some authors argue that growth and financial deepening go hand in hand: as the economy grows there are more opportunities for diversification, and this in turn induces agents to invest in riskier but higher return projects, so the economy grows faster (Acemoglu and Zilibotti 1997). Intermediation, in this view, is a correlate of growth, and thus is influenced by the same institutional environment that promotes or retards growth. In a pessimistic form, this amounts to an extreme version of the induced institutional innovation hypothesis: there is little point discussing institutions, because the institutions that exist are always the ones appropriate for existing technologies and prices. Influential work by Levine and co-authors (Levine *et al.* 2000; Demirgüç-Kunt and Levine 2001; Levine 2001) however, seems to have firmly established the causal importance of financial development for subsequent economic growth.

Finally, the dispersed nature of settlements in many developing countries is another obvious culprit. But low population density seems not to be a sufficient condition. Intermediation was weak and lacking in Bangladesh, a very high-density country, before the recent explosive growth of Grameen Bank and other microfinance institutions. Clearly, there have been very important changes in the technologies of intermediation that have facilitated financial market expansion even in low-density areas. Low population densities have also not hindered the very rapid expansion of mirocredit in Africa, where loan officers on average extend more loans than their Asian counterparts (Lapenu and Zeller 2001).

These observations suggest that the question for this chapter is the following: Holding bad policy, population density, and general growth determinants constant, are there other proximate factors constraining intermediation that integrates local financial markets and safety nets with urban and national financial institutions, and is there room for innovation in public policy to overcome these? Our goal then is to investigate the factors that make intermediation expensive, focusing on factors different from or additional to, those typically used to explain what makes local bilateral contracts expensive. We then explore whether public policy might play a role in reducing the costs of intermediation, with the caveat that proposals for public policy must pass the test of 'surviving' government failure.

We proceed as follows. Section 15.2 outlines what kinds of intermediaries we have in mind, and what kinds of costs and benefits they expect from transactions. Section 15.3 presents some evidence regarding the relative absence of these institutions in many economies. Section 15.4 offers a simple insurance model summarizing how information asymmetries and costly enforcement constrain contracting in agency relationships where side-contracting is possible. Section 15.5 then briefly summarizes recent theories of lock-in and models that incorporate more of the social and political realities of village and slum life. All of these theories place trust and informational closeness at the centre of the problem of intermediation. Section 15.6 discusses policy and innovation. Section 15.7 concludes.

15.2. INTERMEDIARIES

Our focus in this chapter is on innovation in regional and national intermediation. Intermediation implies an intermediary. We are concerned with the person who 'delivers' financial contracts across a geographic space to a locality, acting as the agent of a large-scale regional or national institution, and the incentives they face. At some points, when we speak of an intermediary, we will usually mean the actual person, rather than the institution itself. The 'intermediary', then, is shorthand for 'the agent of the institution that intermediates'.

The intermediary will usually have at least two 'constituencies' caring about his or her behaviour. On one side will be locals who enter into contracts with the institution through the intermediary. On the other side is the institution itself, in whose name the intermediary acts as a delegate. The last few decades have witnessed an explosion of research on how contracts between an intermediary and his village clients should be structured and, somewhat less frequently, on the contractual relationship between the intermediary and the institution. This literature covers both financial markets and safety nets, but shares a common emphasis in modeling the contingent nature of actions that must be taken, or claims that must be settled, and consequent problem of verifying contingent states on the part of the many parties to a transaction.

Table 15.1 exemplifies the kinds of problems an intermediary might expect in carrying out different financial services. Consider first the relatively simple transaction of transferring money to a specified individual. Western Union and other cash transfer services provide a good example of private sector intermediation that is ubiquitous in much of the developing world today. While the intermediation services that they provide link individuals across vast distances, the transacting problem they solve is relatively simple. The intermediary is mainly charged with maintaining proper accounts

Table 15.1. *Moral hazard and intermediaries in financial transactions*

	Action of intermediary	Institutions' concerns about agent	Villagers' concerns about agent	Agents' concerns about institutions	Agents' concerns about villagers
Money transfer	Receive and disburse money over space	Agent might collude with others to disburse funds fraudulently	Agent might miscount or demand bribe		Villager might falsify identity
Savings	Receive and disburse money over time	Agent might not do proper bookkeeping	Agent might deliberately falsify savings entries in passbook	Institution might not pursue sound financial management; might accuse agent of embezzlement	Villager might claim made deposits
Pawning	Receive goods and disburse money over time and subject to conditions	Agent might buy and sell goods on the side	Agent might sell goods early		Villager might pawn stolen goods
Lending	Disburse and collect money over time	Agent might not monitor or enforce repayment, might collude with borrower, or might demand bribes	Agent might not record loan repayments; might disburse less than registered loan	Institution might not pursue sound financial management; might accuse agent of embezzlement	Villager might deliberately default or might undertake riskier action
Insurance	Offer contingent contracts, verify outcomes, disburse claims	Agent might not verify claims, collude with insurer, or might demand bribes	Agent might deny claim arbitrarily, or might demand bribe		Villager might misrepresent state of affairs or might undertake riskier action
Safety net	Verify outcomes, disburse claims	Agent might disburse funds to ineligible recipients, might demand bribes	Agent might deny claim arbitrarily, or might demand bribe	Institution might make proper performance too costly	Villager might misrepresent state of affairs

and with verifying the identity of the recipient of funds, rather than with verifying the applicability of contingent claims. There are clear, verifiable steps that help Western Union monitor the agents within its own network. The public, in turn, has come to trust Western Union in part because of the substantial investments it has made in local offices and publicity. These investments signal that Western Union intends to maintain a long-term presence, and therefore that Western Union is less likely to abscond with their money. The public is also generally aware that Western Union has an elaborate system for tracing and monitoring its offices and agents.

Second, consider the activities of 'pure' savings institutions. Postal savings bank, for example, are common financial intermediaries, often with branches throughout every poor country. They provide the service of trustworthy holding of savings. The main issue is to convince depositors that their investments will be safe, and earn a sufficient rate of return. (Japan's ubiquitous postal savings institution has been criticized for advertising 'too much' the safety of deposits, leading, perhaps, to disintermediation from the broader banking system.) Informal intermediaries also exist, usually in the form of professional 'organizers' of ROSCAs. There are agency issues (intermediary or intermediary institution absconding with the money), and even the comparatively safe savings institution may be vulnerable to runs if financial management is imprudent (as in the savings and loans crisis in the United States). The intermediary does little state verification, and is again concerned more with accounting and identity verification.

Third, consider the pawnshop. Pawning is a combination of lending and insurance with collateral (Skully 1994), and pawnshops may sometimes be important sources of finance (in China, or early nineteenth-century United States, for example). In many of the poorest villages of the world informal pawnshops operate to basically guarantee a market, that is, liquidity, for non-standard commodities (at discounted prices). Household possessions can then become, like livestock, part of a household's buffer stock strategy. The pawnshop intermediates non-standard goods between the village and broader markets. The information problem now extends past identity verification, into assessments of both the origins of the pawned goods (are they stolen?) and valuation of the goods themselves.

Fourth, consider lending and insurance. These are transactions that are much more vulnerable to agency problems, as they are dependent on private information on actions and outcomes and contingencies. We are lumping lending and insurance together because both are state-contingent financial transactions, as loans are almost everywhere subject to possible default renegotiation. Intermediary agents in these transactions play a more complicated role than do intermediaries in the earlier examples. Borrowers and claimants may have incentives to dissimulate their actions and outcomes. For that reason, intermediaries must screen applicants, monitor the actions of insurees and borrowers, verify outcomes, and transmit information and resources collected to the larger organization for which they work. The financial institution employing these intermediaries must not only design contracts to limit strategic behaviours on the part of borrowers and insurees, but must also provide incentives to the loan officers and insurance salespeople they hire to monitor and not collude with clients, in order to protect the value of investments made by savings depositors or outside creditors.

Fifth, consider national or regional safety nets. Very often urban-based social workers will determine whether particular persons meet welfare criteria. Why are these decisions not decentralized to cheaper, local, agents? We have discussed this question at length elsewhere (see Conning and Kevane 2002). Because safety nets are funded through taxation (rather than through contributions) it is the government's money, and because the poor and vulnerable are in this case *recipients* rather than *reciprocators*, it is not clear that intermediaries have incentives to deliver the subsidy to those most in need, the way an intermediary delivers loans to those most able to repay. Redistributive programmes then involve paradoxes of targeting and possible programme capture (Sen 1995; Gelbach and Pritchett 1997).

The discussion above suggests that intermediation of financial contracts and safety nets is impaired because of problems on the supply-side of the market. Private sector intermediary institutions have not stepped in to take advantage of seemingly large arbitrage opportunities. State and local governments, and national non-governmental organizations, have eschewed local intermediaries for targeting available resources for public safety nets and poverty alleviation.

15.3. THE RELATIVE ABSENCE OF INTERMEDIATION

There is ample evidence to suggest that financial systems and local safety nets are not as integrated into the larger financial system as they could be. Many of the intermediary institutions described above have never been observed in villages and rural areas around the world. For example, despite the apparent simplicity of the transactions, Western Union had no presence in sub-Saharan Africa until 1993, when two expatriate Ghanaian financial entrepreneurs convinced the conglomerate to commence operations in Ghana. In the following eight years, Western Union expanded throughout the continent into forty-seven countries, transferring roughly US$1 billion per year. In South Africa alone Western Union processed 3.2 million transactions in 1999, but it was not until 2001 that the company opened a regional office.

Government legislation to regulate and permit microfinance is a major obstacle. South Africa, the most developed financial centre on the continent, only established implementing legislation for microfinance in 1999 (Meagher and Wilkinson 2001). In African countries, even trade credit among manufacturing firms is relatively limited, and credit bureaus are largely absent (Fafchamps 1997, 2000). Government regulations are also hindering the establishment of credit bureaus for microfinance in Latin America (Development Alternatives Inc. 2002). Few microfinance institutions use scoring methods or reputation histories to determine loans or loan conditions (see Schreiner 2002 and Sadoulet: Chapter 17, this volume).

The recent expansion of microfinance institutions throughout the world suggests that supply-side innovations are important. West Africa, for example, has seen an explosion of interest in microfinance in the past decade. Most villages were completely cut-off from even these modest microloans prior to this credit boom (MkNelly and Kevane 2001). Many microcredit institutions now have almost a decade of sustained, and close to sustainable, intermediation. Clients continue to borrow event though it is now apparent that the financial services are the only 'benefit' from participation.[1]

The expansion of South Africa's pension system to black citizens is also telling (Case and Deaton 1998). Clearly, here was a case of widespread demand for pensions, and a politically motivated constraint on supply. The electorate is overwhelmingly in favour of a state-sponsored pension system for the aged. It is more than likely that other African countries have similar voter equilibria where national-level pensions would be demanded. Moreover, existing pension and social safety nets seem to suffer from serious problems of intermediation, in the sense that agents responsible for distribution to individuals in localities do very poor jobs of targeting.

For the informal sector, there is mixed evidence on the relative size and functioning of informal local and regional intermediation for credit and insurance. Self-sustaining credit and insurance networks offer partial insurance because of problems of information or limited commitment, even within the close quarters and repeated interaction of village life (Coate and Ravallion 1993; Fafchamps 1996; Kimball 1988; Ligon et al. 1999). The weight of evidence suggests that informal insurance mechanisms are seriously incomplete (Townsend 1994; Morduch 1995). More recent research rejects even the hypothesis of complete sharing of risks within households (Dercon and Krishnan 2000; Goldstein 2000). As for regional networks, Grimard (1997) presents evidence suggesting that ethnic groups occupying large spaces in Cote d'Ivoire do practice limited consumption pooling. Udry (1994), on the other hand, finds that local state-contingent contracts common in northern Nigeria do not extend to inter-village financial arrangements.

15.4. LACK OF INTERMEDIATION ARISING FROM AGENCY PROBLEMS

In all of the examples of Table 15.1 there are numerous layers of contracting that a financial institution or policymaker must take into account when assessing intermediation possibilities. First, the intermediary institution must motivate and solve asymmetric information problems with its own employees, and its own depositors or creditors. Second, the intermediary institution must find contractual forms that ensure profitability when lending to or insuring clients, or that achieve the desired targeting, in the case of a safety net. Third, the intermediary institution must anticipate and may possibly want to regulate or harness the existing or new local side-contracting arrangements that agents and clients' might strike up among themselves, or with other persons or competing institutions.

Understanding the nature and potential impacts of such side-contracting activities lies at the heart of any theory of financial intermediation because side-contracting with a third party typically changes the incentives faced by the parties to a bilateral

---

[1] Many villagers may have joined microfinance schemes expecting to receive non-pecuniary benefits, or even village public goods such as schools or dispensaries. Most microfinance institutions, however, do not provide public goods; nor do they necessarily do a good job of 'empowering' women through collective mobilization.

contract. The inability to rule out or properly regulate some sorts of side-contracts with third parties may be deleterious to one or both parties to a contract, and therefore may 'crowd-out' certain types of beneficial transactions. In other cases, side-contracts among locals or with other financial intermediaries may well be beneficial to an outside institution transacting with locals; side-contracts may actually serve to 'crowd-in' local or outside resources and build more complex intermediary structures that permit transactions that would not have taken place.

The design of structures to promote financial intermediation involves deciding which side-contracts to allow or to internalize within the institution, and which to exclude or try to regulate. The impact of potential side-contracting and collusion has been discussed in the theoretical literature, for example, in the context of risk-sharing and moral hazard models of Itoh (1993), Holmstrom and Milgrom (1990), Arnott and Stiglitz (1991), and Prescott and Townsend (2002), in the group loan model of Stiglitz (1990), as well as in the industrial organization literature (Laffont and Tirole 1993). Our purpose below is to synthesize and illustrate several key results with a simple model, emphasizing policy relevant lessons for developing countries.

We begin with a standard analysis of insurance in the presence of moral hazard and then progressively complicate the model by allowing for different types of side-contracts amongst agents. Comparing these alternative scenarios clarifies when local contracting crowds out, or crowds in, new outside financial services. The model also offers insights into the use of delegated monitoring and emergence of financial inter-mediation, and effects that monitoring costs, transaction costs, and village power dynamics can have on the shape and welfare consequences of financial contracting.

We use the word 'villager' or 'agent' to describe the clients, and financial institution (FI) to describe the outside provider of financial services, recognizing that the kind of clients we are discussing are also rural dwellers who live from non-farm incomes, or slum dwellers in cities, and that many of our examples concern insurance, rather than loans.

15.4.1. *Elements of a Model*

Think of a very simple economic setting where there are only two villagers or agents. Each villager has access to a single risky production project and the two projects are stochastically independent. The outcome on each project is affected by each agent's effort. If the agent is diligent he incurs disutility of effort D and his project succeeds to yield an outcome X_s with probability p_s or fails with probability $p_f = (1 - p_s)$ to yield outcome $X_f < X_s$. An agent who does not apply effort avoids effort disutility D, but this lowers the probability of success from p_s to $q_s < p_s$. In what follows it will be useful to also define the joint or total project outcome $X_{ij} = X_i^1 + X_j^2$ where $i \in \{s,f\}$ and $j \in \{s,f\}$ together index the four possible joint outcomes or states of the world.

Since villagers are risk-averse there are obvious gains to state-contingent contracting within the village, and between villagers and a risk-neutral outside financial institution (FI). A first-best efficient allocation would have villagers purchasing full insurance from the FI to obtain smooth consumption. Such arrangements will however not in general

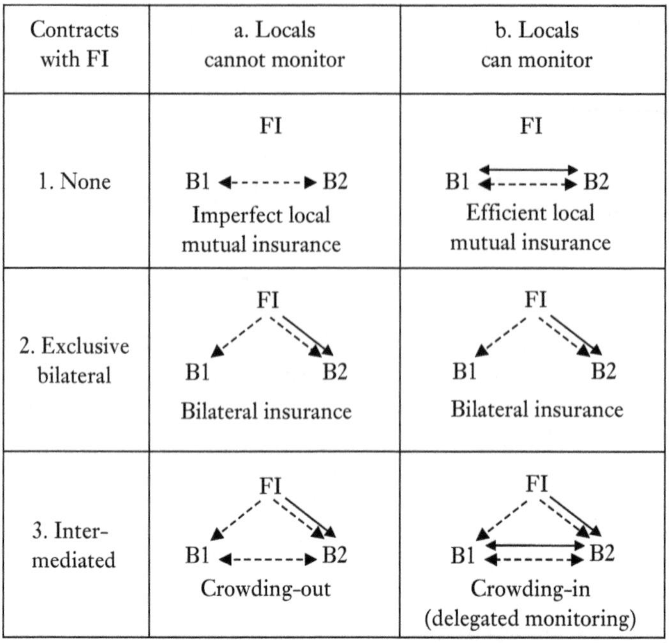

Contracts with FI	a. Locals cannot monitor	b. Locals can monitor
1. None	FI B1 ◄------► B2 Imperfect local mutual insurance	FI B1 ◄═══► B2 Efficient local mutual insurance
2. Exclusive bilateral	FI B1　　　B2 Bilateral insurance	FI B1　　　B2 Bilateral insurance
3. Inter-mediated	FI B1 ◄------► B2 Crowding-out	FI B1 ◄------► B2 Crowding-in (delegated monitoring)

Figure 15.1. *Alternative contract structures for a simple village economy*

Note: Dashed lines indicate outcome-contingent contracting. Solid lines indicate monitored or action-contingent contracting.

be feasible if the FI cannot specify villager 1's effort in a contract. Figure 15.1 portrays six possible alternative contract structures that might become feasible depending on whether local agents can observe and 'monitor' each other's actions to limit moral hazard in local contracts, and whether or not an outside FI can enforce exclusive contract by limiting side-contracts among agents.

The possible contractual structures are:

(1.a) an imperfect local mutual insurance equilibrium where because of moral hazard risk-sharing even among local agents is imperfect and there is no feasible trade with an outside FI;

(1.b) a locally efficient mutual insurance equilibrium where local monitoring allows villagers to get around moral hazard and achieve efficient risk-sharing in local trades but risk-sharing remains incomplete due to an inability to trade with an outside FI;

(2.a, 2.b) equilibria with exclusive bilateral contracts between an outside FI and each of the villagers where insurance is imperfect due to moral hazard;

(3.a) 'crowding-out' equilibria where side-contracting between villagers disrupts insurance that might have otherwise been provided by an outside FI (in the case of complete crowding-out this case collapses to 1.a); and

(3.b) equilibria where an outside FI utilizes local agents or village structures as delegated monitors or intermediaries to provide financial services that otherwise
would have been infeasible.

This last set of equilibrium structures is the most interesting as they illustrate how
'closeness' among locals might be harnessed to leverage or 'crowd-in' outside financial
resources that might otherwise not have been forthcoming. We explore this case in
detail below and in the discussion of costly delegated monitoring. Our aim is to clarify
the conditions under which each of these different contractual structures is likely to
emerge and to compare the volume of trade and welfare in each case.

There are four possible joint project outcomes, or states in this simple village economy. The state-contingent consumption bundle for villager $k \in \{1, 2\}$ is
given by c_{ij}^k or $\{c_{ff}^k, c_{sf}^k, c_{fs}^k, c_{ss}^k\}$. To simplify the analysis further, assume agent 2 always
chooses to exert effort but agent 1's effort level cannot be verified by an outside finan-
cial institution and may therefore be subject to moral hazard. Below we will examine
scenarios where agent 2 can and cannot observe agent 1's action.

In what follows we follow the convention of the literature and focus on the financial
institution's 'implementation problem'. That is, we look for the set of contracts that
implements diligence or effort by the first agent at lowest cost to the principal (in this
case the FI) while providing insurance to the villager(s). How the resulting surplus
is actually divided between the FI and the agents is not that important. We could
just as well be looking at contracts in a market where competition in insurance and
lending means the FI can only break even and leaves all realized gains to trade with the
villagers, or any situation in between. Our goal here is to offer the reader a more policy
relevant synthesis of the general type of results established by Itoh (1993), Holmstrom
and Milgrom (1990), and Arnott and Stiglitz (1991).

Case 1: isolated local mutual insurance
When villagers can monitor each other's efforts (case 1.b) they can enter into locally
efficient mutual insurance or consumption pooling arrangements. This equilibrium is
locally efficient in the sense that the marginal rate of substitution between any two
states will be equalized across agents (i.e. $u_{ij}^2 = \lambda_{ij}^1$ for every state ij, where λ
is a constant) but is not first-best efficient because it fails to take advantage of the
gains to trading with a risk-neutral outside FI who could provide full insurance against
village-wide shocks.

When villagers cannot monitor efforts (case 1.a), moral hazard will stand in the
way of efficient local mutual insurance. The need to provide agent 1 with incentives
will result in more variable consumption patterns and lower welfare. Since moral
hazard applies only to agent 1, this is analysed as a classic moral-hazard problem with
a risk-averse principal (Holmstrom 1979).

Case 2: exclusive bilateral contracts
Assume now that the FI can contract separately with each villager using an *exclusive* contract that prohibits any type of side-contract among agents. The FI seeks to
provide insurance/loans to the agents at minimum expected payout $c_{ij}^1 + c_{ij}^2$. If F is

the cost of funds and transaction, then the FI chooses $\{c_{ij}^1, c_{ij}^2\}$ to induce both agents to participate and provide villager 1 with incentives to be diligent:

$$\min_{c_{ij}^1, c_{ij}^2} \sum_i \sum_j p_i p_j (c_{ij}^1 + c_{ij}^2) + F, \tag{15.1}$$

subject to

$$\sum_i \sum_j p_i p_j u(c_{ij}^1) - D \geq \sum_i \sum_j q_i p_j u(c_{ij}^1), \tag{15.2}$$

$$\sum_i \sum_j p_i p_j u(c_{ij}^k) - D \geq \bar{U}. \tag{15.3}$$

As project returns are independent of one another and agents cannot observe each other's actions, no relative-performance evaluation considerations apply and the optimal contract offered to each agent will be an individual contract in the sense that each agent's payment is not made contingent on the outcomes of the other agent's project (Holmstrom 1979; Mookherjee 1984). An optimal contract will therefore have $c_{ss}^k = c_{sf}^k = c_s^k$ and $c_{fs}^k = c_{ff}^k = c_f^k$ for $k = 1, 2$, since any other feasible contract with the same expected consumption value imposes more risk on the agent. Since villager 2's actions are by assumption verifiable, the FI can provide full insurance and the agent obtains the same fixed consumption level in each state. Agent 1 on the other hand must be given incentives to exert effort. Letting $\Delta = p_s - q_s$, the incentive compatibility (IC) constraint for agent 1 can be expanded and rewritten as:

$$u(c_s^1) - u(c_f^2) \geq \frac{D}{\Delta}. \tag{15.4}$$

This states that an optimal contract must give the agent higher expected utility following project success compared to failure in order for the agent to have incentive to want to raise the probability of success by exerting higher effort. Since for this reason villager 1 must bear risk, the expected cost of providing a contract that keeps villager 1 at his reservation expected utility rises. The feasibility of contracts between the FI and the villager depends therefore on the cost of diligence D (which in turn may depend on monitoring by the FI or its delegates, as discussed below), how diligence raises the probability of success (captured by Δ), the villagers' degree of risk aversion, and the FI's fixed costs F.

Case 3a: side-contracts and crowding-out

The exclusive bilateral contract just examined is the solution to a standard moral hazard problem.[2] This solution rests on the assumption that the FI can costlessly prohibit all side-contracts. Given a large empirical and anthropological literature describing a prevalence of local risk-sharing arrangements this assumption may not be very realistic. Even where local risk-sharing arrangements might not have been extensive prior to the arrival of outside forms of finance, it seems probable that enterprising locals

---

[2] As villager 1's participation constraint and incentive constraint must both bind at an optimum, the optimal contract is easily shown to be $u(c_f^1) = (\bar{U} + D) - pD/\Delta$ and $u(c_s^1) = (\bar{U} + D) + (1 - p)D/\Delta$.

would search for ways to exploit newly created opportunities for financial arbitrage via side-contracts. For example, a borrower who obtains outside insurance or loans might on-lend some of those funds to others, or might call on others for help in the event that he cannot meet a required payment.

Do such side-contracts help or hinder villagers' access to outside financial services? This question has been studied in some depth in the theoretical literature (Holmstrom and Milgrom 1990; Varian 1990; Arnott and Stiglitz 1991; Itoh 1993), but has not frequently been translated into policy relevant lessons. A conclusion that runs throughout these studies is that if agents can side-contract only on the same observable contingencies that an outside financial institution can contract on—in other words, if agents do not possess informational 'closeness' relative to the outsider—then such side-deals can never improve, and may quite possibly harm, villagers' access to financial services. On the other hand, side-contracts can help 'crowd-in' new or additional financial services if an outside FI can design a contract to harness local agent's 'closeness' or ability to side-contract on actions or outcomes that the FI would not be in a position to observe or verify via bilateral contracting. We argue that 'crowding-in' of this sort is at the heart of what financial intermediation is all about.

Consider first the crowding-out scenario. The two agents can now side-contract for the purpose of further mutual insurance but contracts can only be made contingent on the same publicly observable outcomes that the FI relies upon in its own contracts with villagers. Recall that, by design, the optimal individual contracts offered by the financial institution in case 1 above provided full insurance to agent 2 but left agent 1 imperfectly insured in order to provide incentives. This now leaves open the possibility that agents might find it profitable to agree to a mutual insurance side-contract to smooth out agent 1's consumption. Such side-contracting may however disrupt agent 1's incentive to remain diligent and hence might harm the value of the contracts the FI has with agent 1.

If the FI cannot physically or legally forbid such side-contracts, it should at least anticipate its consequences in the design of its own contracts. As the FI can always reproduce whatever side-contract arrangements the agents have in mind, without loss of generality we can restrict attention to contracts that by design provide incentives against further side-contracts or coalition-formation. Following (Itoh 1993) we refer to such contracts as *coalition-proof*. For a contract between the FI and local agents to be coalition-proof requires that the contracts meet an additional set of constraints compared to the case where side-contracts could be costlessly prohibited. This can only reduce the feasible contract set, leading to the possibility of crowding-out.

To illustrate, consider the simple case of a village that organizes a mutual aid programme to meet basic needs, regardless of past actions. The village safety net prevents agents' consumption from ever falling below some feasible minimum threshold. Incentives for an agent to be diligent in a contract with an outside FI will then obviously be dulled if the local safety net provides too much insurance in the event of failures on the financed activity. Contracts with an outside financial intermediary may become difficult or impossible to implement.

This suggests why pre-existing local mutual insurance arrangements might delay the entry of new forms of outside finance, or conversely, why new outside intermediaries might crowd-out pre-existing local insurance arrangements. A significant social science literature has decried the breakdown of such local risk-sharing arrangements in the face of market penetration (Scott 1976), and recent empirical literature has established crowding-out in some cases. In Chapter 13, Albarran and Attanasio analyse evidence suggesting that Mexico's PROGRESA social safety net programme crowded out local private insurance transfers. Morduch (1999) surveys similar findings. Despite these claims, our view is there is not yet enough evidence to decide on how important and pervasive this concern is in practice. It cannot always be presumed that effective local insurance 'existed' prior to intermediation; many NGOs spend considerable effort and resources promoting local mutual insurance, rather than encouraging intermediation. Furthermore, the development of markets has been changing households outside opportunities anyway, leaving some households vulnerable as local sharing networks and institutions have been modified or displaced. To not offer social safety nets, or to not encourage outside private intermediation in such contexts for fear of disrupting local insurance networks runs the risk of romanticizing institutions that may already be weak and risks leaving vulnerable households behind.

More fundamentally, the ability of locals to side-contract can at times be turned into an asset for potentially 'crowding-in' rather than 'crowding-out' new financial services. Financial innovation is about finding ways to harness local information and enforcement mechanisms to help leverage outside resources and expand the range of feasible contracting. To understand these issues we turn next to a variation on the model that can produce 'crowding-in', followed by a discussion of the concept of delegated monitoring.

Case 3b: crowding-in by harnessing local information
Suppose the situation is as in the last section except that now agent 2 can enter into action-contingent side-contracts with agent 1 while the financial institution remains unable to observe or directly contract on agent 1's actions. Can the outside financial institution harness this extra 'closeness' between agents, to enable greater access to financial services?

There are two cases to consider, the first where agents can transfer utility directly among themselves, and the second where they can only contract for state-contingent payments of goods.[3] In the transferable utility case,[3] the FI wishes to minimize the expected cost of implementing diligence (15.1) subject to

$$\sum_i \sum_j p_{ij}\big(u(c_{ij}^1) + u(c_{ij}^2)\big) - 2D \geq \sum_i \sum_j q_{ij}\big(u(c_{ij}^1) + u(c_{ij}^2)\big) - D, \qquad (15.5)$$

$$\sum_i \sum_j p_i p_j \big(u(c_{ij}^1) + u(c_{ij}^2)\big) - 2D \geq 2\bar{U}, \qquad (15.6)$$

$$u'(c_{ij}^1) = u'(c_{ij}^2) \quad \text{for all } i,j. \qquad (15.7)$$

---

[3] Equivalent to assuming agents have quasi-linear utility functions.

The incentive compatibility constraint (15.5) and participation constraint (15.6) reflect the fact that the agents, acting as a coalition, act to maximize the utility achieved by the group, which they will then redistribute according to some efficient side-contracting mechanism internal to the village. The FI cannot legally or physically forbid such side-contracts but it can and will take them into consideration when designing the optimal contract. Since the FI can always reproduce any outcome-contingent side-contract the agents might have chosen, without loss of generality, we can restrict attention to contracts that provide incentive against further side-contracts or coalition-formation (Tirole 1992). The coalition-proof constraints (15.7) capture the fact that agents will always want local mutual insurance within the coalition, and therefore (in the transferable utility case) the marginal utility of consumption in each state must be the same for the two agents.

The FI can take advantage of agents' ability to side-contract on actions to provide better risk-sharing services without disrupting agent 1's incentives to be diligent. The reason is that the individual-level incentive compatibility constraint (15.4) can now be replaced by a coalition-level incentive compatibility constraint (15.5) that is easier to satisfy. Intuitively, the FI can now provide more consumption smoothing to agent 1 without disrupting incentives because agent 2's 'monitoring' keeps agent 1 diligent even in circumstances where the individual IC constraint (15.4) would not be satisfied.

Agent 2 has in effect been hired to be the FI's delegated monitor. To have incentives to 'monitor' agent 2 must however suffer some consequences for agent 1's project failures. This raises the cost of contracting with agent 2 by lowering the risk premium the FI can extract compared to the earlier bilateral contract case. In the transferable utility case this is always worthwhile because agent 2's 'monitoring' increases the risk premium the FI can now extract from agent 1. Itoh's (1993) remarkable paper proves these results more formally; demonstrating also that agent side-contracting on actions can also be of advantage to the principal in the non-transferable utility case.[4]

15.4.2. *Costly Delegated Monitoring and the Role of Intermediary Capital*

The assumption that agents can costlessly observe and side-contract on both outcomes and actions is widely employed in the theoretical literature. Stiglitz (1990), for example, assumes costless side-contracting to model group loans and peer-monitoring, showing that a joint-liability loan works to harness the assumed closeness among borrowers. The assumption is not very realistic however. It means that villagers can perfectly 'collude' or 'cooperate' without cost to coordinate actions, as if the village were a single syndicate or collective household (Chiappori 1988). Taken literally this implies that

---

[4] In the non-transferable utility case, coalition-proof constraints (15.7) are replaced by the more general condition that marginal rates of substitution be equalized across agents, and the coalitional incentive compatibility constraint (15.5) are modified to remain consistent with each agent getting their agreement utility levels. See Itoh (1993) for full details.

efficient local risk-sharing should always hold within the village. But efficient risk-sharing is often rejected empirically even within households (Udry 1996). A collective village seems even less plausible. A more realistic assumption is that locally informed agents may have an advantage compared to outsiders in carrying out *costly* and imperfect monitoring and control activities. Understanding how monitoring and delegation costs vary with different intermediary structures is essential to appreciating the possibilities and limits of financial innovation in developing countries.

Some villagers will naturally be in a better position than others to act as delegates in costly monitoring and control activities. A delegated monitor, as the last section made clear, needs to bear risk to have incentives to monitor, so less risk-averse and/or better-capitalized agents make better delegated monitors. This might suggest why local shopkeepers, landlords, and employers so often fill this role.

Since a less risk-averse agent 2 makes for a better monitor let us for simplicity now assume that agent 2 is risk-neutral. In addition, agent 2 no longer engages in risky production and his/her earnings are now determined simply by the terms of his/her contract as a delegated monitor. In contrast to the last section, we now assume the contract is designed for the benefit of agent 1, as it would be in a competitive financial market. The practical implication of this is that the delegated monitor and the outside FI are now kept at their participation constraints while we aim to maximize agent 1's expected consumption.

To capture the idea that monitoring is a costly and imperfect activity, we adapt a simple specification borrowed from the financial contracting literature.[5] A local delegated monitor can, at monitoring cost m reduce the private benefit that an insured farmer stands to gain from non-diligence from D to $d < D$. Think of m as the labour effort the monitor must expend in frequent visits, inspections, and social work and d as the lower net private benefit that agent 1 gets from being non-diligent when he is monitored and pressured[6] in this way. An outside FI might also try to monitor the insured farmer with their own non-local staff only at a higher cost $M > m$, which in general makes it prohibitive.

The contract design problem can now be stated as:

$$\max_{c_i^1, c_i^2} Eu(c_i^1 \mid p) - d, \tag{15.8}$$

subject to

$$E(c_i^1 \mid p) - d \geq E(c_i^1 \mid q), \tag{15.9}$$

$$E(X_i - c_i^1 - c_i^2 \mid p) - F \geq 0, \tag{15.10}$$

$$E(c_i^2 \mid p) - m \geq 0, \tag{15.11}$$

$$E(c_i^2 \mid p) - m \geq E(c_i^2 \mid q). \tag{15.12}$$

---

[5] See, for example, Holmstrom and Tirole (1997), Hoshi *et al.* (1993), and Conning (1999).

[6] Note that m could include helping actions to help the farmer prevent failure. In general a 'monitoring action' is any action that helps raise the rewards to diligence and/or lower the rewards to non-diligence.

The first three expressions are as in the individual contract design problem except that now d replaces D, to capture the idea that costly monitoring expenditure by agent 2 can directly lower agent 1's gains from moral hazard. Constraints (15.10) and (15.11) are participation constraints for the FI and the delegated monitor, respectively. Since villager 2's monitoring actions cannot be observed by the FI, they too are subject to moral hazard, and the contract terms must provide incentives for agent 2 to monitor. The monitor's incentive compatibility constraint (15.12) can be expanded and rearranged to give:

$$c_s^2 \geq c_f^2 + \frac{m}{\Delta}, \tag{15.13}$$

which states that agent 2 must be sufficiently rewarded for agent 1's successful outcomes and penalized for failures to have an incentive to want to raise the probability of success via monitoring. For a given value of c_f^2, this incentive constraint implies that the intermediary must earn an expected remuneration, net of monitoring cost m, of at least:

$$E(c_i^2 \mid p) - m = pc_f^2 + (1-p)c_s^2 - m = c_f^2 + p\frac{m}{\Delta} - m \tag{15.14}$$

to remain a diligent monitor. If the participation constraint (15.11) is also to be met then this expression must be at least as large as what agent 2 can earn in her next best activity, which has been normalized to zero. Whether this participation constraint binds—in which case total cost of involving a delegate is only m—or remains slack, in which case the monitor earns a rent, depends on how low the contract sets c_f^2.

Define $F^m = pm/\Delta - m$. If the contract sets $c_f^2 = -F^m$ then (15.11) can be shown to bind exactly and incentives maintained, by setting $c_s^2 = -F^m + m/\Delta$. The delegated monitor would then earn remuneration $E(c_i^2 \mid p) = -F^m + pm/\Delta = m$, or exactly her reservation utility plus monitoring cost m. Note, however, that $c_f^2 = -F^m < 0$ as long as $p > q$ so the delegated monitor has to, in effect, be made a co-insurer/loan guarantor, absorbing part of the 'losses' from agent 1's project failures.

Agent 2's willingness to place enough of his/her own capital at risk is what credibly signals his/her incentive to monitor and thereby helps leverage or 'crowd-in' additional financial services from an outside FI who might otherwise have been reluctant to contract at all with agent 1. If we interpret F as the opportunity cost of loan funds needed to fund agent 1's project then we would interpret agent 2 as lending F^m and the uninformed outside FI providing the difference, $F^u = F - F^m$.

Local intermediary capital will however often be in limited supply, and the best monitors of poor people are often the other poor people who live and interact with them but have little working capital. What happens if agent 2 does not have any intermediary capital, so F must be provided exclusively by the FI? In this case $c_f^2 = 0$ so to maintain incentive constraint (15.13) at minimum cost we must set $c_s^2 = m/\Delta$. The delegated monitor will then earn $E(c_i^2 \mid p) = pm/\Delta$ implying participation constraint (15.11) must be slack because $E(c_i^2 \mid p) - m = pm/\Delta - m > 0$ as long as $p > q$. Intuitively, because the delegated monitor cannot be punished for agent

1's failures she must be rewarded better for success to maintain incentives, giving the delegated monitor a strictly positive information rent, or *delegation cost*, pm/Δ which raises the cost of her participation. As this rent reduces the remaining project surplus to be divided, higher delegation costs lead to higher implicit financing costs for agent 1 and clearly reduces the set of feasible arrangements. Delegation costs rise with the severity of the underlying moral hazard for agent 1, as captured by p/Δ and with the size of monitoring cost m, which shapes the scope for moral hazard by agent 2.

If a competitive market for delegated monitors existed in the village, then delegates with more capital of their own to place at risk will be in a position to offer the most attractive financial package because placing intermediary capital at risk lowers the information rent. The dearth of capital or diversification activities in many poor areas suggests that local intermediary capital may be in limited supply. In such a context outside financial institutions may have to recruit local monitors and accept delegation costs as the cost of providing staff incentives.

Diamond's (1984) seminal work on financial intermediation identified an important mechanism for lowering delegation costs.[7] His insight was to note that if a delegate is placed in charge of monitoring several villagers financial projects, and if returns from those different projects are imperfectly correlated, then the monitor could be made to cover the losses on one project out of the 'bonus' received from another project succeeding. For example, if agent 2 with no initial capital of her own were made to monitor n villagers just like agent 1 each with identical but stochastically independent projects, it can be shown[8] that the delegation cost per borrower can be lowered from $(p/(p-q))m > m$ to $(p^n/(p^n-q^n))m$ which falls to m as n tends to infinity. In other words, a delegated monitor with no intermediary capital of her own can in principle lower her costs down to the level of a less diversified monitor who does have intermediary capital. Diamond argued that monitoring is delegated to specialized financial intermediaries such as banks precisely because incentive diversification effects reduce the delegation cost per borrower compared to less diversified financial institutions.

Unfortunately, a local intermediary often becomes a good monitor because he or she knows a lot about a specific area or line of business, but the correlation of project returns within such similar groups is likely to be high, so incentive diversification opportunities of the sort identified by Diamond are likely to remain limited. This may be one reason why microfinance has tended to be more successful in urban settings than rural settings (at least in Latin America). The heavy use local agents and monitored lending in microfinance may also help explain why leverage ratios at microfinance banks have remained far lower than in most other areas of banking (Conning 1999).

15.5. OTHER THEORIES OF THE LACK OF INTERMEDIATION

The above discussion explained how asymmetric information leading to moral hazard could lead to less financial intermediation than one might expect. Models of asymmetric

---

[7] Diamond's original focus was a model of costly state verification, but the essential insight carries over.
[8] See Conning (2000) and Laux (2001) for more detailed related analyses.

information leading to adverse selection would have similar effects. In this section, we consider a group of more eclectic models that explain the slowness in adoption of financial intermediation. The models and discussion emphasize the origins of asymmetric information and trust and how historical factors and non-economic considerations might prevent intermediation.

15.5.1. *A Network Approach*

Network approaches focus on the inertia of a system locked-in to an existing, but perhaps increasingly inefficient, set of overlapping, informal, local insurance arrangements, and safety nets. Gilbert (1999: 7) conjectures that these informal arrangements may deter development of more sophisticated intermediation:

many African farmers are implicitly co-insured within the village or extended family. This makes the purchase of insurance unattractive since the benefits from payoffs would be partially disseminated across the community while the costs remain theirs alone. A move towards the market requires that farmers become more atomistic in their behaviour.

There are two interpretations here. One is that villagers may be implicitly required to participate in a kind of basic needs insurance as part of their membership in the village community. In that case, outside insurance for particular risks (price risk in Gilbert's case) is less valuable for the villagers; they cannot 'opt out' of the broader basic needs insurance. The other interpretation is that while these arrangements may have been the best possible given the constraints on larger-scale intermediation, the inefficiency becomes greater as the constraints on formal intermediation are relaxed through investments in public infrastructure, more effective technology, and improved reputation of formal institutions. Now, given a choice between local, informal insurance, and intermediated insurance, people might prefer intermediated insurance. But the pre-existence of the local insurance network inhibits the switch to the new technology of intermediation.

A coordination problem exists: only if sufficient numbers of local residents make the switch to intermediated insurance will it gain the acceptance of others, but no individual has incentives to make the switch before the others. In the case of publicly subsidized safety nets, many authors have noted that offering such 'free' outside insurance immediately begins an unraveling of the local insurance arrangement. But for private intermediaries it is not clear whether offering initial subsidies will be an equilibrium strategy when the subsequent market for intermediated services is competitive.

Consider a simple model where agents have productive activities that generate one unit of 'extra' consumption goods in alternating years. These goods cannot be saved. Each person also has a stock of illiquid wealth that yields basic consumption (so the marginal utility of consumption in the years when a person does not get extra consumption is not infinite). Obviously, the villagers can work out a sharing arrangement that is self-enforcing, if the game is repeated, where the degree of sharing depends on the degree of impatience of the agents and their relative bargaining power. The agent who gets the extra amount weighs the utility from consuming all of it against the loss of future smoothing. Now further suppose that each successful round of consumption smoothing builds up trust among the members according to a simple, decreasing returns function, and that this trust is a valuable stock that evaporates when someone cheats on the agreement or terminates the arrangement. As trust accumulates, the discount rate required to sustain the arrangement becomes less and less difficult to meet. Then the age of any particular local insurance arrangement determines the penetration capacity of an outside intermediary institution offering consumption smoothing services (through savings, for instance). Since the profitability of the outside institution also depends on the trust that it accumulates, it may not be able to penetrate villages with established local arrangements, even if its trust-generating technology is superior to that of the local arrangement.

It may be the case that imposing regulatory hurdles breaks down these informal, local arrangements and leaves the field clear for larger-scale intermediaries with better finance and trust-building technologies. A number of authors have hypothesized this effect, or even advocated it. Bossone (2000: 19–20) notes that the 'franchise' value of an intermediary, by which he means the value of the reputation built-up through honoring promises for quality service, improves the quality of financial intermediation:

Only a positive net franchise value from intermediation may attract investment in reputational capital from financial institutions. Use of mild regulatory restraints on market competition might increase the franchise value of domestic institutions, especially in least developed countries and in those emerging from long periods of financial repression . . . restraints such as (market-based) deposit rate ceilings and restrictions on market entry may have large rent creation effects that would allow banks to raise profits during the phase of initial reform.

Some economic historians have hypothesized that national regulatory intervention factored in undermining local financial institutions and safety nets.[9] Regulations created a national market, with concomitant costs and benefits. One should not be too optimistic about this line of thinking in terms of actual implementation. The potential for 'government failure' applies, and legislatures or regulators may misread the nature of lock-in and destroy useful trust in a misguided attempt to generate economies of scale or scope.

15.5.2. *Social Norms against Cooperation with Intermediaries*

We may approach from a historical perspective the issue of origins of differential comparative trust in local versus outside financial institutions. Local groups have numerous norms that restrict economic activities. Many African societies have prohibitions on selling land to outsiders. Many have similar restrictions on where and to whom women of the village may marry. It is not too far to imagine that village

---

[9] Even the successful industrialized economies have followed very different institutional development paths, and more than one set of institutional arrangements for finance may emerge as equilibrium in a national economy, as the contrasting experiences of the United States and Germany suggest (Holmstrom 1996).

societies have similar norms against revealing information to outsiders, particularly against selling information for profit.[10]

Such a collusive norm of non-cooperation may have arisen in response to shared experiences with intermediaries in colonial regimes. In peasant societies under colonialism, especially in areas of indirect rule, the 'agent' of the state, often a villager appointed because of his skills at translation, or willingness to curry favour with outside administrators, was able to link intermediation with monopoly over force, and so made people worse off. The relationship between peasants and colonial agent was quite literally a prisoner's dilemma, with the peasants as prisoners and the agent as jailer, and local norms developed to solve that dilemma. One can imagine a repeated prisoner's dilemma game, where villagers know that only randomly does the agent 'offer' a game where cooperation yields high payoffs. A sustainable strategy may be to never cooperate with the agent. And of course, from the villagers perspective the agents of the formal economy and state are one and the same; they collude and act together to extract resources from the villagers.

The state and villagers are continuously bargaining over division of local surplus. A change in relative threat points then changes the outcome of bargaining. A village decision to cooperate with intermediaries, seemingly in their interest, may lead to a change in threat points that could make villagers worse off. The problem here is the state or intermediary cannot credibly commit to refrain from using new information or resources or shift in threat point to extract more resources, rendering the village worse off.

The question then becomes how quickly these village norms against cooperation erode when more and more opportunities for profitable cooperation with intermediaries arise and when the link between formality and abuse of power diminishes. It should be recalled that the distinction between colonial and post-independent regimes has not been sharp, in terms of the exercise of arbitrary power. Contemporary regimes quite often use the same tactics of inviting intermediaries, even business intermediaries, to monopolize force.[11] There are few distinctions to be made, then, between agents of the police and agents of formal institutions; from the point of view of the villagers they work closely together. A villager who becomes an agent of a formal institution comes closer to the locus of power, and comes closer to being able to exercise power himself.

Ironically, much recent public policy on intermediation is premised on the assumption that local social pressure can be used to reinforce the contracts entered into by the intermediary. But social pressure often works in quite the opposite direction: rather than generating peer pressure to repay, local society generates peer pressure not to 'fink' on a recalcitrant non-repayer.

---

[10] Platteau (2000: 12–14) notes that revealing information even within a village may be subject to numerous constraints having to do with face-saving and avoiding retaliation.

[11] Many of the problems of the oil multinationals in Nigeria stem from their willingness to blur the lines between their representative, who intermediate with villagers over contracts and access, and the repressive state military.

15.5.3. *A Standard Local Political Economy Argument for Opposition to Intermediaries*

Local politics is the mechanism through which local public goods are created and distributed and the local economy is regulated. Control over these processes yields benefits to those in power, benefits that are contested in the local political arena. Like any political system, maintaining power depends on relative, rather than absolute, differences in the ability to influence or persuade voters. If the decision about whether to allow or enable an intermediary to enter the village in the first place is a political decision taken locally, the political process may stymie the efforts of the intermediary to enter. This may happen despite the intermediary's potential to improve financial services for most in the village. If the service disturbs the relative balance of power within a village, it may be blocked. Alternatively, relatively disadvantaged members of the community may block programme introduction for the opposite region: they may feel the programme may be captured or misused by elites, giving them even more power in the community. Bardhan and Mookherjee (1998) develop a model that illustrates some of the important parameters that determine the degree and effects of programme capture.

The social distrust and political economy problems of intermediaries perhaps explain why so many microfinance institutions are reluctant to squarely address the fact that their services rely on the unpaid labour of a village president and treasurer, who are entrusted with basic bookkeeping, enforcement, and monitoring tasks. These villagers ought to be the ideal recruitment ground for a new category of intermediary agent placed on incentive contracts. The reluctance of microfinance institutions to hire local people to carry out tasks is strongly suggestive of the seriousness of the problems discussed above.

15.6. PUBLIC POLICY TO IMPROVE INTERMEDIATION

The theoretical discussion of the preceding two sections has some implications for policy. The challenge is to generate institutional innovations that will more quickly address the problem of delivering financial intermediation to the most poor. Such innovations serve two functions of potentially offering self-selecting redistribution with less leakage and also relieving the inefficiencies associated with low asset positions impeding choice of productive activities.

Governments are usually less informed about local economic circumstances compared with private parties. Thus, the main role for public policy in fostering and promoting greater levels of intermediation are twofold. First, removing entrenched restrictions, such as hurdles for the legal establishment of financial providers to the poor, draconian anti-usury laws, etc. At best, these laws often are ignored in the breach, and cause financial firms to obfuscate their records. At worst, they completely stymie formal sector intermediation. Second, providing essential public good inputs, as in a legal system that might facilitate lower cost third-party enforcement of contracts, prudential regulation, or legislation to promote public or private credit bureaus that improve the distribution of verifiable credit histories (Klein 1992). Hernando de Soto (2000) argues that the lack of clearly defined legal property rights for 400–600 million squatters worldwide strongly limits poor people's ability to utilize the assets they control to leverage additional resources.

Unfortunately, the literature is filled with examples of failed imported institutional innovation. The dismal record of credit cooperatives of the 1970s is a case in point. Another is the attempt by colonial government to introduce courts and land as collateral to facilitate the development of credit.[12] More recent property titling programmes in developing countries reveal more mixed results. Studies of the impact of a large-scale Peruvian urban squatter titling programme (designed in part by Hernando de Soto) on credit availability have not found much evidence of a very significant credit supply response, but these markets may take time to develop (Field 2002). Property reforms by themselves do not appear to create deeper financial markets, and some evidence suggests that property titling reforms in contexts where credit markets already fail can contribute to land concentration. Carter and Olinto (2003) report, for example, that the positive impact of a land titling programme on credit in Paraguay was almost exclusively confined to larger farms.

These mixed experiences highlight the need for continued learning and experimentation. Most developing countries have a long way to go in terms of implementing such public policy interventions (or non-interventions as the case may be). Moreover, successful public action along these lines cannot be quick, which is unfortunate for the poor. For infrastructure investments (in legal systems) to promote trust and lower the cost of contract enforcement, they have to become legitimate. They have to become the 'rules of the game' that are no longer contested. Legal capacity and financial institutional infrastructure is developed in the process of making and enforcing real decisions, not just by passing laws and training bureaucrats.

These reforms will not be enough. Even with more efficient private sector intermediation, a large number of poor and vulnerable households would remain imperfectly insured and with limited access to credit. This is because of limited wealth, moral hazard, and adverse selection problems, and the other local social and political problems discussed above. Public policy and pro–competitive policies may reduce these barriers, but irreducible transaction costs and other trading frictions are nonetheless likely to remain.

The lessons of the moral hazard approach to intermediation suggest that policies to support the creation of more financial intermediation should focus on 'growing' intermediary capital. Donors may be encouraged to make equity investments in the funds of microcredit and microinsurance organizations. Similarly, policies by microfinance organizations to build up capital locally though deposit mobilization and new savings instruments can help organizations build up intermediary capital and then leverage outside funds more effectively. The promotion of 'sustainable microfinance' in policy circles in recent years has helped focus attention on the role of hard budget constraints and incentives. But hard budgets are in principle also consistent with subsidies to

---

[12] Kranton and Swamy (1999) examine the experience of India.

the activities of new financial intermediaries, if effective and credible mechanisms for delivering those subsidies can be found.

Government guarantee funds in and of themselves may help local intermediaries to leverage outside funds from private sources. Guarantee funds act as monitors and guarantors of the monitoring intermediaries who try to leverage funds from outsiders. But developing countries have had many very bad experiences with guarantee funds (Levitsky 1997). To be effective, these funds have to themselves engage in intensive monitoring activities. Because the funds are government entities, they usually are prevented from using high-powered incentives to ensure bureaucratic effort and are prone to political capture.

One innovative approach was Chile's Cupones de Bonificacion (CUBOS) programme that auctioned government-funded vouchers among banks willing to lend to small and medium enterprises. Banks and leasing companies purchased these vouchers at auction at an average of about 75 cents on the dollar, but were then able to use these vouchers at par to purchase private insurance against loan non-repayment. The system was set up as a deliberate attempt to stimulate new private intermediation and at the same time target loan resources to small businesses without an explicit government loan guarantee fund (Arrau 1997). It helped foment the entry of new participants in the market for small business loans and private loan insurance.

Non-governmental agencies have had some success in overcoming the problems of intermediation identified above. Some microfinance institutions, for instance, ameliorate the delegated monitoring problem of limited liability by substituting (or more often, complementing) monitoring by a delegate with peer monitoring by a group. They also mitigate moral hazard problems by narrowing the product offering to products where the scope for moral hazard is small. On the lending side, loans are kept small and repayment periods short. Frequent group meetings with regular repayments help identify problem areas where monitoring can become more intensive.

Tentative efforts to intermediate microinsurance are similar. Programmes are sometimes bundling credit provision with death insurance or basic health insurance, where borrowers are obliged to purchase the services of a non-fee based health clinic. The insuree is free of course to seek alternative treatment, but the local health clinic provides a floor of basic health service in case of need. Making this participation mandatory eliminates the adverse selection problem. Most medical costs in developing countries are associated with easily cured or prevented disease, so moral hazard costs are not a large concern.[13]

There would seem to be opportunities for more bundling of this kind. For instance, there are other sources of risk that might be profitably insured. One important one for farmers and microborrowers is commodity price risk. In many microcredit programmes loans are taken for the purpose of stocking commodities on the expectation

---

[13] Providing catastrophic health insurance is another matter altogether. Insuring income losses due to sickness is especially difficult because of possible collusion between doctors and patients. In largely illiterate societies it is hard to see how any system for longer-term or more costly illnesses could be insured in a sustainable way. Families must bear the costs of self-insurance.

that prices will rise, as they generally do. But prices are risky, and sometimes they fall. A microfinance institution might find that instead of small loans where repayment potential is largely independent, its portfolio consists of thousands of people who have bet on the same expected movements in agricultural prices. Offering price insurance seems to be a natural way to increase expected benefits for both borrowers and microfinance institution.

The microfinance institution has to play the intermediary, in the absence of well-developed forward, futures, or options markets. There seems to be little research in understanding the specific reasons why such simple insurance contracts are not offered by existing intermediaries. Gilbert (1999) speculates that rural banks in developing countries lack even the basic expertise needed to price such contracts (estimating future crop prices, monitoring crop developments, analysing historical price patterns). If sold in advance, for small sums to rural microfinance clients, the possibilities of collusion and price manipulation seem small. Demand for such contracts may well be small, but then we are back to assuming that the lack of intermediation really is nothing more than a lack of demand because of relatively inexpensive local intermediation, self-insurance, and crop and activity diversification.

With regards to the distrust of intermediaries, it is worth recalling that microfinance intermediary institutions are usually motivated by low-powered incentives. They are non-profits, and often bundle their services with rhetoric emphasizing social change or with expenditures on local public services. These features give the intermediary more credibility than someone intermediating for profit; they are perhaps perceived as different from the state.

Microfinance institutions also use a 'blanket' approach that potentially mitigates the political economy problems. Because they are invariably regional in scope, the programmes give incentives for elites to embrace rather than undermine projects. Elites are enmeshed in their own political struggles with elites from other regions, for control of regional institutions. Programmes that aid elites in other villages must then be embraced by local elites. While their relative position might suffer within the village, they may prefer that to losing ground in their regional struggles among elite groups.

15.7. CONCLUSION

The financial system of an economy is the nexus of contracts and intermediary structures that comprise an often-complex web of transactions and agency relationships between different parties in the system. Financial systems vary immensely in structure and complexity. In some societies where regional or national level financial intermediation is weak, the financial system may be thought of as a set of islands of local financial transactions, but with few bridges or communication links between islands. Where financial intermediation is more developed, a dense network of actual or potential bridges across islands will be in place.

In the course of the development process financial markets become more integrated, and people benefit from the specialized services of financial intermediaries who are able to bridge the gaps between local informal and national financial institutions. But financial integration can happen rapidly or slowly. We have reviewed some basic explanations of the slowness of intermediation. The first account focused on problems of information asymmetry, lack of intermediary capital, and crowding-out. The second focused on recent literature on lock-in, suggesting that individuals already imbricated in existing financial networks may have few incentives to 'jump ship' to deal with an intermediary from the more anonymous 'national' market. The third offered an anthropological account more appropriate to village and 'closed' societies, where norms against cooperation with outsiders may be strong. The fourth noted a standard political economy model of resistance to new institutions because of possible shifts in relative bargaining power.

We should again emphasize that the kinds of supply-side innovations and issues we have discussed are only relevant once the basic groundwork of enforceability has been laid, through the maintenance of legitimate legal institutions. Given the enormity of that problem for many of the poorest countries, especially in sub-Saharan Africa, and given that we know so little about the empirical relevance of the theories discussed here, policymakers should be prudent at this point, looking to undo the negative effects of bad regulatory policies first rather than introduce new programmes and regulations.

REFERENCES

Acemoglu, D. and F. Zilibotti (1997). 'Was Prometheus Unbound by Chance? Risk, Diversification, and Growth'. *Journal of Political Economy*, 105(4), 709–51.

Adams, D. W., D. H. Graham, and J. D. Von Pischke (1984). 'Undermining Rural Development with Cheap Credit', in D. W. Adams, D. H. Graham, and J. D. Von-Pischke (eds), *Undermining Rural Development with Cheap Credit*. Westview Special Studies in Social, Political and Economic Development Series 1–7. Boulder, CO and London: Westview Press.

Arnott, R. and J. E. Stiglitz (1991). 'Moral Hazard and Nonmarket Institutions: Dysfunctional Crowding Out or Peer Monitoring?'. *American Economic Review*, 81(1), 179–90.

Arrau, P. (1997). 'Evaluation of CORFO's CUBOS-SME Program: 1991–1995'. *The Financier*, 4, 1–2.

Bardhan, P. and D. Mookherjee (1998). *Expenditure Decentralization and the Delivery of Public Services in Developing Countries*. Boston, MA: Boston University.

Bossone, B. (2000). *The Role of Trust in Financial Sector Development*. Washington, DC: World Bank.

Carter, M. R. and P. Olinto (2003). 'Getting Institutions "Right" for Whom: Credit Constraints and the Impact of Property Rights on the Quantity and Composition of Investment'. *American Journal of Agricultural Economics*, 85(1), 173–86.

Case, A. and A. Deaton (1998). 'Large Cash Transfers to the Elderly in South Africa'. *Economic Journal*, 108(450), 1330–61.

Chiappori, P. A. (1988). 'Rational Household Labor Supply'. *Econometrica*, 56, 63–89.

Coate, S. and M. Ravallion (1993). 'Reciprocity without Commitment: Characterization and Performance of Informal Insurance Arrangements'. *Journal of Development Economics*, 40, 1–24.

Conning, J. (1999). 'Outreach, Sustainability and Leverage in Monitored and Peer-Monitored Lending'. *Journal of Development Economics*, 60(1), 51–77.

—— (2000). 'Monitoring by Delegates or by Peers? Joint Liability Loans under Moral Hazard'. *Working Paper*. New York: Department of Economics, Hunter College.

—— and M. Kevane (2002). 'Community-Based Targeting Mechanisms for Social Safety Nets: A Critical Review'. *World Development*, 30(3), 375–94.

de Soto, H. (2000). *The Mystery of Capital: Why Capitalism Succeeds in the West and Fails Almost Everywhere Else*. New York: Basic Books.

Demirgüç-Kunt, A. and R. Levine (2001). *Financial Structure and Economic Growth: A Cross-Country Comparison of Banks, Markets, and Development*. Cambridge, MA: MIT Press.

Dercon, S. and P. Krishnan (2000). 'In Sickness and in Health: Risk Sharing within Households in Rural Ethiopia'. *Journal of Political Economy*, 108(4), 688–727.

Development Alternatives Inc. (2002). *DAI Credit Bureau Initiatives*. Bethesda, MD: Development Alternatives Inc.

Diamond, D. W. (1984). 'Financial Intermediation and Delegated Monitoring'. *Review of Economic Studies*, 51(3), 393–414.

—— (1996). 'Financial Intermediation as Delegated Monitoring: A Simple Example'. *Federal Reserve Bank of Richmond Economic Quarterly*, 82(3), 51–66.

Fafchamps, M. (1996). 'Risk Sharing, Quasi Credit, and the Enforcement of Informal Contracts', mimeo, Department of Economics, Stanford University.

—— (1997). 'Trade Credit in Zimbabwean Manufacturing'. *World Development*, 25(5), 795–815.

—— (2000). 'Ethnicity and Credit in African Manufacturing'. *Journal of Development Economics*, 61(1), 205–35.

Field, E. (2002). 'Entitled to Work: Urban Property Rights and Labor Supply in Peru'. *Working Paper*. Princeton, NJ: Department of Economics, Princeton University.

Gelbach, J. B. and L. Pritchett (1997). 'More for the Poor is Less for the Poor: The Politics of Targeting'. *Policy Research Working Paper* No. 1799.26. Washington, DC: Development Research Group, Poverty and Human Resources, World Bank.

Gilbert, C. (1999). 'Commodity Risk Management', mimeo, Department of Finance and Financial Sector Management, Vrije Universiteit, Amsterdam.

Goldstein, M. P. (2000). 'Intrahousehold Allocation and Farming in Southern Ghana'. Ph.D. thesis, University of California, Berkeley, CA.

Grimard, F. (1997). 'Household Consumption Smoothing through Ethnic Ties: Evidence from Côte D'Ivoire'. *Journal of Development Economics*, 53(2), 391–422.

Holmstrom, B. (1979). 'Moral Hazard and Observability'. *Bell Journal of Economics*, 10(1), 74–91.

—— (1996). 'Financing of Investment in Eastern Europe: A Theoretical Perspective'. *Industrial and Corporate Change*, 5(2), 205–37.

—— and P. Milgrom (1990). 'Regulating Trade among Agents'. *Journal of Institutional and Theoretical Economics*, 146(1), 85–105.

—— and J. Tirole (1997). 'Financial Intermediation, Loanable Funds, and the Real Sector'. *Quarterly Journal of Economics*, 112(3), 663–91.

Hoshi, T., D. Scharfstein, and A. K. Kashyap (1993). 'The Choice between Public and Private Debt: An Analysis of Post-Deregulation Corporate Financing in Japan'. *NBER Working Paper* No. 4421. Cambridge, MA: NBER.

Itoh, H. (1993). 'Coalitions, Incentives, and Risk Sharing'. *Journal of Economic Theory*, 60(2), 410–27.

Kimball, M. (1988). 'Farmer Cooperatives as Behavior Toward Risk'. *American Economic Review*, 78, 224–32.

Klein, D. (1992). 'Promise Keeping in the Great Society: A Model of Credit Information Sharing'. *Economics and Politics*, 4(2), 117–36.

Kranton, R. and A. Swamy (1999). 'The Hazards of Piecemeal Reform: British Civil Courts and the Credit Market in Colonial India'. *Journal of Developmental Economics*, 58(1), 1–24.

Laffont, J.-J. and J. Tirole (1993). *A Theory of Incentives in Procurement and Regulation*. Cambridge, MA: MIT Press.

Lapenu, C. and M. Zeller (2001). *Distribution, Growth, and Performance of Microfinance Institutions in Africa, Asia, and Latin America*. Washington, DC: International Food Policy Research Institute.

Laux, C. (2001). 'Limited-Liability and Incentive Contracting with Multiple Projects'. *RAND Journal of Economics*, 32(3), 514–26.

Levine, R. (2001). 'International Financial Liberalization and Economic Growth'. *Review of International Economics*, 9(4), 688–702.

——, N. Loayza, and T. Beck (2000). 'Financial Intermediation and Growth: Causality and Causes'. *Journal of Monetary Economics*, 46(1), 31–77.

Levitsky, J. (1997). 'Credit Guarantees Schemes for SMEs—An International Review'. *Small Enterprise Development*, 8(2), 4–17.

Ligon, E., J. P. Thomas, and T. Worall (1999). 'Mutual Insurance with Limited Commitment: Theory and Evidence from Village Economies'. *Working Paper*. Berkeley, CA: University of California.

McKinnon, R. (1973). *Money and Capital in Economic Development*. Washington, DC: Brookings Institution.

Meagher, P. and B. Wilkinson (2001). 'Filling the Gap in South Africa's Small and Micro Credit Market: An Analysis of Major Policy, Legal, and Regulatory Issues'. Report submitted to the Microfinance Regulatory Council of South Africa. IRIS Center, University of Maryland.

MkNelly, B. and M. Kevane (2001). 'Improving Design and Performance of Group Lending: Suggestions from Burkina Faso'. *World Development*, 30(11), 2017–32.

Mookherjee, D. (1984). 'Optimal Incentive Schemes with Many Agents'. *Review of Economic Studies*, 51(3), 433–46.

Morduch, J. (1995). 'Income Smoothing and Consumption Smoothing'. *Journal of Economic Perspectives*, 9(3), 103–14.

—— (1999). 'Between the State and the Market: Can Informal Insurance Patch the Safety Net?' *World Bank Research Observer*, 14(2), 187–207.

Nelson, E. (1999). 'Financial Intermediation for the Poor: Survey of the State of the Art'. *African Economic Policy Discussion Paper* No. 10. Bethesda, MD: Development Alternatives Inc.

Platteau, J. P. (2000). 'Community Imperfections'. Paper prepared for the Annual Bank Conference on Development Economics. Centre de Recherche en Economie du Développement (CRED), Department of Economics, University of Namur.

Prescott, E. S. and R. M. Townsend (2002). 'Collective Organizations versus Relative Performance Contracts: Inequality, Risk Sharing and Moral Hazard'. *Journal of Economic Theory*, 103, 283–310.

Schreiner, M. (2002). *Scoring: The Next Breakthrough in Microcredit?* Washington, DC: Consultative Group to Assist the Poorest, World Bank.

Scott, J. C. (1976). *The Moral Economy of the Peasant: Rebellion and Subsistence in Southeast Asia*. New Haven, CT: Yale University Press.

Sen, A. (1995). 'The Political Economy of Targeting', in D van de Walle (ed.), *Public Spending and the Poor: Theory and Evidence*. Baltimore, MD: Johns Hopkins University Press.

Skully, M. (1994). 'The Development of the Pawnshop Industry in East Asia', in F. J. A. Baumann and O. Hospes (eds), *Financial Landscapes Reconstructed: The Fine Art of Mapping Development.* Boulder, CO: Westview Press.

Stiglitz, J. E. (1990). 'Peer Monitoring and Credit Markets'. *World Bank Economic Review*, 4(3), 351–66.

Tirole, J. (1992). 'Collusion and the Theory of Organizations', in J. J. Laffont (ed.), *Advances in Economic Theory: Sixth World Congress*, Vol. 2. Econometric Society Monographs No. 21 Cambridge: Cambridge University Press.

Townsend, R. M. (1994). 'Risk and Insurance in Village India'. *Econometrica*, 62(3), 539–91.

Udry, C. (1994). 'Risk and Insurance in a Rural Credit Market: An Empirical Investigation in Northern Nigeria'. *Review of Economic Studies*, 61(3), 495–526.

—— (1996). 'Gender, Agricultural Production, and the Theory of the Household'. *Journal of Political Economy*, 104(5), 1010–46.

Varian, H. R. (1990). 'Monitoring Agents with Other Agents'. *Journal of Institutional and Theoretical Economics*, 146(1), 153–74.

PART VII

DEVELOPING BETTER PROTECTION FOR THE POOR

16

Can Food-for-Work Programmes Reduce Vulnerability?

CHRISTOPHER B. BARRETT, STEIN HOLDEN,
AND DANIEL C. CLAY

Food-for-work (FFW) programmes are widely touted for their capacity to target poor populations effectively with a reliable safety net, thereby reducing vulnerability due to downside risk exposure, while simultaneously investing in the production or maintenance of valuable public goods necessary to stimulate productivity and thus growth in aggregate incomes. The empirical evidence is mixed, however, as to the efficacy of FFW in any of these dimensions. Proponents cite cases in which FFW appears to have performed as intended, while opponents present evidence of its failures. The development community needs to guard against uncritical acceptance of either naive or hostile claims about FFW and to develop a better understanding of how, when, and why FFW programmes can indeed reduce vulnerability. This chapter aims to advance such an understanding.

There exist two distinct, important layers to the question of FFW's efficacy. First, there is the short-run question of whether FFW effectively cushions people who suffer transitory income shocks. Does FFW, as a mechanism for emergency relief, provide an effective safety net, mitigating the adverse welfare effects of adverse real income shocks, especially those suffered by persons beneath or near the poverty line? The answer here turns largely on targeting and timing. In order to provide effective insurance, FFW has to reach those who suffer serious shocks quickly, before serious undernourishment and associated health problems set in. Yet transitory hunger associated with short-term crises represents a relatively small share of hunger worldwide, with estimates ranging 10–25 per cent (Speth 1993; Barrett 2002). Most malnutrition in the world arises due to chronic deprivation and vulnerability. So insofar as FFW is often aimed, instead, at relieving chronic deprivation and vulnerability, insurance against transitory income shocks may not always be the appropriate benchmark against which to evaluate FFW.

This leads naturally to the second, longer-run question of whether FFW, as an instrument for development, improves livelihoods, either by accelerating recovery

We thank Abdillahi Aboud, Mesfin Bezuneh, Stefan Dercon, Fitsum Hagos, Kevin Heisey, Robin Jackson, Peter Little, Dan Maxwell, John McPeak, Daniel Molla, David Pottebaum, Bekele Shiferaw, and Patrick Webb for past collaborations and conversations on which this work draws as well as for constructive comments on an earlier draft. All remaining errors are ours.

from shocks—as in the case of post-conflict rehabilitation—or by fostering income growth and wealth accumulation among the chronically destitute. Does or can FFW facilitate investment, innovation, and access to new, attractive opportunities?

If the former function is commonly thought of as a safety net to catch those who are falling, the latter function is akin to a cargo net. People can either climb up it or be lifted up by it. The two functions can obviously be effectively linked, as when an effective safety net obviates beneficiaries' need to liquidate productive assets so as to finance essential current consumption, thereby enabling them to resume productive activities soon after the emergency ends and to climb quickly back out of poverty. There is also the less attractive possibility of people becoming ensnared in the safety net, when the relief function undermines the development function by diverting resources. The central questions about FFW are therefore whether it helps individuals, households, and communities in times of stress and whether it (also) facilitates the desired transition from relief to development, that is, whether FFW reduces vulnerability in the short-term, the long-term, both, or neither.

We try to get at this core question through review of our own and others' work on FFW, drawing mainly on empirical evidence from sub-Saharan Africa, especially Ethiopia and Kenya. FFW programmes have been active elsewhere in the developing world, especially in South and Southeast Asia. But the basic features and issues are the same worldwide and we focus on those geographic areas from whence we know the evidence best. We begin by reviewing the context that has given rise to rapid diffusion of FFW schemes in low-income areas around the world and the simple theory that makes it so conceptually appealing. We illustrate the potential with examples of FFW successes. Then we identify conceptual problems with the simple theory of FFW, likewise illustrating these points with empirical evidence of failures. The concluding section draws out the core lessons to be learned.

16.1. THE APPEAL OF FOOD-FOR-WORK: A SIMPLE THEORY AND SOME EVIDENCE

FFW has become increasingly popular over the past decade, especially in sub-Saharan Africa (Devereux 1999; von Braun et al. 1999). The government of Ethiopia, for example, has expressed a commitment to channel 80 per cent of its food assistance resources to FFW programmes (FDRE 1996). Several trends have jointly contributed to food-for-work's sharp growth in popularity over the past generation. These merit brief review.

First, at least since Sen's (1981) seminal work two decades ago, policymakers and researchers have come to understand hunger as being largely determined by individuals' capacity to maintain access to sufficient food to maintain good nutrition, and thereby good health, and much less as a function of local food supply shocks than had been previously believed. Partly as a consequence, FFW schemes have blossomed as regular transfer programmes in chronic food deficit regions as a means of ensuring access to food. Second, in both domestic and international poverty interventions, broad-based concern has emerged about offering benefits without requiring programme participants to work, leading to a gradual shift from transfers to workfare programmes worldwide. Third, increasing distrust of central government and belief in the subsidiarity principle[1] have fuelled decentralization efforts in myriad public activities. Fourth, the end of the Cold War and growing dissatisfaction with foreign aid have led to a sharp decline in development assistance and a rapid rise in the share of overseas aid consumed by emergencies (Barrett and Carter 2001), although some 'emergencies' prove relatively permanent, as in the Greater Horn of Africa region on which we concentrate. Declining foreign assistance volumes have made cash resources increasingly scarce; food is now often the most readily available form of assistance to international charities and developing country governments.

Together, these trends have given rise to 'developmental food aid', of which food-for-work is a primary modality. In essence, FFW aims (i) to provide participants with at least the minimum essential quantity of food necessary to maintain good nutrition, (ii) to require work in exchange for this benefit, (iii) to reduce or decentralize both the targeting of beneficiaries and the prioritization and management of public works projects, and (iv) to harness the few resources available, in the form in which they are available (food), to try to maintain a modicum of development activity in the face of overwhelming relief demands. Among relief and development practitioners, one hears plenty of loose ideas as to how and why FFW should, or does, work. From these, one can fashion a simple, informal theory of FFW that runs as follows.

Assume all individuals consider leisure a normal good (i.e. demand for leisure increases with income), that the opportunity cost of time—as reflected by one's wage or salary rate, for example—likewise increases with income, and that everyone faces the same market prices for food, capital, land, and other goods and services. Under these assumptions, an unrestricted offer of employment at a low wage rate should be self-targeting in the sense that the characteristics of the transfer suffice to create incentives for participation that vary across individuals. In particular, because the cost of participation is made an increasing function of one's pre-participation income or wealth, only the needy should find project participation attractive, even absent any administrative restrictions on programme participation.

By creating demand for otherwise unemployed or underemployed labour, FFW provides an income transfer to such persons. This is the first sense in which FFW serves short-term relief objectives. This familiar, Keynesian function can be important even in the absence of shocks, for example, by smoothing out seasonal fluctuations in labour demand, and therefore wage rates, in rural areas where rainfall patterns and insufficient irrigation preclude year-round crop cultivation.

The open-ended nature of the programme provides insurance against transitory income shocks through the guarantee of a minimum income to all who are willing to work. So for people who lose their jobs, suffer crop failure or livestock loss on their own farms, or otherwise face a sudden decrease in labour productivity and thus income and welfare, FFW offers a plausible safety net. This is the second sense in which FFW

---

[1] The principle of subsidiarity stipulates that authority and responsibility for actions be devolved to the lowest level capable of undertaking them effectively.

has short-term relief objectives. It provides transfers equal to the difference between the (unobserved) next-best option for self-selected programme participants that can be accessed on short notice. Such insurance is especially important for those lacking access to liquid savings or to credit, that is, to most of the rural poor in the world. Absent such insurance, their response to significant transitory income shocks typically involves coping behaviours such as migration, sale of productive assets such as land or livestock, or sharp reduction in consumption of food or health services. These strategies often compromise one's future income prospects, thereby turning what might otherwise be a transitory income shock into a permanent one. Such phenomena give rise to stochastic poverty traps and chronic destitution (McPeak and Barrett 2001; Barrett 2002). Moreover, when agricultural labour productivity falls, small farmers often reallocate labour to activities that adversely affect the natural environment, such as deforestation, wildlife poaching, and soil nutrient mining (Barrett and Arcese 1998; Barrett 1999; Barrett *et al.* 2002). Providing back-up employment to absorb transitorily surplus labour before it generates negative environmental externalities safeguards community assets. This is the first sense in which FFW has a long-term role as a cargo net; people may fall, but they can climb back up without injuring others if insurance in the form of fallback employment is available.

The second sense in which FFW can serve long-term development objectives is similarly linked to its (first) short-run function. By providing predictable transfers, FFW can obviate binding seasonal liquidity constraints. Many small farmers around the world run short of the cash necessary to purchase food, pay hired workers, and purchase inputs in the planting and growing season, popularly termed the 'hungry' season in many areas. The marginal cost of capital can be quite high, sufficient to preclude purchase of high-return inputs such as chemical fertilizer or investment in capital improvements such as improved soil and water conservation structures or labour-intensive cultivation practices exhibiting sharply increased expected crop yields (Moser and Barrett 2001; Barrett *et al.* 2002).

In theory, the self-targeting feature of FFW reduces administrative targeting expenses, thereby allowing not only a higher rate of programme participation, but also greater expenditure on materials that, when combined with the labour elicited by the FFW programme, produce durable assets of value to the community. Insofar as capital scarcity limits the productivity of the poor, production of public capital goods such as roads, natural resources, schools, and health clinics can increase the future income prospects of all community members, FFW programme participants and non-participants alike. The creation of capital goods though FFW programmes is the second potential long-term benefit of FFW; like a cargo net, it can prospectively lift the poor out of poverty.

Some conjecture that collective investment in public goods through FFW programmes may also strengthen community ties and thereby build valuable social capital. Scholars of community development describe collective action, along with trust, reciprocity, and effective networks, as fundamental to the generation of social capital essential to the production and maintenance of public goods (Flora 1997). Flora concludes that the most successful mobilization of collective action will occur when participation is diverse and inclusive, suggesting a silver lining to targeting errors that result in beneficiary diversity. Indeed, as Sharp (1997) reports in her review of food aid targeting in Ethiopia, many communities consciously invite participation from needy as well as non-needy households in their FFW programmes in the interest of developing greater community ownership and commitment.

The preceding logic describes workfare programmes of all types (Clay 1986; Ravallion 1991, 1999; Besley and Coate 1992; von Braun 1995). FFW programmes are effectively workfare with a specific form of payment: food. One of the central questions about FFW's efficacy thus turns on the appropriateness of payment in kind.

There are two conditions under which food seems a desirable form of payment from the beneficiaries' viewpoint.[2] First, where hyperinflation prevails, food can be a very effective payment medium since it retains its real value in the face of rapidly changing nominal prices. Second, by explicitly interlinking labour and food markets, FFW may reduce transaction costs where food markets perform relatively poorly, thereby increasing access to food (Holden and Shanmugaratnam 1995; Holden and Binswanger 1998). This latter condition is most likely to hold in food deficit regions where spatial arbitrage occurs slowly, at best, in response to local increases in demand. In such settings, cash wages may increase food availability for programme participants less than it fuels nominal food price increases—rather than increased food supply— with the dual effect of failing to provide significant net transfers to participants and adversely affecting non-participants locally. Such spillover damages will mostly hurt poorer non-participants because they typically spend a larger share of income on food than do wealthier non-participants. Errors of exclusion of the poor—which we discuss in detail below—are especially damaging if the programme design fuels local food price rises. Payment in food, by contrast, ensures labourers' ability to replenish the energy expended in work without hurting non-participants. So where food markets function poorly and significant numbers of poor people do not participate in public employment schemes, FFW may be a far more pro-poor design than cash for work.

It should also be pointed out that if the food is purchased locally, then the extra local demand stimulus benefits net food sellers in the area.[3] If the food is imported from outside the area—FFW programmes are commonly supplied through international food aid—then FFW distribution almost surely displaces some local purchases, thereby depressing local prices and creating adverse supply disincentives for local farmers. Nonetheless, the trucks that haul food in typically do not return empty, so the additional backhaul transport supply fostered by imported food can provide a *de facto* marketing subsidy to farmers and others who export product from the region, thereby mitigating whatever adverse local food market effects result from FFW

---

[2] Food may be the preferred transfer medium from donors' viewpoint because they wish to stimulate food consumption, whether for commercial or impurely altruistic reasons (Barrett 2002). We ignore those considerations.

[3] We use the term 'net food sellers' rather than 'food producers' in recognition of the fact that a large share of small food producers in the low-income world are net food buyers. Although farming is their primary activity, meagre endowments of land and capital and rudimentary production technologies conspire to leave them unable to meet their own household food demands (Barrett and Dorosh 1996; Weber *et al.* 1988).

distributions. Moreover, induced food price reductions benefit food buyers, especially poorer non-participants because they typically spend a larger share of income on food than do wealthier non-participants.

Whether FFW works as popularly theorized is, of course, an empirical question, and one that has not yet been thoroughly and adequately answered. The simple theory just outlined points to five key testable hypotheses related to:

(i) targeting efficacy—including timing of deliveries—because targeting deter-mines both whether FFW indeed proves a pro-poor transfer, as intended, and, derivatively, the extent of any adverse local producer price effects due to substitution for commercially purchased food;

(ii) the extent to which accurately timed and targeted FFW transfers prove suf-ficient to pre-empt potentially injurious coping behaviours, including liquida-tion of productive assets, long-distance migration, and sharply reduced food consumption that increases the risk of irreversible injury, illness, or death;

(iii) FFW's impact in relieving binding working capital constraints and thereby stimulating participant investment or adoption of improved technologies;

(iv) whether FFW in fact produces durable public goods of value to local communities, which can include not only physical infrastructure, but also a tradition of cooperative activity and development of local leadership and management skills; and

(v) whether or not imported foodstuffs relieve transport bottlenecks, thereby reducing marketing costs for local exporters through a *de facto* transport subsidy.

As yet, there is insufficient empirical evidence on these five hypotheses to be able to make any global statements as to the efficacy of FFW interventions. Sufficient evidence exists, however, to be able to draw provisional conclusions on some of the points, particularly those regarding hypotheses (i), (iii), and (iv). We therefore focus hereafter on those points especially.

16.1.1. *FFW Commonly Generates Pro-poor Transfers*

The workfare literature more generally, including the sub-literature on FFW, finds strong pro-poor effects of public employment programmes, even once one takes the opportunity cost of participants' foregone private employment earnings into consideration. Previous empirical research has found significant pro-poor transfers resulting from employment guarantee schemes in Argentina, Bangladesh, India, Niger, South Africa, and Zimbabwe, among others, as reflected by probabilities of or net trans-fers from participation that decline in income or wealth (Dev 1995; von Braun 1995; Webb 1995; Subbarao 1997; Clay *et al.* 1998; Ravallion 1999; Atwood *et al.* 2000; Haddad and Adato 2001; Jalan and Ravallion 2001). Part of this success appears to be due to the self-targeting feature of these schemes. Part may also arise due to the decentralization inherent to public employment programmes. If local officials have superior access to information regarding prospective participants' welfare, devolution of targeting authority to local levels may well result in better targeting than could be expected on the basis of proxy indicators typically used by central governments (Alderman 2002).

Transfers in the form of food also work well in areas where the cash economy is a man's world while food is the responsibility of women, no matter who procures it. In such cultural settings and if intrahousehold resource competition exists, then food may be a more effective medium than cash for indirect targeting of transfers to needy beneficiaries, particularly children. This matters in many areas, especially where cultural morals dictate that distributions are almost always to men, as in some Islamic communities familiar to us in the Greater Horn of Africa.

16.1.2. *FFW Relieves Liquidity Constraints*

The need for public provision of insurance services, whether through FFW or other means, arises directly from financial markets failures. So part of any salutary effect of FFW transfers should come from their impact on participants' financial liquidity. By reducing households' need to purchase food—and often providing cash indirectly through food that beneficiaries subsequently sell—FFW indeed seems to help foster greater net investment in other productive assets than might otherwise occur, whether in natural capital through new soil conservation investments (Barrett *et al.* 2002) or adoption of improved inputs or production technologies (von Braun 1995; Bezuneh *et al.* 1988). The effect may be subtle, appearing not as increased investment, but rather as reduced disinvestment, whether of valuable natural capital through erosion-inducing deforestation (Barrett 1999) or sale of high return assets, such as livestock, to meet short-term cash requirements for food, medicines, or school fees (Barrett *et al.* 2001). The clear indication of FFW's effect on relieving binding constraints is that the income gains associated with participation exceed the value of the food received, signalling that binding liquidity or subsistence constraints otherwise restricted participants' livelihood choice, as seems to have been true in lower Baringo District, Kenya (Barrett *et al.* 2001). FFW may not be a first-best transfer where cash transfers a feasible alternative (it typically is not politically feasible). Yet, FFW provides a transfer, thereby relieving these constraints and permitting improved livelihoods.

16.1.3. *FFW Projects can Produce Valuable Public Goods*

Ethiopia has the largest FFW programme in Africa, the vast majority of which has been channelled into investment in natural resource conservation and road building. Although there are ample cases of failed projects—more on this below—it is equally true that some projects have generated public goods of lasting value. For example, von Braun *et al.* (1999) report on the multiplier effects of an FFW-built road in the Ethiopian lowlands, where improved market access directly attributable to that road led to the establishment of water mills and fruit plantations and the revival of traditional cotton spinning and weaving in the three years after the road was built. Well-conceived and managed FFW projects that invest in necessary materials to complement labour inputs clearly can 'crowd in' private investment, just as proponents claim.

16.2. PROBLEMS WITH THE SIMPLE THEORY AND SOME EVIDENCE

In spite of clear signs of some successes with FFW, their efficacy has come under increased scrutiny of late as evidence on programme shortcomings accumulates. Beyond providing a helpful reminder that FFW is not a cure-all for vulnerability in the developing world, this evidence helps reveal problems with the simple theory sketched out in the previous section. A more qualified understanding of how FFW operates in the complex settings in which it is deployed can help identify contexts in which it is most likely to prove helpful. The next section addresses those lessons learned. First we examine a series of problems identifiable in the simple theory of FFW.

16.2.1. *Targeting Errors*

While the empirical evidence largely supports the claim that FFW—and self-targeting employment schemes more broadly—generates pro-poor distributions, as discussed earlier, targeting errors can nonetheless be great. One can usefully identify two distinct types of targeting errors: errors of inclusion, wherein benefits are enjoyed by unintended participants, and errors of exclusion, related to target subpopulations' failure to participate. A central problem in project evaluation and the scholarly literature surrounding workfare and FFW programmes stems from the conflation of *ex ante* poverty with the experience of transitory real income shocks. FFW programmes can provide regular, in-kind transfers to poor, food-deficit populations, provide insurance to those suffering short-term welfare shocks, or both. With surprisingly few exceptions (see Dercon and Krishnan 2001), little attention has been paid to targeting efficacy as it relates to the consumption smoothing rather than the poverty reducing effects of FFW. Since most donors and analysts are interested in the efficacy of the insurance function primarily, if not exclusively, as it relates to the poor, the distinction is perhaps not of great importance to most readers. But it is nonetheless worth keeping in mind that finding any transfer programme—be it FFW or some other form—reaches the poor is not the same as finding that it effectively insures against real income shocks, nor vice versa. It is important to have the true objectives of the programme firmly in mind before embarking on analysis of targeting efficacy.

First, we consider the problem of errors of inclusion. Several recent studies have found evidence that many non-poor participate in FFW schemes (Clay *et al.* 1999; Devereux 1999; Jayne *et al.* 1999; Teklu and Asefa 1999; Gebremedhin and Swinton 2001). One common explanation of errors of inclusion is that the FFW wages were set too high, inducing substitution of money wage work in the local labour market for FFW work, and thereby limiting the additionality of the FFW transfer since it largely substitutes for other income that would have been earned in the project's absence (Ravallion *et al.* 1993; von Braun 1995; Teklu and Asefa 1999). Moreover, when wages are set too high, project managers commonly face excess labour supply and have to ration participation in some fashion. There are good reasons to believe that local elites enjoy a higher probability of selection for participation than do outcasts.[4]

Perhaps the most discouraging form of errors of inclusion relate to ghost workers. Unfortunately, FFW programmes (and public employment schemes more generally), have a checkered history of fraud and waste due to lack of enforcement of work requirements under the programme. Project monitoring and evaluation efforts in various countries in Africa and Asia have commonly uncovered evidence of significant numbers of ghost workers who were paid for a day's labour but who never actually reported to work, of idle-but-present workers, and of work days only half the length of the agreed labour requirement.

Errors of exclusion are intrinsically related to errors of inclusion. In some cases this is because intended recipients get crowded out by participating elites. Other times, finite transfer resources limit the geographic reach of the programme to a few administratively selected locations (Devereux 1999; Gebremedhin and Swinton 2001). The common feature of these explanations of the targeting deficiencies of FFW is the suggestion that targeting errors can be corrected by a change in operational methods: a lower FFW wage, closer auditing of employment roles, a larger budget to expand geographic coverage, and so on.

The evidence suggests, however, that errors of exclusion and inclusion in FFW targeting are due at least as much to structural issues as to operational details. For example, results from a study of food aid targeting in Ethiopia in 1995/6 (Clay *et al.* 1999) provide empirical confirmation for a growing body of anecdotal evidence reported by Sharp (1997) demonstrating the frequent inability of Ethiopia's food aid system to target the most needy populations, despite its heavy reliance on FFW.[5] Clay *et al.* (1999) examine the food aid receipts of 4218 rural households in 1995/6 and conclude that food aid targeting exhibits high errors of exclusion and inclusion at both the *wereda* (district) and household levels.[6] The primary beneficiaries of food aid programmes, including FFW, were found to be households at the extremes in terms of *ex ante* food availability: those with the least and those with the most.

---

[4] Herring and Edwards (1993) tell an interesting story of manipulation and corruption that arise due to the many different opportunities for local FFW managers to exercise discretion (e.g. over project duration, location, wage rates, payment terms, and so on) and how this may affect participation profiles, even in a seemingly successful programme like Maharashtra's Employment Guarantee Scheme.

[5] Sharp (1997) provides an excellent, broad-based discussion of food aid targeting in Ethiopia and the circumstances under which different methods appear to be relatively more or less successful, based on case studies of various food aid programmes and projects implemented in Ethiopia over the past several years.

[6] These household data derive principally from the Food Security Survey, implemented in June 1996 by the Grain Market Research Project in collaboration with the Ethiopia Central Statistical Authority (CSA). The sample was randomly drawn as a subset of the CSA's annual agricultural survey. As such, it is a nationally representative sample of rural, agriculturally based households. The survey addressed a broad array of grain marketing and food security issues including: grain production and marketing, food aid use, impacts of food aid programme participation, landownership and use, household labour and demographics, and various farming practices. It also elicited households' willingness to participate in FFW programmes under various payment terms.

Several factors account for the high level of targeting error in the Ethiopian case. First, a disproportionate number of female and aged heads of households receive food aid, irrespective of their food needs. Indicator targeting is an established method in the absence of detailed information on prospective recipients' need and resources, but it commonly leads to significant targeting errors nonetheless (Barrett 2002).

Second, FFW can only assist those physically able to work. Since physical disability is strongly, positively correlated with poverty and vulnerability in the low-income world, FFW by construction cannot serve all the poor. As long as the proportion of the poor who are able-bodied is reasonably large, this is not a serious constraint. In some places, especially in sub-Saharan Africa, work requirements pose an increasing challenge to reaching the poor because of the HIV/AIDS pandemic. As more able-bodied adults fall prey to the disease or need to devote considerable time at home to caring for sick loved ones, this problem is exploding. By sharply increasing the population of poor people unable to work, HIV/AIDS is reducing the potential scope of FFW as both a safety net and as a development intervention. The same is true in post-conflict settings where many of the needy are amputees, blinded, or otherwise permanently incapacitated by the war and where many households are now headed by widows. In Cambodia, the country with the world's highest proportion of population with amputations, errors of omission have proved to be extremely large in FFW projects because the injured and widows typically are unable or unwilling to participate (personal communication with David Pottebaum).

Third, the accuracy of the self-targeting component of food-for-work schemes may be fundamentally limited by factor market failures affecting the nature of local labour supply in low-income agrarian settings. Factor markets in land, labour, and capital are often incomplete in poor, rural economies, so labour and cultivable land does not necessarily move freely between households so as to equalize (quality-adjusted) land/labour ratios. Therefore household reservation FFW wage rates—the threshold wage that induces self-selection into the programme—need not be strongly, inversely related to household pre-transfer income unconditionally, as the conventional wisdom assumes, but rather may increase with income only conditional on other structural factors—in particular, the composition of households' productive asset endowments—that influence shadow wage rates. Barrett and Clay (2003) demonstrate this in the 1995/96 Ethiopia data, showing that elicited reservation wages—which are unrelated to operational details such as programme wage rates or administrative selection criteria—have no significant unconditional relationship to income, but a strong relationship once one controls for (imperfectly tradable) productive asset holdings. The poor are too often assumed to be more 'labour rich' than those with higher incomes. In many settings, this is not true. As a consequence, lowering wage rates induces self-selection out of the programme by the poor. Barrett and Clay (2003) report that even at a daily wage of five kg of wheat—which is higher than the norm in FFW programmes in Ethiopia— nearly half of the lowest income quintile self-selects out of FFW programmes. Many of Ethiopia's able-bodied poor appear to have better uses for their time than participation in low-wage FFW programmes. Yet, raising FFW wages both reduces the number of prospective beneficiaries, due to the budget constraint, and induces increased errors of inclusion. Barrett and Clay (2003) find that the participation probability of a household with income equal to twice the sample median is at least 80 per cent of the participation probability of a household in the lowest decile no matter the FFW wage rate. The tradeoffs between errors of exclusion and errors of inclusion in FFW programmes appear considerable.

Female-headed households are commonly more labour constrained and thus less able or willing to participate in FFW projects, especially those requiring a high minimum level of effort. Although evidence from Bangladesh and India show high female participation rates in employment guarantee schemes in general and FFW projects in particular (von Braun 1995), evidence from elsewhere finds women often miss out on these opportunities (Clay *et al.* 1998; Barrett and Clay 2003). The archetypal case concerns widows with young children. These households commonly have incomes well below the mean but effective labour availability that is even lower.

Fourth, inertia in the food aid delivery system seems to impede its ability to reach households outside of historically deficit areas (Jayne *et al.* 1999, 2001).[7] Regular, in-kind transfers into chronically food deficit areas may be effective as poverty reduction efforts and maintenance of some low level of ongoing activity in areas prone to recurring crises may help donors 'ramp up' in years when need becomes acute. Nevertheless, FFW projects developed legitimately in crisis years have been shown to build momentum that sustains them even during peaceful times and relatively good harvest years. In Ethiopia, for example, one of the strongest determinants of household level food aid receipts is the number of years in the past that communities and households within these communities have received such assistance, independent of the actual need for food in these communities/households (Clay *et al.* 1999; Jayne *et al.* 1999).

It may be that inertia-related targeting errors reflect authorities' redistributive objectives, which may be unrelated to need. Political economy considerations certainly account for a significant share of targeting errors of food distribution at the level of nation states (Barrett 1998, 2001), and surely play a role within countries and communities as well.

It is also likely that inertia can be at least partly attributed to the progressive build-up of institutional capacity in the food aid delivery system over time, notably the investments made by government agencies and NGOs in such things as personnel, contacts, and knowledge of the area, offices, trucks, and institutional reputation. Because of the tremendous flow and momentum built up in the food aid delivery system, altering its course to meet the needs of deficit households in other areas that may not benefit from the same extent of infrastructure and institutionalization, has become a formidable challenge. Given significant sunk costs to food distribution, it may be optimal to limit flexibility to respond to intertemporal changes in need across locations, or even households within a location. It may simply be too expensive to respond to fluctuating needs accurately and promptly. Oftentimes, however, the field staff expert in the

---

[7] Similar inertia is observable in food aid flows at the more aggregate level of individual nations (Barrett 1998, 2001; Barrett and Heisey 2002).

logistics of food distribution, who are essential to run a good short-term safety net operation, remain in place over the longer term and must try to make themselves over as development experts, a process that unsurprisingly often fails.

In some cases, national governments, participating donor organizations, and the NGOs charged with implementing food aid programmes, have sought to legitimize inertia in food aid programming by reengineering programmes originally implemented for purposes of emergency relief into instruments of 'development'. The emergence of FFW programmes in Ethiopia since the 1984/5 drought seems to demonstrate this evolution most aptly. Ethiopia's National Policy on Disaster Prevention and Management (NPDPM) now states that disaster relief should ensure adequate income transfer for disaster affected households, promote self-reliance among beneficiaries, preserve assets to promote speedy recovery, be geared to eliminate the root causes of disaster vulnerability, and contribute to sustainable development (Transitional Government of Ethiopia 1993*a*, *b*). Any one of those aspirations poses serious challenges. Meeting them all is a tall order indeed.

16.2.2. *Timing Errors*

The timing of food provision is an oft-overlooked element of targeting. FFW must be available quickly in response to adverse shocks if it is to function effectively as a safety net, in particular, for it to kick in before beneficiaries are forced to divest themselves of productive assets in their quest to meet current consumption needs. Rapid response depends on getting the administrative and logistical machinery for food distribution in place early. This is another sense in which inertia may be beneficial, although Botswana's successful experiences with FFW projects that expand and contract radically in response to need indicate that administrative capacity is the key, not ongoing FFW programmes (von Braun *et al.* 1999). Nonetheless, inertia in food aid distribution likely helps explain the relatively good performance of FFW programmes in Tigray during the 2000 drought, for they were in place and functional before the rains fell.

The capacity to launch new FFW programmes or to expand existing ones in response to shocks depends on the availability of food in emergency response systems, whether by virtue of advanced positioning of food stocks, as in strategic grain reserves, or by prompt requisition and delivery of food aid in response to early warnings systems, as has occurred in southern Africa during the last two El Niño events. Failure to ensure sufficient supply in emergency distribution channels can lead to serious delays, as has been routinely a problem in Sudan over the past decade. This problem was evident as well in south-eastern Ethiopia during the 2000 drought, when donors upset with the government about the Ethiopia–Eritrea war manifest their displeasure through a delayed and miserly response to an emergency appeal that had been forewarned a year in advance.[8] Food aid in general does not have a track record of timely response

---

[8] A complicating factor in the case of Ethiopia in 2000 is that several recent studies (Clay *et al.* 1999; Jayne *et al.* 1999, 2001) had just highlighted the targeting errors associated with food aid distribution in Ethiopia, which caused donors to question the efficacy of food aid just as the crisis was beginning.

to fluctuating need, although there is evidence that multilateral distribution through the World Food Programme responds reasonably promptly to changing local food production and commercial food import capacity, albeit in modest magnitude due to limited resources (Barrett and Heisey 2002).

Timing matters for at least two reasons. First, untimely food distribution can magnify rather than dampen variability in household dietary energy supply and in local food prices. Unpublished quarterly data collected from 177 pastoralist households in northern Kenya during the devastating 2000 drought indicate that food aid receipts peaked as non-concessional food availability from other sources recovered. Second, disruptions and delays in the provision or distribution of food can undermine participant confidence in the programme—thereby inducing intended beneficiaries to self-select out of FFW—quality of works, or both (Sharp 1997).

16.2.3. *Wages: Flexibility and Form*

We have already discussed how wage rates set too high can induce targeting errors, both by eliciting participation by unintended beneficiaries and by exhausting programme budgets too quickly, thereby leading to errors of exclusion. It is also true, however, that FFW wages must be sufficient to reproduce the physical energy of the labourer. Where private labour demand is weak, prevailing market wage rates may be very low already. Indeed, wage rates for part-time casual labour, especially during the hungry season, may be marginal supplements to households whose average labour productivity is higher due to self-employment on- or off-farm. Under such circumstances, market wage rates may prove insufficient to sustain the health of fully employed FFW labourers.[9] This is of special concern for female programme participants, who may be more likely to share earned rations with family members, especially their children. In a study for CARE in Ethiopia McCaston (1991) found that women on FFW exhibited deteriorating body mass indices—the primary adult anthropometric indicator of nutritional status—because they shared rations calculated so as just to reproduce the worker's energy expenditures.

The other principle issue concerning wages relates to the form of payment. Should workers be paid in food or in cash? Earlier we offered arguments as to when it seems appropriate to pay wages in food. The empirical evidence in favour of payment in kind is limited, however. One issue concerns the extra costs of transport and handling of food, relative to cash wages. Estimates in Bangladesh found that cash wages would reduce total programme costs by 25 per cent compared to food wages (Clay *et al.* 1998). Given binding budget constraints that limit coverage, too often leading to significant errors of exclusion, one must be able to demonstrate that these added costs are worth bearing.

The second issue related to payment form concerns the fungibility premium participants put on cash over food receipts. Barrett and Clay (2003) find that at low wage

---

[9] For example, 3 kg of wheat has been the common daily FFW wage rate in Ethiopia for several years, and is above the market wage rate in many places when food prices are high.

rates, up to the equivalent of 2 kg per day of wheat (less than prevailing market wage rates), households' willingness to participate in FFW projects is invariant to payment form in Ethiopia. Thereafter, however, the premium associated with payment in cash jumps. Above a low threshold, far more people will participate in a programme if the wage is paid in cash rather than its equivalent in food. This premium ranges from 12 to 65 per cent, depending on the wage rate offered. This reflects both the need poor people have for cash for other purposes, such as medicines, school fees, or loan repayments—and the transactions costs they incur selling food to meet these cash requirements—and the errors of inclusion inherent to FFW programmes, wherein food surplus households may be relatively labour rich and therefore willing to work for food wages that merely increase their net sales. Northern Kenyan elders tell us routinely that only 50–80 per cent of received food grain aid is consumed as food. Recipients, they say, use the rest as seed, livestock feed, or to make home brew.[10] Whether FFW is intended as a regular transfer to the chronic poor or as an insurance buffer for those suffering shocks, food is not always the form in which people need most assistance.

16.2.4. *Quality of Public Goods Created*

We previously acknowledged that some FFW projects have been shown to generate valuable public goods. This should not, however, be taken for granted. As any experienced municipal official can attest, production of durable public goods is no simple matter. It takes cooperation within the community, management skills, and significant non-labour inputs. These ingredients are not always available to FFW projects. Where FFW is being used as part of post-conflict rehabilitation, community cooperation can prove especially elusive, as has proved true in Cambodia (Sakko 1999). Since project officers with implementing NGOs are typically selected for their skills at managing food distribution, not at public works project management, necessary human capital is often missing. Moreover, given that one factor driving the rise of FFW has increased the scarcity of non-food resources from donors, finding funds to purchase complementary inputs has grown increasingly difficult for FFW project managers. Finally, there is commonly a tradeoff between locating projects where the need to provide short-term relief in response to shocks or long-term transfers to combat poverty are greatest versus where logistical feasibility (e.g. access to transport infrastructure to deliver food and supplies) and geophysical suitability for resource conservation or road construction projects (Atwood *et al.* 2000; Gebremedhin and Swinton 2001).

As a direct consequence of these factors, the assets created using FFW labour are all too often inappropriate, of poor quality, or not maintained. For example, a review of the Canadian International Development Agency's (CIDA's) FFW programmes in Ethiopia found no evidence of a sustainable long-term increase in household-level

---

[10] In areas of conflict, as in parts of northern Kenya, people would rather hold cash than food because the former is far easier to carry in flight. When people have to evacuate on short notice due to civil strife, they will carry cash but not food rations they have received.

food security due to the assets created by FFW projects, whether due to poor choice, quality, or upkeep of investments (Clay *et al.* 1998). Gebremedhin and Swinton (2001) find evidence of compromises in central Tigray, Ethiopia, 1992–5, with project feasibility typically trumping both needs targeting and expected investment returns in determining project location.

When investments require relatively little in the way of non-labour variable inputs, there may be no tradeoff between the short-run, safety net objective of FFW—to provide insurance to as many people as possible—that depends on employment generation, and the longer run, cargo net objective—to increase incomes and reduce vulnerability—that depends on the efficacy of FFW investments. This has, for example, been an argument used to defend the emphasis placed on construction of soil and water conservation structures in Ethiopian FFW programmes. Indeed, both econometric and simulation results from northern Ethiopia suggest that well-timed FFW projects that invest in soil and water conservation structures both help cushion the poor against yield shocks and induce private investment in land improvements that raise long-term agricultural productivity and incomes (Holden *et al.* 2003).

There is little solid evidence, however, that labour-based methods are either better or worse than equipment-based methods in the construction of public works across the board. In the case of road construction, one of the more common investments of FFW programmes, Stock and DeVeen (1996) conclude that there is broad scope for using labour-based methods. However, the completion time using labour-based methods is often constrained by the availability and willingness of the local labour pool. And even labour-intensive designs commonly need some complementary inputs. In Zimbabwe, insufficient resources for non-wage inputs led to minimal asset creation, much wasted labour and thus negligible longer-term productivity gains from that nation's extensive FFW programmes (von Braun *et al.* 1999). In Cambodia, the scope for labour-intensive public works proved much narrower once programmes were underway than proponents had initially anticipated (Sakko 1999).

16.2.5. *Crowding-Out Private Transfers*

Proponents of FFW often claim that it creates social capital by bringing individuals together in work teams on projects intended for collective benefit. We are unaware, however, of any solid empirical evidence in support of this hypothesis.[11] Indeed, it seems that any observable positive correlation between social capital stocks and FFW performance is more likely due to the need for established community-level participation, leadership and cooperation in project identification, design and implementation. Von Braun *et al.* (1999), discussing relatively favourable FFW experiences in Botswana and Niger, Dev's (1995) study of Bangladesh, and Molteberg's (1997) report on the Relief Society of Tigray (REST), an Ethiopian NGO, all suggest that FFW is most effective in creating durable public investments of value where strong

---

[11] This may be due in part to the fact that empirical measurement of social capital is fraught with myriad conceptual and methodological problems.

community work traditions prevail, local institutions exhibit effective organizational capacity, or both.

One must also worry about the possibility that public transfers through FFW or other interventions may crowd out private transfers, thereby diminishing community cohesion. Albarran and Attanasio (Chapter 13, this volume) find evidence of crowding-out of private transfers by public ones in Mexico and Cox and Jimenez (1992) find similar evidence in Peru. We are unaware of rigorous empirical work on this question in the narrower context of FFW. But our experience in pastoral areas of southern Ethiopia and northern Kenya suggest reason for caution. Where detailed ethnographic among the region's pastoralists in the 1960s and 1970s described extensive, active networks of gifts, loans, and transfers among pastoralists to cushion people against shocks due to climate, disease, or raiding, more recent data from the same areas show that transfers provide very little in the way of insurance against losses (Lybbert *et al.* 2001; McPeak and Barrett 2001). Discussions with elders and long-time observers of the region consistently point to the emergence of ubiquitous food aid distribution, albeit more often as free food than as FFW in this particular region, as giving neighbours and extended family an excuse to reduce support for one another. If FFW and other public programmes do indeed displace private safety nets, a hypothesis still in need of careful testing, then the net benefits of these programmes are obviously less than they might appear through a simple accounting of programme beneficiaries, even after making adjustment for alternative private employment forsaken (Jalan and Ravallion 2001).

The hypothesis that FFW may build social capital, posed in the previous section, may also cut the other way. When participation must be rationed, one all too frequently finds systematic exclusion of migrant returnees, particular ethnic groups, or clans by the authorities responsible for choosing participants, with adverse consequences for social cohesion within the community. Moreover, once individuals have become accustomed to getting paid for contributions to community infrastructure, it can be more difficult to mobilize voluntary labour to contribute to the provision of local public goods, a problem decried frequently by both NGOs and community leaders in the Horn of Africa.[12] An anonymous referee reinforces this point by describing how in Indonesia, customary self-help activities in which people are expected to contribute time to community-based projects (*gotong royong*), may be undermined by public employment programmes that now pay people (in cash or rice) for activities traditionally carried out as a public contribution. FFW activities run the risk of subtly shifting the locus of responsibility for community action from community members themselves to outside agencies or government.

16.2.6. *Disincentive Effects*

Economists and policymakers have long worried about the potential disincentive effects of giving away food, both because transfers may induce beneficiaries to reduce labour supply and that food transfers may substitute for commercial purchases, thereby

---

[12] We thank Patrick Webb for reminding us of this important issue.

depressing local food prices and reducing farmers' incentives to produce and to invest in their land (intensification) and traders' incentives to invest in marketing capital. The latter effect is intimately related to targeting errors because the extent of errors of inclusion directly affects the volume of commercial purchases displaced in the market.

The empirical evidence on disincentive effects is nonetheless quite mixed. Much seems to turn on whether FFW is occasional (a safety net) or chronic (an ongoing employment programme with cash wages), whether it generates productive public goods (e.g. roads or soil conservation structures), and how well it is targeted to the truly needy.

Jayne (1998) and Tschirley *et al.* (1996) find evidence of FFW transfers reducing net food purchases at household level in Ethiopia and Mozambique, respectively. Mohapatra *et al.* (1999) caution, however, against inferences about net incentives to smallholder farmers on the basis of output price movements alone since FFW, and food aid distribution more generally, can also affect factor prices. We are unaware of any direct empirical study of FFW's effect on food producers' net profits.

Using rapid appraisal and participatory ranking techniques in a single project in Damot Woyde, Ethiopia, in 1989, Maxwell *et al.* (1994) found no significant disincentive effects with respect to either labour supply or agricultural intensification. They attribute this favourable result to careful targeting—community targeting combined with self-targeting—and to complementary encouragement of intensification by other means.

In contrast, the 1995/6 national survey data from Ethiopia are consistent with the claim of significant disincentive effects. Table 16.1 shows that labour and land productivity are both sharply decreasing with households' frequency of FFW participation. The differences between groups are highly statistically significant after controlling farm size, level of intensification, livestock ownership, region, rainfall, and characteristics of the head of household such as education, gender, and age.[13] This is true as well for free food aid distribution, which would be consistent with the labour supply disincentive hypothesis. Unlike free food aid receipt, however, FFW is also strongly associated with reduced investment in agricultural intensification, including improved seed, chemical fertilizers, organic fertilizers, pesticides, and irrigation technologies. Comparing mean intensification index scores, FFW non-participant households are far more likely to intensify than are chronic FFW households, with an average intensification score twice that of the chronic FFW participants.

In the absence of defensible instruments we cannot conclusively dismiss the possibility of reverse causality, and it is surely true that poor productivity in some marginal areas causes food aid receipt, in particular chronic FFW participation. Programme placement effects appear significant in related work using different data from Ethiopia (Dercon and Krishnan 2001). We nonetheless think it important not to dismiss the disincentive effect argument entirely for three reasons. First, previous analysis

---

[13] Labour productivity is computed as total household income (in birr) from farm (value of production) and non-farm sources per household unit of labour. Household members aged 15–65 are valued at 1.0 labour units, while children ages 10–14 and the elderly aged 65 and over are valued at 0.5 labour units.

Table 16.1. *Comparison of labour and land productivity, income diversification, and agricultural intensification across levels of food aid use*

Type and level of food aid use	N	Indicators of productivity, diversification, and intensification			
		Labour productivity (Mean income in birr per unit of household labour)	Land productivity (Mean farm income in birr per hectare of land)	Income diversification (Mean % of total income received from off-farm sources)	Agricultural intensification (Mean index score)
Free food aid (FFA) use					
Non–users	2,345	679	2,053	7.8	0.99
Intermittent users	768	586	1,771	6.6	0.72
Chronic users	72	407	1,154	15.4	0.69
ANOVA significance		#0.001	#0.01	#0.001	#0.001
Food-for-work (FFW) use					
Non–users	2,574	679	2,049	7.5	0.94
Intermittent users	567	534	1,658	8.5	0.82
Chronic users	44	457	910	6.1	0.47
ANOVA significance		#0.001	#0.001	#0.052	#0.001
Factors and covariates in ANOVA		Factors: –region Covariates: –farm size –TLU –intensification –inc diversif. –age of head –sex of head –educ of head –rainfall	Factors: –region Covariates: –HHlabour –farm size –TLU –intensification –inc diversif. –age of head –sex of head –educ of head –rainfall	Factors: –region Covariates: –HHlabour –farm size –TLU –intensification –age of head –sex of head –educ of head –rainfall	Factors: –region Covariates: –HHlabour –farm size –TLU –inc diversif. –age of head –sex of head –educ of head –rainfall

Table 16.2. *Comparison of farmer perceptions of change by type and frequency of food aid use*

Perceived change due to food aid use	Frequency and type of food aid received in past five years				
	Intermittent FFA only (%)	Chronic FFA only (%)	All combinations of FFA & FFW (%)	Intermittent FFW only (%)	Chronic FFW only (%)
Household farm labour availability					
Decrease	7.1	11.1	25.1	24.8	25.8
No change	84.1	76.9	68.3	70.4	70.2
Increase	8.8	10.0	6.0	4.8	4.0
Overall crop cultivation					
Decrease	18.0	28.1	26.9	19.0	41.5
No change	63.8	65.5	57.9	65.3	42.3
Increase	18.3	6.5	15.2	15.7	16.2
Use of fertilizer and other variable inputs					
Decrease	7.3	2.0	10.4	7.6	28.1
No change	82.8	92.1	77.1	84.5	65.8
Increase	9.9	5.9	10.4	7.9	6.1
Number of observations	441	28	371	203	38

(Clay *et al.* 1999; Barrett and Clay 2003) shows food aid distribution is not effect-ively targeted on the basis of poverty or household *ex ante* food availability, indicators that are more discernible by community and FFW project leaders than are labour or land productivity or intensification measures. Second, important differences emerge between free food aid and FFW in the level of income diversification and agricultural intensification observed although there is no difference in targeting efficacy between these two modalities. In particular, sustained receipt of free food is associated with greater off-farm employment and higher agricultural intensification than FFW. Third, data on farmer perceptions of their own practices (Table 16.2) show that FFW users are demonstrably more likely to perceive decreased labour availability on their farm and chronic FFW participants are substantially more likely to perceive a decrease in use of fertilizer and other non-labour variable inputs and in crop production overall, relative to recipients of free food aid. On average, in spite of clear, positive cases such that reported by Maxwell *et al.* (1994), Ethiopian farmers perceive and articulate a negative effect of FFW on their farms. Authentic programme placement effects not withstanding, farmers' concerns deserve to be taken seriously.

The same concerns are evident in other Ethiopian data. In a survey of 400 households in sixteen communities in Tigray in 1998, Hagos and Holden (1998) similarly found that 21 per cent of households stated that FFW participation gave them less time to look after their farm and animals, while only 1 per cent said FFW participation gave them more time to look after their farm and animals. Forty-three per cent stated that it reduced their need to produce own food and only 4 per cent stated that it made them able to invest more on their own farms. The main investment effects of FFW are therefore likely to be the direct effects of FFW.

Holden *et al.* (2001, 2003) explore the sensitivity of how household agricultural production and investment behavioural responses to transfers respond to alternative structural assumptions through a bioeconomic household model calibrated to survey data collected in Andit Tid, North Shewa, Amhara Region, and Ethiopia. Andit Tit received food aid for the first time in 1999 after the *belg* season rains failed for the second consecutive year, a very unusual event. Their modelling exercise finds that production and investment incentives—and consequently food production, agricultural labour use, area cultivated, extent of conservation investments, and soil erosion outcomes—vary depending on structural assumptions about the initial yield effects of conservation technologies, households' access to non-farm income, and whether FFW is used for conservation investment or not in the community. When FFW labour is channelled into productive public goods investment in soil conservation (through construction of bunds on farmland) and households enjoy unconstrained access to the labour market, FFW leads to greater agricultural production and increased conservation investment, as well as reduced land degradation due to erosion. When the opposite conditions hold, however, incentives to produce food and conserve the land are comprised by FFW. Although these are merely modelling results, not empirical observations, they are consistent with and help explain the variation one observes in case studies, where FFW appears to create favourable incentives in some settings, but disincentives to agricultural production or on-farm investment in others. The devil indeed seems to be in the local factor market details.

16.3. CORE LESSONS: HOW, WHEN, AND WHY FFW WORKS

So can the competing evidence on FFW be reconciled adequately to generate some useful rules of thumb as to when, how, and why FFW can serve effectively as short-term insurance, a longer-term rehabilitation and development intervention, or both? The evidence suggests a reasonably broad set of conditions under which FFW can perform effectively as a short-term safety net, a much narrower set of conditions under which it can also, or instead, advance longer-term 'cargo net' objectives related to development and rehabilitation.

Reconciling short-run and long-run objectives is a first-order priority in the design of FFW programmes. Clay *et al.* (1998; 1999) assert that 'public works projects cannot effectively achieve both [short-run and long-run] goals simultaneously and should generally have one or other as their primary objective'. There are clear tradeoffs between (i) wage payments and provision of complementary inputs to improve the quality of public works, and often between (ii) selecting project leaders skilled in short-term relief operations or in longer-term development programming, and (iii) selecting programme sites based on logistical feasibility, expected returns to FFW public works, or immediate nutritional needs of local populations. There are circumstances under which food is the primary, occasionally the only, form in which resources are available for development efforts. In such cases, but probably only such cases, long-run objectives might legitimately take priority. As a general rule, however, FFW is most effective as a means of providing short-term insurance against shocks and, when carefully planned and implemented, can help rather than hinder longer-term recovery and development efforts.

Efficacy in meeting short-run insurance objectives basically hinges on the issues of targeting and timing. Three key geographic criteria matter in FFW targeting. First, it is most appropriate in chronically food deficit zones that are relatively poorly integrated into the commercial food marketing network, else food is an undesirable form for making transfers and likely institutional inertia can lead to substantial targeting errors in subsequent years. If local food marketing systems perform spatial arbitrage reasonably efficiently and transport costs are not excessive, transfers in kind will be far more costly to donors and less desirable for most prospective beneficiaries than cash transfers.

Second, FFW works best where private market demand for labour fails to provide a vent for surplus labour released by those who suffer shocks. If employment opportunities exist but food markets are weak, free food distribution will generally outperform FFW, which works best as a means of resolving multiple market failures in food and labour. Nonetheless, frictions caused by high transactions costs in land and capital markets can lead to considerable variation in the reservation wage rates at which households become willing to participate in FFW projects, thereby limiting the potential efficacy of self-targeting. The very market failures that justify the use of FFW also limit its efficacy in reaching intended beneficiaries, a key limitation that must be kept in mind.

Third, since FFW requires able-bodied participants, it is most effective in reaching vulnerable persons in areas with relatively low rates of chronic illness or injury, that is, not in areas with severe HIV/AIDS or landmine injury problems. Together, these points imply subjecting FFW transfers to an initial geographic targeting based on the three criteria of food and labour market performance and general morbidity status.

Both theory and the empirical evidence favour following up this three criteria geographic targeting with community targeting before relying on the self-targeting feature of FFW to determine programme participation. There are at least two reasons for the advisability of community targeting. First, the evidence suggests that although community-level targeting can lead to some errors of inclusion due to political patronage, the greater effect is improved targeting to the poor by taking advantage of local knowledge of households' needs and capabilities that is difficult to capture in measurable indicators (Maxwell *et al*. 1994; von Braun *et al*. 1999; Alderman 2002). Such community targeting can help reduce the targeting errors that result from exclusive reliance on self-targeting in areas where factor market imperfections break down the theorized positive relationship between household income or wealth and reservation FFW participation wage (Barrett and Clay 2003).

The second reason for community-level targeting is that active local participation and leadership in project identification, design, and implementation matter, to the ultimate efficacy of FFW and other employment programmes (Maxwell *et al*. 1994;

Von Braun *et al.* 1999; Haddad and Adato 2001). Mitigation of the potential adverse medium-to-long-term effects of FFW requires that attention be paid to the incentives created for agricultural intensification and labour supply patterns and to the choice and quality of the public goods created by the FFW effort.

We stop short of recommending that community leadership and existing social capital be used as a fourth criterion in geographic targeting of FFW projects because there is insufficient evidence on which to conclude whether FFW and similar projects can create community capacity. Indeed, as previously discussed, public employment programmes can even undermine extant community work norms. Moreover, extant difficulties in the effective measurement of community leadership and social capital, combined with the likely political unacceptability of ranking communities by these characteristics, renders this criterion practically infeasible. Nonetheless, the likelihood of success in reaching intended beneficiaries at reasonable current and future cost is plainly greater in locations that do not suffer dysfunctional local politics.

Timely delivery is crucial to any sort of public transfer scheme intended to insure poor subpopulations against loss of health, productive assets and, in the extreme, life. The experience of countries such as Botswana and of episodes like the last two El Niño events in southern Africa underscore the value of early warning systems and careful pre-planning by responsible government officials and cooperating donors and NGOs. FFW programmes need to be active or cued for operation in response to emerging need. If programme design commences with the onset of an emergency, it is almost surely too late for FFW to prove effective. There is much to be learned as well from the contrasting experiences of the World Food Programme, which relies heavily on local purchases and triangular transactions to source food for delivery to FFW programmes and whose food aid flows demonstrably stabilize food availability in recipient countries (Barrett and Heisey 2002), and the United States' PL 480 programme, from which bilateral flows are procured in the United States, subject to considerable delays, and exhibit no discernible effect in responding effectively to fluctuating needs (Barrett 2001).

Reasonably accurate targeting matters for longer-term development purposes, as well. Otherwise, FFW rations displace commercial food purchases at an unacceptably high rate, driving down local prices and depressing investment incentives for farmers and food traders. Indeed, the disincentive effects of FFW are real threats if care is not taken to counteract them through explicit promotion of agricultural intensification and production of appropriate and durable public goods such as roads, schools, and soil and water conservation structures. Well-targeted FFW needs to be applied to the production or maintenance of public goods (i) in which local or national government would not otherwise be investing at present, (ii) that will be maintained satisfactorily thereafter, (iii) that can be produced at good quality by labour-intensive means, (iv) for which complementary non-labour inputs are readily available, and (v) about which local populations are enthusiastic. This is a tall order, but it is by no means infeasible. There are good cases of where this indeed works. A common denominator is almost always active community participation in the identification of project priorities. Local participation and commitment is essential to overcome moral hazard and information asymmetries between target populations and external agents. Failures of past FFW efforts may largely be due to a top-down approach where the programme administrators lacked the necessary information and local commitment needed to design and implement properly targeted, high quality programmes. A central government with manifest institutional commitment and technical expertise to design and implement effective FFW programmes following clear objectives and a simple design seems necessary to programme effectiveness, but by no means sufficient. Communities cannot run effective FFW projects in a vacuum, but central governments are typically unable to do so either absent strong collaboration with local jurisdictions and civil society.

Looking to the bottom line, these points confirm that FFW is but one piece of the broader puzzle of insuring the poor against catastrophic loss. The heterogeneity of poor, food insecure people and the communities in which they reside necessitates a portfolio approach in which officials, donors, and relief agencies on the ground can draw from a range of different instruments to respond to emerging needs. There is always danger in a 'one size fits all' approach, and this is no less true of food-for-work than for any other type of intervention.

REFERENCES

Alderman, H. (2002). 'Do Local Officials Know Something We Don't? Decentralization of Targeted Transfers in Albania'. *Journal of Public Economics*, 83(3), 375–404.

Atwood, D. A., A. S. M. Jahangir, H. Smith, and G. Kabir (2000). 'Food Aid in Bangladesh: From Relief to Development', in R. Ahmed, S. Haggblade, and T. Chowdhury (eds), *Out of the Shadow of Famine: Evolving Food Markets and Food Policy in Bangladesh*. Baltimore, MD: Johns Hopkins University Press.

Barrett, C. B. (1998). 'Food Aid: Is It Development Assistance, Trade Promotion, Both or Neither?'. *American Journal of Agricultural Economics*, 80(3), 566–71.

—— (1999). 'Stochastic Food Prices and Slash-and-Burn Agriculture'. *Environment and Development Economics*, 4(2), 161–76.

—— (2001). 'Does Food Aid Stabilize Food Availability?' *Economic Development and Cultural Change*, 49(2), 335–49.

—— (2002). 'Food Security and Food Assistance Programmes', in B. L. Gardner and G. C. Rausser (eds), *Handbook of Agricultural Economics*, Vol. 2. Amsterdam: North-Holland.

—— and P. Arcese (1998). 'Wildlife Harvest in Integrated Conservation and Development Projects: Linking Harvest to Household Demand, Agricultural Production and Environmental Shocks in the Serengeti'. *Land Economics*, 74(4), 449–65.

—— and M. R. Carter (2001). 'Can't Get Ahead For Falling Behind: New Directions for Development Policy to Escape Poverty and Relief Traps'. *Choices*, 16(4), 35–8.

—— and D. C. Clay (2003). 'How Accurate Is Food-for-Work Self-Targeting Accuracy in the Presence of Imperfect Factor Markets? Evidence from Ethiopia'. *Journal of Development Studies*, 39(5), 152–80.

—— and P. A. Dorosh (1996). 'Farmers' Welfare and Changing Food Prices: Nonparametric Evidence From Rice In Madagascar'. *American Journal of Agricultural Economics*, 78(3), 656–69.

—— and K. C. Heisey (2002). 'How Effectively Does Multilateral Food Aid Respond To Fluctuating Needs?'. *Food Policy*, 27(5–6), 477–91.

Barrett, C. B., M. Bezuneh, and A. Aboud (2001). 'Income Diversification, Poverty Traps and Policy Shocks in Côte d'Ivoire and Kenya'. *Food Policy*, 26(4), 367–84.

——, F. Place, and A. A. Aboud (2002). *Natural Resources Management in African Agriculture: Understanding and Improving Current Practices*. Wallingford: CAB International.

Besley, T. and S. Coate (1992). 'Workfare vs. Welfare: Incentive Arguments for Work Requirements in Poverty Alleviation Programmes'. *American Economic Review*, 82(2), 249–61.

Bezuneh, M., B. J. Deaton, and G. W. Norton (1988). 'Food Aid Impacts in Rural Kenya'. *American Journal of Agricultural Economics*, 70(1), 181–91.

Clay, E. J. (1986). 'Rural Public Works and Food-for-Work: A Survey'. *World Development*, 14(10/11), 1237–86.

Clay, D. C., D. Molla, and H. Debebe (1999). 'Food Aid Targeting in Ethiopia: A Study of Who Needs it and Who Gets it'. *Food Policy*, 24(3), 391–409.

——, N. Pillai, and C. Benson (1998). *The Future of Food Aid: A Policy Review*. London: Overseas Development Institute.

Cox, D. and E. Jimenez (1992). 'Social Security and Private Transfers in Peru'. *World Bank Economic Review*, 6(1), 155–69.

Dercon, S. and P. Krishnan (2001). 'Informal Insurance, Public Transfers and Consumption Smoothing (or Does Food Aid Reduce Vulnerability?)', unpublished manuscript.

Dev, S. M. (1995). 'India's (Maharashtra) Employment Guarantee Scheme: Lessons from Long Experience', in J. von Braun (ed.), *Employment for Poverty Reduction and Food Security*. Washington, DC: International Food Policy Research Institute.

Devereux, S. (1999). 'Targeting Transfers: Innovative Solutions to Familiar Problems'. *IDS Bulletin*, 30(2), 61–74.

FDRE (1996). *Food Security Strategy 1996*. Federal Democratic Republic of Ethiopia: Addis Ababa.

Flora, C. (1997). 'Building Social Capital: The Importance of Entrepreneurial Social Infrastructure'. *Rural Development News*, 21(2), 1–3.

Gebremedhin, B. and S. M. Swinton (2001). 'Reconciling Food-for-Work Project Feasibility with Food Aid Targeting in Tigray, Ethiopia'. *Food Policy*, 26(1), 85–95.

Haddad, L. and M. Adato (2001). 'How Effectively Do Public Works Programmes Transfer Benefits to the Poor? Evidence from South Africa'. *Food Consumption and Nutrition Division Discussion Paper* No. 108. Washington, DC: International Food Policy Research Institute.

Hagos, F. and Holden S. (1998). 'Incentives for Conservation in Tigray, Ethiopia: Findings from a Household Survey', draft report, Department of Economics and Social Sciences, Agricultural University of Norway.

Herring, R. J. and R. M. Edwards (1993). 'Guaranteeing Employment to the Rural Poor: Social Functions and Class Interests in the Employment Guarantee Scheme in Western India'. *World Development*, 11(7), 575–92.

Holden, S. T. and H. Binswanger (1998). 'Small Farmer Decisionmaking, Market Imperfections, and Natural Resource Management in Developing Countries', in E. Lutz, H. Binswanger, P. Hazell, and A. McCalla (eds), *Agriculture and the Environment. Perspectives on Sustainable Rural Development*. Washington, DC: World Bank.

—— and N. Shanmugaratnam (1995). 'Structural Adjustment, Production Subsidies, and Sustainable Land Use'. *Forum for Development Studies*, 2, 247–66.

——, J. Pender, and B. Shiferaw (2001). 'Land Degradation, Drought and Food Security: A Bioeconomic Model with Market Imperfections'. *IFPRI Discussion Paper*. Washington, DC: International Food Policy Research Institute.

——, C. B. Barrett, and F. Hagos (2003). 'Food for Work for Poverty Reduction and the Promotion of Sustainable Land Use: Can It Work?'. *Unpublished Working Paper*.

Jalan, J. and M. Ravallion (2001). 'Income Gains to the Poor from Workfare: Estimates for Argentina's Trabajar Program', mimeo, World Bank, Washington, DC.

Jayne, T. S. (1998). 'Food Aid Targeting and Household Food Marketing Behavior: The Case of Tigray Region, Ethiopia', paper presented at the 14th Annual Conference of the Canadian Association for the Study of International Development: 'A Future for Food Aid?', Congress of the Social Sciences and Humanities, Ottawa.

——, J. Strauss, and T. Yamano (1999). 'Targeting of Food Aid in Rural Ethiopia: Chronic Need or Inertia', mimeo, Michigan State University.

——, ——, ——, and D. Molla (2001). 'Giving to the Poor? Targeting of Food Aid in Rural Ethiopia'. *World Development*, 29(5), 887–910.

Lybbert, T. J., C. B. Barrett, S. Desta, and D. L. Coppock (2001). 'Pastoral Risk and Wealth-Differentiated Herd Accumulation Patterns in Southern Ethiopia', mimeo, Ithaca, Department of Applied Economics and Management, Cornell University, NY.

Maxwell, S., D. Belshaw, and A. Lirenso (1994). 'The Disincentive Effect of Food-for-Work on Labour Supply and Agricultural Intensification and Diversification in Ethiopia'. *Journal of Agricultural Economics*, 45(3), 351–9.

McCaston, M. K. (1999). 'The Shortcomings of Food Aid Targeting: Food for Work Programmes and Human Energy Expenditure', paper presented at the Society for Applied Anthropology Annual Meetings, April, Tucson, Arizona.

McPeak, J. G. and C. B. Barrett (2001). 'Differential Risk Exposure and Stochastic Poverty Traps Among East African Pastoralists'. *American Journal of Agricultural Economics*, 83(3), 674–9.

Mohapatra, S., C. B. Barrett, D. L. Snyder, and B. Biswas (1999). 'Does Food Aid Really Discourage Food Production?'. *Indian Journal of Agricultural Economics*, 54(2), 212–19.

Molteberg, E. (1997). 'The SSE Programme. Linking Relief and Long-Term Development Activities in NGO Projects of the SSE Programme in Mali, Eritrea and Ethiopia', A report, Agricultural University of Norway, Noragric.

Moser, C. M. and C. B. Barrett (2001). 'The Disappointing Adoption Dynamics of a Yield-Increasing, Low External Input Technology: The Case of SRI in Madagascar', unpublished manuscript.

Ravallion, M. (1991). 'Reaching the Rural Poor through Public Employment: Arguments, Lessons, and Evidence from South Asia'. *World Bank Research Observer*, 6(1), 153–76.

—— (1999). 'Appraising Workfare'. *World Bank Research Observer*, 14(1), 31–48.

——, G. Datt, and S. Chaudhuri (1993). 'Does Maharashtra's Employment Guarantee Scheme Guarantee Employment? Effects of the 1988 Wage Increase'. *Economic Development and Cultural Change*, 41(2), 251–75.

Sakko, J. (1999). 'Access, Transport, and Local Economic Development: The Socio-Economic Impact of Labour-Based Rural Infrastructure Rehabilitation and Maintenance in Siem Rep Province, Kingdom of Cambodia', report to the International Labour Organization, Regional Office for Asia and Pacific.

Sen, A. (1981). *Poverty and Famines*. Oxford: Oxford University Press.

Sharp, K. (1997). *Targeting Food Aid in Ethiopia*. Addis Ababa: Save the Children Fund (UK).

Speth, J. G. (1993). 'Towards Sustainable Food Security', Sir John Crawford Memorial Lecture, Consultative Group for International Agricultural Research, Washington, DC.

Stock, E. and J. de Veen (1996). 'Expanding Labor-based Methods in Roads Programmes'. *Approach Paper, Sub-Saharan Africa Transport Policy Program (SSATP) Working Paper* No. 18. World Bank and Economic Commission for Africa.

Subbarao, K. (1997). 'Public Works as an Anti-Poverty Program: An Overview of Cross-Country Experience'. *American Journal of Agricultural Economics*, 79(3), 678–83.

Teklu, T. and S. Asefa (1999). 'Who Participates in Labor-Intensive Public Works in Sub-Saharan Africa? Evidence from Rural Botswana and Kenya'. *World Development*, 27(2), 431–8.

Transitional Government of Ethiopia (1993*a*). 'Directives for Disaster Prevention and Management', Addis Ababa.

—— (1993*b*). 'National Policy on Disaster Prevention and Management', Addis Ababa.

Tschirley, D., C. Donovan, and M. T. Weber (1996). 'Food Aid and Food Markets: Lessons from Mozambique'. *Food Policy*, 21(2), 189–209.

von Braun, J. (ed.) (1995). *Employment for Poverty Reduction and Food Security.* International Food Policy Research Institute, Washington, DC.

——, T. Teklu, and P. Webb (1999). *Famine in Africa: Causes, Responses, and Prevention.* Baltimore, MD: Johns Hopkins University Press.

Webb, P. (1995). 'Employment Programmes for Food Security in Rural and Urban Africa: Experiences in Niger and Zimbabwe', in J. von Braun (ed.), *Employment for Poverty Reduction and Food Security.* Washington, DC: International Food Policy Research Institute.

Weber, M. T., J. M. Staatz, E. W. Crawford, and R. H. Bernsten (1988). 'Informing Food Security Decisions in Africa: Empirical Analysis and Policy Dialogue'. *American Journal of Agricultural Economics*, 70(5), 1044–52.

17

Learning from Visa®? Incorporating Insurance Provisions in Microfinance Contracts

17.1. INTRODUCTION

One of the important distinguishing characteristics of poor is their exposure and vulnerability to risk. The prevalence of agriculture and accompanying activities (such as seasonal work), the undersupply and poor quality of transportation and communication infrastructures, and the unreliability of the macroeconomic environment tend to create strong fluctuations in income. Furthermore, low-income households, due to their higher consumption requirement as a proportion of their income and their limited capacity to buffer the effects of shocks, find themselves less able to absorb risk without falling below binding subsistence-level consumption constraints (Rosenzweig and Binswanger 1993). Low-income households are thus very *vulnerable* to risk: income shocks have a significant impact on household consumption.

In order to reduce the effect of shocks on their consumption patterns, households engage in strategies to mitigate their exposure to risk and lower the impact of shocks. However, these strategies often induce a reduction in future income growth opportunities. Risk-management strategies reduce household exposure to risk by the choice of less variable activities, but at the expense of more profitable ones (Reardon *et al.* 1994). Risk-coping strategies remedy the lack in income through (often disadvantageous) changes in asset position and resources (Alderman and Paxson 1994;

Paper prepared for the WIDER Conference on Insurance against Poverty held in Helsinki 14–15 June, 2001. Funding for the survey in Guatemala was generously provided by the Mellon and the Ford Foundations and the Financial Research Center at Princeton University. I am deeply grateful to Stefan Dercon, Ian Shelding and an anonymous referee for their extensive and insightful comments, and to the participants of the Helsinki WIDER conference, the Workshop on Theoretical and Empirical Research on Microfinance at the University of Heidelberg, and seminar participants at the Free University of Amsterdam, ECARES, Toulouse, and the National University of Singapore for interesting comments and discussions. The usual disclaimer applies.

Dercon 2000).[1] By reducing households' productive capacity, these risk-management and risk-coping strategies can impart severe and often long-term consequences to even temporary downturns.

In complete information settings, optimal contracts would involve payments contingent on the states of the world and private actions. In the non-anonymous settings of local or 'village' economies, informational asymmetries are small enough to see such (at least partially contingent) contracts exist. This is the case for quasi-credit contracts, in which the repayment conditions of the contract depend on the relative outcome of the contracting parties (Lund and Fafchamps 2003 report evidence for the Philippines, Grimard 1997 for Côte d'Ivoire, and Udry 1990 for Nigeria). This is also the case for remittances (Lucas and Stark 1985; de la Brière et al. 2002; Jensen 1998) and informal insurance arrangements (Coate and Ravallion 1993; Morduch 1999a). However, these risk-sharing arrangements are incomplete even when agents have good information, and households—particularly poor households—remain subjected to substantial uninsured risk (Paxson 1993; Jalan and Ravallion 1999).

Furthermore, when one moves to settings in which agents have substantial private information, contracts with full contingencies become difficult to implement. Arrangements must thus rely on non-manipulable signals of performance, letting rise to long-term contracting and financial instruments in well-developed markets; and to share-cropping (Ackerberg and Botticini 1998), interlinked contracts (Besley 1995), and other such arrangements in less-developed countries.

In a classic paper, Townsend (1982) makes the case for the feasibility of risk-sharing contracts even under private information. These contracts involve several periods with payments based on past reports to induce truthful revelation of private information. While these schemes may require complicated payments in a real-world situations,[2] they still suggest that optimal lending contracts under private information probably involve some mixture of credit and insurance.

In this chapter, we argue that the repeated nature of microcredit contracts can allow the lending institution to set up insurance contracts through the creation of a reputation mechanism. Indeed, the success of microcredit institutions at successfully extending credit to the poor, while maintaining high repayment rates, is widely attributed to the particularities of the contracts offered (Morduch 1999b): the loans are uncollateralized (thus favouring outreach);[3] and incentives to repay are created by granting

---

[1] Examples include pulling children out of schooling (Jacoby and Skoufias 1997), cancelling or postponing investments (Morduch 1999a), overexploitation of local resources (Platteau 2000), diminishing nutritional intake (Deaton 1988; Dercon and Krishnan 2000), and running down relationship-based insurance benefits (Goldstein et al. 2001).

[2] Townsend's (1982) payment scheme has to induce truthful reporting of two possible states of the world. Allowing for more states would induce an exponential increase in the number of incentive-compatibility conditions.

[3] There has been a debate as what types of poor microcredit actually reaches. In particular, there is increasing evidence that it does not directly help the poorest of the poor (Alexander 2001; Navajas et al. 2001).

borrowers access to larger future loans only upon successful fulfilment of current contracts (Stiglitz 1990; Ghatak and Guinnane 1999; Sadoulet 1999*a*).[4] The idea in this chapter is to use the repeated interaction between the banks and clients to allow borrowers to build a credit record, which they can use to insure themselves in case of temporary liquidity shocks. We derive the conditions for the evolution of reputation, of premia, and of the sanctions in case of claims, to protect the financial institutions against adverse selection, moral hazard behaviour and fraudulent claims. These conditions are very reminiscent of the types of conditions put on credit-card contracts in the United States, or car insurance contracts. The caveat is that the contract we propose is not an optimal contract, since we derive sufficient conditions for the insurance contract to satisfy the participation and incentive constraints for borrowers and the financial institution. However, it is a simple and implementable contract that improves the ones currently offered.[5]

Very recently, the microfinance industry has developed an interest in providing insurance products to their clients. The benefit is twofold: reduce borrower vulnerability, and improve the financial sustainability of institutions through a positive impact on repayment rates (Del Conte 2000). While clients are clearly demanding insurance products, the challenge is to understand what types of products are best fitted to their needs. Recently, Brown and Churchill (2000) have detailed insurance contracts in thirty-two institutions (out of the sixty institutions that have been identified worldwide as offering some type of microinsurance product). Their focus has been on the advantages and disadvantages of microcredit institutions at providing insurance products. The advantages of such institutions carry on their experience at the grassroot level, having a client base they know, and their clients know and trust them. Their disadvantages lie in the capacity of the institution to provide insurance, because of the technicality of insurance products (actuarial analysis), and because of the insurability of highly covariate shocks. The solution proposed are alliances with specialized insurance companies, in which the insurer devises the products and the microcredit institution distributes them (referred to as 'Partner–Agent model' in Brown and Churchill). However, most of these initiatives have been cantoned to life, property, health, disability, and catastrophe insurance—insurance for large and verifiable shocks (McCord 2001).[6] The range of insurance product offered remains relatively limited.

The remainder of the chapter is organized as follows. In the next section, we describe microcredit contracts and illustrate the empirical importance of insurance for borrowers using survey data from Guatemala. We then present a basic model

---

[4] To reinforce these dynamic repayment incentives, loans tend to be small short-term loans with frequent payments (to minimize the benefits of deviation from repayment) and display a sharp growth upon repayment (to increase the benefits from repayment of the current loan) (Varian 1990; Jain and Mansuri 2001).

[5] The reason we do not derive the less-restrictive necessary condition is due to a lack of closed for solutions. Necessary conditions for particular examples, however, would be relatively simple to simulate from the expressions we provide.

[6] Even in case programs that provide loan-payment insurance, the insurance payment is made only upon verification of an identifiable shock (e.g. Canadian Cooperative Association (CCA) in China; Del Conte 2000).

which aims to capture the salient features of the observed microcredit contracts, namely individual loans and group loans in which members are jointly liable. This model is used to demonstrate the incentive mechanisms behind microfinance contracts, and how insurance is an important by-product of joint-liability loans. The next section extends the contracts to include insurance provision. The main contribution of the paper is to show the contractual conditions that allow these contracts to be sustainable for the institution and for the borrowers. We close the paper by discussing the historical and regulatory limitations on the implementation of these contracts, and point towards the importance of establishing transparent accounting practices.

17.2. MICROCREDIT AND INSURANCE

Microcredit contracts were introduced in the late 1970s by Muhammad Yunus, founder of the now-famous Grameen Bank in Bangladesh. The idea was to provide working capital for poor entrepreneurs to generate higher incomes and thus break the cycle of poverty that they faced. While many programs have emerged over the past thirty years[7] and have adapted the original Grameen methodology, all rely on the same two basic principles: (i) poor borrowers need credit and are credit-constrained; (ii) institutions can thus use conditional access to future loans as an incentive mechanism for repayment. As described in the introduction, borrowers are offered a sequence of (generally) uncollateralized loans, which grow over time. Loan repayment grants a borrower access to a further loan; any default, however, is punished by a loss of access to these further loans.

Loan contracts have been offered in two general forms: individual loans, in which borrowers are individually responsible for their loans; and group loans, in which borrowers are asked to form groups (typically between three and eight people[8]), each member receives a loan, and members are jointly liable for the entirety of the group loan: if *any* part of a group loan is not repaid, *all* members of the group are considered in default.

There has been a long debate in the literature on the relative benefits of individual versus group loans. Authors have argued that the joint liability in group loans can have positive effect on repayment rates by inducing borrowers to coordinate on safer projects (Stiglitz 1990; Wydick 1995), pressuring each other to repay (Armendáriz 1999), or providing a mechanism for institutions to charge different effective interest rates for different types of borrowers, thus diminishing the adverse selection inherent in contracts with asymmetric information (Ghatak and Guinnane 1999). Others have pointed out that joint liability can actually lead to lower repayment rates both due to voluntary defaults and the (positive) covariance between incomes of group members (Besley and Coate 1995). Furthermore, despite possible improvements in repayment rates, joint liability may lead to inefficiencies. Group members may overmonitor (Varian 1990) or put pressure on partners to take excessively safe and low-return projects (Banerjee *et al.* 1994). Nonetheless, implicitly or explicitly, all these papers recognize

---

[7] The Microcredit Summit Campaign Report (2000) reports 1065 programmes serving 13.8 million clients in the world.   [8] Although some 'village banking' models use larger groups.

the importance of the repeated loans in creating dynamic incentives for borrowers to repay.

Unlike most of the academic work, practitioners have long focused on the 'mutual help' aspect of group lending. Jointly liable borrowers will scrutinize each others' projects and actions, but will also come together and repay loans in case of trouble. As reported on the Grameen Trust's website: 'The Group Model's basic philosophy lies in the fact that shortcomings and weaknesses at the individual level are overcome by the collective responsibility and security afforded by the formation of a group of such individuals.' In this chapter, we concentrate on the insurance aspect of this mutual help in credit groups.

To illustrate the importance of this insurance provision, we turn to evidence from a 1995 survey that we conducted in Guatemala. We interviewed the 782 members of 210 credit groups that were clients of *Génesis Empresarial*, a Guatemalan Non-Governmental Organization (Table 17.1 provides descriptive statistics). They were small informal market sellers, very typical vendors found in markets in low and middle-income countries, characterized by low sales ($400–500 in good weeks) which were quite variable (sales in a bad weeks were around 40 per cent lower on average). They kept low stocks of merchandise and had a high rate of capital turnover as demonstrated by nearly half the sample buying merchandise more frequently than two to three times a week. Their activity was confined to one business, although a large proportion of households had other sources of income (only 40 per cent of the surveyed entrepreneurs were the sole source of household income).

Their access to credit was limited, with only 4 per cent having access to formal banks. Their main credit sources were money lenders and wholesale credit, although these tended to charge very high interest rates (15–25 per cent over the loan). Family and friends were also possible sources of credit, but for small and short-term amounts.

Loans offered by *Génesis Empresarial* were two-month loans for working capital, with regular payment schedules (weekly, fortnightly, or monthly). Loans started off relatively small ($60) but grew rapidly upon successful repayment, typically by 10–30 per cent. On average, loans represented around two weeks worth of inventory. Repayment problems were met with penalties: one late payment resulted in no increase in loan size; two late payments reduced the loan size; and three late payments in a year resulted in permanent exclusion from any further loan. Since payments start after the first week of the loan, a fair share of borrowers (19 per cent) put part of the loan aside in order to make the first one or two payments, to reduce the chance of going into default.

While all borrowers surveyed were in groups—which *Génesis* requires to be between three and eight members—all borrowers (in principle) have access to both groups and individual loans. Both type of loans carried the same monthly interest rate (2.5 per cent, as in the formal banking sector in 1995[9]) and had exactly the same growth paths and other terms. Yet, two-thirds of borrowers *chose* group loans.[10]

---

[9] This amounts to a real monthly interest rate of 1.65% (IFS 1998).

[10] While there is some differential screening in practice, borrowers can opt for an individual loan easily after just a few rounds of group lending. People in older groups who remain in group loans therefore reveal their preference for those groups over individual loans (switching costs are negligible).

Table 17.1. *Descriptive statistics*

Variables	Mean	SD[a]	Median[a]	Min[a]	5%[a]	95%[a]	Max[a]	N
Personal/business characteristics								
Average weekly sales in good weeks (in US$)	531	770	381	14	112	1203	13,333	782
Bad week sales, as a fraction of good week	0.58	0.17	0.58	0.03	0.29	0.84	1.00	782
Buying merchandise daily	0.19	—	—	—	—	—	—	782
Buying 2–3 times per week	0.29	—	—	—	—	—	—	782
Buying once a week	0.35	—	—	—	—	—	—	782
Only one business	0.79	—	—	—	—	—	—	772
Sole income provider to household	0.40	—	—	—	—	—	—	782
Loan characteristics								
Loan size (in US$)	740	555	650	56	167	1700	5000	782
Loan size/average daily purchases	17	20	12	1	2	47	93	647
Weekly payments	0.30	—	—	—	—	—	—	782
Fortnightly payments	0.32	—	—	—	—	—	—	782
Monthly payments	0.38	—	—	—	—	—	—	782
Payment size (in US$)	124	97	93	5	29	276	718	782
Payment/average daily purchase	2.98	3.40	1.92	0.02	0.29	8.73	27.69	647
% keeping loans to make first payments	0.19	—	—	—	—	—	—	780
Number of payments kept	1.88	1.17	1.75	0.10	1.00	5.00	5.00	146
Group characteristics								
Group size	3.7	0.94	3	3	3	6	8	210
Groups of 3	0.50[b]							105
Groups of 4	0.34[b]							72
Groups of 5	0.12[b]							26
Groups of 6	0.01[b]							3
Groups of 7	0.00[b]							1
Groups of 8	0.01[b]							3

[a] Standard deviation, minimum, maximum, median, and 5% and 95% points are not reported for dummy variables.
[b] As a percentage of total number of groups.

A question thus naturally arises: why would borrowers ever choose group loans? The individual and group contracts are similar in every aspect except for the extra joint liability. Part of the answer, we want to suggest, stems from insurance that emerges in these credit groups.

The insurance-need measure that we use records the number of times a borrower in a group declares having had difficulties making a payment in the previous year. As reported in Table 17.2, over 60 per cent of groups report a need for insurance over the past year. Typically, shortfalls in income arise because of low sales or bad planning (74 per cent), or of shocks such as robbery and family illness (23 per cent)—shocks that can be classified as idiosyncratic (although not necessarily exogenous).[11] In 69 per cent of the cases, help came from someone within the group. For 23 per cent of cases, the help came from personal resources: either friends or family outside the group, or from personal savings or borrowing from a moneylender. The help is for non-trivial amounts since it covers around 20 per cent of the payment due by the person who cannot repay.[12]

The evidence from the Guatemalan data suggests that the need for insurance is important and relatively frequent in credit groups. The next section examines how groups contracts are instrumental in the provision of insurance between borrowers. Later we will propose a new contract that improves on the insurance sustained by joint-liability contracts.

17.3. JOINT LIABILITY AND INSURANCE

In order to understand why some borrowers choose group loans over individual loans, we present a simple model (inspired from Sadoulet 1999*a*) which aims at capturing the most important features of microfinance contracts: the repeated loans, the informational advantage that borrowers have over the lending institution, and the sanctions in case of default. While the economic and social environments are somewhat stylized, the simplifying assumptions allow us to clearly identify the precise role joint liability plays in the establishment and sustaining of insurance arrangements.[13] With these results, we will then be able to analyse how to improve the current microfinance contracts by incorporating an explicit institutional insurance aspect to them.

Assume a continuum of individuals, each born with a sequence of one-period projects requiring a unit of capital in every period. Each project in every period has two states of nature: it can succeed and yield a positive return X, or fail and yield a return of zero.

Individuals are distinguished by their exogenous probability of success: in every period, i's project succeeds with an exogenous probability P_i. There is no moral

---

[11] While it is probable that the risk of robbery and family illness varies little from group member to group member, repayment ability being affected by low sales or bad planning is typically the result of borrowers' choices of liquidity strategy. Borrowers who save earlier for the purpose of making the payment encounter fewer problems in case of bad sales the last days before the payment is due. However, this is at a high opportunity cost considering the high turnover of capital (payments represent two to three days of merchandise purchases, with half of the borrowers buying merchandise at least two to three times a week—see Table 17.1). The tradeoff for borrowers is thus between risk and return.

[12] We refer to this 'mutual help' as insurance because we have strong anecdotal evidence that suggest that members of groups pay each other risk premia to compensate for differential risks in the credit groups.

[13] For a complete analysis of repayment strategies and of equilibrium behaviour in this model, the interested reader is referred to Sadoulet (1999*a*).

Table 17.2. *Insurance occurences in credit groups (210 credit groups)*

	N	%	
Insurance need in past year			
(Someone in group has had trouble			
making own payment in past year)			
None	79	0.38	
Once	34	0.16	
2 times	26	0.12	
3–4 times	35	0.17	
More than 4 times	36	0.17	
	210		Total = 468 times in past year
Reason insurance was needed			
Low sales	155	0.63	
Bad planning	30	0.12	
Robbery	7	0.03	
Family illness	49	0.20	
Other	6	0.02	
	247[a]		
Who provides insurance?			
A member of the group	128	0.52	
The whole group	42	0.17	
Someone from outside	49	0.20	
Self-insurance	8	0.03	(savings, moneylender)
Resulted in late payment	20	0.08	(insurance failed)
	247[a]		

How much?

	Amount ($)	As fraction of payment[b]
Mean	28	0.24
Median	17	0.17
5%	5	0.04
95%	88	0.67
Min	2	0.01
Max	167	1.25

[a] The question was only asked for the past two times $(34 + (26 \times 2) + (35 \times 2) + (36 \times 2) = 228$ events) and more than one answer was possible (19 cases) = 247.

[b] As we have only current payment information, and not the payment information at the time insurance was given, these are only approximations.

hazard in effort or choice of projects (there will be moral hazard in the choice of repayment). Individuals have no assets or other sources of income, and cannot save between periods.[14] Projects must therefore be financed by a loan in every period.

Loans are provided by a unique financial institution. The objective of the lending institution is to maximize the number of *repaid* loans, subject to a break-even constraint. It, however, has no information on borrower type or on project returns. It can therefore not price-discriminate across borrowers or provide state-contingent contracts.

The financial institution offers two type of loans: individual loans, and group loans. Both types of loans have the same modalities—same interest rate, same term (one period), and same amount—and operate on the same following principle: if a borrower fulfills the repayment requirements towards the financial institution, he/she is granted a future loan. However, any default is punished by the exclusion of the borrower from access to either types of loan from then on.[15] The only difference between individual loans and group loans is a joint-liability requirement. In group loans, borrowers are asked to form a group; each partner receives a loan; and the members are jointly liable: if *any* part of the group loan is not repaid, *all* members of the group is considered in default.[16] Once borrowers lose access to loans from the financial institution, they have no other source of credit and their future present discounted value is (normalized to) zero.[17]

Repayment strategies are governed by borrowers' ability and willingness to repay. When a borrower's project fails, he/she is unable to repay his/her loan; he/she thus has no choice but to default. When his/her project succeeds, however, he/she is faced with a choice of actions: he/she is able to repay, but is he/she *willing?* In individual loans, willingness to repay has straightforward consequences: if he/she chooses to repay, he/she gets access to future loans; if he/she chooses not to repay, he/she will be considered in default. In the group loan, his/her (simplified) repayment strategies are similar: he/she can choose never to repay his/her share, irrespective of what his/her partners do; repay his/her share only if his/her partners repay their share; or repay

---

[14] Alternatively, we could have assumed that the sequence of loans grow faster than the returns on individual projects. It limits individuals' incentive to default on the current loan and self-finance from then on with the amount they did not repay.

[15] It is clear that this permanent exclusion does not look optimal. However, this is the rule announced clearly by all microfinance projects we are aware of, and it is precisely a modification of this rule that the contract in section 17.4 will call for.

[16] The equality of interest rates on group loans and individual loans is a characteristic that we adopt to replicate what is done in practice. It is clear that since individual loans and group loans are different products, they should carry a different 'price'. In personal communication, the financial manager of Accion International, an organization which provides a microlending methodology to institutions, evoked simplicity and fear of selection effects if each contract was priced differently.

[17] Alternatively, borrowers' fallback option could be to turn to a moneylender. Money lenders typically have information on borrower types and on projects, and are a monopoly source of credit. Moreover, they have recourse to severe punishments to control moral hazard. Evidence from the literature on informal money lenders is that they can extract much of borrower surplus. We could therefore normalize the present discounted value to borrowers of borrowing from this fallback option to zero.

not only his/her share but also his/her partners' share if necessary. We will refer to this third strategy as 'insurance'.[18]

To illustrate why people might choose group loans, we assume that borrowers have perfect information on types and actions of all potential partners, that they have no external sanctioning mechanism, and that borrowers carry a non-verifiable reputation (observable only by other borrowers, but not by the financial institution). These assumptions are extreme but provide stark results as to the benefits of group loans. A weakening of these assumptions simply diminish the benefits of group loans as compared to individual loans.[19]

A few more unimportant technical assumptions are made for simplicity. Borrowers are risk-neutral. We restrict our attention to groups of two to avoid the tradeoff between group size and quality of partners. We assume that $X \geq 2L$ so that borrowers are always *able* to provide insurance when their project is successful. This assumption, while seemingly strong if taken literally (requiring 200 per cent return on projects), is effectively not very restrictive since it is a direct consequence of our assumption that projects yield zero when they fail. In practice, projects rarely fail completely; the assumption is essentially that group members, when successful, are always able to cover the amount by which their partners fall short. When they cannot, it is as if their project had failed. A third assumption is that borrowers can only participate in one loan in each period, to avoid a possibility of self-insurance through investment in several projects. The probabilities of success are assumed to be independent over time and across borrowers to circumvent the potential tradeoff between partner quality and covariance of returns. Borrowers are assumed to be infinitely lived (or to face an exogenous probability of dying). They share the same discount factor $\delta \in (0, 1)$. The borrower types are distributed according to some (discrete or continuous) distribution F and there is a unit mass of borrowers of every type (so that the equilibrium displays equal treatment within each type).[20] Since projects are identically and independently distributed over time, we restrict strategies to be stationary over time.

Under these assumptions, Sadoulet (1999a) shows that all borrowers who are 'safe enough' have an incentive to maintain access to future loans, where 'safe enough' borrowers are defined by

$$P_i \geq \frac{L}{\delta X}. \tag{17.1}$$

[18] The repayment strategies in the group loan are in fact slightly more general than the ones we present in that individuals do not simply repay necessarily their own share but a proportion of the total group loan (see Sadoulet 1999a).

[19] Imperfect information between borrowers entail that intragroup contracts provide less than full insurance, thus diminishing the relative benefits of group lending as compared to individual loans. Similarly, outside sanctions could allow individuals to set up insurance arrangements without joint liability, thus diminishing the role for joint liability loans. If borrowers could become anonymous again after the group dissolve, in the sense that past actions are not remembered, groups would provide less than full insurance, as in the imperfect information case above.

[20] Formally, each borrower is denoted by a pair $\{i, n\} \in [0, 1] \times [0, 1]$ where the first coordinate represents their type and is distributed on [0, 1] according to F. See Sadoulet (1999b).

For individual loans, this condition is straightforward: given that the project succeeds and the borrower *can* repay, as long as the discounted expected value of getting another loan next period and defaulting on it ($\delta P_i X$) is greater than the cost of repaying the current loan (L), then the borrower *will* repay his/her current loan:

$$X - L + \delta\,(P_i X) \geq X \iff P_i \geq \frac{L}{\delta X}.$$

A strategy of repaying loans when successful leads to the same condition. Repaying the current loan and maintaining access to future loans as long as projects are successful outweighs the one period benefit of not repaying a loan (and losing access to future loans) as long as P_i is safe enough:

$$X - L + \sum_{s=1}^{\infty} (\delta P_i)^s\,(X - L) \geq X \iff P_i \geq \frac{L}{\delta X}. \tag{17.2}$$

Similarly, for group loans, borrowers will repay their loans and provide insurance if they are safe enough that the benefit of maintaining access to future loans is worth the cost of repaying. More importantly, group loans provide a forum through which borrowers can set up an insurance agreement in an environment in which they have no other existing insurance opportunity (because of lack of external sanctioning mechanisms to enforce insurance agreements). The new technology allowing the enforcement of insurance agreements is precisely the joint liability: it prevents borrowers from reneging *ex post* on insurance promises, since the borrower not fulfilling the insurance agreement would be considered in default too. In essence, the financial institution, despite being uninformed, provides a punishment for borrowers who do not conform with the insurance arrangement.

This new insurance opportunity, through group loans, offers a valuable service to borrowers who want to maintain access to future loans. This insurance is so valuable, in fact, that borrowers may voluntarily form in groups which are heterogeneous in risk in equilibrium (Sadoulet 1999*b*): safe members join groups with riskier partners and 'sell' them insurance. Both safe and riskier types are better off than in separate homogeneous group since the riskier member increases his inherent ability to repay the loan, while the safer member extracts more surplus from the trade than he/she loses from having a riskier partner.

Sadoulet (1999*a*) shows that the condition for borrowers to repay their loans and insure their partners when necessary is exactly the same as the condition for individual loans (17.1). No borrower riskier than $L/\delta X$ would ever be accepted as a partner in a group loan. Furthermore, borrowers satisfying (17.1) either repay their loans and insure if the risk differential is not too high in their group, or opt for individual loans (which they repay) rather than group loans if they cannot find an acceptable partner.

Tables 17.3 and 17.4 look at the risk composition of groups and insurance flows within these groups.[21] As we see in Table 17.3, not all groups are homogeneous in

---

[21] Borrowers' risk is measured by their liquidity strategy. The interested reader is referred to Sadoulet and Carpenter (2000) for details.

Table 17.3. *Risk heterogeneity in groups*

Lowest risk quantile in group	Number of groups					N
	Highest risk quintile in group					
	1	2	3	4	5	
1	2	18	21	26	33	100
2		5	11	13	17	46
3			2	14	22	38
4				1	17	18
5					8	8
						210 groups

Note: The italics indicate cells with less than five observations.

Table 17.4. *Net insurance provision in groups*

Lowest risk quantile in group	Highest risk quintile in group				
	1	2	3	4	5
1	2.00	0.91	0.67	1.33	0.47
	(0.00)	(0.00)	(0.00)	(0.00)	(0.00)
2		0.75	1.00	1.00	0.00
		(0.00)	(0.00)	(0.00)	(0.00)
3			−0.50	−1.33	1.13
			(0.00)	(0.00)	(0.00)
4				0.00	2.00
				(0.00)	(0.00)
5					-0.50
					(0.00)

Note: (mean # times provided − # times received).
The italics indicate cells with less than five observations.
Bold italics indicates significance at 10% level.
Standard errors of mean in parentheses.

risk. In fact, groups homogeneous in risk are relatively scarce (18 groups out of 210). Furthermore, there exist a significant amount of extremely heterogeneous groups, with members in the two extreme risk quantiles (thirty-three groups) or separated by three risk quantiles (fourty-three groups). While matching frictions may prevent borrowers from finding their optimal partner, it would be difficult to argue that such pronounced heterogeneity would emerge from a homogeneous matching equilibrium, particularly considering how underserved the credit market was in Guatemala.[22]

---

[22] Choice of heterogeneity to benefit from negative covariance does not seem to be an issue in this data. Covariance in sales did not appear to be an important feature in these urban markets, despite our prior intuition that they would be. The major shocks—rain and seasonal variation in buying patterns—tended to

Moreover, within groups, insurance flows from the safer part of the risk *distribution* to the risky part (not only from the safer borrowers to the riskier partners in a group; Table 17.4). Groups are very heterogeneous in risk, and insurance is provided within these heterogeneous group. Unfortunately, the data does not contain information on the payments from the riskier members to their safer partners. Anecdotal evidence, nonetheless, does confirm the existence of such payments.[23]

The evidence from the Guatemalan data suggests that insurance is important and relatively frequent, and that borrowers form groups to maximize gains from trading insurance. Yet, a financial institution is much better able than these small credit groups of absorbing credit risk. Transferring the credit risk from a lending institution to the (certainly more risk averse) borrowers has efficiency and welfare costs.

Furthermore, contracts offered by the lending institution do not take into account borrowers' repayment history. For example, a particular group that had been working with *Génesis* for seven years and suddenly faced repayment difficulties for the first time was evicted from the programme. While the loan officer would have liked to keep the group for future loans, he or she recognized that making an exception would weaken the credibility of rules and could start an avalanche of defaults. Yet, *Génesis* clearly had more information on them than on first-time borrowers. Not using this information in the loan contract suggests an important loss in efficiency. In the next section, we propose a remedy by adding insurance clauses to credit contracts.

17.4. INSURANCE PROVISIONS IN CREDIT CONTRACTS

The environment is as described: individuals need one unit of capital to invest; projects yield an amount X when successful and 0 when they fail; borrowers are only able to repay their loan when their projects succeed. The projects outcome are independent and identically distributed over time for each borrower.

The financial institution introduces an insurance contract tied to the individual loan. The basic idea of the contract is that, since the institution has no information on the actual outcome of projects in any particular period, insurance will be

---

be perfectly covariate across activities and thus uninsurable within the group; and the patterns of sales do not differ greatly according to the products sold (except in case of durable goods).

[23] In Sadoulet (1999a), we report the case of a group composed of four borrowers. The leader of the group was a 50-year-old man with a well-established cloth business, stocked with several rolls of cloth (over $2,500 worth). He had been selling in this market for twenty-six years and was a well-respected figure in that section of the market. The other three members of the group were shoesellers, around twenty-five years old, all in their second year of business. Each of them had no more than thirty pairs of shoes in hand, making them very vulnerable to the fluctuations of the market. It rapidly became clear, in talking to each member of the group, that the younger members of the group were repaying part (if not all) of the group leader's loan at every payment. He essentially repaid only when the younger members needed assistance to repay the group loan. The younger borrowers were therefore ready to pay more than 35% extra in interest in exchange for insurance (they were free to disband the group and form a group among the three of them).

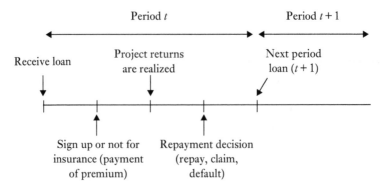

Figure 17.1. *Timing of loan and insurance contract*

awarded conditional on a measure of borrowers' reputation. Through their repayment behaviour, individual borrowers build up a credit record and, as long as borrowers are in good standing with the financial institution, their insurance claims will be honoured, thus protecting them from default.

The timing is as depicted in Fig. 17.1. In each period, borrowers in good standing receive a loan. If they qualify for insurance, they choose whether to subscribe to the insurance contract or not, and pay the according premium out of the loan they just received. They invest the remainder of the money and their project succeeds or not. They then take the repayment decision. The stage game then ends and the game moves to period $t + 1$.

The financial institution starts with some prior distribution of types. Since the institution initially has no information on any particular borrower, all borrowers start at the same reputation, say the mean of the institution's prior on distribution the distribution of types:[24]

$$\mu_i^{[1]} = E^{[1]}(P_i) = \mu^{[1]},$$

where $E^{[t]}$ denotes the expectation taken by the financial institution at the beginning of period t (i.e. before observing i's repayment outcome in time t).[25] As time passes, the institution updates individual borrowers' reputation according to observations of repayment or not. Borrower i's reputation based on his/her repayment behaviour after t loans is thus given by

$$\mu_i^{[t]} = E_t\big(P_i \mid c_i^{[t]}\big), \tag{17.3}$$

---

[24] Recall, borrowers have no assets or other sources of income. They are thus unable to signal their type by any type of investment or bond posting.

[25] The square brackets are used to distinguish the notion of 'at the beginning of time t' from exponential powers.

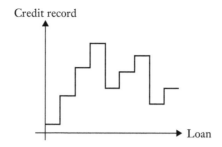

Figure 17.2. *Evolution of borrower reputation*

where $c_i^{[t]}$ represents the number of claims i has made up to the beginning of loan t.[26] An example is depicted in Fig. 17.2. Repayment of a loan increases i's reputation; a claim decreases his/her reputation.

In order to finance the insurance, the financial institution fixes an insurance premium. The premium is charged at the time the loan is disbursed. We constrain the financial institution to charge actuarially fair premia to each subscriber (up to incentive constraints that will emerge below). The premium $\psi_i^{[t]}$ for borrower i in time t depends therefore on his/her reputation $\mu_i^{[t]}$ in time t:

$$\psi_i^{[t]} = \left(1 - \mu_i^{[t]}\right)L. \tag{17.4}$$

From period to period, the premium is updated according to (17.3) as more information becomes available.

The financial institution has to protect itself from two sources of abuse. The first one stems from the borrowers who never repay any loan participating in the insurance scheme; the second one from borrowers filing false claims. We examine each in turn.

17.4.1. *Excluding Undesirable Borrowers*

As we saw in Section 17.3 (equation (17.1)), borrowers of type $P_i < L/\delta X$ are such the cost of repaying a loan outweighs the benefit of maintaining access to future loans. If granted a loan without insurance, they would default after one period. The new possibility of insurance could allow them to default several periods before being evicted from the programme. These risky borrowers would sign up for the insurance contract in order to benefit from a second loan on which to default, as long as the premium is

---

[26] Note that, since the returns for individuals are independent and identically distributed over time, the order of claims does not matter. More generally, this could be written as conditional on the history of repayment $h_i^{[t]}$.

not too large of a cost:

$$- \psi_i^{[1]} + P_i X + \delta(P_i X) > P_i X$$

$$\Longleftrightarrow \quad \psi_i^{[1]} = (1 - \mu^{[1]})L < \delta P_i X$$

$$\Longleftrightarrow \quad P_i > (1 - \mu^{[1]})\frac{L}{\delta X}.$$

Any borrower in $[(1 - \mu^{[1]})(L/\delta X), L/\delta X]$ will thus sign up for the insurance contract and never repay, for any first-period estimate of mean risk $\mu^{[1]}$.[27]

One way to advert this adverse selection is for the financial institution to deny insurance coverage to any borrower who does not have a reputation above a certain threshold $\tilde{\mu}$. As long as the threshold is such that it takes sufficient rounds of successful loan repayment to reach it (say N), the institution can weed out borrowers wanting to strategically default on the insurance contract:

$$P_i(X - L) + P_i\delta\big[P_i(X - L) + P_i\delta\big[\cdots + P_i\delta\big[- \psi_i^{[N]} + P_i X + \delta[P_i X]\big]\big]\big] < P_i X.$$

The longer the waiting period, the fewer the borrowers that will undertake the waiting period rather than default immediately. Note that since the contracts are one-period contracts, borrowers have no incentive to sign up to the insurance until they have repaid sufficient number of loans to reach the threshold reputation $\tilde{\mu}$.

The insurance contract must thus provide some incentive mechanism encouraging borrowers to only claim insurance when they need it, and allow the financial institution to deny claims from borrowers it views as opportunistic. The insurance contract will therefore display the following two properties.

Proposition 1 *When the financial institution has no information on borrower types or project outcomes, to protect itself against adverse selection, the financial institution provides incomplete insurance in the sense that:*

- *No borrowers with reputations below some cut-off $\tilde{\mu}$ are insured;*
- *There is no insurance in the first round of loans:*

$$\tilde{\mu} > \mu^{[1]}$$

The proof is in the Appendix. The intuition is that to keep all undesirable borrowers from participating, the financial institution must put an entry cost to the insurance contract. This entry cost can take the form of several preliminary rounds of successful repayment—or a series of discouragingly high premia—until borrowers establish their reputation as willing repayers.

Do good types participate? Ignoring fraudulent claims for an instance, if the financial institution had perfect information on borrower types, the insurance contract would

---

[27] Futhermore, there exist type distributions such that charging a premium corresponding to the average risk $\mu^{[1]}$ discourages participation of the safer types, leading to participation of only the high-risk borrowers.

be priced such that the premium is exactly the expected cost of insurance, namely

$$\mu_i^{[t]} = (1 - P_i)L.$$

Borrowers' discounted expected return in the insurance contract would thus be given by:

$$\sum_{t=1}^{\infty} \delta^{t-1}(-(1 - P_i)L + P_i(X - L)) = \frac{P_iX - L}{1 - \delta},$$

which, compared to the expected returns without insurance:

$$\frac{P_i(X - L)}{1 - \delta P_i} \tag{17.5}$$

insures that all borrowers with $P_i \in [(L/\delta X), 1]$ would participate, were the institution to have perfect information:

$$\frac{P_iX - L}{1 - \delta} > \frac{P_i(X - L)}{1 - \delta P_i} \iff P_i > \frac{L}{\delta X} \quad \text{and} \quad P_i < 1. \tag{17.6}$$

However, the institution does not have perfect information on types. Nonetheless, as long as the financial institution's assessment of a borrower risk is not too high compared to his/her actual risk, the borrower will participate.

To see this, examine the returns under the insurance contract if the financial institution estimated correctly a borrower's probability of failure, and compare them to the returns without insurance. Suppose that from $T(i)$ onwards, the financial institution correctly estimates borrower i's riskiness. Take the period before the one in which the financial institution has perfect information, $T(i) - 1$. A borrower i satisfying (17.6) will sign up for an insurance contract in $T(i) - 1$ and pay the premium $\psi_i^{[T(i)-1]}$ if the expected return of doing so is greater than the expected return of waiting for one more period before getting insurance (and running the risk of losing access to future loans):

$$-\psi_i^{[T(i)-1]} + P_i(X - L) + \delta\left(\frac{P_iX - L}{1 - \delta}\right) \geq P_i\left(X - L + \delta\frac{P_iX - L}{1 - \delta}\right).$$

This holds as long as the premium does not outweigh the benefit of insurance:

$$\psi_i^{[T(i)-1]} \leq \delta(1 - P_i)\frac{P_iX - L}{1 - \delta}.$$

Working backwards, we show in the Appendix that borrower i will sign up for insurance in period n as long as the premium $\psi_i^{[n]}$ is less than an upper bound $\psi_i^{[n]\,\text{max}}$, where $\psi_i^{[n]\,\text{max}}$ is given by:

$$\psi_i^{[n]\,\text{max}} \equiv (1 - P_i)\delta\frac{P_iX - L}{1 - \delta} - (1 - P_i)\sum_{s=1}^{T(i)-n-1}\delta^s E^{[n]}\left(\psi_i^{[n+s]} \mid F \text{ in } n\right). \tag{17.7}$$

We further show that this maximum premium $\psi_i^{[n]\max}$ is increasing with n: the better the information the financial institution has on borrower i's type, the larger the (temporary) deviation from the accurate premium the borrower is willing to accept. And since the premium that borrowers face before signing up for the first time is decreasing over time and tends to zero– by virtue of borrowers having had to be successful for *all* periods before signing up for insurance or they are considered in default and lose access to loans–, there exists for, each $P_i > (L/\delta X)$, a number of waiting periods $n(P_i)$ such that a borrower i will sign up for insurance in period $n(P_i)$ and not before:

$$\forall P_i \in \left[\frac{L}{\delta X}, 1\right], \quad \exists n(i) > 1 \text{ such that } \psi_i^{[t]\max} < \psi_i^{[t]} \quad \forall t < n(i), \text{ and}$$

$$\psi_i^{[n(i)]\max} \geq \psi_i^{[n(i)]}.$$

Since the premium tends to zero as the number of waiting periods becomes large, and that there are strictly positive net benefits from insurance for all $P_i \in ((L/\delta X), 1)$, all 'good types'—the borrowers with projects which are socially beneficial—will eventually participate in the insurance scheme.

We now turn to the second source of abuse: fraudulent claims.

17.4.2. *Deterring Fraudulent Claims*

Since the financial institution has very little information on borrowers in the first rounds of the loans, the gains and losses in reputation for borrowers are greatest in those rounds. Each repayment or insurance claim represents a large proportion of the information that the institution has at its disposal to assess individuals. However, as the number of loan rounds gets large, this difference in reputation from an extra observation shrinks to the point that it becomes negligible. The effectiveness of the drop in reputation as a deterrent for false insurance claims thus diminishes over time. The insurance contract thus has to rely on additional sanctions to deter false insurance claims.

Proposition 2   *The institution must impose costs beyond simple loss of reputation after insurance claims in order to deter fraudulent claims.*

The formal argument is given in Appendix 17.A3. The intuition is easy to follow in Fig. 17.3, which represents borrowers reputation as a function on the numbers of loans repaid. The top curve is a borrower's reputation with no defaults; the second is a borrowers' reputation after one default; and so on. Any default drops the borrower down one curve.

By filing a false claim, the borrower gains the fact of not repaying the current loan and the insurance premium. The costs are an increase in the future premia due to a loss of reputation, and an increase in the probability of falling below the reputation cut-off after repeated failures. However, after enough loan repetitions, these two losses

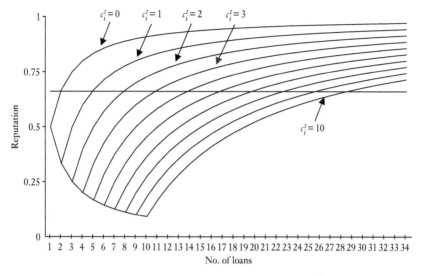

Figure 17.3. *Evolution of borrower reputation* $\mu_i^{[t]}$

effects become infinitesimal. An extra cost of claiming insurance must thus be imposed to discourage borrowers from filing false claims.

One possible form this extra cost could take is one inspired by US-style credit-card contracts. Banks issue credit cards to customers who have stable incomes[28] and a credit record without great blemishes. If a customer were to miss payments early in the relationship, the issuing bank would severely restrict (and even stop) that customer's use of that card. However, over time, responsible use and timely payments is met with increases in credit limits and a willingness from the issuing bank to accept late payments. Credit-card holders are therefore able to use their credit record (i.e. reputation as good payers) to smooth temporary shortfalls in income. The costs to the holder are a late-payment fee and, if the late payments are recurrent, negative entries in the holder's record at various credit rating agencies.[29] These negative entries in the credit record have a sufficient impact that after relatively few missed payments, the financial institution will deny the card holder any further services and the card holder will find it difficult to get access to any other financial services due to the ensuing bad credit record. It takes a long time for a person with a bad credit record to 'rebuild his/her credit'.

While the parallel to US credit-card contracts is not quite exact—credit cards allow *late* payments, not defaults[30]—the reputation and sanctioning mechanisms proposed

---

[28] or to college students with cosigners with stable incomes. Thanks mom!

[29] The idea of sharp important negative effects from reputation upon claims and slow rebuilding of reputation during periods of no claims is also prevalent in auto-insurance contracts. Accidents, speeding tickets, and other signs of hazardous driving are punished by large immediate losses of points that drivers typically need several years of faultless records to erase.

[30] In essence, credit-card companies provide temporary loans to borrowers in good standing to make up income shortfalls.

in this chapter are quite similar to the ones apparently applied in these contracts. Formally, the sanctioning to prevent moral hazard behaviour is equivalent in our model to downgrading a borrower's reputation *and* reducing his/her acquired 'experience' (by which we mean the number of loans he/she participated in). Reducing a borrower's reputation by more than dictated by the Bayesian updating rule (17.3) pushes the defaulting borrower closer to the cut-off below which he/she will be denied insurance; stripping away experience and considering his/her as a newer borrower than he/she actually is (i.e. using a lower t to calculate updates on his/her reputation) increases the risk that he/she will actually reach the cut-off due to repeated failures. Financial institutions can customize these losses in reputation and in experience in order to achieve exactly the punishment they intend. The argument in the Appendix proves the following proposition.

Proposition 3 *There exists a cutoff, a sequence of insurance premia, and a sequence of costs in case of insurance claims such that the insurance contract is a Nash Equilibrium.*

The proof verifies that the contract modalities are sufficient to cover the financial institution's costs, do not exceed the benefits of insurance for participating borrowers, and induce truthful reporting from the part of the participating borrowers.

17.5. CONCLUSION

As documented, insurance is an important by-product of group-lending contracts. However, by the virtue of transferring risk to groups of borrowers less able to absorb it than the lending institution, these contracts entail an important loss in efficiency.

In this chapter, we show that there exists simple credit-with-insurance contracts that financial institutions could implement in environments in which insurance mechanisms are incomplete. While insurance is normally a very difficult industry to enter due to the complicated issues in actuarial analysis, repayment insurance does not seem to require important institutional capabilities: no new information is required; the contract is simple to implement; it is certainly welfare improving since building reputation is less costly than building savings. And furthermore, it maintains some borrowers who would have dropped out after a failure in the system.

The question is then understanding why institutions do not implement such contracts. In one sense, institutions have started to document insurance contracts in a number of institutions worldwide which are experimenting with life, health, and property insurance (Brown and Churchill 2000). Furthermore, implicit insurance arrangements exist, whereby institutions are more flexible on the terms of repayment with older groups.

Nevertheless, explicit repayment insurance has four important hurdles to clear. For microcredit programmes, providing repayment insurance can impact institutional credibility. These programmes are often located in areas in which public targeted credit programmes have failed in the past due to their lax enforcement of rules. If the current institutions are seen as 'soft' on the rules due to the provision of insurance, they may be faced with waves of default, like their predecessors. Furthermore, many of these institutions, in order to increase their credibility and their access to funds, are preparing for an eventual transition to becoming formal banks. Repayment insurance could be viewed by regulators as a 'creative accounting' way to make their portfolio look in good standing, and thus derail the process of formalization. Third, institutions must be able to cover potential large-scale shocks. Since microfinance institutions operate in relatively small geographical areas, they are not immune to a large fraction of their loan portfolio suffering bad outcomes (floods, fire in a market, earthquakes, etc.). While large covaried shocks are easily observable, the ability of the institution to provide insurance is then in question. Institutions must then be able to reinsure these risks. Lastly, while it is often argued that it is unnecessary to regulate credit-only schemes for prudential reasons (Christen and Rosenberg 1999; UNCDF 2002)—the administrative burden can impose high costs and bureaucratic bottlenecks, especially if supervisory capacity is in short supply, while the risk of a badly run credit programme only puts the donors' funds at risk—insurance schemes require supervision since funds taken from their clients are put at risk. The capacity of banking authorities to regulate deposit-taking institutions often imposes barriers for small institutions to offer savings services; the same issue will emerge with the insurance regulation authority.[31]

This suggests a very important direction for policy regarding accounting practices. For institutions to successfully manage loans and insurance, strict accounting rules are needed to separate true instances of insurance from non-performing loans. As we have seen in recent banking sector crises, even developed countries are far from adhering to the standards advocated by the Basel Accords. Transparency, however, is crucial for institutions to gain credibility: in the eyes of their clients, of their national regulatory agency, as well as with potential reinsurers.

Appendix

17.A1. *Proof of Proposition 1*

The financial institution wants to keep all $P_i < L/\delta X$ from participating. At time 1, however, the financial institution cannot discriminate between borrowers; every borrower has the same reputation:

$$\mu^{[1]} = E(P_i) \quad \forall i,$$

where the expectation is taken at the beginning of period 1. This, as we saw in the main text, implies that all borrowers in $[(1 - \mu^{[1]})(L/\delta X), L/\delta X]$ sign up for the insurance contract even though they never intend to repay any loan. The issue is thus to put an entry cost to keep all $P_i < L/\delta X$ out.

When insurance is offered at time $t = 1$, the problem is that the net expected return from the insurance contract is greater than the expected benefit from strategic default

---

[31] With the added problem that it is likely to be even less familiar with microfinance schemes than the banking regulators.

for a range of borrowers:

$$-(1 - \mu^{[1]})L + P_iX + \delta(P_iX) > P_iX$$

$$\Longleftrightarrow P_i \in \left[(1 - \mu^{[1]})\frac{L}{\delta X}, \frac{L}{\delta X}\right).$$

When insurance is only offered first at time $t = 2$, the set of people for whom the net expected return of waiting for insurance in time $t = 2$ and then defaulting is greater than the expected benefit from strategic default in the first loan is as follows:

$$P_i(X - L) + \delta P_i(-(1 - \mu^{[2]})L + P_iX + \delta P_iX) > P_iX$$

$$\Longleftrightarrow \forall P_i \in \left[\frac{1 + \delta(1 - \mu^{[2]})}{1 + \delta}\frac{L}{\delta X}, \frac{L}{\delta X}\right),$$

where $\mu^{[2]}$ denotes a borrower's reputation at the beginning of time t when he/she has repaid all his/her loans, that is

$$\mu^{[2]} \equiv E^{[2]}(P_i \mid c_i^{[2]} = 0).$$

Note that whether the range of potential adverse selection into the insurance contract increases or not depends on the updating from period 1 to 2:

$$\frac{1 + \delta(1 - \mu^{[2]})}{1 + \delta}\frac{L}{\delta X} \geq (1 - \mu^{[1]})\frac{L}{\delta X} \Longleftrightarrow \frac{\mu^{[2]}}{\mu^{[1]}} \leq 1 + \frac{1}{\delta}.$$

If there is a big decrease in reputation from repaying in period 1, it might be worth for some P_i to do so, in order to qualify for insurance in period 2 (even though it would not have been worth signing up for insurance and strategically defaulting in period 1).

Similarly, if insurance is first offered at time $t = T$, the set of borrowers who benefit more from waiting until time T to default twice rather than defaulting in the first period is implicitly given by:

$$\sum_{t=1}^{T-1} \delta^{t-1}(P_i)^t(X - L) + (\delta P_i)^{T-1}(-(1 - \mu^{[T]})L + P_iX + \delta P_iX) > P_iX.$$

$$(17.A8)$$

The threshold reputation at each t is given by:

$$\mu^*(t) > \left((\delta P_i)^{-t} + \frac{(1 - P_i(1 + \delta))}{\delta P_i^2}\right)\frac{(1 - \delta P_i)}{\delta P_i^2(1 - P_i(\delta X/L))}. \qquad (17.A9)$$

If there exists a pair $(t, \mu^{[t]})$ such that this holds for any P_i, then those borrowers will mimic being a 'good borrower' for $t - 1$ periods and repay all their loans (if they can), in order to qualify for insurance in period t and immediately strategically default.

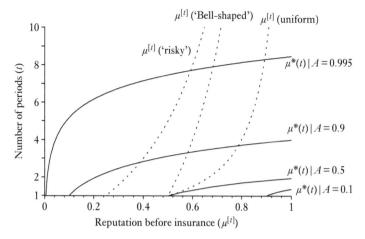

Figure 17.A1. *Bayesian reputations ($\mu^{[t]}$) for different priors, and thresholds (μ^*) for various values of $P_i = A(L/\delta X)$*

The thresholds are depicted in Fig. 17.A1 for borrowers with $P_i = A(L/\delta X)$ for values of A. Take any combination (μ, t). If $\mu > \mu^*(t)$ for a particular borrower i, then he/she will mimic being a good borrower (for at most t periods. It might hold for some earlier combination of (μ, t)).

How many risky borrowers would mimic being good borrowers depends on the insurance premium charged, which itself depends on the financial institution's prior. In Fig. 17.A1, we illustrate the evolution of reputation of borrowers who success-fully repay all their loans (a precondition to qualify for insurance) for three different priors: a uniform distribution, a bell-shaped distribution[32] as an approximate to a normal distribution, and a distribution with a higher mass of risky types[33] to reflect a 'pessimistic' prior. In this illustration, if the financial institution imposes three periods of successful repayment before borrowers can qualify for an insurance contract, only borrowers with $P_i \in [(9/10)(L/\delta X), L/\delta X]$ would mimic good types in order to qualify for insurance and then strategically default.

More importantly, note that, for any prior the institution may have, there will always be some adverse selection:

$$\lim_{P_i \longrightarrow L/\delta X} \mu^*(t) = \infty \qquad \forall t.$$

Borrower with P_i close enough to $L/\delta X$ would require very long waiting periods to discourage them from mimicking good borrowers.

Nonetheless, for the financial institution, if a borrower repays $T - 1$ loans before defaulting on two loans in a row, the expected cost of adverse selection for a borrower

---

[32] A beta(6, 6) distribution.   [33] A beta(2, 6) distribution.

with probability of success P_i is given by:

$$\sum_{t=1}^{T-1}((\delta P_i)^{t-1}(1-P_i)\,L) + (\delta P_i)^{T-1}(-(1-\mu)L + L + \delta L),$$

that is, up to period T, the borrower repays as long as he/she can; and at period T (reached with probability P_i^{T-1} and discounted by δ^{T-1}), the borrower pays a premium $(1-\mu^{[T]})L$ and then defaults on the two subsequent payments. This has to be compared to the cost L if a borrower simply defaults in the first period:

$$\sum_{t=1}^{T-1}((\delta P_i)^{t-1}(1-P_i)L) + (\delta P_i)^{T-1}(-(1-\mu)L + L + \delta L) \le L. \qquad (17.A10)$$

If the waiting period is long enough, the costs engendered by the borrowers defaulting after taking insurance are smaller than the costs of immediate default without insurance:

$$\sum_{t=1}^{T-1}((\delta P_i)^{t-1}(1-P_i)L) + (\delta P_i)^{T-1}(-(1-\mu^{[T]})L + L + \delta L) \le L$$

$$\Longleftrightarrow \quad T \ge 1 + \frac{\ln(((\delta + \mu^{[T]})(1 - \delta P_i) - (1 - P_i))/(1 - \delta)P_i)}{-\ln \delta P_i}.$$

$$(17.A11)$$

For a given value of δ, the right-hand side of (17.A11) reaches its maximum value at $P_i = (L/\delta X)$, $X = 2L$ (since $X \ge 2L$ by assumption), and $\mu^{[T]} = 1$:

$$\max_{P_i \in [0, L/\delta X], \mu^{[T]} \in [0,1]} \left(1 + \frac{\ln(((\delta + \mu^{[T]})(1 - \delta P_i) - (1 - P_i))/(1 - \delta)P_i)}{-\ln \delta P_i}\right)$$

$$= 1 + \frac{\ln(1 + (\delta^2/(1 - \delta)))}{\ln 2}.$$

Note that, for reasonable values of the discount factor δ, the number of waiting periods sufficient for equation (17.A10) to hold is reasonably low, as demonstrated in the table below.

$\mu^{[T]}$	Values of T									
	δ ($X = 2L$)					δ ($X = 1.2L$)				
	0.7	0.8	0.90	0.95	0.99	0.7	0.8	0.90	0.95	0.99
0.25	0	1	2	3	5	0	1	2	3	5
0.50	1	2	3	4	6	1	2	3	4	6
0.75	1	2	3	4	7	1	2	3	4	7
1.00	2	3	4	5	7	2	3	4	5	7

In summary, we have shown that the institution can never completely eliminate adverse selection through waiting periods, as some risky borrowers will mimic the behaviour of safe borrowers to qualify for insurance in order to strategically default twice. However, the financial institution can control how much adverse selection it is willing to endure through the choice of the waiting period. Furthermore, even if there is some adverse selection into the insurance contract, the cost of this adverse selection is smaller than the cost of the original adverse selection in the loan contracts without insurance. Furthermore, repayment rates are improved since borrowers repay a certain amount of loans before defaulting (instead of defaulting on 100 per cent of their loans).

17.A2. *Properties of the Insurance Premium*

Upper bound on premium

In this section, we derive the upper bound on the premium that borrower i is willing to repay at the beginning of period $T(i) - N$.

Take period $T(i) - N$. The expected return of having an insurance contract from $T(i) - N$ onwards is given by:

$$- \psi_i^{[T(i)-N]} + P_i(X - L) + \delta\left(-E\left(\psi_i^{[T(i)-N+1]}\right) + P_i(X - L)\right) + \cdots$$
$$+ \delta^{N-1}\left(-E\left(\psi_i^{[T(i)-1]}\right) + P_i(X - L)\right) + \delta^N \frac{P_i X - L}{1 - \delta},$$

where the expectations are taken at the beginning of period $T(i) - N$. Rewriting,[34] this is equivalent to:

$$- \psi_i^{[T(i)-N]} + P_i(X - L) + \left(-\sum_{s=1}^{N-1} \delta^s\left(E\left(\psi_i^{[T(i)-N+s]}\right) - (1 - P_i)L\right)\right.$$
$$\left. + \delta \frac{P_i X - L}{1 - \delta}\right). \tag{17.A12}$$

Compare this expected return of signing up for insurance in period $T(i) - N$ to the expected return if borrower i waits one extra period before signing up for the insurance contract (which he/she can do only if his/her project succeeds):

$$P_i(X - L) + P_i\left(-\sum_{s=1}^{N-1} \delta^s\left(E\left(\psi_i^{[T(i)-N+s]} \mid S \text{ in } T(i) - N\right) - (1 - P_i)L\right)\right.$$
$$\left. + \delta \frac{P_i X - L}{1 - \delta}\right), \tag{17.A13}$$

---

[34] Using $P_i(X - L) = P_i X - L + (1 - P_i)L$.

where $E(\psi_i^{[T(i)-N+s]} \mid S \text{ in } T(i) - N)$ denotes the expected value (taken at the beginning of time $T(i) - N$) of the premium in $T(i) - N + s$ conditional on the fact that borrower i's project's success in period $T(i) - N$.[35]

To decide whether to sign up for insurance at the beginning of period $T - N$, borrower i compares the expected returns (17.A12) and (17.A13). Signing up for insurance in period $T(i) - N$ yields higher expected returns than waiting one more period if the premium does not exceed the following bound:

$$\psi_i^{[T(i)-N]} \leq \delta(1 - P_i)\frac{P_i X - L}{1 - \delta}$$
$$+ \sum_{s=1}^{N-1} \delta^s \left(P_i E\left(\psi_i^{[T(i)-N+s]} \mid S \text{ in } T(i) - N\right) - E\left(\psi_i^{[T(i)-N+s]}\right)\right).$$

Note that this is equivalent to

$$\psi_i^{[T(i)-N]} \leq (1-P_i)\delta\frac{P_i X - L}{1 - \delta} - (1-P_i)\sum_{s=1}^{N-1} \delta^s E\left(\psi_i^{[T(i)-N+s]} \mid F \text{ in } T(i)-N\right),$$

since

$$E\left(\psi_i^{[T(i)-N+s]}\right) = P_i E\left(\psi_i^{[T(i)-N+s]} \mid S \text{ in } T(i) - N\right)$$
$$+ (1 - P_i)E\left(\psi_i^{[T(i)-N+s]} \mid F \text{ in } T(i) - N\right).$$

Define the upper bound to the premium that i is will to pay for a new insurance contract in period n as:

$$\psi_i^{[n]\max} \equiv (1 - P_i)\delta\frac{P_i X - L}{1 - \delta} - (1 - P_i)\sum_{s=1}^{T(i)-n-1} \delta^s E^{[n]}\left(\psi_i^{[n+s]} \mid F \text{ in } n\right),$$

where $E^{[n]}$ denotes the expectation taken at the beginning of period n. This is exactly equation (17.7) in the text.

Proof that maximum premium $\psi_i^{[n]\max}$ is increasing in n
We want to show that the maximum premium borrower i is willing to pay in period n, namely (equation (17.7) in the text)

$$\psi_i^{[n]\max} \equiv (1 - P_i)\delta\frac{P_i X - L}{1 - \delta} - (1 - P_i)\sum_{s=1}^{T(i)-n-1} \delta^s E^{[n]}\left(\psi_i^{[n+s]} \mid F \text{ in } n\right)$$

is increasing in n.

[35] If the project is unsuccessful in $T(i) - N$, borrower i defaults and loses access to future loans.

For a borrower with a given history up to time n, compare this maximum premium in two successive periods: n and $n + 1$. The difference is given by:

$$\psi_i^{[n]\max} - \psi_i^{[n+1]\max} = -(1 - P_i)E^{[n]}\left(\psi_i^{[n+1]} \mid F \text{ in } n\right)$$

$$+ (1 - P_i) \sum_{s=2}^{n-1} \delta^s \left\{ E^{[n]}\left(\psi_i^{[n+s]} \mid F \text{ in } n\right) - E^{[n+1]}\left(\psi_i^{[n+1+s]} \mid F \text{ in } n + 1\right) \right\}.$$

$$(17.A14)$$

The first term is negative. To compare the terms inside the summation, we note that borrower i's project has to be successful in n to receive a loan in period $n + 1$ since he/she has no insurance in period n. We can thus rewrite:

$$E^{[n+1]}\left(\psi_i^{[n+1+s]} \mid F \text{ in } n + 1\right) = E^{[n]}\left(\psi_i^{[n+1+s]} \mid S \text{ in } n; \ F \text{ in } n + 1\right)$$

$$= P_i \cdot E^{[n]}\left(\psi_i^{[n+1+s]} \mid S \text{ in } n; \ F \text{ in } n + 1; \ S \text{ in } n + 2\right)$$

$$+ (1 - P_i) \cdot E^{[n]}\left(\psi_i^{[n+1+s]} \mid S \text{ in } n; \ F \text{ in } n + 1; \ F \text{ in } n + 2\right).$$

Similarly, we can rewrite

$$E^{[n]}\left(\psi_i^{[n+s]} \mid F \text{ in } n\right) = P_i \cdot E^{[n]}\left(\psi_i^{[n+s]} \mid F \text{ in } n; \ S \text{ in } n + 1\right)$$

$$+ (1 - P_i) \cdot E^{[n]}\left(\psi_i^{[n+s]} \mid F \text{ in } n; \ F \text{ in } n + 1\right).$$

By the fact that premia go up with failures (claims) and down with successful repayments, and that project outcomes are *iid* over time,[36] we have that

$$E^{[n]}\left(\psi_i^{[n+1+s]} \mid S \text{ in } n; F \text{ in } n+1; S \text{ in } n+2\right) < E^{[n]}\left(\psi_i^{[n+s]} \mid F \text{ in } n; S \text{ in } n+1\right)$$

and

$$E^{[n]}\left(\psi_i^{[n+1+s]} \mid S \text{ in } n; \ F \text{ in } n+1; \ F \text{ in } n+2\right) < E^{[n]}\left(\psi_i^{[n+s]} \mid F \text{ in } n; \ F \text{ in } n+1\right).$$

This implies that

$$E^{[n+1]}\left(\psi_i^{[n+1+s]} \mid F \text{ in } n + 1\right) < E^{[n]}\left(\psi_i^{[n+s]} \mid F \text{ in } n\right) \quad \forall s$$

and, thus, that the difference in (17.A14) is negative:

$$\psi_i^{[n]\max} - \psi_i^{[n+1]\max} < 0,$$

that is, $\psi_i^{[n]\max}$ is increasing in n.

17.A3. *Proof of Proposition 2*

Bayesian updating of reputations
When a borrower undertakes his/her first loan, the financial institution has no inform-ation on his/her type. The new borrower's reputation is therefore set at the mean of

---

[36] That is, it is not the order of success and failures that matter but the total number of each.

the institution's prior on the distribution of borrower types:

$$\mu_i^{[1]} = \mu^{[1]} = \int_0^1 g(p)p \, dp,$$

where $g(p)$ denotes the institution's prior. However, as the financial institution gathers information on the borrower's repayment behaviour, it can update its assessment on his/her type. For example, before the second loan, a borrower's reputation is updated by Bayes' rule according to whether he/she repaid or not:

$$\mu_i^{[2]} = \frac{\int_0^1 p^{1-c}(1-p)^c g(p)p \, dp}{\int_0^1 p^{1-c}(1-p)^c g(p) \, dp},$$

where $c = 0$ if i repaid his/her loan and $c = 1$ if i claimed insurance in period 1.

Since the projects are assumed to be independently and identically distributed for each borrower over time, borrower i's reputation in time t depends simply on the number of loans $(t-1)$ and the number of insurance claims $c_i^{[t]}$ that i has filed up to period t:

$$\mu_i^{[t]} \equiv \mu(t, c_i^{[t]}) = \frac{\int_0^1 \binom{t-1}{c_i^{[t]}} p^{(t-1)-c_i^{[t]}}(1-p)^{c_i^{[t]}} g(p)p \, dp}{\int_0^1 \binom{t-1}{c_i^{[t]}} p^{(t-1)-c_i^{[t]}}(1-p)^{c_i^{[t]}} g(p) \, dp}.$$

The prior distribution $g(p)$ determines how much weight the institution puts on the new information for each type.

Eliminating false claims from safe borrowers
In order to gain intuition on the results, we restrict our attention to beta distributions as priors, since they are very flexible distributions that can take various shapes and that they have the advantage of being easy to use (see Rice 1988):

$$g(p) = \frac{\Gamma(a)\Gamma(b)}{\Gamma(a+b)} p^{a-1}(1-p)^{b-1}.$$

Borrower i's reputation at the beginning of period t is then given by the simple formula:

$$\mu_i^{[t]} = \frac{(t-1) - c_i^{[t]} + a}{(t-1) + (a+b)}.$$

Note that the uniform distribution is simply a beta with $a = b = 1$, so that the initial reputation at $t = 1$ would simply be $\mu_i^{[1]} = 1/2$.

The marginal contribution of an extra insurance claim to borrower i's reputation is given by

$$\mu(t, c+1) - \mu(t, c) = \frac{\int_0^1 (1-p)g^{[t-1]}(p)p \, dp}{\int_0^1 (1-p)g^{[t-1]}(p) \, dp} - \frac{\int_0^1 pg^{[t-1]}(p)p \, dp}{\int_0^1 pg^{[t-1]}(p) \, dp},$$

where $g^{[t-1]}(p)$ is the distribution of borrower reputations at the beginning of time $t-1$, given c claims up to the beginning of period $t-1$. Taking the prior distribution to be a beta, this difference works out to:

$$\mu(t, c+1) - \mu(t, c) = \frac{(t-1) - (c+1) + a}{(t-1) + (a+b)} - \frac{(t-1) - c + a}{(t-1) + (a+b)}$$

$$= -\frac{1}{(t-1) + (a+b)},$$

which is negative and of magnitude decreasing in t.[37]

False claims lead to a loss in income due to loss in reputation
This loss in reputation translates to a loss of income (through higher premium) in every period equivalent to

$$(1 - \mu(t, c+1))\delta L - (1 - \mu(t, c))\delta L = \delta \frac{L}{(t-1) + a + b},$$

or a loss of expected income from t onwards (ignoring the increase in the probability of falling below the cut-off) equal to

$$\sum_{k=1}^{\infty} \left(\frac{\delta^k L}{(t+k-1) + a + b} \right). \tag{17.A15}$$

As t becomes large, this cost goes to zero for any beta prior.[38]

False claims lead to a loss in income due to a higher probability of losing access to insurance
In addition to the loss in income due to loss in reputation, there is a loss associated with an increased probability of falling below the cut-off due to repeated failures. Take a borrower with c claims up to time t:

$$\mu(t, c) = \frac{(t-1) - c + a}{(t-1) + a + b}.$$

To reach the limit below which insurance claims are denied—denote it μ_*—it takes a certain amount of further claims. For example, denote by $s_t^c(0)$ the number of claims in a row to go from a reputation of $\mu(t, c)$ to a reputation just below μ_*, where $s_t^c(0)$ is

---

[37] This is where the use of a beta distribution is convenient: the loss in reputation in each period is independent of the number of claims made up to that point.

[38] By virtue of Bayesian updating, it is actually true for any prior. We restrict our attention to beta priors because of what follows.

the first integer such that

$$\frac{(t-1)-c+a}{(t-1)+s_t^c(0)+a+b} < \mu_*.$$

Similarly, it takes $s_t^c(1)$ loans with $s_t^c(1) - 1$ claims (and 1 repayment) to go from a reputation of $\mu(t,c)$ to a reputation just below μ_*, where $s_t^c(1)$ is the first integer such that

$$\frac{(t-1)+1-c+a}{(t-1)+s_t^c(1)+a+b} < \mu_*.$$

More generally, it takes $s_t^c(z)$ loans with $s_t^c(z) - z$ claims (and z repayments) to go from $\mu(t,c)$ to just below μ_*, where $s_t^c(z)$ is the first integer such that

$$\frac{(t-1)+z-c+a}{(t-1)+s_t^c(z)+a+b} < \mu_* \tag{17.A16}$$

and is given by

$$s_t^c(z) = \text{int}\left\{\left(\frac{1}{\mu_*}-1\right)t + \frac{z-c}{\mu_*} - \frac{(1-\mu_*)(1-a)+b\mu_*}{\mu_*}\right\} + 1.$$

Note that $s_t^c(z)$ is increasing in t and $\lim_{t \to \infty} s_t^c(z) = \infty$ since $\mu_* < 1$.

If a borrower makes no false claims, the probability for a borrower with reputation $\mu(t,c)$ of hitting the limit μ_* is thus given by summing the number of ways a borrower can have $s_t^c(z) - z$ failures times the probability of having $s_t^c(z) - z$ failures for all values of z:

$$\sum_{z=0}^{s_t^c(z)} \binom{s_t^c(z)}{z} p^z (1-p)^{s_t^c(z)-z}. \tag{17.A17}$$

Note that, from (17.A16), a borrower with an additional insurance claim at time t (i.e. $c+1$ claims) faces fewer rounds before hitting the limit:

$$s_t^{c+1}(z) = \text{int}\left\{\left(\frac{1}{\mu_*}-1\right)t + \frac{z-(c+1)}{\mu_*} - \frac{(1-\mu_*)(1-a)+b\mu_*}{\mu_*}\right\} + 1$$

$$= s_t^c(z-1).$$

The probability of hitting the limit μ_* with $(c+1)$ claims is then given by:

$$\sum_{z=0}^{s_t^c(z-1)} \binom{s_t^c(z-1)}{z} p^z (1-p)^{s_t^c(z-1)-z}. \tag{17.A18}$$

We note that the difference between (17.A18) and (17.A17) is decreasing in t and converges to zero as $t \longrightarrow \infty$. This is due to the fact that the difference can be written as

$$\text{eqn(17.A18)}-\text{eqn(17.A17)} = \sum_{z=0}^{s_t^c(z)} \left[\binom{s_t^c(z)}{z} - \binom{s_t^c(z-1)}{z} p^\xi \right] p^z (1-p)^{s_t^c(z-1)-z},$$

(17.A19)

where ξ denotes the difference $s_t^c(z) - s_t^c(z-1)$;[39] that each term in the sum is bounded above by:

$$s_t^c(z)^z (1-p)^{s_t^c(z)-z} > \left[\binom{s_t^c(z)}{z} - \binom{s_t^c(z-1)}{z} p^\xi \right] p^z (1-p)^{s_t^c(z-1)-z}$$

(17.A20)

(since the term in brackets is smaller than $\binom{s_t^c(z)}{z}$, which itself is smaller than $s_t^c(z)^z$, and that $p \leq 1$); that the left-hand side of (17.A20) goes to zero as t goes to infinity by the fact that

$$\lim_{n \longrightarrow \infty} n^z p^z (1-p)^{n-z} = 0 \quad \text{for all } z \geq 0$$

(because $p \leq 1$); and that the limit of $n^z p^z (1-p)^{n-z}$ as z approaches n is zero (the sum in (17.A19) hence does not diverge).

The loss associated with the increased probability of falling below the cut-off due to an additional false insurance claim thus goes to zero as the number of loans increases.

Net gains from false claims are positive for t large enough
The gains from deviating, however, remain significant and comprises not repaying the current loan L. As we saw above, the costs of false claims are twofold: (i) false claims decrease future income due to a loss of reputation; and (ii) false claims increase the probability of falling below the cut-off (17.A19) in the future. Since both costs tend to zero as the number of periods increase, and since the cost of deviation remains constant, we have that all borrowers will thus eventually benefit for filing false claims. It is therefore necessary for the insurance contract to impose costs beyond simple loss of reputation after insurance claims in order to deter false claims, as stated in Proposition 2.

17.A4. *Proof of Proposition*

To prove the proposition, we have to show (i) that there exists a cut-off to deter adverse selection; (ii) that there exists a punishment sufficient to deter false claims (moral hazard); (iii) that the insurance premium is sufficient to cover the financial institution's insurance costs; and (iv) that the contract satisfies the borrowers' participation constraint.

---

[39] Note that $\binom{s_t^c(z-1)}{z} = 0$ for $z > s_t^c(z-1)$.

Cut-off to deter adverse selection
In the proof of Proposition 1, we showed that the financial institution can choose a number of waiting periods to make the adverse selection problem as small as it wants.

Sufficient punishment to deter false claims (moral hazard)
In the proof of Proposition 2, we showed that extra sanctions beyond simple loss of reputation were necessary to deter false insurance claims.

The gross benefits from filing a false insurance claim are equal to the cost of not repaying the loan L. To discourage moral hazard behaviour, the sanction for a claim simply has to be equal to the benefit of the moral hazard.

The simple punishment we propose in this chapter is the following. When a borrower files a claim in period t, the institution 'demotes' the period-t borrower to a period-$(t - N_i^{[t]})$ borrower, where $N_i^{[t]}$ is the minimal integer such that

$$\sum_{s=1}^{N} \delta^s \left(\mu_i^{[t]} - \mu_i^{[t-N+s]} \right) L \geq L. \tag{17.A21}$$

The left-hand side of (17.A21) is the premium costs above the current premium cost that borrower i paid in the $N_i^{[t]}$ previous periods. The financial institution chooses $N_i^{[t]}$ such that this extra cost is exactly equal to the benefit of deviation for borrower i in period t in order to avert any false claims.

Does this contract maintain the participation constraint in case of real claims? If borrower i already had an insurance contract in $t - N_i^{[t]}$, his/her participation constraint is clearly satisfied, since it is just a repetition of what he/she did in the past, which took into account this risk of failure. If $t - N_i^{[t]}$ is greater that a borrower's insurance experience (i.e. borrower i did not have an insurance contract in $t - N_i^{[t]}$), then the financial institution considers the borrower in default.

Participation constraint for financial institution
As shown in the proof of how to limit adverse selection above (Appendix 17.A4), the insurance scheme increase repayment rates for borrowers who strategically default. This softens the institutions' participation constraint.

Furthermore, borrowers only participate once the premium charged is 'not too high' compared to the actual cost of insuring the borrowers. On average, the institution thus charges borrowers higher premia than the actual cost of insuring them (although the institution cannot change this because of adverse selection issues).

If the institution offered credit without insurance, offering credit with insurance satisfies its participation constraint.

Participation constraint for borrowers
Participation in the insurance contract of the 'good guys', that is, borrowers with $P_i > L/\delta X$, follows from the argument given in Section 17.4.1. They are willing to repay their loans even without insurance. This means that the waiting periods do not

deter them from participation. They start participating once the premium has gone down sufficiently.

REFERENCES

Ackerberg, D. A. and M. Botticini (1998). 'Endogenous Matching and the Empirical Determinants of Contract Form'. mimeo, Boston University.

Alderman, H. and C. Paxson (1994). 'Do the Poor Insure? A Synthesis of the Literature on Risk and Consumption in Developing Countries', in E. Bacha (ed.), *Economics in a Changing World: Volume 4: Development, Trade and the Environment.* London: Macmillan Press.

Alexander, G. (2001). 'An Empirical Analysis of Microfinance: Who are the Clients'. *Working Paper.* Fordham University.

Armendáriz de Aghion, B. (1999). 'On the Design of a Credit Agreement with Peer Monitoring'. *Journal of Development Economics*, 60(1), 79–104.

Banerjee, A., T. Besley, and T. Guinnane (1994). 'Thy Neighbor's Keeper: The Design of a Credit Cooperative with Theory and a Test'. *Quarterly Journal of Economics*, 109(2), 491–515.

Besley, T. (1995). 'Nonmarket Institutions for Credit and Risk Sharing in Low-Income Countries'. *Journal of Economic Perspectives*, 9(3), 115–27.

—— and S. Coate (1995). 'Group Lending, Repayment Incentives and Social Collateral'. *Journal of Development Economics*, 46, 1–18.

de la Brière, B., E. Sadoulet, A. de Janvry, and S. Lambert (2002). 'The Role of Destination, Gender, and Family Composition in Explaining Remittances: An Analysis for the Dominican Sierra'. *Journal of Development Economics*, 68(2), 309–28.

Brown, W. and C. Churchill (1999). 'Insurance Provision in Low-Income Communities. Part I: A Primer on Insurance Principles and Products'. Microenterprise Best Practices, USAID's Microenterprise Innovation Project.

—— and —— (2000). 'Insurance Provision in Low-Income Communities. Part II: Initial Lessons from Micro-Insurance Experiments for the Poor', Microenterprise Best Practices, USAID's Microenterprise Innovation Project.

Bull, C. (87). 'The Existence of Self-Enforcing Implicit Contracts'. *Quarterly Journal of Economics*, 102(1), 147–60

Christen, R. and R. Rosenberg (1999). 'The Rush to Regulate: Legal Frameworks for Microfinance'. *CGAP Occasional Paper* No. 4. Washington, DC: CGAP.

Coate, S. and M. Ravallion (1993). 'Reciprocity without Commitment: Characterization and Performance of Informal Insurance Arrangements'. *Journal of Development Economics*, 40(1), 1–24.

Deaton, A. (1988). 'Quantity, Quality, and the Spatial Variation of Price'. *American Economic Review*, 78, 418–30.

Del Conte, A. (2000). 'Roundtable on Microinsurance Services in the Informal Economy: The Role of Microfinance Institutions', The Ford Foundation, New York.

Dercon, S. (2000). 'Income Risk, Coping Strategies and Safety Nets'. Background paper for *World Development Report 2000/01.*

—— and P. Krishnan (2000). 'In Sickness and Health: Risk Sharing within Households in Rural Ethiopia'. *Journal of Political Economy*, 108(4), 688–727.

Fafchamps, M. and S. Lund (2003). 'Risk-Sharing Networks in Rural Philippines'. *Journal of Development Economics*, 71(2), 261–87.

Ghatak, M. and T. Guinnane (1999). 'The Economics of Lending with Joint Liability: Theory and Practice'. *Journal of Development Economics*, 60, 195–228.

Goldstein, M., A. de Janvry, and E. Sadoulet (2001). 'You Can't Always Get What You Want: Inclusion and Exclusion in Mutual Insurance Networks in Southern Ghana'. *Working Paper*, June. London School of Economics.

Grameen Trust Website: www.grameen-info.org/mcredit/cmodel.html

Grimard, F. (1997). 'Household Consumption Smoothing through Ethnic Ties: Evidence from Cote D'Ivoire'. *Journal of Development Economics*, 53(2), 391–422.

IMF (1998). *International Finance Statistics Yearbook*.

Jacoby, H. and E. Skoufias (1997). 'Risk, Financial Markets, and Human Capital in a Developing Country'. *Review of Economic Studies*, 64(3), 311–36.

Jain, S. and G. Mansuri (2001). 'A little at a Time: The Use of Regularly Scheduled Repayments in Microfinance Programs'. *Working Paper*, August. University of Virginia.

Jalan, J. and M. Ravallion (1999). 'Are the Poor Less Well-insured? Evidence on Vulnerability to Income Risk in Rural China'. *Journal of Development Economics*, 58, 61–81.

Jensen, R. (1998). 'Public Transfers, Private Transfers and the Crowding Out Hypothesis: Evidence from South Africa'. *Working Paper* R98-08. Cambridge, MA: Harvard University, Kennedy School of Government.

Ligon, E., J. Thomas, and T. Worrall (2000). 'Mutual Insurance, Individual Savings and Limited Commitment'. *Review of Economic Dynamics*, 3(2), 216–46.

Lucas, R. E. and O. Stark (1985). 'Motivations to Remit: Evidence from Botswana'. *Journal of Political Economy*, 93(5), 901–18.

McCord, M. J. (2001). 'MicroInsurance Center Policy Statement'. Micro-Save Africa, Microinsurance Centre, Kampala.

Microcredit Summit Campaign Report (2000). 'Empowering Women with Microcredit'. (www.microcreditsummit.org/campaigns/report00.html).

Morduch, J. (1999a). 'Between the State and the Market: Can Informal Insurance Patch the Safety Net?'. *World Bank Research Observer*, 14(2), 187–207.

—— (1999b). 'The Microfinance Promise'. *Journal of Economic Literature*, 37, 1569–614.

Navajas, S., C. Gonzalez-Vega, and A. Gonzalez (2001). 'Do Lending Technologies Exclude the Poor? The Case of Rural El Salvador'. *Working Paper*, May. Ohio State University.

Paxson, C. (1993). 'Consumption and Income Seasonality in Thailand'. *Journal of Political Economy*, 101(1), 39–72.

Platteau, J.-Ph. (2000). *Institutions, Social Norms, and Economic Development*. New York: Harwood Academic Publishers.

Reardon, T., A. A. Fall, V. Kelly, C. Delgado, P. Matlon, J. Hopkins and O. Badiane (1994). 'Is Income Diversification Agriculture-led in the West African Semi-Arid Tropics? The Nature, Causes, Effects, Distribution and Production of Off-farm Activities', in A. Atsain, S. Wangwe, and A. G. Drabek (eds), *Economic Policy Experience in Africa: What have We Learned?* Nairobi: African Economic Research Consortium.

Rice, J. A. (1988). *Mathematical Statistics and Data Analysis*. Belmont, CA: Wadsworth & Brooks.

Rosenzweig, M. and H. Binswanger (1993). 'Wealth, Weather Risk, and the Consumption and Profitability of Agricultural Investments'. *Economic Journal*, 103, 56–78.

Sadoulet, L. (1999a). 'The Role of Mutual Insurance in Group Lending'. Ph.D. dissertation, Princeton University, Chapter 1.

—— (1999b). 'Non-monotone Matching in Group Lending'. Ph.D. dissertation, Princeton University, Chapter 2.

—— and S. Carpenter (2000). 'Endogenous Matching and Risk Heterogeneity: Evidence on Microcredit Group Formation in Guatemala'. Mimeo. ECARES/ULB, Brussels.

Stiglitz, J. E. (1990). 'Incentives, Information and Organizational Design'. *NBER Working Paper* No. 2979. Cambridge, MA: National Bureau of Economic Research.

Townsend, R. (1982). 'Optimal Multiperiod Contracts and the Gain from Enduring Relationships under Private Information'. *Journal of Political Economy*, 90(6), 1166–86.

Udry, C. (1990). 'Credit Markets in Northern Nigeria: Credit as Insurance in a Rural Economy'. *The World Bank Economic Review*, 4(3), September.

UNCDF (2002). 'UNCDF Strategy for Policy Impact and Replication in Local Governance and Microfinance', United Nations Capital Development Fund, May.

Varian, H. (1990). 'Monitoring Agents with Other Agents'. *Zeitschrift für die gesamte Staatswissenschaft*, 146, 153–74.

Wydick, W. B. (1995). 'Group Lending as a Credit Delivery Mechanism in Guatemala'. Ph.D. dissertation, Department of Economics, University of California at Berkeley.

18

Can Financial Markets be Tapped to Help Poor People Cope with Weather Risks?

JERRY SKEES, PANOS VARANGIS, DONALD F. LARSON,
AND PAUL SIEGEL

18.1. INTRODUCTION

This chapter focuses on private and public mechanisms for managing natural disasters. When many households within the same community face risks that create contemporaneous losses for all, traditional coping mechanisms that may work for managing idiosyncratic risks are likely to fail; local social networks in rural areas are strained to the limit. In developing countries where farming remains a major source of employment, correlated risks are prevalent and pose a real threat to the rural economy.

Two sources of correlated risk are common: market risks (prices for output and inputs); and natural disaster risks (hurricanes, droughts, floods, frosts, earthquakes, volcanic eruptions, and so on). While far from perfect, some market mechanisms are available for managing market-related risks. For example, even in developing countries, futures exchange markets offer some risk management possibilities for internationally traded commodities. However, the traditional market-based instrument for managing natural disaster risk, insurance, is largely underdeveloped and unavailable in most parts of the world. Further, insurance alone will not address the problems faced by rural households when natural disasters occur.

The focus here is on risks that are related to weather events (excess rain, droughts, freezes, high winds, and so on) that have a severe impact on rural incomes. Given the growing interest in weather insurance markets, there are opportunities for innovation that have, as of yet, been largely unexploited. A number of studies are recognizing that markets may more easily provide rainfall insurance than traditional crop insurance in many developing countries (Gautam et al. 1994; Sakurai and Reardon 1997; Skees et al. 1999; Skees 2000). In addition, we discuss using such parametric insurance to cover correlated risks for a community of poor households through formal and informal risk-sharing arrangements. This is a potentially important innovation since instruments for managing correlated risk can complement the approaches for managing

The authors would like to gratefully acknowledge contributions by professionals in Mexico who provided information on Mexico and Jonathan Morduch and Stefan Dercon for helpful comments on the chapter.

idiosyncratic risks. We take our analysis one step further and argue that the basic information and analysis needed to design and value index insurance can also be used to develop a spatial mapping of weather-related risks. In turn, estimates of actually fair premia for classes of natural disaster risks provide a systematic way of pricing risk that can help policymakers determine when and how to intervene to help mitigate such risks or to compensate victims of weather-related events. The capacity to systematically price risk is key, since free or subsidized disaster assistance can provide perverse incentives and often can have unintended consequences. Based on insurance principles, we discuss ways of structuring disaster assistance so that it facilitates rather than crowds out other forms of risk management. Though government interventions are justified for infrequent, high-loss events, more frequent risk events may be more appropriately left to private sector insurance markets if the transaction costs of such insurance can be controlled. Our solution involves segmenting and layering the natural disaster risk to encourage more efficient risk management at various levels of loss.

18.2. RISK AND THE RURAL POOR

Siegel and Alwang (1999) develop a taxonomy of risk-coping strategies for rural households facing risk and these strategies are explored in greater detail in other chapters. Largely, these strategies are informal, based on personal relationships with limited scope for spatially pooling risks (Dercon 2002). Consequently, the range and capacity of risk-coping strategies are limited among the poor, especially when the risks are correlated. In turn, adopted strategies can slow the development process by limiting household incentives to use productivity-enhancing technologies and to specialize in activities where comparative advantages exist. Such risks also affect the credit-worthiness of rural households and constrain credit markets.

Moreover, shocks to local agriculture can have multiplicative effects on incomes in poor rural communities. For example, a widespread natural disaster (drought or flood) that creates significant yield loss for crops and damages grazing lands for livestock can have a devastating impact on all sources of income. Consider the effect of a major drought on a poor rural household. First, crops grown by the household for either household consumption or for sale will be damaged. Further, if the household has livestock, the pasture and other forage sources will also be damaged in a major drought. The household will either be forced to purchase feed, sell the livestock, or move the livestock to a region not impacted by the drought. All of these risk coping strategies will be costly. Mass selling of livestock during a major drought will depress livestock prices. Beyond the commodities grown on the farm, a major drought will also likely hurt the opportunities for selling the household labour to other farmers in the community. For example, opportunities to earn income by selling labour to harvest a crop are generally directly tied to the amount of the harvest. Since non-agricultural jobs are closely tied to the farm incomes in many communities, a major drought may also affect off-farm job opportunities for the rural poor.

When the diversified portfolio of income for the rural poor remains tied to farm production, correlated risk from a widespread natural disaster will still jeopardize the income flows for households even though they have multiple sources of income. In short, correlated risk limit the value of diversification for local households. Since correlated risks also can cause market failure in capital markets and limit access to credit, there are further welfare gains that may be achieved through the use of more efficient systems for managing natural disaster risk.

18.3. PUBLIC POLICY ALTERNATIVES FOR MANAGING AND COPING WITH NATURAL DISASTER RISK

Generally, two major courses have been tried that would give individuals the opportunity to manage or cope with natural disaster risk: traditional crop insurance that gives individuals the opportunity to protect against natural disaster risk *ex ante*; and disaster aid that gives assistance *post hoc*. There are important differences between these strategies that involve access, incentives, and costs to society. Free disaster aid can potentially work at cross-purposes with crop insurance by reducing the incentives for individuals to purchase insurance.

18.3.1. *Problems with Traditional Insurance*

Government supported crop insurance has been touted for years as being an important innovation for helping rural households manage risk since, conceptually, it provides well-targeted compensation for yield-related risks. In addition, crop insurance can be used as collateral for small and medium farmers that would not be able to obtain credit otherwise. These arguments are attractive since credit plays a major role in development and the linkage between credit and the pace of technological development is well documented.

Still, there are no examples of successful crop insurance programmes without heavy reliance on government subsidies (Hazell 1992; Skees *et al.* 1999; Skees 1999*b*, 2001). Providing individual crop insurance requires significant monitoring and some form of farm level inspection to verify crop losses. Further, the use of public funds to support crop insurance is also questionable since these funds tend to have a high opportunity cost in many developing countries. Moreover, crop insurance programmes are directly linked to the amount of crop being grown by individuals. They generally do not allow for others who suffer because of crop losses in the local economy to receive payments.

More fundamentally, the success of crop insurance programmes has been curtailed due to adverse selection and moral hazard problems. Adverse selection means that those who know *ex ante* that their risk are high are the most likely to buy the insurance. Moral hazard occurs *ex post* as farmers change their behaviour in ways that make them more risky to the insurance provider. The dual problems of adverse selection and moral hazard adds to the cost of crop insurance. It also reduces the portion of actual crop value that can be insured since high deductibles or co-payments are used as one way to reduce problems of adverse selection and moral hazard.

Furthermore, since the correlated risk from insuring natural disasters cannot be pooled (especially in developing countries) the primary insurers must rely heavily on traditional reinsurance markets. Reinsurance markets are inefficient, costly, and suffer from pricing cycles that respond to major losses (Noonan 1994; Kunreuther *et al.* 1995; Jaffee and Russell 1997; Stipp 1997; Froot 1999). Access to reinsurance in developing countries is also extremely limited. Reinsurance can be expensive or impossible in many cases as most reinsurers shy away from providing their services for agricultural risk in developing countries. The international reinsurers that understand agricultural risk rightly conclude that there are problems with underwriting crop insurance in developing countries. They also understand that they can make more money concentrating on the heavily subsidized US market.

Finally, the demand for paying for crop insurance is curtailed by the cognitive problem failure problem among individual in assessing catastrophic risk (Kunreuther 1996). Thus, even when a decisionmaker may be able to afford the insurance, they may make the wrong assessment about the real risk and decide that the price is too high. This disconnect is even more pronounced given that crop insurance providers will add extra premium for the catastrophic events.

18.3.2. *Problems with Free Disaster Assistance*

If traditional crop insurance is neither the most appropriate nor affordable means for poor farmers, what else can governments do to help them manage income risks coming from natural disasters? Free disaster assistance is a common response, even among poor countries, as the international community can be quick to respond when there are natural disasters. However, international aid is more likely in the face of major hurricanes and earthquakes and not as forthcoming when the natural disaster is a slowly developing drought. Further, disaster aid is almost always *post hoc* with few rules and no real knowledge about how much will come and who will get the aid. This raises serious equity questions and opens the door for corruption and abuse.

In many developing countries, the *post hoc* disaster aid comes in the form of debt forgiveness. Debt forgiveness does not help the poorest rural residents since most of them do not have credit. For that matter, few countries actually have disaster aid programmes that are targeted at the poor.

Economists are rightly concerned with the incentives embedded in free disaster aid (Dacy and Kunreuther 1969; Kunreuther 1973, 1993, 1996; Anderson 1976; Freeman and Kunreuther 1997; US General Accounting Office 1980, 1989; Rettger and Boisvert 1979; Kaplow 1991). When households come to expect government compensation for natural disaster losses, they will take on additional risks. If they do not bear the consequences of risky decisions, they will engage in activities that expose them to still more risk. For example, in the United States well-intentioned federal relief has likely encouraged further development along geologic fault lines and hurricane prone coastal areas (Rossi *et al.* 1982; Epstein 1996; Noll 1996). Research by Keeton *et al.* (1999) suggests that the federal agricultural disaster assistance and heavily subsidized crop insurance encourages crop production in marginal areas. Disaster relief becomes self-perpetuating when individuals do not get proper price signals about their exposure to losses from natural disasters.

To avoid some of the problems with free disaster aid, risk must be internalized or at least made explicit. Insurance and other risk-sharing markets make risk explicit by pricing risk so that decisionmakers can fully see the real cost of the risks they face in these markets. Even, when free disaster aid is justified, it would be more efficient to have well-defined rules for the provision of such aid.

18.3.3. *Recent Innovations for Supplying Insurance for Natural Disaster Risk*

Recent innovations in the capital markets could provide alternatives for dealing with natural disaster risks. These innovations have the potential to make insurance for natural disasters more affordable and more accessible even in developing countries. A convergence of traditional insurance markets and capital markets is underway (Doherty 1997; Lamm 1997; Cole and Chiarenza 1999; Skees 1999*a*). There are a number of innovations in packaging natural disaster risk into various forms of tradable financial assets. Some of these instruments are packaged as catastrophe bonds; insurance contracts; exotic options; or some other derivative financial instrument, including the advent of an active weather market. Each provides the holder with funding contingent upon the occurrence of some risky event. By purchasing these instruments, those holding the risk share some of their risk exposure with market investors. Those selling the instruments earn favourable returns and are willing to accept the risk as part of a broad-based diversified portfolio. These emerging risk-sharing markets should increase the supply of risk-sharing solutions for natural disaster risk.

While risk-sharing markets have been evolving for some time, the development of risk-sharing instruments based on natural phenomena has escalated rapidly in recent years, largely due to the increase in natural disaster losses suffered by insurers and reinsurers. The result has been a growing market in various types of natural disaster-based financial instruments (Doherty 1997; Skees 1999*a*).

One new instrument used in sharing catastrophic risk from natural disasters is the proliferation of catastrophe or 'cat' bonds—bonds whose coupon and principle payments depend on the performance of an index or pool of natural catastrophe risk. There are successful examples of using cat bonds in Japan and the United States to spread the risks of earthquakes, and expansion of this approach offers a unique opportunity to link world financiers and poor people in a partnership that is mutually beneficial. Many of the cat bond transactions were designed as parametric, meaning that their payments would be tied to some statistic where the probability distribution can be estimated and the event can be measured (such as wind speed for hurricanes or the Richter scale for earthquakes). Since the index being used is an indirect measure of losses, those investing their funds in the catastrophe bonds do not have to worry about adverse selection or moral hazard.

In parallel with the development of catastrophe bonds, an active weather market emerged in the United States in the later part of the 1990s. The weather markets expanded into Europe and Japan during the early part of the new century. While weather markets largely involve using temperature to hedge the revenues of supplies of electricity and natural gas, a number of creative approaches to writing risk instruments based on weather events have emerged. For example, activity in hedging rainfall events has been growing. Such innovation offers potentially affordable insurance for catastrophic risk from droughts and floods. But, even more importantly, as long as the rainfall measures are reliable and secure, insurers and reinsurance have now emerged to write index insurance based on rainfall—even in developing countries. This is highly significant since the due diligence for traditional insurance and reinsurance involves high transaction costs that create major hurdles for traditional reinsurers in developing countries.

18.4. USING WEATHER-BASED INDEX CONTRACTS

Properly designed weather-based index contracts could be used in a variety of ways within a developing country as a:

- means of supplying a form of direct insurance for anyone at risk when there are major droughts, freezes, or floods;
- means of facilitating mutual insurance and collective action whereby the group buys the index and then determines how to distribute payments to members of the group;
- means of providing a form of reinsurance for the private or government agricultural insurance;
- mechanism for providing clearly defined disaster aid in a standing disaster relief programme for the rural poor.

The same infrastructure of relatively low cost measures of weather events and the research needed to design effective contracts that match the risk of individuals in the society could be used for each of these purposes as well. Maintaining quality meteorological services is already viewed as a public good. Using these data to provide for more effective means of risk-sharing enhances the public good arguments for high maintaining high-quality services.

18.4.1. *Using Weather Index Contracts as Direct Crop Insurance*

As mentioned, there is an emerging literature about how rainfall insurance could replace traditional crop insurance. A key advantage of this kind of insurance is that the weather or 'trigger' event (e.g. a rainfall shortage) can be independently verified, and therefore not subject to the same possibilities of manipulation that are present when insurance payments are linked to actual farm losses. And since the contracts and indemnity payments are the same for all buyers per unit of insurance, the usual problems of moral hazard and adverse selection associated with public crop insurance are significantly less. Additionally, the insurance would be easy to administer, since there are no individual contracts to write; no on-farm inspections; and no individual loss assessments. Given that one does not tie the losses to an individual farm, such insurance can be sold to a broad range of people, including agricultural traders, shopkeepers, and landless workers whose incomes are also affected by the insured events.

Weather index insurance would also be easy to market. For example, it could be sold through banks, farm cooperatives, input suppliers, and microfinance organizations, as well as being sold directly to farmers. Weather insurance is not only for producers and rural people. Banks and rural finance institutions could purchase such insurance to protect their portfolios against defaults caused by severe weather events. Rural finance entities aggregate and pool risk. With index insurance contracts one can take advantage of such entities to become the means of mitigating basis risk via loans to farmers who have a loss and do not receive a payment from the index insurance (Mahul 2002; Skees 2003). Similarly, input suppliers could be the purchasers of such insurance. Once financial institutions are able to shift correlated risk out of local areas with index insurance contracts, they would be in a better position to expand credit to farmers, at perhaps improved terms.

There is already some experience with weather-based index insurance in agriculture. There is an insurance plan in Canada in the province of Ontario that uses rainfall indexes to insure alfalfa hay production. In Alberta, rainfall is being used to insure rangeland and temperature is being used to protect against losses in silage corn. A private insurance company in Argentina is offering a rainfall insurance contract to a milk-producing cooperative (there is strong positive correlation between rainfall and milk production). While the overall number of applications is still relatively small, the interest is growing. There are several applications of index insurance in agriculture not based on rainfall (or temperature) but on average area yields. Instead of rainfall, the index that triggers the insurance payments is based on estimates of the average yield for a county or other predetermined area. Area-based yield insurance has similar benefits as weather-based index insurance as long as proper procedures are following in estimating area yields and in the contract design, including setting adequate premium rates. Some of the countries that have developed agricultural insurance products based on area yields are the United States, Sweden, Canada, Brazil, Argentina, and Morocco, the latter still on a pilot basis (Skees *et al*. 1997).

A specially funded project was also awarded to a working group within the World Bank. This project has investigated the feasibility of developing Weather-based index contracts for four countries: Ethiopia, Morocco, Nicaragua, and Tunisia. Since the project began, several of the professionals involved have begun similar investigations in other countries, including Argentina, India, Mexico, Mongolia, Romania, and Turkey. There is clearly a growing international interest in weather insurance. Furthermore, the International Finance Corporation (IFC) of the World Bank group is working towards assisting developing countries in having access to the newly developed weather markets. In this role, IFC plans to take a financial interest in these markets, increasing the likelihood of their success.

Designing a weather index insurance product

An index contract is very different from traditional crop insurance. Unlike traditional crop insurance where it must be tied to a specific crop with a measure of plantings and yield potential, the index contract can be purchased at any dollar value. Ideally this value would reflect some measure of income at risk to avoid taking on undue risk or giving the appearance of gambling. Since no crop acres must be reported or monitored, the poor household can be provided disaster aid based on the portfolio of income. Anyone can purchase additional index contracts to reflect the full array of income that may be at risk for the household when the major drought occurs. For example, if a household earning US$2,000 per year from a mix of sources estimates that half of this income is vulnerable during a major drought, they may purchase US$1,000 of value in the drought index insurance. This would be true even if only a very small percentage of the US$1,000 comes from crops they grow themselves. Traditional crop insurance would never provide such an opportunity. In fact, for subsistence farmers growing crops for home consumption, traditional crop insurance would never be available.

A number of different contract designs might be considered (Skees 2000). In a straightforward proportional contract the payments would be structured as a percentage of the rain below a specified threshold or strike level. For example, let us assume that the average rainfall is 300 mm for the three months most critical for the crop season. Any rainfall below 200 mm creates problems. With a straightforward proportional contract, if rainfall were 100 mm, a 50 per cent payment would be made:

Percentage payment = (Strike − Actual rain)/Strike

Percentage payment = (200 − 100)/200 or 50%

The protection purchased is an individual decision that should be based on value at risk and the amount of funds that are available to pay premiums. Premiums are a direct function of the protection purchased:

Premium payments = protection purchased × premium rate

Indemnity payments are a direct function of the percentage payment when the index drops below the threshold and the protection purchased:

Payment = percentage payment × protection purchased

For example, with a 50 per cent payment rate, an individual who purchased US$1,000 of protection would receive US$500 (50% × US$1,000).

18.4.2. *Using Weather Index Insurance to Facilitate Mutual Insurance*

The introduction of weather index insurance opens numerous possibilities for collective action among small farmers. By removing the correlated risk due to catastrophic weather events, this insurance could aid in fostering mutual insurance arrangements among households and also in the effective delivery of financial services to them. For example, informal arrangements between households could reduce transaction costs of sharing risk once correlated risks, such as weather related risks, are reduced or eliminated. Also, microfinance entities (MFEs) are becoming important in delivering financial services to the rural poor, but can be victims of natural catastrophes (Nagarajan 1998). Moreover, as Morduch (1999) observes generous donor funds have been key to the role that MFEs have played in providing services after the occurrence of catastrophes but he argues that these donations are unlikely to continue. This increases the important role that natural catastrophe insurance can play in both adding to the services that MFEs provide and in adding to their sustainability in light of a local natural catastrophe. Nagarajan (1998) posed the questions on whether MFEs can develop programmes that could serve as a social safety net following a natural catastrophe and whether they could develop products to manage and mitigate natural catastrophe risks to protect their clients and their portfolio. It can be argued that MFEs could perhaps deliver insurance and natural catastrophe aid to their communities if they (MFEs) have access to catastrophic weather insurance. Black *et al.* (1999), Skees (1999*a*), and Zeuli (1999) extend these ideas to the United States by arguing that cooperatives could purchase the area-based yield insurance and become mutual insures.

Introducing weather insurance to mutual insurance or microfinance schemes has the additional benefit of dealing with the problem of basis risk. That is the problem that weather events may not have the same impact on all farmers within a region; not everyone experiences the same loss. Basis risk is an important problem in the use of weather insurance contracts by individual farmers, particularly small ones. However, it is possible to reduce the basis risk if a group of farmers obtain such insurance with *ex ante* arrangements to distribute the payments within the group based upon predetermined criteria. In effect, the group obtains formal insurance to cover systemic and catastrophic risks and relies on informal arrangements to distribute the payments within the group.

A good example of how catastrophic weather insurance could enhance mutual insurance arrangements among farmers can be provided by the Mexican fondos de aseguramiento, or fondos for short. Fondos are groups of farmers formed for the purpose of providing mutual crop insurance to their members. There are about 200 fondos in operation in Mexico having some 70,000 farmers in total as members. They are non-profit, civil associations and they operate in such a way that the collected premiums create reserves to pay indemnities and cover the operational costs. However, in the event of severe weather events, the collected premiums and reserves are not sufficient to cover the losses. This is because natural catastrophes affect all farmers in the fondo simultaneously and their mutual insurance needs to make large payments to all of them at the same time. A World Bank study for the Mexican crop insurance identified drought, excess humidity, and frost as the main weather perils that cause catastrophic risks for the fondos. That is, fondos run out of collected premiums and reserves to pay for losses mainly due to these severe weather events. Thus, obtaining insurance for these weather perils is crucial for the financial viability of the fondos.

18.4.3. *Using Index Contracts for Disaster Funds*

As was established earlier, in countries where the rural poor have been engaged in livelihood diversification, the variety of income sources may still be exposed to risks from major natural disasters. Not only can the own farm income suffer, but the opportunities to earn a wage in various activities that are directly tied to agriculture will also become limited. Further, the link connecting the non-farm economy to the farm economy may also mean that non-farm job opportunities suffer as well during a regional natural disaster. For these reasons, tying a standing disaster aid package directly to weather events may be the most reasonable and clear way to provide assistance to the rural poor during a natural disaster. Goes and Skees (2003) have examined a possible role for indexed catastrophe bonds in providing disaster relief to developing countries in conjunction with *ex ante* charitable donations. This unique mechanism could be structured to address many of the problems associated with traditional sources of disaster relief.

How would a weather-based index catastrophe aid programme work? The first item to consider is designing a contract that would provide roughly equal aid to all low-income households regardless of the regional location. It should be designed to replace only a portion of the lost income. Finding the right weather events that create the most serious losses requires some research.

The value of free aid can be calculated using the same method as one would use if the weather index were being developed as insurance. These calculations can be used to provide the same implicit value of aid regardless of the large differences that may exist among different regions within a country. This is important as most disaster aid rarely involves basic principles of risk assessment, thus creating perverse incentives for risk taking.

A logical threshold may be to provide aid for infrequent events, say, one in twenty or more year events. Using a parametric weather trigger to make disaster payments makes the rules explicit and transparent. It also should improve the timing of payments. Even more important, such indexes could facilitate an insurance market in weather contracts. The government would now have the incentives to maintain a reliable infrastructure to measure the important weather events. Further, there would have been some level of research to perform the analysis needed to establish the parameters for contracts that transfer the same amount to everyone. Private companies could do any number of things with the information and infrastructure; they could match the contract of the government with more money; they could offer a layer of insurance above what the government offers (i.e. for less frequent events); they could both match and offer another layer. The key is that a disaster programme that is structured in this fashion would not crowd out private sector innovations rather it would encourage them.

Unlike regular crop insurance, parametric insurance does not directly compensate for assessed losses, but rather pays out when an agreed upon indicator meets an agreed upon condition—for example, when the temperature recorded at a defined weather station falls below a certain level. Consequently, transaction costs associated with the insurance are lower since field assessments of damage are not required. Parametric insurance is also easier to price, since the expected payouts from the insurance can be estimated by calculating from historic data the probability of the trigger condition being met.

In Mexico's example, we find that the historic Fondo de Desastres Naturales (FONDEN) crop related payouts for drought are in line, but slightly below, rough estimates based on probabilities. This may mean that current FONDEN criteria are triggered too frequently and that the discretionary component of FONDEN has worked to limit expenses. However, it also shows that parametric triggers can generate similar payments. This finding is relevant for all programmes, since parametric triggers could be used for social protection expenditures that are additional to payments for crop-related losses.

Benefits and limits of parametric triggers

If suitable triggers can be found, there are several sound technical reasons for converting to a scheme that pays out based solely on parametric triggers. First, triggers can be derived that provide equal protection to all smallholders. Second, reinsurance becomes straightforward, since payouts are based on historic probabilities that reinsurers can easily understand and price. Third, the process is quick and low cost since field visits are not required.

Designing triggers that have an equal probability of payout regardless of crop type or location would eliminate distortion of payments among farmers. If compensation were to depend on crop damage—as measured by field inspectors—farmers who take preventative action to limit crop losses would be penalized. In contrast, payouts based solely on weather conditions would restore normal incentives to take preventative action. Of course, any free insurance causes distortion by providing marginal compensation without cost. This can also be reduced by designing the triggers so that the payout is only for infrequent events.

If short-term budget issues can be solved, there are often advantages for governments who self-insure. Purchasing reinsurance from private firms converts large lump-sum assistance expenditures into annual premiums that can be more easily budgeted. Doing so, however, will come at a price, which in turn, is related to the probability of payouts. For parametric insurance these costs can be calculated in a straightforward way. In contrast, when payouts include a measure of discretion, reinsurers will have difficulty pricing the probability of payouts and may be reluctant to reinsure.

Breaking the link between payouts and field inspections has a cost as well. The most significant drawback of parametric triggers is the potential mismatch between conditions at weather stations and effects in the field. This basis risk has an analogy with price hedging where local prices may differ from price observed in Chicago or other hedging markets. Whether the basis risk overwhelms the significant benefits of parametric insurance is an empirical question, depending largely upon the spatial correlation of rainfall events over time. For example, in areas with microclimates, the spatial correlation may be too weak and the basis risk too high. Nonetheless, the basis risk problems can be solved if the index insurance is combined with rural finance or mutual insurance (Mahul 2002; Skees 2003).

At the same time, introducing insurance contracts that payout when certain whether events occurs introduces new incentives that create a different type of moral hazard. While beneficiaries may not be able to influence the weather, they may be able to influence those responsible for reporting weather station readings. Poorly paid station workers, especially in remote areas, may be bribed, or unsecured stations tampered with. New technologies that electronically relay weather data can reduce the risk of falsified reports, but require investments. Remote confirmation by satellite is another way to potentially catch false reports, but recent research at the World Bank suggests that current technologies are not yet accurate enough to provide effective safeguards.

18.4.4. *Weather Information as a Public Good*

As discussed, pricing weather risks is a basic step towards designing related insurance projects and in assessing vulnerability to natural disasters. Generally, destructive weather events of the type that trigger significant insurance payouts, or calls for government relief, are relatively rare in a meteorological sense. Assessing the probability of such events requires a long and consistent time series spanning decades. An important question then is how available are such time series.

Experience in the World Bank Group suggests that long time series of temperature and rainfall data are common in many developing countries; however, the series are often associated with specific weather stations and specific parts of the country. In addition, gaps are common due to many reasons ranging from war to misplaced records. In some cases, historic data remains locked in stored paper records. Still, long time-series of meteorological have multiple uses that include pricing risk and many national and international groups are contributing to building up basic climate data. For example, in connection with a famine early warning system, the Government of Ethiopia and international donors are processing and digitizing paper records spanning decades. In the World Bank Group, the International Finance Corporation offers reinsurance for weather insurance and works with countries to analyse domestic meteorological data. The United States National Oceanic and Atmospheric Administration is developing databases that use ground–station and satellite data to create interpolated time series of temperature and precipitation.

18.5. SUMMARY AND CONCLUSIONS

A host of risks face poor rural households in developing countries. Social programmes are needed to address health risk, human capital development risk, and natural disaster risk. Among the more popular risk management strategies used by poor rural households is diversification. However, diversification as a risk management strategy can hinder development since welfare gains may be possible when households specialize. Further, since farming remains a dominant activity in many rural areas, diversification may not actually spread certain types of correlated risk, in particular, weather events that cause widespread loss for crops and grazing lands. These correlated risks may impact a variety of sources of income: own farm, agricultural labour, and non-farm income. In some rural areas, even the non-farm jobs can be tied to the well-being of the local farm economy. Any natural disaster or general downturn in producer prices that hurts the local farm economy may have negative effects on non-farm jobs as well.

If there are no mechanisms available to help households manage natural disaster risk or price risk then financial markets will likely be incomplete. Such incomplete markets will likely mean that inadequate credit is available in the rural economy. If farmers either have no access to credit or exhibit extreme risk aversion and do not borrow, they are unlikely to adopt available technologies that are needed to advance agricultural production. Thus, efforts that combine the dual roles of helping the rural poor recover from natural disasters and aiding in the emergence of market-based risk management strategies are important. However, public disaster assistance is problematic as it can send the wrong signals to those in high-risk areas.

With these issues in mind, this chapter focuses on natural disaster risk policies. Traditional crop insurance is dismissed as a viable alternative for medium and small farmers in developing countries. Given recent developments in international capital markets we turn to the potential of indexing weather events (e.g. shortfalls or excess rain, extreme temperatures, and so on). While there is no single solution, such indexes could facilitate multiple objectives, where they could be used:

- as an objective means of providing disaster aid based on relative risk so as not to favour high risk regions;
- by state governments to fund disaster aid;
- by intermediaries in the economy to help manage natural disaster risk; and
- directly as insurance to households against certain local natural disasters.

Once governments decide to use weather index contracts, any combination of uses becomes possible. The public support of a sound and secure infrastructure to measure weather events is a prerequisite for many of the items discussed above. Governments in developing economies, with the aid of international development agencies, can also process and make historical weather data publicly available. To the extent that the capital markets trust the data for weather events in developing countries, it may be possible someday to create efficient and affordable risk sharing instruments that can be used for multiple purposes.

REFERENCES

Anderson, D. R. (1976). 'All Risks Rating Within a Catastrophe Insurance System'. *Journal of Risk and Insurance*, 43, 629–51.

Black, J. R., B. J. Barnett, and Y. Hu (1999). 'Cooperatives and Capital Markets: The Case of Minnesota-Dakota Sugar Cooperatives'. *American Journal of Agricultural Economics*, 81, 1240–6.

Cole, J. B. and A. Chiarenza (1999). 'Convergence in the Markets for Insurance Risk and Capital'. *Risk Magazine*, July, 9–12.

Dacy, D. C. and H. Kunreuther (1969). *The Economics of Natural Disasters: Implications for Federal Policy*. New York: The Free Press.

Dercon, S. (2002). 'Income Risk, Coping Strategies, and Safety Nets'. *World Bank Research Observer*, 17, 141–66.

Doherty, N. A. (1997). 'Financial Innovation in The Management of Catastrophic Risk', paper presented at ASTIN/AFIR Conference, August, Australia.

Epstein, R. A. (1996). 'Catastrophic Responses to Catastrophic Risks'. *Journal of Risk and Uncertainty*, 12, 287–308.

Freeman, P. K. and H. Kunreuther (1997). *Managing Environmental Risk Through Insurance*. Boston, MA: Kluwer Academic Press.

Froot, K. A. (1999). *The Financing of Catastrophic Risk*. Chicago, IL and London: University of Chicago Press.

Gautam, M., P. Hazell, and H. Alderman (1994). 'Rural Demand for Drought Insurance'. *Policy Research Working Paper* 1383, November. Washington, DC: World Bank.

Goes, A. and J. Skees. (2003). 'Financing Natural Disaster Risk Using Charity Contributions and *Ex Ante* Index Insurance', paper presented at the American Agricultural Economics Association Annual Meeting, 27–30 July, Montreal.

Hazell, P. B. R. (1992). 'The Appropriate Role of Agricultural Insurance in Developing Countries'. *Journal of International Development*, 4, 567–81.

Jaffee, D. M. and T. Russell (1997). 'Catastrophe Insurance, Capital Markets, and Uninsurable Risks'. *Journal of Risk and Insurance*, 64, 205–320.

Kaplow, L. (1991). 'Incentives and Government Relief for Risk'. *Journal of Risk and Uncertainty*, 4, 167–75.

Keeton, K., J. Skees, and J. Long (1999). 'The Potential Influence of Risk Management Programs on Cropping Decisions', paper selected at the American Agricultural Economics Association Meeting, 8–11 August, Nashville, TN.

Kunreuther, H. (1973). *Recovery From Natural Disasters: Insurance or Federal Aid?*. Washington, DC: American Enterprise Institute for Public Policy Research.

—— (1993). 'Combining Insurance with Hazard Mitigation to Reduce Disaster Losses'. *Natural Hazards Observer*, 17, 1–3.

—— (1996). 'Mitigating Disaster Losses through Insurance'. *Journal of Risk and Uncertainty*, 12, 171–87.

——, J. Meszarous, R. Hogarth, and M. Spranca (1995). 'Ambiguity and Underwriter Decision Processes'. *Journal of Economic Behavior and Organization*, 26, 337–52.

Lamm, R. M. Jr. (1997). 'The Catastrophe Reinsurance Market: Gyrations and Innovations amid Major Structural Transformation', *Bankers Trust Research*, 3(February), 1–13 (New York: Bankers Trust Company).

Mahul, O. (2002). 'Coping with Catastrophic Risk: The Role of (Non-)Participating Contracts'. *Working Paper*. Paris: Department of Economics, INRA.

Morduch, J. (1999). 'The Microfinance Promise'. *Journal of Economic Literature*, xxxviii, 1569–1614.

Nagarajan, G. (1998). *Microfinance in the Wake of Natural Disasters: Challenges and Opportunities*. Bethesda, MD: Development Alternatives Inc.

Noll, R. G. (1996). 'The Complex Politics of Catastrophe Economics'. *Journal of Risk and Uncertainty*, 12, 141–6.

Noonan, B. (1994). 'A Catastrophe Waiting to Happen?' *Best's Review*, February, 30–33.

Rettger, M. J. and R. N. Boisvert (1979). 'Flood Insurance or Disaster Loans, An Economic Evaluation'. *American Journal of Agricultural Economics*, 61, 496–505.

Rossi, P., J. Wright, and E. Weber-Burdin (1982). *Natural Hazards and Public Choice: The State and Local Politics of Hazard Mitigation*. New York: Academic Press.

Sakurai, T. and T. Reardon (1997). 'Potential Demand for Drought Insurance in Burkina Faso and its Determinants'. *American Journal of Agricultural Econmics*, 79, 1193–1207.

Siegel, P. B. and J. Alwang (1999). 'An Asset Based Approach to Social Risk Management: A Conceptual Approach'. *Social Protection Discussion Paper* No. 9926. Washington, DC: World Bank.

Skees, J. R. (1999*a*). 'Opportunities for Improved Efficiency in Risk-Sharing Using Capital Markets'. *American Journal of Agricultural Economics*, 81, 1228–1233.

—— (1999*b*). 'Agricultural Risk Management or Income Enhancement?'. *Regulation, The CATO Review of Business and Government*, 22, 35–43.

—— (2000). 'A Role for Capital Markets in Natural Disasters: A Piece of the Food Security Puzzle'. *Food Policy*, 25, 365–378.

—— (2001). 'The Bad Harvest'. *Regulation, The CATO Review of Business and Government*, 24, 16–21.

—— (2003) 'Risk Management Challenges in Rural Financial Markets: Blending Risk Management Innovations with Rural Finance', thematic paper presented at 'Paving the Way Forward for Rural Finance: An International Conference on Best Practices', 2–4 June, Washington, DC.

——, J. R. Black, and B. J. Barnett (1997). 'Designing and Rating an Area Yield Crop Insurance Contract'. *American Journal of Agricultural Economics*, 79, 430–438.

——, P. Hazell, and M. Miranda (1999). 'New Approaches to Crop Insurance in Developing Countries'. *EPTD Discussion Paper* No. 55. Washington, DC: International Food Policy Research Institute.

Stipp, D. (1997). 'A New Way to Bet on Disasters'. *Fortune*, 8 September.

US General Accounting Office (1980). 'Federal Disaster Assistance: What Should the Policy be?'. *PAD-80-39*. Washington, DC: US Government Printing Office.

—— (1989). 'Disaster Assistance: Crop Insurance Can Provide Assistance More Effectively than Other Programs'. *RCED-89-211*. Washington, DC: US Government Printing Office.

Zeuli, K. (1999). 'New Risk Management Strategies for Agricultural Cooperatives'. *American Journal of Agricultural Economics*, 81, 1234–1239.

PART VIII

CONCLUSION

19

Risk, Poverty, and Public Action

STEFAN DERCON

19.1. THE NEED FOR MORE PUBLIC ACTION

This last chapter[1] presents a brief discussion of some of the main lessons from the research published in this book. It will focus on the scope for public action to provide insurance against poverty. There will be no attempt to give a comprehensive overview of the conclusions from the different chapters or a complete general discussion of all the issues involved. Rather, I want to focus on a few questions. First, how strong is the case for public action for more social protection in developing countries? What are its limitations? Second, what lessons have we learned for the form public action could take, given limited budgets? What role, if any, is there for existing non-market institutions, for the state, for the private sector, or for development aid? While discussing these questions, I will point to a number of gaps in the research on these issues.

19.1.1. *Why Public Action for More Insurance and Social Protection?*

The presence of uninsured risk results in welfare losses. For the poor, it is a reason for substantial hardship. At present, many poor people are not offered opportunities to insure themselves against this hardship, while the support offered when shocks occur is often limited. Viewed like this, there is no doubt that more social protection is a good idea, justifying public action to foster more insurance and mechanisms to protect the poor. In the presence of insurance and credit market failures, there is a further problem: the poor may enter into activities and asset portfolios with low-risk, but also low returns. This in turn affects their long-term income and their ability to move out of poverty. Furthermore, shocks may have long-lasting effects: productive assets may be destroyed or sold off to survive, health may be undermined or children may be taken out of school. The result is higher poverty that may persist. This suggests that uninsured risk may lead to poverty traps: there is persistence in poverty, caused by the market imperfections, the presence of risk, and the household's responses to it. Temporary support may avoid households to fall into

---

[1] Some of the ideas and conclusions in this chapter are based on a discussion among all authors contributing to this book. I am grateful to all of them. The views expressed in this chapter are my own as are the errors.

the trap, and may also lift them out; providing a strong case for offering broader social protection.

There is a growing literature on models of the poverty trap. The class of models relevant for our case is what some have called 'historical self-reinforcement' or 'path dependence' models (Mookherjee and Ray 2001).[2] Effectively, the level of well-being and assets at a particular point is having a permanent impact on the options available. For example, in a large number of models, asset inequalities result in some groups (or possibly countries) staying permanently behind others. Some of these models may have multiple equilibria but they do not need to have them; it is just that 'history' matters. Examples are the models in Banerjee and Newman (1993), Dasgupta and Ray (1986), Galor and Zeira (1993), and the like. Typically, credit market imperfections conspire with asset inequality to cause traps.[3] Risk and insurance market failures result in poverty traps via the risk management and coping mechanisms chosen by households to avoid destitution. Alternatively, by wiping out assets, shocks could push households down the asset distribution into these traps as well. The overall result is permanently lower incomes and lower growth for particular households. They could be trapped below some threshold—for example, defined in terms of assets or of nutritional status, as in Dasgupta and Ray (1986). Banerjee (Chapter 3, this volume) presented a model where at low levels of protection, there could be a poverty trap, in which the poor will not invest into profitable but risky activities, while the rich will take up these activities. These different models have in common that there are efficiency losses in the economy, linked to the lack of insurance compounded by existing inequalities. There are high marginal returns from shifting resources towards the poor, and they outweigh the marginal losses to the rich. In short, within particular ranges of transfers, there is no efficiency-equity tradeoff from redistribution. Alternatively, aid-financed social protection would imply both efficiency and equity gains.

For this to justify more social protection for efficiency reasons requires more empirical evidence. Chapter 1 provided suggestive evidence from a number of contexts, with poorer households having low-risk activity portfolios with lower returns. The evidence in Dercon (1996) suggests that the shift into low-risk activities for the poorest quintile relative to the richest resulted in 20 per cent lower incomes per unit

---

[2] Much of the current theory literature focuses on growth traps as coordination failures (the Rodenstein–Rodan model, and its modern proponents, such as in Murphy et al. 1989 and Romer 1986, and so on). Multiple equilibria and low-growth equilibrium are possibilities in this set-up. Shocks can play an important role in these processes. A substantial shock is needed to push one to a low growth or GDP level equilibrium when there are multiple equilibria; a positive shock may push you out again (as in the coordination failure models). As a model of how risk and shocks affect poverty, it is not entirely satisfactory.

[3] Note that you do not have to have vast inequalities to cause 'traps' for some—as long as there is some level of assets needed to avoid a trap, one could get individuals trapped in poverty in most set-ups. In such a context, different outcomes are possible. Overall, growth could be lower, due to some growth trap society is stuck in. Of course, data from one country only could not do much in this respect. However, one could get specific poverty traps—or low-growth/levels of income traps for some groups. For example, there could be a local income and growth trap—for example, a geographical poverty trap as or group-specific traps—where specific characteristics cause the negative externalities to keep the group with these characteristics trapped.

of land in his study area in Tanzania. Extrapolating the results in Rosenzweig and Binswanger (1993), the efficiency loss is even higher for poor households in their Indian sample. Jalan and Ravallion (Chapter 5, this volume) went further and tried to test whether household income dynamics were consistent with the presence of multiple equilibria (where the lower level of income would be the poverty trap equilibrium). Their evidence does not suggest a pure poverty trap, but a relatively slow recovery from shocks, specifically for the poor: incomes may take several years to recover from shocks, and the recovery is slower for the poor. The evidence in Chapter 6 suggests permanent effects on children from drought—lower adult height, poor education outcomes, and therefore lower lifetime earnings. The impact of the drought in Zimbabwe on a particularly vulnerable cohort of children was estimated at about 7 per cent of lifetime earnings. But it could be argued that this is not a wealth of evidence.[4] Furthermore, there is a need to establish much more firmly the quantitative importance of these effects in different context. More empirical work on the short- and long-term consequences of uninsured risk on poverty and growth in the developing world is a priority.

19.1.2. *Some Limits to Social Protection*

If, however, these effects from risk and shocks on the poor are indeed long-lasting and quantitatively as important as the available evidence, then there is a case for intervention in the form of subsidized insurance. The marginal returns of the assets of the poor could be increased to levels similar to those unaffected by the insurance market failure. But one should be aware of the limits to such strategies. The key issue is that market failure and risk conspire to exacerbate any existing inequality—the poor cannot take advantage of opportunities if they cannot bear the risk, contrary to the rich. Providing more insurance removes the risk of worsening poverty or poverty traps—but it does not resolve the initial inequality. As Fafchamps (Chapter 4, this volume) emphasized: full insurance locks agents into persistent inequality. It does not reduce it, nor is there any scope for a lucky agent to escape. In such a world, insurance is no substitute for redistribution.

Banerjee (Chapter 3, this volume) warned for another problem: providing more insurance in the form of protection against downside risk may provide incentives for more risk-taking so that the poor take on high return, risky investments. But this may undermine their access to credit markets, if moneylenders and banks need sufficient incentives for the borrower to repay in case the project fails. Social protection may reduce these incentives, so the poor may become more excluded from credit markets. If they need access to these markets to grow out of poverty, they may become locked in long-term poverty because of social insurance. The empirical significance of these effects is unknown, but worth exploring.

---

[4] Some studies found only limited long-term costs of uninsured risk, including on the poor—Jalan and Ravallion (2001) is an example.

19.2. BUILDING ON EXISTING INSTITUTIONS

19.2.1. *The Strengths and Weaknesses of Informal Risk-sharing Institutions*

In the context of public action to increase social protection, it would seem attractive to build on existing institutions. The presence of informal risk-sharing institutions in communities across the world would offer such an opportunity. Their strengths are well known: the fact that they tend to be nested within relatively well-defined communities and social networks allows one to achieve some risk-pooling without some of the standard information and enforcement problems plaguing market-based systems. In particular, social norms, sanctions, and proximity reduce the problems related to moral hazard, adverse selection, and enforcement. Even though the evidence shows that they may not be able to replicate first-best risk-sharing, they appear to offer at least some protection in contexts where market-based insurance hardly exists.

But we should not be blind to their weaknesses. Three issues are crucial: the type of risk they can handle, the exclusion of marginal groups from these institutions and their apparent inability to handle change. First, their ability to solve some of the standard problems with insurance markets is limited to only specific types of risk. They are typically only able to handle individual-specific (idiosyncratic) risk. Basic reciprocity relations cannot handle common (or covariate) risk. Even though it should be possible for these groups to build-up assets to deal with more covariate shocks—indeed, some types of groups appear to be doing this, for example, funeral societies (*iddirs*) in Ethiopia—in general, savings to cope with shocks are largely kept by households or individuals, not by groups. Similarly, savings groups, such as Rotating Savings and Credit Associations (ROSCAs), may at times allow members to use the group for insurance purposes (e.g. allowing members to borrow or to bid for early disbursement), but their functioning means that they cannot deal with requests from all members for funds at the same time.

Furthermore, informal risk-sharing institutions are best-suited for small disbursements for relatively frequent events. Using these groups for events requiring very high payouts relative to the income of the members would require either large groups or the accumulation of savings by the group. Sustaining reciprocity if the events are very rare is also difficult, since interaction becomes more limited. Enforcement of continued participation in such groups, without strong social sanctions, would require that transfers within the context of a risk-sharing network take the form of quasi-credit, that is, those contributing in net terms over time should be compensated for this, as if some of the transfers were in fact a loan (Platteau and Abraham 1987; Ligon *et al.* 2002). In short, the type of risks these groups can insure is limited, but for good reasons. Providing support to broaden their coverage of risks, for example, by encouraging larger groups to exploit risk-pooling incentives, may lead to the loss of the crucial information and enforcement advantages of the current groups, undermining their sustainability.

We should also not underestimate the inequalities embedded in some risk-sharing institutions. First, as is well illustrated by De Weerdt (Chapter 10, this volume), wealth and other socio-economic characteristics matter for networks: his finding that the poor have less dense risk-sharing networks than the rich is striking, leaving the poor more exposed. The need for insurance on the part of the poor also often leads to unequal or patron–client relations with richer households, and possibly poverty traps (Fafchamps 1992). The fact that some marginal groups are excluded from risk-sharing institutions should not just be interpreted as a reflection of power relations—rather they reflect the inefficiency of the existing insurance arrangements. From an insurance point of view, the benefits of risk-pooling provide incentives to increase group size and diversify its composition. However, even limited asymmetric information or enforcement problems may lead to rationing in insurance, or less than full insurance. Furthermore, credit market imperfections may imply that the poorest members in communities may simply not be able to contribute, even if not affected by 'bad luck', or they may tend to experience persistence in shocks—making them unsuitable candidates to be offered membership of a risk-sharing arrangement, unless purely based on altruistic or redistributive grounds.

Finally, there is little evidence that these informal institutions manage to sustain themselves in periods of change. Platteau (Chapter 12, this volume) documented this for traditional institutions governing access to land and other common-property resources. However, besides much casual evidence, in general there has been little research on whether and how these institutions manage to sustain themselves in the face of rapid change, such as increasing population pressure or market liberalization, or large shocks, such as the AIDS epidemic in Africa. Such change or shocks changes risk distributions, requiring a restructuring in existing arrangements, possibly putting pressure to exclude certain groups or undermining the social norms and sanctions sustaining these mechanisms. However, little is known about how well these institutions cope. Economic research should increasingly shift its focus from the functioning of mutual support in closed 'village' economies to changes in mutual support.

19.2.2. *Scaling up Informal Institutions*

Developing more widespread social protection embedded in more traditional risk-sharing institutions or, more broadly, community organizations would be valuable, if possible. It is bound to assist governance and the smooth functioning of social protection mechanisms. A good understanding of the strengths and weaknesses of these informal institutions is therefore necessary. It is not clear a priori how successful such strategy could be. The key strength of indigenous organizations is their social proximity, allowing social norms and sanctions to partially alleviate some of the key causes of insurance market failure, in terms of monitoring and enforcement, but a key limitation is the type of risks these institutions can address. But in order to broaden the risks covered, more risk-pooling is necessary, either by making the group membership wider (in terms of space, occupations, ethnicity, clans) or by finding effective ways of reinsuring each of the groups. Clearly, this will involve losing some of the informational and enforcement advantages of local social organizations, resulting in lower efficiency, a higher cost structure and ultimately, less insurance unless it becomes subsidized. It would require an active role of intermediaries between the overall insurance system and the local institutions. The serious problems related to this are well documented by Conning and Kevane (Chapter 15, this volume). The problems of exclusion of specific groups from local institutions and power relations in risk-sharing would also need to be addressed when building upon existing institutions, to avoid capture by the rich or powerful of the benefits from expanding protection. Solving these problems may again undermine the sustainability of these institutions.

These constraints on using existing social institutions as models for the design and vehicles of delivery of more social protection would provide a strong argument for the need to develop additional forms of social protection, alongside existing informal institutions. In practice, this seems to be an observed strategy in many of the poorest countries. As a number of contributions in this book emphasized, even in this case, ignoring the existing institutions would result in misleading inference on the net impact of formal social protection schemes. Some crowding-out of the private transfers linked to traditional institutions when public transfers are introduced is widely observed. Traditional schemes may also be undermined by the development of formal schemes.

While the scale of crowding-out is important for the evaluation of the impact of formal schemes, some have commented that in itself crowding-out is really not a problem, provided the emerging formal system provides superior social protection. The weaknesses of existing schemes, in terms of limited coverage of some of the poorest groups and the most catastrophic risks, and the lack of full insurance offered, may be a sufficient reason to let formal social protection crowd out informal systems (Morduch and Sharma 2002). To establish this, more evidence is needed on the efficiency and equity of public systems relative to informal institutions, and the incidence and distribution of crowding-out. But if in the end a public system of universal or targeted coverage can emerge, the loss of these informal institutions may not be a serious problem.

Against this view on the possible irrelevance of crowding-out, however, at least one more issue should be considered. The existing informal institutions for risk-sharing may provide a much broader social function, for example, by encouraging more interaction and trust within these networks. As such, they contribute to the social capital of these communities. These externalities are hard to quantify, but it is possible that crowding-out would have higher welfare costs than could be calculated via standard approaches.

19.3. THE SCOPE FOR PUBLIC ACTION TO PROVIDE BROADER SOCIAL PROTECTION

The case for fostering better social protection seems strong, justifying public action, and the allocation of budgetary resources to its provision. But this does not settle the issue of the form public action should take. State involvement is an obvious option, but encouraging NGOs, local social institutions, and the private sectors to provide more insurance and protection should not be ignored. A general state-run system of universal social insurance and substantial direct means-tested transfers may seem an admirable ideal from an equity point of view, but it is unlikely to be the most cost-effective system, involving high administrative costs and possibly substantial incentive-related inefficiencies. The informational requirements make this generally unfeasible in poor countries with limited budgets and administrative capacity anyway. Still, it does not mean that public action cannot achieve substantial improvements in social protection, even given limited means. On this, what have we learned from the contributions in this book?

Possible measures can be classified into two categories: first, *ex ante* measures that result in the poor and vulnerable taking out more insurance; second, *ex post* measures that provide transfers to the poor when they face bad shocks that remained uninsured. *Ex ante* measures would provide incentives and means to the poor to protect themselves better against hardship: examples are supporting self-insurance via savings, assisting income risk management by providing access to credit, supporting community-based risk-sharing, and encouraging the introduction of insurance products tailored to poor contexts. *Ex post* measures would provide a genuine safety net, appropriately targeted to the poor but large enough in scale and coverage to provide broad-based social protection at some minimally accepted and feasible level of standard of living. It could be part of a more general welfare support system, or specifically targeted for risk-related hardship. In the rest of this final section, I will discuss each of these possibilities further.

19.3.1. *Introducing New Insurance Products*

In recent years, microfinance institutions and even insurance companies in developing countries have started to design and provide insurance products for low-income clients. Life and health insurance are most common. Nevertheless, relative to microcredit programmes, they are typically still relatively limited. What scope is there for experimenting and expanding insurance products? First, it is worthwhile to recall some of the main reasons for the lack of insurance to start with. Market-based insurance requires a high information environment while problems of adverse selection and moral hazard will limit the extent to which insurance providers would be willing to offer insurance. Problems with enforcement of payouts for claims undermine the willingness of clients to take out insurance. A possible solution for this credibility problem requires the establishment of reinsurance markets, but this is not self-evident. Non-market insurance may benefit from a better information environment but there is no scope for insurance of important covariate or infrequent risks. Both market and non-market insurance solve some of the information problems they face by excluding certain groups and individuals from its arrangements.

Could microinsurance, in the form of the provision simple, low-cost insurance contracts, tailored to low-income clients provide a way out? Such contracts need to overcome the same information and enforcement problems as market-based insurance, and the small scale of the contracts will make transactions costs high. Still, just as with microcredit, it could provide a service to low-income clients that otherwise would remain rationed in the market, even if it would mean rather substantial subsidies. It is nevertheless helpful to emphasize some differences with microcredit provision. First, the enforcement problem in credit is faced by the loan provider, but in insurance, it is a problem for the client. Second, with credit, there is repeated interaction between borrower and lender during the repayment period and this implies regular transactions and monitoring costs. In the case of insurance, the information content of the regular payment of the premium is rather limited, while there are only small transactions costs for the provider, since the insurance can be easily withdrawn when the premium is not paid. For the provider, transactions costs are irregular and only high when a claim comes in. Finally, reinsurance is essential to keep the costs of insurance provision low. This implies the need for regulation, high quality of actuarial data, and the certification of events to allow this reinsurance market to function.

The need for reinsurance and the costs of verification of claims imply that the types of risk that can be insured at relatively low-cost are limited. Certain events may be easily verifiable—such as death or serious illness—so that life and health insurance may be obvious contracts to start with. But even in those cases there may be problems. To avoid adverse selection, there would be a need to exclude certain groups, based on disease (such as AIDS) or age—but these are groups that may suffer serious hardship without insurance. Reinsurance would require systems of certification—but what if in certain locations with poor institutions it may be easy to obtain false death or poor health certificates?

In general, there is surprisingly little research on microinsurance, at least compared to the vast microcredit literature. There is also little or no systematic evidence on how existing risk-sharing or other social institutions could be mobilized to provide a basis for more widespread insurance provision for different types of risk. The sceptical discussion in the previous section remains valid. But the main requirement now is to obtain empirical evidence. This also implies the need for experiments combined with research, preferably in the form of 'natural' microinsurance experiments to evaluate its impact.

Alternative insurance products could also be promising. Weather-indexed bonds, as suggested in Skees *et al.*'s Chapter 18 (this volume) is one such example. A key advantage is that claim verification is straightforward: a key source of losses is insured, not the loss itself.[5] Still, given the high covariance of rainfall and other climatic factors across regions and countries, the development of reinsurance markets covering large geographic areas would be particularly important in this case. Whether products for weather or catastrophic risk can be introduced in some of the poorest countries remains to be seen.

---

[5] Developing weather insurance tailored to the poor may be less straightforward. It would require verifiable records on rainfall. But if the poor tend to live in marginal areas with limited agricultural wealth, few rainfall stations are likely to be available at present. Unless the local rainfall is highly covariate with rainfall in 'richer' areas, rainfall insurance would not offer much protection to them.

19.3.2. *Promoting More Self-insurance via Savings and Microcredit*

Besides designing and supplying better insurance products for the poor, there is also scope for assisting the poor in protecting themselves. As was discussed in Chapters 1 and 2, there is substantial scope for more self-insurance provided better savings instruments suitable for the poor can be offered. Key problems with existing self-insurance via assets is that they tend to be risky and may well be strongly covariate with incomes, limiting their effectiveness, while financial savings products are typically not tailored to the poor, offering low or negative returns, and involving prohibitive transactions costs.

As an area for subsidized intervention and regulation, it also does not suffer from the important informational problems affecting credit and insurance. There is no issue of adverse selection or moral hazard, nor any serious reinsurance issues. The main issues are potentially high transactions costs and the need for credibility of the institution (Morduch and Sharma 2002). With few exceptions, such as SafeSave in Bangladesh, initiatives remain relatively thin on the ground. Most savings instruments within microfinance institutions still appear to be mostly used as instruments for accessing micro-credit—for example, as a means of developing reputation and commitment. Flexible savings instruments for precautionary motives are usually not encouraged.

It does not mean that there is no further role for more standard microcredit products, on the contrary. Increasing assets and incomes, which in turn allow savings to increase, offers a virtuous cycle to provide a buffer against future hardship. Furthermore, access to credit can serve as a means of insurance, allowing the poor to borrow in bad years against future incomes. Finally, since profitable sources of income, suitable for diversification purposes in an income risk management strategy often involve important set-up costs, small loans could have a very large impact on income risk exposure. Overall, however, this requires that microfinance institutions offer flexible products that allow the poor to enter into credit despite being faced with substantial risk. One possible route would be to provide interlinked contracts, which typically offer more efficient outcomes than separate credit and specific insurance contracts—a standard solution for mortgage lending products in developed countries. An example would be to link credit with health insurance. There is substantial room for more experimentation and research on such products.

19.3.3. *The Role of Targeted Transfers*

Ex ante measures may provide substantial protection, but ultimately they cannot fully insure individuals and families. Informal mechanisms only offer limited insurance. Micro-insurance products will have to be simple, insuring only specific, highly observable risks, while high-risk groups may have to be excluded by design. The existence of certain risks, for example, catastrophic risks, can hardly be anticipated beforehand. Self-insurance fails if shocks happen to materialize in successive periods. All self-protection strategies require some outlay beforehand, at times high to guarantee the sustainability of the institution, and the poorest households may not be able to afford this, while credit to pay for insurance may not be available. In short, some *ex post* measures, providing transfers to those affected by uninsured risk, would still be necessary as part of a social protection system.

This is not the place for an exhaustive discussion on the scope and form of a transfer-based safety net (see Drèze and Sen 1989; van de Walle and Nead 1995). A few issues are relevant for our discussion. For example, targeting support is probably the most efficient solution given limited means, but one should be aware of the potential errors of targeting, especially for those requiring support but excluded due to imperfections in the targeting design. Self-targeted programmes may seem most attractive, where the design of the programme ensures incentives for participation only by the target group and not by others, so avoiding costly identification of the beneficiaries. Workfare programmes such as food-for-work are often designed in such a way, but the return to the beneficiaries has to be kept low to ensure incentives for others not to participate. Coverage is typically not complete: certain groups may not be reached by such programmes, for example, women that have took after children may not find the time to take part. Alternative targeting schemes, such as allowing community leaders to select beneficiaries or schemes based on observed characteristics (such as nutritional status or livestock ownership) have their own costs and problems (Conning and Kevane 2000; Ravallion 2003). In the case of uninsured risk transfers, the question of who should be targeted is also not self-evident. In principle, for an efficient safety net, one should be most concerned with reaching those for whom protection will avoid poverty traps or persistence, via their effects on investment and activity choice. Given the problems of identifying those currently poor, it is unlikely that one can identify these using any of the possible targeting methods.

In setting up a transfer-based safety net, it is definitely worth exploring whether existing local risk-sharing institutions could be scaled up. As discussed before, whether the informational advantages outweigh their weaknesses is not clear. But the question of who should be covered by the safety net should also be based on an assessment of its full impact, including existing informal institutions. Crowding-out may reduce the welfare impact, even though if the safety net breaks down power relations, this may be welfare increasing as well. As discussed in Chapters 9 and 14, targeting issues may also have limited relevance if risk-sharing is taking place: informal arrangements could even help to compensate fully for targeting errors. This is an illustration of a more general point: formal safety nets cannot exist in isolation. Any public action to increase social protection will have to take into account existing risk management and coping mechanisms.

19.3.4. *Institutions, Credibility, and Public Action*

Allocating resources for social protection programmes is not enough to ensure their success. There is also a need for sustainable institutions that can fulfil the commitments implied in the *ex ante* and *ex post* social protection measures discussed before. Insurance or savings contracts need to be honoured, and transfer schemes operational in all contingencies. Different agents, including NGOs, community organizations, or the private sector, could play a significant role in the delivery of these social protection measures. There is a crucial role, however, for the government to develop and support an appropriate regulatory and institutional framework for such programmes. But this is not self-evident.

Recall that a key objective for the provision of insurance against poverty is to make sure that risk is not a reason for persistent poverty, by ensuring that uninsured risk does not force the poor to invest in activities and assets of low profitability to limit their own exposure to risk. Social protection measures can only ensure this if they are fully credible to the poor: in other words, they can be sure that the protection is available, so that they do not have to change their behaviour towards even less-risky livelihoods. Ultimately, sustainable and transparent institutions are required to deliver this credibility.

This implies that the safety net must be available at clear, pre-announced terms at all times—even if a highly covariate shock implies that large numbers will require it, and irrespective of the budgetary costs in such a case. This requires substantial planning, organization, and commitment of resources. Furthermore, if microinsurance contracts are offered, then they must be honoured at all times, requiring well-developed reinsurance mechanisms, or forms of state or similar guarantees. Institutions are also unsustainable if the enforcement of contracts becomes too costly. One issue is that there must be credible ways of proving claims. Developing easier ways of verification, and establishing records and actuarial data would cut transactions costs and assist the development of reinsurance markets. Savings institutions need deposit insurance schemes or strict regulations on their use of the clients' savings. Savers require a low-risk environment, including credibility about macroeconomic stability and inflation, or protection from embezzlement.

Fostering credibility in social protection is therefore an important task. Governments in developing countries not only have limited means to establish broader social protection. Their institutions are often not sustainable and therefore well-intentioned social protection measures may lack credibility. Credibility is not easily gained, and governments in poor developing countries face an uphill struggle to acquire it. This identifies an important role for aid and the donor community: by supporting and guaranteeing the enforcement of these measures it would allow social protection to provide genuine insurance against poverty.

REFERENCES

Banerjee, A. and A. Newman (1993). 'Occupational Choice and the Process of Development'. *Journal of Political Economy*, 101(2), 274–98.

Conning, J. and M. Kevane (2002). 'Community Based Targeting Mechanisms for Social Safety Nets: A Critical Review'. *World Development*, 30(3), 375–94.

Dasgupta, P. and D. Ray (1986). 'Inequality as a Determinant of Malnutrition and Unemployment: Theory'. *Economic Journal*, 90, 1011–34.

Dercon, S. (1996). 'Risk, Crop Choice and Savings'. *Economic Development and Cultural Change*, 44(3), 385–514.

Drèze, J. and A. K. Sen (1989). *Hunger and Public Action*. Oxford: Oxford University Press.

Fafchamps, M. (1992). 'Solidarity Networks in Pre-Industrial Societies: Rational Peasants with a Moral Economy'. *Economic Development and Cultural Change*, 41(4), 147–174.

Galor, O. and J. Zeira (1993). 'Income Distribution and Macroeconomics'. *Review of Economic Studies*, 60, 35–52.

Jalan, J. and M. Ravallion (2001). 'Behavioral Responses to Risk in Rural China'. *Journal of Development Economics*, 66, 23–49.

Ligon, E., J. Thomas, and J. Worrall (2002). 'Informal Insurance Arrangements with Limited Commitment: Theory and Evidence from Village Economies'. *Review of Economic Studies*, 69(1), 209–245.

Mookherjee, D. and D. Ray (2001). 'Introduction', in D. Mookherjee and D. Ray (eds), *Readings in the Theory of Economic Development*. London: Blackwell.

Morduch, J. and M. Sharma (2002). 'Strengthening Public Safety Nets from the Bottom Up', *Social Protection Discussion Paper Series*. Washington, DC: Social Protection Unit, Human Development Network, World Bank.

Murphy, K., A. Shleifer, and R. Vishny (1989). 'Industrialization and the Big Push'. *Journal of Political Economy*, 97, 1003–1026.

Platteau, J. P. and A. Abraham (1987). 'An Inquiry into Quasi-Credit: The Role of Reciprocal Credit and Interlinked Deals in Small-Scale Fishing Communities'. *Journal of Development Studies*, 23(4), 461–490.

Ravallion, M. (2003). 'Targeted Transfers in Poor Countries: Revisiting the Tradeoffs and Policy Options'. *Working Paper No. 3048*. Washington, DC: World Bank.

Romer, P. (1986). 'Increasing Returns and Long-run Growth'. *Journal of Political Economy*, 92, 1002–1037.

Rosenzweig, M. and H. Binswanger (1993). 'Wealth, Weather Risk and the Composition and Profitability of Agricultural Investments'. *Economic Journal*, 103, 56–78.

van de Walle, D. and K. Nead (eds). (1995). *Public Spending and the Poor: Theory and Evidence*. Baltimore, MD: Johns Hopkins University Press.

Index

Lightning Source UK Ltd.
Milton Keynes UK
UKHW020636100223
416739UK00003B/290